Readings in
MENTAL RETARDATION

Special Learning Corporation

42 Boston Post Rd. Guilford, Connecticut 06437

SPECIAL LEARNING CORPORATION

Publisher's Message:

The Special Education Series is the first comprehensive series designed for special education courses of study. It is also the first series to offer such a wide variety of high quality books. In addition, the series will be expanded and up-dated each year. No other publications in the area of special education can equal this. We stress high quality content, a superb advisory and consulting group, and special features that help in understanding the course of study. In addition we believe we must also publish in very small enrollment areas in order to establish the credibility and strength of our series. We realize the enrollments in courses of study such as Autism, Visually Handicapped Education, or Diagnosis and Placement are not large. Nevertheless, we believe there is a need for course books in these areas and books that are kept up-to-date on an annual basis! Special Learning Corporation's goal is to publish the highest quality materials for the college and university courses of study. With your comments and support we will continue to do this.

John P. Quirk

©1978 by Special Learning Corporation, Guilford, Connecticut 06437

All rights reserved. No part of this book may be reproduced, stored, or communicated by any means--without written permission from Special Learning Corporation.

First Edition
1 2 3 4 5

ISBN No. 0-89568-002-5

Manufactured by the Redson Rice Corporation, Chicago, Illinois

SENIOR AUTHOR

HERBERT GOLDSTEIN, currently at New York University and formerly of Yeshiva University, is a professor of Special Education and Director of the Curriculum Research and Development Center in Mental Retardation. He received his Ed.D from the University of Illinois and was a Fulbright Scholar and Lecturer in Mental Retardation at the University of Oslo. A coauthor of the Illinois Curriculum Guide for Mentally Handicapped Children, Professor Goldstein has written extensively about special education. He also has served as an editorial consultant for the American Association on Mental Deficiency and the Council for Exceptional Children.

Special Education Series Content Specialists

Dr. Judy Smith
Director, Special Education
Teacher-Training Program
Alexandria, Virginia

Ms. Carlene Van Etten
Dept. of Special Education
University of New Mexico
Albuquerque, New Mexico

Dr. Gary Adamson
Dept. of Special Education
University of New Mexico
Albuquerque, New Mexico

Dr. Malcolm Norwood
Director of Dissemination
Bureau of Education for the
  Handicapped
Washington, D.C.

Advisory Board

Ann Fabe Isaacs
Chief Executive Officer
The National Association for
  Creative Children and Adults
Cincinnati, Ohio

Joseph Sullivan
Area Cooperative Educational
  Services
Director, Village School
North Haven, Connecticut

Judith Kaufman
Associate Professor
Ferkauf Graduate School of
  Humanities and Social Sciences
Yeshiva University, New York

Theodore Bergeron
Former Executive Director
Shoreline Association for the
  Retarded and Handicapped
Chapel Hill, North Carolina

Lorraine H. Marchi
Founder, National Association for
the Visually Handicapped
New York, N.Y.

E. Eugene Black
Division of Special Education,
State Department of Education
Sacramento, California

Cecil Bobo
Consultant
Exceptional Children and Youth
State Department of Education
Montgomery, Alabama

Conwell G. Strickland
Department of Special Education
Baylor University
Waco, Texas

Field-Testing and Reviewers

Ms. Eida Lynn Hinson
Infant Intervention Specialist,
Shoreline Association for Retarded
  and Handicapped,
Guilford, Connecticut

Ms. Dona Chiappe
Director, Shoreline Learning Center
Guilford, Connecticut

Ms. Mary Ellen Ryan
Early Education Instructor,
Department of Mental Retardation,
Waterford, Connecticut

International Advisory Board

Sweden
Karl Gustav Stukat
Goteborg, Sweden

Lars Alin
Professor, Psychological Institute
Göteburg University
Göteburg, Sweden

France
Madame Grandrut
Secretariat aux Handicap

United Kingdom
Christopher Jones
Professor of Special Education

Mexico
Jean de-Blumeville
Director of Special Projects
Mexico City, Mexico

Puerto Rico
Sra. Virguinia Stgo Udo Torres
Department of Health
Santurce, Puerto Rico

Norway
Karl Evang M.D.
Director of General Health Services
Oslo, Norway

Barbara Halstromm
De Blindas Forening
Enskede, Norway

Trygve Bore
Head of Division for Special Schools
Oslo, Norway

SPECIAL EDUCATION SERIES

- Autism
* - Behavior Modification
  - Biological Bases of Learning Disabilities
  - Brain Impairments
  - Career and Vocational Education
  - Child Abuse
  - Child Development
  - Child Psychology
  - Cognitive and Communication Skills
  - Creative Arts
  - Curriculum and Materials
* - Deaf Education
  - Developmental Disabilities
* - Diagnosis and Placement
  - Down's Syndrome
- Dyslexia
  - Early Learning
  - Educational Technology
* - Emotional and Behavioral Disorders
- Exceptional Parents

* - Gifted Education
  - Hyperactivity
* - Learning Disabilities
  - Learning Theory
- Mainstreaming
* - Mental Retardation
  - Multiple Handicapped Education
  - Occupational Therapy
* - Physically Handicapped Education
  - Pre-School and Day Care Education
* - Psychology of Exceptional Children
  - Reading Skill Development
  - Research and Development
  - Severe Mental Retardation
  - Slow Learner Education
  - Social Learning
* - Special Education
* - Speech and Hearing
  - Testing and Diagnosis
* - Visually Handicapped Education

- Published Titles   * Major Course Areas

CONTENTS

Glossary of terms   ix
Topic matrix   xi

1. History and Theory

Overview   2

1. **"Who Are All the Children?",** Wayne D. Lance, *Exceptional Children,* Vol. 43 No. 2, October 1976.   4
The author brings us a complete view of educational services for exceptional children beginning in 1817 and advancing to present day strides within the field.

2. **"Introduction to Mental Retardation,"** U.S. Government document.   13
An overall breakdown as to the specifics of mental retardation, such as: causes, prevalency, and a future outlook of available services.

3. **"Mentally Retarded People: 200 Years in America,"** Gary B. Mesibov, Ph.D., *Journal of Clinical Child Psychology,* Vol. 5, Winter 1976.   17
Dr. Mesibov has compiled a 200 year view of the history of mental retardation within the United States bringing us up to 1976 views of attitudes and trends.

4. **"Ten Years in the Ark,"** Joseph J. McHugh, *America,* Vol. 132 No. 17, May 3, 1975.   22
A look at a communal living federation of mentally handicapped citizens with communities in France, Canada, Belgium, England, Africa, India and the United States.

5. **"Mental Retardation: What It Is."**   24
A factual chart showing levels of retardation, educational programs, and rehabilitation services as compiled by the president's panel on mental retardation.

6. **"Facts on Mental Retardation,"** National Association for Retarded Children.   26
This article contains a complete point by point analysis of retardation facts which include causes, needs, and available services within the United States.

7. **"Affective Reactions of Retarded and Nonretarded Children to Success and Failure,"** Charles Hayes, Robert Prinz, *American Journal of Mental Deficiency,* Vol. 81 No. 1, July 1976.   31
Classroom techniques are evaluated with using success and failure performance for retarded children as compared with nonretarded subjects.

8. **"The Strange Child,"** Thomas J. Cottle, *America,* November 15, 1975.   33
The warmly told story of a family with 3 normal sons who experience the birth of a retarded daughter and her affect on their lives.

9. **"Katherine Wants to go to School Saturday, Sunday, and All Through Summer,"** Katherine H. Berg, *The PTA Magazine,* Vol. 69, No. 1, September 1974.   38
A mother's view of her brain damaged daughter's progress in special education classes.

10. **"Designing a Special Playground,"** Pamela Gillet, *Children Today,* Vol. 6 No. 1, January/February 1977.   39
An innovative view of the planning and execution of a special education playground with its implications and usefulness to retarded children.

11. **"Whose Child Is This?",** Anonymous, *Redbook Magazine,* Vol. 143 No. 4, August 1974.   44
True happenings of a mentally retarded boy's effect on a neighborhood who experiences the importance of love and need for each other through his being.

2. Research, Diagnosis and Assessment

Overview   46

12. **"Mental Retardation, Research and Education,"** *JAMA,* Vol. 191 No. 3, January 18, 1965.   48
A stimulating overview of current research into the causes, therapy, and education of the mentally retarded from a medical standpoint.

13. **"Early Identification of Handicapped Children Through Frequency Sampling Technique,"** *Exceptional Children,* Vol. 43 No. 7, April 1977.   52
The author's discuss their collaboration on a pilot study which stresses the importance of early childhood identification programs for special education classes.

14. **"Diagnosis,"** (chapter one) Mental Retardation, *American Medical Association/A Handbook for the Primary Physician.*   56
Mental retardation diagnosis is viewed in detail, giving biological, neurological, physical, psychological, and historical views.

15. "Brief Reports - Predictive Value of Infant Intelligence Scales with Multiply Handicapped Children," Rebecca F. DuBose, *American Journal of Mental Deficiency*, Vol. 81 No. 4, 1976. ...64
The results of infant intelligence tests are discussed as reliable predictors of later intellectual development of the multiply handicapped.

16. "The Retarded Child - Checking Out Facilities for Care," Mary Alderman/staff editor, *Patient Care*, May 15, 1972. ...67
An open evaluation of guidelines of assistance describing the basic steps of placement for retarded children.

17. "Application of Piaget's Theory to the Study of Thinking of the Mentally Retarded," Nancy K. Klein, Ph.D., Philip L. Safford, Ph.D., *Mental Retardation*, 1976. ...72
This article contains research into inellectual growth from sensorimotor intelligence through adult logic of the mentally retarded from Piaget's studies.

18. "Elements for Developing Competency Based Programs for the Mentally Retarded," Robert C. Sauter, *Mental Retardation*, Vol. 15, No. 1, February 1977. ...84
Educational principles of curriculum planning affecting student behavior of the mentally retarded are approached and laid out in this program for special education.

3. Prospectus on Causes and Preventions

Overview ...88

19. "We Can Do More to Prevent the Tragedy of Retarded Children," *Psychology Today*, Vol. 10 No. 7, December 1976. ...90
The Koch's point to society's obligations to the retarded which can be enlightened through understanding and acceptance of their potential in all aspects of life.

20. "Lead and Mental Retardation," *Science News*, Vol. 107 No 14, April 5, 1975. ...94
A short discussion of the affects of lead poisoning of children who suffer neurological damage as a result of drinking tap water.

21. "Prevention," *American Medical Association/A Handbook for the Primary Physician*. ...95
The medical view of the aspects of early diagnosis and treatment to modify or reverse the course of the occurrance of retardation and its ultimate prevention is discussed.

Focus I ...104
"Jimmie"
A photographic essay of a day spent with a young Down's syndrome child.

4. Educable Mentally Retarded

Overview ...106

22. "Integration Programs for the Mildly Retarded," Gilbert R. Guerin, Kathleen Szatlocky, *Exceptional Children*, November 1974. ...108
This study examines programs which integrated mentally retarded students in 8 California school districts and its ramifications.

23. "Reading Comprehension Skills Vis-A-Vis the Mentally Retarded," Oliver L. Hurley, *Education and Training of the Mentally Retarded*, Vol. 10 No. 1, February 1975. ...114
A comprehensive review concerning reading comprehension skills of EMR children with questions and answers as to its validity.

24. "Developing the Creative Potential of Educable Mentally Retarded Students," Barbara Gay Ford, Joseph S. Renzulli, *The Journal of Creative Behavior*, Vol. 10 No. 3, 3rd Quarter 1976. ...119
Creative behavioral training is discussed with regard to mentally retarded youngsters might.

25. "Vocabulary Development of Educable Retarded Children," Arthur M. Taylor, Martha L. Thurlow, James E. Turnure, *Exceptional Children*, Vol. 43 No. 7, April 1977. ...125
Valid methods of competency factors of verbal elaboration for educable retarded children are laid out from findings in basic research.

26. "The Child With Minimal Brain Dysfunction — A Profile," Sam D. Clements, Ph.D., *A Symposium-Children With Minimal Brain Injury*, 1964. ...128
A psychogenic view of a child with minimal brain dysfunction including causes, diagnosis, educational alternatives and medical evaluations.

27. "Functional Similarities of Learning Disability and Mild Retardation," John T. Neisworth, John G. Greer, *Exceptional Children*, Vol. 42 No. 1, September 1975. ...140
This paper suggests that the special education field must expand its role along the lines of an interactive model.

28. "America's Needs in Habitation and Employment of the Mentally Retarded," The President's Committee on Mental Retardation and The President's Committee on Employment of the Handicapped. ...142
A discussion of the overlapping of "the retarded" and "the learning disabled" through scientific pedagogy which applies for all children.

29. "Special Education Services for the 'Mildly Handicapped': Beyond a Diagnostic and Remedial Model," Phyllis L. Newcomer, Ed.D., *The Journal of Special Education*, Vol. 11 No. 2, 1977. 146
This report stresses the vocational needs of the retarded through the involvement and caring of all the citizens of America.

30. "I Think I Can," *Good Housekeeping*, September 1974. 156
The warmly told story of a courageous little girl whose triumph over massive brain injury is related through her father's words.

5. Trainable Mentally Retarded

Overview 160

31. "Assessment of Counseling Practices at the Birth of a Child With Down's Syndrome," Siegrfied M. Pueschel and Ann Murphy, *American Journal of Mental Deficiency*, Vol. 8, No. 4, January 1977. 162
Since institutionalization of newborn Down's syndrome children is generally undesirable, families of these children often are in need of appropriate community services.

32. "Your Down's Syndrome Child... You Can Help Him Develop From Infancy to Adulthood," David Pitt, M.D., National Association for Retarded Citizens. 167
Beginning with a basic look at Down's syndrome and its causes, this article traces the development of these children from birth to maturity.

33. "Review of Drug Treatment for Down's Syndrome Persons," Jack B. Share, *American Journal of Mental Deficiency*, Vol. 80 No. 4, January 1976. 178
To date, no medication treatment has demonstrated any marked improvement in the development of Down's syndrome individuals.

34. "No Stars Please, For Teaching the Retarded," *Today's Education*, Vol. 61 No. 3, March 1972. 182
For every person who has been showered with praise for teaching the retarded, the author addresses this article.

35. "The Gift of Susy," Nancy Lee Riffe, *McCall's Magazine*, Vol. C11 No. 2, November 1974. 184
Told to accept her Down's syndrome daughter as she was born, and not to think about what she is not, the author traces her own courageous fight to provide her daughter with the best opportunities available.

36. "My Twin Sister Isn't Just Like Me," How One Girl Learned A Very Special Lesson in Love," Sandra Ann Lambert, 189
Seventeen, December 1972.
The author tells a personal story of mental retardation, relating the feelings, insights, and fears that come from having a handicapped sibling.

37. "Counseling Parents After the Birth of An Infant With Down's Syndrome," Deborah A. Golden, Jessica G. Davis, *Children Today*, Vol. 3 No. 2, April 1974. 191
Learning that their new baby has Down's syndrome can be a frightening, confusing experience for parents.

38. "Training the Mentally Retarded: A Progress Report," *American Education*, November 1975. 196
A close look is presented of the innovative model preschool center for handicapped children at the University of Washington.

Focus II 200
A comprehensive listing of the various types of mental retardation, the characteristics, causes, and preventions.

6. Severely and Profoundly Mentally Retarded

Overview 202

39. "The Severely/Profoundly Handicapped: Who Are They? Where Are They?", Ed Sontag, Ed.D., Judy Smith, M.S.Ed., Wayne Sailor, Ph.D., *The Journal of Special Education*, Vol. 11 No. 1, 1977. 204
Contained in this article is an examination of approaches to the problems of definition and categorization of the severely/profoundly handicapped.

40. "Training Teachers for the Severely and Profoundly Handicapped: A New Frontier," *Exceptional Children*, Vol. 42 No. 4, January 1976. 210
A basic examination of the components to be integrated within existing teacher training program structures

41. "Language Training for the Severely Retarded: Five Years of Behavior Analysis," Lee K. Snyder, Thomas Lovitt, James O. Smith, *Exceptional Children*, Vol. 42 No. 1, September 1975. 216
A timely series of 23 studies which raises hopes for two-way communication avenues to be opened to those who have been shut out for too long.

42. "Breaking Down the IQ Walls-Severely Retarded People Can Learn to Read," Renee Fuller, *Psychology Today*, Vol. 8, No. 5, October 1974. 220
A ball-stick-bird reading program which is considered to be a valid "scientific system of teaching for those who are ready or not."

43. **"Optimizing Test Performance of Moderately and Severely Mentally Retarded Adolescents and Adults,"** Milton Budoff and James L. Hamilton, *American Journal of Mental Deficiency,* Vol. 81 No. 1, 1976. — 225
A study of learning potential assessment procedures involving a train-within-test model for severely retarded adolescents and adults.

44. **"Background Music for Repetitive Task Performance of Severely Retarded Individuals,"** Joel S. Richman, *Exceptional Children.* — 232
Environmental manipulation in the form of specific tempo background music is used to assist in habitation of the severely retarded with improved performance results.

45. **"Teaching the Unteachables,"** John Fleischman, *Human Behavior,* Vol. 5 No. 5, May 1976. — 236
A caring view of how the profoundly retarded can learn to lead useful and happy lives in spite of their retardation.

46. **"Behavioral Training Strategies in Sheltered Workshops for the Severely Developmentally Disabled,"** Paul Wehman, Adelle Renzaglia, Richard Schutz, *Education and Training of the Mentally Retarded,* — 243
A 3 section behavioral analysis of learning and behavior problems.

7. Emerging Directions

Overview — 250

47. **"Opening More Doors for the Nation's Retarded,"** *U.S. News and World Report,"* Vol. LXXXI No. 9, August 30, 1976. — 252
A hopeful view of the strides of living and working condition improvements and expectations for America's mentally retarded.

48. **"New Hope for Retarded Children,"** Sara Stutz, *Reader's Digest,* Vol. 105 No. 632, December 1974. — 254
The importance of early special training is discussed from a psychological view.

49. **"Role Playing and Behavior Modification: A Demonstration with Mentally Retarded Children,"** L. Gerald Buchan, Sally Teed, Craig Peterson, *The Clearing House,* Vol. 50 No. 2, October 1976. — 256
A teaching tool of role playing and behavior modification programs is laid out for teaching.

50. **"A New Life for the Retarded,"** Susan Charnelle, *McCalls,* Vol. C1 No. 7, April 1974. — 260
Looking at an experiment in community living in the Boston, Massachusetts suburb of Wakefield, of mildly retarded young adults.

51. **"One Person Makes a Difference,"** Eunice Kennedy Shriver, *Parks and Recreation,* Vol. 10 No. 12, December 1975. — 261
Eunice Kennedy Shriver stresses the difference one person can make in voluntarism through the Special Olympics.

52. **"Sex Education of the Mentally Retarded Child in the Home,** Evalyn S. Gendel, M.D., National Association for Retarded Citizens. — 264
A compassionate overview of how sex education might best be motivated for the parents and mentally retarded within the home setting.

53. **"How Retarded Children Can Be Helped,"** Evelyn Hart, *Public Affairs Pamphlets,* 1959. — 268
Current trends and avenues for provision for the mentally retarded are studied in this article.

54. **"To Defend the Rights of the Helpless,"** Eunice Shriver, *Redbook Magazine,* Vol. 146 No. 6, April 1976. — 276
Eunice Shriver through her vitality has reached thousands of handicapped individuals. Here she speaks of her experience with the National Special Olympics.

55. **"Classroom Techniques,"** Lou Brown, Barbara Huppler, Laura Pierce, Nancy Scheuerman, Ed Sontag, *Education and Training of the Mentally Retarded.* — 278
Described within is a program which attempts to develop and/or improve basic communication skill of young trainable students.

56. **"A Haven for Steve,"** Veronica Dolan, *McCalls,* Vol. XCIX No. 7, April 1972. — 284
A brief look at a hostel program in Colorado for mentally retarded persons which offers an alternative living experience as they approach adulthood.

57. **"The 6 Point Program,"** U.S. Department of Health, Education, and Welfare Social and Rehabilitation Services. — 285
A model system of services for the mentally retarded.

58. **"Enabling the Disabled,"** *AS and U,* November 1976. — 290
Brief views of what California state has done with their campus facilities for the handicapped.

59. **"New Hope for the Retarded Child,"** Walter Jacob, U.S. Government Document. — 291
A detailed overall view of the future for retarded persons.

Index — 299
Appendix of Organizations — 302

GLOSSARY OF TERMS

amniocentesis A diagnostic procedure in which several diseases which cause mental retardation in utero may be detected. Insertion of a needle through the abdominal wall into the uterus, for extraction of amniotic fluid, results in the obtaining of free-floating cells for observation in a laboratory.

amniotic fluid Fluid surrounding the fetus in utero.

anencephaly Absence of portions of the brain, or the brain in its entirety.

anomaly An abnormality or malfunction.

anoxia A cause of mental retardation in the unborn infant, brought on by a lack of oxygen on the mother's part.

Apert's syndrome A condition characterized by a fusion of the toes and fingers, coronal synostosis, and a cleft palate.

aphasia Inability to understand and/or use language meaningfully.

aura A sensation which is experienced just prior to an epileptic seizure.

behavior modification The technique involved in altering undesirable behavior to a more appropriate state.

brain injury A general term refering to any damage to the brain.

chromosome The structures in the cell nucleus which carry the genes.

cleft palate A congenital defect due to a failure in development of the roof of the mouth.

congenital Present from birth on.

cretinism Characterized by small stature, dry skin, and sparse hair, this is due to an absence of the thyroid hormone. Treatment involves administration of thryoid extract to the infant.

Down's syndrome Named for Dr. John Langdon-Down, who first identified it in 1886, this condition is caused by an extra number 21 chromosome in each cell of the body making a total of 47 chromosomes. This disorder occurs in all degrees of retardation severity. Those affected have similar physical characteristics.

educable mentally retarded Those individuals whose I.Q. range is approximately between 50 and 70. This population is able generally to learn elementary school skills.

electroencphalogram The record produced by an electroencephagram, an instrument used to record changes in electric potential between different areas of the brain.

encephalitis Inflammation of the brain resulting from a virus.

fontanel Space between the cranial bones which is covered by a membranous structure. This appears as a soft spot on the top of a normal infant's head at birth.

galactosemia Progressive physical and mental degeneration due to a mataoblism defect win the enzyme which converts galactose to glucose. Detection takes place through blood tests and treatment is dietary.

gene Those parts of the chromosome which transmit hereditary characteristics.

genetic Pertaining to or transmitted by genes.

Hurler's disease Characterized by a swarf-like stature, with shortness of neck and trunk, and depression of the bridge of the nose. There is no treatment. Prevention is only through prenatal diagnosis.

hydrocephalus Caused by the growth of a tumor or subdural hematoma which results in the blockage of fluid at the base of the brain and collection in the ventricles. This disease is characterized by an exceptionally large head.

hyperactivity Disorganized, disruptive, and unpredictable behavior overreaction to stimuli.

intrauterine growth retardation -also called Warkany's syndrome, a condition characterized by an abnormally small placenta and low birth weight.

mainstreaming The placement of handicapped students into educational programs with normal functioning children.

mental retardation Subnormal intellectual development beginning in childhood, resulting in deficiencies in social functioning.

microcephaly An abnormally small cranium.

mosaicism A condition in which an individual has an abnormal number of chromosomes in some cells and a normal chromosomal complement in other cells.

myoclonic seizures One form of epileptic seizure in which the head is repeatedly dropped and the arm is extended.

neonatal The period of time between the onset of labor and six weeks of age.

phenlketonuria Caused by the absence of certain enzymes which are necessary to convert phenylanine to tyrosine. Detected by a blood test at birth, dietary treatment can eliminate harmful proteins.

placenta previa The separation of the placenta from the uterine wall during the birth process, resulting in the deprivation of food and oxygen to the fetus.

post natal After birth.

prematurity Children born weighing less than 5 pounds and 8 ounces at birth. Associated with 15 to 20 percent of all cases of mental retardation.

prenatal Before birth.

psychomotor Pertaining to the motor effect of psychological processes.

rubella A disease which, if contracted by the mother during the first three months of pregnancy, can cause congenital defects in her offspring. Commonly known as German measles.

severe retardation Those persons whose IQ falls approximately between 0 and 29. They will in most cases, require constant, lifelong care.

social learning Increasing a child's competence in making relevant decisions and exhibiting appropriate behavior.

syndrome A collection of specific symptoms.

Tay Sachs disease Manifested by the first 4 months of life, this hereditary disease occurs in children of Askenazi Jewish descent. It is characterized by convulsions, spasticity and progressive blindness. There is no treatment currently, however early detection is possible through amniocentesis.

time-out from reinforcement A therapeutic intervention in which a reinforcing condition is removed or altered for a period of time immediately following the occurrence of an undesirable response.

toxemia A condition developed by some women during the last three months of pregnancy, in which the blood contains toxic substances. The cause is unknown, however the symptoms are high blood pressure, albumin in the urine, dizzy spells, and in some cases, convulsions.

trainable retardation Those persons whose IQ falls approximately between 30 and 49. They can be taught simple speech and self-help skills.

trisomy 21 The most common form of Down's syndrome in which there is a trisomy of three individual number 21 chromosomes where there should be one pair. All of the cells of this individual will have 47 chromosomes.

tuberous scherosis Characterized by mental retardation, convulsions, skin changes, and possibly brain tumors. No treatment is known.

tyrosine Amino acid which is found in protein substances.

Wilson's disease Characterized by abnormal copper deposits in several body organs.

TOPIC MATRIX

Readings in Mental Retardation provides the college student in special education an overview of the nature, needs and educational techniques in teaching the mentally retarded.

COURSE OUTLINE:

Teaching the Mentally Retarded

I. Characteristics and needs of the mentally retarded
II. Appropriate educational programs
III. Education materials for the retarded
IV. Classroom management
V. Teaching techniques for the retarded

Readings in Mental Retardation

I. Mental Retardation: An Historical Overview
II. Research, Diagnosis and Assessment
III. Prospectus on Causes and Prevention of Mental Retardation
IV. Educable Mentally Retarded
V. Trainable Mentally Deficient
VI. Severely and Profoundly Retarded
VII. Emerging Directions

Related Special Learning Corporation Readers

I. Reading in Special Education
II. Readings in Behavior Modification
III. Readings in Psychology of Exceptional Children
IV. Readings in Mainstreaming

PREFACE

In 1968, the Assembly of the International League of Societies for the Mentally Handicapped adopted a declaration of the general and special rights of the mentally retarded. The opening statement declares, "The mentally retarded person has the same basic rights as other citizens of the same country and same age." The statement clearly outlines the ideology behind the status of mentally handicapped people today. In reality, the situation is not always one of acceptance by society. During the past decade, monumental changes in both attitude and provision of services for the mentally handicapped have occurred. Unprecedented federal subsidies and court decisions have spurred this change. Increased exposure and education of the public has improved attitudes toward the retarded. Certainly progress has emerged since the founding days of our nation, when the first hospital for the mentally retarded was built in Williamsburg, Virginia, in 1773. More like a prison than a hospital, the inmates were chained in tiny cells without heat or proper food. As more public awareness develops and appropriate services are increased, it is hoped that the closing statement of the declaration of the rights of the mentally retarded will become a reality, "Above all — the Mentally Retarded Person Has the Right to Respect."

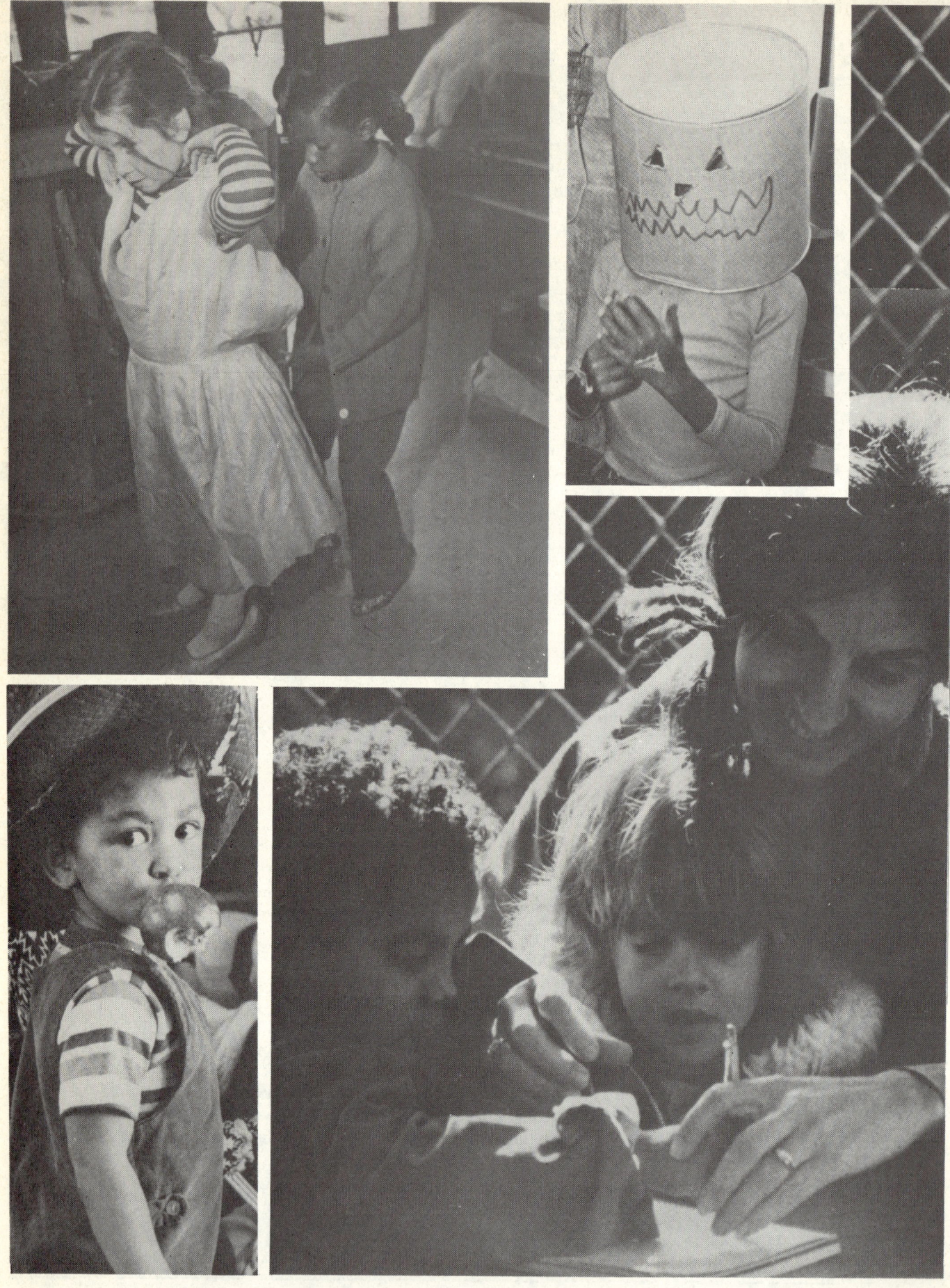

History and Theory

Concern and interest in mentally retarded children was lacking for several hundred years previous to the dawning of the twentieth century. Jean Itard brought mental retardation to French public attention in the eighteenth century when he attempted to "civilize" a young boy who had previously lived a savage and wild life in the French woods...thus he came to be called the Wild Boy of Aveyron. Itard met with little success in his attempts to educate this 8 year old "wild boy", but the fact that he did attempt this undertaking brought the eyes of the world to rest on the concerns of mental retardation. Europe took the lead in establishing some schools for the mentally retarded built upon known theories of the time and based on the fact that mental defects were considered accountable to education. With practical application and growth, it soon was realized that limits of how much these children could actually grasp had to be accepted by educators.

Misconceptions among the public at large and professionals ran the gamut at this time. It was popular theory that mental deficiency was a disease and direct consequences were criminal and delinquent behaviors.

Mentally retarded beings had to be closed within prisons and homes for paupers with education being of no real consequence in treatment.

With the first part of the twentieth century, attempts of segregation and special education began to make headway. The development of intelligence tests in France in 1904 by Alfred Binet and Theodore Simon brought new inroads for further possible success. With these tests, measurement and detection accuracy brought about more and better education programs around the world. With the outbreak of World War I it became apparent that the intelligence test would further serve special education, when the United States learned that nearly half of all army recruits possessed a mental age of 12 years and less... a country with a half "feebleminded" population of young people... How could this be? It was then established that intelligence alone could not remain adequate proof of mental retardation. Other factors would have to be considered in new areas of research... racial differences in intelligence, inherited mental capacity factors, and IQ in relation to occupational levels came into play.

New attitudes and concepts toward mental retardation brought new and specialized programs for training to meet the unique problems of the retarded. Parents began to realize their place in their child's education, killing the old theory that the major cause was hereditary. The parents became a strong and influential group in bringing about more understanding of the problems at hand and refused to doom their children to institutional lives.

Franklin D. Roosevelt initiated new programs with the outbreak of World War II to combat poverty. Through these programs it was learned that rejection rates of over 700,000 men were directly related to the incidence of being classified mentally deficient. Theory was further developed by John F. Kennedy when he appointed his panel on mental retardation. That panel concluded: "Accumulating evidence that a host of social, economic, and environmental factors — often categorized as cultural deprivation — are correlated, or associated to a high degree with the incidence of mental retardation, especially in its milder manifestations..."

The National Association for Retarded Children was formed in 1950 by a group of forty two concerned parents. They helped bring about new legislation, research and programs... now with over 100,000 members in local chapters throughout the United States, they make strides of greatness through their efforts of positive thought and action.

We presently continue to strive for new and better approaches through education and science... we can still do more.

Who Are *All* the Children?

WAYNE D. LANCE

WAYNE D. LANCE is Professor of Education, University of Oregon, and Director, Northwest Area Learning Resource Center, Eugene.

Education for *all* exceptional children! Two hundred years as a nation, and as we embark on the third century, we have declared through our laws and by personal commitment that, at last, none shall be excluded. The fact of education for all, meaning equal educational opportunity, has yet to catch up with the intent. Yet, there is satisfaction in knowing that the intent has been expressed in so clear a manner. As in any great endeavor, the beginnings were small, the result of vision and of personal dedication, born out of a love for humanity manifested in the actions of men and women. Vignettes selected from the history of special education serve as reminders that recent achievements may not be claimed as tributes to this generation alone, but are the fruit of seeds planted long ago by a few in recorded history and by many who never made the printed page.

Revolutionary Strides

• *Hartford, Connecticut, April 15, 1817:* The Rev. Thomas H. Gallaudet, principal of the Connecticut Asylum for the Education and Instruction of Deaf and Dumb Persons, announced today that seven pupils were enrolled on this opening day. Mr. Gallaudet returned from Europe last August where he had studied the art of instructing the deaf and dumb for nearly 15 months. The new asylum is the first permanent school for the education of deaf-mutes in this country and is supported by both private charity and an appropriation of $5,000 from the Connecticut Legislature (Fay, 1893).

• *Boston, August 18, 1831:* The New England Asylum for the Blind, incorporated over two years ago, finally has a director, it was announced today. Dr. Samuel Gridley Howe, a physician, plans to travel to the continent later this year to observe programs for the blind and to engage teachers. The school is scheduled to open sometime next year once space has been found and staff employed (Farrell, 1956).

• *Boston, October 1, 1848:* An experimental school for idiotic children opened in a wing of the Perkins Institution today. Ten children are enrolled and James B. Richards has been assigned as the teacher. An amount of $2,500 per annum has been appropriated by the Legislature following the receipt of a report from a special commission chaired by Dr. Samuel Gridley Howe. The commission sees the school as a model for the rest of the country. Quoting from Dr. Howe's report "... it would be demonstrated that no idiot need be confined or restrained by force; that the young can be trained for industry, order, and self-respect; that they can be redeemed from odious and filthy habits, and there is not one of any age who may not be made more of a man and less of a brute by patience and kindness directed by energy and skill" (Kanner, 1964, pp. 41–42).

• *Chicago, September 17, 1900:* Demands by parents for day school classes for their blind children were realized today as a special classroom opened in a regular school in this city. Mr. John Curtis, the teacher, indicated that the program is considered to be an experiment to see if blind children can be educated nearer to their homes rather than having to reside at the state school in the southern part of the state (Farrell, 1956).

• *Worcester, Massachusetts, September, 1901:* Preparatory schools for gifted children opened in Worcester this month, initiating a new concept in education. Believed to be the first such school in the United States specifically for the benefit of unusually bright children, these schools provide seventh, eighth, and ninth graders with opportunities to accelerate their studies in Latin, French, German, and algebra, in addition to the usual studies. After two years in the preparatory school these students will enter high school with a full year's credit in these special subjects (McDonald, 1915).

• *New York City, September 1908:* Public School No. 2, under the direction of principal J. F. Reigart, began a new program for children with defective speech this month. Mr. Reigart stated that the teacher of the class has engaged in special study to prepare her to help these children overcome their speech problems. According to City School Superintendent Maxwell, "The experiment ... demonstrates that the attempt to cure serious speech defects, which interfere with success and satisfaction in life is possible and well worth while" (McDonald, 1915, p. 88).

• *Anystate, USA, September 15, 1980:* In a special news release from the office of the State Superintendent of Public Instruction, the Superintendent announced that the goal of providing full educational opportunity to all children within the state has been achieved. He issued an invitation to anyone knowing of a child with a learning problem who is not receiving an appropriate education to please contact his office immediately. "The measure of success," said the Superintendent, "is nothing less than 100%."

The first six vignettes reflect the facts of recorded history—the last encompasses a hope and confidence in the efforts of a myriad of par-

1. MENTAL RETARDATION

ents, educators, legislators, and others during the remaining years of this decade.

Changing Attitudes and Changing Children
Establishment of Special Education

The recognition of the need to provide different treatments to individuals with obviously differing capacities for benefiting from the traditional educational practices led to the establishment of special education. From an historical perspective, special education may be viewed as developing through three successive stages: "(1) treatment through the segregation and restriction of resources for survival appropriate for people called different, (2) caring for people regarded as different by providing resources required for their physical existence, and (3) instructing such people so that they may be incorporated into existing, dominant social systems" (Heiny, 1971, p. 344). While examples from contemporary history may demonstrate that we have yet to fully pass from stage one, pronouncements abound that our goals have passed beyond segregation and restriction, through mere caring, to an attempt to assist the exceptional individual to be able to meet certain cultural standards. Whether those standards should be those of the dominant society or of pluralistic cultures is a much debated topic and one in which there is little consensus among special educators.

Recognition and Labeling

The vignettes from the 19th century illustrate rather nicely how special education began in this country with a recognition of the exceptional individual as a homogeneous element of the population and with labels to legitimate the classifications (Heiny, 1971). Bartel and Guskin (1971) supported the thesis that the process of identifying and so labeling individuals not only creates a handicap, but also exacerbates the condition as people so marked are treated differently. It seems that the very process which enabled large numbers of children to be educated, first in residential institutions and later in day schools and classes, often led to increasing segregation continuing into the adult years. As one reviews the early history of special education in the United States (Frampton & Rowell, 1938; Wallin, 1924), it is apparent that advances in our abilities to diagnose led to greater homogeneity in populations assigned to special programs and less opportunity for exceptional individuals to participate actively with nonhandicapped individuals.

Social Indictment

Looking back upon the early years of this century it appears that the more society became aware of the extent of handicapping conditions, especially in the area of mental retardation, the greater the alarm expressed through various forms of social indictment (Davies, 1959). This indictment, manifested in various forms of discrimination and segregation nevertheless caused an awakening among educators regarding the responsibilities public schools should assume for the education and rehabilitation of handicapped children and youth. Leaders like Wallace Wallin directed educators' attention to a more comprehensive view of factors, both "intrinsic and extrinsic," to use Wallin's words that tended to "mar" the development of the handicapped individual (Wallin, 1914).

"Happiness First" Motto

Following such leads, pupils began to be viewed as functioning members of their *total* environment. Educators expanded their concepts of what education was really all about and the result was a broadening of the curriculum especially in day schools and day classes for the exceptional, to include a variety of training in the practical arts along with a continuing emphasis on the basic academic

1. Who Are All the Children?

skills. The curriculum developed by the special class teachers of Boston prior to World War I exemplified this trend (*The Boston Way*, 1924). The "happiness first—all else follows" motto imported from abroad (Bridie, 1917) began to permeate the philosophies of special educators about this same time in our history, and while segregation of the handicapped was the order of the day, the emphasis was nonetheless one of making education a pleasant, and hopefully, practical experience.

Mainstreaming Is upon Us

This "caring attitude" on the part of educators led to a reexamination of the curriculum for the exceptional and a definite movement toward an individualization of instruction. Schwartz and Oseroff (1975) reviewed some 100 years of literature pertaining to individualized instruction and concluded that the developmental phases of this movement have led to rather highly structured systems for individualizing instruction. Thus we moved from a "happiness first" philosophy to a prevailing attitude that pupils should be able to demonstrate competency in any number of areas appropriate to their career objectives. This appears to coincide with Heiny's (1971) stages of development and we find ourselves pressing rapidly into stage three, namely providing programs such that the exceptional individual will be incorporated into the dominant social system. Mainstreaming is upon us—woven into our laws, our policies, and the very attitudes underlying the way in which we approach the development and implementation of programs for the exceptional individual.

Far More than Placement

The complexities of mainstreaming become evident as one considers the implications of a definition supplied by Kaufman, Gottlieb, Agard, and Kukic (1975):

> Mainstreaming refers to the temporal, instructional, and social integration of eligible exceptional children with normal peers based on an ongoing, individually determined, educational planning and programming process and requires clarification of responsibility among regular and special education administrative, instructional, and supportive personnel (p. 4).

As described by The Council for Exceptional Children, mainstreaming is far more than the placement of a child into a regular program for a period of time each day (Caster, 1975). The interactions of the instructional variables with social and temporal factors must all be accounted for in conjunction with the process of planning and the delineation of role responsibility. As the implications of mainstreaming become more evident, the prevailing attitudes seem to return to social innovation rather than social perpetuation. Heiny (1971) hypothesized that, "Social reformers seek redistribution of resources in favor of those who are labeled different, and social perpetuators seek efficient and effective use of resources within the distributions obtained by reformers" (p. 348). The goal of full educational services for all children and the concept of mainstreaming embedded within that goal requires social innovation rather than a reliance on a mere perpetuation of the principle of maintenance.

A Long Time in the Making

The call for full services to all children is not a product of this decade alone. It is interesting to note the parallels in statements issuing from the executive branch of government following the White House Conference on Children and Youth in 1930 and the writings of Elsie Martens of the US Office of Education in 1944. Such statements as,

1. MENTAL RETARDATION

"The concept of free public education for all children admits of no exceptions," and "no State program of services for exceptional children is complete *until it includes them all, with preference for none*" (Martens, 1944, pp. 1, 13) are evidence that the goal of full service to all exceptional children has been a long time in the making.

Professional organizations, like The Council for Exceptional Children, have been long time advocates of a full service concept. The Council has offered considerable assistance to education in such matters as the establishment of model legislation (Weintraub, Abeson, & Braddock, 1971) and in offering conferences and other platforms for the promotion of innovations. Organizations such as the National Association for Gifted Children have generated considerable grass roots support for specific exceptionalities, the result often being a focusing of attention on the needs of all children.

Evidence for Needed Changes

Comprehensive studies and reviews of special education programs as exemplified by the "Project on the Classification of Exceptional Children" (Hobbs, 1975a, 1975b) and the Rand Report (Kakalik, Brewer, Dougharty, Fleischauer, Genensky, & Wallen, 1974) have also begun to have impact on the attitudes regarding exceptionality as held by various segments of the public sector. Such studies, along with results of applied research, have been used as evidence for needed changes.

Equally compelling as a force to change attitudes has been the actions of the courts. Not only have the courts said that appropriate education for the handicapped is an inalienable right (Gilhool, 1973; Weintraub & Abeson, 1972), but they have also spoken out regarding the classification of students (Kirp, 1974) and due process requirements. (Abeson, Bolick, & Hass, 1975).

Responsibility of the Advocacy Function

Even as the results of litigation have been felt at every level—federal, state, and local—so too have advocates for the exceptional individual begun to organize in the form of national, state, and local advisory groups and councils. Councils on developmental disabilities are becoming active in every state (Stedman, 1976), and child advocacy systems at the local level are involving parents and neighborhood groups (Reynolds, 1974). While advocacy may usually be defined as "an independent movement of consumers (e.g., parents, people with disabilities, and children) and their allies to monitor and change human service agencies" (Biklen, 1976, p. 309), it may also be a function performed by a public agency such as the public schools.

Among the recommendations from the "Project on the Classification of Exceptional Children," which could have tremendous impact on public school programs for the handicapped if implemented, is one dealing with assignment of responsibility for the advocacy function. The recommendation reads as follows: "The public schools should be the institution with primary advocacy responsibility for providing or obtaining educational and related services for all children in need of special assistance whose condition or life circumstances does not require their institutionalization" (Hobbs, 1975a, p. 250). Such responsibility should begin, according to the authors, as early as children are identified after birth and should continue at least through the usual school years. Schools should provide, or arrange to be provided, not only the usual educational services, but therapy, special diets, prosthetic devices, drugs, and medical and health care. The educational program should include recreational programs, halfway houses, sheltered vocational settings, and a full

1. Who Are All the Children?

range of activities covering all aspects of the handicapped individual's life space.

In this, our country's bicentennial year, we find ourselves on the threshold of achieving a goal that the Rev. Gallaudet and Dr. Howe would certainly have endorsed as they commenced their heroic efforts with a mere handful of children requiring special help. Where they talked in terms of educational programs for a few, we now look to providing full services to more than 9 million mentally or physically handicapped children and youth aged 0 to 21 (Kakalik, et al., 1974). Our changing attitudes are evident—it seems well to ask, "Who are all the children?"

A Dynamic Concept of Exceptionality

The concept of exceptionality is not a static one. Over the decades as our society has moved from a position characterized by segregation of the severely handicapped and neglect of the mildly and moderately handicapped to a position marked by integration and acceptance, we have seen an expansion of the range of ages for which we believe society should assume some responsibility as well as demonstrations of responsibility for individuals who in some way have difficulties in adjusting or learning (such difficulties not being limited solely to the traditional handicaps). But the expanding concept of exceptionality goes beyond learning and adjustment problems per se to a concern for any individual for whom the usual educational program is not entirely appropriate.

Thus, over the years, the schools have periodically recognized that the needs of gifted children were not being met by the traditional instructional programs, and sporadic and isolated attempts have been made to adjust curriculum and methods for these students. Recognition that children who have been abused by parents and guardians may require adjustments in the typical school program is another example of a dynamic concept of exceptionality. Children from minority groups who are gifted or who have handicapping conditions often have unmet needs stemming not only from their difficulties in benefiting from a typical school program because of their giftedness or handicap, but further compounded by the cultural inappropriateness of materials, methods, and educational technology.

Three Dimensions

Perhaps we can best picture the expanding concept of exceptionality along three dimensions, each exerting an interactive influence upon the other: (a) chronological age, (b) degree of variation from the norm in educational related performance, and (c) environmental and cultural factors impacting on the learner's accommodation to school programs. In this decade, we are experiencing a movement to broaden the schools' responsibility up and down the age range (to wit, programs for preschool handicapped youngsters and young adult handicapped) to include the severely handicapped formerly considered the responsibility of residential institutions, and to accommodate programs to a pluralistic society and to children affected adversely by home and community influences.

Noteworthy Progress

An encouraging aspect of this expanding concept of exceptionality is a move away from rigid labels and categories toward a focus on the learning characteristics of children and the accommodation of educational programs to these characteristics. The most noteworthy progress in arriving at an understanding of the issues involved in classifying and labeling children was achieved through the "Project on the Classification of Exceptional Children" under the direction of Nicho-

1. MENTAL RETARDATION

las Hobbs (Hobbs, 1975a, 1975b). Sponsored by 10 federal agencies, 93 experts from various disciplines summarized existing knowledge relating to the topic of classification of children which was used in developing a set of 40 recommendations presented to the Secretary of Health, Education, and Welfare. A number of these recommendations are given vitality in the recently enacted "Education for All Handicapped Children Act" (Public Law 94-142).

Who Are They?

Who are all the children? They are the more than 9 million physically or mentally handicapped children and youth in this country, ages 0 to 21 who need services not required by "normal" youth (Kakalik, et al., 1974). They are the gifted and talented who usually manage to survive within traditional classroom settings but often fail to achieve their potential during the school years. As The Council for Exceptional Children declared in a resolution adopted in 1974, they are the tens of thousands of abused and neglected children for whom educators have responsibilities to assist in prevention of further injury and to provide programs to remediate the damage that has occurred (Soeffing, 1975). They are the handicapped persons from minority groups whose educational problems are compounded by failure of the curriculum and methodology to adapt to language and culture factors that impinge on the educational process (Norris & Overbeck, 1974). In short, a dynamic concept of exceptionality encompasses all the children for whom regular school programs must be adapted in order to help the children achieve in accordance with their potential, regardless of the degree of deviance from the norm or the effects of environmental influences.

Achieving the Goal

Education for *all* exceptional children. Is this goal really within our reach? What are the resources upon which we can rest our hope for such a noble objective? What evidence exists that we are ready to move forward at an unprecedented rate? We can point to a number of encouraging trends that give substance to what could easily become an elusive goal beyond our grasp.

Federal Support

According to a recent study completed by the Rand Corporation for the Department of Health, Education, and Welfare, the annual federal expenditures for programs for all handicapped youth was in excess of $1 billion (Kakalik, et al., 1974). Of this amount, the federal government expended about $314 million for special education programs, constituting about 12% of the total amount spent nationwide by all government agencies. This evidence of federal support is only a beginning as we view the intent of Public Law 94-142 which was adopted by the Congress and approved by President Ford late last year. This law, which assures a free appropriate public education to all handicapped children, authorizes federal expenditures exceeding $3 billion annually by 1982.

Local Assistance

Proposed rules being promulgated by the Department of Health, Education, and Welfare put teeth into the Rehabilitation Act of 1973 by requiring annual efforts to locate individuals requiring special assistance and subsequent provision of as suitable an education as that provided to nonhandicapped persons (HEW, 1976). Through federal and state efforts, national, regional, and state learning resource systems are being established to provide assistance and support to exceptional children and their teachers (Lance, 1975). Smaller school districts are combining resources to better muster the resources needed to provide full educational services (Colella & Foster, 1974).

Regional direction services are being established in several states to bridge the gaps between agencies serving the handicapped. Systematic representations of the concept of full educational services have been developed and disseminated (Crosson, 1975).

The Role of Technology

On another front, one is encouraged by the developments in technology which have already impacted on our ability to better serve the exceptional. The application of technology to meet the seemingly overwhelming obstacles imposed by sensory handicaps can be traced into antiquity, probably even predating Jerome Cardan's advocacy of using the sense of touch for the blind and a system of signs for the deaf in the 16th century (Farrell, 1956). It was the efforts of the brilliant blind Professor Louis Braille, however, who perfected a system of raised dots during the 1830's that was later to become such an integral part of educational programs for the blind. While this tactile system of reading has served the blind so well for over a hundred years, the potential for the application of modern technology tickles the imagination.

Already the OPTICON reader is in use in many countries (Telesensory Systems, Inc., 1976). This compact device allows the reader to move an optical scanner across a page and to receive tactile impressions representative of the printed letters on the index finger of one hand. A blind individual, once trained to use this device, is no longer limited in the scope of reading to only those materials which have been put into braille. The "Talking Calculator," which "speaks" when the buttons are depressed and provides an audio as well as visual output, permits the blind to perform complex mathematical calculations as easily and rapidly as the seeing. Initial experimentation with the Vocoder, a device that translates auditory signals into tactual impressions for use by hearing impaired individuals, is equally exciting in its implications for improving educational opportunities for the sensory handicapped (Engelmann & Rosov, 1975). The use of microfiche readers and devices such as the Optiscope Enlarger (Hellinger & Berger, 1972) for immediate enlarging of the printed page by partially sighted individuals holds promise for bypassing the slow and expensive process of printing materials in large type. Other applications of technology, including the use of computers and specialized media, have been described (Lance, 1973), many of which can enhance the instructional process for the handicapped learner.

Commitment of the Individual

Yet, the achievement of the goal of full educational services for all exceptional children will not be a product merely of federal and state assistance or of the applications of systems and technology. Rather it depends upon the commitment of individuals ready and able to devote themselves to the demanding requirements of being an effective teacher of the exceptional individual. Anne Mansfield Sullivan exemplifies this commitment, the ability to appraise a situation and to demonstrate a caring attitude and innovative teaching style so necessary if we are to reach *all* the children. Upon arriving in Tuscumbia on March 3, 1887, Miss Sullivan found Helen Keller, an untaught, quick tempered, willful child, waiting to be guided to a full achievement of her potential. As Miss Sullivan handed Helen a doll and slowly spelled "d-o-l-l" in her hand, a relationship was begun that would eventually result in a deaf and blind child blossoming into a creative adult (Keller, 1904).

While much has changed since Rev. Gallaudet opened a school for the deaf in 1817 and Miss Sullivan held out a hand to a little girl in 1887, one constant remains: Success in helping any exceptional indi-

1. MENTAL RETARDATION

vidual to achieve a full measure of the potential which is uniquely his is dependent upon the expression and demonstration of a loving concern by those adults who have been given the opportunity to devote themselves as teachers of exceptional children. Because this constant is still apparent in so many individuals today, the goal of a full and appropriate education for *all* exceptional children appears to almost be within our grasp.

References

Abeson, A., Bolick, N., & Hass, J. *A primer on due process: Education decisions for handicapped children.* Reston VA: The Council for Exceptional Children, 1975.

Bartel, N. R., & Guskin, S. L. A handicap as a social phenomenon. In W. M. Cruickshank (Ed.), *Psychology of exceptional children and youth* (3rd ed.). Englewood Cliffs NJ: Prentice-Hall, 1971.

Biklen, D. Advocacy comes of age. *Exceptional Children.* 1976, 42, 308-313.

The Boston way: Plans for the development of the individual child. Concord NH: Rumford Press, 1924.

Bridie, M. F. *An introduction to special school work.* London: Edward Arnold, 1917.

Caster, J. What is "Mainstreaming?" *Exceptional Children.* 1975, 42, 174.

Colella, H. V., & Foster, H. BOCES: A delivery system for special education. *Phi Delta Kappan,* 1974, 55(8), 544-545.

Crosson, J. E. *Full educational services for handicapped children and youth: A planning guide.* Eugene OR: Northwest Learning Resource System, University of Oregon, 1975.

Davies, S. P. *The mentally retarded in society.* New York: Columbia University Press, 1959.

Engelmann, S., & Rosov, R. Tactual hearing experiment with deaf and hearing subjects. *Exceptional Children.* 1975, 41, 243-253.

Farrell, G. *The story of blindness.* Cambridge: Harvard University Press, 1956.

Fay, E. A. (Ed.). *Histories of American schools for the deaf. 1817-1893* (Vol. 1). Washington DC: The Volta Bureau, 1893.

Frampton, M. E., & Rowell, H. G. (Eds.), *Education of the handicapped* (Vol. 1) *History.* New York: World Book, 1938.

Gilhool, T. K. Education: An inalienable right. *Exceptional Children.* 1973, 39, 597-609.

Heiny, R. W. Special education: History. *The encyclopedia of education* (Vol. 8). New York: Macmillan & The Free Press, 1971.

Hellinger, G. O., & Berger, A. W. The optiscope enlarger: A report of initial field trials. *New Outlook for the Blind,* 1972, 66, 320-322.

Hobbs, N. *The futures of children: Categories, labels, and their consequences.* San Francisco: Jossey-Bass, 1975. (a)

Hobbs, N. (Ed.). *Issues in the classification of children* (2 vols.). San Francisco: Jossey-Bass, 1975. (b)

Kakalik, J. S., Brewer, G. D., Dougharty, L. A., Fleischauer, P. D., Genensky, S. M., & Wallen, L. M. *Improving services to handicapped children with emphasis on hearing and vision impairments: Summary and recommendations.* Santa Monica: The Rand Corporation, 1974.

Kanner, L. *A history of the care and study of the mentally retarded.* Springfield IL: Charles C Thomas, 1964.

Kaufman, M. J., Gottlieb, J., Agard, J. A., & Kukic, M. B. Mainstreaming: Toward an explication of the construct. *Focus on Exceptional Children,* 1975, 7(3), 1-12.

Keller, H. *The story of my life.* New York: Grosset & Dunlap, 1904.

Kirp, D. L. Student classification, public policy, and the courts. *Harvard Educational Review,* 1974, 44, 7-52.

Lance, W. D. *Instructional media and the handicapped.* Stanford CA: ERIC Clearinghouse on Media and Technology, Stanford University, 1973.

Lance, W. D. Learning resource systems for special education. *Theory into Practice,* 1975, 14(2), 90-98.

Martens, E. H. *Needs of exceptional children.* Washington DC: US Office of Education, 1944.

McDonald, R. A. F. *Adjustment of school organization to various population groups.* New York: Teachers College, Columbia University, 1915.

Norris, P., & Overbeck, D. B. The institutionalized mentally retarded Navajo: A service program. *Mental Retardation,* 1974, 12(3), 18-20.

Introduction To Mental Retardation

What is Mental Retardation?

Mentally retarded persons are those who mature at a below average rate and experience unusual difficulty in learning, social adjustment and economic productivity. The most generally accepted technical definition describes mental retardation as "significantly subaverage general intellectual functioning existing concurrently with deficits in adaptive behavior, and manifested during the developmental period." In terms of IQ, mentally retarded individuals score below 70. This means that the measured intelligence of 97% of the general population is greater than that of mentally retarded persons. All areas of abilities are affected, and the condition exists from childhood.

Mental retardation is not a disease, nor should it be confused with mental illness. Mentally retarded children grow into mentally retarded adults; they do not remain "eternal children." The big difference is that they learn more slowly and with much greater difficulty.

How Prevalent is the Condition?

Mentally retarded persons constitute one of the largest single handicapped groups in America. They include more than six million persons, and slightly more than 100,000 newborn children are likely to be added to this group each year unless far-reaching preventive measures are discovered and employed. Today, one out of every ten Americans has a direct involvement with the problem by virtue of having a mentally retarded person in his or her family.

Mental retardation is four times more common than rheumatic heart disease and nine times more prevalent than cerebral palsy. It affects 15 times as many people as total blindness and 10 times as many children and adults as polio did before research provided the Salk vaccine.

Who are the Potential Victims?

Mental retardation can strike individuals of every race, religion and nationality, every educational, social and economic

Introduction to Mental Retardation. ©U.S. Government document.

1. MENTAL RETARDATION

background. Some of our nation's leading figures have had mentally retarded family members. As a matter of fact, hereditary components are known to account for only a fraction of the cases of retardation.

What are the Causes of Mental Retardation?

Mental retardation can be caused by any condition which impairs development of the brain before birth, during birth or in the early childhood years. Well over 250 causes have already been discovered, but they account for only about one-fourth of all known cases of mental retardation. In three-fourths of the cases, the specific cause remains unknown.

Some of the most common causes include:

- Genetic Irregularities -- These result from abnormality of genes inherited from the parents, or from disorders of the genes caused during pregnancy by infections, over-exposure to x-rays, and other factors. Inborn errors of metabolism which may produce mental retardation, such as PKU (phenylketonuria), fall in this category. Chromosomal abnormalities have likewise been related to some forms of mental retardation, such as Down's Syndrome ("mongolism").

- Problems During Pregnancy -- Malnutrition, as well as german measles, glandular disorders and many other illnesses of the mother during pregnancy frequently result in a child being born retarded. Physical malformations of the brain or other organs originating in prenatal life may also result in retardation.

- Problems at Birth -- Extraordinarily prolonged labor, pelvic pressure, hemorrhages--any birth condition of unusual stress--may injure the infant's brain. Likewise, any reduction in the supply of oxygen to the infant's brain during birth may impair mental development. Rh factor incompatability between mother and child, if not promptly treated, can also lead to retardation.

- Problems After Birth -- Childhood diseases like whooping cough, chicken pox, measles, meningitis, scarlet fever, encephalitis and polio can damage the brain, as can accidents, such as a blow to the head. Glandular imbalance or malnutrition may prevent normal development, while substances such as lead and mercury can produce irreparable damage to the brain and nervous system.

- Environmental Factors -- The President's Committee on Mental Retardation has concluded that 75 percent of our nation's mentally retarded citizens come from urban and rural poverty areas. In addition to malnutrition, lead poisoning, disease-producing conditions, inadequate medical care and other health hazards associated with poverty situations, children in disadvantaged areas are likely to be deprived of many common day-to-day experiences of more fortunate youngsters. Recent research suggests that such understimulation can result in irreparable damage and can serve as a cause of mental retardation.

What are the Degrees of Mental Retardation?

About 89 percent of mentally retarded persons are mildly retarded and, in many respects, quite similar to their non-retarded peers. They differ primarily in rate and degree of intellectual development. While still young, their retardation is not readily apparent, and these children are not usually identified as retarded until they enter public school. With proper education and training, these individuals can enter the competitive labor market and the mainstream of daily community life.

Moderately retarded persons, who comprise about six percent of the mentally retarded, are more obviously handicapped. Their retardation is usually apparent before school age. However, appropriate educational opportunities throughout the developmental years can prepare these individuals for satisfying and productive lives in the community.

The remaining five percent of retarded persons are severely or profoundly retarded. In addition to obvious intellectual impairment, they frequently have other handicaps, such as cerebral palsy, epilepsy, blindness or deafness. Recent technological advances have demonstrated that most severely and profoundly retarded persons can learn to care for their basic needs. They also can perform many useful work activities, with supervision, and can otherwise adapt satisfactorily to normal patterns of life.

Can Mental Retardation be Prevented?

Recent scientific developments have led some authorities to conclude that 50 percent of the cases of mental retardation could be prevented if current knowledge were fully implemented. Unfortunately, many of the known preventive approaches are not yet in wide use. Obviously, there is an urgent need not only to implement what is already known, but to discover means of preventing those many causes of mental retardation for which effective prevention is still unknown. Examples of specific approaches to prevention include:

- Damage due to Rh-factor incompatibility can be prevented by blood exchange in the infant at the time of birth and special immunization of the mother.

- Quick treatment in cases of lead poisoning or, preferably, action to prevent children from eating paint containing lead can also be effective in preventing some cases.

- Measles vaccine--developed to combat rubella--can help if widely used.

- Early detection and dietary treatment is effective in some forms of inborn errors of metabolism, such as PKU and galactosemia.

- Improved nutrition of pregnant women and young infants can reduce the dangers of retardation from malnutrition.

- Surgical techniques have proven effective in preventing retardation resulting from accumulation of cerebrospinal fluid in the brain (hydrocephalus) and premature fusion of the cranial sutures (craniosynostosis).

- Better pediatric care, including antibiotics that control the high fever formerly associated with many of the dangerous children's diseases, also works to limit mental retardation.

Can Mental Retardation be Cured?

No means have yet been found to repair damaged brain tissue or to artificially increase the number of brain cells. In that sense, no "cure" for mental retardation is known today, and research in this area is desperately needed.

Can Mental Retardation be Ameliorated?

Almost all mentally retarded individuals have the capacity to learn, to develop and to grow. The great majority can become economically productive, fully participating members of society.

1. MENTAL RETARDATION

All retarded children and adults need the same basic services which other human beings need for normal development. These services include education, vocational preparation, health services of all types, recreational opportunities, religious services and many more. Unfortunately, many retarded persons have been denied access to these services or have been provided with inappropriate services, often at exhorbitant costs to their families.

In addition to basic generic services, many retarded persons need specialized services to meet extraordinary needs. Examples include vocational rehabilitation, sheltered workshops, work activity centers, diagnostic and evaluation centers, day training, pre-school classes and all types of residential services. Traditionally, many of these services have been unavailable or of questionable quality.

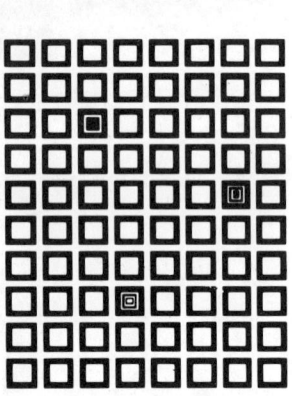

PSYCHOLOGY OF EXCEPTIONAL CHILDREN

Designed for the introductory courses of study in special education, this book provides an overview of the exceptional child. The social, emotional, linguistic and cognitive development of handicapped children are looked at, along with a special section dealing with support systems for the exceptional child, specifically family relationships.

For more information about this book and other materials in special education, contact Joseph Logan,

Special Learning Corporation
42 Boston Post Rd. Guilford, Connecticut 06437 (203) 453-6525

Mentally Retarded People:

200 Years In America

The author received his A.B. from Stanford University, his M.A. from the University of Michigan, and his Ph.D. from Brandeis University. He taught psychology at the University of Guam for three years and had a year of postdoctoral training in Clinical Child Psychology at the Division for Disorders of Development and Learning at the University of North Carolina. Currently he is a Staff Psychologist and Assistant Professor at the University of North Carolina.

Gary B. Mesibov, Ph.D.

Attitudes of Americans toward mentally retarded people have fluctuated considerably during the 200 years of our country's existence. Beginning with the earliest years, attitudes have changed back and forth from ignorant to supportive to protective to apprehensive. Although there are numerous aspects to the multifaceted questions involving mentally retarded people, most Americans are unaware of these subtleties, having only vague and general attitudes toward "the mentally retarded" as a group. For this reason no attempt will be made to differentiate attitudes toward different degrees of mental retardation or toward different subgroups (e.g. adults and children), and the phrase mentally retarded person will be used throughout this paper.

Although degrees of mental retardation will not be emphasized, a word about classification is necessary for an understanding of the terms that will be used. For many years the words "moron," "imbecile" and "idiot" were used to describe the different levels of mental retardation. The term "moron" referred to an IQ of about 50-70, "imbecile" referred to an IQ of about 30-50 and "idiot" referred to an IQ of about 0-30. Later the term "feebleminded" replaced "moron" in many places, especially Europe. These terms were used until 1954 when the World Health Organization recommended the terms "mild subnormality," "moderate subnormality" and "severe subnormality" to describe the degrees of mental retardation. This classification system was never widely accepted and was soon replaced by the current system proposed in the 1973 manual of the AAMD. The current system includes 4 categories of mental retardation: mild, moderate, severe, and profound. In this paper the terms quoted will reflect the authors' periods.

It is difficult to find information concerning the attitudes of colonial Americans and the earliest fathers of our Republic toward mentally handicapped persons. According to Wolfensberger, "In colonial America, handicaps were looked upon as the consequence of a stern providence meting out judgment for wickedness" (1969, p. 79). Deutsch (1938) writes that some mentally retarded citizens remained at home, some wandered about the countryside and some went to jails where they were not treated particularly well. He also describes a colonial practice of having private citizens charged with keeping retarded citizens in their homes at the public's expense.

Although the stern judgments of handicapped people described by Wolfensberger were no doubt true in some cases, the prevailing attitude toward retarded citizens seems most accurately described by Kott (1971) as ignorance. Most mildly and moderately retarded individuals probably fit

1. MENTAL RETARDATION

quite easily into an early, agrarian American society that was primarily untrained and unschooled. Crissey (1975) supports this position: "In an almost wholly illiterate population, functioning at the simplest vocational level, the group we now label 'educated retarded' no doubt was indistinguishable" (p. 800). The intellectual demands of our pre-industrial society were minimal and consequently, mental handicaps were minimal as well.

The first indication of a general awareness of mental retardation was in 1845 when Dr. Amariah Brigham called for an institution in New York state to train "idiots." Brigham was most certainly influenced, as were most people in those years, by the famous work of Itard in France with "The Wild Boy of Aveyron (1801)." Itard's pioneering efforts at training this apparently retarded child aroused the interest of many professionals in training those with limited capacity. Responding to these forces and to the fact that the 1845 New York State census had found about 1600 "idiots" in the state, Brigham wrote, "We are of the opinion that much may be done for their improvement and comfort; that many, instead of being a burden and expense to the community, may be so improved as to engage in useful employments and to support themselves; and also to participate in the enjoyments of society" (Deutsch, 1938, p. 341).

Brigham's remarks foreshadowed the trend that would prevail for the next 25 years in the United States. Under the leadership of Samuel Howe, who believed that training mentally retarded persons was a public responsibility, and Edouard Seguin, Itard's student, 1850 marked the beginning of the residential school designed to equip all mentally retarded citizens with the skills needed to integrate themselves into society. The 100 years beginning with the residential school in South Boston are well documented by numerous excellent historical summaries (Crissey, 1975; Haskell, 1944; Kanner, 1964; Sloan, 1963; Wolfensberger, 1969); however, for those not familiar with these works, a brief review will follow.

The director of the residential training program in South Boston, Edouard Seguin, had brought two very important things to this country from his native Europe. One was a technique called the physiological method. This technique had been adapted from training programs for the deaf (and dumb) by Itard for use with his famous boy from Aveyron. The physiological method emphasized intensive sensory training utilizing many principles of the method currently called behavior modification. In addition, the programs of Doman, Delacado, Kephart and Frostig were foreshadowed in Seguin's physiological method (Crissey, 1975). Along with this technique, Seguin also brought with him a capacity to lead and excite. A large number of residential programs were developed along his model beginning with New York (1851), Pennsylvania (1852) and Ohio (1857). By 1890 14 states had separate mental retardation facilities (Kott, 1971), all operating on systems similar to Seguin's.

Seguin's leadership not only provided the model that was followed by most of the mid-19th century residential schools, but he was also the main force behind the first organization for those working with mentally retarded people. In 1866 Seguin suggested that "Every year the Superintendents of the various schools should meet, to impart to one another the difficulties they have encountered, the results of their experience, and mostly to compare the books containing their orders and regulations" (Deutsch, 1938, pp. 345-346). Ten years later, during America's centennial celebration, officials of the Elwyn Training School invited all officers of similar institutions to go to Pennsylvania for the purposes outlined by Seguin. On June 6, 1876, the superintendents gathered at Elwyn and decided to form an organization called The Association of Medical Officers of American Institutions for Idiots and Feebleminded Persons. The name was changed to The American Association for the Study of the Feebleminded in 1906 and finally to its present name, The American Association on Mental Deficiency in 1933. The organization began publishing its proceedings in 1896 in the *Journal of Psycho-Asthenics* which later became the *American Journal of Mental Deficiency*. Seguin's leadership and profound influence were acknowledged by his election as the first President of this organization.

The goals of the mid-19th century training centers following Seguin's model were quite noble and ambitious. This was a period of "unrestrained optimism" (Kott, 1971, p. 26). The prevailing attitude was that with training and education all mentally retarded persons could be returned to the community. Although it was acknowledged that some were untrainable, this was believed to represent an extremely small percentage who were only untrainable because they had not been reached early enough. The therapeutic goal of these early institutions is underscored by the fact that those few thought to be untrainable were not admitted.

Not only were the goals of these residential training schools different from most of the institutions that followed, but so was the general lay-out and setting. First of all, these institutions were rather small with from 150-200 children "so that the children could be well known to the staff thoroughly diagnosed, and the proper education devised" (Crissey, 1975, p. 802). Instead of ignoring these residential programs, legislators seemed inclined to watch them closely in order to monitor their progress. Not only were these programs located in the community, but their activities directly related to those of the community. The overall plan was for the child to stay at home during the early years with the parents receiving suggestions and consultation from the institution. Later special training of specific skills took place in the institution after which the retarded individual returned to the community where he/she would be able to function as a responsible member.

Unfortunately the enthusiasm and optimism engendered by Seguin and his followers were short-lived. As early as 1869, reservations were expressed by some of Seguin's staunchest advocates, "the degree and extent for the education for the idiot may not have been as great as was first predicted" (Haskell, 1944, p. 111). These early doubts increased and finally developed into widespread disappointment as expressed in 1902 by Dr. Martin Barr of the Elwyn school in Pennsylvania, "Without formal expression emanating from our association as a body there is yet, I believe, a consensus that abandons the hope long cherished of a return of the imbecile to the world" (1976, p. 101).

The main reason for this discouragement appears to be because the initial claims of Seguin and the environmentalists were a bit too strong and unrealistic. Consequently, they were quickly proven to be unfounded. The wave of disappointment and discouragement resulted from expectations that had been raised yet unfulfilled. Professionals had been told that their hard work would be rewarded by the return of their clients to the community. What they found instead was that "a very small proportion of the feebleminded could be returned to the community, even after years of training, on a self-supporting basis" (Davies, 1923, p. 35).

Several other factors accelerated the changes that were occurring. The Seguin programs had established for the first time that the state would assume some of the responsibility for training and caring for its mentally retarded citizens. Previously this responsibility fell almost totally on the families. Consequently, when Seguin and his followers were unable to deliver on their promise to teach these citizens to function independently in society, many parents demanded that the residential training schools continue to maintain their mentally retarded children indefinitely. This resulted in increasingly larger institutions, a development that was necessitated by financial exigencies.

As a result of the perceived failure of the residential training school program, the entire complexion of our country's mental retardation services began to change. The residential training centers slowly became places of refuge for mentally retarded people who were now thought to be unable to live in modern society: "Institutions have changed their character, largely to furnish a permanent residence with congenial surroundings for these unfortunates" (Wolfensberger, 1969, p. 96).

These changing circumstances created a new role for the institutions of the late 19th century. They became places of refuge, designed to protect instead of train mentally retarded citizens. Regrettable though this new emphasis on protection may seem today, this was nothing in comparison to what was to follow. This period of protective isolation was only the "lull before the storm". Several factors in the early 20th century would plunge most mentally retarded citizens into a nightmare of frightening proportions.

Most historians agree that two factors helped trigger what is now referred to as "the alarmist stage." The first was the rediscovery of the Mendelian Laws of Heredity and the new emphasis that was placed on heredity and eugenics. While Seguin had stressed parental and accidental causes of mental retardation, the emphasis around 1900 shifted to heredity as the major factor producing mental retardation. As Goddard stated in 1912, "Feeblemindedness is hereditary and transmitted as surely as any other character" (Wolfensberger, 1969, p. 107).

This new emphasis on heredity helped stimulate the tracing of family histories, the most famous of these being Dugdale's study of the Juke family, Goddard's study of the Kallikak family and Tredgold's study for the British Royal Commission. These studies reinforced the belief in hereditary transmission by revealing that mental retardation had existed in some families for generations. In his report for the British Royal Commission Tredgold wrote, "In 90 per cent of patients suffering from mental defect, the condition is the result of a morbid state of the ancestors . . ." (Davies, 1923, p. 39).

As if the evidence for the herditary basis for mental retardation wasn't enough to worsen the plight of most mentally retarded persons by suggesting that mental retardation was immutable, the family studies revealed that families with a high incidence of mental retardation also committed many crimes. This was probably the single piece of evidence that most alarmed the populace during this period.

A second trigger for this alarmist period was the development of intelligence tests. The arrival of the IQ reinforced the assumption that intelligence was immutable. Intelligence tests also made possible the first large scale testing of the general population which identified large numbers of mentally retarded persons who had previously been undetected. This new finding, along with the concerns that the eugenic studies of Dugdale and Tredgold had elicited, pushed a nervous society beyond its limits. During this period it was not only learned that mentally retarded families were the source of most crime and degeneracy; but, in addition, the IQ data suggested that there were many more of those mentally retarded "criminals" than had previously been realized.

The ugly mood of the alarmist period can best be captured by the following quotations of professionals who were probably more positively inclined toward mentally retarded citizens than the average citizens: Butler in 1907, "While there are many anti-social forces, I believe none demands more earnest thought, more immediate action than this. Feeblemindedness produces more pauperism, degeneracy and crime than any other one force" (Wolfensberger, 1969, p. 102); Goddard in 1915, "For many generations we have recognized and pitied the idiot. Of late we have recognized a higher type of defective, the moron, and have discovered that he is a burden; that he is a menace to society and civilizaion; that he is responsible to a large degree for many, if not all, of our social

3. 200 Years in America

problems" (Wolfensberger, 1969, pp. 102-103); and from Johnson in 1901, "I do not think that, to prevent the propagation of this class it is necessary to kill them off or to resort to the knife; but, if it is necessary, it should be done" (Wolfensberger, 1969, p. 106).

The concerns raised during the alarmist period led to two suggested solutions to the problem of mental retardation: sterilization and segregation as outlined by Barr of the Elwyn School, "One cannot fail to recognize the necessity for the enforcement of measures which experience has demonstrated as absolutely needful steps toward prevention, viz: The separation, sequestration and asexualization of degenerates . . ." (Wolfensberger, 1969, p. 108). In 1907 Indiana passed the country's first sterilization law and many other states followed closely. Separation was accomplished by institutionalization. The institutional movement had now come full cycle. Originally begun by Seguin to prepare mentally retarded citizens for society, institutions were now being used to keep them away from society permanently.

Fortunately, the policies of sterilization and total separation soon proved unworkable and were discontinued. In 1915 Cornell summed up the reasons why sterilization was not the solution:

The sterilization of feeble-minded is now universally acknowledged to be impracticable, principally because the line of demarcation between feeble-mindedness and normality is not definite, because the hereditary influence in this field has not been quantitatively determined, because the operation is dangerous, the idea more or less revolting and, possibly, because it is not in consonance with the religious thought of a certain portion of the community. Sterilization, therefore, need not be further discussed at this time. (Wolfensberger, 1969, p. 112).

The failure of the separation policies were due to several factors. First, many parents objected to institutionalizing their mentally retarded children and "the courts are seldom willing to utilize even existing commitment laws without the consent of the parents, except in extreme cases" (Wolfensberger, 1969, p. 128). Second, financial considerations began to enter into decision making when it became apparent that institutionalization was not as inexpensive as was once believed. To institutionalize all mentally retarded citizens would have greatly increased costs. Third, new data began to reveal that IQ was not as fixed as was once thought (Doll, 1940). People were learning that it was often extremely difficult to identify mildly retarded persons. Finally, new data also revealed that the relationship between mental retardation and crime was not as strong as was once believed; "We have begun to recognize the fact that there are good morons and bad morons" (Murdoch, 1917, p. 41).

The failure of sterilization and separation along with the new data on IQ and crime led to still another change in attitudes: "the pendulum . . . had gone too far and is coming back" (Murdoch, 1917, p. 41). The end of the horrors of World War I also marked the end of the alarmist period. This does not mean that the post World War I era ushered in a return to the enthusiasm and optimism of the 1850's. The depression and hard times that followed would have precluded that, even if our leaders had been so inclined. However, during the postwar period this overwhelming fear of mentally retarded persons and the idea of eliminating or totally secluding them subsided. Even though these persons were still mostly ignored in their institutions, the worst was behind them.

The stagnant period between the wars was followed by renewed interest in mentally retarded citizens following World War II. Perhaps this revived interest occurred because of America's collective revulsion at the Nazi's mass slaughter of mentally retarded citizens in Germany. It might also have been part of the post World War II interest in the biological and social sciences. But whatever the source of this renewed interest, it was undoubtedly intensified by the rise of a par-

1. MENTAL RETARDATION

ents' organization, The National Association for Retarded Children (NARC) which advocated for mentally retarded citizens and has since become one of the most effective citizen advocacy groups in the world (Lippman, 1972).

As a result of these and perhaps other factors as well, programs for mentally retarded persons began to spring up again. One of the first projects of the NARC was to establish day care centers for retarded children so that parents who wanted to maintain their retarded children at home could have some relief and support. In 1957 Delaware passed the country's first legislation establishing state-supported centers for mentally retarded persons. In the early 1960's President John F. Kennedy's keen interest in civil liberties in general and mentally retarded citizens in particular led him to commission a panel to propose a nationwide plan. In 1962 the panel presented to Kennedy and the country the plan that was to shape our public policies toward mentally retarded persons for the next 15 years. Among the recommendations of the panel were the following:

1. Establishment of research centers for the study of mental retardation with special emphasis on its causes and prevention.
2. Improvement of health and welfare services for all, especially those with the greatest need.
3. Appropriate educational programs for all and the extension of the definition of educational beyond simply academics.
4. Training of professionals to work in all aspects of mental retardation, especially at the leadership level.
5. Development of comprehensive community-centered services on a continuum to meet all of the needs of mentally retarded persons and their families.

The 1960's brought about a revival of the programs and enthusiasm of the 1850's. However, unlike the Seguin model the programs of the 1960's and 1970's emphasized community-based instead of residential services. The report of Kennedy's Presidential Commission served extremely well as a model for guiding effective actions and programs; "One can think of few governmental reports and recommendations that have had such an impact and that have served so well as a guideline" (Crissey, 1975, p. 805).

In summary, America's mentally retarded citizens have seen many changes during the 200 years of our Republic. For the first 75 years they appeared to be virtually ignored and easily absorbed into an uneducated, agrarian society minimizing their handicaps. Mid-19th century programs took them out of their homes and provided training designed to return them to function as independent citizens. Between 1870-1890, the failure of these attempts to "normalize" retarded persons became obvious and an era of protective isolation followed. Retarded persons remained in institutions for protection from the cruel outside world. The following 20 years reversed the roles of the protector and the protected. Mentally retarded persons remained in institutions during this time, but they became the danger and society the innocent victim in need of protection. The period between the two World Wars saw movement away from concerns with mentally retarded persons because of the more pressing problems of the depression and the post-depression years. Following World War II came the second major effort to train and improve the lives of mentally retarded citizens. This effort was formalized and guided by a report of the President's Commission.

All of which leads to what? Why study history anyhow? It appears that there are at least two benefits to be gained from this historical discussion of our attitudes and programs involving mentally retarded persons: one is to better understand our situation today, and the second is to gain perspective and fresh insights.

This historical review should enable us to have a better understanding of today's issues because each of the historical trends has remnants that are very much alive today. The pre-1850 era of ignorance and inattention to the problems of mental retardation is still with us in many ways. Many citizens have had limited contact with mentally retarded people and know nothing about them. A recent study by Hill and Hill (1976) revealed that even among the more educated college population there are still many misunderstandings about mental retardation, although today's students are somewhat better informed than their predecessors. Not only are people often uninformed about mental retardation but they are also uninformed about available services. In Nebraska, an area nationally recognized for its programs for mentally retarded persons, Kelly and Menolascino (1975) found that the primary referral agents for mentally retarded persons, local physicians, were generally unaware of these exemplary local programs.

In certain ways the present era resembles the optimistic and enthusiastic 1850's and 1860's. A new Presidential Committee has recently completed its report, and new programs are proliferating. There are probably more competent professionals working on more programs for mentally retarded persons than ever before in the history of our nation. Recent efforts are succeeding in developing community programs for all retarded citizens. However, amidst the present euphoria, we must guard against promising too much.

Unfortunately in the 1970's there are still tendencies to shelter mentally retarded citizens from society and society from these citizens. As in the late 1800's, thousands of mentally retarded citizens still reside in residential institutions. Even though Perske's (1972) excellent article has pointed out the dignity of risk, many professionals and parents are not allowing many mentally retarded persons to take the risk necessary for them to achieve their maximal potential.

The pre-World War I notion of protecting society from its mentally retarded citizens is also, unfortunately, with us. A Gallup Poll commissioned by the President's Committee on Mental Retardation (1976) revealed that 14% of the American population fear mentally retarded people. A recent survey of physicians' attitudes in San Francisco showed that 22% favored euthanasia for children with Down's syndrome and 50% favored it for Down's syndrome with intestinal blockage, even though this blockage entails only a relatively simple operation ("Bay City Poll," 1976). Although the survey reflects the attitude that these children are less than human much more than that they are to be feared, this other attitude is every bit as dangerous.

The fact that most of the historical trends in attitudes toward mentally retarded persons are still very much with us today does not mean that nothing has changed during the 200 years of our Republic. Certainly the emphases have changed and it would be hard to deny that considerable progress has been made. But the fact that the adverse historical trends cited have not yet disappeared should make us pause from time to time to consider exactly how we got to where we are.

A second purpose of this historical analysis was to use historical trends in order to develop fresh insights. One such insight is the realization that 200 years of programs have focused almost entirely on mentally retarded citizens and not at all upon the members of the society who must learn to accept them. Although several reports and papers have expressed the view that society must be prepared to accept mentally retarded persons (President's Committee on Mental Retardation, 1976), none have translated this notion into programs having a significant impact. Perhaps a reasonable goal for us now is to begin encouraging and aiding our citizens in providing a dignified place for the mentally handicapped persons among us.

Some leaders argue that the best place to begin integrating mentally retarded citizens into society is in the public schools. They are advocating mixing mentally handicapped and normal children in regular classroom settings hoping that greater contact will facilitate greater understanding and mutual compatibility. Unfortunately this strategy ignores the extensive literature on racial integration which demonstrated

3. 200 Years in America

that putting people together is simply not enough (Amir, 1969). Extensive planning and programming must be done in order to prepare each group for the other. When adequate preparation is missing, the result can be increased tension and intolerance.

Successfully training society and its mentally retarded citizens to live together with one another might enable us to return to the spirit of the pre-1850 era when mentally retarded people lived in their local communities without creating a great deal of attention. Although there is often a tendency to glorify the past, it seems appropriate to look back during this bicentennial year. Our society is of course not as simple now and will never be, so our task of finding a place for those with mental handicaps is much greater than it ever was. However, we have available to us 200 years of growth and progress with which to accomplish what needs to be done. As Davies astutely observed in 1923:

In short, the feebleminded quite truly reflect in their behavior the kind of environment in which they find themselves. In that way they are an index of social conditions. If the community finds large numbers of delinquent, socially menacing feebleminded in its midst, let it look at itself and ask: "What kind of community have we here, what kinds of neighborhoods, of homes, of recreation, etc.?" The trouble must be sought somewhere beyond the feebleminded. (p. 195)

What better way to begin our second 200 years than by looking "beyond the feeble-minded" and asking "What kind of people are we and what kind of community have we here?"

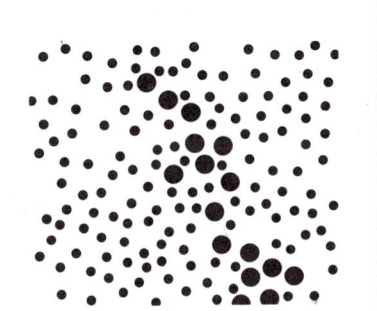

Mainstreaming

Taking an in depth look at the controversy of mainstreaming versus special education classes for the exceptional child, this book presents an overview of the problems and methods involved. The history of mainstreaming, along with future trends are discussed.

For further information concerning this book and other special education materials, contact:

Joseph Logan, Editor
Special Learning Corporation

Special Learning Corporation
42 Boston Post Rd. Guilford, Connecticut 06437 (203) 453-6525

Ten Years in the Ark

JOSEPH J. MC HUGH

[Joseph J. McHugh, S. J., *is completing his theological studies at Weston College School of Theology, Cambridge, Mass.*]

They knew best of all they were unclean, feared and unwanted. And yet, while lepers were excluded by law from the Jewish community, some openly sought out Jesus for healing. Jesus dared to be with these outcasts, to touch them, to heal them and to restore them to human community. An encounter with Jesus restored a sense of value and self-respect to the socially excluded leper.

Ten years ago, Jean Vanier began living with the mentally handicapped in a community he called L'Arche—the Ark—in Trosley-Breuil, France. After seeing how a society either ignored the needs of the handicapped completely or packed them away in institutions to deal with them effectively, the former Royal Canadian Navy officer, doctor of philosophy and son of Georges P. Vanier, 19th Governor-General of Canada, decided to share his life with the handicapped. The name L'Arche captured Mr. Vanier's vision. Instead of excluding the mentally handicapped from the human community, he wanted to gather them together into an accepting, caring and joyful fellowship. In a world intoxicated with strength and yet incapable of dealing effectively with weakness, the Ark hoped to restore a sense of value and self-respect to the handicapped. The Ark's vision was, and still is, the hard business of seriously living the gospel.

From this initial vision and single community in France, L'Arche today has become a federated movement with communities in France, Canada, Belgium, England, Africa, India and the United States. As the sites multiply, the vision remains clearly focused. Each house in the federation provides a communal living situation for the mentally handicapped, who would otherwise be institutionalized or without care at all. Certainly not without suffering and difficulty, Mr. Vanier's L'Arche has brought the handicapped and their "normal" assistants together as equals in a Christian atmosphere of respect, care and genuine joy in being together. L'Arche respects and cherishes in joy the unique gift each person can bring to community.

In an age characterized by contempt for human life, talk of the ethics of triage and the deep insensitivity of the powerful debating the price of grain while the powerless starve to death, L'Arche is a concrete sign that the Kingdom of God is alive and preached to the poor. Mr. Vanier is a serious Christian, and his ten years in the L'Arche movement demand our respect, our support and our reflection.

What has Mr. Vanier's decade at L'Arche meant? A civilization like ours, mesmerized by rationality, efficiency and productivity, cannot deal effectively or vitally with those who are judged useless by these same values. L'Arche, however, preaches gently, without fanfare, that power, efficiency and productivity are not the only human values worth cultivating. We suffer from a philosophic prejudice against being handicapped. Our civilization rests on a description of the self that focuses narrowly on the concepts of intelligence, self-reflection and control. Although Mr. Vanier would admit that the handicapped may lack a high degree of rational and productive ability, he is demonstrating that they are capable of being happy in an environment that protects their weakness and sustains the less pragmatic values of respect, care and joy.

L'Arche serves in our time to remind us of the importance of cultivating human community. Just as we have narrowly defined being human, so we have formed an idea of community that is exclusively based on the values of rationality and productivity. L'Arche refutes such an exclusive view and stands for the just inclusion of all—even the weak and powerless—in the community of God's people. L'Arche treats all persons as created in the image of God.

The message of Mr. Vanier's first decade at L'Arche reflects a commitment to justice. We can quite conveniently give the handicapped "things" and institutions to keep them occupied and out of our way. The mentally handicapped, however, do not want our philanthropy, our extras or any part of our abundance. They ask to share in our substance. The gospel demands solidarity with the poor, the willingness to share our lives and communities with them. Jean Vanier and the L'Arche movement live this gospel mandate.

Jean Vanier has shown Christian concern to many persons in the past decade, and although we are humbled before the untiring scope of his generous and concerned ministry, he remains a hopeful sign of the power of gospel values in shaping and transforming at least small pockets of human society. Mr. Vanier's first decade at L'Arche challenges our own handicaps of relying exclusively on our autonomy and control in judging persons and designing our communities. The first ten years of L'Arche can also teach us to accept and cherish more tolerantly the weakness in others and in ourselves.

1. MENTAL RETARDATION

Mental Retardation: What It Is

Mental retardation too often is thought of in terms of the severely retarded who look and act "different." In reality, most of the retarded are mildly affected, with no obvious symptoms. Through education and training, the majority can become self-sufficient citizens.

They are children with few enriching early experiences, youths with levels of functioning too low for employment; adults unable to cope with the demands of sustaining themselves in society.

The retarded in disadvantaged neighborhoods often receive less service from public and private agencies than do the retarded living in other neighborhoods. Services could be greatly improved with the proper planning and leadership.

Some two million retarded persons capable of learning to support themselves need job training and placement services. Even at minimum wages, they have a potential annual earning capacity of $6 billion.

Education:

Public school provisions for the mentally retarded have taken the form of special classes with small pupil-teacher ratios, specially trained teachers and the utilization of a curriculum designed for these specific needs. These educational programs have focused primarily on the trainable (moderately) and the educable (mildly) retarded. The scope has typically included children of school

Facts About Mental Retardation

Level	Age 0-5 — maturation and development	Age 6-21 — training and education
Mild	Often not noticed as retarded by casual observer, but is slower to walk, feed self, and talk than most children.	Can acquire practical skills and useful reading and arithmetic to a third to sixth grade level with special attention. Can be guided toward social conformity.
Moderate	Noticeable delays in motor development, especially in speech; responds to training in various self-help activities.	Can learn simple communication, elementary health and safety habits, and simple manual skills; does not progress in functional reading or arithmetic.
Severe	Marked delay in motor development; little or no communication skills; may respond to training in elementary self-help, e.g., self-feeding.	Usually walks barring specific disability; has some understanding of speech and some response; can profit from systematic habit training.
Profound	Gross retardation; minimal capacity for functioning in sensori-motor areas; needs nursing care.	Obvious delays in all areas of development; shows basic emotional responses; may respond to skillful training in use of legs, hands and jaws; needs supervision.

Adopted from the President's Panel on Mental Retardation. A National Plan for a National Problem: Chart Book, U.S. Department of Health, Education, and Welfare, Washington, D.C., 1963, p. 15.

age, with the program culminating in vocational training preparatory to employment.

In some slum neighborhoods, a large percentage of regular school enrollment will have educational and vocational training needs similar to those of the educable mentally retarded. In these situations the need may not be for more or better special classes but for a generally improved situation in the school. This would include teachers with special training, low pupil-teacher ratios, appropriate materials and equipment, and the addition of supportive services such as psychological and speech therapy services. At the secondary level, primary attention should be given to vocational training for the educable mentally retarded.

Rehabilitation

Although a number of rehabilitation services are needed by the mentally retarded at different stages of life, the sheltered workshop represents the major rehabilitation service with the most general application. Many mildly retarded adults can, with assistance, obtain employment. Others will require the service of a rehabilitation counselor. Still others will need further training prior to entering the competitive world. Few moderately retarded persons will independently obtain employment. In general, they will rely on sheltered workshop employment and/or training.

Adult—social and vocational adequacy	Environmental factors contributing to MR
Can usually achieve social and vocational skills adequate of self-maintenance; may need occasional guidance and support when under unusual social or economic stress.	Lack of early detection. Absence of certain developmental experiences during early childhood.
	Poor health and diet.
	Ineffective education.
	Lack of vocational training and guidance opportunities.
	Inadequate parental stimulus directed toward school.
Can perform simple tasks under sheltered conditions; participates in simple recreation; travels alone in familiar places; usually incapable of self maintenance.	Insufficient education of parents concerning methods of working with their retarded child.
	Inadequate relief to enable the mother to cope with the child's demands.
	Lack of day care facilities which focus on child development.
	Lack of rehabilitation facilities.
	Absence of group living programs for young adults.
	Poor general health of mother.
Can conform to daily routines and repetitive activities; needs continuing direction and supervision in protective environment.	Lack of prenatal care.
	Insufficient medical attention at time of birth.
	Lack of pediatric care during childhood illness.
May walk, need nursing care, have primitive speech; usually benefits from regular physical activity; incapable of self-maintenance.	Lack of pertinent knowledge of child-rearing practices.
	Insufficient access to specialized service of social agencies.
	Failure to apply suitable corrective measures.
	High incidence of accidents.

Facts On Mental Retardation

To What Extent Do the Mentally Retarded Differ from Other People?

Current practice is to classify mentally retarded persons by degree of retardation, using both intellectual and social criteria.

For descriptive convenience the range of possible retardation has been divided into four levels—mild, moderate, severe and profound.

Mildly retarded persons are highly similar to their nonretarded peers, differing primarily in rate and degree of intellectual development. While still young, their retardation is not readily apparent, and these children are not usually identified as retarded until they enter public school. During adulthood, they again tend to lose their identity as mentally retarded when they are absorbed into the competitive labor market and daily community life.

The retardation of moderately retarded persons is more obvious. The developmental delay shown by this group will usually be apparent before they reach school age. However, appropriate opportunities for community-based education throughout the developmental years can prepare moderately retarded individuals to live a satisfying and productive life in the community.

Severely and profoundly retarded persons exhibit the most pronounced developmental delay and frequently have handicaps other than mental retardation. Not many years ago, it was believed that persons in these classifications were destined to a life of complete dependency and helplessness—that they could not learn. However, systematic training efforts have demonstrated clearly that—with few exceptions—severely and profoundly retarded persons can learn to care for their basic needs. They also can perform many useful work activities, with supervision, and can otherwise adapt satisfactorily to normal patterns of life.

How Prevalent Is Mental Retardation in the United States?

An estimated three per cent of the population of the United States—or more than six million individuals—are believed to be mentally retarded.

Slightly more than 100,000 babies born each year are likely to join this group. By 1980, natural population growth is expected to increase the total to more than 6.8 million, unless far-reaching preventive measures can be discovered and employed.

Mentally retarded persons are found among every race, religion and nationality; every educational, social and economic background. The condition is four times more common than rheumatic heart disease and nine times more prevalent than cerebral palsy. It affects 15 times as many people as total blindness. It disables 10 times as many children and adults as polio did before research provided the Salk vaccine. And one out of every 10 Americans has a direct involvement with the problem by virtue of having a mentally retarded person in his or her family.

The vast majority of mentally retarded persons are mildly retarded. They are handicapped members of our society. However, if they are helped to achieve a satisfactory degree of social and vocational independence, they may no longer be labeled as mentally retarded during adulthood.

Although a significant number of moderately, severely, and profoundly retarded children are found and given help in early childhood, many more are overlooked or improperly diagnosed. The infant mortality rate among these groups is suspected to be high but is difficult to document since, frequently, a baby may not clearly show his retardation. Indeed, he may not for months or even years after birth.

Once a mentally retarded child has reached the age of five or six, he has a good chance of achieving a normal life expectancy. In fact, the life expectancy today of mildly retarded persons is about the same as that of nonretarded individuals. For the other levels, particularly profoundly and severely retarded persons, it is substantially less. However, even this trend is being reversed, thanks to antibiotics and other modern lifesaving treatments. For example, statistics concerning the life expectancy of children with Down's Syndrome indicate much greater life expectancy for this group today than 20 or 30 years ago.

ESTIMATES OF RETARDATION BY AGE AND DEGREE—1970

1970 Census	All Ages	Under 21 Years	21 Years and above
General Population	203.2 million	80.5 million	122.7 million
3% General Population Retarded	6.1 million	2.4 million	3.7 million
Profound (IQ below 20) About 1½%	92 thousand	36 thousand	56 thousand
Severe (IQ 20-35) About 3½%	214 thousand	84 thousand	130 thousand
Moderate (IQ 36-51) About 6%	366 thousand	144 thousand	222 thousand
Mild (IQ 52-67) About 89%	5.4 million+	2.1 million+	3.3 million+

What Are the Causes of Mental Retardation?

Mental retardation can be caused by any condition that hinders or interferes with development before birth, during birth or in the early childhood years. More than 200 causes have already been identified, although these account for only about a fourth of all identified cases of mental retardation.

Among the specific identified causes are: rubella (German measles) in the mother during the first three months of pregnancy, syphilis, meningitis, toxoplasmosis, Rh-factor incompatability between mother and infant, lead poisoning in young children, malnutrition and chromosome abnormalities. Among the most common and best known of the latter is Down's Syndrome (Mongolism) which occurs in one out of every 600 babies born and usually results in moderate to severe mental retardation.

A number of inborn errors of metabolism have been identified which, if not treated, can cause damage to the nervous system and hence mental retardation.

6. Facts on Mental Retardation

Physical malformations of the brain or other organs originating in prenatal life may also result in mental retardation directly or indirectly. Examples include hydrocephalus (a blocking of ducts resulting in an accumulation of fluid in the brain) and craniosynostosis (a premature closing of the sutures of the skull).

Inflammation of the brain associated with childhood measles is another cause, now preventable.

As time goes on, more people who were originally placed in the "undifferentiated" category are found to have specific diagnosable causes of their mental retardation. However, even today, no clear diagnosis of cause can be made in the majority of cases, and in most of these there is no demonstrable pathology of the nervous system.

Undoubtedly among the mildly retarded there are many people whose development has been adversely affected by non-specific influences such as inadequate diet, inadequate prenatal and perinatal care and lack of adequate stimulation toward growth and development through learning opportunities.

Mental development, like physical development, is promoted by the right kind of activity and stimulation, and is retarded when it is lacking. Indeed, the two tend to interact. In this process the years of early childhood, when the nervous system is maturing and language developing, are very critical.

How Many Mentally Retarded Persons Are Actually Brain Damaged?

The term "brain damage" has not been adequately defined and is used differently by different people.

Destruction of brain tissue or interference with brain development in the infant or young child frequently produces mental retardation as well as cerebral palsy, convulsive seizures, hyperactivity and perceptual problems.

Such damage accounts for a substantial fraction of moderate, severe and profound mental retardation. Although it cannot be definitely shown in most cases of mild mental retardation, the extent of its contribution is not known, and expert opinion is divided.

Several factors may be at work in the same individual. For example, the premature infant is more vulnerable to brain damage. Prematurity is more common among mothers who receive inadequate prenatal care, and inadequate prenatal care in turn is more common in the underprivileged groups in our society. These same children are also more frequently exposed to inadequate postnatal opportunities for growth and development and to other factors contributing to psychological and cultural deprivation.

The extent of psychomotor, perceptual and sensory handicaps among mentally retarded persons points to common causation in many cases. Most severely and profoundly retarded individuals have pronounced motor handicaps or impairment of hearing, vision or speech, or a combination of these. Although the

1. MENTAL RETARDATION

majority of mildly retarded persons would not be readily identified as physically handicapped, their general level of motor coordination is below average, despite the occurrence among them of a few remarkable athletes.

Is Mental Retardation Preventable?

Progress is being made in the prevention of mental retardation, but it is proceeding, as might be expected, through a succession of small advances across the broad front, rather than by any singular spectacular breakthrough.

Each of the many contributing causes must be analyzed specifically and specific preventive measures devised when the cause has been found.

Progress is being made against some of the more serious forms by such techniques as corrective surgery for malformations of the skull and for the diversion of excess fluid in the brain.

Children who have inadequate blood sugar in the first few critical days after birth are now more readily identified and given corrective treatment.

Damage due to the Rh-factor incompatibility can be prevented by blood exchange in the infant at time of birth and special immunization of the mother.

Quick treatment in cases of lead poisoning or, better yet, action to prevent children from eating paint containing lead can also be effective in preventing some cases.

The measles vaccines — including the vaccine for rubella — can help if widely used.

Some progress is being made in identifying the characteristics of mothers most likely to give birth prematurely, so that this indirect cause of mental retardation may be reduced.

Thus far, however, all of these steps have been effective in eliminating only a relatively small fraction of mental retardation. Increased attention to relevant basic research and to the prompt application of new discoveries is essential to carrying forward this initial progress. Moreover, some of the forms of retardation which stem from physical, emotional or cultural deprivation will yield only to basic social reform.

What Can Be Done for Those Who Are Retarded?

Where prevention has not been effective and retardation has already been established, specialized training and rehabilitation are necessary.

Of the estimated six million retarded persons of all ages who need mental retardation services at sometime during their lives, about three million can be considered "substantially handicapped" in that they have a long-term, continuing need for special services.

Secondary handicaps such as impairment of speech and hearing, seizures, emotional maladjustment and the like must be treated and reduced to the minimum.

Special educational and vocational opportunities must be made available, and help and advice given to parents in managing day to day problems.

All of these efforts must be based on accurate diagnosis at the earliest age level possible.

Among the services which should be available are specialized diagnostic facilities, home nursing programs, parent counseling, specialized nursery and day care centers, special classes in public and other day schools, religious nurture, camping and other recreational programs, vocational training, sheltered workshops, specialized employment services, income maintenance where necessary, foster homes and boarding care, and specialized living arrangements.

Thus, as a cause of lifetime disability and as a social, educational and medical problem of unique extent and complexity, mental retardation presents an outstanding challenge to science and society in the United States and throughout the world.

What Provisions for Mentally Retarded Persons Exist in Residential Institutions?

Approximately 200,000 mentally retarded children and adults now receive around-the-clock supervision, training, and care in residential institutions, most of them under state auspices, in the United States.

There are one or more publicly administered residential facilities in each state, but the quality of care, as well as the capacity, in relation to need, varies markedly from state to state.

Some mentally retarded children and adults are also mentally ill and are therefore cared for in mental hospitals, but in some states admission of mentally retarded persons to mental hospitals has been forced by the shortage of facilities especially designed for retarded individuals. This practice works a hardship not only on the retarded person, but on the program of the mental hospital.

There is a continuing need to improve the quality of care and habilitation provided to residents as well as a need to prevent or terminate institutional care for those for whom community arrangements are more suitable.

The vast majority of the retarded are, and should be, living outside of institutions. They need a wide array of services.

What Other Specialized Services Are Being Offered to Retarded Individuals?

Special classes for retarded persons are known to have reached the million mark. However, we must still conclude that only about 40 per cent of those in need are receiving education services.

Vocational rehabilitation services to retarded individuals have been intensified in recent years. During 1972 about 43,700 mentally retarded persons were employed through the federal-state vocational rehabilitation program.

There are now about 2,500 sheltered workshops

6. Facts on Mental Retardation

in the United States which accept mentally retarded clients. These workshops provide opportunities for training and for long-term sheltered employment which were virtually unavailable to retarded individuals before 1953. There are many communities, however, where this service is still unavailable.

Several hundred specialized diagnostic clinics have been established since 1949. The majority provide specialized diagnostic service using a team of specialists in child development. Most provide for continued parent counseling and some also have adjunctive nursery school and group programs for continued observation and optimal stimulation of the young child.

The provision for day care for children of school age and for activity centers for adults who are too severely handicapped to fit into the special class programs or into competitive or sheltered employment are relatively new and rapidly expanding components of the service system.

What Urgent Steps Are Required Now To Meet the Needs?

1. Research in biomedical fields relevant to prevention and treatment.
2. Research in the behavioral and social sciences relevant to prevention of socio-cultural forms of mental retardation and relevant to techniques of education which will more effectively develop the fullest potentials of which each retarded individual is capable.
3. Orientation of physicians to the early diagnosis and positive management of mentally retarded youngsters in their care.
4. Extension of parent education services to provide practical assistance to mothers in the everyday problems of rearing a mentally retarded child.
5. The extension of specialized diagnostic facilities so that they are reasonably accessible to all population groups in all parts of the country.
6. Extension of public school programs for all retarded children, especially in those states which have heretofore provided inadequate legislative and financial bases for these programs.
7. Recruitment and effective training of approximately 50,000 new teachers.
8. Development of improved techniques for selective placement of the mildly and moderately retarded youth and adult in gainful employment, tied with interpretation to employers of the assets and limitations of the mentally retarded employee.
9. Extension and improvement of opportunities for sheltered employment of those incapable of entering the competitive employment market.
10. Modification of laws governing the civil status of mentally retarded persons.
11. New approaches to protective services, guardianship, social guidance and economic security for the mentally retarded adult who cannot contribute substantially to his own support.
12. Development of diversified residential facilities close to the main stream of community life and professional service and adapted to the various individual needs apparent among the mentally retarded children and adults in need of residential care.
13. Effective planning and coordination of major public and private activities at national, regional, state and local levels.

How Much Is Being Spent on Mentally Retarded Persons Today in the U. S.?

The direct cost to the taxpayer in support of schools, residential institutions and related specialized services amounts to more than $1½ billion a year, a sum which does not include the costs borne by the families of retarded individuals.

Direct subsistence costs in the form of welfare and Social Security payments made to adults disabled by mental retardation exceed $400 million.

These welfare maintenance costs, together with the expense of operating special schools and residential facilities, point up the urgent need for more vigorous preventive measures and efforts to rehabilitate those retarded persons now dependent on such programs and services.

Additional amounts are invested by the federal government in research and professional training, in demonstration projects, and in grants to the states in the service areas. There are now 12 mental retardation research centers which were initiated with federal funds.

The total of $425 million granted in these areas during fiscal year 1972 was matched directly and indirectly by state, local and private funds.

Increasing interest has been shown by many of the governors of the various states in improved planning and diversification of service, with participation by all major departments of state government, in collaboration with local government and with voluntary organizations. This phenomenon is being accelerated by the formation of state planning and advisory councils on developmental disabilities under the federal Developmental Disabilities Services and Facilities Construction Act of 1970. Mental retardation is the most prevalent form of developmental disability.

What Was the President's Panel on Mental Retardation?

In October 1961, President Kennedy appointed 27 professional and civic leaders to make recommendations concerning the scope of the problem of mental retardation in the United States, the major areas of concern that offer the most hope, the resources that must be mobilized, and the relationships between the federal government, the states, and private resources in promoting prevention and amelioration.

1. MENTAL RETARDATION

In response to this mandate the panel presented a report to the President in October of 1962. The report was entitled "A Proposed Program for National Action to Combat Mental Retardation."

The report covered broadly the topics of research in scientific manpower, prevention, clinical and social services, education, vocational rehabilitation and training, recreation, residential care, planning and coordination, legal problems, and public attitudes.

It inaugurated an era of increased federal action in research, prevention, professional training and construction of facilities for the retarded.

What Is The President's Committee on Mental Retardation?

The President's Committee on Mental Retardation was established in May, 1966. The Secretary of Health, Education, and Welfare is chairman; members are the Secretary of Labor, the Director of the Office of Economic Opportunity and 21 distinguished men and women.

The executive order establishing the President's Committee on Mental Retardation assigned it three tasks: 1. To advise and assist the President on evaluation of the adequacy of the national effort to combat mental retardation, coordination of federal activities in the field, liaison between federal activities and those of other public and private agencies, and development of public information to reduce the incidence of mental retardation and ameliorate its effects. 2. To mobilize professional and general public support for mental retardation activities. 3. To report to the President at least annually.

For more information, write directly to: The President's Committee on Mental Retardation, Washington, D. C. 20201.

What Is NARC?

NARC, the National Association for Retarded Citizens, is a voluntary nationwide organization devoted to improving the welfare of mentally retarded persons without regard to race, creed, geographical location or degree of retardation. It provides help to parents, individuals, organizations and communities in jointly solving the problems caused by mental retardation.

It was organized in 1950 by a dedicated group of parents and friends of mentally retarded persons. By mid-1973 it had grown to include more than 245,000 members affiliated with 1,500 state and local member units.

NARC works on the local, state and national level in fostering the advancement of research and ameliorative services, creating increased public awareness of the needs and potential of mentally retarded persons, working with governmental agencies to encourage progressive legislation and its proper implementation, furthering the development of improved residential facilities and employment opportunities for mentally retarded persons, offering guidance to those who need help and those who want to help, reminding all concerned that retarded persons are entitled to the full range of human and civil rights.

What Is Youth-NARC?

Youth-NARC is a national volunteer organization of young people pledged to serve as friends to mentally retarded persons in their own communities and to work in cooperation with the local Association for Retarded Citizens toward the acquisition of services and total citizenship for retarded children and adults.

Organized in 1967, Youth-NARC now has more than 20,000 members between the ages of 13 and 25 in its 43 state member units.

Youth-NARC has focused primarily on direct personal service to mentally retarded individuals. But it also has had as its aims public education, career motivation, governmental affairs and leadership development.

At present, Youth-NARC is trying to effect change in the lives of thousands of mentally retarded individuals. As Youth-NARC has stated in its creed, "We are joined together to learn how to live better, how to work with others and to give of ourselves to serve mentally retarded persons. We believe in the worth of each other and have fun in proving it."

Affective Reactions of Retarded and Nonretarded Children to Success and Failure

CHARLES S. HAYES AND ROBERT J. PRINZ

After performing a simple motor task, 208 mildly retarded and nonretarded girls and boys pointed to photographs of modeled affective facial expressions to indicate how they felt, wished to feel, and thought their teachers would feel about their performance. Children in both IQ groups frequently attributed positive affect to themselves and their teachers after success, although younger retarded children were less positive than were nonretarded children in teacher affect attributions. Following failure, retarded subjects were generally less frequently negative than were nonretarded subjects in affect attributions to themselves and particularly to their teachers. Emphasis on success and minimization of failure in classrooms for retarded children was offered as one possible explanation for the IQ group affect differences following failure.

Zigler (e.g., 1973) has postulated that high levels of failure by retarded persons can affect personality development adversely. The purpose of this study was to examine emotional reactions of retarded and nonretarded children to task performance through use of a nonverbal technique similar to that used by Miller and Gottlieb (1972). Their procedure involved measurement of affect of retarded and nonretarded children through their identification of photos of a boy modeling affective facial expressions. This occurred after their cooperative participation in a ring-toss game with a peer partner and in the presence of the experimenter. A nonretarded child could choose either a retarded or nonretarded child as a partner in the game. A monetary prize was offered for a certain performance level on the game. The children were asked to guess which photo was taken just after the boy pictured completed the task (other frame of reference), indicate which photo represented the way they personally felt after task completion, and which one showed the way they wished they had felt. Actual performance on the game was related to photo choice for the retarded subjects only when they were indicating how the boy in the picture felt and not how they personally felt; the opposite was true for the nonretarded subjects.

Miller and Gottlieb (1972) suggested that retarded persons may be more sensitive to, and capable of identifying, others' feelings toward them than they are in indicating their own feelings. This notion was further examined in the present study. In contrast to the procedure in Miller and Gottlieb's study the children in the present study participated individually on a task, performance outcome was manipulated by the experimenter, and a teacher frame of reference replaced other frame of reference. After performing a simple motor task (coding), 104 educable mentally retarded children from self-contained classes and 104 nonretarded younger and older children (8 to 11 and 12 to 16 years, respectively) pointed to photographs of a 12-year-old boy modeling affective facial expressions (two demonstrating positive affect, three demonstrating negative affect) to indicate how they felt, wished to feel, and thought their teachers would feel about their performance. Equal numbers of girls and boys were each given success and failure trials which were manipulated by the experimenter. In the success condition, the child was allowed to complete the task and receive two

---

This project was supported by a U.S. Public Health Service Grant No. FR05372 awarded to the first author.

1. MENTAL RETARDATION

pieces of chocolate candy. In the failure condition, the child was stopped at a predetermined point before task completion and told he did not finish in time; hence, he could not receive any candy. It was anticipated that the retarded children would show higher performance-affect correspondence (positive affect after success, negative affect after failure) in attributing affect to their teacher than to themselves, as suggested by Miller and Gottlieb (1972). This prediction was not supported, although the pattern of results was informative. After failure, negative self-affective attributions were 93 and 72 percent for nonretarded and retarded subjects, respectively. When the child was asked how he thought his teacher would feel regarding his performance, negative affective choices were 89 and 54 percent for nonretarded and retarded subjects, respectively. When IQ groups were compared according to same sex and age categories through chi square and Fisher's Exact Probability Test, all differences were significant ($ps < .05$), except in the case of older girls for the self- and teacher attributions. Following success, there were no significant IQ-group differences in frequency of affective choices in self-attributions, although younger retarded subjects were significantly less positive in teacher attributions than were chronological age (CA) matched nonretarded subjects in teacher attributions ($p < .05$). Positive affect choices in the self-attribution frame were 91 and 89 percent and in the teacher frame were 96 and 85 percent for nonretarded and retarded subjects, respectively.

There were no significant age or sex differences within each IQ group in affective attributions after success or failure. Effects of order of success and failure trials on affective choices were minimal (2 of 48 comparisons were significant at the .05 level).

After 11 months, the task was repeated with 52 randomly selected retarded subjects (26 girls and 26 boys) to assess stability of findings. A pattern of results emerged which is consistent with that found in the original study. After success, most subjects assigned positive affect to themselves (100 percent for girls and 96 percent for boys) and their teachers (81 percent for girls and 100 percent for boys); but following failure, subjects were not consistently negative in affect attributions to themselves (69 percent for girls and 77 percent for boys) or their teachers (62 percent for girls and 38 percent for boys). Statistical analyses of association (coefficient of contingency, lambda symmetric) were used to determine within-individual consistency of affective choice but yielded equivocal results and were deemed inappropriate because of such factors as small sample size and restricted variance. Thus, only descriptive results follow. Within-individual consistency of affective choices, as assessed by percentages of subjects showing same affective choices (positive or negative) on original measurement and 11 months follow-up, was highest in the self-attribution frame under the success condition (self frame = 92 percent for girls and 89 percent for boys; teacher frame = 73 percent for girls and 77 percent for boys). Consistency of affective choices was generally lower after failure (self frame = 62 percent for girls and 73 percent for boys; teacher frame = 77 percent for girls and 35 percent for boys, the latter being below chance level). A number of factors may account for the lower consistency levels after failure: e.g., low reliability of the measure, changes in the children over the period between measurements, and, in the case of the teacher frame, the problem of youngsters acquiring new teachers. It is impossible to determine the operative variables from these data.

The major finding of an IQ-group difference in reactions to task failure suggests that failure may have less negative impact on retarded than on nonretarded children. Because of the emphasis on success and minimization of failure in classrooms for retarded children, these children may be less inclined to perceive teacher upset or discouragement with their failed performances. It is also possible that some retarded subjects may have denied their actual feelings. Such tendencies have been suggested by Harrison and Budoff (1972). A general inability by many retarded persons to comprehend instructions for photo identification following failed performance does not seem to be a likely explanation of the results in view of the high frequency of positive affective choices by retarded subjects after successful performances. More definitive conclusions, however, await further related research in which investigators should take into account the social-status variable (not systematically controlled in the present study due to sampling restrictions) and attempt to disentangle children's reactions to failure (noncompletion of a task) from reactions to being denied a tangible reward.

Child Development Clinic
University Hospital School
University of Iowa
Iowa City, IA 52242

The Strange Child

After three normal sons, the Ritchies had Gloria. Here is an account of one family's care, loyalty and strains, and of the burden our society puts on such middle-class families

THOMAS J. COTTLE

As a girl, Caroline Ritchie made a promise to have four children like her mother and grandmother. Ideally, there would be two boys and two girls, but it did not matter so long as they were healthy. Every woman probably thinks that way, she used to say, especially when something went wrong with a child in her family. Although no one ever confirmed it, it was said that her mother's mother gave birth to a strange child. Its head, the story went, was enormous, its nose was flat, and its eyes were set so far apart it was difficult to imagine the child being able to focus them. No one in the family, however, knew the fate of the child. Caroline asked her mother many times but answers were not forthcoming. "They had ways of dealing with those kinds of children then," her mother replied. "And besides, why's a little girl like you so interested in things like that? Look at life and be thankful about what's good, what grows up healthy, like you." It was clear from her mother's evasiveness that such a child had been born, but her mother gave no information. "Think about the good, Caroline," she always said. "The bad is for the devil and gossips."

As the years passed, the mystery of the strange baby assumed less importance for Caroline. By the time she married, at 19, she had forgotten about it. Not even her first pregnancy a year later caused the memories to return. In her last month of pregnancy, she was struck by the fear that her child would be born blind. At night, her husband, Charlie Ritchie, had to hold her and try to convince her there was only the slightest chance of blindness.

Charles Ritchie Jr. was born on the day Caroline's doctor had predicted months before. He weighed a little over seven pounds and was in perfect health. He even had a full head of hair.

Maintaining her wish to have four children and buoyed by the easiness of the delivery, Caroline waited barely a year before getting pregnant again. A steelworker, Charles Ritchie protested that his salary was not increasing fast enough to support two children, but Caroline insisted. She warned her husband of the dangers of waiting too long before having children. She was already 21, and most doctors agreed that women should have children before the age of 25. Charles said he thought women could have babies until they were 40.

A second son, Ronald, was born 20 months after Charlie Jr. A healthy, robust baby, his early visitors knew he was destined to become an athlete. Charles was especially pleased by the arrival of his second son. A small salary raise helped in paying doctor bills, and there was talk of the Ritchies moving to a larger apartment.

The move came when Ronald was two. The new apartment was larger and brighter and in a better neighborhood. Everyone in the Ritchie family recognized that Charles and Caroline were moving up. With some of their money problems solved, few were surprised to learn that Caroline was pregnant again. Charles joked that he was aiming for a basketball team; Caroline said she wouldn't quit until they had a girl.

For no apparent reason, Caroline wondered more about this baby than the others. Perhaps it was because she was approaching 25, or because she felt different inside. The doctor tried to assure her that he could find nothing wrong, but one day the recollection of her grandmother's strange child returned. Unable to hide her fright, she began shaking. She felt her heart speeding, and tears rushed into her eyes. Finally, she broke down and cried.

The last two months of pregnancy were filled with fits of anxiety, terrifying dreams and loss of appetite. Charles had to force her to eat and drink enough milk. On several occasions her children found her sitting alone weeping. Their confused looks only made her feel more troubled.

A third son, Howard Riley, was born without problems. Six pounds, bald, red-faced, Howard cried so loudly it made the nurses laugh.

Caroline's relief was almost as exhilarating as the birth itself. She thanked God, her doctor, her mother, her grandmother, even though the woman was dead, her sons and, of course, Charles, the manager of the Ritchie's own baseball team, who already was talking of a fourth. "I may not get the basketball team," he told the doctor,

The Strange Child, Thomas J. Cottle, America, November 15, 1975. ©1975 America Press, Inc.

1. MENTAL RETARDATION

"but one more and I'll have my infield."

Apparently, the talk of a fourth child was serious, for a year and a half later Caroline was pregnant again. The boys were doing well, Charles' job was holding up, so why not try to stretch the luck one last time. But no more children, even if the fourth wasn't a girl.

As with the previous pregnancy, the fantasies of the strange child returned. Afraid to bother anyone, she hid the anxiety and used the concealment of these feelings and her work around the house to account for her excessive fatigue. At last, it was time for the delivery.

Caroline was put to sleep without pain. She awoke hearing the voices of her husband and doctor. A nurse was handing her a daughter, Gloria Myra, and her heart beat quickly.

"You lost your infield," she said to Charles.

"It's better like this. Infields are cheap to get. It's outfields you pay a helluva lot for."

"What about that guy at work with eight boys?"

"Bernardi? I'll tell him it's quality, not quantity. Besides he's only got two boys."

The next morning, with Charles lounging at the end of the bed, he told her what the doctor had said. "There was a chance," Charles began, "that Gloria had sustained a certain amount of brain damage. There was a chance that no noticeable damage had occurred. But there was also the chance that something could go wrong, that development wouldn't be totally normal."

"Like what?" Caroline asked, feeling herself wanting to cry out.

"Like speech, or learning. We have to wait. It could also be nothing. No one knows. The worst it could be is special schools, that's all. It's not the end of the world."

Caroline lay still, her eyes dry, her body feeling as though it had gone dead. "It's the end of the world for that baby," she whispered. "If you aren't normal, there's no sense being alive. Little things are different, even missing a finger or a toe. But, when your brain isn't working, you're a vegetable. No matter what anybody

> 'The child's . . . capabilities were . . . "flawed". . . . It was Caroline's wish that they visit medical specialists, but Charles reminded her that their income allowed for infrequent consultations'

says, you're either a human being or a vegetable, and she's a vegetable!"

Charles tried to comfort her. "It's not true."

"I gave birth to a vegetable."

"We don't know the extent of anything."

"I know. I'm the mother of that child." She wanted to say "strange child."

"I'm the baby's father," Charles said gently.

"It's not the same. You'll never know. There's only one way you know. That child doesn't have a chance. You better face it, we're three for four. Oh, God," she moaned. "What do you tell people? And what do you tell the child? 'You're really fine, baby. It's that all the other kids in your class are weird.' Why didn't they tell me months ago?"

"How could they know?"

"They know! They just don't like doing abortions. They make sure the baby comes out. What do they care if it's a vegetable? Once that baby leaves the hospital, they don't give a damn about it."

"I doubt it," Charles snapped.

"I don't. I know."

"Yeah," he said bitterly, "you're the mother."

"Of a vegetable."

"We don't have the faintest idea what's going to be with her," he said at last. "There's a lot of kids with problems, you don't even know there's anything wrong with them."

"You remember I told you about having babies after 25?" she continued, not hearing a word he said. "It was my mistake. I pretended it wasn't true. I should have called a halt to that idea of four children. It was this whole childish thing with me. I had to have four children."

"What do you want to do?" Charles finally exploded. "You want me to go in there and kill the baby? How about I kill the kid *and* the nurse. That make you feel better?"

"You want to know something? It might be the best thing we've ever done. It sure is better than spending the rest of your life mothering a vegetable."

"Anybody can be a mother when the baby is healthy," Charles said before leaving. "Anybody can be good with kids like ours. Real mothers are made when things like this happen. I made my peace with it the second I knew. You're going to have to do the same."

There was nothing in Gloria's first year that signaled trouble. Early in the second year, Caroline noticed that the child's utterances seemed peculiar. Certain reactions too were slow. By the end of two years, it was evident that the child's language and learning capabilities were, in Caroline's word, "flawed," but the Ritchies had to wait until the child's development unfolded more. It was Caroline's wish that they visit medical specialists throughout the city, but Charles reminded her that their income allowed for infrequent consultations.

Gloria turned four in the same year that Caroline reached 30. The child seemed happy, although her speech was slow and often incomprehensible. Ronald acted as an interpreter, but he, too, became exasperated when he could not understand his sister. Charles remained constant. The seriousness of his daughter's condition distressed him, but he hid his fright and sadness. He began investigating various placement possibilities, but, without state support, he had to settle for a public school.

Unable to decide on an appropriate course of action, Caroline kept Gloria from school until she was five, when she entered the neighborhood kindergarten her brothers had attended. Pleased that the school accepted Gloria, the Ritchies barely fretted over Gloria's discomfort in the first weeks of kindergarten. Gradually, she hardly noticed her mother leaving the kindergarten room.

By Christmas, however, it was obvious that she needed more help than the school could provide. The kindergarten class had been unusually large, the principal told Caroline and

8. The Strange Child

Charles. Perhaps everyone had underestimated how handicapped the child actually was. Caroline heard the word "handicapped" as though someone had shot her in the face. She had never used the word to describe Gloria, and yet she could not disagree with the principal. The child was handicapped.

Inevitably, the Ritchies withdrew Gloria from school. The child seemed unperturbed by the action. Caroline, waiting for some response of disappointment, fell into a sadness on recognizing Gloria's inability to demonstrate normal emotional responses. Until that point, she and Charles had concentrated on the muscular and cognitive weaknesses. They simply had not seriously considered the possibility that the damage to Gloria's brain had affected her feelings.

The kindergarten experience represented the first tangible failure. Believing school would reveal the problems that would haunt Gloria's life, Caroline had bypassed the opportunity to send the child to a neighborhood nursery, despite the urging of its director. "Many mothers," the director had said, "are afraid of retardation and brain damage. But, more than anything, they're afraid to watch their child in school. As long as they keep the child at home, nobody's around to make comparisons. You can always say the child's behind her older brothers because she's younger. Parents even tell themselves: 'Maybe she's all right after all. Maybe I just forgot how long it took my other children to talk and read.' But, once they get the child in school and pit her against normal boys and girls, they realize where they stand."

Caroline trusted the director but never enrolled Gloria in the school. So nursery school was forfeited, and a year later the kindergarten experience, too, had ended. Caroline could justify Gloria's not going to school by claiming she had more time to strengthen the child's confidence. Charles, however, accused Caroline of being relieved that the school had rejected the child. Caroline denied it, but she had reached the point of wishing that Gloria would stay small, so that people would think she was too young for school.

When it was time for first grade,

> **'Everything was shabby and an ugly odor filled the room. Charles retired to the men's room where he vomited on the floor. . . . He left the hospital without seeing the schoolroom again'**

Caroline again registered Gloria in kindergarten. This time, she was openly refused admission. The Ritchies would have to try elsewhere. Upset by the rejection, Caroline tried to get Gloria admitted into other kindergartens, but administrators wondered why she had waited so long. One school rejected Gloria on the grounds that it was not in the Ritchies' home district. Another said there was space for Gloria but withdrew their acceptance when they saw the child was handicapped. A third school offered a tentative acceptance for the following year. The only remaining options were two private institutions with exorbitant tuition fees. When Charles heard what his share would be, even after partial state support, he never bothered to call either school. Gloria would remain home another year and face the possibility of never attending any school.

Hiding his last hope from his wife, Charles Ritchie called several mental hospitals. He visited one of them and found it to be more pleasant than he had imagined. But when he inquired about costs, he heard a figure of over $6,000 a year. He had been misadvised. The school was not public. Driving home, Charles found himself weeping.

A week later, he visited another hospital. This time he called in advance and inquired about expenses. The grounds of the second hospital were especially lovely, the offices not unlike the public school he himself attended. When offered to be shown around, Charles insisted on seeing only the school for special children. "It's like college," Charles told himself. "Like these big colleges with famous football teams."

After passing through locked corridors, high-walled courtyards and rooms that looked like dormitories, he reached the classroom. The room was huge, poorly lit and empty of color. Many of the children were sick in a way he had never seen. Some, wearing helmets, sat in the middle of the room on little chairs rocking. Others sat on the floor perfectly still. Some paced aimlessly back and forth, and one boy kept running into a padded wall. Everything was shabby and an ugly odor filled the room. Charles retired to the men's room where he vomited on the floor. He refrained from washing his face and rinsing out his mouth for fear of touching the sinks. He left the hospital without seeing the schoolroom again.

There was no need to visit the last hospital on his list if it was worse than this one. Nor would he tell Caroline of his excursions. She had made the right decision, he told her. Hospitals weren't for them unless they had a million dollars.

"Does that mean" she asked, "you don't disapprove of me as Gloria's mother?"

As was now his practice, Charles drank with friends after work. Caroline never mentioned this new behavior, but it was clear to everyone in the family. Charles, of course, was aware of the frequency of his drinking. The experiences involving Gloria had begun to eat away at him. He felt hopeless, not only about her, but about his own life as well. Night after night, he lay awake barely able to endure the anxiety and restlessness. Playing with the boys, once a source of pleasure, had become a burden. Just watching Gloria tediously working on a puzzle made him feel angry and useless. Within a short time she would turn seven. In all these years, she had attended school less than four months.

"I sit there night after night and watch her," he said to me, a friend of several years, on the eve of Gloria's birthday. "I dread the weekends when I have to be home with the four of them all day. Anybody can see why I drink. I told my wife the day the child was born I'd made peace with her condition. The doctor could have told me, by the time she was four, she'd be a vegetable, a hulk, lying in the middle of the living room, and I would have said that's all right with me. She isn't that bad off. Next to the children I

1. MENTAL RETARDATION

saw that day in the hospital, she's normal. You can't believe how terrible those kids out there look. There are degrees to this thing, you know.

"You can live with a retarded, brain-damaged, handicapped child, whatever you want to call them. My boys live with it. Believe me, I see it. They don't want to tell you how they're feeling, but every once in a while they'll say: 'Daddy, is she ever going to be all right? Is she ever going to get better?' They have the courage to ask questions their parents would like to ask. So I can live with it. But, when something like this school business happens, it's not only the child you think about. That's only part of the situation. *You're* the situation. If you're strong, there's no sick child in the world can make you see yourself any other way. You just stick it out as long as it takes, the rest of your life, if need be. The birth of my sons was like a sign that everything was good. Marriage was good, my job was good. But Gloria's coming into the world—and we wanted her—she was a sign that things weren't going to be so good anymore.

"That child came, seven years ago tomorrow afternoon. Know what I was thinking about in the hospital? How's your wife, how's the child and how you going to pay the bills? God forbid something could happen to your wife or your child—you could be faced with burying both of them, but you'd have to come up with the money. Somebody hits me with a couple of thousand dollars in bills, where do I go? And let's say you come up with this money. Where do I get the money for the next bill? Here comes a retarded, handicapped kid into my home, here she is, day after day showing us how bad it's really going to be. The doctor knew what we'd be getting, only he didn't think it was best to tell us. So there she comes and I'm sick about it inside, and my wife is sick about it. But she comes into the world and every day now is a reminder that *I'm* the one who's handicapped. She's the one everybody can see having problems, but I'm the one who's less well off than most of the men in this world.

"The days I visited those hospitals were what settled everything. When I saw those kids banging their heads against the walls, that was it. If you don't have the money for a good situation, you end up putting your kid in a room like that one, which I swear wasn't good enough for an animal. So now I walk around wondering what to do with my kid. When someone asks, I tell them Gloria goes to school, and she's happy, and we're real pleased. Nothing less than that. I lie, and I drink. We've denied the problem with that child from the beginning. We both had in mind that you can pretend either there's nothing wrong with her, or whatever is wrong will go away. Magic. One day everything's supposed to turn out fine. So here we are with a seven-year-old kid who's handicapped. I hate the word, but you can't pretend things are different. Children pretend, adults deny, somewhere in between is the man who drinks!"

Caroline Ritchie would not say she had denied "the problem," although she admits to wishing she could run away from it. She berates her husband for his weakness, but she understands his sense of failure and hopelessness. The seven years with Gloria have had their moments of happiness, confusion, bitterness. She wants to love the child, but she wants to blame her, too.

"In the beginning," she said soon after Gloria's seventh birthday, "I reacted foolishly. I confess to wishing the baby had been born dead. I told Charles but he refused to listen. The nurses hated me for saying it. They must have thought I was deranged. It was strange, because, even though I was saying it, I really didn't mean it. It was like I felt I had to let people think, not only was she not a part of me anymore, she'd never been a part of me. If I pretended to kill Gloria, I could kill myself, or the part of me that made her what she was.

"Then there was the part about the strange child, my sweet little leftover from childhood. It was like the reason I held onto that memory was because it was being arranged that *I* would have the strange baby. All during my third pregnancy, something inside me told me that I had to keep thinking something would happen so that nothing *would* happen. It was like I had to let all these little demons dance around so I could kill them. But I knew nothing would happen. At least deep down inside I didn't think anything would.

"But the fourth child brought out too many old superstitions. First was the feeling that I'd had three and things had gone too well. Then I decided that the 'strange child' memories and my desire to have four children was going to produce the bad magic. There are times when I still have the wish that Gloria had never been born, but then there are times when I'm glad she was born—retarded, I mean. I took her to the circus about a year ago. I remember at intermission we went to buy food and I felt great, like I had discovered a new source of energy in myself. She was six then, and everybody who looked at us could see there was something wrong. But it didn't bother me. In fact I was glad she was like that. It was like I was saying to them, you think she's handicapped, but I think she's special. I wouldn't trade her for all the healthy children in the world. I wouldn't even trade her for a healthy her. This is the way she was born, this is the way she was meant to be.

"Those feelings don't last long, though. Sometimes I'll imagine making Gloria famous. You know the ads with

8. The Strange Child

a movie star and a crippled child? I imagine that Gloria could do that. Or sometimes I'll pretend that I've started a crusade for brain-damaged children and people vote me the mother of the year. One minute I want her dead, the next minute I'm using her to become famous. Maybe both these feelings are part of the same thing. Maybe they're signs that I was shocked, disappointed. But you can't blame anybody, and you don't like telling people what's happened. You tell your husband, 'It's you and me, Buster, how do you like what we just made? Pretty super, isn't she?'

"I suppose the worst people are the ones in school. I always think they're blaming me for the way I'm treating her. I always want to tell them, I'm really a good mother. You should see me when I'm alone with her. Why don't you blame her? She makes my life hard, too, you know. I don't put her out of my head like you teachers can do with students. You go home in the afternoon and forget the children, but we're with them all the time. I could have taken Gloria to the doctor more often, but every time I go he always says there's nothing I could have done any different. The big things they advise cost a lot of money, so, we do what we can. But I don't see where these school people have the right to judge us the way they do, or at least the way I imagine they do. They don't take her. They've got all the excuses in the world why she doesn't fit in. Everywhere I go they have all the best advice for me, but nobody says, sure, we'll take her and help her to learn.

"I think about having more children. I'd like to know whether it would happen again. I know that statistics say I'd probably have a normal baby, but we'll never find out. I used to have a fantasy that Charles and I would have a baby. Nobody would know that I was pregnant. We'd go away where nobody knew us. Then the baby would be born, and it would be a girl and we would name it Gloria, naturally. Then we'd wait a few years and come back and show everybody our real daughter Gloria. I don't know what we'd do with a seven-year-old girl, so nobody would see us with two daughters. Maybe we'd put her in a hospital somewhere and let the state take care of her, like you see those people with psychotic children doing. They don't want their children, so they deposit them in these horrible places and tell the people they'll come back and pick their children up when they're cured, but everybody knows they'll never come back.

"I don't have to hide the fact that I was crushed by this. I'm a good mother. I got over the first shock. You never forget about a handicapped child's situation, but you live with it until it only bothers you at certain times. At night sometimes, when I'm alone, it gets bad. Or sometimes when I'll see a large family pile out of station wagon I'll find myself watching, waiting for the handicapped one to get out. Anyway, most of the time I've got everything under control. You have four children and a husband and an apartment that's too small, and not enough money. You have a tough job. But I had it licked. You know what set me back? The schools. I'd always counted on them. I assumed, when we took Gloria to get her registered, there'd be no more problems. I even waited. I didn't send her to nursery school, thinking it would be easier to have her home. I thought a child like her is especially sensitive, and I didn't want her to feel people were shipping her off so they didn't have to be with her. But school lasted a few months and fell apart. Actually, they kept her out. They could have kept her, but they didn't want to. They said they didn't have the proper facilities. That's a lot of bunk if you ask me. If you want somebody, you take them; if you don't, you don't.

"I go up and down with Gloria. Sometimes I feel everything's going to be fine, but sometimes I'm ready to quit. I read all the books on retardation and brain-damaged children, technical books along with the magazine articles on parents like us. I know there are experts all over, especially in cities. If Gloria were in good hands, I'd feel optimistic. It's like when the man comes to fix the stove. You know it's going to cost something, but the moment he comes you begin to feel better. Just his coming makes you feel better. I'd feel the same way if we could get Gloria placed somewhere. God, anywhere. Right now, nothing's being done. Doctors can't do anything. Schools have all kinds of excuses. So you feel it inside. You're the person who broke the stove, and the stove's still broken. Gloria's being loved, but she's not making progress. Our whole family's not making progress.

"I suppose what gets me more than anything is what she thinks about. You can tell she understands a lot. We're careful about what we say in front of her. I mean, we don't talk about her condition to her face. But once I'd like to know: Does she really understand how she is? She has to be in school. Someone has to accept her, or she'll never know anything, not only about the world, but about herself. And also, I won't think I'm doing my best until she's in the right place. I always tell myself that none of this with school would have happened if we were rich. But maybe that's not true. Maybe that's what brings people together. Rich or poor or like us, in between somewhere, we can all share this thing. Then again, the rich find places for their children, and here we are having every school say no. So we're doubly worse off. It's like we're lepers that people are afraid to let come near them.

"My child deserves a lot more than that. *We* deserve a lot more. We have a right to have that child in school. I won't bring up the 'we pay taxes too' argument, but we have a right by token of living where we live. Our child has a right, too, although some people seem to think she doesn't. They're adding to her handicap, you know. People can carry on by themselves for a little while, but then they need the society to help them the rest of the way. This child needs even more help than most children, and all they're doing is pulling away from her. And we're running after anybody who'll help. It's so absurd it's almost laughable. I wonder why we don't laugh. If we started laughing Gloria would laugh. She laughs a lot."

[Thomas J. Cottle *has written several articles that have appeared in* **America** *including "A Child's Evolution" (3/29). He is affiliated with the Children's Defense Fund of the Washington Research Project, Cambridge, Mass.*]

KATHERINE WANTS TO GO TO SCHOOL SATURDAY, SUNDAY, AND ALL THROUGH SUMMER

By Katherine H. Berg

If you're a "polite person," you won't ask, "How can you stand having a retarded child like Katherine?" You'll smile quietly as you watch her run like a penguin, using her arms for balance. And as you try to make sense out of her jumbled speech, you'll think, "I'm glad she's not mine."

Katherine is a curly-haired, affectionate six-year-old who functions like a four-year-old because of brain damage. She was five when she learned to climb on the toilet by herself. At that age she also learned how to put a sentence together. "Keep doggie in gate," she said one day. "He get out, be dead."

Have I always loved her? No. When she was two I used to get very depressed watching her play with Raphael and Michael, the twins next door. As they dashed after rubber balls and climbed fences, Katherine would curl her shoulders, squint her eyes, and sit in the sandbox sucking her thumb. Obviously she was different, and her apathy hurt me. And when I felt tired, frustrated, and worried about her, I would cry. Then I'd feel her small hand touch my tears and pat my cheeks.

It's this tenderness of Katherine's that makes me love her. Her stutters and contorted words sometimes bring pain, which is mixed with joy as I watch her struggle patiently with knee socks in the morning before she climbs on the school bus.

Until five years ago retarded children were pretty much forgotten and unloved by everyone except their parents and certain medical and educational specialists. Thoughts like "we don't want our kids going to school with them," or "they have the brains of a fly, so why spend money trying to teach them?" prevailed.

Retarded children between three and five years of age invariably played at home; few nursery schools or kindergartens would have them.

Then, when a retarded child turned six, he or she could go to school only if the school system was large enough and progressive enough to have special education classes. (Children with IQs of 50 to 70 attend EMR classes — Educable Mentally Retarded; those with IQs between 30 and 50 attend TMR classes — Trainable Mentally Retarded; those with IQs of 30 or below are severely retarded and, after three to five years on a waiting list, usually enter a state school and hospital.)

In the last five years parental and professional pressure on state and federal governments has spurred new laws. For instance, at the national level, we now have a Supreme Court decision that says local school systems must provide classes for retarded children. And in Georgia, our home state, two other relatively new laws have begun to make a difference.

"The Mandatory Education Law of 1969" said that by 1975 all retarded children in Georgia must be in public school programs. And "The Mandatory Community Services Act of 1972" created day-care centers for the severely retarded and those with emotional and behavioral problems.

Most states, happily, now have similar laws. And most school systems are now seeking financial assistance to set up preschool programs for the retarded, who learn slowly and require constant repetition of new material. For them, an early start is necessary.

Katherine started attending her school and training center for TMR children when she was four. In the three years she has been there she has learned to recognize colors and the letters of the alphabet, and to read twenty words. She knows her full name, sings songs like "Row, Row, Row Your Boat," and can play, though not perfectly, with jumping jacks and other toys. These are tremendous achievements for her, deeds she'd have difficulty accomplishing without school.

But Katherine has also learned other things, far more important than reading, at school. She has discovered, you see, that she is a little girl whom people *love*.

Most teachers who work with retarded children create a classroom steeped in praise, love, and patience. There's little pressure for perfection.

For example, Katherine and her classmates are applauded when they count to ten and it sounds like "one-do-tee-our-ive-six-even-ate-nine-den." There is a speech therapist who works with each child, but inside the classroom self-confidence and self-direction are stressed.

The classroom is like a mini-neighborhood or maxi-family group, and Katherine learns a lot about social interaction there. If Chris hits her, she cries. And when Chris hears her sob, he runs over to hug her. But his initial blow will probably keep her from taking his mittens again.

Is your initial question still lingering? Are you thinking that, no matter how good it is, school will never make Katherine speak or act normally?

You're right, of course.

But if school is filled with happy experiences for her, and if it helps her prepare for a job when she reaches sixteen, then the school is doing its job. It's creating a happy retarded child — and that's all I, her mother, can ask.

Katherine H. Berg is on the executive committee of the Monte Sano Public School PTA in Augusta, Georgia.

DESIGNING A SPECIAL PLAYGROUND

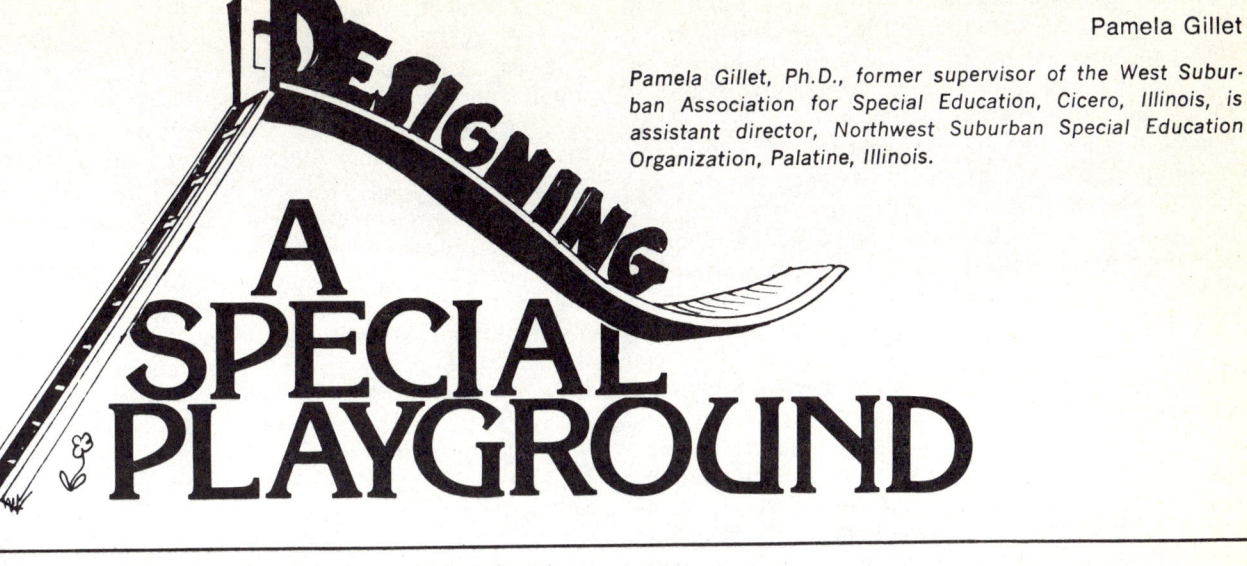

Pamela Gillet

Pamela Gillet, Ph.D., former supervisor of the West Suburban Association for Special Education, Cicero, Illinois, is assistant director, Northwest Suburban Special Education Organization, Palatine, Illinois.

Student architects begin construction of the special playground they designed for children at the West Suburban Center for Special Education.

In recent years many innovative techniques have been employed to enhance children's school environment. Classrooms for special education and open space learning environments have been designed, and new teaching aids and devices have been developed to help teachers individualize instruction to meet the needs of each child. However, these imaginative advances have focused primarily on the classroom environment, while the outdoor environment—the playground where children also learn and play during the school day—has remained largely unchanged.

After a series of faculty discussions, teachers in one specialized suburban Chicago school decided that it was time to focus on transforming the traditional asphalt playground, with its few remote, concrete structures, into an innovative, outside learning area. The school, the West Suburban Center for Special Education in Cicero, Illinois, is supported through eight public school districts in the western suburbs of Chicago. Any trainable mentally handicapped child or any preschool multiply-handicapped child living within these school districts can attend the Center. In February 1974, when plans for the playground were being formulated, there were 108 children enrolled.

Staff members felt that the use of the new playground should contribute to achieving the objectives of the school's curriculum, yet allow each teacher the

1. MENTAL RETARDATION

flexibility to incorporate his or her individual goals and creativeness. We believed that the playground, in addition to providing an inviting atmosphere for recreational and creative play, should also be designed to foster the children's intellectual and social development and strengthen their physical abilities. Children's playground experiences should enhance the development of receptive and expressive language skills, too, and facilitiate their use of verbal communication to express their needs and feelings. Finally, we felt that it should be structured to promote the children's independence by enabling them to manipulate their environment.

After these ideas were formulated, we directed our attention to the actual physical plan and structural components of the proposed playground. How would we prepare a ground plan for the placement of the playground structures? How would the structures be built? What construction materials would best meet our standards for safety, durability and ease of maintenance? Architectural assistance was definitely needed.

As is true in most school districts, the allocated playground budget was minimal and prohibited our using a professional architectural firm. We decided to contact the Department of Architecture at the University of Illinois, Chicago Circle Campus, which had consulted with other groups who were developing community outdoor recreational areas. R. Thomas Jaeger, an instructor in the Architectural School, agreed to give us assistance in developing the special playground and, a few weeks later, the first orientation meeting was held with our staff, Professor Jaeger and the 80 freshman architecture students who elected to work on this project.

Center staff members conducted a series of short lecture and discussion classes for the students to familiarize them with the characteristics of the children at the center in terms of their language and social, motor and intellectual development, and to discuss the objectives of the school's curriculum in relation to playground activities. The students also visited the Center in small groups, to observe and interact with the children in their daily routine. Staff members and student architects also accompanied the children on field trips to various parks and playgrounds to note the children's reactions to the various structures and to see how they negotiated activities on them.

After several more discussion sessions, the students built and presented to staff members a variety of models for the playground. Each student explained the anticipated uses of the structure he or she had designed and the reason for its layout. Discussion covered such considerations as fire ordinance restrictions; composition and variety of the materials used; height, strength, safety, durability and maintenance re-

A stationary, wood fire engine, painted bright red, is one of the most popular areas of the new West Suburban Center playground.

10. A Special Playground

quirements of the structures; landscaping of the play areas; feasibility of staff supervision of the children on the playground; and the provision of safe and attractive pedestrian walks throughout.

The students then spent several weeks working to combine their existing models into three final projects. Again, the staff was invited to meet with the students and a final playground plan was decided upon. It called for a creative structure approach to allow the children freedom of choice to negotiate the structures at will—for example, being able to crawl under steps as well as to walk up them. Traditional swings, ropes and seesaws were incorporated in the plan to enable the children to transfer learned skills on the school playground to playgrounds in their own communities. Materials and structures which would facilitate instruction in tactile differentiation and sensory stimulation, as well as academic and motor experiences, were included.

To supplement the allocated budget, Center staff members solicited donations of lumber, gravel, shrubbery, paint and other materials from various community sources. Many generous persons answered our requests and we were able to begin the actual construction in May 1974. The architecture students and several staff members worked weekends to turn railroad ties, 2 x 4s, gallons of paint, gravel, sand and an assortment of trees into an appealing playground that would delight all the children.

The completed playground is divided into six distinct areas; an asphalt bicycle path, along which appropriate traffic signs are mounted, harmoniously connects and integrates the separate areas. This arrangement permits some children to ride on vehicles while others use the stationary structures without interfering with each other's activities. The six areas include:

☐ A large fort made from railroad ties with many levels of steps for climbing and crawling and ample space underneath for crawling and digging. A platform on the structure may be used for play productions, singing and other activities.

☐ A stationary, wood fire engine painted bright red, which encourages climbing, role-playing and manipulating.

☐ Two small, open-sided, wooden play houses, which provide gathering areas, opportunities for hide and seek and role-playing activities—or a quiet place for a child to be alone.

☐ A sun-shaded area, equipped with a large wooden clock and a variety of colorful, labeled cutout shapes—an ideal place to conduct a group art or language activity or to have a quiet class luncheon.

☐ A traditional playground area, with swings, seesaws, ropes and cement animals, to enable the children to learn motor skills and to provide opportunities

Student volunteers in the Department of Architecture at the University of Illinois, Chicago Circle Campus, designed and built new structures for a play area at the Center for Proviso Area Exceptional Children.

1. MENTAL RETARDATION

Above and opposite page: The large, brightly-colored numbers on the Proviso Area Center playground form structural supports for the equipment—and also enclose good hiding places.

10. A Special Playground

for developing interpersonal relationships (learning to share and to take turns, for example).

☐ A small structure made of railroad ties for the youngest children so that they can begin developing such skills as climbing, riding, running, jumping, crawling and bending in an environment that is not threatening to them.

A planted area complements the overall landscape design. Here children can also take part in horticultural activities and observe the growth of plants and seasonal changes in plant life.

Throughout all areas of the playground a wide variety of textures and materials can be examined and contrasted.

These six areas make the playground more than a play area. It is an extension of the total classroom. Teachers can prepare plans that will involve children in activities to enhance their motor skills and sensory perception, stimulate langauge development and understanding of concepts and help them develop greater self-awareness. Shapes, colors, textures, positional and functional words, time concepts, numbers, letters and traffic signs can all be taught through the use of the various areas of the playground.

Activities to develop social awareness and interpersonal relationships do not have to be "planned"; they just naturally occur on the playground, which also provides a healthy outlet for a child's tension.

Specific lesson plans for use with this special playground can be developed. The lesson plan can include, for example, the specific objective and the skill to be taught, generally in the motor area; the playground area and structures or other materials involved; the procedure; the reinforced learning aspects (counting, telling time, reading signs, identifying textures, etc.); and evaluation activities.

The playground at the West Suburban Center has also served as a model for others who are interested in creating special play areas. For example, at the request of a teacher who had visited the West Suburban Center, Professor Jaeger and 50 architecture students designed and recently completed an outdoor play area for the Center for Proviso Area Exceptional Children in Maywood, Illinois. One unusual feature of this playground is the use of large, brightly-colored numbers to form the structural supports for slides, stairs, ramps and suspension bridges.

Our original objective of providing a special playground has been fulfilled—and the playground has provided many hours of fun and instruction for children at the West Suburban Center. As teachers modify the playground, based on evaluations of its use, it is hoped that the special playground will continue to amuse, stimulate and delight all the children.

Whose Child Is This?

Anonymous

Dooter was a strange, solitary, proud little boy who seemed different from the others. Yet like all the children who played in our back yard, he needed love and had love to give. Unlike them, Dooter had a very special lesson to teach us all

Children's voices, shrill and taunting, cut through the sleepy summer afternoon. They momentarily drowned out the contented bird chatter and lazy crow calls, falling like stones around the heels of a small boy beating a dogged retreat across our front lawn.

"Go home, Dooter!" "Doo-oo-ooter's retarded! Doo-oo-ooter's retarded. . . ."

At the far end of the lawn the boy dropped to the ground beneath the sickly pine tree we had planted there. He was small; I judged him to be about eight years old. From my window I could see his sturdy shoulders wrenched with sobs. I ran out to him.

"Honey, are you hurt?"

He looked up, his tear-filled blue eyes defensive.

"Are you hurt, honey?" I repeated, but he did not answer. He dropped his eyes to his dirty bare feet, kicked his toe brutally hard against the grass for a full minute and then solemnly and with great dignity rose and walked away.

That was my introduction to Dooter. His family had moved into a house two doors from us a few days before. I knew nothing about them, but apparently the neighborhood children had lost no time in getting acquainted.

My husband and I love children—the troublesome little creatures. Our brood of six healthy and active youngsters, from our two-year-old to our 13-year-old, make up a gregarious clan. It was inevitable, therefore, that our back yard had become the unofficial playground for the street. I had fallen into the role of neighborhood baby sitter, dispensing endless handouts of water, cookies, bandages and tissues. (There were, I admit, rare occasions when I would feel a twinge of envy on glancing from my window to see a group of mothers quietly enjoying coffee on a neighboring patio while their children created havoc in our back yard.)

My first encounter with Dooter left me disturbed. I had become judge and jury in cases of outright hostility, and no one questioned my supreme right to command. Only occasionally did I have to resort to the old "If you can't get along, you'll have to go home" routine. In Dooter's case, though, matters had been taken out of my hands.

The second encounter with Dooter was even less auspicious than the first. The older boys had a game of miniature golf going in the back yard. The girls were playing with the baby in the sandbox by the kitchen window.

Dooter entered the yard. Roy, our eldest son, asked if he wanted to play. Dooter glanced stoically at the boys, shrugged and darted off. He soon returned, carrying his own golf club. He stepped into the game abruptly, struck viciously at the ball, missed it entirely and cut into the ground.

"Hey, wait your turn!" someone protested.

Dooter turned without a word and walked away.

Only moments later I heard the baby shriek. A wave of loud and vociferous indignation rose as the back-yard world rushed to her rescue. I ran outside as our ten-year-old daughter staggered toward me, carrying the shrieking baby.

"He just hit her! For no reason, he just hit her with the golf club!"

My heart pounded from fear, indignation, disbelief. I examined the baby. There was a small bump on the side of her forehead where the club had grazed her.

Trembling at the realization that a fraction of an inch had averted tragedy, I turned to Dooter. The children were still shrieking in outrage. Through it all Dooter stood impassively, his eyes inscrutable, emotionless. But his small frame seemed to be braced for resistance from whatever corner attack might come at him.

I was both horrified and angry.

"Why did you do that, Dooter?" I demanded.

He did not answer.

"You hurt the baby. Why would you do that?"

He stood stiff, silent. I stared at him. Now that I knew the baby was safe, I was becoming calm enough to be anxious about his attitude.

"Are you mad at the baby?" I asked.

"No," he said. It was the first word I had heard him speak, and his voice was surprisingly deep and gruff.

"Then why would you hit her? She wouldn't hurt you. Do you understand, Dooter?"

His gaze never faltered. Unblinking, unyielding, he studied me a moment longer. Then he turned and majestically stalked away. His attack had been without malice; somehow I knew that.

The next day when Dooter came, I could hear some of the neighborhood children ordering him to go home. "You can't play with us. My mother said you're retarded."

I will never fathom the mind of a mother who can tell her child such a truth without explanation. To do so is to arm him with a weapon of which he has no understanding. Before I could reach the yard Dooter was gone—a solitary but strangely proud little figure trudging heavily down the street, looking straight ahead.

That was the day I held a powwow with our children, my stanch allies. When I told them my conclusions about Dooter and that I believed he had not meant to hurt the baby, their sympathy for him was quick in coming. I have found that children have an infinite capacity for compassion.

Then we called the other children to the patio. I tried to explain that we all are born different, and described Dooter's problem to them as simply as I could. We let them know that Dooter could play in our yard and that those who wanted to play there also would have to be responsible for seeing that he hurt no one and was not hurt himself.

As time passed, the children accepted Dooter more and more fully. It grew increasingly evident that he did not understand pain or seem to feel it as keenly as others. One day our ten-year-old rushed breathlessly into the kitchen.

"Mama! Dooter's hurt. He fell off his bike and he won't go home. He's bleeding all over."

I rushed outside. There was Dooter, stretched on the lawn chair, blood oozing from one side of his forehead, an elbow angry and raw, one knee cut and bleeding.

"Oh, Dooter." I surveyed the damage. "You really hurt yourself."

11. Whose Child Is This?

"Don't hurt," Dooter growled in his strangely mature voice.

"You'd better go home and let your mother put some medicine on those places," I advised him.

"Ain't there," Dooter muttered.

The children explained that both his mother and his stepfather worked and that his grandmother was watching him.

"Well, go let your grandmother doctor you," I said.

"Don't hurt," he said firmly, unmoving.

The outcome was that we "doctored" Dooter, amid great outpourings of admiration and sympathy from the children. Dooter sat unflinchingly through my ministrations. He did not shrink even when the Merthiolate hit his raw knee.

After that Dooter seemed to welcome his frequent skirmishes with fate—bruises from a bicycle spill, a nick from his pocket knife, a fall from a tree. He would appear at the door, bruised and bleeding, waiting confidently for expressions of consternation and ministering, pointing with an air of triumph and then announcing brusquely, "Cut myself" or, "Hurt my hand."

Dooter was not an eight-year-old, as I had first surmised, but 12. In the two years that he lived near us, we all grew to love this gruff-voiced little boy, and to our children he became a solemn, challenging part of the family. They did not give in to him on matters of "social conscience," however. He had to abide by the same rules as everyone else. In games and sports he began to prove unexpectedly dexterous, and was soon a vital part of any game.

And he learned to hold his own in a civilized fashion, appearing at the door from time to time like all the others with complaints that, "They ain't playin' fair—I didn't get to bat enough times," or, "Bill gets on the swing first and then won't get off. He ought to share."

Regardless of handicap, anyone who wants to be a participant in society must live by its rules. Dooter had a lot to learn, mostly because he never before had had an opportunity to participate.

The week Roy got his crystal radio set, our yard was a beehive of activity. When the earphones brought the first broadcast to assorted sets of ears, the event was greeted with the enthusiasm accorded a walk in space. The following weekend we went out of town. Roy had left his crystal set in the workshop. When we returned the workshop door was open, the earphones to the set were lying on the floor, broken, and wires and parts were scattered over the table. Dooter plodded up to the door.

"Dooter, do you know who did this?" my husband asked.

"Yeah. I did. Tried to fix the thing . . . wouldn't work . . ." His hand hammered at the doorframe vindictively.

"But you know you aren't supposed to come in the workshop and you know Roy doesn't let anyone touch his set unless he's there," my husband said sternly. "Now, for doing that, you can't play here for one week. When the week is over, you come back—but you're not to come into our yard for a week. Do you understand?"

Dooter's expression was unchanged; he did not seem to comprehend. But he turned slowly and walked away.

Dooter's stepfather came down a few minutes later to apologize and offered to buy Roy a new set. It was another first for Dooter, we learned; usually he was uncommunicative with his mother and stepfather about his scrapes away from home. But this time he had told them that he had been sent home and why.

It was our first meeting with Mr. Johnson, who unmistakably was concerned about Dooter—something we already had guessed from the boy's appearance and from the fact that he was always well supplied with toys, books and games. We assured him that the damage to the set could be repaired but we felt Dooter needed a lesson. Mr. Johnson was full of appreciation. In the past, he said, people just got angry when Dooter misbehaved and told him and his wife to keep their boy at home.

We all suffered through the week, watching Dooter sidle by on the street, observing us from the corner of his eye. Never once did he attempt to approach the house, however. Saturday finally came. I heard the children gather at the telephone and Roy saying, "Hey, Dooter, your week's up. Come on down and play ball!" It seemed that Roy had barely put down the phone before Dooter was at the door, flushed and smiling, with his ball, bat and glove.

As the weeks went by we found that Dooter was capable of great love. He was no longer the fearful, unspeaking little soldier who had raised his own battlements for self-preservation.

One day he marched up to our ten-year-old daughter and handed her a handful of sad-looking flowers. Then he turned around to where I was hanging clothes on the line and stated manfully, "I brought her some pretty flowers. Picked 'em myself out there." He waved vaguely toward the cow pasture. Then he stood waiting for the approval he knew would come, shoulders rigid, chest out—a soldier at parade rest.

Another time the doorbell jangled and there was Dooter, holding the baby by the hand. "She was too close to the street," he said almost accusingly. "She shouldn't get close to the street." And with this chastisement he released her hand and stalked away. He was learning rules, even if they were our rules.

It was not unusual to find Dooter sitting on the porch with our mite of a first grader while she instructed him from her primer. Proudly and laboriously he would read after her, "See Spot. See Spot run." Then he would smile and wait for her admiration.

The boys helped him cut grass and allowed him to help them weed our small garden. They also waged a continuing battle to teach him not to be cruel to his large German shepherd—another instance of his inability to comprehend the pain of others. He would yank at the dog's collar and beat the friendly animal with a stick. Strangely, despite this rough treatment, Dooter's dog tagged along devotedly after the small, determined boy through every swamp and ditch, and went into a frenzy of excitement at the slightest hint that Dooter wanted to play.

Eventually even Dooter's rough treatment of his dog eased under the pressure of the boys' disapproval. He was not afraid to compete for love now. He worked, listened and learned in a new freedom of being. He was transferred from a school for the retarded to public school. Although he was not the mental equal of children his age, it was felt that he would be more at home with them and that he was capable of social adjustment. The teachers were understanding and he was not a disciplinary problem. He responded openly and readily to the good in others and instinctively recognized the bad. I never saw Dooter cry from physical pain, but an unkind act filled his eyes with tears.

Dooter's development did not come about solely because of our back-yard playground. His mother and stepfather gave him love and every advantage. But the companionship of his peers could not be bought. When his family moved from the neighborhood, his mother and stepfather, concerned about losing Dooter's friends but encouraged by his developing abilities, told us how much they thought we had helped him.

They gave us their lasting gratitude. But what did Dooter give to our neighborhood?

He gave us an opportunity for new understanding, new awareness, a common bond. He was Dooter; he was different in his own right but his difference was no longer of great consequence—he also was just one of the kids. In the most important way he was like the rest of us—he needed love and he had love that needed to be given.

Whose child is Dooter? Ours. Yours. Mine. The brother of our children. Can we learn to accept Dooter and others like him so completely that our children immediately sense our acceptance and make it their own? Can we learn to give him love, that intangible necessity that money cannot buy? And will the next Dooter be received similarly in our neighborhood? I believe so.

Dooter comes back to visit often. When his stepfather's station wagon pulls up at the door and he alights with the supreme assurance of a visiting monarch, you can hear the kids yelling across the yards down the street, "Hey, come on down. Dooter's back! Ha-a-a-ay, Doo-oo-ooter's back!"

THE END

EDITORS' NOTE: *To protect their privacy, the names of the individuals and families in this story have been changed. The events, however, happened as described.*

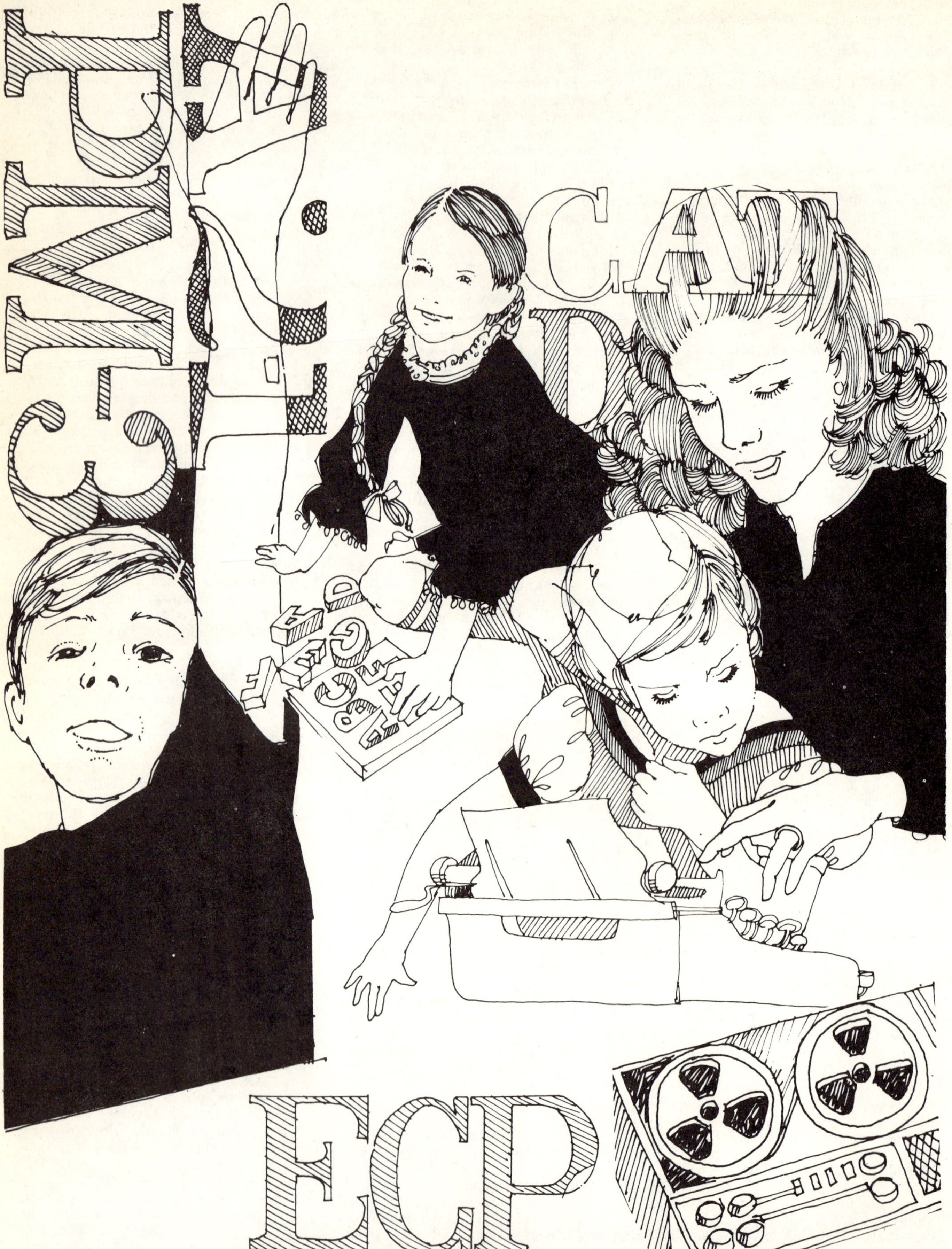
CAT
ECP

Research, Diagnosis and Assessment

Diagnosis and identification of mental retardation is made difficult due to the fact that over 200 causes are known to exist. The American Association on Mental Deficiency defines it thusly:

"Mental retardation refers to significantly sub-average general intellectual functioning existing concurrently with deficits in adaptive behavior and manifested during the developmental period."

Orderly classification is difficult, as the degree of intellectual insufficiency and social adaptability combined with physical handicaps and emotional problems require close scrutiny. Intelligence-quotients are helpful in defining a "mildly" retarded child at 50 to 70; "moderately" retarded at 35 to 50; "severely" retarded at 20 to 35, and "profoundly" retarded at below 20. Educational assessment identifies retarded children in "educable", "trainable", and "totally dependent" categories, taking into consideration academic competence levels, social adjustment levels, and degree of self-help skills and their atainment. The most current research shows that prevalenc will vary with age, making early observation so necessary and important to remedial and treatment follow-up, especially in the case of so-called "disadvantaged" children.

Prime causes of mental retardation are thought to stem from biological factors affecting the neural matrix, and experimental factors affecting functions of the central nervous system during the post natal period. 10% to 25% of the total retarded population are classified as being moderately, severely or profoundly handicapped and are diagnosed accordingly. Diagnostic classification includes, Down's Syndrome, cranial anomalies, tumors, cerebral palsy and genetic defects. Other considerations include physical handicaps of ambulatory arm and hand use, malformations, organic aspects, and sensory impairment. The remaining 75% to 90% are classified as "mildly retarded", having IQ quotients above 50. Psychogenics and biological factors are considered to be contributors, with special education bringing new adjustments in their lives.

Research has shown us that from birth to the end of the first year is crucial to assessment, with preschool years highlighting delayed development. Other forms of diagnosis include biological syndrome, parental developmental history, social history observation, and medical assessment by a physician through neurological evaluation taking into consideration general body proportion, the size of the head, tongue, hair, eyes, ears, skin, and extremities. Gross and fine motor skills are also considered, along with neurological analysis. This is achieved through the use of X-rays, electroencephalograms, and dermatoglyphics. Dental diagnosis and psychological testing are other tools of assessment available for the necessary process of proper diagnosis.

However, the fact still remains that in a great majority of cases the causes are still unknown. We can only take comfort in the fact that we have considerably improved our understanding of etiological factors of mental retardation up to now, with future research and new findings in the fields of anthropology, neuropathology, biochemistry of brain tissue, immunologic genetics, and neurophysiology bringing us further necessary information to meet the needs of retarded children the world over we must go a long way before we can take any comfort in the fact that we are even beginning to really meet those needs.

MENTAL RETARDATION

RESEARCH AND EDUCATION

Editors, second edition:
Julius B. Richmond, M.D., Chairman
George Tarjan, M.D.
Robert S. Mendelsohn, M.D.

With developments mushrooming in every aspect of mental retardation, the physician may feel confused. However, he may take comfort in the knowledge that he is far from atypical, no matter what the date on his medical diploma. Significant new advances in the biological and behavioral sciences are apt to outdate today what was learned a year or ten years ago. Every expert in the field shares the physician's struggle to keep abreast of the new knowledge pouring from laboratory, clinic, and consulting room. The physician can only take as much advantage as possible of each opportunity for continuing education as it presents itself. His most stimulating learning experiences, however, may well come as he keeps up with current research. Finally, he should keep in mind that much of the new knowledge and new advances gained by research deals with the rarest of conditions (PKU, biochemical disorders, etc.). Knowledge about the prevention and management of the overwhelming majority of cases of mental retardation has been available for many decades, awaiting only to be applied.

Promising Areas of Research

Major research efforts are now being directed toward (1) increased understanding of the causes of retardation, including both biomedical and experiential factors, (2) improved methods of identification, (3) progress in treatment and education, and (4) development of more effective preventive techniques.

Research into causation. Research into biological causation now focuses not only on the physiological processes of pregnancy and childbirth but also on specific diseases and disease conditions. These include maternal, fetal, and neonatal infections; trauma during and after birth; disorders of metabolism, growth, or nutrition, including those that are genetically determined; and abnormal growths in the central nervous system.

A major recent undertaking is the Collaborative Perinatal Project, a joint endeavor by the National Institute of Neurological Diseases and Blindness, with 51 major medical centers. A prospective study of 50,000 pregnant women, the project is attempting to determine the relationships between factors affecting women during pregnancy and the neurological, sensory, and mental disorders of their offspring. Undergirding the study is the hypothesis that factors resulting in abortions, fetal death, and neonatal mortality or morbidity may also be those responsible for mental retardation, cerebral palsy, and other neurological disorders.

Several clues to the origins of neurosensory defects have already developed from the study. Analysis has disclosed an association between anoxia at birth and the infant's abnormal psychological performance at 8 months. Investigators may eventually be able to search previously stored data for possible etiologic factors pertinent to a specified degree of retardation or type of neurological disorder. These are typical of the kinds of results that may develop.

In other studies over the country, a number of investigators are searching for better ways to identify and control the causes of premature labor and delivery, often associated with retardation. Studies are underway to delineate the structure and function of uterine and cervical musculature in various stages of pregnancy and delivery, both in normal and premature births. Other studies essay a more detailed assessment of placental function.

The role of toxemias and infections, both bacterial and viral, is attracting heightened interest. A variety of bacterial infections have been implicated in placental disease as the cause of a number of abortions and fetal deaths. Viral research has identified certain agents responsible for fetal and infant damage and death, including the viruses of rubella, herpes simplex, cytomegalic inclusion disease, etc. An immunization antigen against the rubella virus is now available.

Research continues into the role of toxic medications and high-energy radiation during pregnancy, as well as the possible effects of fallout, background, and other indirect radiation in producing fetal disease.

In studies of stress, experimental evidence is accumulating to demonstrate that infant rhesus monkeys subjected to controlled asphyxia and resuscitation at birth develop various degrees of neuromotor and behavioral handicaps including retardation. These studies strongly indicate that anoxia near the end of the gestational period can cause permanent damage in the brain. Many investigators in complementary studies are exploring safer methods of oxygenating the cyanotic newborn.

12. Research and Education

The physician may also expect results from current investigations including improved diagnostic tests, post-natal passive immunization and phototherapy in the prevention and treatment of erythroblastosis fetalis.

Genetic research is producing increasingly distinct concepts of hereditary patterns of disease in which retardation is a primary sign. An abnormal number of unusual arrangements of chromosomes has been associated with retardation in such diseases as Down's syndrome. New information on the role of abnormal chromosomes is rapidly becoming available.

The elaboration of the genetic code continues. Investigators have demonstrated that the store of genetic information is replicated and passed on from generation to generation by means of the DNA in the nucleus of each cell. The RNA elaborated by information from DNA is perhaps the chemical factor determining memory, learning and recall, all involved in the intellectual process. The work on the role of RNA in synthesis of brain protein and in memory induction and retention has only begun to expand the vast field of basic brain biochemistry. Now that research has linked the genetic code to the formation of protein by means of RNA, the physician may expect even more interesting findings relating brain function to proper intellectual development.

Phenylketonuria is only one of several genetically determined errors of metabolism for which recent research has provided not only means of detection but methods of prevention as well. Further biochemical research in individuals who fail to develop normally will probably provide clues to the discovery of other genetically determined types of retardation.

Dental research in proper preventive and reparative care for the mentally retarded, and the physically handicapped, will come only when medical schools recognize that the teeth and oral cavity are an integral part of the body, and not a thing apart, and insist upon the development of a department of stomatology or dentistry within the format and climate of the medical school. Dental schools are goal-oriented towards the 200 million "normal" population. It is at the present time not feasible for them to undertake research and care for the 5 million mentally handicapped.

Future research should include the possibility of using specifically tailored antibiotic lozenges or adhesive ointments to remove the pathogenic bacteria adhering to the tooth surfaces and thus arrest the caries process and reduce the gingivitis. Pilot studies in this direction show good promise. The use of fluoridated water and fluoride mouth rinses can do much to increase enamel resistance to caries attack. Preventive practices suited to mass control and prevention of dental diseases, based on techniques which do not require patient cooperation or even the expensive services of specially trained dental personnel, must be sought if proper dental care is to become a reality for the retarded—if not for the general population. Such research must be based in hospitals, institutions, and medical schools, preferably connected with dental schools with their rich resources in specialized knowledge and specialized skills in preventive dental care and dental repair.

In addition to biologically oriented investigation, research is probing the nature and role of experiential factors. Evidence is accumulating to demonstrate that varied sensory stimulation, opportunity for unhampered motor activity and for progressively more complex behavior in the form of response is necessary for development of the nervous system and for behavioral adjustment. Environmental stimulation develops perceptual discrimination which—appropriately rewarded by increased opportunity for pleasurable stimulation and response—eventually provides for more complex mental activities such as concept formation, including concrete, abstract, and symbolic categorization. Such mental activities constitute the basis for problem solving, for thinking, and for creative activities characteristic of the higher behavioral levels and social adjustment.

Since adaptation to the environment is in essence normal intellectual behavior, it follows that an individual deprived of this rich experience will develop less adequate bases for discriminative adjustment.

As the child grows, social and cultural stimulation become increasingly essential to the development of cognitive function, which characterizes the higher levels of intellectual development.

Current research is elaborating ways in which children reared in institutional or depressed settings, urban or rural, are apt to be deprived of appropriately constituted social and cultural experience and therefore subject to retardation in social and intellectual adaptation. Experimental projects are now attempting to reverse this cultural process by special enrichment programs, remedial classes, and introduction to a wide variety of stimulating experiences.

Current investigations indicate that lagging language development in the retarded reduces their problem-solving skills in both verbal and nonverbal tasks. Investigators are measuring the profile of language (encoding, integrating, and decoding) of retardates with different etiologies. Others are developing and testing new programs to stimulate language development. Physicians can look to psychologists to use the recently devised Illinois Test of Psycholinguistics in an intensive study of language patterns in retardation.

As yet behavioral scientists have not found precise methods of measuring hearing vocabularies of the more severely retarded, or methods to develop their language to a functional level. Limited research indicates that existing techniques of speech therapists are effective only in special cases.

Research in identification and therapy. The World Health Organization has held conferences on the classification of mental retardation. Advances in the taxonomy of this group of disorders are desirable. Research concerning the differentiation of the major emotional disorders of childhood as well as their relationships and overlaps is clearly indicated.

Research in methodology for identifying various degrees of retardation is now aimed at weighing and refining the various items so that better prediction of future function may be possible. Investigators currently differ as to how early in infancy mental retardation can be recognized and with what reliance subsequent behavior and development can be predicted. Further research may enable investigators to further delineate certain kinds of functional behavior in the infant at least as signs, if not certain indicators, of possible malfunction.

Measurement of intelligence in children and adults is further advanced than that of infants. Studies indicate that a few children may advance slowly through childhood with progressively lower IQ's, while others develop more rapidly with increasing IQ's over a period of years. There is also evidence of continued mental growth into early adulthood. Persons retarded as children may approach normal intelligence on reaching the age of 20 or 30.

More basic research on learning of the retarded has been conducted in the last decade than in all of our past history; still, only a beginning has been made in this complex field. Developmental theorists continue to investigate cognitive structures, as well as emotional and motivational factors, and their differential influence on performance. There is also increased appreciation of the importance of past experiences determining performance. Recent application of computer methods to the study of the average evoked response of the cortex recorded via EEG through scalp and skull, however, has provided significant promise of being able to use the magnitude and latency of response to differentiate between signals attended to and signals not attended to.

Thus there is promise that the attention and vigilance of the retarded may be more adequately studied and thus related to modern neurophysiologically oriented theories of brain function.

2. RESEARCH, DIAGNOSIS, AND ASSESSMENT

It may be possible to determine whether a part of the brain is pathologically impaired or merely functionally incompetent and subject to training and rehabilitation. Thus there is promise that eventually investigators may be able to ascertain whether an existing malfunction depends on structural or functional inadequacy, whether it is dependent upon biochemical, physiological, or psychological factors, and whether it is modifiable by proper retraining.

Investigation has long been underway in teaching methods for the retarded. As early as 1856, educators were observing with interest the methods of Dr. Harvey Wilbur at the New York State Idiot Asylum in Syracuse to see what could be learned from idiot education that would be pertinent to the needs of all children.

At present the need continues for more research into the problems of educating the retarded. Further investigation is needed into the process of teacher selection for the "educable" retarded. Educators also need to know more about the most appropriate settings for educational programs in order to determine whether these programs are more effective within the regular schools or in special schools. The comparative merits of institutional and community settings in programs for the "trainable" also require further investigation. At the present time almost nothing is known about effective instructional procedures for the severely retarded.

The rather popular behavior-shaping techniques have produced significant, at times dramatic results. However, until more is known about the generalizability of behaviors acquired through operant conditioning, this method of management must not be considered a panacea. Therefore, critical evaluation of the many specific techniques and their results should go on in order to place these techniques in appropriate perspective.

In the area of remediation, there is need for intensive research to improve methods of psychotherapy for handling psychiatric disorders among the retarded. Also needed is further research into autism, its causation, and possible therapy.

Retarded children often acquire a series of diagnoses including early infantile or childhood autism and childhood schizophrenia. The relationships between the diagnoses of early childhood psychoses and mental retardation remain obscure. No firm scientific conclusions can be drawn, and the argument continues on a semantic and philosophic level.

The physician may wish to participate in the research that should be a part of every continuing clinical program and community effort. He can encourage the organizations and institutions with which he is affiliated to increase the support of all research, both basic and applied. At the same time, he must be sure that the legitimate interests of the patient are protected and that proper ethical standards are maintained. The institutionalized retardates, like prison inmates, constitute a captive population. Opportunities for exploitation in the name of research are always present. In addition to the personal integrity of the researcher, other safeguards are needed. All research efforts, from the planning stage through the actual investigation and later publication, should be conducted only with the full knowledge and approval of the individual families. Parents' organizations should be kept informed of developments in research. In addition, an independent review board of other professionals, citizen members, clergy and community representatives is advised to prevent any possible abuses and to arrange for proper compensation for any patients damaged during the research process.

Poor people, including Blacks, Chicanos, Appalachian whites, Puerto Ricans, American Indians, and others have for some time demonstrated increasing resistance to participating in research and in survey efforts. The Navaho Indians, in an apocryphal story, describe the typical family on a reservation as consisting of a father, mother, 3 children and a cultural anthropologist. These same attitudes have been extended to include medical scientists. This kind of antipathy has been effectively articulated by parents' organizations of the retarded. They call for a reordering of priorities, for an increase in service, if necessary at the expense of research: They insist that the discoveries of older research be promptly applied and that new research clearly demonstrate its relevance in understandable language.

This is destined to become an important political issue that will affect every physician interested in patient care and research.

Just as our country is behind other modern industrialized nations in infant mortality, so it lags behind other countries in its care and concern for the mentally retarded. Any research effort should include comparison with foreign, particularly European, approaches to the care of the retarded. Science and medicine are universal and transcend national boundaries, and consideration of better methods in other countries should in no way reflect on the patriotism of the physician.

Communicating information to the physician is not as simple as it appears. Any educational effort faces the built-in resistance of many physicians, both because of their pessimistic attitude toward mental retardation in general and because of the personal feelings of anxiety and guilt such patients may arouse.

Much of the formal education in the field has limited appeal: The lecture method can be dull and stilted, and some courses provide too many exhortative generalizations and too little practical advice. And, finally, the outpourings of medical literature make problematic the amount of information actually conveyed, by any given printed page. As with most education, the people who might profit most are the last to seek it out.

There are, however, ways of circumventing these natural barriers. Information can be provided to the physician as he goes his course. Problems of retardation may be introduced into existing perinatal mortality and morbidity conferences and into hospital staff meetings which the physician normally attends. A discussion of the topic can be included in society meetings devoted primarily to other topics.

Specialists in rehabilitation and specifically in mental retardation can be added to hospital staffs and their activities made apparent to the physician as he makes his customary rounds. There is a critical need to reinstitute some exposure to dental problems within the pre-doctoral education of the physician and to expand the educational functions of the dental department in the hospital so that interns and residents acquire a better orientation towards preventive dental practice for their patients to replace the current practice of referring patients to the dentist only when disease is rampant and almost beyond repair. Most importantly, programs and seminars can be designed to be attractive, immediate, and practical, featuring the give and take and the active problem-solving approach of the panel, the case discussion, and the demonstration rather than relying exclusively on the lecture.

Responsibilities for Education

The physician with a continuing interest in retardation may well assume responsibility for helping with the education of others. He may take an active role in organizing postgraduate learning opportunities for himself and his fellow physicians. He may exert his influence as a member of a specialty society, as clinical teacher, or as medical school alumnus on the undergraduate and graduate learning in this field.

The medical student needs education specifically related to his operational role. Preparation of the physician for effective

12. Research and Education

service to the retarded must include attention to all his responsibilities in prevention, diagnosis, treatment, and mobilization of the resources of family, community, and environment. Ignoring the study of mental retardation in the medical schools, internships, and residencies may subtly bias the young physician against further learning in the field.

The physician may find that he exercises his most potent influence over medical education by the requests he makes of the medical schools for postgraduate education for himself. Continuing pressure on the schools from the physician for more education in retardation will do much to alert educators to the necessity of incorporating just such teaching in the program for medical students. A need recognized by men in the field is apt to be reflected shortly in education for this field.

Vehicles for Continuing Education

The formal postgraduate course sponsored by medical school, society, or specialty organization is only one of several ways to obtain continuing education. A physician may absorb a good deal of information from his professional journals, from conferences with colleagues, and through regular meetings of medical societies. His education may continue in the community mental-health clinic or the residential facility.

In smaller communities traveling clinics and visiting specialists who will discuss his cases with the physician can be helpful. A new proposal is that for a regional consultant, rather like the venereal disease-control officer, who might provide information, particularly for physicians in smaller communities. In some areas state health officials expert in maternal and child welfare can provide this same service.

In the large communities a central information service may prove helpful to physicians as may directories of existing services and facilities.

The American Association of Mental Deficiency, with a multi-disciplinary membership of 8,000, publishes two journals, encourages many research endeavors, and can be a valuable source of information.

Finally, the physician who would facilitate education for his colleagues may work through the medical societies and other organizations enlisting the greatest physician interest and support.

By thus attending to his own continuing education and encouraging that of others, the primary physician may make his conclusive contribution to the welfare of the retarded and to the prevention of this affliction in others during the years to come.

LAURA
SOUND FILMSTRIP-HANDICAPPED

This true story serves as excellent role-model for those who are handicapped. It tells the story of a woman with Spina Bifida and her everyday experiences, problems, and activities. It's purpose is to illustrate for teachers of special education practical and social learning experiences of handicapped individuals.

Filmstrip and cassette and teacher's guide $14.95

For further information contact:

Joseph Logan, Editor
Special Learning Corporation

Special Learning Corporation
42 Boston Post Rd. Guilford, Connecticut 06437   (203) 453-6525

Early Identification of Handicapped Children through a Frequency Sampling Technique

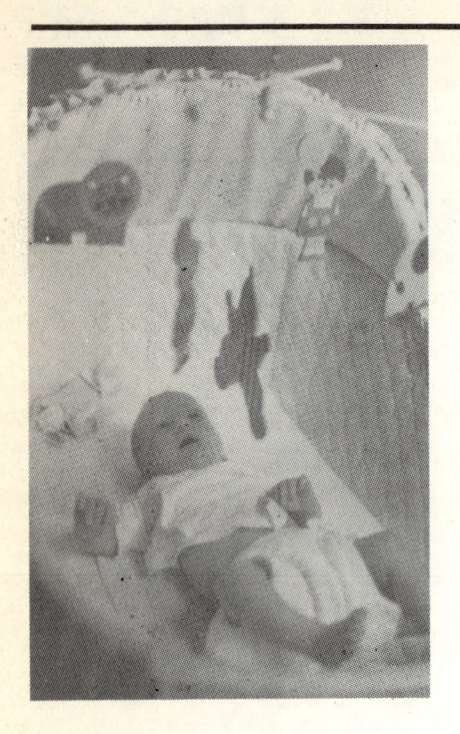

LARRY A. MAGLIOCCA
ROBERT T. RINALDI
JOHN L. CREW
HAROLD P. KUNZELMANN

LARRY A. MAGLIOCCA is Research Associate, Faculty for Exceptional Children, Ohio State University, Columbus; ROBERT T. RINALDI is Assistant Superintendent, Area for Exceptional Children, and JOHN L. CREW is Superintendent of Public Instruction, Baltimore City Public Schools, Baltimore, Maryland; and HAROLD P. KUNZELMANN is Director of Consulting Services, International Management Systems, Kansas City, Missouri. The research reported herein was supported in part by Grant No. OEG-0-74-2709 from the Bureau of Education for the Handicapped, US Office of Education. Contractors undertaking such projects under Government sponsorship are encouraged to express freely their professional judgment in the conduct of the project. Points of view or opinions stated do not, therefore, necessarily represent official Office of Education position or policy.

A top priority of congressional action for the promotion of programs for handicapped children is termed child find. The child find concept is based on at least two major conclusions about children who are disabled. First, many handicapped children are not detected until their late primary years in the second or third grade. Second, when the children are found and diagnosis is completed, much of the information is not directly related to daily instructional plans of remediation.

The roots of the delivery of special education services are founded in the early detection of any form of handicapping condition, rapid remedial assistance in learning, and return to or placement in the least restrictive educational environment. The referral process available for teachers becomes the initiation point for causing special education services to become operational.

The early childhood program is a key area from which a child find concept may evolve.

As part of the project entitled Baltimore Early Childhood Learning Continuum, project personnel selected three classes in early childhood education to determine if children who had learning problems could be identified and assisted while remaining in a regular program placement.

Channels of Investigation

It was determined that at least three channels of identification were open to investigation:

- *Alternative 1:* Children would be identified when the teacher felt the child could profit from special education services. This meant waiting until the teacher had enough interaction with each child to feel comfortable in the referring process to initiate the referral actions.

- *Alternative 2:* A second means of identification considered was ability testing either through an achievement test or a battery of standardized instruments. The two factors that were considered obstacles to this approach were (a) that such testing was prohibitive in terms of cost and (b) that there are serious questions as to the cultural free aspects of tests that are available. In addition, the norming processes used to standardize the ability tests for young children are highly questionable.

- *Alternative 3:* The third identification alternative was to devise a screening process that has the following characteristics: (a) it should be easily administered by classroom teachers, (b) it should provide the earliest possible means of inschool identification of at risk children with a high correlation to teacher identification of at risk children at the end of the school year, and (c) it should have direct instructional relevance for remedial actions.

While each of the above was a viable alternative for early identification of handicapping conditions, it was determined that alternatives 1 and 3, teacher referral and screening process, would be combined to produce a pilot project. The conclusion was based on a review of the available literature relating to the identification of handicapping conditions in young children.

Review of the Literature

An Educational Resources Information Center search of related literature based on descriptors such as *Identification, Preschool Programs,* and *Education* revealed 32 current studies. The primary mode of identification within these studies was equally distributed over academic, social behaviors, developmental patterns, language development, and visual motor development categories. Not only does the mode differ, but as Glidewell and Swallow (1969) pointed out, the screening methods vary considerably from the interview, to full diagnostic batteries, to symptom surveys. However, only a small number of studies addressed themselves to the crucial issue: predictive validity. Keeping this deficiency in mind, there still remain significant guidelines currently in the literature to assist in the development of early identification instruments and procedures.

Bradley (1974) reported that when a team approach to learning problem identification was used for devising a learning profile and modifying kindergarten curriculum, a degree of difference was found favoring the experimental groups for more child improvement. The implication is that some form of identification will be slightly better than relying solely on the referral process.

A contrasting view was given by Keogh and Becker (1973). They have raised questions concerning the relevancy of any identification procedures depending upon criteria from outside the actual school environment. Their questions serve as cautions in the development of identification instruments: (a) How valid are the identifying or predictive measures? (b) What are the implications of diagnostic data for remediation or educational intervention? (c) Do benefits of early identification outweigh possible damaging or negative efforts of such recognition?

The validity question cited in this critique is the most important in the development of early identification procedures but remains unanswerable. There are few clear corresponding relationships between the identification of learning disabilities from screening procedures and subsequent school achievement. The reasons for a lack of successful progress in educational programs on the part of some children are complex. In addition, as Haring and Ridgway (1967) have indicated, a failure to progress satisfactorily in learning may be as much the fault of the learning environment as a function of the organism. However, Keogh and Becker (1973) postulated a most important guideline: Predictive validity will increase when the screening

13. Early Identification

material is relevant to the immediate school environment in which the child will function.

The above studies conclude contrasting views which may be interpreted to mean that some combination of teacher identification and screening with materials of immediate consequence to the school environment is the best means of finding handicapping conditions and effecting instructional change.

The two predictive validity studies reviewed yielded one correlational design and one longitudinal study. The correlational study (Amundson, 1972) was based on the Metropolitan Readiness Test and the Wizard of Oz Preschool Screening Program (Amundson, 1972) and showed $r = .90$ with an N of 23 pupils. The longitudinal study (Rubin & Krus, 1974) indicated the School Behavior Profile found the same identified problem kindergarten pupils in the fourth grade 42% of the time. Both studies tended not to use acceptable predictive criteria. However, it can be concluded that a need exists for identification instruments which have firm predictive validity.

Generally, the research literature indicates consensus on some important points: (a) Teachers of preschool children should be the basic identification agent of finding handicapping conditions of children in their charge, (b) any means of finding children who may need learning assistance that avoids standardized testing should be considered, and (c) no child should be labeled as at risk based on any previously administered standardized test in light of the inadequate reliability and validity of such instruments (Dykstra, 1967; Severson, 1972; Proger, 1972). The remaining potential seems to lie in some procedure that insures teacher agreement and predictive outcome of immediate program change.

Based on a pragmatic approach, the administration and staff of the Baltimore Learning Continuum Project, which provided comprehensive special services to young handicapped children within regular preschool and first grade classrooms, designed and field tested a screening instrument. The instrument attempted to identify children 4 and 5 years of age early in the school year while having a high correlation with teacher referrals of children needing some type of special education service.

Procedures

The basic measurement used for the investigation of the screening device was frequency. Frequency is defined as counts per unit time. The counts were academic performances such as writing letters and numbers and saying names, words, and letters. The fixed time unit was 1 minute. The frequency score was the correct number of responses per minute. The consistent measurement plan insured complete reliability when counts were accurate. The staff of the project did the counting and timing to insure high reliability.

Children were individually screened on 5 consecutive days. Screening stations were manned by two project staff members in an area adjacent to the early education classroom. During the first day of screening, children received assistance in relational and directional concepts such as *alike* or *different* and *top* or *bottom*. The actual 1 minute timing of the task began when the child started the task rather than on the signal of "go" by the tester.

The selected population was based on children enrolled in an early education program within a lower socioeconomic area of the City of Baltimore. The population included children from three classrooms, 35 females and 30 males for a total of 65 children.

Table 1 includes the subtests that were used and the purpose of each subtest. Also included are descriptions of the materials used, task descriptions, and scoring.

The screening procedures were initiated in February, which was somewhat late in the school year. However, this was a pilot effort in preparation for the coming school year in the fall. Teachers' classification of their children into at risk and low risk categories was completed in May.

The most useful reference in the literature involving a frequency sampling procedure in early identification was the *State of Washington Screening Booklets* (Kunzelmann, 1972). Under this system several subtests are similar to their procedures: the X's in Circles, the See-Say Letters, the See-Say Numbers and the See-Write Letters. However, in the present study several changes were initiated. First, several subtests were added to reflect a younger population of pupils: Naming Pictures, Naming Number Sets, Color Matching and Hear-Touch (body parts). Secondly, to reduce the typical great variability of performance at this early age, children were tested individually on all subtests rather than including a mixture of group and individual sessions. Finally, subtests were eliminated from consideration that did not have immediate curricular implications of performance for the child.

Rationale for Subtest Selections

Subtest design was based on several factors. Measures were developed on the basis of their face validity to the immediate school environment in which the child functioned; that is, the content of the measure reflected an important curricular goal or performance skill that the child was expected to exhibit. The frequency score yielded the child's relative proficiency in the performance of each specific task. In addition, the visual, auditory, and kinesthetic modalities were all tapped in the design of various subtests. The first seven subtests were administered to the 3 and 4 year olds; all nine subtests were administered to the 5 year olds.

The first two subtests represented a measure of proficiency with the child's basic tool in the early education program, the primary pencil. The X's in Circles provided the opportunity to assess eye-hand coordination with the primary pencil within the spatial requirements of a small circle. In the second subtest, XO Pattern, the child's developing skill with the pencil was employed in the reproduction of patterns of visual stimuli. This subtest was included after behavioral analysis of the mainstream classroom revealed an increasing

TABLE 1
Subtest Selections

Subtests	Purpose	Task	Materials	Scoring
X's in Circles	Test eye-hand coordination when using a pencil	Mark X in each circle	40 3/4 inch circles on grid	Total no. of X's inside circles
XO Pattern	Test ability to produce and imitate a pattern	Continue XO pattern	Paper divided into 88 squares	Total no. of X's and O's in correct pattern
Counting Number Sets	Test ability to count	Count objects on each card	20 cards; Objects 1 to 10	Total no. of correct counts
See-Say Letters	Test ability to name letters	Name letters	Chart with upper and lower case letters (114)	Total no. of letters named
Matching Colors	Test ability to match colors	Match colored blocks to colored boxes	46 blocks and 6 matching boxes	Total no. of blocks matched
Naming Pictures	Test ability to name picture symbols of objects	Name pictures objects	77 pictures mounted on a chart	Total no. of pictures named
Hear-Touch (body parts)	Test auditory discrimination and locating body parts	Touch body parts named	Audiotape with 40 cues	Total no. of responses
See-Write Letters	Test ability to reproduce letters	Reproduce letters underneath samples	Paper with upper case letters	Total no. of letters copied
See-Say Numbers	Test ability to name numbers	Name random numbers from 1 to 20	78 numbers on a chart	Total no. of numbers named

Note: Time = 60 seconds.

2. RESEARCH, DIAGNOSIS, AND ASSESSMENT

emphasis on the child's skill to reproduce visual patterns via the chalkboard, overhead projector, and practice worksheets.

Counting in sequence is viewed in many early childhood programs as a primary mathematics skill. Within this particular program, children also identified the counted objects as a set. In the Counting Number Sets subtest, a chart of objects and geometric shapes in sets of 1 to 10 was developed. The child was to count the number of objects or shapes on the card and specify the number in the set.

The names of the letters of the alphabet were emphasized as a preliminary activity to reading. In this school environment, both upper case and lower case letters were used. The See-Say Letters subtest measured the child's facility at naming upper and lower case letters from a chart.

Colors were an important learning task not only in simple discrimination of one color from another but also as cues to learning other instructional tasks. The Matching Colors subtest involved the matching of blocks of six different colors with a colored box of the same color. The child was not required to name the color.

A child's expressive language within any educational program is critical to most learning activities, especially prereading instruction. The Naming Pictures subtest was devised to measure a child's verbal facility in naming simple object drawings without any background to distract from the object. Special consideration was given to selecting objects for the drawings that were in high frequency use in the classrooms and appropriate to the children's background of experiences.

The last subtest administered to the 3 and 4 year olds was the Hear-Touch. In this subtest, a voice on a prerecorded tape named a part of the body every 1.5 seconds as the child listened and touched the correct part of the body. The specific body parts were derived from curricular objectives: head, ear, eye, nose, neck, shoulder, elbow, hand, waist, knee, ankle, and foot.

Two additional subtests were administered only to the 5 year olds. Both subtests reflect the cognitive emphasis of this specific curriculum on proficiency in letters and numbers. In the See-Write Letters, the child copied randomized alphabet letters (upper and lower case) in a box directly beneath the model letters. The last subtest was the See-Say Numbers. The child named randomized numbers from 1 to 20 from a number chart.

Results

Upon completion of the screening, a mean score was computed for the 5 days of frequency scores per each subtest yielding seven scores for 4 year olds and nine scores for 5 year olds.

The frequency scores for each subtest were ranked from highest to lowest score for each age group. Children were identified as at risk when three or more of the subtest scores fell below a certain cutoff level. Initially, three different cutoff levels were established. However, as shown in Table 2, the 25% cutoff level was verified later as possessing the highest predictive value. Applying the 25% criteria as the cutoff for ranked scores, 15 children were identified as possible at risk learners.

TABLE 2

Comparison of Three Cutoff Levels to Year End Teacher Identification of At Risk Children

Cutoff criteria	Number of children identified
37.5%	17 (13% overidentified)
25%	15 (1% underidentified)
10%	12 (8% underidentified)

Study of the cumulative records of the 65 children following the screening found that 8 of the 15 children identified by the screening instrument had already been referred for special instructional assistance by the classroom teacher. One child had been referred for assistance whose frequency scores were above the cutoff domain.

The issues raised from the research literature indicated predictive validity as the most critical outcome of an early identification procedure. Teacher judgment is cited as one of the most reliable means of identifying at risk children when teachers have sufficient time to observe their children (usually a minimum of 4 months or more). Predictive validity of an early identification procedure can be established, therefore, by comparing the results of early identification screening with teacher judgment.

Near the completion of the school term (third week in May), the three classroom teachers participating in this study were interviewed. On the basis of their judgment, the 65 children were classified as either at risk or low risk for the upcoming school year. The teachers indicated that in addition to the 9 children previously referred, there were 7 other children who, in the teachers' opinions, could be classified as at risk. Using teacher judgment as the criteria for accuracy, Figure 1 summarizes the findings. At the 25% cutoff level, there is a high correlation between teacher judgment and identification through the frequency sampling technique as to the classification of 65 children into low risk or at risk categories.

	At risk	Low risk		
Teacher judgment Low risk	0	49	Agreement	= 64 (99%)
Teacher judgment At risk	15	1	Disagreement	= 1 (1%)
			Total	= 65 (100%)

Frequency sampling instrument

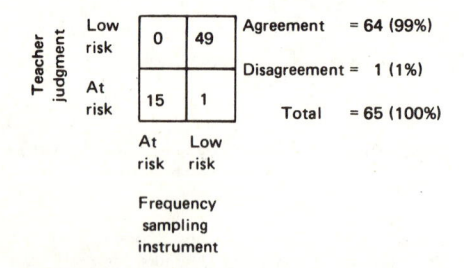

FIGURE 1. Comparison of identification by teacher judgment to results of instrument identification.

While the results of this screening are strong, it should be noted that only 65 children were included in this pilot study. The power of the screening device is questionably high. There is a need to repeat the procedures with a larger population.

Administration of High Predictive Subtests

Although subtests were designed to represent major instructional emphases and performance skills within the extant early education program, the nine subtests did not function equally well at discriminating at risk learners from low risk learners. In Table 3, the nine subtests are ranked by their predictive value. Each subtest's predictive value was established by correlating teachers' judgment of at risk learners at the end of the year with each child's position in the ranking of the mean scores per each subtest. A brief perusal of Table 3 indicates that the see-write subtest and see-say subtests seem to have the most predictive value.

There were a number of empirical findings that improved test administration reliability. First, administration of the subtests should be on an individual basis. It is generally agreed that children at this age level do not perform consistently in most testing situations. Factors such as attending to directions, on task behaviors, and motivation are school related skills beginning to develop during kindergarten and first grade; it is difficult to obtain reliable results in a group administration situation. To accommodate these developmental factors, three screening stations, with furniture suitable to the children's age, were used to test individual children.

Second, children should receive a practice session for all subtests on the first day of screening. It was found that some children needed assistance with making marks such as X or did not understand key directional and relational concepts used in the screening procedures.

Third, although children are started on the subtest with the traditional "Ready, get set, go" type of direction, timing should not begin until the child actually begins the task. This procedure makes the stopwatch a necessity during testing.

Careful preparation of subtest materials also insures reliable results. A packet of subtest materials for each child should be kept in a large envelope with a cover sheet stapled to the front to record identification data and all subtest scores for the 5 days of screening. Practice sheets may be covered with laminating material so that they are reusable; confusion of practice materials with scored materials is also prevented in this way. To design

TABLE 3

Ranking of Subtests by Highest Predictive Value

Subtest	4 year olds	5 year olds
X's in Circles	1	3
XO Pattern	2	2
Counting Number Sets	4	6
See-Say Letters	5	1
Matching Colors	3	4
Naming Pictures	6	8
Hear-Touch (body parts)	7	9
See-Write Letters	—	7
See-Say Numbers	—	5

standard charts, press type letters and numbers were used. In this way the materials were prepared with a standard appearance without requiring the services of a draftsman.

Conclusions

Three major conclusions have evolved from this pilot study: (a) The amount of instructional months of savings for children by using screening is critical, (b) the teacher variable was not an issue in the screening, and (c) the predictive validity of screening through a frequency sampling technique is high.

The first conclusion is the most critical to the children who may be identified by teachers during a school year. Given that teacher referrals are the best means of identification when teachers know the children, any means of speeding the process is advantageous to the children. By waiting for teacher referrals to evolve, many instructional months are lost. From the pilot study reported here, it is estimated that over 144 months of needed instruction were wasted because of not identifying children earlier in the year.

The second conclusion, the teacher variable issue, which is found in most testing, is not a factor based on the independent judgments of three project staff members. Table 4 indicates the ranking of the three classroom teachers from the sample screening classes on various instructional issues. The teachers are clearly different in their approach to instruction. Without question they agreed with the screening results when the 25% cutoff level was used.

The third conclusion, high predictive validity, must be replicated because of sample size of this study; however, the predictive validity of the screening is a guarded conclusion on which the above two conclusions are based. Based on the findings in this pilot study, the early identification techniques described here will be expanded to six elementary schools for the 1975-1976 school year with a total student population of approximately 800 students in kindergarten and first grade classrooms. If the predictive validity holds at or above .90, then it will be recommended that the screening techniques be implemented systemwide.

TABLE 4
Teacher Instructional Strategies

Area observed	Teachers A	Teachers B	Teachers C
Class control	2	3	1
Attention to children	2	3	1
Individual testing	2	1	3
Group work	2	3	1
Noise level	2	3	1
Class organization	2	3	1
Curriculum materials	2	3	1
Extra activities	3	2	1
Student motivation	2	3	1
Teacher motivation	2	3	1
Use of school resources	3	2	1

Note: Scale of 1 to 3, with 3 as highest.

References

Amundson, M. S. *A preliminary screening program to identify functioning strengths and weaknesses in preschool children.* ERIC ED 071743, August, 1972.

Berger, S., & Perlman, E. *A model for prevention: A kindergarten screening program.* ERIC ED 085083, 1973.

Bradley, E. *Identification of Learning Problems—Adjustment in kindergarten curricula.* ERIC ED 095995, 1974.

Dykstra, R. The use of reading readiness tests for diagnosis and prediction: A critique. In T. C. Barrett (Ed.), *The evaluation of children's reading achievement.* Newark DE: International Reading Association, 1967.

Glidewell, J. C., & Swallow, C. S. *The prevalence of maladjustment in elementary schools: A report prepared for the Joint Commission on the Mental Health of Children.* Chicago: University of Chicago Press, 1969.

Haring, N. G., & Ridgway, R. W. Early identification of children with learning disabilities. *Exceptional Children,* 1967, *33,* 387-395.

Keogh, B. K., & Becker, L. D. Early detection of learning problems: Questions, cautions and guidelines. *Exceptional Children,* 1973, *40,* 5-11.

Kunzelmann, H. *Child service demonstration project.* State of Washington: Department of Public Instruction, 1972.

Proger, B. E. Test review no. 9: Tests of basic experiences. *Journal of Special Education,* 1972, *6,* 179-184.

Rubin, R. A. & Krus, P. H. *Predictive validity of a school behavior rating scale.* ERIC ED 090276, April, 1974.

Severson, R. A. Early detection of children with potential learning disabilities: A seven year effort. *Proceedings, 80th Annual Convention, American Psychological Association,* 1972, *7,* 561-562.

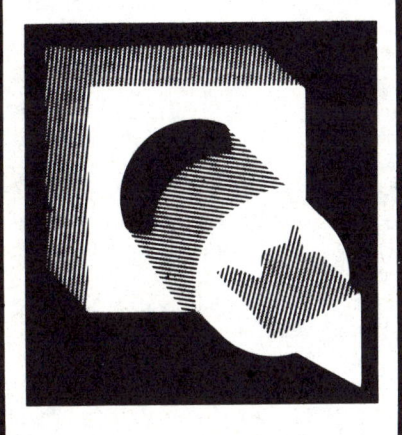

Diagnosis and Placement

Current trends in diagnostic procedures, along with a detailed look at medical assessment of exceptional children are discussed. The controversy of mainstreaming versus placement in self-contained special education classes is also featured.

For further information about this book and other special education materials, contact:

Joseph Logan, Editor
Special Learning Corporation

Special Learning Corporation
42 Boston Post Rd. Guilford, Connecticut 06437 (203) 453-6525

Mental Retardation: Diagnosis

The identification and diagnosis of mental retardation is one of the most challenging problems confronting the physician. Although about 200 causes of retardation have been identified, in most cases the physician can make no specific etiologic diagnosis.

He can define retardation only in terms of functional characteristics, of significant impairments in intellectual functioning and in the social adaptation of the individual.

A definition of mental retardation as defined by the American Association on Mental Deficiency is as follows:

Mental retardation refers to significantly sub-average general intellectual functioning existing concurrently with deficits in adaptive behavior and manifested during the developmental period.

The nature of impairment varies with the age of the individual. Below school age it is a lag in self-help, locomotion, eating and communications skills; in school, disability in learning; and at the adult level, inability to remain independent or to meet employment requirements. Hence, the process of evaluation and provision of services is a dynamic one, and the physician's role changes with the advancing age and individual needs of each retarded individual.

Retarded persons, like all other patients, must be considered as individuals. The retarded do not fall neatly into any classification. They vary widely in degree of intellectual deficit and social adaptability. Some have associated physical handicaps and emotional problems; some do not. Some require protective care; others achieve a striking degree of independence. Some remain identified as retarded; others slip back into the general population without occasioning any further special concern.

Because of the difficulty in classification, the physician may wish to become familiar with the commonly used definitions. The "mildly" retarded child is generally defined within the intelligence-quotient range of 50 to 70; the "moderately" retarded, 35 to 50; the "severely" retarded, 20 to 35; and the "profoundly" retarded, below 20.

In terms of educational potential, retarded children are described as "educable," "trainable," or "totally dependent." The educable individual may achieve an academic competence of fourth- or fifth-grade level, a moderate amount of social adjustment, and a satisfactory degree of self-support via occupations not requiring abstract thought. The trainable child may attain an acceptable level of self-care, social adjustment to home and neighborhood, and a degree of economic usefulness via the home, residential facility, or sheltered workshop. The totally dependent child requires assistance in personal care and usually requires permanent residential care outside the home.

Three percent of newborn infants will probably be diagnosed as being retarded at some time during their lives. However, there is widespread agreement that this figure represents a substantial overdiagnosis. Possibly the majority of this 3% include cases of so-called "functional retardation" particularly among the poor, cases of so-called "minimal cerebral dysfunction," cases of learning disorders and cases of emotional disorders. It is likely that the true prevalence of mental retardation is less than 1% of the population.

Figures on incidence may not be readily translated into equivalent figures on prevalence. We do not know exactly how many mentally retarded individuals there are in a community of 100,000 at any given moment, and diagnostic difficulties hamper such studies. While it is relatively easy to measure intelligence, diagnosis also requires consideration of impairment in adaptation, a characteristic much harder to quantify.

Present evidence indicates that prevalence varies with age. Only during the school years do general adaptation and measured intelligence correlate to a high degree since the major expectation of school age children is school performance. Therefore most retarded children, particularly the mildly impaired, become clinically visible only upon school entrance and become asymptomatic again in adulthood. In the more severely affected groups, increasing mortality with age takes many.

The identification of lag in development, based on accurate, early observation, is vital to success in both treatment and remedial action. In an increasing number of instances, detection and diagnosis of an underlying biological abnormality can lead to the prevention of brain disease and consequent retardation.

Early diagnosis is equally important for children born and raised in poverty, having experienced what has been termed "environmental deprivation." Evidence indicates that exposure to nursery school and other stimulating experiences may enhance the learning process as well as the social adjustment of many "disadvantaged" children. Many do become self-supporting and productive adults. Many more could become equally or even more productive if discovered early enough, given adequate protection from neglect, and provided with the social and cultural milieu for intellectual growth.

Early diagnosis of problems which interfere with the development of the child in the comparatively privileged home may help prevent a situation in which parents—unaware of the handicap—make unrealistic demands on the child, exacerbating his condition and further depressing his function.

Early identification of any child as possibly retarded enables the physician to extend his observation period, permitting careful data gathering and deliberate appraisal as well as preventive action. Early screening procedures in hospitals, clinics, or private practice (as part of continuing, comprehensive child health service) can help to develop a roster of high-risk patients for careful follow-up.

The role of the physician may be crucial at this point. He is often the chief professional person who contacts children in the preschool period. He is the primary professional person with the clinical training and skills to evaluate biological determinants. His relationship to the family may designate him as the most appropriate person to coordinate and evaluate various diagnostic procedures, interpret findings to the parents, plan for comprehensive care and treatment, and see to it that the family gets to the proper social resources.

The physician's own expanding knowledge of patterns of growth and development, his skill in diagnostic method, and his acuity in dealing with high-risk groups can all facilitate early diagnosis. His alertness to implications of new research can speed their transfer from professional journal to clinical action.

The physician carries a heavy responsibility in early identification and management. Many parents report that they had to see two, three or more physicians before finding one who would believe in their observations. This early necessity to "shop around" leads almost inevitably to further shopping for medical and extramedical opinions later.

The initiative of the physician is important to the development of community resources. He is often the key person to encourage the use of screening devices in hospitals, to establish diagnostic teams and clinics, and to alert other disciplines to possibilities of early identification. He may also effectively lend his support to social agencies and school systems to whom retardation may first become known in their frequent contacts with high-risk families.

The physician may approach identification in different ways: (1) by causation, (2) by place of identification, (3) by age of child, or (4) by biological syndrome.

Causation

The primary causes of mental retardation may be considered to originate from the *biological* factors which influence the biochemical and structural organization of the neural matrix, or from *experiential* factors which influence the organization of function in the central nervous system during postnatal maturation, or from varying combinations.

Biological and experiential etiologic factors may have two orders of relationship with mental retardation: a *primary* or initiating relationship, and a *secondary* or compounding and perpetuating relationship. A time scale and a quantitative scale are implied in this organization. When the physician is not able to modify a primary cause therapeutically, he may be able to intervene on a secondary level and thus enhance the adaptational capacities of the individual.

The physician's responsibilities in relation to the biological aspects of retardation include (1) preventive diagnosis through the early recognition of disorders which may be predisposing to retarded functioning; (2) early identification of deviant development and the appraisal of its biological determinants; and (3) identification of biological influences in children recognized and referred by nonmedical sources or by other physicians.

Equally important but less well defined are the physician's responsibilities in relation to the experiential aspects of retardation. The physician may be alerted to these factors: (1) birth and early infancy in extreme poverty situations, (2) lack of sensory stimulation in the first six months of life, (3) distortion in patterns of parental care, (4) the effects of rearing in an institution, and (5) the role of influences, such as child abuse, long-term foster care, failure to thrive, and accidents.

During the diagnostic process the physician may remain alert to preventive opportunities through identification of high-risk individuals whose circumstances indicate an increased potential for the development of retardation, through the treatment of predisposing diseases before retardation appears, through modification of adverse psychosocial factors, and through treatment of superimposed neuroses or psychoses.

Diagnosis by Place of Identification

The physician may group the retarded in two major categories according to type of retardation and probable place of identification.

Those in the first group—the moderately, severely or profoundly handicapped—represent between 10% and 25% of the retarded population and are most apt to be identified first in the physician's office. Specific diagnoses include Down's syndrome (mongolism), cranial anomalies, genetic defects, tumors, and cerebral palsy, as well as sequelae of traumata, infections, and neurotropic poisons. Organic components, malformations, physical handicaps of ambulation and of arm-hand use, and sensory impairments are common. The IQ is usually below 50. Developmental milestones are grossly delayed and behavior is consistent with the degree of mental defect. A trainable segment of this group can benefit from special education programs which some schools provide. The family background is similar to that of the general population.

The second group includes 75% to 90% of the retarded. Degree of retardation is mild, ie, the IQ is above 50. The child is most apt to be identified in the school and later referred to the physician for evaluation. The physician may encounter difficulty in making a specific diagnosis. These children usually look normal; physical handicaps and congenital malformations are uncommon. Multiple factors, psychogenic and biological, may interact to produce this syndrome. Because these unfavorable factors tend to cluster in underprivileged socioeconomic groups, the term "cultural-familial" has been used by some. After testing, at present these patients are often placed in classes for the educable. Few are ever institutionalized and the majority remain in the community. After the school years, most join the semi-skilled and unskilled labor force, but some achieve higher professional and managerial positions. Many achieve relatively good adjustment and their identity as retarded individuals is lost.

Diagnosis by Age

A more detailed analysis of types of retardation according to age at which they become evident may be of assistance.

From Birth to End of First Year. Diagnosis is most likely in children exhibiting an obvious physical defect associated with deficiency. Signs of organic damage and extreme retardation are often identifiable before the age of 12 months in children with

2. RESEARCH, DIAGNOSIS, AND ASSESSMENT

Down's syndrome, microcephaly, hydrocephaly, etc. Intellectual deficit is often severe or profound, ie, IQ less than 35, although children with Down's syndrome may early in life manifest relatively high IQs. At this age the mildly retarded are often difficult or impossible to assess because of variation in developmental patterns and the absence of stigmata. Children who will develop familial retardation usually remain within normal ranges in their first year.

The Preschool Years. At this stage, previously undiagnosed conditions may become apparent through delay in walking, speech, habit training, and poor coordination. Such signs as simplicity of play, inability to combine words into sentences, lack of imagination, and choice of younger playmates may be among presenting complaints. Intellectual deficit may be moderate, ie, IQ of 35 to 50. Physician or parent may make the initial observation of delay.

Teachers in nursery schools, day care centers, and Head Start centers often play an important role in identifying children with delayed development.

The School Years. The mildly retarded with an IQ of 50 to 70 will become apparent at this age through academic failure, often accented by behavior patterns of aggressiveness, withdrawal, or negativism. Teachers or school officials frequently refer these children to the physician who demonstrates a capacity to work cooperatively with these individuals, their families and the schools.

Diagnosis by Biological Syndrome

The presence of certain biological syndromes indicates a certain probability of retardation. These syndromes are varied enough, however, to preclude the inevitability of retardation in every case. Although the steady increase in understanding of these syndromes is impressive, as a group these disorders are relatively rare. Clinical clues are of two types: particular morphological or anatomical stigmata, and progressive developmental deterioration.

The list of known metabolic retardations and progressive central processes—eg, the cerebral lipidoses of which infantile amaurotic familial idiocy (Tay-Sachs disease) is representative, the variants of mucopolysaccharidoses (Hurler's syndrome), leukodystrophies, hypothyroidism—has grown so large that the physician, before undertaking appropriate laboratory procedures, must refer to medical texts and literature to determine those diseases possible in a particular child.

As in all other aspects of medicine, the physician employs the history as an exceedingly important tool. Items particularly significant in retardation are developmental data, social data, and medical history.

History

Developmental Information. Parents, grandparents and other family members can provide significant material via comparisons between the child's development and that of siblings or peers. They can also provide helpful recollections of delay in reaching the usual norms in habit training and coordination, as well as delay in comprehension and use of language. Because quality and quantity of vocabulary are highly correlated with individual intelligence, an underdeveloped comprehension and speaking vocabulary provide possibly the best single index of retardation in the child with normal visual and normal auditory capacities.

The normal child will vocalize a simple word or two meaningfully between 9 and 12 months of age, use simple words to make his wants known by 18 months, and speak in two- or three-word sentences by the age of 2 years. By 7-9 years, he usually overcomes his last errors of fluency and articulation. Significant deviation from these norms provides a valuable clue to possible mental deficit.

Social Data. The observant physician notes family interactions and their possible effect on the child's behavior. He can also detect evidences of environmental deprivation, lack of appropriate stimulation, and signs of social or economic deprivation.

Medical History. The physician will find it helpful to explore (1) relevant genetic information; (2) fertility history of mother and experiences of mother in this pregnancy; (3) history of labor and delivery: blood group incompatibilities, stressful labor, etc.; (4) significant episodes in the life of the child: infections, accidents, responses to therapy; (5) seizures: myoclonic, grand mal, staring episodes, unexplained crying bouts, apneic and cyanotic episodes, stiffness and limpness, behavioral disturbances; (6) progressive developmental or neurological deterioration. He should also, insofar as possible, secure records of the birth, previous medical and surgical care, and previous hospitalizations.

Physical Examination

Developmental Assessment. Developmental delay must exist before retardation can be identified; developmental appraisal, therefore, is the fundamental technique underlying diagnosis. The physician familiarizes himself with developmental milestones in normal children, and makes their assessment an integral part of every well-baby examination. The teaching of developmental appraisal is increasingly incorporated into the educational program of medical students and into postgraduate teaching.

In developmental evaluation, the physician may find a simple assessment form helpful (see Appendix A).

A satisfactory "shorthand" for assessment might go as follows: a child sits with support from 6 to 8 months, sits alone from 8 to 10 months, walks from 12 to 18 months, talks from 18 to 24 months, rides a tricycle at 3 years, and copies a square at 4 years. These items are most likely to be remembered by parents.

Toilet training is an important issue to the family of the retarded and is influenced by socio-cultural environment.

At present there is a difference of opinion as to the usefulness of these scales in predicting the *subsequent* development of any given child. However, they do provide objective and measurable estimates of *current* behavioral functioning, and the value of such information is not to be minimized.

The physician is primarily concerned with the child's present status. If the infant is slow to reach and grasp, to hold his head up, sit, walk, vocalize, and talk, if he does not cry or respond at a minimal level, the doctor has cause for concern. He may initiate a more intensive study or request consultation.

The physician who records these developmental observations and describes the behavior observed will be able to compare the child's earlier performance with his later abilities. Such records, kept consistently, will enhance the physician's own abilities to identify not only the retardate but also more specifically the child who might profit by immediate remedial procedures.

Neurological Examination

Neurological examination in the evaluation of the mentally retarded individual requires not only a careful assessment of nervous system function but a complete physical examination. General observation may provide very important clues that will relate to the specific neurologic deficit.

General body proportions. Shortened extremities suggest *chondrodystrophy*. Body asymmetry associated with short stature with occasional syndactyly may suggest *Silver's syndrome* (mental retardation usually not present).

14. Diagnosis

The history at birth may alert one to certain types of disorders, such as dysmaturity syndromes (low birth weight at term) and intra-uterine growth retardation, which are associated with a higher incidence of neurological difficulties.

Head. Careful examination of the head can provide many clues, if not the specific diagnosis, in many problems (Table 1). A very small head may indicate *microcephaly* which may be familial, secondary to anoxia or damage due to intrauterine infections. Many disorders are associated with a small head.

Increased biparietal diameter of the head may be seen in chronic subdural hematoma. Many of these problems are related to physical abuse and are associated with other evidence of physical trauma. Radiographic examination of skull may reveal fractures.

Large head may indicate: *hydrocephalus, cerebral gigantism, generalized gangliosiodosis, Hunter's disease, Hurler's disease, Tay-Sachs disease,* or *achondroplasia.* The doll-like facies seen in Tay-Sachs disease is often characteristic.

Tongue. Large tongue may be seen in *cretinism, Down's syndrome, hypoglycemia, Trisomy 17-18, Hurler's disease, Hunter's disease, generalized gangliosidosis, Sanfilippo's syndrome.* Furrowed tongue may be seen in *Down's syndrome.* Lobulated tongue may be seen in *oral-facial-digital (OFD) syndrome.*

Hair. Sparse, coarse, kinky hair *(Menkes' syndrome)* devoid of pigmentation may suggest *neurodegenerative* disease with *monilethrix* (varying diameters of the hair shaft) often associated with seizures, spasticity and clinical downhill course.

The hair is coarse, brittle and scanty with the hairline far down on the forehead in *cretinism.*

The confluence of the eyebrows and hypertrichosis is seen in *de Lange's syndrome.*

A white forelock suggests the presence of *Waardenburg's syndrome.* Mental retardation is usually not present but may be considered because of unrecognized nerve deafness.

The appearance of a low V-shaped frontal hairline may suggest the *median, cleft face syndrome* in which there is an associated median cleft palate.

Eyes. Confluent eyebrows are characteristics of the *de Lange's syndrome.* Hypertelorism is seen in many variations from normal to abnormal. Congenital cataracts: *Hallerman-Streiff, rubella, oculo-cerebral-renal syndromes.* Deviations of slant of eyes are seen in *Down's syndrome, de Lange's syndrome, cerebral gigantism, Apert's syndrome,* and many others. Coloboma of the pupil may be seen in *oculo-auriculo-vertebral dysplasia, Trisomy 13-15, Trisomy 17-18* and several other disorders.

Ears. Abnormalities of the ears may be due to many disorders. Ex.: prominent anti-helix—*Down's syndrome;* preauricular appendages and atresia of external meatus—*oculo-auricular-vertebral dysplasia.*

Low-set ears are seen in the following syndromes and other disorders: *Apert, Crouzon, Hallerman-Streiff, Pierre-Robin, Trisomy 13-15, 17-18, Rubinstein-Taybi, Cri-du-Chat.*

Extremities. Syndactyly of fingers and toes—*Apert's syndrome.* Broad thumbs and toes—*Rubinstein-Taybi syndrome.* Tapered fingers—*new dominant syndrome.* Polydactyly—*Laurence-Moon-Biedl syndrome.* Syndactyly of toes and overlapping toes—*Ring chromosome 18.*

Fifth finger overlapping the fourth, polydactyly, syndactyly, retroflexed thumbs and "rocker bottom" feet seen in *Trisomy 13-15.* Flexion of hand with overlapping of the index finger over the third, "rocker bottom" feet, short sternum—seen in *Trisomy 17-18.* Polydactyly, syndactyly associated with cryptorchidism and/or hypospadias suggests the *Smith-Lemli-Opitz syndrome.*

Skin. Acrocyanosis may be seen in the *Marinesco-Sjögren syndrome.* (Mental retardation associated with cerebellar ataxia, bilateral congenital cataracts and short stature.)

Adenoma sebaceum, with characteristic butterfly distribution over nose and cheeks, is seen in *tuberous sclerosis,* in which these may also be fibromas of gums, nails, forehead and scalp. Cafe-au-lait spots, depigmentation, orange peel appearance trunk with decreased pigmentation and hemangiomas, and graying hair may also be seen.

The port-wine hemangioma, usually over one side of the face and forehead, suggests the *Sturge-Weber syndrome.* Telangiectasia of the skin of the ears and conjunctiva of the eyes suggests the *ataxia-telangiectasia Barr's syndrome.* Blotching of the skin may be seen in Familial Dysautonomia. Ichthyosis may be seen in *Chondrodystrophica Calcificans Congenita* and the *Sjögren-Larsson syndrome.* Cafe-au-lait spots may be seen in *neurofibromatosis, tuberous sclerosis* and *ataxia-telangiectasia.*

Soft neurological signs. Ex.: Gross and fine motor awkwardness including gait, hopping, etc., handwriting, minimal choreothetoid movements, subtle asymmetry of deep tendon reflexes, asymmetrical clonus; right-left disorientation, i.e., inability or difficulty in differentiating right from left; isolated extensor toe sign—not associated with other significant findings.

These findings may or may not represent a significant abnormality. They may or may not be associated with clinically significant problems. In themselves, they do not specifically indicate the presence of a clinical syndrome, but as a generalization, one is more likely to observe such findings in the more severely mentally retarded individuals.

The neurological examination is an attempt to assess clinically and in terms of neuroanatomy and neurophysiology certain information which will allow a physician to reach a decision as to the existence of a disturbance of function of the nervous system, its location within the nervous system and its nature. A complete examination requires not only competence on the part of the examiner, but also an awareness of the problem and ability to cooperate on the part of the patient. It is apparent that with young infants and children and patients who are unable to be cooperative professional observation will be the critical part of the examination. One must use a number of techniques which are not necessarily familiar or orthodox when working with older, cooperative individuals. One of the most critical areas of the neurological examination of infants and children is to assess their overall level of development including mental status. The patient's overall level of activity, his cooperation, his social responsiveness, and his awareness to the situation are all reviewed. Many of the tasks are evaluated in regard to the expectations for a given chronological age. Certain abilities to function increase with chronological age, and what may be perfectly normal at one age may be abnormal at another. For this reason, the concept of developmental neurology is most critical in the assessment of

Table 1.—Head Circumference for Boys and Girls During the First 7 Years of Life*

Age	Boys No.	Boys Mean, Cm	Boys SD	Girls No.	Girls Mean, Cm	Girls SD
1 mo	295	37.3	±1.54	282	36.5	±1.41
3 mo	229	40.7	±1.43	230	39.8	±1.39
6 mo	275	43.6	±1.45	262	42.5	±1.42
9 mo	247	45.7	±1.40	259	44.6	±1.41
1 yr	289	46.8	±1.40	275	45.6	±1.22
1½ yr	255	47.9	±1.40	255	47.0	±1.30
2 yr	264	49.1	±1.47	260	48.0	±1.32
2½ yr	219	49.8	±1.39	221	48.8	±1.35
3 yr	216	50.4	±1.35	227	49.5	±1.35
3½ yr	226	51.0	±1.40	222	50.1	±1.45
4 yr	233	51.2	±1.41	229	50.7	±1.46
4½ yr	220	51.6	±1.45	217	51.0	±1.48
5 yr	224	51.8	±1.47	225	51.2	±1.50
7 yr	187	52.7	±1.48	194	52.2	±1.37

*From Westropp, C.K., and Barber, C.R.: Growth of the Skull in Young Children. J Neurol Psychiat 19:52, 1956. (Reprinted by permission of the authors, the editor, and publishers, B.M.A. House, Tavistock Square, London, W.C.1.)

2. RESEARCH, DIAGNOSIS, AND ASSESSMENT

children.

Diverse methods are used to assess the function of the nervous system. It is important to remember that the physician is attempting, through a careful examination, to interpret systematically the structure and function of the nervous system. Following an overall assessment of the development, including handedness, the physician will attempt to assess the function of rather clearly defined areas.

Examination of the cranial nerves gives information concerned with the sense of smell, vision, eye movements, pupillary function, sensation about the face and head, muscles of mastication, muscles of facial expression, taste, hearing, equilibrium, swallowing, ability to speak, tongue movement and some movements of the neck. These areas can generally be examined with precision both physiologically and anatomically.

The next level of examination concerns motor (or voluntary muscle) function. The components responsible for these functions range from high centers in the brain to the muscle itself. A disturbance at any level may cause some impairment of function. In general, the motor system can be assessed with greater accuracy than some other parts of the nervous system. One can usually establish whether a given disturbance of motor function is due to some impairment of brain, spinal cord, peripheral nerve or muscle. Areas of the nervous system that also participate in the control of movements (such as the basal ganglia and cerebellum in the brain) can also be identified with some accuracy.

There are a number of reflexes which are elicited during a neurological examination. They vary from knee-jerks to pupillary reflexes of the eye. Some reflexes, such as sucking and grasp, are present at birth and disappear with maturation.

Examination of the sensory system is difficult at any age and requires considerable cooperation from the patient. It is very difficult for the young child to cooperate sufficiently to give meaningful information. Information concerning the ability to perceive pain (pin-prick), temperature (hot-cold), light touch, position sense (direction of movement in fingers, toes, limbs) and vibration may be important. Some complex aspects of higher brain sensory function such as visual, auditory or complex exteroceptive (pain, temperature, light touch) and proprioceptive sensations (movements) are difficult to assess in young children. This is particularly true for those higher order sensations at the level of the brain concerned with visual and auditory perception. These functions are vital for reading and language. There are many ways that can be used to aid in assessing these areas of function. All require some ability of the patient to cooperate in this assessment.

The ability of children to read, copy geometric designs, draw figures, calculate and other such tasks must be carefully assessed in certain problems. Although the physician may screen these functions, it should be recognized that an accurate assessment may require a qualified psychological examiner.

Other aspects of the neurological examination will identify directionality (the ability to differentiate right from left), gait, coordination, language and communication. The physician also makes an overall estimate of the patient's mental state and behavior.

Special Tests

The decision to perform special tests or procedures should always be preceded by a clinical examination and complete appraisal of the patient. Only tests that will clarify the problem should be performed, and the performance of extensive and irrelevant procedures must be avoided. Specialized studies can be valuable adjuncts in an overall clinical neurological assessment. As with all laboratory studies, they must be evaluated by the physician in terms of the overall clinical problem. These studies alone generally will not clarify a given clinical problem, but are of value when interpreted in terms of the overall clinical problem.

X-rays of the skull can be helpful in some clinical probems. This is particularly true when one is dealing with possible injuries, maldevelopment of the skull, previous infection or other factors that might contribute to calcification of brain or blood vessels, erosion of bone due to some abnormal growth. As it might be expected, they are not generally helpful in the assessment of disorders of learning and/or behavior.

The electroencephalogram (EEG) can be a most valuable laboratory aid in the assessment of many clinical problems. Patients with many clinical manifestations of nervous system disease (ex. cerebral palsy, epilepsy, severe mental retardation) have a higher incidence of EEG abnormalities. The significance of the presence or absence of such abnormalities must be evaluated by the physician.

However, the EEG is often used and overused in the assessment of learning and/or behavioral difficulties. It does not measure intellectual level or specifically correlate with behavioral disorders. The question of establishing the presence or absence of "brain damage" is often posed. The EEG only measures the electrical activity of the brain. Abnormalities in these recordings mean little unless they are correlated with specific clinical problems by a physician qualified to do so. Attempts have been made to correlate EEG deviations with abnormal learning and/or behavior, but there are many problems in this application. Many studies have been done, but each investigator has approached the problem somewhat differently and there is little consensus. Thus far, there does not appear to be any specific EEG abnormality that correlates with a specific aberration in learning and/or behavior.

Findings on clinical examination may indicate additional laboratory investigations, but should be done only when indicated. Specific biochemical studies of blood and/or urine (Tables 2 and 3)—examination of the spinal fluid, chromosome studies—may sometimes be needed. Brain scan (studies of uptake of radioactive substance by the brain), angiograms (special X-ray techniques using injections of radiopaque dyes in blood vessels to the brain), pneumoencephalograms or ventriculograms (air in the ventricular system of the brain) are rarely indicated in learning and/or behavioral disorders.

Dermatoglyphics. Abnormal patterns are present not only in Down's syndrome, but also in rubella and in many cases of mental retardation of unknown cause.

Dental Aspects

Diagnosis. There are a few conditions (such as dental decay and poor oral hygiene) that are more frequently found in the teeth and mouth of mentally retarded children than in normal children. In a few specific syndromes, such as in Down's syndrome and kernicterus, one can observe more specific signs characteristics of the condition.

In general, mentally retarded children suffer from excessive dental decay and gingivitis. Both are related to poor oral hygiene. Caries *frequency* (except in Down's syndrome) is about the same as in normal children; but once initiated, the process of decay tends to progress more rapidly and destructively. This may be related to the excessive amounts of sweets (sucrose-containing candies and cookies) given to these children by indulgent parents and relatives "to keep them happy." The general lack of oral hygiene, especially in institutionalized children, is directly related to inability to manage a toothbrush effectively, the protein-poor high-carbohydrate soft diet, and inattention to oral cleanliness in the

14. Diagnosis

TABLE 2.—IDENTIFIABLE BIOCHEMICAL DISORDERS OFTEN ASSOCIATED WITH MENTAL RETARDATION, CHARACTERIZED BY ELEVATED BLOOD AMINO ACIDS

Disease	Amino Acid Increased in Blood	Clinical Features
Phenylketonuria	Phenylalanine (o-hydroxyphenylacetic acid, other phenolic acid compounds in urine)	Mousy odor, eczema, seizures
Homocystinuria (vitamin B₆ sensitive and B₆ insensitive forms)	Methionine (homocystine in urine)	Dislocated lenses, malar flush, generalized osteoporosis, thromboembolic phenomena
Histidinemia	Histidine	Retarded speech development, articulatory defects
Maple syrup urine disease	Alloisoleucine, isoleucine, leucine, valine	Maple syrup odor of urine, hypertonia, seizures
Prolinemia type II	Proline, hydroxyproline, glycine in urine	(?) association with seizures, (?) mental retardation
Glycinemia, non-ketotic	Glycine	Seizures, spasticity, opisthotonos
Lysinemia, persistent	Lysine	Growth failure, absence secondary sex characteristics
Hyperammonemia type I (Carbamyl phosphate synthetase deficiency)	Glycine, glutamine	Episodic vomiting, irritability, lethargy, coma, seizures, hyperammonemia
Hyperammonemia Type II (Ornithine transcarbamylase transferase deficiency)	Glutamine (plus orotic acid in urine)	As above with hepatomegaly, SGOT hyperammonemia
Citrullinemia	Citrulline	Attacks of vomiting, post-absorptive hyperammonemia
Argininemia	Arginine (arginine, cystine, lysine, and ornithine in urine)	Spastic diplegia, seizures, hyperammonemia
Argininosuccinicaciduria	Argininosuccinic acid	Seizures, hepatomegaly, vomiting, coma, intermittent ataxia, abnormal hair, postprandial hyperammonemia
Lesch-Nyhan syndrome (hypoxanthine-guanine phosphoribosyl transferase deficiency)	Serum urate elevated (urinary uric acid excretion increased)	Self-mutilation, choreoathetosis, spasticity

Prepared by Sterling Garrard, M.D.

child. The build-up of thick tenacious microbial colonies and carbohydrate-containing debris on the teeth of such children is obvious upon even cursory examination as is the fetor ex ore. These microbial masses are inhabited by cariogenic microorganisms (usually cariogenic strep.) resulting in severe and deep carious lesions; and also by toxin producing microorganisms which produce a severe and progressive gingivitis leading to periodontal disease. The latter is especially prominent in children with Down's syndrome.

Hypoplastic pits in the enamel occur more frequently in brain damaged children, especially in those with cerebral palsy, than in normal children, but are not pathognomonic. Enamel hypoplasias reflect the exact *time* of a metabolic disturbance, usually a disturbance in calcium metabolism. The incidence is low in normal children and much higher in brain-damaged children. Hypoplastic pitting of the enamel may occur as a result of birth trauma and poor neonatal adjustment (frequent in cerebral palsy). These are seen at the gingival line of the primary incisors and at the incisal ⅓ of the permanent incisors.

In kernicterus one may note a greenish color in the enamel of the primary (baby) teeth as a result of pre-natal or neonatal incorporation of bilirubin.

In persons with fructose intolerance or diabetes, the caries attack rate is very low as a result of severe restrictions of sugars.

In Down's syndrome, the characteristic oral picture is: macroglossia with fissured tongue, thick ropy saliva with drooling at early ages (diminished swallowing reflex?) and severe progressive periodontal disease with early loosening and loss of teeth. In general, the caries attack rate in Down's syndrome is less than in other mental retardates. These children often show small or peg-shaped lateral incisors and/or congenital absence of these teeth.

This is not a characteristic of Down's syndrome, but merely an increased frequency.

In children with cerebral palsy, bruxism (night-grinding) is very common. Although annoying to those sleeping in the same room, bruxism is not as destructive to the attaching tissues in children as it can become in even normal persons during middle age.

Special Procedures

In attempting to determine the specific etiologic diagnosis in a patient with mental retardation, the physician is confronted with a bewildering number of syndromes. Because many of these syndromes are seen infrequently and because many of the clinical features are not specific, the physician cannot always depend on clinical observation alone to establish the diagnosis.

The laboratory, properly utilized, can be an extremely useful adjunct to the physician. Diagnostic procedures have been increasing at a fantastic rate and no physician or laboratory can possibly carry out all of the procedures useful in the diagnosis of mental retardation. The clinician dealing with mental retardation should be able to select those tests likely to be positive in a specific case. In order to do this, the physician should have at his disposal certain simple "screening" tests. Every child with undiagnosed mental retardation should have the following laboratory studies performed:

Phenistix — PKU.
Clinitest — reducing substance (galactose-galactosemia).
Labstix — pH, ketones, glucose, occult blood, protein.

If the child's history and physical examination are suggestive of a metabolic disorder, the following types of compounds can be detected in blood or urine samples by utilizing sample laboratory procedures.

(1) Amino acids: colorimetric tests, chromatography or electrophoresis; primary amino acidurias such as hyperglycinuria or secondary amino acidurias such as in infantile cirrhosis or Lowe's syndrome.

(2) Sugars: colorimetric tests, chromatography; galactose in galactosemia or pentose in pentosuria.

(3) Mucopolysaccharides: spot tests, colorimetric tests, increased urinary glycosaminoglycans in mucopolysaccharidoses (Hurler's, Hunter's) and related disorders (Farber's, fucosidosis).

(4) Organic acids: colorimetric tests, chromatography; phenylpyruvic acid, phenyllactic acid in PKU; -keto acids in maple syrup urine disease; methylmalonic acid in vitamin B dependency syndromes; lactic acid in Leigh's encephalopathy; and uric acid in Lesch-Nyhan syndrome.

(5) T_4 and cholesterol: hypothyroidism.

Chromosomal analysis should be performed on any child with three or more congenital malformations which do not form a recognizable syndrome.

If any of these simple tests are positive, further diagnostic tests are usually required from a specialized center. If the above tests are negative but the history or physical is suggestive of a specific biochemical abnormality, referral should be made to a center for specific enzymatic investigation.

Psychological Tests

Careful psychological tests are often necessary to define a degree of retardation that may not be evident on clinical examination. When the question of organic vs. emotional problems is raised, these tests will often provide clues to aid in diagnosis, family counseling and treatment.

The physician must remember that the IQ is not a diagnosis. Caution is required because the results and interpretation of

2. RESEARCH, DIAGNOSIS, AND ASSESSMENT

TABLE 3.—IDENTIFIABLE BIOCHEMICAL DISORDERS ASSOCIATED WITH MENTAL RETARDATION, CHARACTERIZED BY INCREASED URINARY AMINO ACID BUT LITTLE OR NO INCREASE IN BLOOD CONCENTRATION

Disease	Amino Acid on Excess in Urine	Some Additional Clinical Features
Cystathioninuria	Cystathionine	Features inconstant, may be a benign disorder of metabolism (?)
Hartnup's Disorder	Specific pattern of aminoaciduria (monoamino-monocarboxylic amino acids)	Pellagrous rash, intermittent ataxia, short stature

QUALITATIVE SCREENING TESTS OF URINE*

Test	Phenyl-ketonuria	Homo-cystinuria	Histidi-nemia	Maple syrup disease	Galactosemia (transferase and kinase deficiency)	Hurler's
Ferric chloride and/or buffered dip stick	+	−	+	−	−	−
2,4-dinitro-phenylhydrazine	+	−	±	+	−	−
Cyanide-nitro-prusside	−	+	−	−	−	−
Benedict's (reducing substance)	−	−	−	−	+	−
Glucose oxidase test	−	−	−	−	−	−
Acid albumin turbidity	−	−	−	−	−	+
Spot tests: toluidine blue, Alcian blue	−	−	−	−	−	+

*These are simple screening tests for urine which can be done for older children in the office. However, blood screening tests, such as the Guthrie for elevated phenylalanine level in PKU, may be the preferred screening procedure especially in the new-born.
Prepared by Sterling Garrard, M.D.

various tests may differ, testing situation and examiner may be variables, the child's classroom success may not parallel the test results, and tests are not equally applicable to all children. Inappropriate labeling of a child on the basis of one observation may foster a self-fulfilling prophecy: parents, teachers and others may begin to treat the child as retarded and thereby reinforce the perception that he is retarded and they may also render more likely poor performance on subsequent tests.

Information from these tests can be used as a basis for training and for planning the child's educational program, since they measure both weaknesses and strengths in learning skills. However, intelligence tests should be used only as one among several means of assessment.

Too rigidly used, the IQ may become the determining factor in diagnosis, evaluation and management with the concomitant danger of committing a child, if even for a short time, to a program above or below his potentialities. The physician may wish to confer with the psychologist responsible for testing to obtain a more balanced perspective on the child than the IQ alone can give.

Furthermore, a therapeutic trial of programs may be the best indicator of what the individual can accomplish.

It is important to remember that psychologists are trained to look for deficiency states and abnormalities. Psychological reports often begin by describing what the child cannot do. Yet, it is far more important to determine what the child can do and where his strengths lie. A successful therapeutic approach can be constructed upon these assets and abilities. In addition, the psychologist and the mother may disagree on the child's achievements. The mother usually claims more than the psychological tests have revealed, and the physician should give appropriate weight to the testimony of both the parent and the professional.

Many psychologists are in the habit of excluding parents when children are being examined. This is done in order to be able to "standardize the procedures." However, the purpose of clinical testing is to determine the child's optimal functioning. Therefore retesting, utilizing the mother's presence and assurance, may be appropriate in some cases. In many instances where a discrepancy exists between the reports of parents and psychologist, judgment will simply have to be deferred pending therapeutic trial and the passage of time.

IQ and other intelligence tests have been shown to be influenced by culture, financial status, and other nongenetic factors. Furthermore, they have been misused in many school situations to the possible detriment of the pupil. There are some scales that measure adaptation but they are not in common use and not as well standardized as those available for intelligence. Because of the inherent defects of these tests as well as their wide misinterpretation and misapplication, some have recommended that they be dropped altogether. Most physicians are not qualified to reach carefully considered decisions on this important matter, but they should be aware and, insofar as possible, informed about the various arguments regarding intelligence testing.

The physician may make many valid observations of the influences in any given patient and family, but frequently he may find helpful the trained social worker's evaluative techniques in determining personal and social needs and possible etiologic factors in these areas. The physician may also find useful an educational study to determine the degree of educational disability, or an assessment of vocational potential and skills in the young adult.

In many cases the physician himself may complete a satisfactory evaluation. However, in many others, he may wish to refer the patient and family to appropriate clinics or medical centers, or he may call in consultants or make referrals on an individual basis to pediatricians, psychiatrists, neurologists, orthopedists, otolaryngologists, ophthalmologists, social workers, educators, speech therapists or vocational counselors.

Other Learning Handicaps

Mental retardation is not the only depressant of learning capacity. A child who seems retarded may be suffering from defective hearing or vision, cerebral palsy, communication or language disorder, emotional disorder, perceptual handicap, another chronic illness or from chronic malnutrition.

A condition known generally as "perceptual handicap," also ascribed a dozen or so different names (including "minimal brain damage"), has been the subject of considerable dispute for the last decade. There is little agreement on its cause, management, or even whether there indeed is such a disease.

The consensus seems to favor considering the entire question as primarily educational, rather than medical, although occasionally drugs, such as dextroamphetamine, methylphenidate and others, seem to offer some assistance. The etiologic role of socioeconomic and obstetric factors also needs further clarification. Proper treatment demands consultation with other disciplines such as social work, psychology and education.

Additional Considerations

Mental retardation is one of the atypical crises which require cautious appraisal and mature, deliberate consideration. The physician must not allow his frustrations and anxieties or those of the family to impede his deliberate and meticulous assessment. The physician tends to associate crisis with an inevitable need for speed. He may feel compelled to make a rapid evaluation in order to announce an early diagnosis to the parents of the affected child. Haste, however, resulting in an inaccurate diagnosis and too early labeling of the child may add to the distress of the parents and the detriment of the child.

It may be advisable, in the case of newborns with suspected Down's syndrome and other similar conditions, to have one or more physicians called into consultation even before the mother and father are initially informed by the family physician. In this way, the danger of hasty action can be further minimized.

During the process of diagnosis, the physician must provide support to the family. He may find it appropriate to suggest a flexible attitude to the parents, indicating that the child may be delayed in development but that a certain amount of time may be necessary for evaluation. The brain of the young child, he may indicate, may have unrealized potentialities for development, and it would be a mistake to make a hurried diagnosis without following the child for a period of time to measure the capacity of this more slowly developing individual.

The physician and family may use this period of evaluation to institute helpful management procedures. Appropriate handling in home, nursery school, or early school training program will maximize the child's potential and make possible a more intelligent prognosis as to the child's future social and vocational adjustment.

Such a period of grace can permit careful gathering of data and minimize parental shopping for other opinions. A time in which family and physician develop mutual confidence can make the decision easier when it comes and lay the groundwork for a sustained relationship between family and doctor necessary for the optimum management of the retarded child.

FINDING AND HELPING HANDICAPPED CHILDREN
Lee Cross and Kennith Goin (eds.)

This is a basic handbook for professionals and volunteers engaged in early identification of handicapped children from birth to the age of eight—a rapidly expanding national effort under the new Education for All Handicapped Children Act.
 A comprehensive guide to casefinding, screening, diagnosis, assessment, and evaluation, this timely book provides a wealth of practical information that will enable teachers, pediatricians, nurses, psychologists, language therapists, social workers, and community leaders to work together effectively. An annotated bibliography describes the best materials currently available for screening, diagnosis, and assessment.

160 pages; 6" x 9"; annotated bibliography; index;
cloth—ISBN: 0-8027-9041-0, $9.85
paper—ISBN: 0-8027-7111-4, $7.65

PLANNING PROGRAMS FOR EARLY EDUCATION OF THE HANDICAPPED
Norman E. Ellis and Lee Cross (eds.)

Comprehensive handbook for the thousands of professionals currently building statewide and district programs for the early education of the handicapped. Chapters are written by Samuel A. Kirk, James J. Gallagher, John Melcher, Norman E. Ellis, Wayne Spence, Wayne B. Largent, Tealy L. Collins, David L. Lillie, and others. Appendix A is an overview of federal legislation that will aid in the development of funding proposals. Appendix B focuses on the pertinent literature about the development of early intervention services.

125 pages, 6 x 9", appendices, index,
ISBN: 0-8027-9039-9, $9.85

To order these books or for more information on these and other college and professional books, contact Joseph Logan, Special Learning Corporation.

SPECIAL LEARNING CORPORATION
42 Boston Post Rd. Guilford, Connecticut 06437 (203) 453-6525

Brief Reports

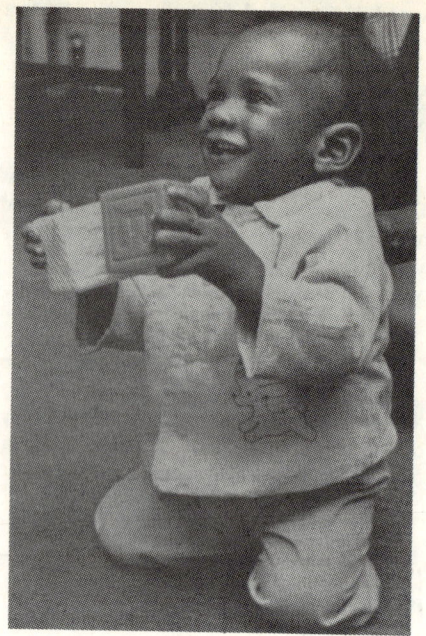

Predictive Value of Infant Intelligence Scales with Multiply Handicapped Children

REBECCA F. DuBOSE
George Peabody College for Teachers

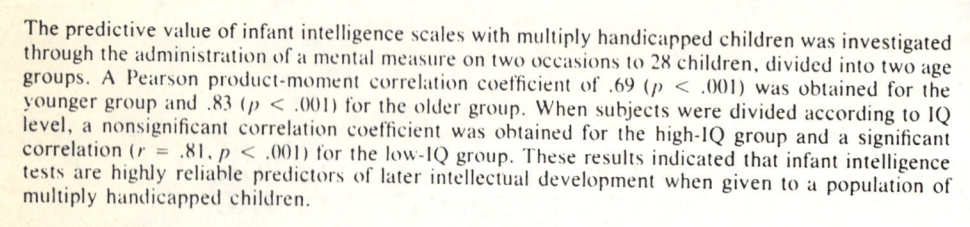

The predictive value of infant intelligence scales with multiply handicapped children was investigated through the administration of a mental measure on two occasions to 28 children, divided into two age groups. A Pearson product-moment correlation coefficient of .69 ($p < .001$) was obtained for the younger group and .83 ($p < .001$) for the older group. When subjects were divided according to IQ level, a nonsignificant correlation coefficient was obtained for the high-IQ group and a significant correlation ($r = .81, p < .001$) for the low-IQ group. These results indicated that infant intelligence tests are highly reliable predictors of later intellectual development when given to a population of multiply handicapped children.

While tests of infant development are notoriously poor predictors of later intellectual functioning in nonretarded populations (Bayley, 1970; Goffeney, Henderson, & Butler, 1971), a number of researchers have recognized their value with severely delayed children (Cavanaugh, Cohen, Dunphy, Ringwall, & Goldberg, 1957; Erickson, Johnson, & Campbell, 1970; Illingsworth, 1961; Werner, Honzik, & Smith, 1968). Illingsworth, for example, kept records of 122 infants who were labeled as mentally retarded after rough developmental assessments during well-baby examinations, although they did not possess obvious characteristics associated with mental retardation. One year later, 75 percent of the children performed on a retarded level. Using the Bayley Scales of Infant Development, VanderVeer and Schweid (1974) identified 23 children (ranging in age from 18 to 30 months) as retarded. When tested 1 to 3 years later, 75 percent of the 15 infants initially found to be in the moderately to profoundly retarded range remained in that category. None of the children initially identified as retarded were "normal" at the later testing. These results suggest that infant intelligence tests can be useful in predicting later developmental functioning when mental retardation is suspected.

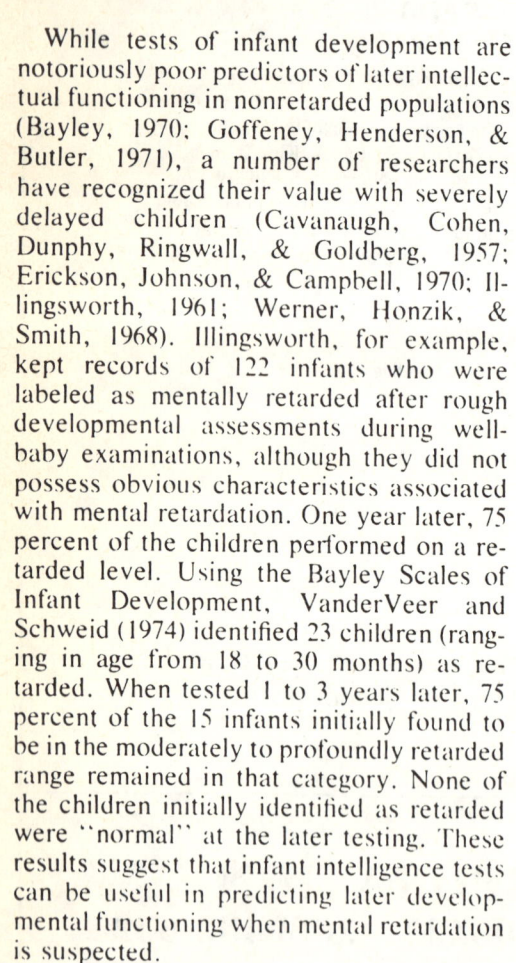

Predicting the course of development in severely retarded children will become increasingly important as mandatory education laws bring these children into the public-education classrooms. Long-term plans are essential if local, state, and federal funds are to be used to cover educational costs. If these youngsters are to be served, then guidelines to plan short-term intervention strategies are needed. Determining where to begin and what objectives to set requires some form of assessment. Assessment should include a battery of tests covering every facet of information needed for planning the youngster's educational program. Some form of a valid and reliable mental measure should be included in the battery.

Additional sensory and physical impairments cause many of these children to be considered untestable (Dodrill, Macfarlane, & Boyd, 1974). Kiernan and DuBose (1974) found that severely and profoundly impaired, including deaf–blind, children can be assessed using infant scales with slight adaptations in the presentation of items. If scales of early mental development are found to be reliable predictors of later development in severely handicapped children, then data can be provided for preparing immediate and long-term goals. The present study was designed to investigate the predictive value of infant intelligence tests when given to deaf–blind–retarded youngsters.

Subjects were 28 (17 males, 11 females) multiply handicapped children evaluated over a 5-year period by members of a diagnostic team from George Peabody College for Teachers. Each subject was evaluated at least twice as a part of a comprehensive psychological–educational assessment. All but 5 subjects had an etiology of rubella syndrome with significant auditory and visual impairments. Of the other 5 subjects, 2 had myleomemingoceles, and 3 had chromosomal abnormalities of unknown origin. All but 2 subjects were nonverbal; however, those two had significant hearing deficits and could not be tested as though they were hearing children. The mean chronological age (CA) at the time of first testing was 72 months (range 32 to 117) and 104 months (range 63 to 135) on the second testing.

Examiners administered the Infant Intelligence Scale (Cattell, 1940), the Mental Scale of the Bayley Scales of Infant Development (Bayley, 1969), or the Merrill–Palmer Scale of Mental Tests (Stutsman, 1948) based on each child's suspected impairments and abilities. These three instruments are heavily loaded with performance tasks and require very little usable vision. When needed, signs and gestures were substituted for oral instructions. Totally blind youngsters were permitted to feel a model before being requested to replicate the model.

The age and estimated ability of each child was the major factor in test selection. The Merrill–Palmer was given to all children estimated to have skills on at least an 18-month level. For subjects below this estimated ability, the Bayley or Cattell was selected. Where possible, mental ages (MAs) and IQs were determined using scaled norms in the manual of each test. In cases where CAs exceeded norms, it was necessary to arrive at an MA score and to then convert this to a ratio IQ, a procedure which unfortunately introduces unknown sources of error.

A mean of 29 months elapsed between first and second testings. During the intervening period, all subjects were enrolled in educational programs. Six were enrolled in full-time residential programs, and the remaining 22 subjects participated in self-contained special-education classes in their home communities.

A total of 28 children were given the same mental measure on two occasions. Table 1 presents the means and standard deviations (SDs) of the test results. Pearson product-moment correlation coefficients were .69 ($p < .001$) for the younger group (mean CA = 51 months) and .83 ($p < .001$) for the older group (mean CA = 101 months). For the group as a whole, the mean MA on initial testing was 29 months; on the second testing, 36 months.

TABLE 1
IQ Means and Standard Deviations (SDs) on Testing Occasions for Younger and Older Groups

Group[a]	First testing Mean	SD	Second testing Mean	SD
Younger	34	15	30	15
Older	43	23	39	20

[a] $N = 14$ in each group.

Table 2 presents the means and SDs for the two groups when divided according to IQ level. The Pearson product-moment correlation for the high-IQ group was .44 ($p > .05$) and .81 ($p < .001$) for the low-IQ group. This finding suggests considerably greater stability for the low-IQ group.

TABLE 2
Means and Standard Deviations (SDs) on both Testing Occasions for High- and Low-IQ Groups

Group[a]	First testing Mean	SD	Second testing Mean	SD
High IQ	55	11	46	15
Low IQ	21	10	23	12

[a] $N = 14$ in each group.

The results of this study strongly support the findings of Illingsworth (1961) and VanderVeer and Schweid (1974) concerning the utility of infant intelligence tests in predicting later mental development in severely handicapped children. All children labeled as retarded on the first testing were also found to be retarded on the second testing occasion. Only one child found to be severely or profoundly retarded on the first testing occasion was found to be above that range on the second occasion. Two children thought to be only moderately retarded on the basis of the first test fell in the severely retarded range at the later testing. Of all the children tested, 81 percent remained in the retardation classification range of their first evaluation. With this group, which ranged in age from 2.5 to 9.5 years at first testing, CA was unrelated to predictability of IQs.

The finding that the low-IQ children were more stable than the high-IQ children deserves further attention. A few extreme differences were noted (-25, -28, -23) upon closer examination of individual scores. Several explanations are offered. In testing very young children with known sensory

2. RESEARCH, DIAGNOSIS, AND ASSESSMENT

deficits, particularly deaf-blind individuals, examiners are extremely careful to allow the benefit of any doubt. Perhaps this occurred more frequently on the first testing occasion. Certainly the test demands at higher levels became more strenuous, requiring a substantial language base in contrast to the sensory motor schemas dominating tests at earlier levels. The higher scoring abilities were apparently more variable and thus more difficult to assess accurately. These results indicate a need for an expanded study using a larger subject pool so that test predictions for high- and low-IQ groups can be compared under more favorable conditions.

In conclusion, results of this study have shown that infant intelligence tests are highly reliable predictors of later intellectual development when given to a population of older multiply handicapped retarded children. These findings are in no way generalizable to all infant intelligence scales or to other populations; however, the results offer strong support for previous findings of the predictive value of infant developmental tests with severely handicapped children. It is recognized that these youngsters will make only minimal gains even in excellent educational programs; therefore, scores will remain predictably stable and can be reliably included in the planning for their immediate and future needs.

Readings in Physically Handicapped Education

This book provides a detailed and thorough foundation for those interested in the many facets of the physically handicapped. The etiology of physical defects along with a special section on educational and occupational mainstreaming are included.

For further information about this book and other special education materials, contact:

Joseph Logan, Editor
Special Learning Corporation

Special Learning Corporation
42 Boston Post Rd. Guilford, Connecticut 06437 (203) 453-6525

The retarded child
Checking out facilities for care

Mary Alderman

Their mentally retarded boy was "doing fine at home," the parents repeatedly assured their doctor. Then, at a Thanksgiving dinner, he pulled on the tablecloth and dumped everything on the floor. The normal children gave their parents an ultimatum to "do something" about this child whom they felt was ruining their lives.

Community pressures can also push a family to a reluctant decision about care of a retarded child. Among the many misconceptions is that retardates are sexually promiscuous. While, in fact, the libido of a retarded individual is usually quite low, a family may be faced with threats or an actual crisis when the child reaches adolescence.

When parents decide that they are unable to care for their mentally retarded child at home, it's natural for them to turn to their family doctor for help. Quite realistically, most parents are afraid of overcrowded and understaffed public residential facilities and hope to find an alternative. Others may be ready to dump their children anywhere, so long as they can shed the responsibility. Even those parents who reject their child will, however, react with guilt and horror if the facility they have chosen turns out to be a dehumanized lockup.

A previous article, "Counseling techniques: Guiding the family of a handicapped child" described parental reaction to severe disability in a child, how and when to tell the parents of the diagnosis, long-term support for the family, and the parents' responsibility for making the important decisions. In that article, the consultants agreed that all babies should go home from the hospital with the mothers so that parents can make a well-considered decision about residential placement of a severely retarded infant, rather than decide while in the initial shock of diagnosis.

The following article is designed to help when you are called upon to help parents in their attempt to find a solution to their problems. Prepared with the assistance of experts conversant with all types of facilities, the article briefly outlines the basic steps parents should take before they reach a final decision about placement. In addition, you'll find a checklist of what to look for in a

2. RESEARCH, DIAGNOSIS, AND ASSESSMENT

residential facility. You may want to give it to parents to aid them in their decision, or use it yourself to check out facilities.

---EXPRESS STOP---

Decision factors: Assess the child's needs and the family situation. Search for alternatives to residential care. The "Porter-Sargent Directory" may provide a starting point. Refer the family to a specialty center familiar with the possibilities of care. With guidance, a family may be able to work out private rather than public care.

Assuming the child has had a thorough diagnostic workup, it's the parents' responsibility to decide on the type of care their child needs. You can help by spelling out the decision factors and exploring the possibilities of care. In so doing, four important areas that you want to investigate are:

1. What are the child's needs and disabilities? What are his strengths? Isolate the contributing factors to the problem. Assess the child's physical, intellectual, social and emotional status.

2. What is the family situation? How old are the parents; how is their health? How old are their other children? Are there babies, toddlers or other handicapped children who require more care? Has the family enough money to hire a sitter or extra help? Explore the family situation, and its stability, to determine if their inability to care for the retarded child is short-term and likely to be relieved or if it's a long-term problem.

3. What are the community's resources? The family should thoroughly evaluate the available services: homemakers, home health aides, public health nurses, infant development centers, infant stimulation home visitors (sometimes called "home-chance visitors"), pre-nursery and nursery school programs for the multihandicapped, daycare centers for the retarded, and special day schools. There may even be "respite homes" where the child can board during family emergencies, vacations, or just a break. The best way to find out about the possibilities in local services is through knowledgeable people in the community. Local branches of the following agencies may be helpful:

»American Association on Mental Deficiency

»American Psychiatric Association

»Council for Exceptional Children

»National Association for Retarded Children

»United Cerebral Palsy Associations.

Since parents often move to communities to be close to a child placed in a residential facility, it's a good idea to urge them to search out possibilities for daycare in other geographical areas.

The "Porter-Sargent Directory" (*Directory for Exceptional Children*, edited by D. R. Young and Porter Sargent, 1971) may be helpful as a starting point in locating services, particularly for the family moving to a new area. This directory, which may be found in some medical libraries, provides a national listing of special schools, day and residential, according to category of handicap. Material is printed as submitted, so parents should evaluate a school carefully.

In addition to facilities for the mentally retarded, the "Porter-Sargent" lists schools and treatment centers for the emotionally disturbed and socially maladjusted; psychiatric and guidance clinics; tutoring and remedial schools; facilities for the orthopedically handicapped; facilities specializing in cardiac, asthmatic, tubercular, and epileptic disorders; and schools and clinics for the blind, the deaf and the speech handicapped.

When the family is exploring possibilities of placement of an adult, they need to look into a wide range of alternatives. There is now a strong drive throughout the country to develop smaller facilities in local communities. Families should discuss living arrangements with local resource people. Some of the alternatives are: foster homes, shared apartments, nursing homes, hotels, half-way houses.

4. What do the parents want? Because guilt is a part of committing any family member to an institution, most parents need to choose residential care only as a last resort; they need the knowledge that they have done everything possible to care for their child themselves. If possible, it may be very helpful to refer the family to a university-affiliated specialty center, such as a child development or mental retardation center. Then parents can get help in reaching a decision on the type of care they want for their child in consultation with experts familiar with the great range of possibilities. These experts may also be able to help the parents work out their ambivalent feelings about placement.

The parents may learn that

they have access to sources of help of which they were unaware. For instance, most parents are afraid of what will happen to their retarded child when they die. In some areas publicly funded guardianships are being developed where someone comes into the home to visit and help the retarded individual, even when he grows old himself.

Experts in care of the retarded may also be able to provide guidance in the financial planning required to assess accurately the possibilities of care. It may be possible, for example, to work out aid through provisions of the Social Security Act which would allow for private rather than public care.

If either parent has accrued benefits under Social Security there are childhood disability benefits for individuals who are disabled prior to age 18. If the individual doesn't have a family, it may be possible to obtain financial aid through Aid to the Permanently and Totally Disabled, based on welfare amendments to the Social Security Act. Adults over the age of 18 qualify if they have a permanent and total disability and have total assets of not more than $300 and earn less than $50 per month. Funds can be used for long-term care in the individual's own home, foster home, residence club, etc. The aid comes in three ways:

1. Monthly payments for food, shelter and lodging
2. Payments for medical care and appliances
3. Social service help and protective supervision.

Veteran's benefits are still another avenue for financing private care. Financial assistance is available to "helpless" children of deceased veterans. For children age 14-23, funds may be used for training or restorative treatment in programs approved by the V.A.

Benefits continue as long as the condition exists and financial assistance is needed, or until the

Evaluating care of the retarded in a residential facility

	YES	NO
1. Are you welcome at any time?	☐	☐
2. Are the children dressed?	☐	☐
3. Do clothes fit?	☐	☐
4. Do socks match?	☐	☐
5. Do shoes fit?	☐	☐
6. Are the children fed in a different place than the sleeping quarters?	☐	☐
7. Are back wards as well kept as front wards?	☐	☐
8. Are the beds long enough?	☐	☐
9. Are the children out of bed? Is adaptive equipment in use?	☐	☐
10. Are braces on the children, or are they stacked in a corner?	☐	☐
11. Is medical care available?	☐	☐
12. If the facility is large, is there an infirmary or hospital with services such as a laboratory and physical therapy?	☐	☐
13. Is the dental hygiene program effective?	☐	☐
14. Do the children go outdoors almost every day, even the most severely afflicted?	☐	☐
15. Look at the children's facial expressions. Are the children responsive to human contact?	☐	☐
16. If the children are under 13, is the number cared for by one adult not more than eight?	☐	☐
17. Are nights and weekends adequately covered by regular and medical staffs?	☐	☐
18. Is there an educational program including physical education?	☐	☐
19. Is there an appropriate training program for young people who may someday be able to live outside the residential facility?	☐	☐
20. Is there a recreational program?	☐	☐
21. Does the staff try to create the world of a child?	☐	☐
22. Are there toys?	☐	☐
23. Do the children have access to the toys?	☐	☐
24. Do the toys look used?	☐	☐
25. Is there a rocking chair in the nursery?	☐	☐
26. Do the toilets have seats?	☐	☐
27. Is privacy in the bathroom provided?	☐	☐
28. Are there curtains, flowers, or pictures?	☐	☐
29. Are snacks and juice or milk available between meals?	☐	☐
30. Is there a place to keep personal possessions?	☐	☐
31. Do the older children have family pictures displayed?	☐	☐
32. Are visits encouraged, both at the facility and at home?	☐	☐
33. Do you feel that you've visited a cheerful place where individualization and human dignity are cherished?	☐	☐

*This material has been prepared for your use with your patients. It may be reproduced on your office copying machine and distributed.

2. RESEARCH, DIAGNOSIS, AND ASSESSMENT

"helpless" child marries. While benefits are higher if the veteran's death was service connected, neediness is an important factor in the determination of level of assistance.

---EXPRESS STOP---

Selecting the facility: JCAH accreditation of residential facilities will be operational by July 1972. Accreditation will provide a baseline for selection, but will not replace personal visits by physician or parent to assess the quality of care. Quality checks are similar to judging a local hospital, such as a look at the back stairway. You should be welcome at all times at a facility for the retarded. Children should be out of bed and dressed. Are toys used? Is there a rocking chair in the nursery? Do the toilets have seats? Do the older children have personal possessions?

Even the most severely retarded children grow and develop, and it is the parents' responsibility to obtain care which satisfies three objectives:
 »meets the child's developmental needs
 »maximizes human qualities, and
 »provides as normal a life as possible.

When a parent asks you to recommend a facility which meets these objectives, you'll need facts based on an up-to-date appraisal.

To avoid condemning a child to incarceration rather than care, it's really necessary to have direct knowledge of an institution before recommending it. If you can't visit the facility yourself, send the parents. You may be able to share your professional responsibility for visiting care facilities for the retarded through a medical society committee.

You'll have some help in your job of steering families to facilities which offer good care through the Joint Commission of Accreditation of Hospitals which has recently adopted standards for accreditation of residential facilities for the mentally retarded. Operational by July 1972, this voluntary program of accreditation should improve the national level of service.

About half of all facilities providing 24-hour service should be accredited within five years, JCAH staff estimates. Right now, JCAH has a comprehensive listing of all residential facilities—public and private, large and small.* JCAH standards for community services and day schools for the retarded, providing less than 24-hour service, will go into effect by April 1973. A listing of day facilities is not available at this time.

While accreditation will provide the baseline for selection, the range in quality among accredited residential facilities will continue to be wide for a number of years. Consequently, tell the parents that even though a facility is accredited, a visit is still essential to judge the quality of care. In addition, despite the fact that either you or the parents may have previously checked out a facility, investigative visits should be current since staff changes can alter the whole tone of care within a year or two.

Judging the quality of care in a facility for the mentally retarded is somewhat like judging the quality of care of a local hospital. Beyond the basic requirement of accreditation, there are subtle ways to evaluate the general morale and caliber of the staff. Many physicians have personal criteria for selecting a hospital with which they want to become affiliated. Are the back stairways clean, or do they smell of urine? Do people hold doors open, or do they allow them to slam against people?

Be cautious about judging a facility on the basis of up-to-date architecture. The building plan should facilitate training programs and, in older buildings this can be accomplished by incorporating ramps and other adaptations, so long as the building meets fire safety standards.

A key appraisal is that of the overall activity; no child has to stay in bed all the time unless there is danger of death from change of position. There is adaptive equipment available, even for hydrocephalics.

A look at the specifics of care provides the answers as to whether or not a facility meets the three basic objectives in care. The checklist on page 100 lists the specifics. To zero-in on the unit where their child would live, encourage parents to ask questions. Many parents of retarded children are shy of professionals and may feel like second-class citizens because they view their child as defective.

Other parents are so angry at the world that they're apt to make enemies wherever they go. A checklist can serve to elicit as well as restrict questions.

Warn the parents against making a snap judgment. You may want to suggest that they plan to study the answers on the checklist at home where they can telephone you if they have more questions.

Parents will need some counseling prior to their first visit to a residential facility; the impact of

16. Checking Out Facilities

seeing a large group of handicapped individuals can be devastating. When they see adolescents and adults, it's like a sudden look into the future for their child, and is more than most people can handle without mental and emotional preparation.

Parents' associations can be very helpful to the family, through emotional support and practical assistance. The National Association for Retarded Children has a special program to train parents on what to look for in residential facilities.

This article was prepared in consultation with:

Roger Freeman, M.D., director of services for handicapped children; associate professor, department of psychiatry, University of British Columbia, Vancouver

Una Haynes, R.N., associate director, professional services program department, United Cerebral Palsy Associations, Inc., New York City

Lewis B. Klebanoff, Ph.D., S.M.Hyg., psychologist; director, Massachusetts Department of Mental Health, Boston University, Joint Center for Developmental Research; editor, *The Exceptional Parent*, Boston

Dorothy F. Ohrenstein, A.C.S.W., chief social worker, Handicapped Children's Unit, St. Christopher's Hospital for Children, Philadelphia

Gerald Solomons, M.D., pediatrician; professor of pediatrics and director, child development clinic, University of Iowa, Iowa City

Ted Taylor, staff officer, Accreditation Council for Facilities for the Mentally Retarded, Joint Commission on Accreditation of Hospitals, Chicago

APPLICATION OF PIAGET'S THEORY TO THE STUDY OF THINKING OF THE MENTALLY RETARDED: A REVIEW OF RESEARCH

Nancy K. Klein, Ph.D.
Cleveland State University

Philip L. Safford, Ph.D.
Kent State University

The developmental theory of Jean Piaget describes intellectual growth, from sensorimotor intelligence through adult logic. Although Piaget has not dealt with mentally retarded (MR) persons per se, his theory has been applied to that population by many researchers. Results of investigations into this application of Paget's stage theory of development indicate that the stages of development in the MR parallel those described by Piaget but appear at later chronological periods. Because of the tremendous variability in cognitive MR task performance within IQ categories, identification of specific aspects of concept learning holds promise for enhancing the school performance of MR children through individualized instruction.

The developmental theory of Jean Piaget deals with the process of intellectual development. The theory focuses on the evolution of abstract thinking from its origins in the sensorimotor behavior of infancy through the intermediate forms (Woodward, 1963). Piaget is not concerned with success or failure, right or wrong, but rather with the kinds of psychological operations comprising intellectual development. His purpose is not to make an inventory of behavior; it is to interpret behavior in terms of its origins and to predict what will grow from it at successive stages.

Piaget suggests that the central nervous system, as a result of its interaction with the environment during the early years, "constantly forms levels of integration which are both quantitatively and qualitatively different from the synthesis out of which they evolved" (Robinson & Robinson, 1965, p. 356). Moreover, his conceptions of psychological development are very different from those generally espoused by theorists who view learning mainly in terms of an associationist model; thus, they have far-reaching ramifications for the study of nearly every area of child development.

The phenomenon of mental retardation poses many questions of critical importance conerning both the universality and the individuality of mental development (Kessler, 1970). The study of this phenomenon from the perspective of Piagetian theory offers promise of increased understanding — both of mental subnormality and of the processes and sequences of mental development. Therefore, the purpose of this review is to analyze some of the major areas in which Piagetian theory has contributed toward better understanding of the development of thought in mentally retarded children.

LEARNING AND DEVELOPMENT

The "child development" tradition of preschool education espoused by Gesell (1954) and Isaacs (1933) is consistent with many of the ideas of Piaget. This tradition encouraged educators to let cognitive abilities develop naturally and to concentrate on social-emotional growth. The fundamental difference between Piaget and Gesell is that Piaget sees the child's total development resulting from varied interactions with the environment. His view assigns both more importance to the environment and a much more active role to the learner than does the pure maturationist conception. "Letting it happen" is not enough; the child must be an active participant with his or her surroundings.

Piaget disregards the dichotomy between maturation and environmentally determined learning. He insists that cognitive processes do not emerge through direct learning but through a reorganization of psychological structures resulting from interaction with the environment (Elkind, 1967; Flavell, 1963; Piaget, 1964). He similarly disregards the dichotomy between cognitive and social-emotional processes. According to Piaget (1964), self concept, social development, play, and art all have cognitive structural components.

Kohlberg (1968) outlined a detailed interactional argument for the shared role of experience and maturation, which raises a question about the effect of specific teaching on cognitive structural development. In a practical sense

the interactional view suggests that limited specific training experiences cannot replace the massive general types of experience accruing with age. Both views, interactional and maturational, then, agree in the factual importance of age readiness, but disagree in their interpretation of this fact. (Kohlberg, 1968, p. 1030)

Gesell and Thompson (Gesell, 1954) found that an untrained twin became as adept at tower building and stair climbing after a week of practice as the trained twin after many weeks of specific training. This has been interpreted as supporting the maturational position. Piaget would say that practice is part of the learning process.

THE ISSUE OF STAGES OF COGNITIVE DEVELOPMENT

Piaget posits a stage-dependent theory of cognitive development. "Stage dependent theories maintain that for the child to arrive at stage B in his development, he must first have reached and passed through stage A. The order is fixed; stage B cannot be arrived at until stage A has been mastered" (Sigel, 1975, p. 71). Thus, the stage of cognitive development is at issue, not the age of the child. Transition from one stage to another necessitates integration and new levels of performance. The roots of stage B are germinated in stage A but reach maturity in the subsequent stage B. Interaction with the environment by a dynamically developing young child is the process that nurtures and fosters cognitive development.

Piaget's position that progression through successive stages occurs in an invariant sequence, combined with his insistence that transitions from one stage to the next involve qualitative rather than quantitative change, has given rise to many studies. What Piaget has referred to as "the American question" — whether development can be accelerated — while of some interest to educators, does not constitute the critical test of Piaget's stage theory. Of greater importance, theoretically, is the question of whether development proceeds in a continuous or a saltatory fashion.

Recent papers by Flavell (1971, 1972) have proposed a reconsideration of invariant sequence, qualitative stage differences, and the nature of transitions. Recognizing that there are qualitative differences in the intellectual tools children bring to bear in dealing with their environments, Flavell notes that the

2. RESEARCH, DIAGNOSIS, AND ASSESSMENT

strict invariant stage theory probably has not been sufficiently documented through empirical evidence. According to Flavell (1971),

Stage-to-stage development is most conspicuously marked by genuinely qualitative changes in the child's repertoire of cognitive "items" (cognitive skills, rules, strategies, etc.). Such development also entails cognitive modifications of a more quantitative sort, however, and these may play an important role in the genesis of the more dramatic, stage-defining, qualitative changes. (p. 450)

Rather than insisting on the criteria of *abruptness* of change and *concurrence* of change (of "items" within a stage), Flavell asserts that "the typical item probably does not achieve its final level of 'functional maturity' . . . until *after* the conventional termination age of the stage in which it is supposed to begin its development" (1971, p. 450). Flavell's (1972) view of "cognitive developmental sequences" attempts to take into account (more adequately than is possible within an invariant stage model) reciprocal interactions within and between developmental sequences resulting in progressively changing and improved cognitive skills.

TRAINING IN PIAGETIAN CONCEPTS

There is much evidence to support the position that specific training cannot substitute for age-linked general experience, as evidenced by the fact that "teachability" of Piagetian concepts has produced conflicting research results. Sigel and Hooper (1968) reported that direct teaching of conservation through verbal instruction did not produce stable conservation concepts. Formal schooling also seems to have little effect upon conservation. Goodnow and Bethon (1966) studied children in Hong Kong who were attending school and who were not in school. There were no significant differences between the unschooled children and comparable-IQ children attending school in many types of conservation tasks. Mermelstein (1964) and Mermelstein and Shulman (1967) compared responses of 6- and 9-year-old Negro children who had been deprived of school on a variety of conservation tasks with Northern urban children of the same age who were attending school. Again no significant differences were found. Wohlwill (1960) and Wohlwill and Lowe (1962) attempted to train children in number conservation but were unsuccessful. Beilin and Franklin (1962) attempted to train for conservation of area and were also unsuccessful. A great many studies have been conducted by Jan Smedslund (1961a, 1961b) involving the acquisition of conservation of weight. He varied the training procedures, and in one situation reinforced trials in conservation of matter. His results were essentially negative with respect to the influence of training.

On the other hand, Sigel, Roeper, and Hooper (1966) reported success in inducing conservation in gifted 5-year-old children. These authors criticized the other investigators for trying to teach conservation directly rather than building toward it by taking the child through the prerequisite steps of multiple classification, multiple relationality, and reversibility. Using 5-year-old gifted children, a training program was developed to take the child through the necessary prerequisite steps leading to conservation. The results showed that each child in the training group could solve at least one more conservation task in the posttest situation than the control children, two of whom were unable to solve any tasks. Parker, Speer, and Rieff (1972) reported a successful training program with 7- and 8-year-old children who were taught multiple classification.

In his comprehensive treatment of methodological issues in the study of psychological development, Wohlwill (1973) addressed the topic of training in conservation. He concluded that studies attempting to induce conservation in nonconserving children have limited value because "the attainment of conservation constitutes a general phenomenon of cognitive development, which, given only certain minimal supportive environmental conditions, will run its course predictably" (p. 331). While the training approach can serve a useful function by tracing the course of development of conservation, the major limitation of training studies is that they have typically not shown that training conditions were either necessary or sufficient for the development to occur.

The vast number of conservation training studies soon diminished, and Brainerd and Allen (1971) traced their decline. They proposed that demonstrations of reversibility — the factor that induces conservation — undercut the validity of the studies. Kuhn (1974) challenged this explanation and pointed instead to inherent methodological limitations of studies within this genre. She suggested that if training studies in conservation are to be undertaken, they should be within the context of "a careful longitudinal assessment of the natural development of that concept" (p. 598). Calling for the systematic incorporation of experimental manipulations within a longitudinal assessment design, she argued that data could thereby be obtained concerning: the length of time during which the development being studied actually takes place, the effects of experiential variation of specific sequences, and the relationships between these sequences and patterns of development of other cognitive behaviors.

REPLICATION STUDIES

Although the training results have been inconclusive, partly because of the methodologies employed, repeated studies of Piaget's work in the development of number and space concepts have borne out his theory. Hyde (1959) investigated number concepts among European, Arab, and Indian children and found responses made in English and Arabic which were almost a direct translation of the responses in French reported by Piaget. Lovell (1966) observed similar responses in English children aged 8–18 years to problems described by Piaget and Inhelder (1958). He found high consistencies in the type of thinking shown by the same subject for various combinations of experiments replicated from the research of Piaget and Inhelder. Similarly, Elkind (1961) found an invariant sequence of the development of substance, weight, and volume conservation.

APPLICATION OF PIAGET'S THEORY TO THE MENTALLY RETARDED (MR)

The diagnostic tools and techniques devised by Piaget and Inhelder (1958) to explore cognitive processes are distinctive in that they allow the experimenter to gain insights into the thinking of children. The most important aspect of Piaget's theory is that it postulates an invariant sequence of intellectual stages of development. Of further importance is the notion that the order of the steps is the issue, rather than the age at which the steps appear or the speed at which they are attained. It is reasonable, therefore, to employ the Piagetian stage model in research with children who are developing at a rate slower than normally expected. The stages of development are placed along a continuum, or ordinal scale of development, from birth onward. The investigator's focus is on the type of thinking shown in problem solving rather than on specific right or wrong responses.

It is somewhat paradoxical that although Piaget was relatively uninterested in individual differences, and in mental retardation per se, he generated ideas which have caused something of a minor revolution in the approach of workers in the field of mental retardation (Robinson & Robinson, 1965). An important aspect of Piaget's orientation is that it enables one to shift from the "deficit" notion described by Zigler (1966) to understanding where the retarded may be in terms of developing cognitive structures. This positive view enables us to look at what retarded children are rather than what they are not; what they know rather than don't know. In addition, we can specify successive stages of development for the individual retarded child.

The "medical model" approach to the MR has historically dominated and has

2. RESEARCH, DIAGNOSIS, AND ASSESSMENT

impeded the application of Piaget's theoretical principles to that population. As the move away from that perspective grows in strength and the "defect" notion diminishes, more and more professionals are beginning to study the thinking of the MR from the theoretical position of Jean Piaget. This movement seems to parallel the trend toward mainstreaming (Dunn, 1968; Lilly, 1970) and the normalization principle espoused by Wolfensberger (1972).

One of the earliest studies which applied Piaget's theory to the study of the MR was done by Mary Woodward (1959) in England. She observed a group of 147 young idiots and imbeciles (the English classification for profoundly and severely retarded individuals) in light of Piaget's stages of sensorimotor development. All subjects failed to reach the lower limit of the Revised Stanford-Binet Intelligence Scale, Form L. They were classified by the problems they solved in terms of the stages of sensorimotor intelligence. All problems of all stages were administered to 65 subjects; 60 of them solved all the problems of the stages lower than that at which they had been classified. This, according to Woodward, suggests that the sequence of sensorimotor development which Piaget observed in normal infants also occurs in low-grade mental defectives. When the stage of sensorimotor intelligence, based on problem solving, was compared with the stage reached in the development of a concept of permanent objects, 87% of the total group of 147 were at the same stage for both aspects. Hand movements and manipulations of toys were readily classifiable as primary, secondary, derived secondary, and tertiary circular reactions, which should occur at stages two, three, four, and five respectively. Only 43% of the subjects in stages one through five showed this correspondence, but in all six of the noncorresponding cases, the discrepancy was found in the fact that manipulations were at a lower stage than problem solving.

Woodward (1963) later pointed out that the significance of the 1959 study lies in its implications for interpreting the behavior of MR children. For example, the primary circular reactions of stage two are defined as repetitions of hand movements by the child, a kind of twiddling of the fingers in front of his face. Profoundly retarded children commonly show this type of behavior, which is regarded as bizarre. According to Woodward (1963):

The hand movements of the profoundly retarded individual are the same as those of the infant of two or three months, and the bizarre quality is due to the much greater size of the retardate and to the discrepancy between his size and his behavior. It was concluded that these mannerisms originated as in the infant, in the course of coordinating vision and grasping. Thus Piaget's approach offers an explanation of the origins of certain manneristic behavior. Following this lead, the suggestion was also put forward that other mannerisms (shaking hands about, banging on a table) are continuations, in the absence of objects, of behavior patterns developed in the first place in relation to objects (shaking them and banging them). (p. 321)

Inhelder (1968) proposed a method to order adult retardates according to stage. In her classificatory system "idiot" (profoundly and severely retarded) is viewed as fixed at the level of sensorimotor intelligence; "imbecile" (moderately retarded) is seen as incapable of surpassing the pre-operational stage; "moron" (mildly retarded) is seen as unable to progress beyond concrete operations; and the borderline adult retardate is seen as able to use only the simpler kinds of formal operations (p. 351). She does not explain why this fixed situation occurs.

An assessment procedure based on Piaget's descriptions of major areas of intellectual growth during the sensorimotor period was developed by Uzgiris and Hunt (1975). This procedure provides a means of charting developmental progress vis-à-vis ordinal scales for each of the following areas of infant development: (a) visual pursuit and permanence of objects; (b) means for achieving desired environmental events; (c) gestural and vocal imitation; (d) operational causality; (e) object relations in space; and (f) schemas for relating to objects. Systematically constructed and tested over an extended period of time before it was introduced as a mental measurement tool, this scale promises to be of particular value in the assessment of cognitive development among young and/or very limited MR children. It may also prove valuable in determining the effects of early intervention programs in enhancing cognitive growth.

Some investigators have studied the role of mental age (MA) of the MR child as a predictor of performance on Piagetian tasks. Stephens, McLaughlin, and Mahaney (1971) obtained data for 75 normal and 75 retarded (IQ range 50–75) individuals, evenly divided into three age groups: 6–10, 10–14, and 14–18. Their purpose was to determine the MA levels at which Ss successfully performed each of 21 discrete measures of reasoning and concept information. Their study has value, even though Piaget has consistently stressed that the rate of progression through stages and substages of cognitive development is a function of interactive individual difference factors. Also, the vicissitudes of mental age as a predictor variable has been pointed out (Ellis, 1963), but in the case of the retarded, it seems essential to take into account some index of intellectual equivalence rather than chronological age (CA) alone.

Another British study involving retarded subjects has supported Piaget's notion of stages in the development of number concepts. Hood (1962) selected normal children aged 4 through 8, drawn from four schools in the Northwest of England. In addition, 40 MR subjects were studied, of whom 23 were called educationally subnormal (ES) and 17 were classified as mentally defective (MD — equivalent to the trainable classification in the United States). The ES group ranged in age from 10 to 15 years. The MD group ranged in age from 9 to 41 years. The Terman-Merrill Scale "L" was used to assess each subject's mental age. Eight of Piaget's experiments were selected for study. These included conservation of continuous quantity, one-to-one correspondence, and establishing correspondence spontaneously. Other tasks aimed at revealing the presence of prenumber concepts. For the normal subjects, prenumber concepts appeared to develop as the child gained in years, and for most of those children studied, the concepts were not developed until the child was 6 or 7 years of age. Mental structure, as well as age, was apparently important. For example, in Experiment 2, involving one-to-one correspondence, 64% in the under-5 age group who were at Stage 2 had a mean MA of 5–7, more than a year above the 28% of the same CA group who were at Stage 1, whose mean MA was only 4–3. Except for Experiments 2 and 8, 100% of the mentally under-5 were at Stage 1. Beyond the 8-year-old level, although 90–100% of the responses were generally found to be at Stage 3, the evidence suggested that the concepts of seriation and class inclusion were still not fully understood by 50% of the retarded subjects. This suggestive study should be replicated in the United States because of the inherent curriculum implications.

Gruen and Vore (1972) studied the development of conservation in normal and retarded children. They selected 10 familial MR children of three different MA levels: 5, 7, and 9 years. The subjects were matched with 60 normal children and given tasks involving: (a) conservation of number; (b) continuous quantity (water); and (c) weight. Differences in performance on these tasks were primarily attributable to MA but not IQ. As expected, conservation of weight was generally more difficult than conservation of water, and the latter was more difficult than conservation of numbers for both the MR and normal subjects. There were, however, some exceptions to this order. Conservation of inequality was typically less difficult than conservation of equality for all concepts.

Richards and Stone (1970) used material reinforcement and concrete teaching materials to teach 7–12-year-olds nonconserving retarded subjects. Contrary to Piaget's position that learned conservation skills would not transfer to other areas of performance, they found that these subjects did in fact transfer conservation to other task areas. However, there was a significant developmental lag in attainment of conservation by the MR subjects in comparison to normal children of the same MA.

The clinical experiments conducted by Piaget, many of which were later rep-

2. RESEARCH, DIAGNOSIS, AND ASSESSMENT

licated by Inhelder (1968) with retarded subjects, allow both clinicians and teachers to better understand the mental operations of a particular child. The discrepancy between MA and CA of the more severely retarded child has given rise to many questions regarding the best predictor of behavior. For Piaget, living is learning. For example, although a child with an IQ of 50 and a CA of 10 has an MA of only 5 years, he has had many experiences which cannot be inferred from his MA.

Boland (1972) attempted to determine the best predictors of conservation behavior and explanation by deriving composite scores for: conservation of two-dimensional space, conservation of substance, conservation of continuous quantity, and conservation of weight for retarded and nonretarded subjects. She found that CA appeared to be the best predictor for conservation of continuous quantity by nonretarded subjects, while MA was the best predictor for conservation of continuous quantity for retarded subjects. MA appeared to predict best for conservation of substance by nonretarded subjects, while there was no consistent predictor for retarded subjects. This study appears to confirm Piaget's findings that conservation is related to the intellectual maturity of the child and that MA seems to be related to the ability to conserve.

Lister (1972) studied the development of educationally subnormal children's understanding of conservation. The subjects were divided into three groups matched for age and IQ. One group was instructed on conservation of a variety of attributes, the second group was instructed on conservation of area only, and the third group was given practice in reading. After 14 months, 30 of the 34 subjects who had been instructed in conservation recognized, generalized, and gave reasons for conservation. None of the initial subjects showed an improved understanding of conservation. However, this study supports the notion that conservation skills can in fact be taught to retarded subjects.

Marchi (1971) explored the relation of a diagnostic procedure based upon Piaget's theory and using the Wechsler Intelligence Scale for Children (WISC). His sample consisted of 106 EMR students ranging from 7 to 16 years of age. All subjects received a WISC, and each subject was individually given conservation tasks related to mass, weight, and volume. He found that stages of conservation were not, in fact, bound to CA and that EMR subjects follow a sequence in the development of conservation similar to that of normals. He also found that the ability to conserve is significantly related to intelligence as measured by the WISC and that there was a positive correlation between various subtests on the WISC and conservation.

Other studies (Mannix, 1960; Woodward, 1961) found that although children entered the stage of concrete operations at varied MAs, no child with an MA of less than 6 performed at the level of concrete operations in all tests, and no child with an MA of more than 6½ was at the pre-operational stage in all tests. Following the pattern of normal children, the retarded child's ability to conserve quantity and number is arrived at gradually, and a period of nonconservation or perceptual domination is followed by a transitional stage before conservation becomes consistent (Kessler, 1970). Teachers' efforts would perhaps be enhanced were they given information on the individual child's cognitive level. Such data would also prevent the child from experiencing excessive failure, since he could be provided with tasks at which he could succeed.

McManis (1969) reported that retarded subjects showed a marked lag in transitivity development, a finding in conflict with Piaget's hypothesis that conservation and transitivity occur together with respect to a given dimension such as weight or length. While a majority of normal children with MA of 8 displayed transitive thinking, the MA level of the majority of retarded subjects who were able to make transitive inferences was 10 to 11. Also, a substantially greater proportion of retarded than normal subjects displayed conservation without transitivity. Since performance by normal and retarded subjects of MA 5 and 6 was comparable on conservation and seriation tasks, these results were interpreted as indicating that a slower rate of transitivity development exists in the retarded subject between MA of 8 and MA of 10 years than for normal controls. The finding of nonconcurrence of transitivity and conservation lends support to Flavell's (1972) argument cited earlier.

In the follow-up study, McManis (1970) reported that the predicted transitivity among retarded subjects was confirmed. In addition, this study indicated a hierarchical relationship among the operations of conservation and seriation performances by the same subjects and supported Piaget's hypothesis that conservation is a necessary but not sufficient prerequisite for seriation.

Assuming that intellective functioning requires an individual to categorize and classify information, Stephens (1966) compared category usage by normal and MR boys. The task required that the subject look at a test card with seven items, four belonging to a category and three being irrelevant. Responses of the retarded group to the naming tasks revealed that even when they were able to use the proper category for grouping test items, they had relatively greater difficulty in naming that category. The retarded subjects appeared to understand the category well enough, but often their comprehension of categories was not sufficiently developed to permit them to conceptualize the relationship between the functional category and its verbal description. Stephens concluded were primarily attributable to MA but not IQ. As expected, conservation of weight was generally more difficult than conservation of water, and the latter was more difficult than conservation of numbers for both the MR and normal subjects. There were, however, some exceptions to this order. Conservation of inequality was typically less difficult than conservation of equality for all concepts.

Richards and Stone (1970) used material reinforcement and concrete teaching materials to teach 7–12-year-olds nonconserving retarded subjects. Contrary to Piaget's position that learned conservation skills would not transfer to other areas of performance, they found that these subjects did in fact transfer conservation to other task areas. However, there was a significant developmental lag in attainment of conservation by the MR subjects in comparison to normal children of the same MA.

The clinical experiments conducted by Piaget, many of which were later replicated by Inhelder (1968) with retarded subjects, allow both clinicians and teachers to better understand the mental operations of a particular child. The discrepancy between MA and CA of the more severely retarded child has given rise to many questions regarding the best predictor of behavior. For Piaget, living is learning. For example, although a child with an IQ of 50 and a CA of 10 has an MA of only 5 years, he has had many experiences which cannot be inferred from his MA.

Boland (1972) attempted to determine the best predictors of conservation behavior and explanation by deriving composite scores for: conservation of two-dimensional space, conservation of substance, conservation of continuous quantity, and conservation of weight for retarded and nonretarded subjects. She found that CA appeared to be the best predictor for conservation of continuous quantity by nonretarded subjects, while MA was the best predictor for conservation of continuous quantity for retarded subjects. MA appeared to predict best for conservation of substance by nonretarded subjects, while there was no consistent predictor for retarded subjects. This study appears to confirm Piaget's findings that conservation is related to the intellectual maturity of the child and that MA seems to be related to the ability to conserve.

Lister (1972) studied the development of educationally subnormal children's understanding of conservation. The subjects were divided into three groups matched for age and IQ. One group was instructed on conservation of a variety of attributes, the second group was instructed on conservation of area only, and the third group was given practice in reading. After 14 months, 30 of the 34 subjects who had been instructed in conservation recognized, generalized, and gave reasons for conservation. None of the initial subjects showed an improved understanding of conservation. However, this study supports the notion that

2. RESEARCH, DIAGNOSIS, AND ASSESSMENT

conservation skills can in fact be taught to retarded subjects.

Marchi (1971) explored the relation of a diagnostic procedure based upon Piaget's theory and using the Wechsler Intelligence Scale for Children (WISC). His sample consisted of 106 EMR students ranging from 7 to 16 years of age. All subjects received a WISC, and each subject was individually given conservation tasks related to mass, weight, and volume. He found that stages of conservation were not, in fact, bound to CA and that EMR subjects follow a sequence in the development of conservation similar to that of normals. He also found that the ability to conserve is significantly related to intelligence as measured by the WISC and that there was a positive correlation between various subtests on the WISC and conservation.

Other studies (Mannix, 1960; Woodward, 1961) found that although children entered the stage of concrete operations at varied MAs, no child with an MA of less than 6 performed at the level of concrete operations in all tests, and no child with an MA of more than 6½ was at the pre-operational stage in all tests. Following the pattern of normal children, the retarded child's ability to conserve quantity and number is arrived at gradually, and a period of nonconservation or perceptual domination is followed by a transitional stage before conservation becomes consistent (Kessler, 1970). Teachers' efforts would perhaps be enhanced were they given information on the individual child's cognitive level. Such data would also prevent the child from experiencing excessive failure, since he could be provided with tasks at which he could succeed.

McManis (1969) reported that retarded subjects showed a marked lag in transitivity development, a finding in conflict with Piaget's hypothesis that conservation and transitivity occur together with respect to a given dimension such as weight or length. While a majority of normal children with MA of 8 displayed transitive thinking, the MA level of the majority of retarded subjects who were able to make transitive inferences was 10 to 11. Also, a substantially greater proportion of retarded than normal subjects displayed conservation without transitivity. Since performance by normal and retarded subjects of MA 5 and 6 was comparable on conservation and seriation tasks, these results were interpreted as indicating that a slower rate of transitivity development exists in the retarded subject between MA of 8 and MA of 10 years than for normal controls. The finding of nonconcurrence of transitivity and conservation lends support to Flavell's (1972) argument cited earlier.

In the follow-up study, McManis (1970) reported that the predicted transitivity among retarded subjects was confirmed. In addition, this study indicated a hierarchical relationship among the operations of conservation and seriation performances by the same subjects and supported Piaget's hypothesis that conservation is a necessary but not sufficient prerequisite for seriation.

Assuming that intellective functioning requires an individual to categorize and classify information, Stephens (1966) compared category usage by normal and MR boys. The task required that the subject look at a test card with seven items, four belonging to a category and three being irrelevant. Responses of the retarded group to the naming tasks revealed that even when they were able to use the proper category for grouping test items, they had relatively greater difficulty in naming that category. The retarded subjects appeared to understand the category well enough, but often their comprehension of categories was not sufficiently developed to permit them to conceptualize the relationship between the functional category and its verbal description. Stephens concluded that the retarded subjects did understand categories but that they were not as well delineated as those of the normal subjects. The relationship of expressive language to thought in the MR needs further investigation because of the inherent psychoeducational implications.

In order to devise the classificatory system based on stage acquisition described earlier, Inhelder (1968) designed experiments to determine the presence of conservation of weight, quantity, and volume in retarded subjects. Inhelder found that every subject who showed conservation of weight also showed conservation of volume and conservation of quantity. These findings confirmed the Piagetian stage hypothesis of the development of conservation in retarded as well as normal children. The findings of Marchi (1971) support Inhelder's work.

Stephens and McLaughlin (1974) reported data on reasoning by retarded and nonretarded subjects. They included assessments in conservation, logic-classification, operativity and symbolic imagery, and formal operations for three age groups (6 to 10, 10 to 14, and 14 to 18) of both nonretarded and retarded subjects. During the initial 2-year phase of the study (cited earlier), developmental trends across age groups were observed in the reasoning of nonretarded persons. The performance of retarded subjects in the 6–10 and 10–14 age groups reflected developmental trends, but statistically significant developmental change did not continue on 27 of the 29 reasoning tasks for the 14–18 age group. Stephens and McLaughlin also found that no retarded person achieved the level of formal operations, which substantiates the clinical findings of Inhelder (1968). When MA and CA were held constant, significant differences did occur between the performance of nonretarded and retarded subjects on 20 of the 29 reasoning tasks. Comparisons of the two groups indicated the performance of retarded subjects generally was characterized by insufficiencies in the grouping, flexibility, and reversibility required in concrete operational thought. The 50–75-IQ group had particular difficulty in tasks dealing with shifts in categorical sorting.

Stephens and McLaughlin (1974) also reported on Phase II, comprising the third and fourth years of their study. They found that both retarded and nonretarded subjects generally showed significant development. None of the three groups of retarded subjects achieved significant gains for dissolution of sugar (volume), changing criterion, and conservation of liquid. Over a 2-year period, the younger group of retarded subjects showed significant improvement on 22 of the 29 variables; the middle group showed significant improvement on 18 variables; and the older group improved significantly on 8 variables. The data revealed a lack of differences between the middle and older group of retarded subjects which, according to Stephens and McLaughlin, may suggest a possible decelerating tempo of cognitive development in the older group ages 16 to 20. The findings in Phase I were generally substantiated during Phase II:

Significant differences which are not accounted for by CA or MA do exist between the operational thought of non-retarded and retarded persons. These differences appear to involve the categorization, flexibility and reversibility required in tasks involving conservation and classification. (p. 126)

CLASSIFICATION — RESEARCH AND TRAINING

In Ripple and Rockcastle (1964), Piaget explains how he differentiates knowledge and learning. For Piaget, learning is limited and focused, but

knowledge is not a copy of reality. To know an object, an event, is not simply to look at it and make a mental copy or image of it. To know an object is to act on it. To know is to modify, to transform the object and to understand the way the object is constructed. An operation is thus the essence of knowledge; it is an interiorized action which modifies the object of knowledge. For instance, an operation would consist of joining objects in a class, to construct a classification. Or an operation would consist of ordering or putting things in a series. In other words, it is a set of actions modifying the object, and enabling the knower to get at the structure of the transformation. (p. 8)

Thus, selecting classification skills for basic research is sanctioned by Piaget's position that such skills are central to cognitive development in general and to logical thinking in particular. Classification skill means the ability of the individual to organize similar and dissimilar materials into logical groups by defining an attribute of the group. The individual must comprehend the rules governing grouping to accomplish classification. It is that comprehension (Piaget's "interiorized action") which has become the foundation for the development of classification skills. With increasing age, the basis of classification shifts from a perceptual to a conceptual one.

Classification performance is influenced by a number of factors. The indi-

2. RESEARCH, DIAGNOSIS, AND ASSESSMENT

vidual's psychological characteristics as well as his previous experiences will have a bearing on the selection of particular attributes. Emphasis on a particular dimension as a basis for grouping has been referred to as cognitive style, a consistent preferential mode of categorization (Kagan, Moss, & Sigel, 1963). The symbolic level of the materials presented also influences classification performance. The existence of a classification skill may well be influenced by both the nature of the stimuli and the type of representation interacting with the developmental and experiential status of the child (Sigel, 1972). When meaningful materials such as animals are used, children aged 7, 9, and 11 tend to focus on the meaning of the item (Sigel, 1964). Sigel (1975) describes studies in which media, dimensionality pictures, words, and items depicting animal figures have an influence on how children categorize.

Klein and Safford (1976a) employed TMR subjects (aged 6–14) and taught them to classify on the dimensions of form, size, and color. When meaningful toys were used, the experimental group was able to classify on the three criterion dimensions. However, when abstract blocks with the same dichotomous color and size dimensions were used, no subject was able to classify.

Classification skills have been studied with various populations, and the research has shown that classification competence will vary with age, sex, and type of child (Kagan et al., 1963; Sigel, Jarman, & Hanaesian, 1967; Sigel & Olmsted, 1967). Furth and Milgram (1965) found that EMR children performed as well in conceptual classification tasks as MA normal controls when the task permitted them to demonstrate conceptual knowledge by a nonverbal response. This may explain in part Stephens's (1966) results. O'Connor and Hermelin (1957) found that severe retardates are unable to verbalize even those concepts which they could successfully employ as principles of classification. Milgram (1968) studied verbalization and conceptual classification with trainable mentally retarded children. On a picture sorting task, the TMRs did as well as MA controls whose IQ was approximately 30 (EMR) and 60 (normals) IQ points higher. There were no significant differences among the normal, educable, and trainable retarded children of approximately MA 6 on the conceptual task.

The TMRs, however, were poorer than the other two groups on concept verbalization. Milgram concluded that the greater the severity of mental defect, the greater the deficiency in verbal formulation of conceptual performance. The trainables were found to be significantly poorer in providing verbal statements accounting for conceptual classification, although none of the subjects was nonverbal. Klein (1972) found similar results in an unpublished study with 8-year-old TMR children. This line of research has obvious implications for workers in the field of mental retardation.

Nye, McManis, and Haugen (1972) reported on research with 20 trainable retarded adults in the training and transfer of categorization. The subjects receiving training improved to a significant extent. Examination of the findings for the separate category scores showed that the training procedure was effective in facilitating categorization skills.

Klein and Safford (1976b) conducted a 6-week individualized cognitive intervention study with TMR children aged 6 to 14. Each experimental subject was taught first to explore and manipulate materials (small toys), then to classify them on the basis of three dimensions: form, size, and color. The experimental group was able to classify materials significantly better than controls on all three dimensions. In addition, subjects in the experimental group completed a double classification, while some of the older subjects completed the triple classification tasks. None of the control subjects was able to complete a triple classification task. They found, however, that the verbal behavior of the subjects paralleled that described by Milgram (1968). Although the subjects could classify in three dimensions, they were frequently unable to provide verbal statements to describe what they had performed. Milgram (1973) cited evidence for nonequivalence of language and cognition in the MR person. He suggests that MR cognitive capacity is not accurately assessed when there is an overreliance on verbal aspects of learning. This position is also supported by Furth (1970). Stephens (1968) found that EMR subjects could employ conceptual stategies in a problem solving situation without being able to provide a verbal label to describe the categories used.

Wolinsky (1970) proposed that Piaget's approach to the analysis of behavior be used as a model for the ongoing evaluation required in diagnostic teaching. Such an approach provides the teacher with an opportunity to analyze a child's approach to a task and tailor an intervention for each child's cognitive level. Classification tasks, as described by Wolinsky, provide the child with a variety of cognitive activities individually organized for each learner.

According to Moss and Mayer (1975),

The notion that concepts are powerful tools with which to organize, understand and react to the environment is valuable as a frame of reference from which to investigate human functioning and in particular to determine the necessary elements for normal functioning. Strategies of concept attainment and a breakdown of components should prove valuable for the teaching and training of the mentally retarded. (p. 281)

Sigel (1964) concluded from his summary of attempts to apply Piaget's theory of development to the study of mental retardation that the research which had been conducted tended to indicate "that the order of the stages is present but they appear at different chronological periods, and that the rate of change varies from that of normal children" (p. 212). He added that the level of conceptualization is directly related to the degree of retardation.

The fact that people can change and the notion of "educability of intelligence" have dominated the thinking of those advocating cognitive-based intervention programs for young children (Furth, 1970; Furth & Wacks, 1974; Kamii, 1972; Weikert, 1972). Applying the child development literature, particularly the theoretical work of Jean Piaget, to the study of the MR child holds a great deal of promise for increasing our understanding of the retarded child as a learner. Psychometric information in combination with a Piagetian clinical cognitive assessment can potentially provide insights into the developing cognitive structures of MR individuals and their learning process.

Gallagher (1975) believes that the confluence of child development literature and present knowledge in mental retardation dovetails with some of the changing views in special education, namely mainstreaming. This new trend — to integrate the MR into general education — puts less emphasis on categorical labels and requires a diagnostic–prescriptive approach to teaching.

The theoretical work of Piaget and the subsequent work by many of the authors cited in this article demonstrate the feasibility and value of such research endeavors. Because of the tremendous variability in cognitive MR task performance within IQ categories, research should attempt to identify specific aspects of concept learning and the cognitive processes involved. Such research may be expected to yield new approaches in planning and implementing individualized teaching of MR children.

References

Beilin, H., & Franklin, I. C. Logical operations in area and length measurement age and training effects. *Child Development*, 1962, 3, 607–616.

Boland, S. K. Assessment of conservation of two dimensional space, substance, continuous quantity and weight with retarded and average children. *Dissertation Abstracts*, 1972, 33, 1040.

Brainerd, C., & Allen, T. Experimental inductions of the conservation of "first-order" quantitative invariants. *Psychological Bulletin*, 1971, 75, 128–144.

Dunn, L. Special education for the mildly retarded — Is much of it justified? *Exceptional Children*, 1968, 35, 5–24.

Elkind, D. The development of quantitative thinking: A systematic replication of Piaget's studies. *Journal of Genetic Psychology*, 1961, 98, 37–46.

Elkind, D. Piaget and Montessori. *Harvard Educational Review*, 1967, 37(4), 327–335.

Elements for Developing Competency-Based Programs for the Mentally Retarded

Robert C. Sauter

Author: ROBERT C. SAUTER, Director of Research in Pharmaceutical Education, University of Southern California, Los Angeles, 90033.

Education, or teaching and learning, is synonymous with change in student behavior. Although change can take place by accident, it is more likely that improvement or change for the better will result by design. Having the end product or objective in mind is an orderly and logical approach to instructional planning.

An orderly development of a competency-based training program for the mentally retarded requires one to be concerned with principles of curriculum planning. This is so, regardless of the expertise, specialty or profession engaged in the educational effort—e.g., teacher, physician, nurse, therapist, aide, program director, etc.

Curriculum planning has, as its purpose, the specification of ends, objectives, or competencies to be achieved as a result of an instructional treatment. Most educators would not quarrel about the use of several terms that mean "statements of educational intent"— objectives, ends, purposes, guidelines, goals, or competencies. Disagreement and confusion result, however, from using terms interchangeably. A behavioral objective should be more specific than a goal or guideline, for example. Communication problems among professionals arise from disregard for common language and dissimilar definitions of terms.

The term, competency, is used in this paper to mean "a demonstrated learner outcome of instruction." This definition calls for a visible, physical act on the part of a learner as evidence of achievement.

Planners of competency-based programs for retarded learners must include these essential components:

1. Define terms—all program participants must be working from the same baseline of understanding.

2. Formulate objectives or competencies—plan for the desired effects.

3. Develop content, instructional materials, and learning experiences related to the stated competencies—planners should know where they are going (objectives) before determining the "what" (content) and the "how" (methodology) of the instructional program.

4. Evaluate—this process allows judgments to be made about the worth of an educational undertaking.

Each participant in program planning must assume responsibility for knowledge about and ability to incorporate these components in the planning process.

Because fuzzy purposes have fuzzy effects, the first step in instructional development is the preparation or selection of clearly stated and specific competencies. These have been identified by other names, particularly "behavioral objectives," as the most specific statements of instructional intent. When analyzed, a competency at this level of specificity embraces four constituents: "A" for audience, "B" for behavior, "C" for condition, and "D" for degree. When a competency contains all four parts, it represents a high order of communicability, both for planners and the target audience—students.

As an example, the following statement consists of all parts: *With the aid of a visual display of eating utensils, the student will locate and name a cup, plate, fork, and spoon.* Students comprise the *audience*; the *behavior* is to locate and name; and the *condition* in which the behavior manifests itself is a visual display of eating utensils. A basis for reassessment is provided because the competency statement calls for a display, and the *degree* set as a desired proficiency level requires identification of four items.

Each competency must be clear and understandable to all instructors engaged in program planning because they serve to guide and direct what is taught and learned, how it is presented, and how much and in what order the content is arranged. The latter two considerations are referred to as "score" and "sequence."

Successful attainment of a competency is dependent upon collaboration among instructional planners, all directing their respective segments at the same target. Specificity or lack of it, planning or lack of it, communication or lack of it, and more, contribute to a difference between a fragmented collection of learning experiences and an educational program.

A competency-based program, therefore, requires the cooperative preparation of competencies. In turn, content, teaching-learning activities, instructional materials, and evaluative tools are devised that provide for and give evidence of competency achievement.

It follows, then, that the end product of the program guides the tasks or subject matter, its form, and sequencing—not vice versa. A competency-based program requires systematic instruction which can result only from coordinating program components.

Classification of Educational Objectives

Based on the assumption that objectives or competencies can be specified best when outcomes are prepared as behavioral changes in learners, a Taxonomy of Education Objectives has been prepared in two volumes (Bloom, 1956; Krathwohl, 1964). At this writing, development of the psychomotor domain handbook is incomplete.

The taxonomy classifies educational objectives into three domains: cognitive or intellectual, affective or feeling, and psychomotor or physical and manipulative. Each domain classifies intended outcomes of the educational process by student behaviors—ways in which learners think, feel, and act. Further, the major classifications of learning outcomes are arranged in hierarchical order, from simple and concrete to complete and abstract types. The categories within each domain subsume the preceding category(ies). For example, the cognitive achievement classifications include knowing, comprehending, applying, analyzing, synthesizing, and evaluating. Thus comprehending assumes knowledge, while applying includes behaviors of both comprehension and knowledge, and so on up and down the scale.

Operationally, the taxonomy handbooks enable instructional planners to make decisions about the kind of learner behavior to promote as well as the type of measurement tool to be used in obtaining evidence of the degree of student success. When clear and specific competencies or objectives are lacking, there is no foundation for developing content, instructional materials, learning activities, or testing devices. Planning a competency-based program for the retarded begins with formulating or selecting objectives. Through a system of classifying outcomes of the educational process, the taxonomy facilitates communication by providing precise definitions and classifications of terms commonly used to identify intended learner behaviors.

Given that the first step in the process of instructional planning is defining goals and objectives, how can a classification of educational objectives guide the deliberations of planners? Recalling that defining terms and formulating objectives or competencies made up the first two components in the educational planning process, the taxonomy defines and classifies terms used to identify learner behavior. If a decision were made to expect the MR student to be competent in using eating utensils, a logical outcome is that the student knows how to use tableware when eating.

Communication problems arise from various interpretations of knowing. Does simple knowledge mean recognize, understand the functions of each utensil, or demonstrate correct usage in eating? What will the student do to give evidence of recognizing or understanding? What degree is set as an acceptable level for demonstrating correct usage? Such questions and others infiltrate the planning stage and affect program outcomes. Unless the competency is clear at this point, all other ingredients of the teaching-learning situation are vague. It is assumed, here, that those engaged in planning take this initial step. If planning is done intuitively or by some other perception that avoids the conscious use of reasoning, certain fundamental questions probably will not be asked, and program development will lack direction for any desired learning effects.

At this point in the planning process the taxonomy becomes an indispensable resource. All possible terms are defined; knowledge includes behaviors of remembering and recalling, comprehension emphasizes demonstrating knowledge or making some use of it by translation, interpretation or extrapolation, and so on throughout the classifications in the domains of the taxonomy.

The task next becomes one of refining the agreed upon outcome to specify the behavior that can be observed and give evidence of achievement. It is now that formulation of behavioral objectives becomes a *sine qua non.*

All behavioral objectives have at least one common ingredient: each specific learning outcome includes a verb to describe a behavior that is observable and measureable by the instructor. Table I illustrates sample verbs as identifiable behaviors. Each verb is representative of one overt manifestation of a behvaioral change. The term "define" is less subject to interpretation than the term "know." Any choice of a term will vary with content or task and the level of expectancy. The higher order of objectives elicits more complex terms, and the same term or verb may be appropriate at different levels depending on relevancy to the objective it is defining and the criterion of acceptable performance.

Gonlund (1970) offers a sample of behavioral terms.

For purposes of clarity, the three domain scheme can be separated. Even though most education is directed toward cognitive achievement, it is conceivable that identified behaviors embrace more than one classification within a domain as well as all three domains of the taxonomy.

Reviewing the previously stated behavioral objective, four observations should be made. First, the prepared statement resulted from a deductive process whereby a broad term, know, was reduced to a specific behavior less subject to varied interpretations. Second, by use of a behavioral term, the objective is phrased in terms of what the learner, not the teacher, will do. Third, the "A", "B", "C", "D" components of a well stated objective can be viewed in proper perspective—for whom is the instruction intended? What should the student do to demonstrate achievement? In what setting should the behavior be demonstrated? What is the desired level of acceptable performance? Fourth, a

2. RESEARCH, DIAGNOSIS, AND ASSESSMENT

TABLE 1
CLASSIFICATION OF EDUCATONAL OBJECTIVES AND ILLUSTRATIVE BEHAVIORAL TERMS

COGNITIVE DOMAIN	VERBS
Know (Remember)	Define, describe, identify, label, list, locate, match, name, outline, reproduce, select.
Comprehend (Interpret)	Convert, defend, distinguish, estimate, explain, give examples, infer, paraphrase, predict, rewrite, summarize, translate.
Apply (Use)	Change, compute, construct, demonstrate, manipulate, modify, operate, predict, prepare, produce, relate, show, solve, use.
Analyze (Break down)	Diagram, differentiate, discriminate, identify, illustrate, infer, outline, point out, relate, select, separate, subdivide.
Synthesize (Put together in new form)	Categorize, combine, compile, compose, create, devise, design, explain, formulate, generate, integrate, modify, organize, plan, rearrange, reconstruct, relate, reorganize, revise, rewrite, summarize, write.
Evaluate (Judge value)	Appraise, compare, conclude, contrast, criticize, describe, discriminate, explain, justify, interpret, relate, summarize, support

AFFECTIVE DOMAIN	VERBS
Receive (Attending)	Ask, choose, describe, follow, give, hold, locate, name, select, sit erect, reply.
Respond (React)	Answer, assist, comply, conform, discuss, greet, help, label, perform, practice, present, read, recite, report, select, tell, write.
Value (Internalization)	Complete, describe, differentiate, explain, follow, form, initiate, invite, join, justify, propose, read, report, select, share, study, work.
Organize (Building a value system)	Adhere, alter, arrange, combine, compare, complete, defend, explain, generalize, identify, integrate, modify, order, organize, prepare, relate, synthesize.
Characterization (Philosophy of life)	Act, discriminate, display, influence, listen, modify, perform, practice, propose, qualify, question, revise, serve, solve, use, verify.

PSYCHOMOTOR DOMAIN	VERBS
To date, a classification system for this domain has not been completed.	Assemble, build, calibrate, change, clean, compose, connect, construct, correct, create, design, dismantle, drill, fasten, fix, follow, grind, grip, hammer, heat, hook, identify, locate, make, manipulate, mend, mix, nail, paint, sand, saw, sharpen, set, sew, sketch, start, stir, use, weigh, wrap.

well defined objective includes content, gives clues about appropriate instructional activities and materials, and provides a performance standard against which to test learner success.

In summary, the answers to three questions will form the basis for developing competency-based programs—Where are you going? How will you get there? How will you know you've arrived?

References

Bloom, B. S. (Ed.) *Taxonomy of educational objectives, handbook I: Cognitive domain.* New York: David McKay Company, 1956.

Gronlund, N. E. *Stating behavioral objectives for classroom instruction.* New York: The Macmillan Company, 1970.

Krathwohl, D. R., Krathwohl, D. R., Bloom, B. S., & Masia, B. B. *Taxonomy of educational objectives, handbook II: Affective domain.* New York: David McKay Company, 1964.

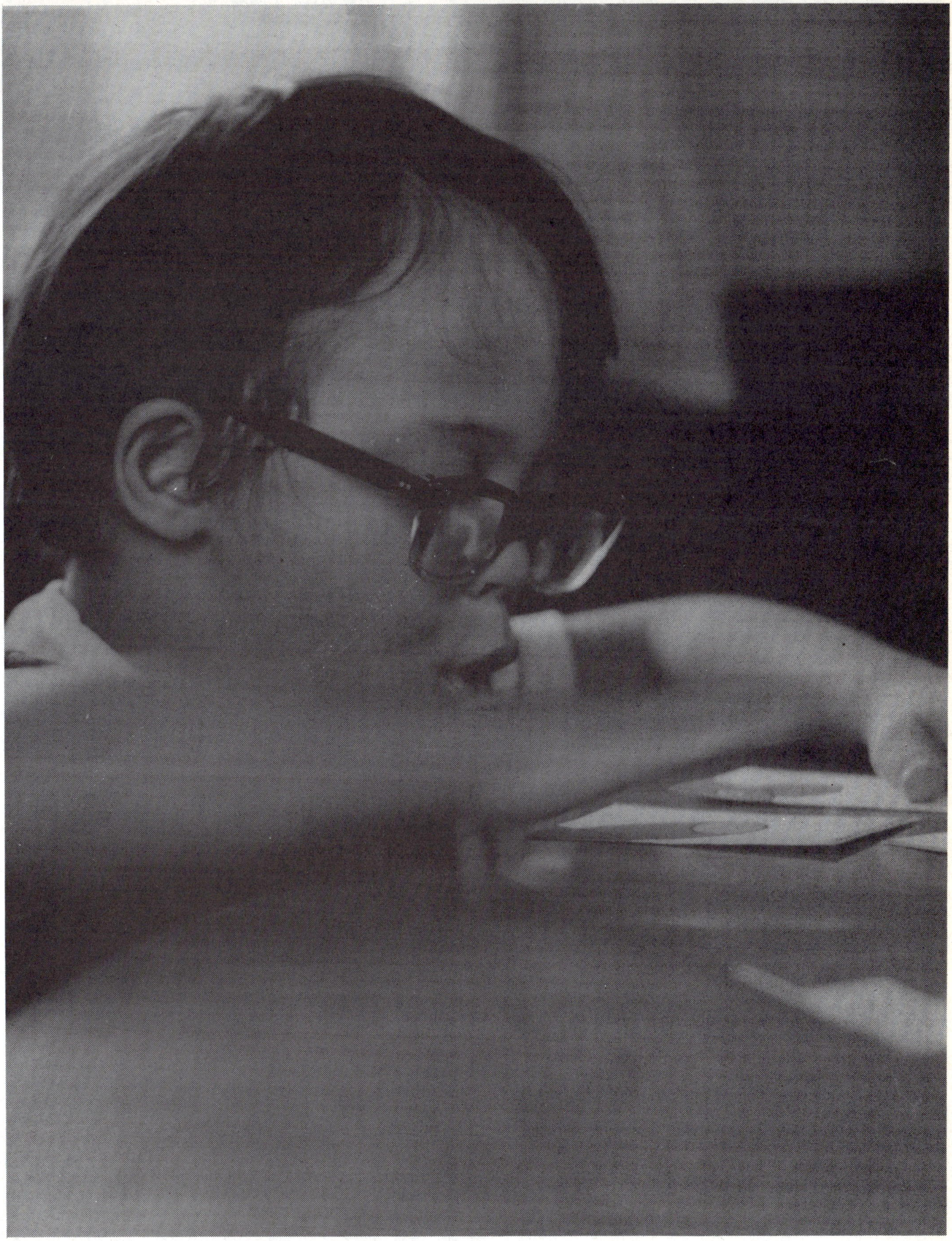

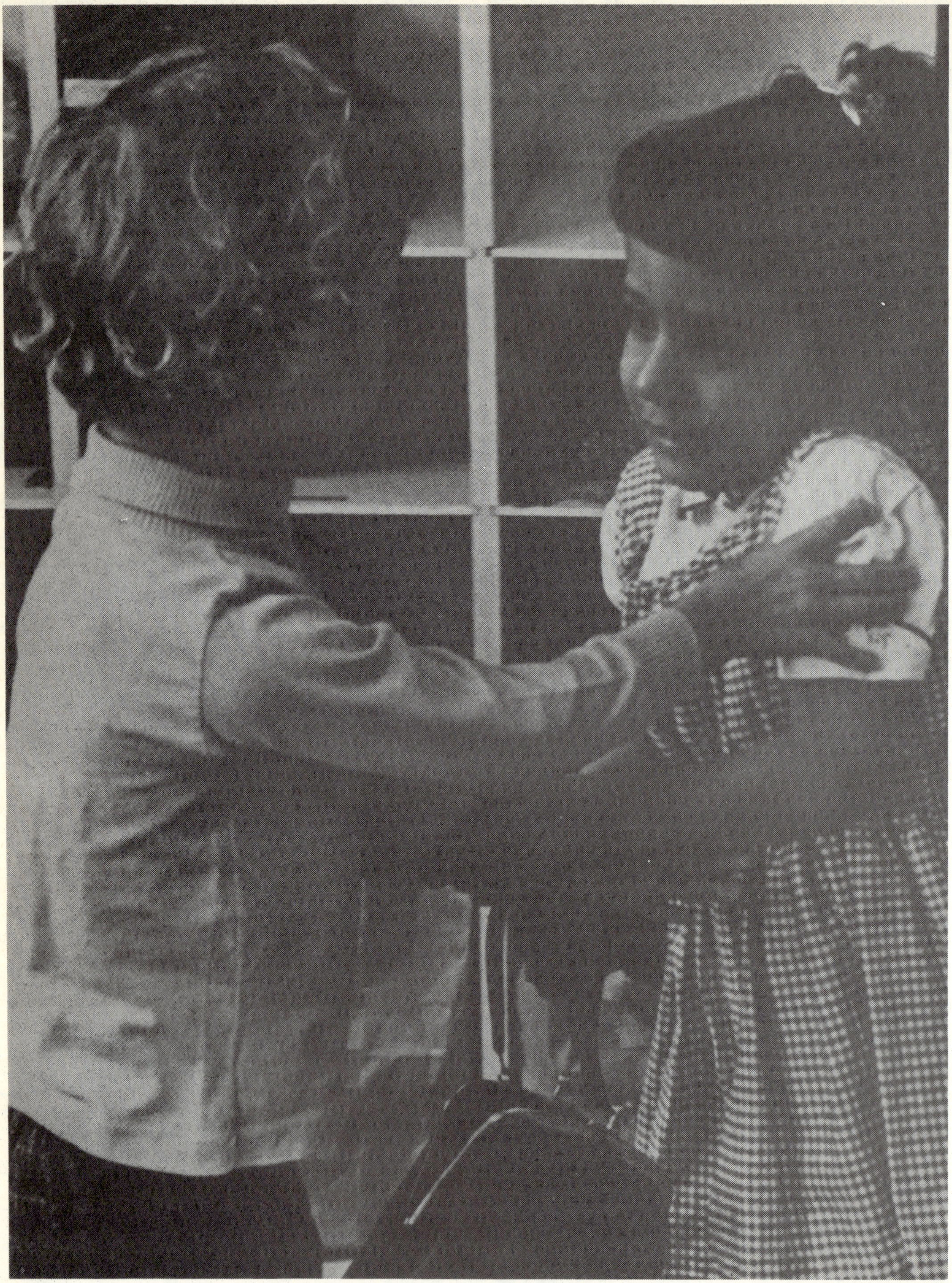

Prospectus on Causes and Prevention of Mental Retardation

The worst cause of mental retardation in children up to now has been lead poisoning through mercury and thallium intake, but establishment of new poison centers has lessened this threat. Radiation exposure during the prenatal period is also a contributing factor to mental retardation which is now recognized and curbed. At the present time we are faced with a relaxed attitude on the part of the American public about the immunization of our children against measles and rubella, which contribute to the brain damage of children, and can be prevented through the use of very inexpensive available vaccines. Public education must be further advanced in this area.

Other causes such as, Tay Sach's disease, Down's syndrome, Klinefelter's syndrome and Turner's syndrome have previously resulted in subnormal intelligence levels, are now all treatable through genetic couseling.

Experiments are being carried out further than within the limits of biological research. It has been recognized that (1) maternal care (2) poverty and (3) institutionalization are further causes of mental retardation which can be made preventable through public awareness. Parent-child relationships can be treated when deviations occur. Disadvantaged classes within our society can obtain help from outpatient clinics, visiting nurse associations, day-care centers and sheltered workshops. Hospitalizm can also be prevented through new federal support of deinstitutionalization programs. Alternatives include smaller residential facilities and foster parent programs. Our priorities and attitudes must change in this country in order that we might correct our previous wrongs in this area.

Progress to now has indeed been exemplary, but we can do more. We must find new methods of training and research. We must reexamine previous research, methodology and educational programs to further understand the needs of each and every unique retarded person. We can only do this through renewed understanding with depth and caring on the part of the public at large.

Mental retardation is not a disease, but is comprised of symptoms of various numbers of disorders. Accidental abnormalities which develop during the prenatal period, birth injuries, defects of genes, childhood illness and environmental deprivation all lead to damage which is not really reparable.

In the United States alone, 30,000 retarded children are born yearly for various reasons. Why? Lack of enlightenment and understanding? First, proper prenatal care can and does lessen the danger of bearing a mentally retarded child. Second, if the first step is closely followed, fewer premature infants will be subject to possible brain damage through neonatal care, thus preventing 90 to 95 percent of all present brain damage. Third, tests are readily available to pinpoint metabolic disorders and diseases which may not be obvious upon birth; 44 states have made PKU blood tests mandatory thus saving infant lives by the hundreds.

New research has brought about further tests to more quickly diagnose other causes — such as maple-syrup urine disease, galactosemia, hypothyroidism, and mocystanuria. New advances in neurosurgery have eliminated "soft-spots" on baby's skulls. Hydrocephalus operations have eliminated the chances of early death for this previously untreatable brain malfunction, while blood clots at birth can now also be treated and corrected.

We Can Do More to Prevent the Tragedy of Retarded Children

Richard Koch and Jean Holt Koch

MORE THAN 60,000 mentally retarded babies will be born in the United States this year. One-fourth will be moderately or severely handicapped. Each of these infants brings untold heartbreak, financial hardship, and anguish to his family, and each one who ends up in a state mental institution will cost taxpayers, on the average, more than a quarter of a million dollars to support. Each one who is so retarded that he cannot work will cost society another $650,000—the money he might have earned during an average lifetime. This need not be, for we now have the knowledge and technology to cut the incidence of mental retardation in half.

Mental retardation is not a disease, but a symptom of any of a number of disorders. Defective genes, abnormalities that develop accidentally during pregnancy, birth injuries, childhood illnesses, even a deprived environment can damage the brain. Once the damage is done, it is irreversible.

Society's obligation to the retarded rests in several areas, one of the most important being an enlightened, understanding attitude. Most people realize that the retarded are people with the same feelings, rights, and responsibilities as all people. True, they are people with handicaps, just as a person born with a clubfoot or impaired eyesight is handicapped. We do not send the person with a physical handicap off to an institution behind locked gates where he can be hidden away, as we have done with the retarded for many years. Instead, we use all the latest medical knowledge to correct his handicap so that he may live a normal life. The retarded deserve to have their physical handicaps corrected. They deserve an education so that they can develop to their highest potential. And they deserve respect so that they can live with dignity and self-confidence. The other area in which society must be involved is in the prevention of mental retardation. It is inexcusable that in the United States, more than 30,000 needlessly retarded children are born each year.

Prenatal care. First, we must insure that all pregnant women and their babies receive good prenatal and neonatal (newborn) medical care. One out of every four women who gives birth in public hospitals has never seen a physician during her pregnancy. In rural and poor areas, the proportion is even higher. We estimate that approximately 350,000 American women give birth each year without prenatal care, and a like number of newborns receive no medical attention.

Every woman needs medical guidance through pregnancy. Many conditions can arise that may cause retardation in the child of a normal expectant mother, and prenatal care can detect and treat some of them before they damage the fetus. Women who plan to give birth at home should have medical supervision during pregnancy and a physician on call in case problems develop during labor.

We have known for years that a woman with Rh-negative blood who marries a man with Rh-positive blood runs a risk of having a mentally retarded child. Although both parents have normal blood types, the mixture causes trouble. In most cases, the fetus inherits the father's dominant Rh-positive blood. This causes no problems during a first pregnancy because the circulatory systems of mother and baby are separate and their blood usually does not mix. But at delivery, if some of the fetal blood in the placenta inadvertently mixes with the mother's blood, her system will begin forming antibodies to this foreign substance. During her next pregnancy, these antibodies may cross the placenta, enter her baby's circulatory system, and systematically destroy the developing red blood cells. This causes the release of bilirubin, one of the pigments in the red blood cells. This substance interferes with the ability of some brain cells to utilize the oxygen carried by the blood. As a result, the affected brain cells are literally starved for oxygen and die.

When such a baby is born, its tiny liver cannot cope with the continued destruction of blood cells. As the bilirubin level rises, the infant's skin becomes jaundiced. Such an infant may become mentally retarded or have cerebral palsy or convulsions.

Prompt exchange transfusions, in which a newborn is given an entirely new supply of blood, can usually prevent brain damage. But the problem need never develop. A new vaccine, given to the Rh-negative mother immediately after the birth of each child, can keep her system from developing antibodies and ends the possibility of an infant incurring brain damage due to Rh incompatibility.

Some women are more likely than others to bear a defective child, but proper prenatal care can lessen the danger. High-risk women include diabetics and those suffering from chronic diseases of the heart, lungs, liver, kidneys, or from metabolic disorders. Women younger than 17 or older than 37 and women who are carrying more than one fetus also are considered high-risk cases. Women who have deficient diets may contract viral diseases that can damage an unborn child.

When a physician monitors a pregnancy, he is alert to signals that warn of possible complications. For example, the baby may lie in a transverse or breech position, indicating labor will be difficult. In such cases, the doctor can plan to do a Caesarean section, averting the possibility of brain damage that sometimes results from lack of oxygen due to a difficult delivery. If every pregnant woman had good prenatal care, the

19. We Can Do More

incidence of mental retardation would probably drop by 10 percent.

Problems of prematurity. Each year 330,000 premature babies are born in the U.S. As birth weight decreases, mental retardation goes up. Ninety percent of newborns weighing less than a pound will be mentally defective, 40 percent of the three-pounders, and 10 percent of the four-pounders. Among babies who weigh six or seven pounds, only from one to three percent will be retarded.

Poverty-stricken women and those who lack prenatal care bear most of the premature babies. Among the poor, there are up to five times as many premature births as among middle-class suburban women; among the medically unsupervised, up to three times as many. Universal prenatal care, coupled with nutritional supplements for women in poverty areas, could drastically reduce the number of premature births. How incongruous it is for society to pay for, say, 30 years of care in an institution at $18,000 a year for each retarded person, but to be unwilling to pay the comparatively small cost of good prenatal care that would prevent mental retardation in the first place. Not all undersized babies are born to poor, malnourished mothers. Heavy smokers also are in danger of bearing babies who weigh less than five pounds, either because the babies are born early or because excessive smoking has retarded the growth of the fetus. And one of the most recent studies indicates maternal alcoholism is a significant cause of mental retardation.

Expert care for these tiny infants can prevent most brain damage. In first-rate hospitals, premature babies are put in intensive-care units, under the supervision of neonatologists and specially trained nurses. Blood is drawn from the babies every few hours to measure their metabolic balance, and their oxygen level, heartbeat, temperature, and respiration are regularly monitored. The incubators have radiant heat and are equipped with mattresses that cause an alarm to ring if the infant stops breathing. Hospitals in many large cities now have such facilities. This care costs about $1,000 a day, but the price is small when compared with the enormous amount of money society pays when a child is severely brain damaged. And this does not even consider the grief and sorrow of the parents involved.

Recent studies show that excellent neonatal care could prevent 90 to 95 percent of all brain damage now suffered by premature babies, even among the tiny one-pounders. It would reduce the annual toll of retarded babies significantly. Similar procedures can minimize or prevent brain damage due to lack of oxygen or to hyaline membrane disease.

One family's experience shows what good medical care can do. Just before Mrs. J. went into the delivery room, her nurse detected a slowed, irregular fetal heartbeat. She summoned the obstetrician, who found that the umbilical cord had descended into the vagina, and was squeezed between the mother's pelvis and the baby's head. While preparations were being made for a Caesarean section, the physician pushed the baby's head back up the birth canal to relieve pressure on the cord and restore the flow of blood to the baby's brain.

At birth, the infant's skin was blue and he was not breathing. The obstetrician suctioned mucus from the baby's air passages, placed him in an incubator, placed a tube in his windpipe to facilitate breathing, and massaged his chest to inflate his lungs. Within three minutes the baby breathed on his own, his pulse became regular and strong. He did well and was discharged from the hospital four days later.

As her son grew older, Mrs. J. noticed that he developed more slowly than her other babies had. He was slightly retarded, but able to attend a regular kindergarten and special classes in public schools. It is likely that, with the special educational opportunities now available, this child will be able to learn a trade, marry, and become a productive member of society. With less skilled care, this child would have suffered severe brain damage and, instead of being able to lead a relatively normal life, he would have been hopelessly retarded and probably institutionalized.

The newborn. Many metabolic disorders and diseases that may cause mental retardation are not obvious at birth. But simple, effective, inexpensive tests can now uncover these ailments.

One of the best-known metabolic disorders that damages brain tissue is phenylketonuria (PKU). It is an enzyme disorder in which the baby cannot use the amino acid phenylalanine, found in all foods that contain protein. Robert Guthrie, a physician in Buffalo, New York, has developed a blood test that identifies these babies within three days after birth, too soon for accumulated phenylalanine to cause brain damage. Once the disorder is detected, physicians can put the baby on a special diet that is low in this amino acid. The child will nearly always have normal intelligence. Without the diet, severe mental retardation is almost a certainty.

Since the newborn PKU blood test is now mandatory in 44 states, it saves almost 250 infants each year. Similar

---

The Degrees of Retardation

When a doctor says that a child is mentally retarded, he is saying that the child will probably have an IQ score of less than 70, compared to the average score, among normal children, of 100. The extent of a child's handicap and its effect on his behavior and development will depend upon the severity of the retardation. All retarded children develop more slowly than normal children.

Mild Retardation: Mild cases of mental retardation often are not detected for several months or even years. Such children make IQ scores of 50 to 70. They are considered educable and can learn simple academic skills. With proper education, many can fit into the normal population, marrying and holding simple jobs. Seventy-five percent of the retarded fall into this category.

Moderate Retardation: Such children make IQ scores of 30 to 49. They can learn simple speech and are considered trainable. Although they need supervision all their lives, they can be toilet trained, taught to dress and feed themselves and keep themselves clean. They can often take jobs in sheltered workshops. They generally do not have to be institutionalized. Twenty-one percent of the retarded fall into this category.

Severe Retardation: Such children make IQ scores of 0 to 29. Most cannot be toilet trained. Few will ever walk or talk. They need constant, lifelong care, which families can rarely provide. Most of these children enter institutions before adolescence; many are placed soon after birth. These children frequently die in early adulthood from physical ailments that accompany their severe mental disorders. Only four percent of the retarded fall into this category.

—Richard Koch and Jean Holt Koch

3. CAUSES AND PREVENTION

tests can detect galactosemia, maple-syrup urine disease, histidinemia, homocystinuria, and hypothyroidism. Unfortunately, very few states mandate newborn screening for all these diseases, although, on a mass basis, the cost would be only about $2.00 for the additional procedures, and the testing could be done on the same blood sample used for the PKU test. All these diseases can cause mental retardation, and all can be treated. Universal screening of newborns would reduce the incidence of mental retardation by at least another five percent.

Advances have also been made in the treatment of other conditions that invariably lead to mental retardation. Craniosynostosis is a condition in which the sutures of the skull are fused together at birth so that there is no "soft spot" at the top of the baby's head. Such a child may become mentally defective because the brain has no room to grow. Today, neurosurgeons can create sutures across the top of the head, enabling the skull to expand.

Operations can also correct hydrocephalus, a condition in which cerebrospinal fluid is trapped in the skull, eventually filling the space the brain should occupy. Without treatment, these babies suffer an early death or develop enormous skulls, have severe mental retardation, and generally spend their lives in an institutional bed.

Sometimes during an especially difficult delivery, or as a result of an accident, there may be bleeding into the lining of the brain of the newborn child. This is called a subdural hematoma. Surgeons can remove these potentially dangerous blood clots before the damage occurs. Accidental poisoning is another cause of brain damage in children. The worst offender as far as mental retardation is concerned is lead poisoning. Parents should be aware of the nearest poison center in case of emergency, as most heavy metals, such as mercury and thallium (an ingredient in roach poison) can cause mental retardation.

Another cause of brain damage in newborns is the exposure of the fetus to radiation. This was demonstrated by the sharp rise in mental retardation among offspring of Japanese women exposed to the atomic bomb blasts of World War II. As a result, doctors are careful not to X-ray the abdomens of women during the first three months of pregnancy. With this knowledge of the effects of radiation on future genera-

> The public has become lax about immunizing children. In some states, as many as one in four children is not inoculated for German measles.

tions, many scientists feel we should use extreme caution in any expansion of nuclear facilities.

Menace of measles. Controlling the spread of contagious diseases would further reduce mental retardation. Of the contagious diseases, regular measles and German measles (rubella) are the heaviest contributors to brain damage.

The complications of regular measles at one time left 2,000 children each year with neurological handicaps, seizures, cerebral palsy, mental retardation, and speech handicaps. When a mother contracts three-day (German) measles during the first three months of pregnancy, her baby may have multiple handicaps, including blindness, deafness, and heart defects as well as seizures, cerebral palsy, and mental retardation.

Inexpensive vaccines ($1.50 per dose when purchased in volume) can prevent both diseases, yet children are still being damaged by measles. Recent data suggest that the public has become lax about immunizing children. In some states as many as one in every four children is not inoculated for German measles. At present, some states require each woman's premarital blood specimen to be tested for German measles. If no evidence is found indicating the person has had the disease, she is encouraged to have this immunization.

If the public were properly educated regarding the serious damage that can be caused by common childhood diseases, not only to the present generation, but to those as yet unborn, it is hard to imagine that this relaxed attitude toward immunization would persist. A possible solution would be for health departments to provide free vaccine to any child. Also, insurance rates could be reduced for families practicing good preventive health measures. If we immunize every well child completely, it has been estimated the savings would approach $1 billion annually.

The newest advance in the preven-tion of retardation is in the area of genetic counseling. A variety of genetic and chromosomal anomalies such as Down's syndrome (mongolism), Tay-Sachs disease, Turner's syndrome, and Klinefelter's syndrome usually result in subnormal intelligence. In the past we knew little about what causes them, how to treat or prevent them, or what to tell parents about the future of their afflicted child.

The situation is brighter today. We know, for example, that Down's syndrome, characterized by Oriental-looking eyes, flattened nasal bridges, short stature, and mental retardation, is a chromosome disorder. Persons with Down's syndrome have an extra chromosome in each of their body cells.

Down's syndrome occurs among all races, and the risk of bearing such a child increases with the age of the mother. Few are born to young women, and those under 35 have only one chance in 1,000 of having such a child. When a woman is between 35 and 39, she has one chance in 300 of having a baby with Down's syndrome. For mothers who are between 40 and 44, the odds go up to one in 100, and between 45 and 49, up to one in 50.

Most of these persons will be moderately retarded and will need special care. Obviously those who are severely retarded may need institutional care. At present, one in every 10 institutionalized patients in the U.S. has Down's syndrome.

Physicians once thought Down's syndrome was inherited and counseled the parents of an affected child not to have more children. We now know that only about one in 20 cases is inherited. The other 19 come from a simple error in cell division. Today, a laboratory blood test can single out hereditary disorders, and parents of a baby with Down's syndrome can safely have additional children.

The tell-tale needle. Amniocentesis, a technological advance, is now helping many parents who carry genetic defects to have healthy children. During the 13th to 16th week of a pregnancy, a physician inserts a sterile needle through the woman's abdominal wall into the uterus, from which he withdraws a small amount of amniotic fluid. Because the fluid always contains a few free-floating cells from the fetus, the cells can be studied for genetic defects such as chromosomal abnormalities, Tay-Sachs disease, and a number of other disorders. Should any serious defect turn up, the parents then have the option of requesting that the pregnancy be terminated.

All high-risk mothers should be aware of this technique and consult their doctors about it. Although abortion should never be forced on anyone, neither should a woman be forced to bear a defective child against her will. This decision is one that must be made by the couple involved with the advice and counseling of their doctor. In the past, high-risk families were usually discouraged from having another child, but with the advent of this new technique, the couple can be reassured that each pregnancy can be monitored by amniocentesis and they need not fear the birth of a retarded baby.

In September Congress voted to prohibit federal funding of abortions for low-income women except when "the life of the mother would be endangered if the fetus were carried to term." This is a step backward in the prevention of mental retardation, as it completely negates the role of amniocentesis and therapeutic abortion for high-risk women who have committed the sin of being poor. Low-income women are those least able to pay for the abortion or the care of a retarded child.

Because Tay-Sachs disease is an inherited recessive genetic defect, screening, counseling, and amniocentesis can wipe it out. The disease occurs predominantly among Ashkenazi Jews. One in every 30 is a carrier of Tay-Sachs, and on the average one in every 3,600 Ashkenazi infants has the disease. When two carriers marry, chances are one in four that their child will inherit the disease and one in two that the child will be a carrier.

We can detect carriers with a simple blood test. If every Jew knew whether he was a carrier, then couples where both are carriers could have amniocentesis performed during each pregnancy, and a defective pregnancy could be terminated so that a normal child could later be born. A Tay-Sachs baby degenerates rapidly, both physically and mentally, becoming blind, helpless, and mentally retarded, and usually dies before it is three years old. Each case costs society $30,000 to $50,000, and causes untold anguish to the family involved.

Dollars and sense. Americans have never made preventive health care a national priority. Our neglect shows in U.S. maternal and infant death rates, which are among the highest in the Western world. Despite our wealth and advanced technology, we do a poorer job than 14 other countries.

The quality and quantity of prenatal and neonatal care vary widely across the country. One way to improve our medical system might be to liberalize federal and state subsidies and private insurance benefits for maternal and neonatal care. Government agencies and insurance companies could simply refuse to pay benefits to hospitals with inferior standards of care.

Because medical services are poorly distributed, with cities having a surplus of physicians and rural areas desperately in need of doctors, we might do well to follow the example of Mexico and several other countries, where every medical-school graduate must serve a specified length of time in a rural area. The problem is aggravated because the U.S. has a glut of medical specialists and a scarcity of general practitioners.

If we made universal preventive health care a reality, we could save thousands of lives each year and halve the rate of mental retardation. When one considers that in California alone, taxpayers spend about $900 million annually to care for the mentally retarded, it becomes obvious that prevention is not only humane but that it makes good economic sense as well.

Richard Koch received his M.D. from the University of Rochester School of Medicine. He is a professor of pediatrics at the University of Southern California School of Medicine and Senior Attending Physician, Childrens Hospital, Los Angeles. The author of over 100 articles, Koch was formerly President of the California Council for Retarded Children and the American Association for Mental Deficiency.

Jean Holt Koch graduated from San Jose State College. She was Chairperson of the Westchester Human Relations Council and is now Secretary of the Mineral King Task Force of the Sierra Club. With Richard Koch, she wrote Understanding the Mentally Retarded Child.

For more information, read:

Conley, Ronald. The Economics of Mental Retardation; Johns Hopkins, 1972, $17.50.

Koch, Richard and Kathryn J. Koch. Understanding the Mentally Retarded Child; Random, 1975, $8.95.

Prevention Handbook, The National Association for Retarded Citizens, P.O. Box 6109, Arlington, Texas 76011.

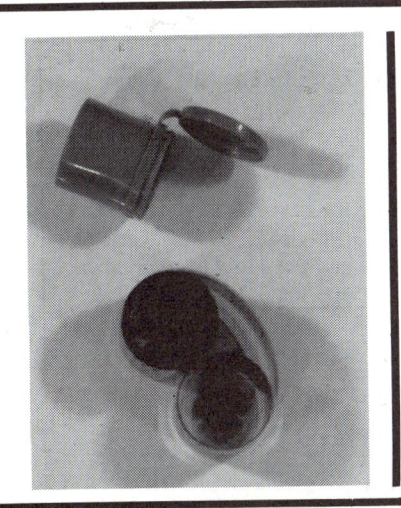

DON'T LABEL ME!

SOUND FILMSTRIP - MENTAL RETARDATION

This poignant filmstrip illustrates the story of a retarded individual's day by day life. It is excellent to show as a role-model. It should be used in an introductory course for exceptional children, a course in mental retardation, or for those teachers now involved in Mainstreaming and teaching the retarded.

Filmstrip and cassette and teacher's guide   **$14.95**

For further information contact:

Joseph Logan, Editor
Special Learning Corporation

Special Learning Corporation
42 Boston Post Rd. Guilford, Connecticut 06437   (203) 453-6525

Lead And Mental Retardation

It has been well demonstrated in children, experimental animals and tissue culture studies that lead exposure can lead to neurological damage. For instance, it has been known for many years that children suffer neurological damage, often permanent, from lead poisoning. Hyperactive children have been diagnosed as having significantly higher amounts of lead in their blood and urine than control children (SN: 12/19/72, p. 377). Feeding lead to suckling rats made them hyperactive and depressed nerve transmitters in their brains (SN: 2/15/75, p. 104). In tissue culture, lead inhibited brain enzymes.

So it should come as no surprise that a group of investigators in Glasgow has found a firm correlation between ingestion of lead from drinking water and mental retardation in children. A. D. Beattie of Stobhill Hospital and his team report their findings in the March 15 LANCET. They conclude that "lead contamination of water may be one factor in the multifactorial etiology of mental retardation and that every effort should be made to reduce the lead content of drinking water."

The subjects of their study were 154 children between the ages of two and five years. Seventy-seven of the children were attending clinics in Glasgow because of retardation in mental development, and 77 were nonretarded healthy children forming a control group matched for age, sex and geographic location within the city. The intelligence quotient was below 70 in each of the mentally retarded children being studied.

Beattie and his team collected water samples from the taps of the homes where the children lived. Then they collected blood samples from their subjects. As they report in LANCET, the amount of lead in the water was significantly higher for the retarded group than for the control group—up to 2,000 micrograms per liter versus a ceiling of 800 micrograms per liter. And the probability of mental retardation was markedly increased when the lead in water exceeded 800 micrograms per liter. The 11 children from homes with the highest levels belonged to the group who were mentally retarded. The levels of lead in the blood of the retarded children were also much higher than in the blood of the control children, strongly suggesting that lead from tap water could get into the children's bodies and exert brain damage and lead to retardation.

But how might lead in tap water trigger brain damage? Although the investigators aren't sure, they have some theories. For instance, they suggest that "an increase in lead in the blood may be associated with biochemical abnormalities in the child brain. The energy requirements of the infant brain are greater than those of the mature brain, and it seems probably, therefore, that a substance such as lead, which inhibits enzymes and mitochondrial respiration, will be harmful to the development of the infant brain."

Since lead is capable of crossing the placenta to the fetus, and brain development in intrauterine life is of paramount importance, Beattie and his colleagues also attempted to see whether tap water lead might threaten children as much, if not more, before birth as after birth. However, they were unable to come up with an answer because the water their subjects were exposed to after birth was usually the same as the water they were exposed to before birth.

Although lead is probably only one of many causes of mental retardation, Beattie and his team believe that lead's importance lies in the fact that lead contamination can be eliminated or at least reduced. "The amount of lead in drinking water," they explain, "can be reduced by removing lead from plumbing systems (eg., water tanks and pipes). This is the most satisfactory solution, but will take several years to achieve. The alternative short-term solution, already initiated in Glasgow, is to treat the water supply in the holding reservoirs with calcium salts such as lime at 2-4 parts per million."

Prevention of Mental Retardation

Prevention, hopefully, can obviate the necessity of people becoming patients. The physician occupies a uniquely favorable position from which to initiate and assist in the development of preventive measures. He may act on the primary level to prevent the occurrence of retardation, on the secondary level through early diagnosis and treatment that may modify or reverse the course of the disease, and finally through treatment of superimposed handicaps.

Prevention at the Biological Level

The physician may conceptualize opportunities for prevention at the biological level by relating them in time to the prenatal, natal, and postnatal periods.

Prenatal period—maternal 'infections' (Table 4)

Acute bacterial infections during the third trimester may induce premature labor; they should be treated promptly and vigorously. Although tuberculosis is not commonly seen during pregnancy, transmission of the infection to the fetus can occur. Congenital tuberculosis must receive early recognition and treatment. The infant should be immediately separated from the mother with the disease in active form.

The majority of acute infections occurring in pregnant women are viral in origin. Any severe viral illness within the first trimester —and particularly in the first eight weeks of pregnancy—may possibly injure the fetus. In the last trimester, a severe viral infection may precipitate premature birth.

The rubella virus is teratogenic during the first trimester, even in the case of inapparent maternal infection. The 1963 rubella epidemic resulted in thousands of malformed infants. The rubella vaccine has recently become available and is currently recommended for use in all children; it is generally contraindicated in women of child-bearing age. If this vaccine fulfills its promise, it will become the prime agent of prevention. Prevention of the "rubella syndrome" has sometimes included deliberate exposure of young girls to rubella to produce a permanent immunity. The physician who recommends this procedure must realize he is increasing risk of further spread of the disease in the community and of increased exposure of women already pregnant. He is also running a small, but definite, risk of exposing a child to a disease with some serious complications such as encephalitis. The protective effect of gamma globulin is variable; a number of studies indicate it does not prevent viremia. Gamma globulin and deliberate exposure may well be of historic interest only, with the increasing use and success of the vaccine.

Because of the high risk of a defective fetus, therapeutic abortion may be recommended. Methods for obtaining permission for abortion vary with state laws, community practices, etc.

No reliable evidence indicates that the influenza virus is teratogenic. Consequently, routine immunization during pregnancy need not be carried out. However, during an epidemic, immunization may be advisable, with the use of a vaccine corresponding to the infecting virus. An influenza infection occurring during the last trimester may lead to premature birth.

The viruses of poliomyelitis, measles, mumps, chickenpox, and herpes simplex have not been implicated as teratogenic agents. However, the viral infection may be transmitted to the fetus. Herpes simplex in the newborn is associated with a high mortality; it can be transmitted from the mother in the postnatal period. The newborn infant should be isolated from the mother with a herpetic infection.

Measles may lead to abortion or stillbirth, and hopefully this disease will be eradicated with the new live vaccine. Generalized vaccina in the fetus has followed smallpox vaccination of the mother. Pregnant women therefore should not be vaccinated routinely. During an epidemic of any kind, the physician should consult with public health officials.

The cytomegalovirus diseases may be transmitted from an asymptomatic mother to the fetus.

No satisfactory therapy or preventive measure is known.

The frequency of congenital syphilis is again increasing. A routine serological study is mandatory during the prenatal period. Antisyphilitic therapy, even if started in the third trimester, will protect the infant against infection.

Toxoplasmosis, a protozoan infection, is also acquired by the fetus from the asymptomatic mother. No therapy or preventive measures are known. Subsequent offspring are not affected.

3. CAUSES AND PREVENTION

TABLE 4.—MATERNAL INFECTIONS WHICH MAY BE ASSOCIATED WITH FETAL OR NEONATAL DISEASE AND CENTRAL NERVOUS SYSTEM SEQUELAE

Agent	Effects on Fetus or Newborn	Prevention
Syphilis	Congenital syphilis	Prenatal serology and treatment
Tuberculosis	Tuberculosis	Separation from mother with active disease; BCG or INH prophylaxis
Toxoplasmosis	Chorioretinitis, intracranial calcifications, hepatosplenomegaly, jaundice, micro or macrocephaly	None
Cytomegalovirus	Subclinical-mild-severe; microcephaly, chorioretinitis, petechiae, hepatosplenomegaly, jaundice, anemia, penumonia, low birth weight	None
Rubella	Subclinical-mild-severe; petechiae, penumonia, hepatosplenomegaly, bone lesions, congenital heart disease, cataracts, deafness	Active immunization of childhood population (?)
Herpesvirus hominis (simplex)	Fulminating disease, vesicular skin lesions, keratoconjunctivitis, hepatosplenomegaly, jaundice, penumonia, encephalitis, chorioretinitis, microcephaly	Isolate asymptomatic infant, especially premature, from mother with genital herpesvirus hominis, type 2, and from anyone with symptomatic herpes
Coxsackie B	Fulminating disease, myocarditis, hyper and hypothermia, hepatomegaly, CNS signs, aseptic meningitis	None
Other picornaviruses ECHO	Diarrhea, rashes, aseptic meningitis	None
Poliovirus	Congenital polio	Active immunization of mother in childhood
Varicella-zoster	Congenital varicella-zoster	Isolate asymptomatic infant from mother; possibly give human immune serum globulin
Pox virus Smallpox	Congenital smallpox, abortion	Isolate asymptomatic infant from mother; possibly give human vaccina immune globulin
Vaccina	Congenital generalized vaccina, abortion	Isolate asymptomatic infant from mother; possibly give human vaccina immune globulin
Myxoparamyxovirus Measles	Congenital measles	Active immunization of mother in childhood
Mumps	Endocardial fibroelastosis	None
Arbovirus Western equine encephalitis	Congenital encephalitis	None

Adapted from Overall, James C. Jr., and Glasgow, Lowell A.: *Virus Infections of the Fetus and New-Born Infant.* The Journal of Pediatrics, 77(2):315-333 (Aug.), 1970. Modified by Sterling Garrard, M.D.

Metabolic Disorders

Several metabolic or endocrinologic disorders in the mother may affect the newborn infant. These maternal diseases include diabetes mellitus, myasthenia gravis, phenylketonuria, idiopathic thrombocytopenic purpura, and hypothyroidism.

The infant born to the mother with diabetes mellitus has a higher neonatal morbidity and mortality and increased frequency of congenital malformations. Suggestive evidence indicates that neurological sequelae may occur in some of these infants. It seems reasonable to suggest that good control of the maternal diabetes and the anticipation of problems in the newborn can decrease neonatal morbidity and mortality.

The mother with hypothyroidism should be adequately treated during pregnancy. Protein-bound iodine (PBI) and butanol-extractable iodine (BEI) levels should be maintained within the normal range if congenital malformations and mental retardation are to be avoided.

Teratogenic Agents

The fetus may react differently to drugs than children and adults. For this reason, self-medication by the mother should be discouraged and medications during the first trimester of pregnancy kept at an absolute minimum. (A recent study revealed that 70% of pregnant women receive two or more medications.)

While the majority of drugs do not lead to malformations in the fetus, nevertheless unpredictable idiosyncracies exist. The fact that a drug has been given in one case during the first trimester without any serious side effects does not imply that this medication is safe for all mothers. Table 5 summarizes the drugs which may have a teratogenic effect on the fetus.

Weight reduction drugs are risky; aspirin may adversely affect blood clotting in the newborn; the excessive use of multivitamin preparations is generally discouraged. The latter are not to be regarded in any sense as a substitute for a good nutritious diet.

Therapeutic radiation to the uterus is damaging to the fetus throughout pregnancy. The low levels of radiation encountered with diagnostic x-ray films carry small hazard. However, elective x-ray study should be performed only in the first ten days following onset of a menstrual period, and the pelvis and gonads should be properly shielded. Routine x-ray pelvimetry is not recommended. The amount of radiation in diagnostic procedures can be reduced through the use of ultrasensitive film, image intensifiers, etc. The use of radioactive isotopes for diagnostic study is not recommended in the pregnant woman.

During premature labor maternal analgesia and anesthesia should be avoided. Furthermore, their use has been questioned even in the delivery of full-term infants. A depressed, cyanotic apneic baby may be a high price to pay for maternal "comfort." The incidence of this kind of history seems to be higher in children with perceptual handicaps, learning disorders, and other forms of retarded development.

The practice of "holding back the baby until the doctor comes" or of inducing labor for the convenience of the physician are mentioned only to be condemned. This kind of obstetric history is commonly elicited from parents of retarded children. Such practices have no legitimate place in medicine.

Genetic Factors

Genetic counseling is a skill requiring considerable training and sensitivity. Many physicians are relatively unschooled in this field and therefore should approach this subject with the greatest of caution in order to avoid oversimplification in an area that demands a subtle blending of multiple factors. In helping guide family decisions in genetic counseling, the physician should consider risk figures as only one aspect. He must also consider family beliefs, convictions, response to stress, religious beliefs, etc.

The physician should make an effort to determine whether the condition is genetic or nongenetic in origin. There is a low risk of recurrence after one affected child when all the following conditions are satisfied: (1) the family history, carefully taken, is negative; (2) both parents are free of the disorder; (3) there is no evidence of abnormal pregnancy wastage; and (4) the affected child does not have any known genetically determined condition such as gargoylism, Tay-Sachs disease, phenylketonuria, etc., and (5) the child and parents have no chromosomal aberration, and (6) a relatively young maternal age. It may be extremely difficult to determine if the cause of the mental retardation is a rare autosomal recessive disorder, an X-linked recessive

21. Prevention

TABLE 5.—EFFECTS OF DRUG INTAKE UPON THE FETUS AND NEWBORN PATIENT

Maternal Drug Intake	Fetal or Neonatal Effect
Potassium iodine, Propylthiouracil, Methimazole	Goiter and mental retardation
Aminopterin, Methotrexate, Chlorambucil	Anomalies and abortions
Coumarin derivatives	Fetal death; hemorrhage (?)
Nicotine, tars	Low birth weight
Reserpine	Sedation, nasal congestion
Diethylstilbestrol	Adenocarcinoma of the vagina after puberty
Salicylates (large amounts), Phenobarbital (excess amounts)	Neonatal hemorrhage
Quinine	Thrombocytopenia
Progestogens, Androgens	Virilization
Antibiotics	
Chloramphenicol	Gray syndrome; death
Novobiocin	Hyperbilirubinemia
Sulfonamides	Kernicterus
Tetracyclines	Inhibition of bone growth; discoloration of teeth
Diuretics (in excess)	Electrolyte disturbances
Vitamin K analogues (excess amount)	Hyperbilirubinemia (?)
Phenothiazines	Hyperbilirubinemia
Intravenous fluids (unphysiologic quantities)	Electrolyte abnormalities
Heroin and morphine	Neonatal hypoxia

Updated by Kathryn S. Huss, M.D.

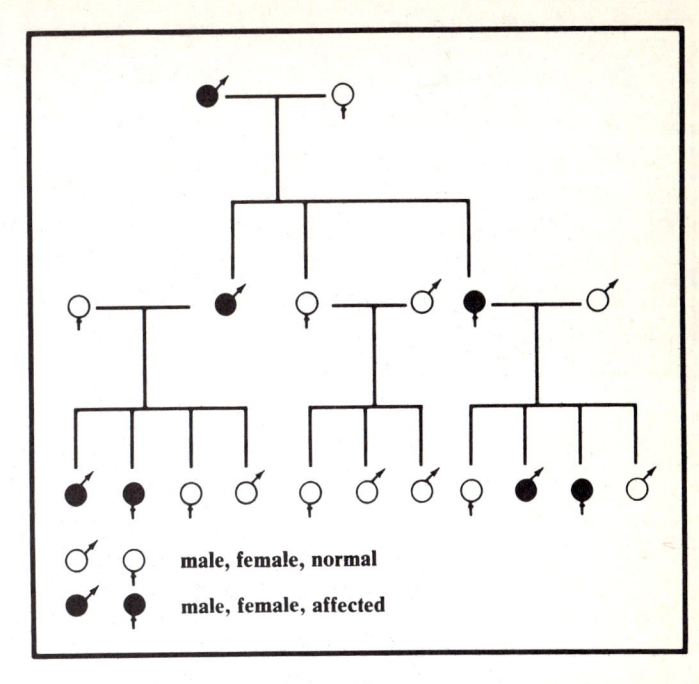

FIGURE 3. Pedigree illustrating simple dominant inheritance, eg, chronic progressive hereditary (Huntington's) chorea. Note (1) transmission of trait through affected persons; (2) both sexes equally affected; (3) appropriate ratio of 1:1 for affected to unaffected. (Prepared by Stanley Wright, MD).

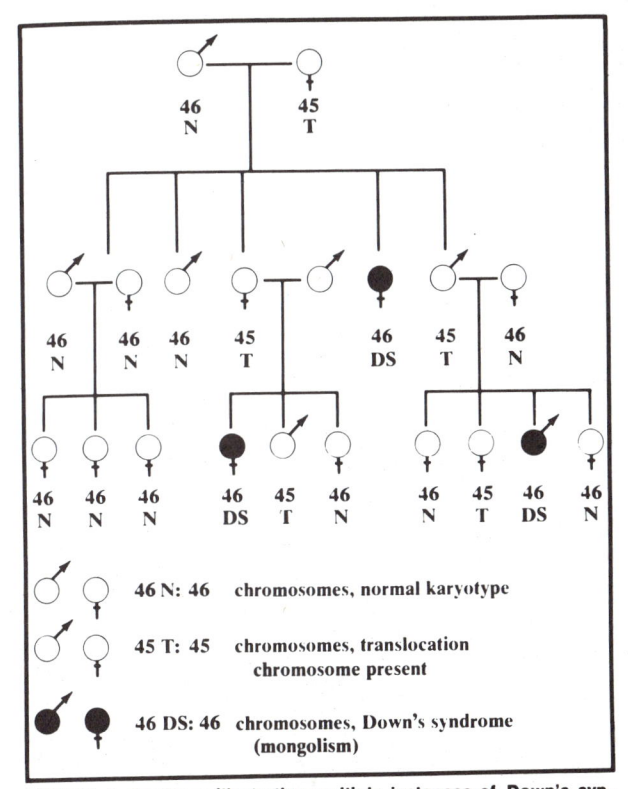

FIGURE 2. Pedigree illustrating multiple instances of Down's syndrome (mongolism) associated with translocation chromosome, eg, 13-15/21. Note three types of offspring from mating of normal (46 N) individual with phenotypically normal carrier parent (45 T). (Prepared by Stanley Wright, MD).

46 N: 46 chromosomes, normal karyotype
45 T: 45 chromosomes, translocation chromosome present
46 DS: 46 chromosomes, Down's syndrome (mongolism)

disorder or a chromosomal aberration and, therefore, the screening tests referred to earlier should be used to help establish a precise diagnosis.

If family history is positive and careful investigation indicates that the disorder in the child and the affected relative are similar, the parents require advice from a genetic counseling facility. Genetic counseling is now available through major medical centers and a directory of genetic counseling centers is available from the National Foundation. The physician should provide the counselor with all relevant information about family history and confirmation of relevant diagnosis. Pedigree charts are shown in Figures 2, 3 and 4.

For recessive disorders, there is a 25% chance for recurrence with each succeeding pregnancy. Dominant disorders can generally be recognized by the transmission of the disorder through several generations, by the fact that both sexes may be affected, and that in most instances an affected child will have an affected parent. In some dominant disorders, ie, tuberous sclerosis and neurofibromatosis, the parents and their family history are often normal. In such instances, the disorder may be due to a new mutation, and the risk for recurrence is less than 10%. New mutations should be considered *only* after the physician has carefully examined both parents and found no evidences of the disease. Even then he may be faced with a parent in whom essentially no manifestations of the disease are present but who may transmit the disease to one-half his children. A sex-linked recessive trait can generally be recognized by the typical pattern of transmission with normal females and affected males. For many autosomal recessive conditions, methods have been developed to detect carriers: Tay-Sachs disease, PKU and galactosemia are three such examples. Identification of high-risk couples is one method of primary prevention.

3. CAUSES AND PREVENTION

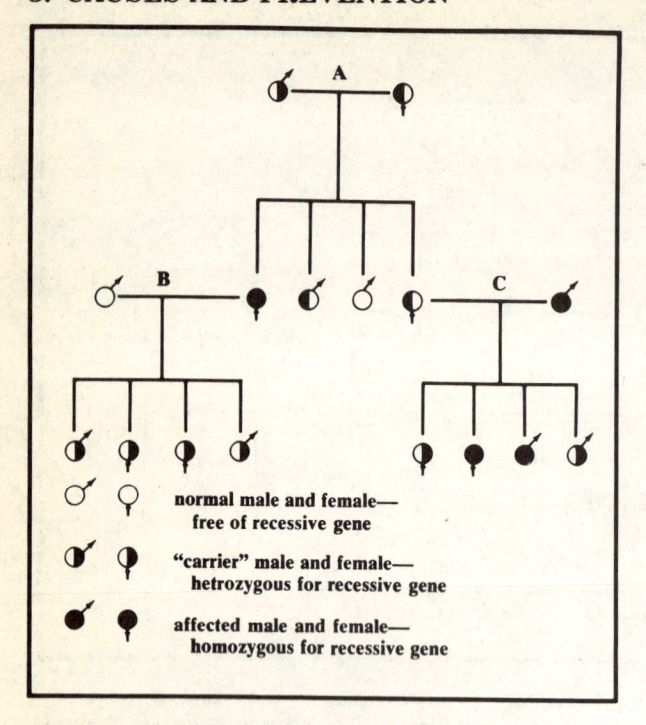

FIGURE 4. Pedigree illustrating simple recessive inheritance, eg, phenylketonuria. "Carrier" parents of affected children have no clinical evidence of disease (A), but one of four of their children may be affected. When affected individual marries person free of recessive gene (B), children will be carriers and have no clinical evidence of disease. If affected individual marries carrier (C), one half of offspring will show the disease and one half will be carriers of the trait. Carrier state for a recessive gene is seldom detectable.

TABLE 6.—MAJOR VIABLE CHROMOSOMAL ABNORMALITIES WHICH MAY BE ASSOCIATED WITH MENTAL RETARDATION, NEUROLOGICAL DISORDER, OR BEHAVORIAL DEVIANCY

Chromosomal Type	Clinical Name	Frequency
AUTOSOMAL ANOMALIES		
47, 21+	Mongolism, Down's Syndrome	1/600 liveborns
47, 18+	E-trisomy, Edward's Syndrome	1/4500 liveborns
47, 13+	D-trisomy, Patau Syndrome	1/4500 liveborns
46, 5p−	Cri-du-Chat Syndrome	1/2000 liveborns
46, 18q−	Long arm 18 deletion syndrome	?
46, 18p−	Short arm 18 deletion syndrome	?
SEX-CHROMOSOME ANOMALIES		
45, X	Turner Syndrome	1/4500 liveborns
47, XXX	The Triple-X Female	1/800 liveborn females
47, XXY	Klinefelter Syndrome	1/800 liveborn males
47, XYY	The XYY Syndrome	1/500 liveborn males

Prepared by Sterling Garrard, M.D.

Chromosomal Disorders

The field of chromosomal disorders is developing at such a rapid pace that frequent consultation with research workers and up-to-date medical literature is mandatory (Table 6). One of the most important clinical conditions associated with a chromosome abnormality is Down's syndrome (Figure 5). All patients are trisomic for chromosome 21, and the majority have 47 chromosomes. Recurrence risks are very low in the group with 47 chromosomes—less than 1/100. Approximately 5% have chromosome counts other than 47. These include (1) the rare individual with double trisomy, ie, both Down's syndrome and Klinefelter's syndrome, chromosome count 48 with an XXY sex chromosome complement; (2) mosaicism, ie, cell lines containing different chromosome numbers, eg, 46 and 47; and (3) those with 46 chromosomes and a translocation, ie, an exchange of chromosome segments between two nonhomologous chromosomes.

Translocation Down's syndrome (3 above) has implications for genetic counseling. This form of Down's syndrome, although clinically similar to the others, is unrelated to maternal age and shows a familial trend in some families. Approximately one-third of families in whom there are two or more individuals with Down's syndrome have been shown to have a translocation as cause of the anomaly.

Approximately 4% of children with Down's syndrome have a translocation. About 70% of these translocations have arisen de novo, ie, as new mutations, and the parents will have a normal chromosome complement, 46. The recurrence risk is low in this group; perhaps 1/100 to 1/200. In the remaining 30% one parent will carry the translocation. There is an empiric risk in this in-

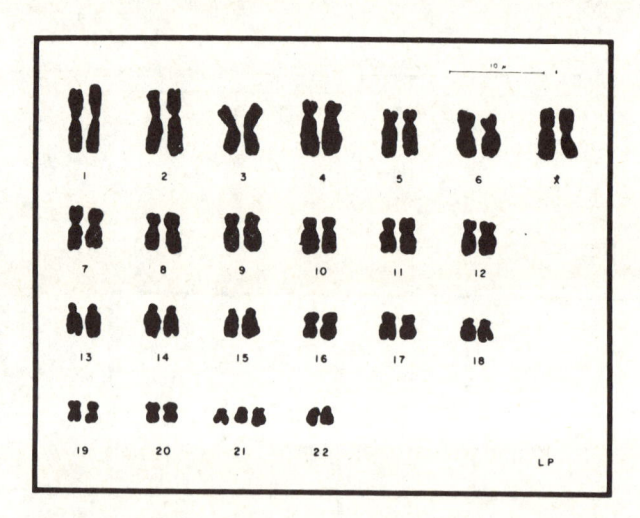

FIGURE 5. Typical karyotype of female patient with Down's syndrome, chromosome No. 47. Note trisomy 21. (Courtesy of Lytt I. Gardner, MD).

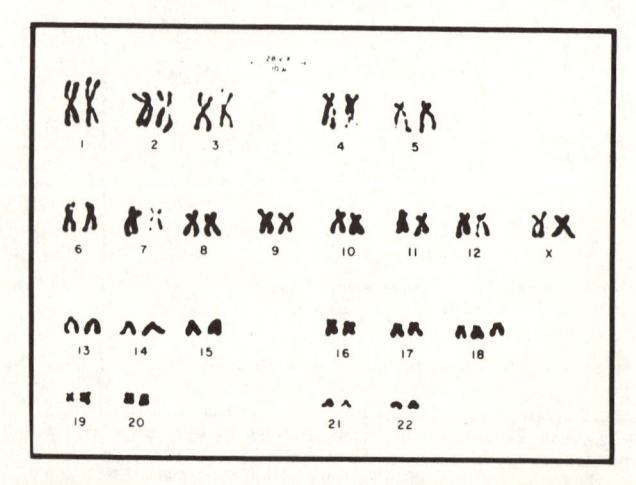

FIGURE 6. Typical karyotype of female patient with trisomy 18. (Courtesy of Lytt I. Gardner, MD).

stance of one-third for a child with Down's syndrome, one-third for a normal child carrying the translocation ("translocation carrier") and one-third for a clinically and chromosomally normal offspring. This figure may be modified according to the parent who carries the translocation as well as the type of translocation.

The most frequent situation in genetic counseling for Down's syndrome arises in the mother less than 30 years old who has one child with Down's syndrome.

At first, there were few facilities able to perform chromosome studies, and they were time-consuming and expensive. Recently, many new specialized centers and laboratories have been developed, and improvements in technique have significantly decreased the time and expense required. However, many physicians may still have to counsel without the benefit of such studies. In cases where the family history is normal, this parent can be informed that empirically, the risks for recurrence are in the range of 1 in 50 to 1 in 100. This figure will, in general, hold true for maternal ages up to 40 years.

Two other autosomal trisomy syndromes have been described, ie, trisomy 13-15 (trisomy D) and trisomy 18 (Figure 6). Both are associated with multiple congenital malformations and can often be suspected from the typical pattern of malformations. There is little indication that these tend to recur in subsequent sibs, and risk figures are probably low. There is no evidence to indicate that abnormalities involving the sex chromosomes, eg, Klinefelter's syndrome (XXY) (Figure 7), Turner's syndrome (XO) or the triple-X syndrome and XYY recur in subsequent sibs. These disorders can be diagnosed in most instances with the aid of a buccal smear sex chromatin test. Chromosome studies are rarely indicated. Klinefelter's syndrome should be suspected in young men of military age who show retarded development of secondary sex characteristics.

Other syndromes of congenital malformations have been found to be associated with a chromosomal abnormality only rarely. Thus, chromosome studies on children who appear to have "some syndromes," multiple congenital malformations, or who seem "odd looking," etc, will probably not prove rewarding.

Natal Period—Fetal Monitoring

The physician should be alert to "high-risk" situations in which either a maternal disorder or an abnormality within the fetus or newborn may produce neurological sequelae (Table 7). Fetal monitoring may offer a valuable new tool. Fetal monitoring today denotes the use of various biochemical and electrophysiologic sensors which may be used to increase our knowledge of fetal well-being during maternal labor.

Electrophysiologic continuous monitoring includes the fetal heart rate (FHR), which may be obtained with the placement of sensors on the maternal abdomen or directly against the fetal scalp in the birth canal. This allows one to observe the beat-to-beat heart rate changes of the fetus. However, to be more useful, the fetal heart rate must be correlated with maternal in utero pressure measurements (labor contractions). These contractions act almost as a "stress test" and provide earlier information about fetal distress than when heart rate is used as a single parameter.

The pressure sensors may be applied abdominally or transvaginally. Both for heart rate and in utero pressure, the vaginal application of sensors gives information that is clearer of electrical monitoring problems and therefore less confusing to interpret.

TABLE 7.—HIGH-RISK INFANTS

FAMILY HISTORY	
Presence of mutant genes	Previous defective sibling
Central nervous system disorders	Parental consanguinity
Low socioeconomic group	
PRECONCEPTIONAL MEDICAL HISTORY	
Irradiation	Cardiovascular or renal disease
Nutrition	Thyroid disease
Hypertension	
OBSTETRICAL FACTORS	
Maternal age <16 or >40	Size of infants
Elderly primipara; prolonged infertility	Fetal loss, perinatal death, stillbirth, premature delivery
Excessive parity	Miscarriage immediately preceding pregnancy
Age of 30 with short interpregnancy interval	Pre-eclampsia; eclampsia
PRESENT PREGNANCY	
Unwanted pregnancy	Narcotic addiction
Diabetes mellitus	Medications (those known to be contraindicated)
Hypertensive cardiovascular disease	Pre-eclampsia, eclampsia
Hyperthyroidism under treatment	Multiple birth
Poor nutrition	Oligohydramnios
Pyuria, pyelonephritis	Rh isoimmunization with rising anti-Rh titre
Infectious diseases: rubella, syphilis, tuberculosis, hepatitis	Indication for caesarean section
Irradiation	
LABOR AND DELIVERY	
Absence of prenatal care	Abruptio placenta
Precipitate, prolonged, or complicated delivery	Hemorrhagic complications
	Fetal heart aberrations
Abnormal presentation or breech	Meconium staining
Prolonged rupture of membranes	Scalp blood pH 7.2 or lower
Low birth weight, especially <1500 grams	Low Apgar score 1 minute, 5 minutes, and 10 minutes
Gestational prematurity	
Small for dates	
PLACENTA	
Single umbilical artery	Placentitis
Massive infarction	Amnion nodosum
NEONATAL	
Hyperbilirubinemia	Fever
Hypoglucosemia	Congenital defects
Apneic episodes	Severe hemolytic disease
Convulsions	Survival following meningitides, traumatic intracranial episodes
Sepsis	
Asphyxia	

FIGURE 7. Typical karyotype of patient with Klinefelter's syndrome. Note XXY chromosomes. (Courtesy of Lytt I. Gardner, MD).

Prepared by Sterling Garrard, M.D.

3. CAUSES AND PREVENTION

These techniques of electronic monitoring, when used correctly, are practical, provide improved observations of the fetus, and the information correlates closely with the neonatal condition of that fetus after birth. All patients with increased risk factors, such as maternal illness or observed clinical signs of fetal distress, such as meconium, should be monitored. At present fetal monitoring suggests that it may lead to the birth of healthier infants and avoid unnecessary caesarian sections, and therefore should be available.

Maternal Health

A high frequency of maternal complications of pregnancy has been found among mentally retarded children. Bleeding and toxemia, often associated with premature birth, result in a significant number of children with cerebral palsy, epilepsy, and mental retardation. In the absence of prematurity, minor degrees of cerebral damage, including behavioral and specific learning disabilities, are present. Mechanical injuries at birth are less significant, ie, those resulting from cord prolapse, malpresentations, and mid- and high-forceps deliveries. Prenatal or natal factors producing anoxia and fetal distress appear to be of more importance than mechanical injury in relation to postnatal neurological sequelae.

Prematurity

Some follow-up studies indicate that 70% of premature infants weighing less than 1,500 gm (3 lb, 5 oz) at birth have various physical and mental disorders, eg, spastic diplegia, mental retardation, speech and hearing difficulties, visual disorders, and behavioral problems. Others feel this figure is high and gives an unnecessarily gloomy picture of the prognosis of prematurity. In any case, prevention of prematurity has high priority in prevention of mental retardation.

Two principles should be kept in mind in the care of the premature. First, prematures may be more sensitive to the actions of medications, eg, oxygen, sulfonamide compounds, chloramphenicol, etc. Second, because of the high frequency of physical and mental handicaps, the physician should perform growth and developmental evaluations regularly.

Prematurity has a much higher incidence in poverty populations. Also, serious infections are much more common in populations that suffer from malnutrition, poor sanitation, slum housing, and racial discrimination. The specific role of socioeconomic class, prenatal, and perinatal complications urgently requires clarification and greater emphasis at all levels of medical education and practice.

Infants with intra-uterine-growth retardation have birth weights less than 2,000 gm (4 lb, 7 oz) and a gestation of 36 weeks or more. They are "low birth weight" infants born at term. Clinically, these patients range from "extreme microcephaly with dwarfism and mental defect" to "mild growth deficiencies with eventual favorable mental and physical development." Cardiovascular, skeletal, ocular, and renal defects are frequent.

The role played by poverty and malnutrition may be of extreme importance in etiology, but unfortunately, most medical research has not concerned itself specifically with these factors. The physician should realize that these are not premature infants, but that they do represent a "high-risk" group, and he should assess their development carefully.

Postmaturity and Dysmaturity

The role of postmaturity or dysmaturity in relation to permanent neurological sequelae has not been adequately studied. The postmature infant has a gestation of 42 weeks or longer. His appearance and development are more mature than that of a term infant. His weight and length may be increased. Early induction of labor is not recommended. The dysmature infant usually has an increased gestation; he shows evidence of wasting, respiratory distress, neurological signs, and an increased neonatal mortality.

Pharmacologic Problems

Premature and full-term infants react differently to drugs than do children or adults. Table 5 summarizes the more important effects of frequently used drugs on the newborn.

Metabolic, hematological, hormonal, or neurological disturbances are common. *Overdosage* is the most frequent cause of toxicity. For example, vitamin K in therapeutic doses of 1 to 2 mg causes no damage; amounts in excess of 50 mg may be toxic. Little is known of the processes of biochemical maturation in the brain of the fetus and the newborn. The vulnerability of this system to the action of certain drugs is established, eg, kernicterus, related to sufonamide compounds. Less obvious neurological sequelae may follow exposure to drugs causing respiratory depression and cyanosis, or drugs which may interfere with normal enzyme activity through competitive inhibition or may alter the permeability of the blood-brain barrier. Any drug which lowers maternal blood pressure to hypotensive levels (ie, hypotensive agents, tranquilizers, and anesthetics) may potentially cause hypoxic damage to the fetus. The recording of the one-minute and five-minute Apgar score can alert the physician to the presence of hypoxia or natal distress (Table 8). Assessment of the heart rate, color, muscular tone, respiratory rate, and cry will indicate infants in immediate danger whose developmental status should be followed carefully.

Erythroblastosis

Early diagnosis and exchange transfusions when indicated will reduce to less than 1% the frequency of kernicterus among infants with Rh or ABO incompatibility. An Rh-negative mother should be delivered in a hospital offering facilities for immediate exchange transfusion. The physician should be familiar with the prognostic value of serial hemoglobin and bilirubin determinations. He should regard jaundice within the first 24 hours as due to erythroblastosis until proved otherwise.

TABLE 8.—EVALUATION OF THE NEWBORN INFANT

SIGN	0	1	2
Heart rate	Absent	Below 100	Over 100
Respiratory effort	Absent	Slow, irregular	Good, crying
Muscle tone	Limp	Some flexion of extremities	Active motion
Response to catheter in nostril (tested after oropharynx is clear)	No response	Grimace	Cough or sneeze
Color	Blue, pale	Body pink, extremities blue	Completely pink

Sixty seconds after the complete birth of the infant (disregarding the cord and placenta) the 5 objective signs above are evaluated, and each is given a score of 0, 1 or 2. A total score of 10 indicates an infant in the best possible condition.

Modified from Virginia Apgar: "Current Research in Anesth. & Analg.," 32:260, 1953. Nelson, W., *Textbook of Pediatrics*, 9th edition, p. 357, 1969.

Hyperbilirubinemia in the premature infant demands special attention. A bilirubin level of 20 mg/100 cc or greater within the first 72 hours of life, or a rapidly rising level, indicates the need for an exchange transfusion. Multiple exchanges may be necessary to keep the level under 20 mg/100 cc.

The entire problem of hyperbilirubinemia and erythroblastosis may be solved by newer measures aimed at prevention rather than treatment. These include the use of ultraviolet light and also the injection of high titre Rh antibodies to the Rh-negative mother after the birth of her first Rh-positive baby.

Intrauterine exchange transfusion has had some favorable results in the hands of specially trained physicians. Its role in the overall picture is problematic and will depend on the success of the methods described above as well as others yet to be discovered.

Amniocentesis

Prenatal detection of genetic disorders resulting in mental retardation has become possible in the past few years. Chromosomal aberrations and many biochemical defects can be detected in cultivated amniotic fluid cells obtained early in the second trimester of pregnancy. Indications for amniocentesis in early pregnancy for conditions causing mental retardation would include the following: (1) women pregnant above the age of 38 years, (2) parent is a known carrier of a chromosome translocation, (3) known carriers of autosomal recessive disorders in which *in utero* diagnosis is possible, (4) known carriers of X-linked recessive disorders, and possibly, (5) women who have previously given birth to children with chromosomal aberrations.

These procedures are difficult and should be performed only by physicians and laboratories skilled in transabdominal amniocentesis, cultivation of amniotic fluid cells and the specific diagnostic tests.

Postnatal Period—Congenital Anomalies

Surgical procedures are available for treatment of infants with premature fusion of the cranial sutures. Early detection is necessary in these disorders to prevent irreversible damage. Routine head measurements should be recorded for all infants during the first year of life. An increased frequency of neural deficits and other anomalies has been found in infants with one umbilical artery.

Metabolic Errors

In the case of inborn metabolic errors, early detection is vital to early treatment and genetic counseling regarding future pregnancies. The diagnosis of phenylketonuria is important in the newborn, in presumably healthy infants, and in the infant or child with a neurological disorder.

This has been legally recognized by a number of states, and laws requiring compulsory PKU testing of newborns have been enacted. Suspicion of phenylketonuria is raised for any infant with an affected sibling. In such an infant, a serum phenylalanine determination should be obtained after the fifth or sixth day of life. The routine use of the ferric chloride "diaper test" or ferric chloride impregnated paper strips has been widely recommended for phenylketonuria detection in early infancy and before suspicion of retardation is raised. Phenylalanine metabolites may not be detected in the newborn's urine until as late as five weeks; hence diaper testing may be of limited value in detection during the first month of life; therefore, this test is of historical interest only and not recommended for routine use.

The physician should test any infant or child in whom he suspects a neurological disorder. Vomiting, irritability, eczema, seizures, and a peculiar odor to the urine are frequently early signs of phenylketonuria. Final diagnosis is based on an elevated serum phenylalanine, together with careful consideration of newer and more sophisticated laboratory biochemical determinations.

The physician should encourage detection of phenylketonuria in high-risk populations, ie, in institutions for the retarded, special education classes, cerebral palsy clinics and schools, etc. Identification of affected families can result in intelligent genetic counseling and early detection of the disease in future infants.

Even though a negative finding is recorded with a test such as the Guthrie test in the newborn period, it is important that urine testing should be continued between 1 and 3 months of age because of the possibility of false-negatives.

The value of the low-phenylalanine diet in the prevention of sequelae is fairly well established, although a few children do poorly despite good dietary control. Early initiation of treatment correlates generally with later measured intelligence, and a trial of dietary therapy is recommended for all PKU children.

The physician should suspect galactosemia in any infant with failure to thrive. Cataracts, hepatomegaly, and jaundice may be present. Large amounts of reducing substances are found in the urine if the child is on a milk diet. The urine must be tested with an agent which will detect reducing substances, eg, tablets containing copper sulfate, hydroxide, and heat-producing agents (Clinitest) or Benedict's reagent. Glucose oxidase strips should be used only as a secondary test. Absolute diagnosis is based on the absence of the transferase enzyme in the red blood cells. Early treatment with a galactose-free diet has been very successful.

The physician should be alert to the insidious onset of the signs and symptoms of cretinism. Lethargy, irritability, anemia, constipation, and retardation of growth are among the earliest signs. Early and aggressive therapy is necessary. Continuous follow-up with determination of bone-age, PBI values, and growth is essential. A small group of cretins, perhaps 5% to 10%, have nonendemic familial goitrous cretinism and genetically determined defects in thyroid synthesis. This is a recessive trait with one-quarter probability of the disease occurring in future siblings. They can be distinguished from nonendemic athyreotic cretins by the finding of a normal or increased uptake of ^{131}I.

Meningitis and Encephalitis

There is an unfortunate tendency in modern medicine to regard the patient as cured once the acute crisis is over and he has exited through the hospital doors. Yet, the bacterial meningitides (Escherichia coli and Hemophilus influenzae) may be followed by permanent neurological sequelae. Tuberculous meningitis frequently shows such sequelae. Chronic encephalopathies which follow some routine immunizations are occasionally reported. Also reported are viral encephalitides and prolonged seizures during acute infections such as roseola.

Preventive measures include the use of measles vaccine, early recognition and prompt treatment of the bacterial meningitides, and tuberculosis case-finding by routine tuberculin tests, especially among high-risk groups. Conversion of the tuberculin reaction at any time in childhood indicates need for treatment.

Accidents and Poisons

Mental retardation due to head trauma from automobile accidents may be prevented. The use of automobile seat belts and provision of day-care centers and proper play areas for children will do much to reduce these accidents. Proper parental education will help prevent others. Of greatest importance is the promotion of better inexpensive public transportation as well as

3. CAUSES AND PREVENTION

better design of cities and highways. Here, again, the responsible physician may be able to exert leadership in his local community and in the nation.

Lead poisoning is clearly preventable. It is associated with low socioeconomic status and is frequently found in large cities. Some patients recover completely, but many are left with permanent brain damage. Improved methods of diagnosis and treatment have been of some value. Again, the physician should press for slum clearance and other anti-poverty measures, as well as work cooperatively with lawyers in order to secure adequate compensation for lead poisoning victims.

Battered Children

Many children have been identified who have suffered brain damage from physical beatings about the head. Concern is increasing over this "battered child syndrome." Statutes have been enacted in some states and are under consideration in others requiring medical reporting of physical abuse of children; they may facilitate preventive measures and contribute to an understanding of the epidemiology of particular types of abuse. Such laws may also have provisions which protect the physician against lawsuits emanating from the care of these patients. The physician need not wait for such legislation to report to proper officials and appropriate social agencies incidents in which he sees reasonably clear evidence of abuse or neglect. This condition, again, is more common in families raised in generations of poverty, social neglect, and discrimination, but no social and economic group is immune.

Other Causes

Increasing evidence suggests that the occurrence of two or more febrile seizures may indicate a predisposition to later seizures. Further, prolonged febrile seizures with asphyxia may produce brain damage. The physician should consider placing such a child on anti-convulsant medication, eg, diphenylhydantoin (Dilantin) sodium or phenobarbital, for a 2- to 4-year period or until the danger of febrile seizures has passed. Consultation with a neurologist may be helpful.

Hypernatremia frequently occurs in infants with diarrhea who are treated with skim milk or proprietary electrolyte solutions. Experimental and clinical evidence suggests that the elevated serum sodium may cause brain damage. The use of one-half strength skim milk or one-half strength isotonic electrolyte solution or human milk for the treatment of infantile diarrhea can prevent hypernatremia.

Prevention at the Experiential Level

The human interrelationships experienced by the child, normal or retarded, make a major contribution to his progress. These relationships may be modified by factors intrinsic to the child as well as by those that impinge on him from the environment. When these conditions are unfavorable, they may modify normal progress so that a functional retardation appears, characteristic of the experiential group. The child already handicapped by a previously existing biological disability may find his progress further slowed by these unfavorable experiential factors.

These factors can be categorized: (1) poverty, (2) institutionalization, and (3) distorted patterns of maternal care.

Poverty: sociocultural deprivation. A majority of the mildly retarded are children of the more disadvantaged classes of our society, characterized by low income, limited educational opportunity, unskilled occupation, and generally impoverished environment. These families must concentrate their meager energies on keeping body and soul together; they have neither means nor skills to provide their children with stimulating conversation, books, music, travel, or other intellectual and cultural advantages, those bestowed almost automatically on many children of the middle- and upper-income groups.

Children of these less fortunate families arrive at school age equipped with neither the experience nor the skills necessary for formal learning. They are backward in language and in the ability for abstract thinking necessary for reading, writing, and counting. From these children come many individuals who perform at the dull borderline and who fill the special classes. Their failure to learn becomes complicated by frustration and anxiety; they may graduate to the streets and ultimately to the institution. (In contrast to this mild form of retardation prevalent in the lower sociocultural groups, severe retardation appears spread more evenly throughout the population.)

In working with families from a wide variety of social classes and cultural groups, the physician may find it helpful to remain alert to the health values and child rearing practices peculiar to the group from which the family comes, recognizing that the family in question may not, however, share all the common characteristics of its social group.

The physician must also be cognizant of possible conflict in matters of health maintenance between his point of view and that of the patient. Areas in which conflict may arise include birth control, sterilization and abortion.

In addition to his concern for the care of the individual patient, the physician may serve as a community leader in development of resources for disadvantaged families unlikely to obtain care from private sources. There is need to emphasize continuity of care and to concentrate particularly on the adolescent girl, the woman with fertility problems, and other high-risk pregnancy groups. Establishment or expansion of outpatient clinics may reduce childbearing risks in these vulnerable groups. In addition, and perhaps of greater importance, the physician may serve as a community leader in bringing about the necessary economic and political changes in an attempt to eliminate poverty altogether.

Retardation in the lower socioeconomic groups is frequently associated with malnutrition and inadequate prenatal care, eg, prematurity, the toxemias, and high perinatal mortality. This inadequate attention stems mostly from lack of money and resources. However, several other considerations may be involved, including limited understanding of the importance of prenatal care; social and ethnic attitudes depreciating medical care generally; and restrictive administrative policies (residence and economic eligibility requirements, etc.) in social- and health-agency practice.

Of major importance is the unattractiveness and indignity of the services provided. Clinics are frequently understaffed and overcrowded, and little time is spent with the patient after a long wait. It is important to provide high quality care. It is also important to consider doctor-patient relationships, staff attitudes, a timely efficient flow of patients, and the appropriate use of existing facilities.

In helping to develop these resources, the physician may also give consideration to locating them near individuals to be served, open at hours convenient to the patient. Assistance should be offered the mother in care of other children.

Education of both physician and mother is vital to prevention. The physician may talk with the mothers regarding prenatal care, family life, ghetto conditions and reasons for unacceptability of medical care. Both can learn from this kind of

21. Prevention

equal interaction.

The physician may also help in establishing such needed new facilities as visiting nursing services, day-care centers and sheltered workshops.

Institutionalization. A child resident for long periods in an institution may display the effects of sensory deprivation as well as other effects of the absence of normal mothering. Such children may appear withdrawn and apathetic and may display characteristics measurably below those typical of their particular age. Similar characteristics may sometimes appear in the child who has been immobilized for long periods because of other physical handicaps, or in the child who because of sensory defect is not capable of receiving normal stimuli.

The physician's opportunities for management may involve suggestion of arrangements for substitute parenting either by special assignment to mother-figures within the institution or by provision of care in a smaller residential facility or foster home. The foster-grandparent program has been an effective and successful contribution in the prevention of "hospitalism." This was initiated as a federally supported anti-poverty effort that provides funds for the assignment (and payment) of older people to work with little children. These children are selected from state hospitals, day-care centers, county and other public hospitals, and similar institutional settings. The physician who observes evidence of deprivation resulting from lack of motor activity or sensory deficit may devise other ways in which stimulation may be provided.

Of greatest importance is the funding of programs that will enable children to be cared for in their own homes. This requires major changes in our spending priorities as well as in public attitudes. The challenge to the physician who claims leadership capacities is obvious.

Distorted patterns of maternal care. Every child has a major need for sensory stimulation of adequate amount and quality. The neonate with an immature nervous system and lack of experience responds only to simple or gross changes in visual, auditory, and tactile stimulation. As his nervous system develops and he accumulates experience, he responds to and seeks out increasingly complex stimuli. By 5 or 6 months of age, his own movements together with caretaking activities of adults may offer sufficient stimulation for growth. By the second year it becomes increasingly important for the child to receive meaningful stimuli from others so as to learn how to respond to them.

In his earliest years, this sensory stimulus is provided by the mother or other caretaker; a stimulating kind of mothering—holding, fondling, and endearment—is necessary to normal growth. An interrelationship mutually stimulating to mother and child promotes optimal development.

The child also has a major need for motor activity, for opportunities to utilize other emerging capacities such as speech and play, and later for a stimulus to the development of acceptable social skills and further intellectual maturity. All of these needs are initially provided for within the family framework and depend to a critical degree on the adequacy of the mother or mother-figure.

The quality of mothering offered the child may be affected, however, by the emotional, economic, and social resources of the mother. Children with teen-age, unwed, or working mothers may be deprived either by an absence of conventional mothering, or a mothering complicated by an inadequate knowledge of how to care for a child. The response of the child may also affect the kind of mothering offered. A handicapped child may predispose to parental overprotection or rejection, thus interfering with the normal processes of stimulation or responsive growth.

A social problem may be encountered in the psychologically withdrawn mother who appears apathetic or unable to stimulate her child. She may offer little of the necessary emotional support and physical care. The depressed mother, for example, may find it difficult to interact with her child and may prefer to leave him alone. The psychologically disturbed mother may be so disorganized as to give ambiguous stimulation to the child. Her verbal signals may contradict the physical messages she conveys. She may handle her child roughly while declaring how much she loves him. The ambiguity of these messages may render the child unable to apprehend, evaluate or respond appropriately to his social environment. Children who suffer these varying deprivations may appear apathetic, unresponsive, and functionally retarded.

Such an appearance should prompt the physician to investigate the child's capacity and the care which he is receiving. The physician may function in a direct medical capacity by encouraging the mother to stimulate her child more actively or to enter into more satisfying relationships with him. He may make such simple suggestions as, for example, that the mother spend an hour a day playing with the child or engaging in other mutually satisfying activity.

If, however, the physician sees a major illness in the mother rendering her unable to care for her child, he may refer her for specialized care and he may suggest arrangements for a mother-substitute for the infant.

At a later stage if a child seems to lack the customary social contacts with other children, or if his family exhibits minimal use of language and social interaction at a low ebb, the physician may suggest peer contacts such as those possible in a nursery school or day-care center.

Prevention, then, in the experiential areas grows from the ordinary contacts of a physician as he observes a young infant and the manner in which the parent cares for him. The physician has an opportunity to determine whether motor activity is fostered, whether the child is capable of receiving environmental stimuli, and whether parent-child relationships are adequate and comfortable. The physician's attention to these factors can be as important as the specific medical care he provides. Prevention in this area of the child's growth and development is most effective in its earliest stages, and therefore the physician's opportunities to see the relationships of the infant and very young child provide him with the maximum chance to perform this very proper function. Correction of deviation in such relationships becomes a major kind of prevention.

FOCUS

Jimmie...

Photography by Simon C. Key

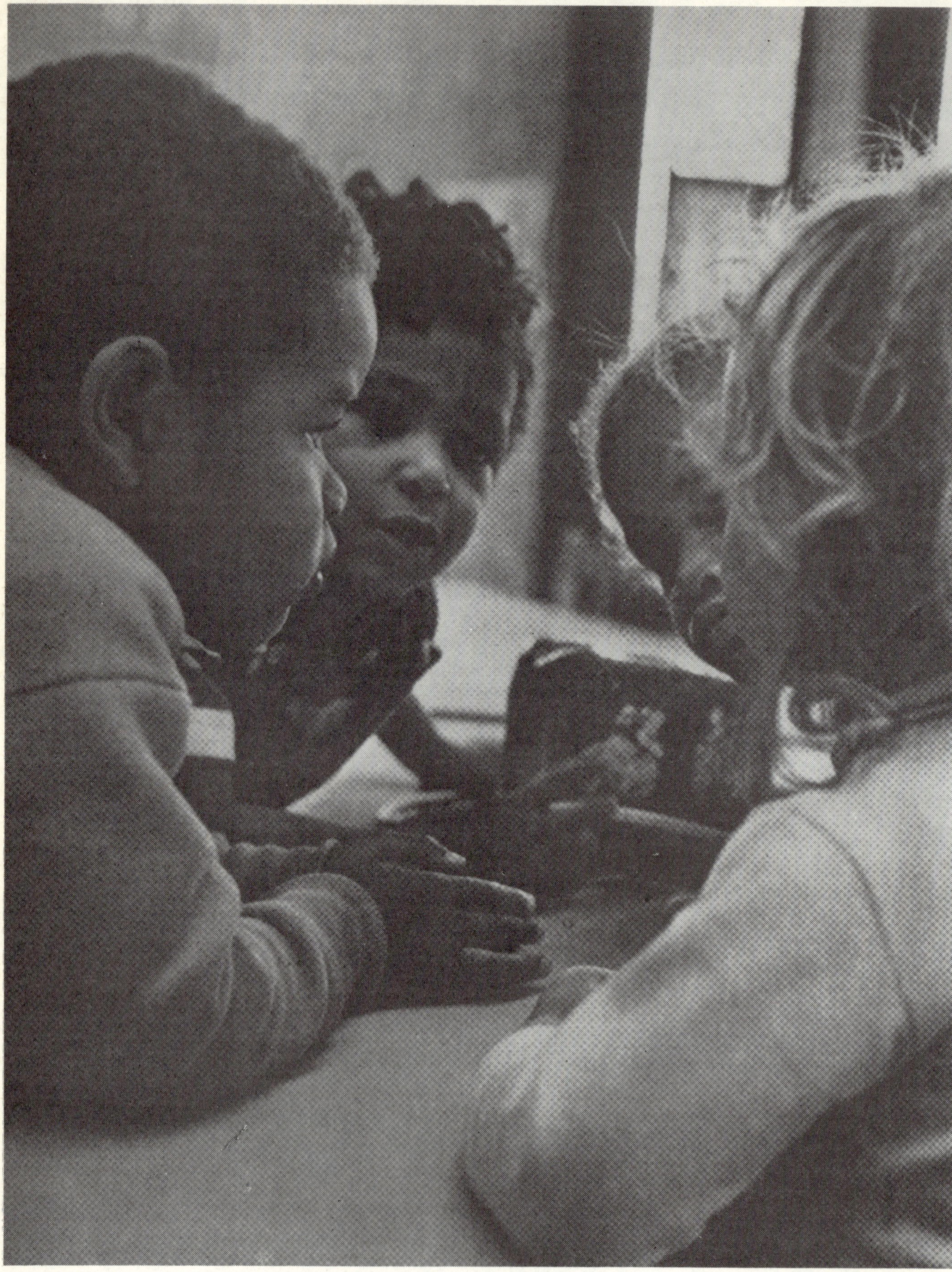

Educable Mentally Retarded

A little over 100 years ago in Springfield, Massachusetts in 1897, special education classes for the mentally retarded came into being. Until this time attitudes reverted back to ancient times when mentally retarded persons were termed "idiot" from the Greek term with a meaning of "peculiar." Hostility and persecution reigned supreme...

With the advent of special classes, education was provided with extremely specialized instruction by specially trained teachers with small classes for one to one instruction, which has come to be known as mainstreaming. In setting up and educational program for the educable mentally retarded, goals must be established. The development of abilities and life skills are crucial to their assured progress in personal and social competence processes. Three objectives had to be included in their curriculum: (1) to develop interaction with their environment (2) to develop social, personal, and vocational skills to make them self-sufficient occupationally and (3) to provide them with general well-rounded information to achieve these goals.

Each step takes into consideration the capability of learning of the child, with the ultimate goal of complete acceptance from the world at large. Vocational training enables the retardate to possibly become a meaningful and contributing member of society. They learn social skills and gain needed self-respect for their own being, even eventually maintaining and owning their own homes and automobiles as a result.

Initially, the foundation is laid through effective use of preschool programs where interpersonal communication, language development, eye-hand coordination, gross motor skills, and sensorimotor functions are established. Then basic readiness skills are introduced and facilitated, all the while taking into consideration individual characteristics of the retarded child. His learning ability level, his general overall long-term retention skills, and his willingness to want to succeed in daily life skills bring him that much closer to a "normal" standard of living. He will also learn arts, crafts, music and even physical education.

Work training programs allow them the dignity of learning a trade, while also becoming a breadwinner. Many employers readily hire retarded citizens because they find that they are not easily bored by repetitive tasks, they stay at their job longer than other workers, and they can be trusted to carry out their job without frequent absenteeism.

In all, special education benefits go hand in hand with vocational training of the educable mentally retarded to bring them out of the home and into the mainstream of life, living on their own, working and contributing to society, meeting new friends and experiencing new activities, and perhaps someday marrying and thus sharing a new found life and a way of living. In achieving all this, they too can become educators. . . to these people already in the mainstream of life, who have had little or no exposure to retarded citizens. Through this integration, they learn that people can and must adapt to the broad trends of life and living, both "normal" and the "mentally retarded" alike . . . we must learn from one another.

Integration Programs for the Mildly Retarded

GILBERT R. GUERIN
KATHLEEN SZATLOCKY

*Gilbert R. Guerin is Coordinator of Research, Center for Research in Special Education, the University of California, Berkeley; and **Kathleen Szatlocky** is a researcher in special education, the University of California, Berkeley.*

Abstract: The study examined programs that integrated mentally retarded students in 8 California school districts. Interviews were conducted with 17 administrators and 31 teachers. Regular classroom observations were made of 27 retarded pupils and 54 randomly selected nonretarded pupils. Four program models were identified and an index of integration was developed and applied to each program. The attitudes of administrators toward integrating programs was, with only one exception, positive; and the majority of teachers also held positive attitudes. The behavior of retarded students was essentially similar to that of regular students.

The regular class placement of the mildly retarded is a fact that can no longer be dismissed as an abstract concept or an experimental intervention. A number of studies (Bradfield, 1973; Christoplos, 1973; Flynn & Flynn, 1970; Renz & Semenson, 1969) attest to the interest shown by school districts in the regular class placement of the retarded student. Barngrover's (1971) study indicated that nearly half of the educators that she interviewed favored regular class placement for the exceptional child. In California, for example, there has been a steady growth in the number of integrated programs. There were estimated to be less than 10 school districts in that state with integrated programs in 1971. Formal applications to the California state department of education for approval of intergrated programs, however, more than doubled for the 1972-1973 school year, and a number of other school districts operated programs that did not require state approval.

Although many studies have focused on the efficacy of special versus regular class placement virtually none have examined the various ways of educating the retarded child with his nonretarded classmates. The controversy between regular and special classes has nearly obscured the fact that there are a wide variety of ways that integration can be accomplished. Rather than a single, simple model there are major program differences in such areas as who is integrated, how long they are in the regular classroom, what educational system is involved, what teaching strategies are used, and what support systems are employed.

Purpose

This study investigated the ways in which the integration of the mildly retarded student had been implemented in the public elementary schools of California. The study was designed to identify similarities and differences between the various programs and the degree of integration that had been achieved. It examined the history and conditions that influenced the programs and observed the behavior of the retarded children while they were in regular classrooms.

Grades 4, 5, and 6 were included in the study. At these levels the full day, self contained class was the most common educational procedure for both nonretarded and retarded students. Schools that had found ways to integrate retarded pupils at these grade levels were selected in order to determine the method used in regular class placement.

School achievement and achievement growth were not included in this study. It was assumed that the retarded student, by definition, would have an achievement significantly lower than his nonretarded classmates. Five of the eight school districts had conducted evaluation studies on their programs and reported that the growth rate in school achievement for integrated students was equal to or greater than the growth rate that these students had experienced in self contained special classes. Further evidence on this question was not considered critical to this study.

The major questions in this study were related to the types of programs in existence, the factors that influenced the degree of integration, and the behavior of students within these programs. The research was designed to answer the following questions:

1. What program models were involved in the integration of the mildly retarded?
2. What amount of integration existed in each program and for each model?
3. What differences were there in the behavior of retarded pupils and regular pupils in regular classrooms?
4. What attitudes did the teaching and administrative staff hold toward the integrated programs in these schools?

Method

Eight school districts participated in this study. Districts were selected which had a district sanctioned commitment to place most or all their retarded students in regular classrooms for part or all of the school day. Programs were included if they, in fact, did place students in regular classrooms on some planned basis. The students selected for study were in the same age range as students generally eligible for grades 4, 5, and 6.

All the school districts that could be identified as appropriate for this study were located in suburban, small city, and rural areas. At the time of this study the large metropolitan schools in California had no integrated programs which placed retarded students in regular classrooms on a planned basis. Districts were selected from those identified by state consultants in special education, the State School Psychologist Association, and reports of federal and state funded projects.

The students included in the study were those who were registered in elementary special education programs and who ranged in age from 9 to 13 years. Intelligence scores were those obtained by psychologists on the *Stanford-Binet Intelligence Scale* or the *Weschler Intelligence Scale for Children*. IQ's ranged from 54 to 72. One district withheld specific IQ scores but did identify students who fell within the designated range. This district was not included in the tabulations on IQ distributions. All students included in this study had been judged by admission committees to be educable mentally retarded within the guidelines of California law.

Student behavior was determined by direct observation and rated on Spaulding's *Coping Analysis Schedule for Educational Settings* (CASES) (1967). This schedule included the following 13 categories: (a) aggressive behavior, (b) negative (inappropriate) attention getting behavior, (c) manipulating and directing others, (d) resisting authority, (e) self directed activity, (f) paying rapt attention, (g) sharing and helping, (h) social interaction, (i) seeking support, assistance, and information, (j) following directions passively and submissively, (k) observing passively, (l) responding to internal stimuli, and (m) physical withdrawal or avoidance.

Data were collected and based on 20 to 30 ten-second observations taken on each special student and on two randomly selected students of the same sex in the same classroom and during the same time period. In this manner data were collected on 27 educable mentally retarded students in regular classrooms and 54 nonretarded students in the same regular classrooms.

Interviews were conducted with 11 special class teachers, 20 regular class teachers, and 9 psychologists, all of whom were directly involved with the integrated programs. Interviews were also held with the 8 central office administrators who were directly responsible for special education within the school districts and with the 8 building administrators at the schools with integrated programs.

Three of the programs in this study operated with some federal project funding. About half of the schools used paid aides and half of the programs ran in classrooms with ordinary classroom instructional procedures. The average class size of the districts in this study was 27.5, slightly below the 28.2 state average reported by the California Teachers Association (1972).

Results

Models

The eight school districts included in this

4. EDUCABLE MENTALLY RETARDED

study used four different methods for the integration of mildly retarded students. These methods fit four descriptive models. Two of these models were evident in two or more schools; a third model was found in one school. The fourth model was also observed in one school but because of limited enrollment it is included in the descriptive but not in the statistical analysis.

In Figure 1, programed partial integration (model I), all the retarded students were assigned to a special class and then programed into regular classrooms for a specific block of

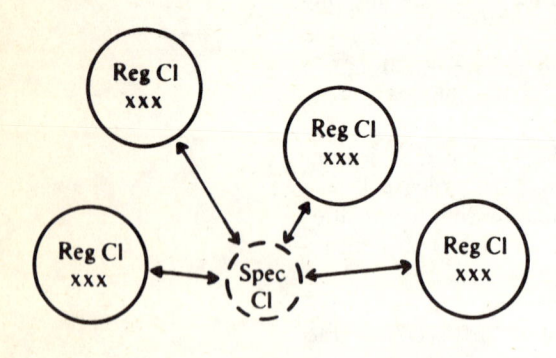

FIGURE 1. Programed partial integration (model I). Students who have been assigned to special class are programed into regular classrooms for blocks of time and by subject areas.

time. Three districts used this procedure; each of these districts had a full time special class teacher who taught only the retarded students. Variations included a district where all special pupils, grades 1 to 3, were integrated into regular classes all morning, and all pupils, grades 4 to 6, were integrated all afternoon. Other districts made selective integrations, attempting to match the student with specific regular class teachers and for specific subjects. In this model students were usually carefully selected for integration and participation part of the school day in a regular classroom.

In Figure 2, combination class (model II), all retarded students were in regular classrooms all day. Three to six retarded students were assigned to each of three regular classrooms in a central school. Funds usually used to support a special classroom were used to reduce the class size of the three regular rooms and to provide supplementary aides and materials. In the district which used this model, one of the three regular classroom teachers held a special credential in addition to her regular teaching credential. This teacher acted as a resource person to the other teachers in the program. This model

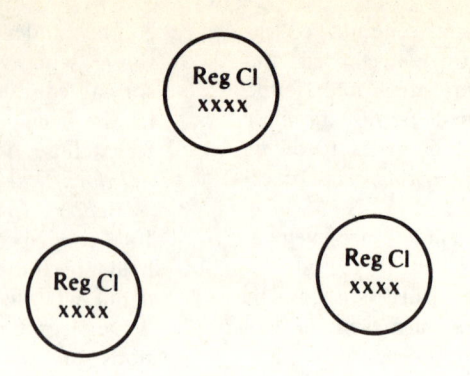

FIGURE 2. Combination class (model II). Special students are enrolled in small sized regular classrooms. Special materials are available, and aides may be provided.

integrated all retarded pupils for the entire school day.

In Figure 3, learning resource center (model III), all of the retarded children were assigned to regular classrooms in centralized schools. This school operated a learning or diagnostic resource center for their regular school population. Special education teachers were added to those who manned the centers

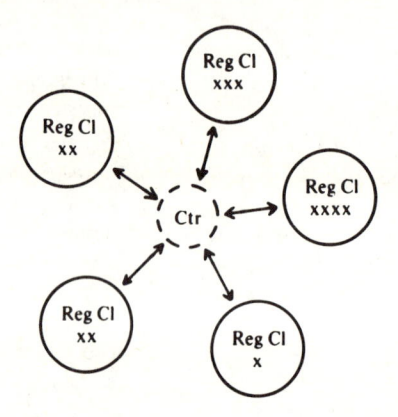

FIGURE 3. Learning resource center (model III). The special teacher functions in a resource center. Exceptional students from regular classrooms use the center for evaluations, prescriptive planning, and tutorial assistance.

and the special teachers saw the retarded pupils for one or two hours a day alone or in small groups. The special teacher provided educational evaluations, prescriptive planning, and tutored assistance. This model integrated all of the retarded pupils for most or all of the school day.

In Figure 4, learning disability groups (model IV), all of the retarded pupils remained as regular class members in their local school. They were seen by a special teacher in a small learning disability group or individually for an hour or two a day. The teacher could move from school to school on

110

an itinerant schedule. This program was used in a district that also used the model I approach. Model IV provided local integration for all retarded pupils for most or all of the school day.

Amount of Integration

School districts differed in both the number of eligible students that they integrated and the portion of the school day that the students spent in regular classrooms. In order to compare the amount of integration for each district an index of integration was established based on the following formula:

$$\text{Index of integration} = \frac{\text{Total hours of integrated instruction per day}}{\text{Total } N \text{ of retarded students} \times \text{total number of instruction hours in the school day}}$$

This formula reported the portion of instructional hours spent in an integrated setting. An example of a computation with the formula follows.

School X has 10 retarded students, 6 are integrated part of the day and 4 are in a special class all day. The 6 integrated students spend different amounts of time in the regular room: student A is integrated 1 hour; student B, 2 hours; students C and D, 4 hours; and students E and F, 5 hours each.

$$\text{Index of integration} = \frac{1(1\text{hr}) + 1(2\text{hr}) + 2(4\text{hr}) + 2(5\text{hr})}{10 \text{ students} \times 6 \text{ hrs per day}} = \frac{21}{60} = .35$$

Table 1 is a report of the amount of integration for each of the schools in the study. It includes the number of students available for integration and the number of integrated students listed by the hours of integrated instruction. The index is given as well as a rank for each school.

Student Behavior

The observations of student behavior were recorded in terms of the 13 variables of the CASES scale. This scale reports the type and frequency of student involvement with school work, peers, and teacher. It includes behavioral characteristics such as passivity versus assertiveness and helpfulness versus disruptiveness. Four separate analyses were made on the data. The Mann-Whitney U-test was used to establish the significance of differences.

In the first analysis the behavior of retarded students in regular classrooms was contrasted with that of nonretarded students.

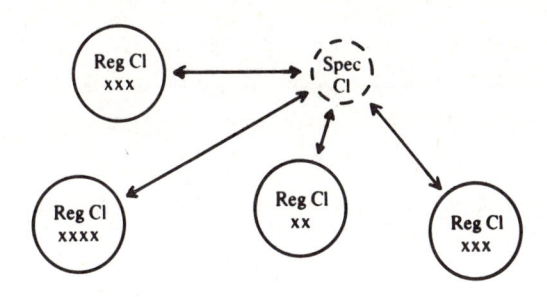

FIGURE 4. Learning disability group (model IV). The student is a member of a regular classroom and is seen by a special teacher for supplementary education. Aides and special materials may be provided.

Only one of the variables was found to be significant and that variable related to the demonstration of manipulating and other directing behavior. A second analysis was made after the groups had been divided by sex. The original difference that occurred between the retarded and nonretarded groups was found to exist primarily among girls. The item indicated that the retarded girls in this study were more manipulative and other directed than nonretarded girls. There were no other significant differences between the girls and no significant differences between the boys.

The third and fourth analyses of the student behavior involved the comparisons of different groups of retarded students. First, the classroom behavior of retarded students who were integrated for most of the day (integration indexes of .71 to 1.00) was compared with the behavior of retarded students in programs with limited integration (integration indexes of .55 to .24). Those students in programs that integrated for most of the school day exhibited significantly more self directed behavior than students with limited integration.

In the second comparison the classroom behavior of students who had been carefully selected for integration was compared with the behavior of integrated retarded students who had been placed without careful selection. The latter group included the students in programs where all the students had been placed in regular classrooms. There were no significant differences in the behavior of these two groups of students.

Attitudes Toward the Program

The attitudes of the staff toward the integrated program are reported in Table 2. Regular as well as special teacher reports

4. EDUCABLE MENTALLY RETARDED

TABLE 1

Amount of Integration for Each of the Districts Studied

District	Model[1]	Available students	0 hrs	1 hrs	2 hrs	3 hrs	4 hrs	5 hrs	6 hrs	Index of integration	Rank by index
1	I	9	2	1	2	2	2			.35	6
2	I	4	1	1	1			1		.33	7
3[2]	III	10				1	5	4		.71	3
4	I	3			2	1				.55	4.5
5	I	9	6	1					2	.24	8
6	II	6							6	1.00	1.5
7	I	10	5	2			1	2		.55	4.5
8	II	5							5	1.00	1.5

[1] For descriptions of the models, see Figures 1 - 4. A fourth model was observed in one school, but because of limited enrollment it is not included in the statistical analysis.
[2] Two schools are represented.

and school and central office administrator responses are included. The table contains the interviewers' report as to the expressed attitudes of staff members toward the program. Also included in Table 2 are the integration model and the average class size.

All but one of the administrators interviewed in this study held positive attitudes toward integration. In the one exception, the administrator expressed neutral views toward the program. Teachers, however, were less consistent. Positive attitudes were held by 62 percent of the teaching staffs. Another 19 percent held neutral attitudes, while 19 percent were negative.

There was also a trend toward a similarity of attitudes among those teachers who worked on the same staff. Hence, a negative attitude on the part of a special teacher was associated with negative attitudes on the part of regular teachers in the school. Attitudes seemed to follow even more specific associations. When special teachers on the same staff held different attitudes, the regular teachers held attitudes similar to those of the special teacher with whom they directly worked (see Table 2, districts 3 and 5).

Discussion

This study identified four program models, each representing a different procedure in the integration of mildly retarded students. These models differed in the amount of time that the special student spent in regular class and in the method by which he was selected for integration. The amount of integration practiced by a school district was found to be related to the type of plan that was chosen and the attitudes of the staff rather than either the behavior or the overall intellectual ability of the retarded students in the school. The general classroom behavior of the retarded students in all the programs in this study was essentially similar to the behavior of regular students in the same rooms.

While programed partial integration was the method most frequently employed, it offered the retarded student the least amount of integration. This method also enjoyed the least amount of regular and special teacher support. The methods of combination classes and learning resource centers provided the student with a maximum amount of integration and also received the strongest regular and special teacher support. Although the learning disability group model was not included in the attitude comparisons, the similarity of this procedure to other procedures of full integration suggest that this model might also receive a maximum amount of teacher or administrator support.

Contrary to common expectations retarded students who were integrated without careful selection behaved as "normally" as their regular classmates and as well as carefully selected retarded students. In fact, in the one significant difference that did occur, the retarded students in nonselective fully integrated placements were more self directed than retarded students in selected, partially integrated placements. These findings raise serious questions about the efficacy of eliminating students from integration on the basis of current, untested screening procedures.

TABLE 2
Attitudes Toward Integration

District	Model	Teachers Regular	Teachers Special	Administrators School	Administrators Central	Average class size
1	I	negative	negative	positive	positive	25.9
2	I	neutral	positive	positive	positive	28.9
3[1]	III	positive neutral	positive neutral	positive neutral	positive	29.9
4	I	positive	neutral	positive	positive	27.8
5[2]	I	negative positive	negative positive	positive	positive	24.9
6	II	positive	positive	positive	positive	28.3
7	I	positive	positive	positive	positive	26.7
8	II	positive	positive	positive	positive	27.7

[1] Two schools are represented.
[2] Staff was split between negative and positive attitudes.

Interview data indicated several differences between fully and partially integrated programs and these may provide the explanations for the greater success of the fully integrated programs. The staffs of these programs had the highest degree of "normal" expectations for their special students. Special assistance in these programs was more frequently designed to complement and enhance regular classroom instruction rather than to parallel regular classroom instruction. The students in the fully integrated program were nearly always seen by their regular teachers as full classroom members; the partially integrated students were more frequently seen as visitors.

Staff attitudes toward the integrated programs were generally positive and supportive. These attitudes followed a pattern similar to that found by Barngrover (1971). Those staff members who were most distant from the students (central administration) were most positive toward integration, while those closest (teachers) had the greater incidence of negative attitudes.

The existence of a central administration with strong positive attitudes toward the integrated program was so characteristic of these programs as to suggest that it was a critical factor in both the programs' creation and maintenance. Interview data supported this premise. Building-level administration strongly supported the program in all but one instance. Again, the results suggest that this support was important, perhaps essential to the success of the programs. Interview data indicated that building principals not only expressed personal support but encouraged support among their teaching staffs.

Teachers were somewhat less supportive of the programs, and the attitudes of the special teachers appeared to be critical to the regular teacher reaction to the program. Classroom teacher attitudes were nearly always identical to those of the special teacher. This trend was so strong that in one school where two special teachers held opposite attitudes toward the program the regular teachers held attitudes similar to the special teacher who sent them the integrated child.

Conclusions

It was demonstrated that there were a variety of program procedures that were used for the integration of the educable mentally retarded into regular classrooms. The majority of the teaching staffs who were associated with these programs approved of the integration and were supported in their attitudes by both their central office and building administrators. The general behavior of the special pupils in these programs was nearly identical to that of their regular classmates, and in fact, the more favorable behavior was found among those pupils placed in the regular classrooms for most of the school day.

These positive findings cast doubts on the argument that the separation of the retarded is necessary because of staff attitudes and student behavior. The apparent success of these integrated programs challenges the nearly universal practice of segregated, self contained classrooms for the retarded.

Researchers and program designers need to examine the requirements of both the special pupil and the teacher in the integrated classroom. Advanced methods for delivering services to the special pupil and the teacher should further improve the integrative programs.

Reading Comprehension Skills vis-a-vis the Mentally Retarded

OLIVER L. HURLEY

Abstract: A comprehensive review of the literature concerning reading comprehension skills of EMR children was made. The search yielded six items which provided only embryonic answers to three guiding questions concerning which comprehension skills should be taught to MR children, the age or level at which these skills should be taught, and the hierarchy of these skills. The paper discusses what the literature says in answer to these three questions and poses others.

In preparation for a study of reading comprehension skills of educable mentally retarded (EMR) children, a comprehensive review of the literature was undertaken. We sought the answers to three interrelated questions: (a) Which reading comprehension skills are taught or believed should be taught to mentally retarded children? (b) What is the age or level at which these skills should be taught as revealed through research or advocated by experts? and (c) What is the hierarchy of skills as shown empirically through research, or advocated by experts based on theory or experience or both?

The term "comprehension" seems to be one of those terms which few people find it necessary to explain. (See Jordan, 1969; Kirk, 1940; Smith 1968). This results in a dearth of specificity, as evidenced by comparing the delineation of skills in the Scott-Foresman basal readers with textbooks in the field of MR. For our research purposes, specificity was necessary, since one objective was to develop techniques for the teaching of skills which, as a composite, could be called, comprehension. This article is a report of the results of our search.

Results

A review of textbooks, curriculum guides and courses of study, and a search of the total ERIC file yielded about 75 pieces of literature, six of which began to provide answers to the questions posed.

The St. Coletta Schools Reading Curriculum for the Mentally Handicapped and the Cincinnati Public Schools Curriculum Bulletin #119 both specified comprehension skills and suggested some sequence of level (primary, intermediate, junior high, senior high) and within level. Table 1 summarizes the scope of those skills listed in the St. Coletta Schools curriculum. The check marks in the columns simply indicate whether the particular skill was listed by name for that level. The Table does not present a complete listing since some items had sub-topics which were omitted.

This is a fairly comprehensive list of skills, with an implied hierarchy of skills. It is not clear, however, whether those skills not checked at the higher levels are no longer to be taught or simply subsumed under a more general, higher level skill. The lack of uniformity of terminology and organization between levels makes it hard to answer this question. Nevertheless, the St. Coletta Schools curriculum provides a partial answer to all three questions asked. It is interesting to note that "abstract meanings" is not mentioned until the advanced level while perceiving associate relationships begins at the readiness level. Since one can conceive of such

23. Reading Comprehension

TABLE 1

Summary of Comprehension Reading Skills from the Reading Curriculum of the St. Coletta Schools

Skills	Readiness	Primary I	Primary II	Intermediate I	Intermediate II	Advanced
Literal Meaning	X	X	X	X	X	X
Pictures		X				
Words				X	X	
Phrases			X	X		X
Sentences		X	X	X	X	X
Paragraphs			X	X	X	X
Longer Selections					X	
Sequence	X	X	X	X	X	
Action		X	X	X	X	
Time		X	X	X	X	
Organization	X	X	X	X		
Main Ideas	X	X	X	X	X	X
Significant Details	X	X	X	X	X	X
Classification			X			
of ideas				X	X	
of words				X		
Following Written Directions		X	X	X	X	X
Perceiving Relationships	X	X	X	X	X	X
Association	X	X	X	X	X	X
Cause and Effect	X	X	X	X	X	X
Drawing Conclusions	X	X	X	X		X
Related Ideas				X		
Word Meanings			X			
Pronouns			X	X	X	
Contrasting Meanings			X	X		
Abstract Meanings						X
Prepositions			X	X		
Synonyms and Antonyms					X	X
Homonyms					X	X
Simple Definition					X	X
Family Relationships					X	X
Distinguishing fact from fancy	X	X	X	X	X	X
Emotional Reactions and Motive	X	X	X	X	X	X
Figures of Speech					X	X

relationships calling for abstract meanings, the question of definition and/or degree of mastery is elicited. The question of expected degree of mastery and level of task difficulty is raised with regard to skills like "emotional reactions and motive" and "figures of speech."

The sequence in the Cincinnati guide is embedded within the reading outcomes for the age levels specified. Those listed by name and the levels at which listed are shown in Table 2. This sequence is not as specific as that of the St. Coletta Schools' guide. There is a sequence stated but specificity is lacking.

McCanne (1963) lists a fairly comprehensive set of reading skills taught to migratory pupils who were not EMR. The skills are listed roughly in the order of their introduction to pupils within each of 10 categories. As with the curriculum guides the sequence is not based on any research data but rather an expert opinion. This list of comprehensive skills is contained in Table 3.

As with the Cincinnati Guide, McCanne lists

4. EDUCABLE MENTALLY RETARDED

TABLE 2
Summary of Reading Comprehension Skills Listed in the Cincinnati Public Schools Curriculum Bulletin #119

CA Level	Skill
6–9	following simple directions finding information
10–12	reads in thought phrases grasps essential meanings in sentences or short unit of words anticipates sequence of ideas and events enjoys stories with plot, sequence and sentence structure appropriate for his MA begins to acquire techniques for locating information follows simple written suggestions reads independently for comprehension of plot and characterization
13–15	uses context clues interprets plot and moods of characters uses techniques for locating information
16–18	reads for information reads and interprets traffic regulations, signs, labels, and instructions reads and interprets simple diagrams knows how to locate information

TABLE 3
Comprehension Reading Skills Listed by McCanne (1963)

following instructions
classifying things and ideas
understanding sequences
comparing and contrasting
visualizing characters, settings, events
discriminating phrases, sentences, paragraphs
selecting the right meaning of words
understanding adverb and pronoun references
using punctuation as an aid to meaning
suggesting title of story
finding main idea of story
finding part of story for specific purpose
making and using questions
distinguishing narrative from conversation
identifying declarative and interrogative sentences
finding major thought units
finding details to support main ideas
recalling information for objectives
recognizing relevant and irrelevant parts
generalizing on given information
identifying time and place
discerning literal vs. figurative
finding main idea of a paragraph
deciding on sub-titles
understanding maps
understanding diagrams
understanding graphs
understanding schedules

other comprehension sub-skills under other headings. He admits to the arbitrariness of his classification scheme which only highlights one of the problems in arriving at a list of comprehension skills and then orders them into a hierarchical sequence. The problem is that all of the skills are interrelated and manifest themselves on many levels of competence while also being multifaceted.

The validation of these three sets of reading comprehension skills is one of experience, of intuition, of knowledge of reading, et cetera. Since the lists are similar with minor differences in terminology, categorization, and sequencing, they could serve as an index of expert opinion relative to the three questions indicated above.

There are three research studies which bear on these questions (Blake, Aaron, & Westbrook, 1967; Meyen, 1968; Myers, 1967). Myers studied the ability of elementary children to (a) predict outcomes and actions, (b) discriminate between fact and fiction, and (c) discriminate between fact and opinion. This dissertation was a sub-study of the larger Blake *et al.* study which identified sequences among basal reading skills, trends in achievement of these skills (including certain comprehension skills) over reading instructional levels, and achievement levels of retarded, normal, and superior groups (levels and rate of skill acquisi-

TABLE 4

Comprehension Skills Studied in the Blake, Aaron and Westbrook (1967) and Myers (1967) Studies

1. Identifying cause-effect relationships directly stated in sentences
2. Identifying details in stories
3. Identifying main ideas directly stated in paragraphs
4. Identifying main ideas directly stated in stories
5. Identifying cause-effect relationships implied in sentences
6. Identifying main ideas implied in paragraphs
7. Identifying main ideas implied in stories
8. Interpreting similes
9. Interpreting idioms
10. Interpreting hyperboles
11. Interpreting personification
12. Interpreting metaphors
13. Predicting outcomes and actions
14. Discriminating between fact and fiction
15. Discriminating between facts and opinion

TABLE 5

Summary of Meyen's (1968) Data

Skill	Total No. of Items	Age to Begin Instruction	Age at which 60% EMR Correct
Recognizing & understanding important facts & details	4	11.6 years	13.3 years
Recognizing & understanding implied facts & relationships	5	12.7	13.0
Recognizing the main idea of a paragraph	3	12.3	15.5
Developing generalizations from a selection	2	12.3	14.1

tion). In addition to Myers' three comprehension skills, this study reports findings on 12 other reading comprehension skills, as shown in Table 4. The first seven listed are in the sequence "corroborated" by a statistical analysis (simplex) of the order of complexity. The last eight were not analysed because there was no logical reason to expect them to differ in complexity.

The sequence was based on the responses of 108 retarded (50-80 I.Q.), 108 normal (90-110 I.Q.), and 92 superior (above 120 I.Q.) children being taught at the 2, 3, 4, 5 reading instructional levels. The retarded group could respond in all skill areas. These studies, then, supply answers to both questions one and three posed earlier.

Meyen (1968) investigated 204 reading skills, each illustrated by a test item. Five curriculum experts and 60 teachers judged each item in terms of importance to the curriculum for educable mentally retarded children and the age level at which they recommended instruction in the skill to begin. The same items were then grouped into tests and administered to 1405 EMR children (CA 9-18) and to a representative sample of 2187 normal pupils in grades 3-8. There were basically 6 comprehension skill areas tapped by varying numbers of specific items. For each item, in addition to the CA levels indicated by the judges, Meyen also reports the percentage of pupils at each age level in both sample groups who got the item correct. Thus, his tables are quite extensive. Therefore, the summary of data given in Table 5 represents means computed across items, grouped into categories specified by the author of the present paper. For each skill area is given (a) the number of items tapping this skill, (b) the average expert opinion of when initial teaching should begin for EMRs, (c) the average age at which 60% of the EMR group got the items correct (for those items where 60% was reached).

Discussion

In answer to the first question posed, the answer would seem to be that almost all reading comprehension skills are, and should be, taught to the EMR. However, when one considers some of the skills often called "literary criticism" (e.g. appreciating literary style, reacting to literary moods and emotions), or "dictionary skills," the question of degree comes in. To what degree should we try to develop a skill like "Emotional reactions and motive" (Table 1) or "discerning literal vs. figurative?" (Table 3) What should be the level of difficulty or complexity of the similes, hyperboles, metaphors (Table 4) that EMR children should be asked to comprehend? While some may argue that such skills as these

4. EDUCABLE MENTALLY RETARDED

should receive no emphasis with EMR children, how can a child enjoy fiction without some degree of these skills? But, how much is enough?

The second question asked at what age or level specific skills should be taught. At first, Meyen's data seem to answer this question. His data show that there is a close correspondence between the age at which his experts said instruction should begin and the age at which 60% of the children passed the item; the latter occurring 2-3 years after instruction began. This suggests the possibility that for some of the items skills mastery might have been achieved at an earlier age if the skills had been taught at an earlier age. Are we fulfilling our prophecies made on the basis of M.A. scores; if so, to what extent? While Meyen's data thus reflect the status quo and are useful in this regard, much more research is needed before we will be able to answer our second question.

Research on the hierarchical ordering of reading comprehension skills (the third question) can be found only in Blake *et al.* but too few skills were sampled. "Expert" opinion, as found in the curriculum guides seem to offer some help but also reveal the difficulty of putting the skills in some sort of logical sequence or of even identifying the skills: differences in terminology and order and classification abound, non-linear reciprocal relationships between and among skills are evident. One example would suffice. Blake *et al.* found that identifying cause-effect relationships was lower in the hierarchy of complexity than identifying details in stories or main ideas stated in the selection. Yet, on a logical basis would not a person need to identify details before being able to identify a cause-effect relationship contained in the reading selection? If yes, then identifying details should occur earlier in the hierarchy. Possibly, both skills are on the same hierarchical level: if so, which one do we teach first? Probably, there is more than one hierarchy, only two of which are involved here — one of complexity, the other of teaching order. Certainly, there is a need for some definitive research in this area.

Conclusions

The purpose of this article was to highlight an area of instruction in which there is very little hard information, an area most of us take for granted, an area in need of much research. This reviewer was surprised at the dearth of specificity and research relative to reading comprehension skills of the EMR. We believe the readers will be too.

References

Blake, K. A., Aaron, I. E., & Westbrook, H. R. Learning of basal reading skills by mentally handicapped and non-mentally handicapped pupils. U. S. Office of Education, Project No. 5-0391, Final Report. Athens, Georgia: University of Georgia, 1967.

Cincinnati Public Schools. *The slow learning program in the elementary and secondary schools.* Curriculum Bulletin No. 119, 1964.

Jordan, L. J. Promoting reading comprehension. *Education and Training of the Mentally Retarded*, 1969, **4**, 132-140.

Kirk, S. A. *Teaching reading to slow-learning children.* Cambridge, Massachusetts: Houghton Mifflin, 1940.

McCanne, R. Use of checklist of reading skills with migratory children. Mimeo reprint. Boulder: Colorado State Dept. of Education, 1963.

Meyen, E. L. Age-placement, difficulty, and importance of basic skills in the curriculum for educable mentally retarded students. Unpublished doctoral dissertation, University of Iowa, 1968.

Myers, S. D. A comparison of selected critical reading skills possessed by elementary children of selected reading and intellectual levels. Unpublished doctoral dissertation, University of Georgia, 1967.

Sisters of St. Francis of Assissi, St. Coletta Schools. *Reading curriculum for the mentally handicapped.* Milwaukee: Department of Special Education Cardinal Stritch College, 1962.

Smith, R. M. *Clinical teaching: Methods of instruction for the retarded.* New York: McGraw-Hill, 1968.

Developing the Creative Potential of Educable Mentally Retarded Students

BARBARA GAY FORD
JOSEPH S. RENZULLI

A number of research studies dealing with creativity indicate that this trait exists to some degree in all persons regardless of their other abilities; and since intervention studies have also shown that creative performance can be modified through training (Meadow & Parnes, 1959; Olton & Crutchfield, 1969), a logical application of previous research would be to provide all learners with experiences that show promise of developing their creative thinking potential. Assuming the value of such thinking as a major component of the adaptive behavior necessary for independence, it is surprising that such a limited number of intervention studies in creativity have been carried out with mentally retarded youngsters.

RELATED RESEARCH It is well known that persons in almost all career areas must be ready to adapt to changes resulting from factors such as technological advances, changing consumer demands, and shifts in the need for marketable skills. A major concern in an era of unprecedented change is the need to introduce an element of flexibility into the training of all persons who will enter the world of work. This need is equally apparent in the education of retarded youngsters because, as Deno (1964) has pointed out in *Work Education for Educable Retarded Youth,* flexibility helps further the aim of maximum self-sufficiency. Results of a study dealing with the vocational success of retarded students by Barrett, Relos, and Eisele (1965) indicated that the successful group could be distinguished by behaviors that emphasized abstract reasoning. The potential carry-over of such training in flexibility and abstract reasoning has serious implications for the education of retarded youngsters, which has traditionally focused on a more concrete and convergent approach to learning.

4. EDUCABLE MENTALLY RETARDED

Evidence from recent literature suggests that all children, regardless of measured intellectual capacity, may exhibit some degree of creativity. Dacey and Madaus (1971), Iscoe and Pierce-Jones (1964), and Yamamoto (1967) have all reported little or no significant correlation between creativity and intelligence in extensive comparisons of heterogeneous populations. Ripple and May (1962) found even less correlation between IQ and creativity in homogeneously grouped children, and have advised caution when comparing the two traits.

When studying the creative thinking abilities of educable mentally retarded (EMR) youngsters and intellectually normal children, Smith (1967) observed no differences between the two groups on nonverbal measures of creative thinking. The work of Kelson (1965), Richmond (1972), and Stern (1963) yielded similar results. In another comparative study Buffmire (1969) found that retarded children might actually score higher than nonretarded students on measures of nonverbal creativity; and an investigation by Cawley and Chase (1966) found no significant differences between retarded and intellectually normal students on selected creativity measures.

A few studies have indicated that the creative abilities of retarded children may possibly be developed through systematic training programs. Tisdall (1962) reported improvements in creativity with EMR populations through the use of a "discovery" method of instruction. Other research has involved practice in free association (Penney & McCann, 1962) and work with a series of brainstorming lessons (Rouse, 1965; Ladner, 1971). Although all of these studies showed increases in creative thinking ability on the part of retarded subjects, the absence of a systematic and readily available set of training activities may very well be the reason why such studies have had little or no influence on actual classroom practice. The present study has attempted to overcome this problem by using an experimental treatment program that is commercially available and easy to administer. The *New Directions in Creativity Program* (NDC) (Renzulli, 1973) consists of 50 activities and accompanying teacher's guides that were developed in accordance with the divergent production "slab" of Guilford's Structure-of-Intellect Model (1967).[1] Previous research (Callahan & Renzulli, 1974) has established the effectiveness of the materials with general populations; however, the present study was designed to answer the following three questions with EMR students:

1. Will work with a systematic set of creativity training materials help educable mentally retarded children to achieve higher scores on creativity tests?
2. Will exposure to these creativity training materials improve EMR children's attitudes toward school?
3. Will EMR children who have worked with these materials earn higher scores on ratings of creativity characteristics?

SUBJECTS

The subjects for the present study consisted of 30 groups of middle-grade and high school level EMR children who attended urban and suburban schools in Connecticut and Illinois. Of these 30 classes, 18 were randomly assigned to the experimental group and the remaining 12 classrooms were designated as the control group. Some of the groups were enrolled in self-contained special education classes and others attended resource rooms for a fixed period of time each day. The IQ range of the sample population was 50 to 80 and the children ranged in age from 10 to 16.

Teachers of the classes assigned to the experimental group were provided with the NDC *(Mark I)* book, a set of three rubber stamps (one happy, one neutral, and one sad face) for the students' use in evaluating their reactions to the activities, a tally sheet to tabulate student response, and a form entitled "Teacher Reaction to Individual Activities." Each teacher was asked to use the NDC activity sheets in the classroom at the rate of two per week for a period of 12 weeks. Classes in the control group carried out regular classroom activity during the experimental period.

At the end of the 12-week experimental period, teachers of both groups were provided with creativity tests, scales, and questionnaires for each of the students in their classes. Previous experience with retarded students prior to this research suggested that the fixed time limits of the creativity tests would greatly reduce the children's quantity of responses. Such students often generate many ideas, but are frequently handicapped by their inability to write and spell and therefore may respond poorly on written tests. In consideration of this verbal handicap and the lack of established norms for retarded students, it was decided that the time limits for all creativity measures would be removed. Teachers were instructed to allow the students as much time as they needed for each section of the four instruments, and to give writing and spelling assistance to individuals when requested. All other standardized instructions for the testing situation were retained.

EXPERIMENTAL DESIGN A posttest only control group design (Campbell & Stanley, 1963) was used to compensate for the reactive effect that has been found to be present in creativity tests (i.e., if a prepost design is used, the pretest may influence subjects' scores on the posttest). Because of the major influence of classroom teachers on the performance and attitudes of any group, it was determined that an objective evaluation would require a comparison of individual classroom mean scores as the statistical unit. The success or failure of instructional programs often hinges on the effectiveness of the teachers involved in an intervention study (Turner & Denny, 1967); however, the use of classroom means helps to avoid errors by providing a more reliable estimate of research findings. Thus, the data reported in the tables that follow represent the mean scores of each set of group means for the 18 experimental and 12 control groups.

MANOVA and discriminant analyses were applied to the data in order to determine the most effective combination of variables distinguishing experimental from control groups. In addition to these analyses, responses to a teacher questionnaire and student questionnaire were tabulated and summarized for the experimental group in order to gain further information regarding teacher and student responses to the use of the training materials.

RESULTS
Scores on Creativity Tests
Christensen and Guilford's tests of *Ideational Fluency, Word Fluency, Alternate Uses,* and *Consequences* were used to investigate the effect of the NDC program on measures of creativity. Table 1 presents the means and standard deviations for the four

4. EDUCABLE MENTALLY RETARDED

predictor variables for both groups. As this table indicates, the ranges on all four creativity tests were very wide, with the experimental group attaining the greatest mean score in every case. When a MANOVA was conducted with the two criterion groups for the four creativity variables, the F ratio indicated that the two groups differed significantly on the battery of four creativity tests ($F = 8.81$; $p < .0002$; d.f. $= 1,28$), with the experimental group exceeding the control group across all four measures. The greatest mean difference between groups was seen in the *Alternate Uses* test, followed by *Consequences*, *Word Fluency*, and *Ideational Fluency* in that order. Based on the factors these tests measure, it can be concluded that the NDC program had the greatest effect on the subjects' flexibility, with significant effects on originality and fluency.

Attitude Toward School

It was hypothesized that EMR students who worked with NDC materials would have better attitudes toward school than students who had not worked with these materials. Erlich's (1969) *Inventory of Attitude Toward School* was scored for the

TABLE 1

Means and standard deviations for experimental and control groups on four measures of creativity.

	Alternate Uses Mean	S.D.	Ideational Fluency Mean	S.D.	Consequences Mean	S.D.	Word Fluency Mean	S.D.
Experimental	7.56	5.12	29.91	14.84	8.87	5.92	33.05	14.23
Control	1.07	1.04	14.96	2.74	1.54	1.01	16.14	4.46
Total	4.96	4.05	23.93	11.69	5.94	4.66	26.28	11.44

Note: Each figure represents the grand mean and standard deviation for 18 Experimental Group means and 12 Control Group means.

TABLE 2

Means and standard deviations for experimental and control groups on four factors and total score of the inventory of attitude toward school.

	Total Score Mean	S.D.	Factor 1 Mean	S.D.	Factor 2 Mean	S.D.	Factor 6 Mean	S.D.	Factor 10 Mean	S.D.
Experimental	94.21	19.07	8.53	2.62	14.86	4.75	10.24	1.86	2.97	1.36
Control	113.41	16.68	12.68	3.16	13.03	4.33	14.63	3.65	4.93	1.92
Total	101.89	18.17	10.19	2.84	14.13	4.59	11.99	2.71	3.75	1.60

following four of twelve possible subfactors: $F_1 =$ Generalized Negative Affect, $F_2 =$ Generalized Positive Affect and Enthusiasm, $F_6 =$ Attitude Toward Teacher(s), and $F_{10} =$ Attitude Toward Emotional Security or Anxiety. Table 2 presents the means and standard deviations for the four subfactors, and the total scores for each group. Again, means differed widely between the two groups, with the experimental group consistently attaining the lower score. Since a smaller score indicates a better attitude toward school, the differences appear to favor the experimental group. The MANOVA for these five predictor variables for the two criterion groups yielded an F ratio of 6.95 ($p < .0004$;

d.f. = 1,28) indicating that there was indeed a significant difference between the two groups in general attitude toward school and on the four sub-factors of the Inventory.

Characteristics of Creativity

The third research question proposed that EMR students who had experienced the NDC creativity training program would exhibit more characteristics of creative behavior than would those students of similar ability who had not worked with the program. Teacher evaluations using the Scale for *Rating Creativity Characteristics* (Renzulli, 1971) yielded an experimental group mean of 23.62 (s.d. = 4.65) and a control group mean of 18.96 (s.d. = 3.28). An analysis of variance comparison of these data resulted in an *F* ratio of 9.01 (d.f. = 1,28) which was significant beyond the .01 level. These data indicate that students who participated in the NDC program received higher ratings on the Renzulli scale than control group students by exhibiting more of the behavioral characteristics of creativity measured by this scale. It should be pointed out, however, that experimental group teachers were aware of the treatment condition and hence subject to the bias that is typically present when rating scales are used to evaluate known treatments.

A MANOVA was performed on all eleven predictor variables and yielded an overall *F* ratio of 9.70 ($p < .0001$; d.f. = 1,28). Following the significant outcomes of this MANOVA, a stepwise discriminant analysis evaluated each of the eleven variables with respect to its contribution to the total discrimination between groups. The five optimum predictor variables included the *Scale for Rating Creativity Characteristics, Alternate Uses, Word Fluency,* the *Inventory of Attitude Toward School* (factor 6 and factor 10 respectively). In other words, these five variables had the greatest impact on the discrimination between the two comparison groups. A plotting of the individual (classroom) means and group centroids based on the discriminant analysis of all eleven variables revealed an absence of overlap between the experimental and control groups. This procedure supports the conclusion that the set of variables discriminated clearly between the two groups and that the NDC materials had a powerful effect in changing the behaviors of EMR youngsters. Considering the outcomes from the stepwise discriminant analysis, it is apparent that the treatment influenced all three of the general categories of dependent variables: divergent or creative production, attitude toward school, and creativity characteristics.

The student and teacher questionnaires and other instruments used to assess experimental group reaction to the NDC program showed a generally positive response to the creativity activities. None of the teachers and very few students (12 percent) gave completely negative evaluations of the materials, and the constructive criticism seen in these data provided valuable suggestions for further study in this area.

DISCUSSION

Some of the most dramatic outcomes of this study were related to the differences in creativity test scores between the experimental and control groups. The comparative mean difference between groups was greatest on the *Alternate Uses* test, a measure of the factor of flexibility. Since it was precisely this trait that was mentioned as a necessary attribute for adjustment to job changes and the attainment of self-sufficiency, such positive results from the short-term implementation of the NDC creativity training

4. EDUCABLE MENTALLY RETARDED

program lend support to the further use of such a program with EMR students. If long-term creativity training consistently resulted in flexibility gains on the part of these children, it should assume an important place in the special education curriculum. It should be pointed out, however, that there are undoubtedly many kinds of "flexibility," and the type measured by Guilford's *Alternate Uses* test may bear limited relationship to that which is required for job adjustment and self-sufficiency. For this reason, the results relating to flexibility should be viewed with caution.

Indications that the experimental group's attitude toward school was significantly more positive than that of the control group were noteworthy. One must be cautious in viewing the outcomes of this or any other attitude questionnaire, since the affective realm is difficult to measure empirically, and results from such a measure may be influenced by several extraneous variables. Although the obtained differences between experimental and control groups' attitude toward school was relatively small, they were highly reliable. Thus, the value of creativity training in improving attitude and lessening anxiety may be enough in itself to justify the implementation of such programs in special education classes.

The findings with regard to observed creativity characteristics of students were important in that they represented teachers' subjective judgments of students' creative abilities. Significant differences favoring the experimental group added further support to the validity of the creativity test results. A question requiring further research would be whether or not a child could acquire more of these behavioral characteristics during the course of extensive creativity training. Data in this area would be a valuable addition to the fund of knowledge dealing with creative growth.

The lasting effects of a creativity training program on the creative abilities of mentally retarded children can only be assessed through long-term implementation of such a program accompanied by periodic evaluation of results in terms of creative growth and carry-over to other subject areas. The outcomes of the present study should give impetus to this type of research, since information regarding this aspect of the retarded child's abilities is limited at this time.

Vocabulary Development of Educable Retarded Children

ARTHUR M. TAYLOR
MARTHA L. THURLOW
JAMES E. TURNURE

ARTHUR M. TAYLOR is Supervisor of Programs for the Mentally Retarded, Special Education Department, St. Paul Public Schools, St. Paul, Minnesota; and MARTHA L. THURLOW is Research Fellow, and JAMES E. TURNURE is Professor of Educational Psychology, Department of Psychoeducational Studies, and RD&D Center in Education of Handicapped Children, University of Minnesota, Minneapolis. This research was supported in part by a grant to the University of Minnesota Research, Development and Demonstration Center in Education of Handicapped Children (OEG-0-332189-4533-032) from the US Office of Education.

BASIC research involving the procedure of verbal elaboration has shown that the learning of paired items is greatly facilitated when the items are presented within a verbal context and that the procedure is particularly effective for young children (Turnure, Thurlow, & Larsen, 1971) and retarded children (Jensen & Rohwer, 1963; Turnure, 1971; Turnure, Larsen, & Thurlow, 1973). In fact, Rohwer (1973) has concluded that elaboration is the main process necessary for efficient associative learning.

Although elaboration, the embedding of information within verbal contexts, appears to be a naturally occurring process and one that is necessarily involved in most instruction, an analysis of the use of elaboration in instructional materials reveals it is not used as consistently or as efficiently as possible. For example, elaboration appears in vocabulary instruction, where a single sentence commonly is used to present the meaning of a single vocabulary word. The use of single sentences for elaborations, however, does not recognize recent research findings that suggest extended elaborations (e.g., paragraphs) have even more impressive effects than simple sentences (Turnure, 1971). The idea of presenting the meaning of a vocabulary word in isolation is also inconsistent with recent research that indicates elaboration facilitates learning mainly because it provides stronger relations between two or more words or concepts learned together in a single context (Bender & Taylor, 1973; Rohwer, 1971; Turnure & Thurlow, 1973).

Despite the potential educational applicability of elaboration, only a few studies have demonstrated that extended elaboration can successfully be used as a vehicle for effective classroom learning. Ross (1971) has developed math concepts via elaboration based instruction, and Bender and Taylor (1973) have used elaboration as a basis for developing social studies instruction for retarded children. Other instructional materials using elaborational techniques have been prepared by individuals interested in vocabulary development (Ammon & Ammon, 1971; Draper & Moeller, 1971). Ammon and Ammon (1971) demonstrated that elaborations involving story themes could be used effectively to develop vocabulary, and Draper and Moeller (1971) successfully used thematic elaborations (i.e., myths and fables) to develop and interrelate new vocabulary words for children in the fourth through sixth grades. Unfortunately, the benefits of using the thematic instruction were not compared to the benefits of nonthematic instruction. Furthermore, neither investigation examined the effectiveness of elaboration in vocabulary instruction for retarded children. While vocabulary instruction has long been a major focus in the education of children, such instruction is particularly critical with retarded children since these children seem to progress more slowly in vocabulary development than expected (Beier, Starkweather, & Lambert, 1969).

Purpose

The purpose of this study was to examine the effectiveness of nonrelational, relational, and mixed approaches to vocabulary instruction for educable mentally retarded children. The nonrelational condition was developed to represent traditional approaches to vocabulary instruction. In this condition, nonrelational elaborations were used during the initial presentation of words and during a final summary. The relational condition was developed to reflect the implication of recent research that the success of elaborations is primarily due to relations, at least in paired associate learning (Thurlow & Turnure, 1972; Turnure & Thurlow, 1973). In this condition, relational elaborations were used in the initial presentation of words and in a thematic summary. The mixed condition represented a blending of the other two conditions. Nonrelational elaborations were used during the initial presentation of words, but major relations between words were presented in a thematic summary.

This investigation allowed for the comparison of the two types of elaborations and the two types of summaries. The two types of elaborations were referred to as relational and nonrelational. Relational elaborations were contexts that developed specific relationships between two or more vocabulary words, and nonrelational elaborations were contexts that expanded the meaning of a single vocabulary word without relating it to the meaning of any other vocabulary word. The two types of summaries were designated as thematic and nonthematic. Thematic summaries were single integrative stories that emphasized a thematic relationship among the vocabulary words in a lesson, and nonthematic summaries were a series of single nonrelational elaborations (one for each vocabulary word in a lesson).

In addition to studying the effects of these factors on vocabulary growth, the study also assessed the spontaneous use of elaboration and related strategies by children receiving the various combinations of elaborations and summaries.

Method

Subjects

Nine self contained classes for primary age educable mentally retarded children ages 8 to 11 participated in the study. The 107 children were pretested on two instruments, the Peabody Picture Vocabulary Test (PPVT) (Dunn, 1961), and the Minnesota Picture Vocabulary Test (MPVT) (Taylor, Thurlow, & Turnure, 1974), which is a test for experimental words that was modeled after the PPVT.

The mean PPVT pretest scores were used to assign the classes to the instructional conditions. The nine classes were grouped in blocks of three, such that the first block contained the three classes with the highest mean PPVT scores, and so on. The three classes within each block were then randomly assigned to the three instructional conditions. This assignment procedure not only resulted in similar mean PPVT pretest scores for the three instructional conditions but also similar MPVT pretest scores. The mean chronological ages and IQ scores were not significantly different; the overall mean chronological age was 10.0 years ($SD = 0.7$) and the overall mean IQ was 74.4 ($SD = 5.6$).

Materials

Three versions of each vocabulary lesson were written to correspond to the three experimental conditions. The lessons for the relational condition involved the use of a relational elaboration in the initial presentation of the vocabulary word and the use of a thematic summary at the end of the lesson. In the nonrelational condition, nonrelational elaborations were used during the initial presentations and also during the nonthematic summary. The mixed condition included nonrelational elaborations followed by a thematic summary.

Of the 15 vocabulary lessons written, 4 each were for the money, time, and written word units, and 3 were for the airplanes unit. Five vocabulary words were taught in each lesson. Lessons were presented on cassette tape recordings while the students followed in textbooks consisting of pictures. The content of the tapes and pictures varied among the three conditions in accordance with the experimental manipulations.

All vocabulary lessons were written in the same format, with the content of the elaborations and summaries being the only source of variation between conditions. (More specific descriptions of the make up of lessons can be found in Taylor, Thurlow, & Turnure, 1974.)

Tests

In this study, the following testing instruments were used to measure either vocabulary development or the use of instructional strategies: PPVT, MPVT, weekly tests, and utilization tests.

The PPVT was used to measure general vocabulary development (i.e., vocabulary not taught in the experimental lessons). For this study, the test was adapted for group administration by using score sheets, and all subjects were tested on the same subset of items. These 44 items were administered as both a pretest and a posttest.

The MPVT was a group administered test containing 27 items, a representative sample of the 75 vocabulary words taught. Changes in MPVT scores from pretest to posttest were used to measure vocabulary growth related to the specific words presented in the instruction.

Weekly tests were group administered tests given at the end of each week to assess the effectiveness of that week's instruction. Each weekly test had two parts—picture recognition and grouping. The picture recognition test required the children to identify pictures of words taught during the week's instruction. The grouping test evaluated the children's ability to remember the words taught in each lesson by asking them to pick from an array made up of two to four pictures of intraunit and/or extraunit intrusions the pictures showing words learned on the same day as a given stimulus picture.

The utilization test was administered individually as a structured interview in which the subject was given a 60 × 40 cm picture of a city scene (Taylor, Thurlow, & Turnure, 1974) that included representations of all 20 words taught in the city unit. The first part of the interview was designed primarily to determine how many of the 20 vocabulary words the subjects would use. The second part of the interview was used to investigate the types of contextual responses the subjects used to describe the picture. Each subject's overall response was judged as to whether or not it was thematic. In addition, all elaborational responses containing vocabulary words were classified as to the type of elaboration represented (relational or nonrelational).

Procedure

Each class was pretested on the PPVT and the MPVT, and then instruction was started. Lessons from each unit that lasted from 30 to 50 minutes were presented the first 4 days of the week. The weekly tests (picture recognition and grouping) were given at the end of each unit by a trained tester.

Instruction was presented over a period of 4 weeks, and all lessons were presented in the same manner. As the children listened to the tape, they referred to their pictures. At the same time, the teacher followed the tape script and monitored student responses.

After all units were completed, each class was posttested on the PPVT, the MPVT, and the utilization test. The utilization test was administered to 54 of the 107 subjects in the study about one month after all other testing. These subjects were the 6 subjects from each class for whom the most complete data were available.

Results

Vocabulary Development

Data related to vocabulary development are presented in Table 1. Changes in PPVT scores were used to assess the hypothesis that all conditions would show general vocabulary development as a result of instruction. The data indicated, however, that only the relational condition showed the expected significant gain from pretest to posttest ($t(28) = 1.80$, $p < .05$, one-tailed test). (See Taylor, Thurlow, & Turnure, 1974, for the rationale and derivation of the general and specific hypotheses presented in this section.)

MPVT scores, shown in Table 1, were used to assess specific vocabulary growth. Repeated measures t tests revealed that the gains were significant in all conditions ($ps < .001$), thus supporting the hypothesis that all conditions would result in specific vocabulary growth.

The data from the weekly picture recognition tests provided information related to the relatively short term effects of the instruction on vocabulary development. Tests on these data confirmed the findings from the MPVT. (See Taylor, Thurlow, & Turnure, 1974, for a discussion of these results.)

Usage of vocabulary was assessed by the first part of the utilization test. One measure of usage taken from this part of the test was the mean number of different vocabulary words used by subjects to describe the picture (maximum = 20). The prediction that subjects in the relational and mixed conditions would use significantly more vocabulary words arose from the assumption that an emphasis on relations would make vocabulary words more available for long term retention. A one-tailed t test of the mean numbers of different words (4.83, 5.55, and 6.06 in the nonrelational, relational, and mixed conditions, respectively) confirmed the hypothesis ($t(52) = 1.80$, $p < .05$).

A second measure of vocabulary usage was the total number of vocabulary nouns (including repetitions) used in relation to the total

TABLE 1
Means and Standard Deviations of PPVT [a] and MPVT [b] Pretest and Posttest Scores

Test Condition	Pretest X	SD	Posttest X	SD	Gain
PPVT					
Nonrelational	32.19	4.51	32.23	4.84	0.04
Relational	31.75	4.76	33.07	3.97	1.32
Mixed	31.79	5.21	32.68	4.28	0.89
MPVT					
Nonrelational	16.71	2.43	22.57	2.42	5.86
Relational	16.96	2.21	22.39	3.07	5.43
Mixed	16.87	2.00	22.60	2.37	5.73

[a] PPVT = Peabody Picture Vocabulary Test
[b] MPVT = Minnesota Picture Vocabulary Test

number of all nouns used by subjects in their descriptions. It was hypothesized that subjects in the relational condition would use relatively more vocabulary nouns than nonvocabulary nouns in their descriptions. This hypothesis was supported by planned comparisons ($F(1,51) = 3.79$, $p < .05$, one-tailed test). The percentages of the total nouns that were vocabulary words were 36.6% in the nonrelational condition, 38.3% in the mixed condition, and 49.6% in the relational condition.

Use of Instructional Strategies

The use of grouping strategies following instruction was partially assessed by means of the weekly grouping test. The mean percentages of pictures correctly grouped on each of the four tests are presented in Table 2. In

TABLE 2
Mean Percentages of Pictures Grouped Correctly on Four Weekly Grouping Tests

Weekly test	Instructional condition		
	Relational	Mixed	Nonrelational
City	70.9	69.0	55.9
Written word	92.7	89.2	90.0
Money	76.2	81.2	74.4
Airplanes	80.1	80.1	75.9
Mean percentage	80.0	79.6	74.1

separate t tests conducted to determine if subjects in the conditions receiving thematic summaries (relational and mixed conditions) were better able to group pictures of the vocabulary words according to the lesson within which they were presented than were subjects in the nonrelational condition, 3 of 4 tests revealed significant differences: city—$t(89) = 3.56$, $p<.01$; money—$t(89) = 1.90$, $p<.05$; and airplanes—$t(94) = 1.68$, $p<.05$. The relational and mixed conditions were not found to be significantly different from each other on any of the weekly grouping tests.

The main instrument for assessing strategy usage resulting from the instruction was the second part of the utilization test. The mean number of relational elaborations used to describe the picture was 0.94 ($SD = 1.20$) in the relational condition, 1.22 ($SD = 2.04$) in the mixed condition, and 1.11 ($SD = 1.49$) in the nonrelational condition. As suggested by these means, the number of relational elaborations did not differ with the conditions, and thus, the data failed to support the hypothesis that subjects in the relational and mixed conditions would use significantly more relations than the subjects in the nonrelational condition.

The mean numbers of nonrelational elaborations used in the relational, mixed, and nonrelational conditions were 1.22 ($SD = 1.16$), 3.44 ($SD = 3.43$), and 1.89 ($SD = 1.67$), respectively. Orthogonal t tests were used to test the hypothesis that subjects receiving nonrelational elaborations (mixed and nonrelational conditions) would use significantly more nonrelational elaborations than subjects in the relational condition; this hypothesis was supported ($t(52) = 2.08$, $p<.05$). The remaining orthogonal t test confirmed that this difference was due to the large number of nonrelational elaborations used by subjects in the mixed condition rather than the nonrelational condition ($t(34) = 1.68$, $p <.05$, one-tailed test).

The use of an integration strategy was measured by scoring each subject's complete response to the picture as to whether or not it represented a single integrated (i.e., thematic) story. The proportions of subjects giving an integrated story in the relational, mixed, and nonrelational conditions were .28, .39, and .11, respectively. As hypothesized, a significantly greater proportion of subjects in the two conditions receiving thematic summaries (relational and mixed conditions) told an integrated story about the picture than in the nonrelational condition ($z = 1.74$, $p<.05$, one-tailed test).

Discussion

This study represents an important link between laboratory research on learning strategies and the development of instruction. Although laboratory studies of elaboration have done much to help refine knowledge of this important learning process, investigators have only vaguely intimated ways in which elaboration can actually be applied to classroom materials. This study made a direct attempt to investigate the types of elaborations and the ways in which elaborations can be used more effectively in education. A major purpose of the study was to delineate the effects of elaboration on the development of vocabulary. The finding that subjects in all instructional conditions showed considerable increases in the experimental vocabulary replicates the findings of Ammon and Ammon (1971) and extends their findings to the population of educable mentally retarded children.

The grouping and utilization tests provided measures of whether subjects from the relational and mixed conditions used their experience with different types of summaries and elaborations. The hypothesis that subjects in conditions containing thematic summaries would perform better when asked to group the vocabulary was supported on 3 of 4 weekly grouping tests. The results from the utilization test supported the hypothesis that significantly more of the subjects who had been exposed to integrative stories in the summaries would use such themes in their own responses. Utilization data also indicated that relational elaborations seldomly occurred in this test format, with no significant differences across conditions. Nonrelational elaborations (contexts that expanded upon the meaning of a single vocabulary word without relating that word to a second vocabulary word), however, were used significantly more often as descriptive statements by subjects who had received instruction based heavily on nonrelational elaborations.

The findings from this study have their most important implications as they relate to the three instructional conditions, conditions which have direct applicability to the classroom. The subjects in the nonrelational condition, a condition that presented vocabulary instruction in a manner similar to the approach often taken in the classroom, performed essentially as well as subjects in the other conditions on measures of specific vocabulary development but less well on indices of strategy usage and generalized vocabulary development. Subjects in the mixed condition, who received a combination of nonrelational elaborations and thematic summaries, performed better than subjects in the other conditions on the following two measures: number of vocabulary words, and number of nonrelational elaborations used. Relational condition subjects showed higher performances on other measures (PPVT gains, proportion of vocabulary nouns to other nouns). Both the relational and mixed conditions surpassed the nonrelational condition on organization measures (weekly grouping tests). On the basis of these differential findings, it appears that perhaps the approach selected for vocabulary instruction in the classroom should vary depending upon plans for subsequent usage (e.g., creative expression versus introduction of new subject matter areas) and even on the characteristics of the children being taught. Further study should be undertaken to explore these possibilities.

Recommendations

Several specific recommendations regarding the nature of elaboration based vocabulary instruction can be made as a result of this study. First, the combination of pictorially presented elaborations and audio tape descriptions seems to make an excellent instructional package for the population of educable mentally retarded children. However, the instruction appears to be greatly enhanced when the pictures are simple, easy to read, and present only a single context or relation. Second, it seems that 5 new vocabulary words may be too many to be introduced within one elaboration based vocabulary lesson. Two or 3 new vocabulary words appear to result in the optimal length elaboration based lesson in which adequate development of definitions and relations can be made. However, if previously learned words (i.e., ones that have been defined and elaborated upon) are to be integrated, it would seem that 5 words would result in an appropriate length lesson, a lesson containing only relations designed to summarize previous learning.

With respect to the context of elaboration based vocabulary instruction, it would appear that, for retarded individuals, concrete words are far easier to develop than abstract words. Further, in presenting any one word, only one definition of the word should be presented within a single lesson. Thus, words with multiple definitions (e.g., penny—the only brown coin, the coin that buys less than all the other coins, and the coin equalling one cent) would require several lessons to teach.

Finally, the instruction should have valid testing methods and instruments to identify the current competencies of the children and to properly sequence the instruction. Tests of both expressive and receptive vocabulary, as well as tests for related skill development, should be given to adequately evaluate progress made by the students. Research on these types of assessment methods and instruments is a crucial requirement for promoting the implementation of transitional research, research that is a necessary guide to the appropriate and efficient application of findings from basic research.

The Child With Minimal Brain Dysfunction— A Profile

Sam D. Clements, Ph.D.

Dr. Clements is assistant professor in the Departments of Psychology and Pediatrics, and director of the Child Guidance Study Unit of the University of Arkansas Medical Center, Little Rock.

In a small town in central Arkansas, lives a ten-year-old boy. His parents are intelligent, college-educated, financially secure, and very concerned for and warmly interested in the welfare of their only offspring. After a stormy first four years, marked by frequent visits to the family physician because of the boy's high degree of irritability, disturbed sleep pattern, his feeding problem, and frequent outbursts of unpredictable temper, they were assured that he was a "normal" youngster with overly-anxious parents.

Dissatisfied with this continual and hackneyed explanation of the child's unusual behavior, they began to make the rounds of professional experts, determined to find the answer for the child's general discontent before the time when he would be entering school. They traveled thousands of miles and spent thousands of dollars. At age five, the boy was diagnosed as "adjustment reaction of childhood," due to parental mishandling; at age six as mentally retarded; at age seven as a "schizophrenic" child; at age eight as a child with minimal brain dysfunction.

Now, at the ripe old age of ten years, he is a child of above average general intelligence, progressing nicely in school, both academically and behaviorally, and is the pride and joy of his parents and community.

I would like to give you a soliloquy written by the father of this youngster, which he presented publicly at a recent organizational meeting of parents of similar children. I present it with his permission.

"How many of you men have come home from work in the evening to find your son having a tantrum because he has to take a bath? After a terrific struggle, your wife gets him into the tub, walks into the living room, and you ask, 'Why don't you discipline that child during the day so that when

26. Minimal Brain Dysfunction

I come home at night, I can have some peace and quiet?'

How many of you have had old friends avoid visiting in your home after your child's third or fourth birthday because they could not endure the noise, confusion, and irritability of your child?

Have you ever come home to find your wife in tears because a neighbor has told her to keep your son out of their yard?

How many of you parents have made the rounds from the family physician, to the pediatrician, to the psychiatrist, and back again, only to be given such earth-shaking advice as, 'Don't worry, he'll grow out of it,' or 'If you parents would sleep in the same bed, the child would feel more secure?'

Have you been called for a conference by your child's teacher, knowing full well what she is going to say?

How many times have you thought, 'There's nothing like this in *my* family!'

Have you and your wife had many late hour discussions about 'What have we done as parents to fail our child?'

After more behavior problems and failure at school, you try again for professional help. But, this time it is different. You have found the right diagnostic facility, and oddly enough, right in your own backyard.

This time you are told that your child has minimal brain dysfunction, or is mildly neurologically handicapped, or is perceptually impaired. Whatever term is given the condition, it means that your child *is* different and cannot help most of the things he does. And, with the proper help and management, these problems can be overcome.

Then comes the period of acceptance, and this too, is as difficult as any previous problem. With the acceptance, however, the home situation begins to improve—for the first time in eight years! No longer do you and the teacher pressure the child to work at tasks which he is unable to perform. Then, the miracle happens. With the correct teaching methods and home handling, your child experiences success for the first time.

At this point, you are not concerned with cause. You are only elated by the fact that your child is being helped. You know for the *first* time what it is like to have a normal, happy home.

These experiences I share with you as a parent."

This, I feel, exquisitely portrays some aspects of the child with minimal brain dysfunction from the viewpoint of a parent. Since, however, it is our duty to survey such children from many angles, perhaps a more apt description would be a "series of silhouettes," rather than a single profile of the child with minimal brain injury.

It is imperative that we clearly understand what is meant by the term "minimal brain dysfunction." The following definition is offered: The diagnostic categories subsumed under the rubric of minimal brain dysfunction refer to children of average or above general intelligence with learning and/or behavior difficulties ranging from mild to most severe, which are due to subtle deviations arising from genetic variations, bio-chemical irregularities, perinatal brain insults, and/or illnesses and injuries sustained during the years critical for the development and maturation of those parts of the central nervous system having to do with

4. EDUCABLE MENTALLY RETARDED

perception, language, inhibition of impulses, and motor control.

The accompanying symptom picture, or some of its parts, has been referred to by such terms as: mild neurologic handicapping; perceptual impairment; the brain-damage behavior syndrome; the Strauss-Lehtinen syndrome; mild organic compromising; and others.

These subtle organic deviations of brain function can be conclusively diagnosed provided the proper time, techniques, and attitudes are utilized.

There is a constant flow of children referred to child psychiatry clinics and other diagnostic centers, who are apparently of good intelligence, yet who fail to progress in academic skills at the expected rate. Some of these youngsters are relegated to the special education classroom designed for the mentally retarded; others are retained in grade for a year or more in hopes they will catch up; most are passed along automatically with their age group even though it is known that the child cannot compete academically with his peers. Not only do these children experience learning difficulties, but they exhibit behavioral differences which are a source of irritation and bewilderment to parents, teachers, and playmates.

The less astute observer might refer to such a child as lazy; immature; undisciplined; a slow-learner; emotionally-blocked; or an under-achiever. Projecting such a youngster into the future, we would usually find that once he had been labeled by one or more of the above-mentioned ambiguous terms, he would be allowed to drift aimlessly through school, passed along grade after grade, meeting defeat after defeat, getting more and more behind in academic skills, until the time he becomes sixteen years of age and can drop out of school. He then attempts to find his place in the economic market only to discover that he is no more able to meet the qualifications for gainful employment than he was to achieve at school. He then joins the legion of the misfits. He may drift into delinquency; spend some time in a "correctional" institution; or end up in a state hospital.

If, somewhere along this line, his behavior becomes *too* disordered because of frustration and failure, he may be referred for professional help. What happens to him at this point will depend upon the adequacy of training of these diagnostic experts as colored by their personal attitudes and beliefs concerning the causes of learning and behavior problems of children.

One would like to believe that our graduate schools of psychology, medicine, social work, and education are teaching future diagnosticians and therapists all that is really known about children who deviate. Such, however, is not the usual case, and represents one of the most flagrant and harmful examples of poor communication among professionals, because in the end, it is the children and their parents who must suffer.

In the majority of present day training centers and institutions charged with teaching our future clinicians regarding maladjusted children, most of the emphasis is given to one side of the story only—the psychogenic side. The course material is steeped in the traditional stereotypes of sibling rivalry, rejecting parents, repressed hostility, oedipal conflict, repressed sexuality, and the like. These are presented as being the major causes of deviant behavior, with only casual reference to the spectrum of organic factors which are primary to all learning and behavior. It is very like a child's game of make believe and we are playing like nothing new has been learned about human behavior over the past fifty years.

This vogue among child guidance workers of attributing the behavioral and learning deviations seen in children almost exclu-

26. Minimal Brain Dysfunction

sively to the rearing patterns and interpersonal relationships experienced by such youngsters has created a long time obstacle to the understanding of and most useful therapeutic aid for a countless number of misunderstood children who grow up to be a countless number of misunderstood adults. This is not meant in any way to belittle the importance of environmental factors as they contribute to any child's difficulty. This is simply a plea that they be placed in their proper perspective. I *am* saying, however, that this lopsided approach to the explanation of disorganized behavior has impeded progress in our efforts to help troubled children because of the closed-shop atmosphere that prevails in psychiatry, social work, education, and psychology.

Past and recent studies have indicated that as many as 70 percent of the youngsters referred to child guidance clinics for whatever reason, can be shown to have mild neurologic differences which form the basic etiology of their difficulties. This leaves but a relatively small percentage whose problem behavior can be explained on a purely psychogenic basis. These facts and view points, however, are not shared by all clinical child workers. One is usually received with a deaf ear and a closed mind if an attempt is made to recall for such professionals that the environment is still only *one* of the major determinants of behavior and that *we are guilty of having given but cursory consideration to the organism which is reacting to that environment.*

What are the discernible and diagnosable features of this child with mild organic impairment, or mild brain injury, or minimal brain dysfunction?

Here is a list of the outstanding characteristics associated with this syndrome, in which only a few or many of the symptoms may appear in a given child:

1. *NORMAL OR ABOVE GENERAL INTELLIGENCE* (as determined from either the Verbal or Performance Scale of the WISC) Characteristic WISC patterns have been isolated for these children and will be discussed later. The important consideration here is that the results of intelligence evaluation clearly indicate that although achievement is variable depending upon the nature of the task, the overall level of intellectual functioning is within normal limits and that we are *not* dealing with a child who is generally mentally retarded, that is, deficient in all areas of endeavor.

2. *SPECIFIC LEARNING DEFICITS*—Child cannot read at grade or age level; a mildly stressful situation may bring forth typical dyslexic errors; spelling poor; difficulty with arithmetic; difficulty with abstractions and whole-part relationships; difficulty in mastering tasks which are dependent upon intact visual-motor-perceptual integration.

3. *PERCEPTUAL-MOTOR DEFICITS*—Printing, writing, and drawing poor; poor and erratic performance when copying geometric figures (Bender Visual Motor Gestalt test); often attempts to compensate for the latter by task-perseverance and/or innumerable and meticulous tiny strokes of the pencil; often has difficulty in reproducing geometric designs with blocks; difficulty with figure-ground and/or whole-part discrimination.

4. *GENERAL COORDINATION DEFICITS*—Child often described as awkward or clumsy; this may appear in either fine muscle performance or in overall coordination, or both.

5. *HYPERKINESIS* (or less frequently, hypokinesis)—Child appears to be in constant motion, flitting from one object or activity to another, or may be merely restless and fidgety;

4. EDUCABLE MENTALLY RETARDED

we have considered that the child's "drivenness" may manifest also as voluble, uninhibited speech, or as disorganized thinking, even in the absence of outward hyperactivity. Some children with learning and behavior symptoms and one or more "equivocal" neurological signs do not show hyperkinesis, but instead can be described as "slow as molasses," since they move, think, and talk at a very reduced rate. Frequently, this slow-responding child will have an "aphasoid" quality in his speech.

6. *IMPULSIVITY*—The child cannot keep from touching and handling objects, particularly in a strange or overstimulating environment; he frequently speaks without checking himself; he may curse, be insulting, or eagerly relate all the family secrets. His impulsivity easily leads him into conflict with the demands of conformity as established by family, school, and society. Some children may commit striking anti-social acts, to the point of fire-setting, stealing, and even murder, with only a modicum of provocation.

7. *EMOTIONAL LABILITY*—The child may be "highstrung," irritable, aggressive, or easily moved to tears; he will have quick changes of emotional behavior from high temper to easy manageability and remorse; he may be panicked by what would appear to others as a minimally stressful situation; however, some are again at the opposite end of the continuum in that they are consistently sweet-and-even tempered, cooperative, diligent, and display a very high frustration tolerance.

8. *SHORT ATTENTION SPAN AND/OR DISTRACTIBILITY*—The child is unable to concentrate on one thing for very long; he especially fades out when abstract material is being presented. Even with this symptom, some show a tendency to become locked in a simple repetitious motor activity or preoccupation with one verbal topic. Some children show fair attention span when their interest is aroused, but when not so engaged, display marked distractibility to casual stimuli.

9. *"EQUIVOCAL" OR "SOFT" NEUROLOGICAL SIGNS*—Among the most frequently seen of such signs are: transient strabismus; dysdiadochokinesis; poor coordination of fingers; mixed and/or confused laterality; speech defect, or a history of slow speech development or irregularity; and general awkwardness.

10. *BORDERLINE ABNORMAL OR ABNORMAL E.E.G.*—Although agreement in this area is not complete, the high frequency of borderline or abnormal brain wave test records reported is felt to be significant.

It is important to reemphasize that a given child may not have symptoms in all or even many of these areas since each child has his own particular cluster of symptoms. The level of his intelligence and nature of his underlying temperament determine to a great extent the form and excellence of his maneuvers to compensate for deficits or deviations.

It is probable that certain general principles underlie the above symptoms. For example, most may be due to perceptual defects having to do with the capacity to receive, hold, scan, and selectively screen out stimuli in a sequential order; to sustain a repertoire of background gestalten as compared with foreground gestalten; to perceive subtle and often abstract behavior gestalten which permit proper socialization to take place. Proprioception may be one of the perceptual areas at fault in some of these children, i.e., manifesting as a deficiency in the ability to perceive, discriminate between, and retain images or sequential body movements in space. It may be that there is a deficiency in inhibitory functions having to do with checking and suspending verbal or motor activity until the incoming sensory data are compared with stored information. When the fantastic complexity of the brain is considered, with its myriad interlocking circuits and groupings of circuits, it is not surprising that in the presence of any disordering of stimuli-monitoring, each child should manifest a unique cluster of symptoms, and that he should be handicapped in learning and in adaptive behavior if the environment is sufficiently trying relative to the magnitude of his defect.

To continue the series of silhouettes, I would like to present a brief case history of such a child which will illustrate dramatically some of the areas in which he is different. First, let us follow his attempt to read a paragraph of third grade material. The correct paragraph, on the right, is from the Gray Standardized Oral Reading Paragraphs:

One there was a little cat and a mouse. They . . . never . . . in the same house the cat did of the mouse tail. "Party passed," said the mouse, "have me my tail came." "No," said the cat, "I will not give you your tail tail you me some mike."	Once there was a cat and mouse. They lived in the same house. the cat bit off the mouse's tail. "Pray puss," said the mouse, "Give me my long tail again." "No," said the cat, "I will not give you your tail till you bring me some milk."

Retarded? Lazy? Undisciplined? No! One cannot be mentally retarded and have a Verbal I.Q. of 120! Lazy? This youngster is trying his heart out—not only to please his teacher and parents, but also he *wants* to be able to read as well as his classmates. Frustrated? *Yes!* And wouldn't you be if you were a fifth grade student like he is who could barely manage second grade reading?

Now, let us compare the intelligence evaluations on our reader, whose name is Dwight, and another boy, Wesley, of the same age, from an equivalent socio-economic background, and in the same fifth grade classroom. These are the results of the Wechsler Intelligence Scale for Children (W.I.S.C.):

	WISC PATTERNS Sub-test	Wesley	Dwight
VERBAL	Information	11	15
	Comprehension	12	18
	Arithmetic	10	5
	Similarities	11	16
	Digit Span	10	12
PERFORMANCE	Picture Completion	11	11
	Picture Arrangement	10	10
	Block Design	11	6
	Object Assembly	10	4
	Coding	12	5
	VERBAL I.Q.	105	120
	PERFORMANCE I.Q.	106	80
	FULL SCALE I.Q.	106	104

The WISC is divided into two main types of tasks—verbal and performance. It is so designed that a score of 10 would indicate "average" ability for age. Note the evenness of achievement in the various tasks by Wesley. Not so with Dwight. His achievement is "spotty" or "scattered" and he is particularly deficient in tasks requiring intact visual-motor-perceptual ability. Of particular diagnostic significance is the 40-point discrepancy between the Verbal and Performance I.Q. scores of Dwight. The Full Scale I.Q. scores, however, are both in the "normal" range.

4. EDUCABLE MENTALLY RETARDED

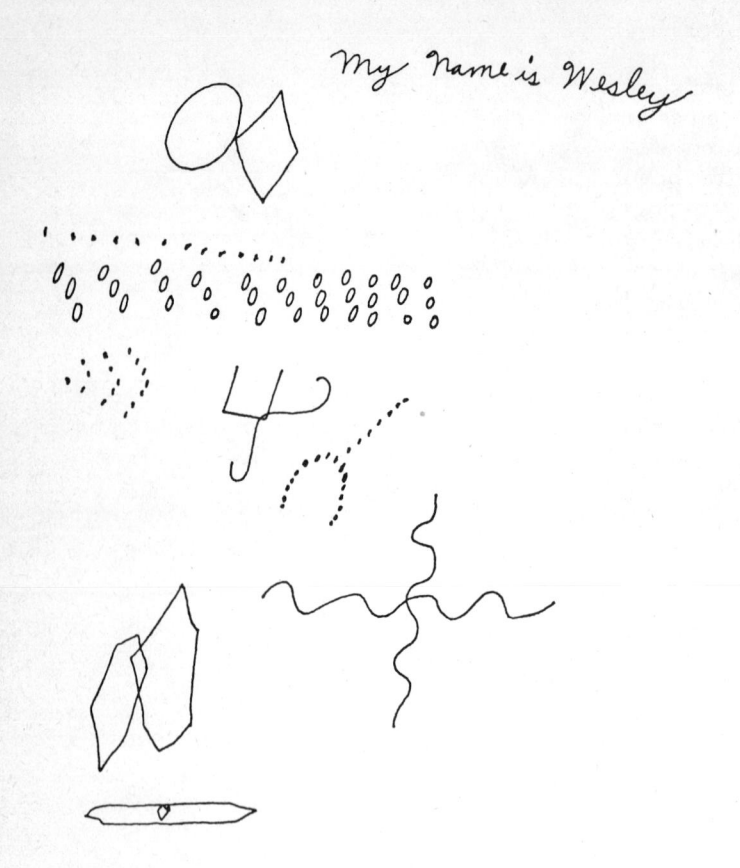

Wesley is considered a very good student, while Dwight is failing, and has since he entered school, although he has been passed year after year.

Now, let us compare their drawings of the Bender Visual Motor Gestalt figures and also a sample of handwriting and spelling. The Bender reproductions of Wesley are well executed, with smooth lines, intact figures. Note his writing at the top. The same figures reproduced by Dwight are considered typical of an "organic" Bender with poor spatial arrangement; lack of closure; "dog ears" when attempting to draw angles. Note in particular Dwight's handwriting and spelling. A typical dyslexic error is the reversal of the letters in the word "is."

The routine child guidance diagnostic workup on children referred for learning and behavior problems, divides into four main categories: 1) pediatric physical examination; 2) medical, developmental, and social history, plus a school report containing both academic and behavioral information; 3) psychological evaluation; and 4) an expanded neurological examination. Let us assume that the child has been given a recent conventional pediatric physical examination, and that gross conditions such as cerebral palsy, mental retardation, eye and ear defects, etcetera, have been ruled out. We have at our disposal an entire department of pediatrics, however, if we desire further physical workup, a careful gestation and developmental history must be obtained, first by means of specially prepared forms which are sent to parents prior to the visit to the clinic, and then elaborated through personal interview. This history must include virus illnesses during pregnancy, bleeding, premature contractions, rupture of membranes, birth weight, etcetera. Diseases and illnesses sustained by the child must be located as to age and severity. The usual interviews with parents and child must be obtained to determine specific interpersonal dynamics, particular emotional stresses and traumata. A special school report containing behavioral and academic observations by the child's teachers and principal is obtained before the child is seen in the clinic.

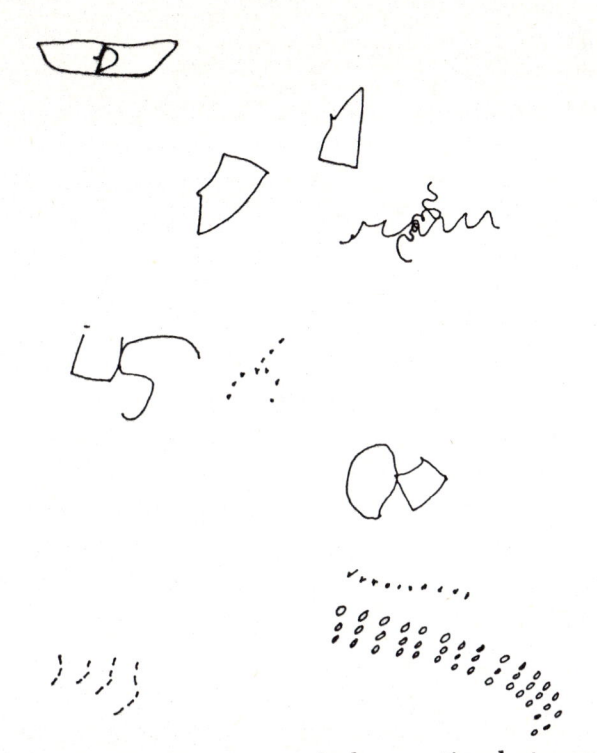

The minimal psychological test battery for any child being evaluated is the complete Wechsler Intelligence Scale for Children, the Bender Visual Motor Gestalt, and the Gray Standardized Reading Paragraphs or similar test. Personality assessment is not considered as a separate and distinct entity, since clues and indicators are constantly being produced by the child, and hence are apt to occur at any time during the workup. We do not routinely use the standard projective techniques, since we feel that in most cases straight-forward interviewing and observing during all contacts with the child yields more than adequate information. A small number of appropriate picture cards from the Michigan Picture Test may be used for some children. We depend most heavily on the WISC, the Bender, and a reading evaluation. The final test battery must await further research and applications from the field of perception.

Of great concern to us is the prevalent use of relatively unrelated tests and techniques to assess intelligence. Items such as drawings of persons or objects, Rorschach and other projective techniques, or 20-minute interviews are considered inadequate, even as screening devices, in approximately the intellectual functioning level of children, and in particular, the child with minimal brain dysfunction.

The complete Wechsler, consisting of a minimum of five Verbal subtests and five Performance subtests, should be administered

4. EDUCABLE MENTALLY RETARDED

routinely. There is no combination of three or four WISC subtests which can substitute for the entire scale, since specific deficiencies may go undetected by the omissions.

Other investigators have searched in vain for a single subtest pattern within the WISC which would be diagnostic for brain damage. Thus far, we have isolated three principal patterns. The most common is characterized by scatter in achievement in either or both the Verbal and Performance Scales (WISC Pattern I). Low scores (relative to others) most frequently occur in Arithmetic and Digit Span in the Verbal Scale; and Block Design, Object Assembly, Coding, and Mazes in the Performance Scale. Frequently with WISC Pattern I, the final Verbal and Performance I.Q. scores turn out nearly equal and the internal variation in subtest scores is ignored by the individual interpreting the results.

The second most frequent WISC pattern (WISC Pattern II) is that in which the Verbal I.Q. is 15 to 40 points higher than the Performance I.Q. If the Arithmetic subtest score is excluded, the difference is more pronounced since number concepts are based on symbols. In this instance, the child's achievement on the other Verbal tasks is sufficiently high that such a drop in Arithmetic is obscured or compensated for in the total Verbal I.Q. score. On the other hand, the child experiences great difficulty with most of the Performance Scale items, but, particularly, the pure visual-motor-perceptual tasks, which include Block Design, Object Assembly, Coding, and Mazes. The end result, however, is that the Performance I.Q. often falls into the mentally deficient range while the Verbal I.Q. is in the normal or above range. In such cases, the Full Scale I.Q. score (the one usually quoted) is virtually meaningless as an indication of over-all intelligence, since it is a composite of these two extremely variant dimensions of intellectual functioning.

The third and least frequent pattern (WISC Pattern III) is the reverse of WISC Pattern II, i.e., the Performance I.Q. is 10 to 30 points higher than the Verbal I.Q. Such a child has difficulty in expressing himself verbally. He must actively search for the words necessary to express his usually concrete solution to a "thought" problem. On the other hand, he is quite proficient at the subtests which constitute the Performance Scale. It is our experience that the child with WISC Pattern III invariably has reading disability.

Now, the claim is often made that "anxiety" will lower subtest scores. It is then indeed noteworthy that "anxiety" can be so selective, and rather suggests that the perceptual systems involved for accomplishment of that task are fragile or impaired.

The Bender Visual Motor Gestalt is used as a measure of perception and visual-motor coordination. The common errors made by children with brain injury are distorted spatial arrangements, perseveration, "dogears," rotations, incomplete closure, etcetera. The child's total approach to the task, the time he takes, as well as the final reproductions must be taken into account. The over-all "organic" Bender stands out strikingly when compared with the norms provided by Bender in her original monograph, which can serve as a frame of reference in lieu of long clinical experience with the instrument.

Gray's Oral Reading Paragraphs are used as a measure of sight reading ability because of their simplicity of administration and content. The child is usually asked to read aloud beginning with paragraph two grade levels below his present grade placement. The time of the school year should be taken into consideration when determining reading level. The number and type of errors are noted as well as smoothness, speed, approach (phonetic, or not), and comprehension of material. There are many other excellent tests available which can be used to assess reading ability.

As usually performed, the conventional neurological examination is reported as "normal" in the type of child we are considering. The physician has his mind set on clear, unequivocal signs and is not sensitive to the value of "soft" signs.

Complex integrated behavior is rarely observed or specifically tested for by a referring physician or even in the usual child guidance workup. The physician often does not synthesize in this thinking the fact that these neurological signs, general behavior, and intellectual functioning are all manifestations of the nervous system. Somewhere between the specialties of medicine and psychology, this important synthesis gets lost or neglected. A special neurological examination designed for child guidance usage is contained in detail in our article dealing with diagnosis and treatment of children of school age with minimal brain dysfunction.* It is an expansion of the work done by many people, and in particular from the pioneering work of Dr. Lehtinen and Dr. Strauss in their classical book, *The Psychopathology and Education of the Brain-Injured Child*, published in 1947.

The neurological items most often found to be present in our child guidance population have been: irregularities in gross coordination; perceptual-motor difficulties; defect in fine coordination; strabismus; dysdiadochokinesia; reading difficulties; mixed laterality; some degree of ambidexterity; and the presence of or history of speech defect. Of the behavioral manifestations, the most frequent are: short attention span; distractibility; hyperactivity; and impulsiveness.

Such a diagnostic procedure can best be done in a medical center setting or in a facility that has at its disposal the various specialists particularly trained to work with children. This type of comprehensive workup can rarely be obtained in the office of a psychiatrist or psychologist in private practice. For one thing, it is very time-consuming, but each procedure is deemed absolutely necessary—nothing can be omitted—if our desire is to help the child.

The treatment plan must include the areas of home management, educational planning, possible medication, and interpretation to and counselling of the parents.

Once the diagnosis of minimal brain dysfunction has been confirmed, the parents are given an "organic" interpretation of the learning and/or behavior problems of their child. We insist that both parents be present for this conference. The relief they feel and lessening of guilt associated with the possibility of being "bad" parents is obvious. This explanation makes parents more understanding of the child's condition and paves the way for a different set of attitudes in handling him. We attempt to answer all questions they pose concerning the past, present, and future. We assure them we will be here to help them in all future planning. We may schedule several such conferences if we feel it is necessary.

We feel that proper medication can be a most important adjunct to the treatment plan. The drugs we have found most helpful thus far in reducing hyperactivity and irritability, and in increasing attention span are captodiamine hydrochloride (SUVREN); thioridazine hydrochloride (MELLARIL), and the amphetamines, (DEXEDRINE and BENZEDRINE). Since children vary in response to various drugs and dosages, there is often the necessity of a period of experimentation with different medica-

---

*"Minimal Brain Dysfunction in the School-Aged Child, Diagnosis and Treatment" by Sam D. Clements and John E. Peters. Arch. Gen. Psychiatry, March 1962.

4. EDUCABLE MENTALLY RETARDED

tions and dosages to reach the best and most useful prescription for a given child. After the drug is regulated, the child is assigned to one of our "medication management" clinics. These children are seen at two to three month intervals for checkups and blood studies.

There has been some talk that physicians are waging "chemical warfare" against our children and adults as well. I would be the first to agree that the indiscriminate use of drugs is a dangerous and perhaps unethical practice. For this reason, medication is used only when it can be helpful, and is most carefully prescribed, supervised, and controlled.

The child's teacher is informed that he is on medication and she is asked to assess its value as it applies to the child's behavior at school.

We are most gratified by the number of children who improve markedly and immediately on a regimen of medication, special teaching, and infrequent counselling of parents. This fact is important in answering the complaint often heard that child guidance clinics bog down in a few intensive psychotherapy cases. The community stands to gain by the utilization of all methods that are successful.

The diagnosis of minimal brain dysfunction is made on the basis of clinical behavior, history, psychological evaluation, and neurological signs. The accumulated weight of various signs and symptoms or the singular specificity thereof, e.g., hyperactivity, reading disability, scatter or discrepancy between Verbal and Performance scores on the WISC, guide us in making the diagnosis. These must be evaluated against a background of environmental and interpersonal determinants. At this stage of our knowledge, it is logical to assume that any disorganization of brain function due to injury or naturally occurring constitutional deviations, places a hardship on the developing child. The accidentally or naturally occurring organic deviations exist in a scale from the gross to the subtle and to different degrees in the various functional and interlocking units within the brain. To deny this premise is to deny that the brain is the organ of the mind and that brains can have important variations from individual to individual.

These conclusions concerning minimal brain injury were influenced by the following factors:

1. Similarities between perceptual defects and symptoms of children and adults with known brain damage and children in which a history of brain damage cannot be firmly established, yet who have similar symptoms.

2. The fact that symptoms cluster together to make recognizable entities. This is especially true of the hyperkinetic syndrome and specific reading disability, but is also true of the more subtle variations that do not fit precisely into these categories.

3. Statistical studies which show a positive correlation between complications of pregnancy and the incidence of later appearing learning and behavioral symptoms. One study indicated such a correlation between the childhood virus diseases occurring under age three years and reading difficulty.

4. Studies which have shown that there is a heredity basis for some cases of dyslexis.

5. Organicity as the primary basis for the clinical entities under discussion is lent support by the high ratio of males to females for hyperkinesis, dyslexia, impulsive acts, etcetera. This could be on the basis of "normal" developmental lag in males making them more susceptible to the disorganizing effects of brain damage and stresses during the years critical for learning

symbol behavior and for acquiring self-inhibiting patterns.

6. The excellent response of these children to medication and educational planning *without benefit of psychotherapy.*

7. The ever present and oft disparaged fact that innumerable siblings reared under sufficiently equivalent conditions do not show these particular learning and behavior symptoms and that countless children reared under psychopathogenic conditions from the mildest to the most severe do not develop learning and behavior symptoms.

Much too often we have seen parents who are "good" parents and who have a child who cannot learn to read, or who is a behavior problem, or is impulsive and hyperactive, or whose speed of mentation is distinctly different from his siblings, for us to jump to the conclusion that the parents must have mishandled the child. The prevailing climate of opinion in both professional and "magazine" psychiatry is such as to create in these parents the conviction that they are somehow, by some magical, subtle aberration in their attitudes and behavior, to blame for the child's condition.

It is necessary to affirm again that psychiatry and psychology must take into account the full spectrum of causality from the unique genetic combination that each individual is, to his gestation and birth experiences, to his interaction with significant persons, and finally to the stresses and emotional traumata of later life after his basic reactions patterns have been laid down. If we cannot at present measure, say, the contribution of the child's genes to his emotional characteristics, then we must leave a large, empty space on the formula of causality until we can. It is all too easy, if one is committed by bias and habit, to detect in almost any mother or father, attitudes and behavior which can be envisioned as causing the reading difficulty, destructiveness, or difficulty in concentration on studies.

Insofar as the diagnostic procedure is concerned, we hold that all areas must be evaluated for each child referred to a child guidance clinic regardless of reason. The psychologist or psychiatrist can no more elect to omit one or more of his basic procedures than the pediatrician can fail to listen to his patient's heart or lungs. We also hold that the prevailing fashion in child psychiatry, psychology, and social work of turning a deaf ear to organic etiology unless it is grossly obvious and of being interested in and attentive only to the intrapsychic and interpersonal factors has placed such professional workers in the position of poor acceptability by the general public which we attempt to serve.

It is my feeling that we are on the threshold of a revolution in the child guidance field. At this point, our foot is just inside the door, but the ranks of feet-on-the-ground type child workers have swelled over the last 15 years, and we come well-armed. In time, this poorly constructed psychogenic obstacle course must fall by the wayside. But, rather than curse the darkness, let us busy ourselves lighting candles wherever we can.

Functional Similarities of Learning Disability and Mild Retardation

JOHN T. NEISWORTH
JOHN G. GREER

JOHN T. NEISWORTH is Associate Professor, College of Human Development, The Pennsylvania State University, University Park; and JOHN G. GREER is Assistant Professor, Department of Education and Rehabilitation, Memphis State University, Memphis, Tennessee.

Many disciplines outside special education (e.g., medicine, clinical and developmental psychology, psychometrics, and sociology) have greatly influenced the criteria and categories used to classify exceptional children. Differing disciplines, of course, have their own foundation, perspective, and focus. *Mental retardation*, especially *educable mental retardation*, is basically defined in psychometric terms, i.e., by scores on standardized psychological (intelligence) tests. *Brain injury, minimal cerebral dysfunction, neurological impairment*, and other terms often associated with learning disability obviously suggest a biomedical approach.

However, many special educators now agree that descriptions of children based on noneducational criteria do not aid the primary task of educators (Kirk, 1966; Bateman, 1967; Hewett, 1968; Neisworth, 1969; Smith, 1971; Haring & Phillips, 1972; Reynolds, 1972; Wallace & Kauffman, 1973). It would seem more productive for educators to describe children in terms of manifest performance liabilities crucial to educational achievement.

Describing Problems: A Conceptual Distinction

Stuart (1970), in discussing the efficacy of psychotherapy, has employed the terms *genotypic* and *phenotypic* to differentiate two ways of describing problems and their resulting implications for intervention. Use of these terms within the context of mental retardation and learning disability may also be useful in discussing separate versus overlapping classifications of mental retardation and learning disability.

The genotypic approach attempts to explain problems by reference to theoretical and general circumstances and describes what a person *is*: A child is retarded, disturbed, or learning disabled. Such an approach views the individual concerned as being affected by a condition which predisposes him to behave in certain ways. A child is slow in social, academic, and motor skills due to a condition of mental retardation, or he exhibits disordered behavior because of an emotionally disturbed state. Performance or behavioral diagnoses are viewed as merely symptomatic of the general condition.

In contrast to the genotypic approach, a phenotypic analysis deals with the surface dimensions of behavior, with focus on what a person *does*. Little, if any, reference is made to presumed condition and such distinctions are avoided. Problems are described in terms of objectively assessed behavior. For example, specific educational problems, defined in terms of measurable competencies, are considered to be sufficient bases for the development and selection of effective remedial programs.

A Tentative Schema

A tentative schema is presented to depict several dimensions which illustrate suggested relationships between learning disability and mental retardation (see Figure 1).

Genotypic Dimension

The genotypic dimension (right to left) displays the presumed independent conditions of organically based mental retardation, mild mental retardation, and learning disability (minimal brain dysfunction and brain injury). Organically based mental retardation is differentiated from mild or educable mental retardation on the basis that gross biological or genetic disorders are present in organic retardation but are generally absent or minimal in mild retardation. The research literature fails to identify any definitive basis for most cases of mild retardation except for polygenetic, environmental, cultural-familial, or other nebulous sources.

Learning disability is shown as comprising two subgroups: minimal brain dysfunction and brain injury. The distinction between these classifications rests on the medically authenticated evidence of abnormal structure or function in brain injured persons as opposed to the inference of such in the minimal brain dysfunction group.

Turning now to the contrasts between mild mental retardation and learning disability, the presumed differences in underlying conditions are far less clear. This distinction is difficult due to the varied and hypothetical, rather than factual, nature of explanations for mild mental retardation and minimal brain dysfunction. Nevertheless, mild mental retardation and learning disability are shown as separate and independent entries along the genotypic dimension to satisfy existing definitions and groupings based on presumptions of differences in underlying (genotypic) conditions.

Phenotypic Dimension

There is no necessary correspondence between condition and measurable (phenotypic) behavior. That is, diverse causes or conditions can produce the same or similar problems in functioning. Similar problems in task persistence, for example, may be attributable to various basic causes. Additionally, the same underlying problem may result in a variety of observable problems. In this case, children may be said to be suffering from the same condition, e.g. cerebral palsy, even though their performance problems may be quite different. Even if an underlying condition has been documented, there is no invariant expression of it.

Focusing more closely on mental retardation and learning disability, there has been no convincing evidence that mild or educable mental retardation is associated with organic dysfunction (APA, 1970). Likewise, research on relationships between brain injury or dysfunction and learning disability is characterized by inconclusive and contradictory findings (see Grossman, 1966). Too often, when an inference of brain injury cannot be authenticated, it is then called *minimal cerebral dysfunction*. This insistence of organic disorder on the basis of the inference that it must be present reflects the assumption of a necessary, one to one correspondence between condition and outcome. Further, psychological tests cannot logically prove underlying problems since such tests are only samples of observable performance.

With the present state of knowledge, it would seem most productive to concur with Grossman (1966), who stated, "Actually, there is no syndrome, no aggregate of neurological signs, that can be correlated with any specific learning and/or behavior disorder" (p. 623). The "Strauss Syndrome," coined by Stevens and Birch (1960), provides an early example of the attempt to describe observable problems without necessitating reference to a real or assumed basic cause.

In general, such genotypic terms as *altered learning processes, decreased potential, minimal cerebral dysfunction, generalized incapacity to learn,* and myriad similar terms are descriptions of conditions or dispositions of children. They are attempted diagnoses of what a child is or is not as opposed to what a child does or does not do. At the phenotypic level, however, are descriptions or assessments of competencies, such as problems in auditory, visual, or tactile discrimination, reversals in reading, short term recall deficits, motor awkwardness, hyperactivity, distractibility and other behaviors that define the psychoeducational repertoires of children.

The overlap depicted in Figure 1 (shaded area) suggests significant phenotypic similarity between educable retardation and learning disability. That is, regardless of real or hypothesized differences in underlying conditions, the overlap portrays an array of performance problems shared by both groups. The degree and nature of such overlap depends, in part, upon the measures employed to describe performance. Intelligence tests are placed at a point along the phenotypic dimension to indicate minimal correspondence between educable retarded and learning disabled groups. This is in accord with existing definitions which differentiate between the educable retarded and learning disabled on the basis of general intellectual performance. In contrast, the assessment of specific learning problems within both groups yields considerably greater correspondence.

It is important to note the increasing area of overlap as a function of decreasing severity of mental retardation and learning disability. One can thus speculate that the two groups increase in phenotypic similarity, i.e., in their psychoeducational profiles, as they approach normality.

Remedial Dimension

A decade ago, Lindsley (1964) discussed the fallacy of *similia similibus curantur,* "like is cured by like." This means that the treatment mode must be related to the cause of a problem. This supposition apparently persists in some areas of psychotherapy and special education, although it is no longer accepted in medicine (Lindsley, 1964). For example, even if documented organic injury were highly correlated with specific behavior disorders, the treatment of choice would not necessarily be organic in nature (see Barrett, 1962; Lindsley, 1962).

If the "like cures like" dictum is cast aside, there would appear to be no need for proponents of medical treatment, such as neurologists or educators of a neurological bent, to insist that the original cause or condition must also be organic to warrant medical intervention. For example, drugs are employed to minimize distractibility even though the cause may be environmental. Likewise, champions of environmental intervention need not argue for environmental origins of problems treated environmentally. It would be advisable for special educators to view psychoeducational behavior as important in its own right and to employ strategies, whatever their theoretical origin, that have empirical support for their efficacy.

Figure 1 also displays increasing overlap of observable educational problems and their responsiveness to instructional strategies. It is suggested that a continuum of tactics of expanding generalizability exists, ranging from relatively disability-specific procedures to more comprehensive treatments. Considering the expanding variety of successful applications of behavior modification, it is located at a point on this continuum to indicate its general utility.

Stevens (1962), Quay (1968), and Iscoe and Payne (1972) have suggested frameworks for conceptualizing instructional organization around phenotypic rather than genotypic dimensions. These frameworks have several characteristics in common:

1. Language systems are based on a common foundation, education, as opposed to terminology coming from various non- or paraeducational perspectives.
2. Labels for children based on cause or condition are avoided.
3. Categories are based on educational variables that facilitate pinpointing of educational objectives and that suggest guidelines for feasible educational grouping and intervention.

When educational objectives are pinpointed and derived from specific skills assessment, considerable overlap between educable retardation and learning disability problems can exist. As illustrations, both groups display problems in distractibility, auditory and visual discrimination, motivation, and retention. The study of learning disabilities seems to lead in the movement to pinpoint deficits more closely. For example, *visual discrimination deficit* provides guidelines and specification to instructional intervention, unlike terms such as *mental retardation* or *neurophrenia*. The term *visual* zeroes in on the sensory mode, while *discrimination* focuses on a specific competency deficit.

Concluding Comments

An instructional paradigm focuses not only on specification of educational deficits but also on specification and management of instructional tactics. At a global level, instructional techniques may bear quite different names, depending on their theoretical basis. However, all instructional techniques are manipulations of stimulus input and consequences. That is, instructional recommendations phrased in varying terminology overlap considerably when analyzed. Input variables within the control of the teacher include manipulation of stimulus organization, intensity, duration, sequence, rate, and frequency of presentation. Management of response consequences involves provision of appropriate contingencies and schedules of reinforcement. When children have difficulty in discriminating a *b* from a *d* (the same phenotypic problem), the same or highly similar instructional strategies are indicated.

Thus, finer and finer analyses of the learning difficulties of "the retarded" and "the learning disabled" will yield a clearer picture of the actual overlap of these two groups and bring educators closer together in refining and sharing their techniques. In essence, this article reiterates Bateman's (1967) conviction:

> One who believes in the learning disabilities approach to teaching quickly finds that it applies to all children everywhere. Thus we have not really been talking about mentally retarded children [or about the learning disabled] but about a scientific pedagogy for all children. (p. 302)

References

American Psychological Association. Psychology and mental retardation. *American Psychologist,* 1970, *25,* 267-268.

Bateman, B. Implications of a learning disability approach for teaching educable retardates. *Mental Retardation,* 1967, *5,* 23-25.

Barrett, B. A. Reduction in rate of multiple tics by free operant conditioning methods. *Journal of Neurosis and Mental Retardation,* 1962, *135,* 187-195.

Grossman, H. J. The child, the teacher and the physician. In W. M. Cruichshank (Ed.), *The teacher of brain-injured children.* Syracuse: Syracuse University Press, 1966.

Haring, N. G., & Phillips, E. L. *Analysis and modification of classroom behavior.* Englewood Cliffs NJ: Prentice-Hall, 1972.

Hewett, F. M. *The emotionally disturbed child in the classroom.* Boston: Allyn & Bacon, 1968.

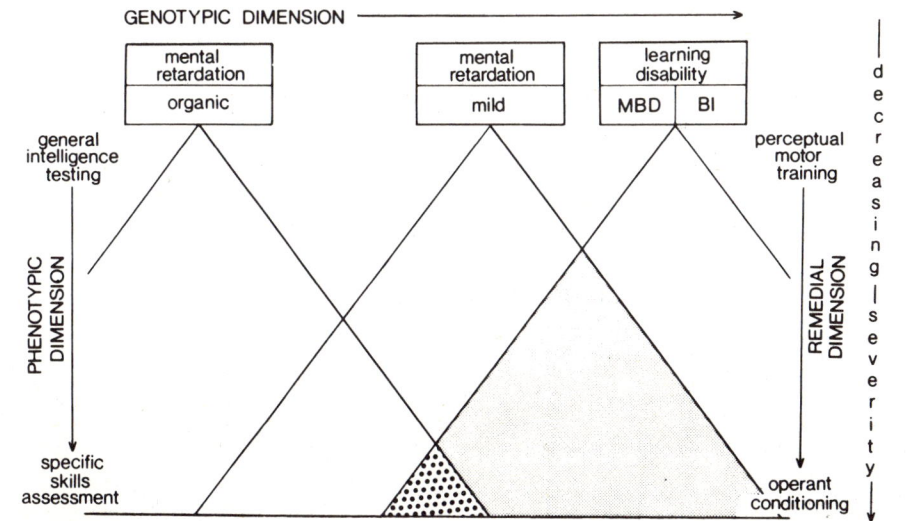

FIGURE 1. A tentative schema of relationships between learning disability and mental retardation.

These, Too, Must Be Equal

America's Needs in Habitation and Employment of the Mentally Retarded

The President's Committee on Mental Retardation
The President's Committee on Employment of the Handicapped

America's Needs in Habitation and Employment of the Mentally Retarded. ©The President's Committee on Mental Retardation and the President's Committee on Employment of the Handicapped.

28. Habilitation and Employment

vocational objectives for their retarded children. To do this, it is necessary to inform not only parents, but also persons to whom parents might turn for counsel (physicians, teachers, vocational rehabilitation counselors, ministers, psychologists, others). These professions should be provided with material dealing with training and employment of the mentally retarded, with the stress placed on the innate value of all work, skilled or unskilled.

The American Association on Mental Deficiency, the American Personnel and Guidance Association, the National Rehabilitation Association, the National Education Association, and the American Psychological Association are among the many professional organizations whose assistance would be essential to carry out this type of program.

3 The Handicapped Children's Early Education Assistance Act (Public Law 90-538) calls for model programs to develop new ways of assisting preschool handicapped children, including the mentally retarded. Preschool years are most critical for the retarded. Therefore, local planning is needed now, to build effective model programs under this Act.

The Approach

This report does not take the easy way of merely asking for new laws, new money, new government involvement.

There already are many laws on the books that can serve the vocational needs of the retarded. These must be implemented. The retarded must be kept in mind in their implementation.

The answer to the vocational needs of the retarded—if there is a single answer—lies in everybody's involvement.

This report, then, stresses the roll of *all* the citizens of America in meeting the employment problems of the mentally retarded.

Building A Highway

Properly preparing the mentally retarded for the world of work is like building a highway. Each mile of the way leads us closer to our goal. On the way we pass these guideposts:

Early preparation

Education and training

Medical habilitation

Employment

Independent or sheltered living

Vital to the entire journey, public promotion and education, to build acceptance of the retarded.

What follows is a discussion of each guidepost with some proposals for future action.

Early Preparation

What does it take to hold a job in the world of work? Ability to perform certain tasks, yes; but far more. It takes certain attitudes: appreciation of, and respect for, a job; willingness to accept responsibility (even if it is for mopping floors or loading trucks); ability to get along with others; capacity to manage the details of life (getting places, being on time, handling money, etc.).

Also, parents of the retarded must impart to them a concept of dignity of all work, regardless of its nature, as well as a sense of dignity of self.

Too often, positive attitudes and work habits are not taught early enough to the retarded. They usually are added as afterthoughts to a curriculum. Rather, they should weave their way through the education of the retarded, from his earliest days onward.

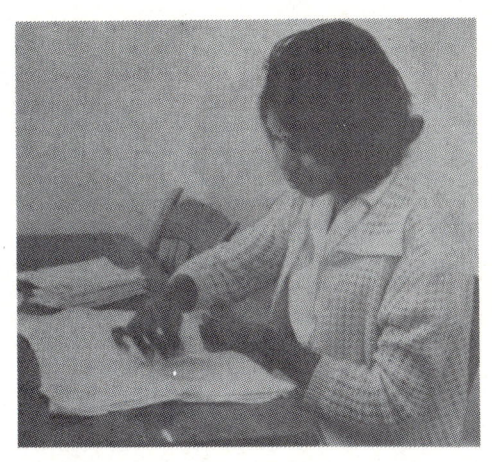

Proposals for Action

1 President Nixon recently called for national action to serve the needs of young people in America up to age 6. Such a national program should include in its charge a specific plan of action for the mentally retarded.

As a beginning in this direction,

A "Head Start," a child development program, should contain specific provisions for the enrichment of mentally retarded children; only through specific provisions can the retarded be assured of equal consideration.

B All "Model Cities" programs should include provision of services for the mentally retarded, to assure earliest possible development of their potential.

2 Parents should be encouraged to accept realistic

Education and Training

Realism must be the key to the education and training of the mentally retarded. The retarded are going to have to enter a real world not truly made for them; get a real job that may be alien to their concepts of work; face up to real social and interpersonal situations that may not always be pleasant; handle real personal problems (money, transportation, living quarters, the like) that for us might be routine but for them are crisis-sized.

Early in life, education and training must prepare them for the world of useful work. And it must prepare them for the world of useful living outside of work.

The education and training resources in the United States are vast, mighty, and innovative. But they have not fully been brought to bear in the lives of the mentally retarded.

Proposals for Action

4 A set of curriculum guidelines should be prepared for every level of education of the mentally retarded, from earliest years onward. Guidelines should include stress on vocational and social preparation for work and for life.

Individual communities could develop their own curricula, based on these guides, to meet local employment conditions.

Preparation of the community guides should be a joint responsibility of private organizations concerned with the retarded, vocational rehabilitation, public employment service and education.

5 More materials on vocational and job-related subjects should be simply written for the mentally retarded themselves. Teachers' guides also should be prepared so that these booklets can be introduced into special education classrooms.

The booklets might contain realistic material dealing with work attitudes, job habits, problems of daily living, etc.

6 New concepts of vocational education that bring students out of the classroom into work-a-day situations should be encouraged. This can come about by increased use of voluntary

3. MENTAL RETARDATION

organizations in arranging of out-of-classroom instruction.

7 There is a need for many more work experience centers with living facilities. The Social and Rehabilitation Service should give special emphasis to the development of such facilities.

8 The "Job Opportunities in the Business Sector" program of the National Alliance of Businessmen should be broadened somewhat to state specifically that mentally retarded applicants are to be included. Also, special realistic entrance requirements should be established for the mentally retarded.

At present, many unidentified retarded persons undoubtedly are entering the JOBS program. With proper identification and proper consideration, many more might benefit from this program.

9 Centralized contract procurement systems should be encouraged fro sheltered workshops, either within individual communities or within regional areas. Centralized contracting can funnel contracts to workshops best equipped to handle them, and can properly assign contracts too large for any single workshop.

10 Many sheltered workshops for the retarded face problems of operations, productivity, safety, and management. There should be strong cooperative efforts among these workshops themselves to meet their common problems and to work together to solve them.

Standards for workshop operations are essential and should be considered in all phases of planning.[1]

11 Vocational education should play a far more meaningful role in meeting the educational and employment needs of the mentally retarded.

A report by the Office of Education shows that 10 percent of America's school population needs special education services. Yet less than 1 percent of vocational education funds have been used in behalf of those with special needs.

Vocational education should be a right to which every American student is entitled, retarded or not retarded, so long as he may reasonably benefit. Funds are needed to extend this right to all. The vocational education amendments of 1968 opened the door to extensive, quality vocational education for the handicapped and the retarded— but full and immediate implementation is necessary, otherwise the amendments are but empty promises.

Meaningful cooperative agreements must be developed among vocational education, vocational rehabilitation, the public employment service, and special education.

12 At least 600 new sheltered workshops that include the mentally retarded are needed today, according to state facility plans. These should be located not only in nonprofit workshop facilities as we know them today, but also within private industrial plants.

13 Special attention must be given to the needs of the mentally retarded in rural communities. Special attention should be given the mentally retarded in families of migrant workers and American Indians. They are often found living in sparsely settled areas. It may be necessary to bring retarded persons quite some distance from home for services. No matter where they are sent, their rural backgrounds and interests should be considered.

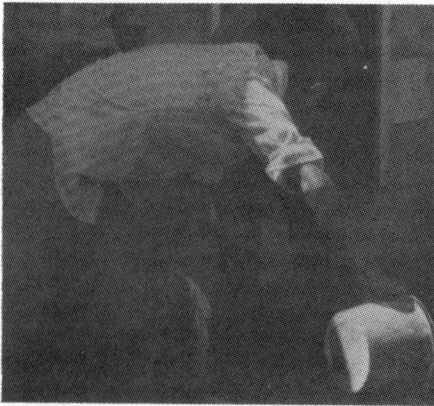

County agents should be given material to acquaint them with mental retardation, so they can advise families of the retarded about sources of assistance.

14 More professional and supportive manpower is needed in the entire field of education and training of the mentally retarded, so that greater numbers of retarded persons can be made ready for employment. Careers in retardation should be promoted in all ways possible, including subsidies for needy students.

The Medical Profession

It is not enough to consider only the vocational rehabilitation needs of the mentally retarded. For them to reach their highest aspirations and lead the fullest lives possible, their medical rehabilitation needs must be met as well.

Yet America has largely overlooked these needs.

There are some 79 medical schools in the United States with grants ranging from $30,000 to $100,000 a year for training in rehabilitation medicine. However, there is but little opportunity for medical trainees to be exposed to concepts of medical rehabilitation of the mentally retarded.

Medical rehabilitation of the retarded must keep pace with advances in other fields. Otherwise the retarded can never hope to share fully in their America.

Proposals for Action

15 Rehabilitation Services Administration must make strong efforts to encourage medical schools

28. Habilitation and Employment

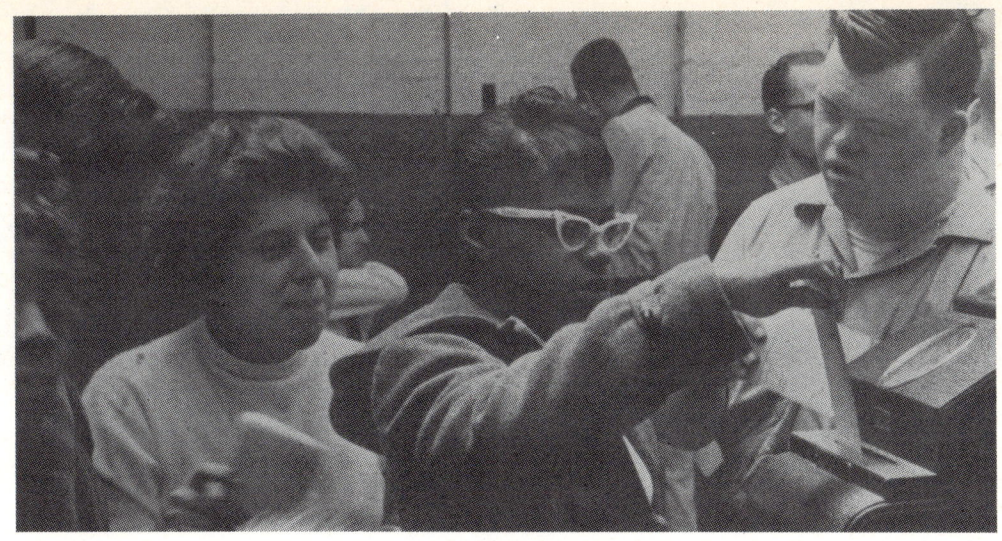

after work will be as full and meaningful as their lives during work.

A recent study by John Hopkins University, sponsored by the President's Committee on Mental Retardation, covered the economic side of preparing the retarded for work. Although the benefits and costs varied widely, many situations were found showing that the benefits greatly exceeded the costs. We know, for example, that when a retarded person is unable to work, he will, in many cases, eventually be institutionalized. Institutional care costs taxpayers about $40,000 per bed in construction costs and the yearly maintenance of the retarded may range from $2,000 to $10,000. In contrast, even at the minimum wage of $1.60 an hour, a retarded person will earn over $3,000 per year and instead of becoming a burden to taxpayers, he will actually lessen their tax burden since about $600 of his earnings will be paid to the community in the form of state and local taxes. The total cost of providing vocational training to the retarded so that they might become employable will probably range between $1,000 and $9,000 in the great majority of cases. It appears that the average cost to taxpayers of preparing the retarded for employment will be about the cost that they would incur for the provision of only 1 year of institutional care for the retarded. (A copy of this study may be obtained from The Johns Hopkins University Press, Charles & 34th Sts., Baltimore, Md. 21218.)

Proposals for Action

29 Living facilities for the mentally retarded should be established in the vicinities where they work. These facilities can include hotels, group homes, halfway houses, cooperative apartments, community homes or farms.

30 Independent living facilities in institutions should be encouraged when possible. These facilities go hand-in-hand with the development of sheltered workshops on the premises.

31 There are some retarded persons for whom competitive employment is not feasible; yet they are fully able to perform in sheltered workshops. Everything possible should be done to encourage more workshops to serve their needs—including financial assistance when necessary.

For example, up to $1,500 per year should be provided for each retarded person in such workshops operated by nonprofit organizations.

Also, retarded workers in these workshops should be subsidized, if need be, to make it possible for them to remain in the community and at work. Workshop employment for the retarded has two advantages: it is more economical than institutionalization, and it is better for the retarded than institutionalization, and it is better for the retarded than institutional life.

32 Retarded persons in institutions, with employment potential as determined by rehabilitation counselors assigned there, should be given every possible service to "graduate" them into jobs and independent living in the community. They should be referred to a vocational rehabilitation counselor no later than their 18th birthday.

33 All living facilities for the mentally retarded should provide for full recreational, medical, vocational, and social needs. Facilities never should be mere living shells; they should offer total living environments.

Promotion and Education

It is not enough to stop short with the preparation of the mentally retarded for employment. America must be told, and told again, of their abilities. We must constantly emphasize their capacity to work, their assets, what they can do rather than what they cannot do.

There can be no end to mass promotion and education. America's memory is short. Unless we repeat ourselves constantly, she is likely to forget.

Proposals for Action

34 The President's Committee on Employment of the Handicapped, the President's Committee on Mental Retardation and the National Association for Retarded Children, the Manpower Administration of the Department of Labor and the Social and Rehabilitation Service of the Department of Health, Education, and Welfare, should continue to work closely to promote jobs for the retarded. It is realized that all three organizations also have other programs to promote, but employment of the retarded should retain a position of high priority.

35 Labor unions should be encouraged to exampt low echelon jobs from ususal "career-ladders," so that the mentally retarded might fill them—without having to face upward steps to jobs beyond their capabilities.

36 State and local governments should be encouraged to establish special hiring procedures for the mentally retarded similar to those of the federal government. Only a dozen states have such procedures at present.

37 An information center should be established to gather data on training and employment of the retarded and to serve as a national focal point for its dissemination. This could be a joint venture of the President's Committees on Mental Retardation and on Employment of the Handicapped.

38 Promotional efforts should be directed to top management to encourage written policy statements favoring jobs for the retarded; to middle-management to encourage implementation of these policies; to rank-and-file workers to gain their acceptance of the retarded as fellow workers.

39 There should be more employer conferences on utilization of lesser-skilled manpower in the labor force, with special reference to the retarded.

Prototype for such conferences might be one held recently by New York University and the President's Committee on Employment of the Handicapped, attended by some 200 leading employers in New York City.

SPECIAL EDUCATION SERVICES FOR THE "MILDLY HANDICAPPED": BEYOND A DIAGNOSTIC AND REMEDIAL MODEL

Phyllis L. Newcomer, Ed.D.
Beaver College, Glenside, Pa.

This paper takes the position that the use of a diagnostic–remedial model to provide special education services to the "mildly handicapped" is often inappropriate. The inadequacies inherent in the diagnostic–remedial approach are presented from both philosophical and operational perspectives. At a philosophical level, the fallacious assumptions associated with the model are presented. Operational ramifications of these assumptions (e.g., the techniques and functions of assessment) are critiqued. The thrust of the argument is that special education must expand its role along the lines of an interactive model. In this vein, the teacher consultant role is suggested as a viable alternative to diagnostic–remedial services.

The rapid growth of special education within the last 15 years has produced programs for large numbers of children who have often been referred to as "mildly handicapped," a label which, for the most part, is a gross misnomer. In many cases, children so labeled lack obvious indications of any handicap, since they appear reasonably intact sensorily, perceptually, emotionally, and cognitively. In a descriptive study of children receiving special education services in resource rooms, Elkins and Kirk (1974) concluded that the common problems which the "mildly handicapped" share are usually their nonachievement in academic subjects, particularly reading, and their tendency to engage in disruptive behaviors. In many cases, it is their characteristic nonconformity or disinclination to respond to group instruction as most of their peers do which causes educators to use such terms as "slow," "immature," "poorly motivated," among other more graphic labels to describe them and designate them as deviant. Notably, such children are usually considered increasingly deviant the longer they are in school. And with each passing year, their ranks swell: Some educators estimate that as many as 30% of their school population display learning and behavioral problems severe enough to warrant special education intervention.

An essential but often overlooked point regarding these children is that the learning difficulties which most of them exhibit are intricately related to the caliber of their educational experiences. Variables over which they have little control, such as the competence of their teachers and their compatability with their classmates, act to shape their attitudes toward themselves as learners and toward school in general.

Moreover, many of their "deviant" behaviors reflect nothing more than the wide range of difference embodied in the concept of normalcy. In other words, some variability in children's behavior is typical rather than atypical; it is only considered deviant because of educators' relatively unrealistic and inflexible expectations. In any event, it has become customary for regular educators to largely ignore the school-related conditions which contribute to children's learning problems and to attend primarily to the child's deficiencies. In so doing, they tacitly accept some or all of the following assumptions: (a) that children who have learning problems are disabled or disordered in some manner and therefore are different from "normal" children; (b) that these deficiencies or deficits are discrete conditions which exist within the child, much as physical disease does; (c) that, after the manner of physical medicine, it is important to isolate the etiology or underlying nature of the problem and to categorize children for the purpose of applying appropriate remediation; (d) that the diagnostic devices currently available are capable of delineating the causes of learning problems and providing information useful for remedial instruction; and (e) that since the child's learning problem is a discrete condition, it can be diagnosed, prescribed for, and remediated in relative isolation with minimal involvement on the part of regular educators.

Partially owing to their conceptualization of deviance, regular educators have generally looked to special educators for convenient solutions to the problem of educating the nonachieving, nonconforming child and have made only token commitments to participate or cooperate in programs designed for this purpose. Special educators have generally responded by accepting the premise that such children are deviant or defective in some way. They demonstrate this by routinely conducting elaborate diagnostic workups which culminate in assignment to a particular disability group (e.g., educable mentally retarded, emotionally disturbed, learning disabled, etc.) and inclusion in either self-contained special education classes or resource programs. This approach to the children not only confirms the regular educator's conceptualization of deviance but largely absolves him of responsibility for the child. The self-contained classes are often totally segregated from regular education programs. Resource programs maintain the child's placement in the regular class, but all too frequently operate concurrently rather than coordinately with the regular program. There is often little relationship between the special educator's instructional strategies and the instructional activities which occur within the regular class, despite the fact that common sense dictates the necessity of interrelated programs when a child's principal problem is with academic achievement.

Presumably the popularity of diagnosing children, assigning them to segregated placements, and/or providing relatively isolated remedial programs reflects the special educator's belief that services of this type are necessary and sufficient to help most children overcome learning problems. The validity of this assumption does not depend upon the appropriateness of these activities per se, since they are obviously useful in many instances, particularly with seriously handicapped children. The key issue is the applicability of these procedures with significant numbers, perhaps even the majority, of children currently involved in special education programs. I take the position that many of the customary, isolated diagnostic and remedial activities may not constitute the most efficient or expedient approach to children in public school special education programs. The predominant use of these techniques may reduce the effectiveness of special education intervention.

In the first place, since many special education students characteristically differ little from their peers, there is no reason to assume that they have internal deficits which prevent learning. Consequently, efforts to discover the etiology which underlies their learning deficits are largely superfluous.

Second, while some of the diagnostic instruments used with special education students are useful to understand children's learning problems and to prescribe instructional activities, many are not. They are simply not related closely enough to academic competencies to be used as designators of specific teaching

4. EDUCABLE MENTALLY RETARDED

activities for nonachievers. The attempts of various diagnosticians to base educational prescriptions on the rather esoteric results of many of these tests has generally done little more than confuse teachers and unfortunately widen the gulf between special and regular educators.

Third, the focus on learning problems as child-centered disorders ignores or at least de-emphasizes the fact that learning is an interactive phenomenon and that failure to learn is often intricately associated with breakdowns in a child's relationship with teachers and peers. More specifically, it may not be sufficient to diagnose and remediate children's academic difficulties in settings removed from the regular classroom if the problems interfering with learning relate primarily to the experiences the child has within the regular classroom. Resolution of these problems cannot take place unless the special educator becomes involved in the regular classroom activities.

I am suggesting that in order to help many children currently involved in special education programs, special educators must expand their role beyond the diagnosis and treatment of children in relative isolation to include activities aimed at altering the general educational environment. They must function to a much greater extent as teacher consultants. I shall attempt to support this position by briefly discussing the limitations of diagnostic–remedial services and by presenting some advantages of the teacher consultant model.

DIAGNOSTIC–REMEDIAL SERVICES

A typical diagnostic test battery administered to children referred for special education programs includes both informal assessment devices and an impressive number of standardized psychoeducational tests. These include measures of intelligence, e.g., the Wechsler Intelligence Scale for Children (Wechsler, 1949), visual perception, e.g., the Frostig Developmental Test of Perception (Frostig, Lefever, & Willesey, 1964), auditory perception, e.g., the Wepman Test of Auditory Discrimination (Wepman, 1958), psycholinguistic ability, e.g., the Illinois Test of Psycholoinguistic Abilities (Kirk, McCarthy, & Kirk, 1968), language development, e.g., the Northwest Syntax Screening Test (Lee, 1969), school achievement skills, e.g., the Wide Range Achievement Test (Jastak, Bijou, & Jastak, 1946), and personality development, e.g., the California Test of Personality (Thorpe, Clark, & Tiegs, 1953).

The objectives of these assessment activities include: (a) identifying the etiology of learning handicaps, often for the purpose of classification; (b) gleaning diagnostic information about children's underlying learning styles and psychological processes; and (c) diagnosing academic content needs for instructional purposes. The rationale underlying all three of these objectives is that the accrued information will enable educators to provide an optimal educational program for each child. Therefore, the extent to which each fulfilled objective improves school experiences for the so-called "mildly handicapped" children determines the value of many of the assessment activities used with that particular population.

Assessment of etiology

Using assessment tools to determine the etiology of learning problems often involves the assumption that poor test performances are generally caused by specific pathological conditions. For example, perceptual–motor deficits as measured by such tests as the Frostig DTVP may be attributed to central nervous system dysfunction; low scores on such tests as the California Test of Personality may be interpreted as reflecting emotional disturbance; and a low intelligence quotient (IQ) is usually seen as indicative of mental retardation. Although this type of test interpretation might be valid when it substantiates more obvious indices of pathology in severely handicapped children, it is often fallacious when applied to most nonachieving children. The causes of academic failure are complex and usually cannot be isolated with available standardized tests. For one thing, the abilities which they measure represent but a very narrow portion of the broad spectrum of possible variables which contribute to the problem. Additionally, most of the available tests simply lack the reliability and validity to be used as the primary indices of etiology. As with academic failure, there are multiple causes for poor performances on standardized tests. Even the most reliable and valid of measures, the intelligence test, lacks the predictive power to be used confidently as the sole index of mental retardation.

Consequently, using test results to assign most nonachieving children to disability categories based on common etiology is often unwarranted. In effect, the test data are often interpreted in an arbitrary manner simply to justify particular special education placements. The inappropriateness of this sort of labeling and classification can be confirmed by its impermanence. Children classified as mental retardates often have ceased to be retarded upon leaving school (Farber, 1963). Others labeled emotionally disturbed were not so identifiable 2 years after their initial diagnosis, despite the fact that they received no treatment (Glavin, Quay, & Werry, 1971). Children designated learning disabled because they appear divergent when compared to their peers may be considered normal when they are grouped with similar nonachieving children (McCarthy, 1974). The adverse effects of disability labeling of this type have been thoroughly discussed by Dunn (1968), Christopolos and Renz (1969), and Iano (1972), among others. Several of these authors have also explored the fact that the categorical self-contained special education classes frequently created for these labeled children have also proven to be educationally ineffective. If in fact assessment does not actually uncover the etiology of learning problems, but simply results in labeling and categorization, these procedures seem to be a waste of time and money when used with nonachieving children.

Assessment of learning processes

The second objective of assessment is to diagnose individual patterns of specific strengths and deficits in the processes which underly learning, i.e., learning style, cognitive functioning, psycholinguistic abilities, perceptual development, etc. The rationale behind this type of assessment is that deficits in these areas are responsible for academic failure. Therefore, remedial teaching should be designed to improve a child's specific deficits, while classroom instruction should take advantage of his underlying strengths. For example, a child with a reading problem who performs poorly on common tests of visual perception and fine motor coordination such as the DTVP, as well as visual–motor subtests from the ITPA and the WISC, but is adequate on auditory subtests, might be diagnosed as requiring remedial training in visual–perceptual skills and be recommended for an aural-based phonics program in reading. Presumably, remediation of his visual–perceptual processes will eventually increase his capacity to learn academic materials.

There are certain difficulties inherent in the generalized use of this approach towards assessment with nonachieving children. The most important problem lies in developing measures of the processes which relate significantly with academic achievement. Although a particular psychological process such as visual perception may appear logically related to the development of certain academic competencies, the very act of reducing a global construct such as visual perception to a specific test task may alter its meaning to the point where the logical relationship no longer applies. For example, the ability to complete the tasks which comprise the DTVP constitutes at best a small segment of the complex process which, for the sake of linguistic convenience, is labeled "visual perception." The relationship of these specific tasks to academic achievement is by no means assured. Thus, not only is it risky to make generalizations which equate poor scores on the DTVP subtest with a global deficit in "visual perception" (since the child may do well on other types of visual perceptual tasks), but there is no reason to assume that a child who fails these particular tasks will also fail academic tasks. In other words, children who do

4. EDUCABLE MENTALLY RETARDED

poorly on tests of psychological processes may have no difficulty learning to read or write. In addition, the fact that a nonachieving child may fail tests of this nature does not imply that process deficits are responsible for his poor achievement. Consequently, there is no reason to assume that diagnosis and remediation of underlying mentalistic processes will improve a child's ability to do academic work.

In fact, reviews of the literature relating several of the most popular tests of psychological processes to academic achievement have generally reported discouraging results. For example, Sedlak and Weener (1972) and Newcomer and Hammill (1975) found inconsistent and practically insignificant predictive relationships between ITPA subtests and academic achievement. Wiederholt (1971) reported no evidence of a significant relationship between the DTVP and academic functioning. Hammill and Larsen (1974) found similar conclusions from their investigations of auditory perception. In short, the inability to establish the educational relevance of these tests — i.e., a consistent relationship between the abilities they measure and school achievement — suggests that the entire elaborate procedure involved in their administration to most children with academic problems may be inappropriate. It further suggests that remedial programs based on these tests may be largely useless, a statement essentially substantiated by reviews of the efficacy of certain popular training programs, such as those for the ITPA (Hammill & Larsen, 1974) and Frostig (Widerholt & Hammill, 1971) tests.

Another issue related to the use of these tests is incidental to the main question of their worth but warrants mention. Much of the language and terminology associated with tests of psychological constructs ("psycholinguistics," "perceptual deficits," "cognitive dysfunction," etc.) is esoteric and difficult for regular educators to understand. Not only does professional jargon of this type serve to reduce communication between the special educator and the regular classroom teacher, but it may also increase the use of other types of inappropriate disability labels, e.g., perceptually deficient, poor auditory learner, etc., among educators.

Assessment of academic content

The third purpose of assessment is to diagnose academic deficits and develop specific criteria for instruction. Logically, this purpose is best served by assessment instruments which relate specifically to academic competencies. These include such standardized diagnostic tests as the Durrell Analysis of Reading Difficulty or the Monroe Reading Aptitude Test. Even more useful than standardized instruments, however, are informal criterion-referenced devices which are particularly valuable in pinpointing specific academic weaknesses. Since these instruments can be created to measure any particular academic skill of interest to a teacher, they never lack educational relevance. For example, if a child were learning to add, the teacher might obtain a precise measure of his particular competencies by developing and administering a test of the skills in addition. As these tests are designed to tap each child's particular criterion abilities, comparison with peers is not essential. A child simply demonstrates mastery of the skill in question at a level which is satisfactory to his teacher. Criterion tests are obviously closely related to remediation, since they clearly reveal areas where the child lacks competence and needs instruction. Consequently, criterion-referenced devices appear to have value for use with children whose main problem is academic failure, i.e., the so-called "mildly handicapped." The remedial activities which they inspire are undoubtedly helpful in overcoming specific academic skill deficits. However, it would be fallacious for special educators to assume that these types of activities, no matter how beneficial they may be, are sufficient to reverse the pattern of learning failure demonstrated by many children. An infinite number of specific skill deficits might be diagnosed and remediated in isolated settings without making a significant impact upon the child's abilities to benefit from the major portion of his school program.

Summary of assessment

Generally, it appears that many standardized tests are being misused in the educational assessment of nonachieving children. Few would deny their value when they are used to gather descriptive information about the general learning characteristics of groups of children, since that information serves to increase understanding of the complex phenomena related to learning. For example, standardized tests might be used to attempt to isolate certain behavioral characteristics common to severely retarded children. However, the use of most tests either to assess the precise causes of any individual's school failure — the etiology or specific learning process deficits which cause nonachievement — or to plan precise instructional programs is generally unwarranted.

LIMITATIONS OF THE DIAGNOSTIC–REMEDIAL MODEL

Since the ability to use informal criterion-referenced devices to measure academic skills is a competency expected of any good teacher and constitutes good instruction, one might conclude that the diagnostic activities which are most valuable for use with nonachieving children need not be restricted to an isolated diagnostic center but could take place within the regular classroom. Not only would this sort of activity open new avenues for the special educator's intervention, but it would reduce certain disadvantages which are components of diagnosis and remediation done in isolation.

The primary limitation on performing most diagnostic and remedial activities in an environment separate from the regular class is that it reduces opportunities for interaction of the regular and special educator. This is true despite the fact that resource room and other "mainstream" special education programs make minor commitments to such interaction. Unfortunately, these relationships are often limited to recommendations from the special to the regular educator involving the use of certain materials or activities with particular children enrolled in the special education program. Rarely does the resource room teacher's role definition plan for the necessary degree of interaction with the regular classroom teacher to establish a coordinated instructional program. The fact that the special educator is infrequently alloted time for classroom observation, teacher conferences, staff meetings, etc. suggests that the teacher consultant aspects of resource room operations are low priority activities, even when lip service is paid to their importance.

Consequently, contact between professionals is usually so superficial and mutual understanding so nonexistant that the special educator's opinions are frequently resented and ignored. It is also true that in many resource or itinerant programs even this minimal level of teacher interaction is absent, and the instructional activities are not integrated at all. The mere existence of a resource or itinerant program to serve children does not change the special educator's typical focus on uncovering the deviance within children, since most of his activities continue to involve delineating and remediating children's deficits. If he is to deal with those factors which act upon the child, those which occur within the classroom, a much more concerted effort is required to institute definitive relationships with regular educators. Although this approach to providing services to children is fraught with difficulty, a lack of effort in this direction may cause problems which can severely limit the special educator's efficiency.

First, the lack of opportunities for interaction with the regular teacher or for observation within the regular classroom will limit the special educator's

4. EDUCABLE MENTALLY RETARDED

ability to understand the many important aspects of a child's learning problem, i.e., the complex experiences which affect his behavior within the regular class. For example, certain kinds of problems which really relate to the child's inability to function independently within a large group are nonexistent in a small group or tutorial situation.

Second, even if a special educator is able to establish a workable remedial program within the resource room, there is little assurance that the regular teacher will cooperate and work with the child in a similar fashion. Consequently, remediation may be "undone" when the child returns to his regular environment. Motivation to learn which is readily stimulated by the special educator may disappear in the classroom when the child is faced with situations that are discouraging and frustrating.

Third, diagnosis and remediation of selected children outside the classroom is expensive and time consuming. The numbers of children seen must be limited; consequently, those children receiving remedial attention are often indistinguishable from the many others with similar problems who are ignored.

Fourth, those educational problems created by faulty teaching techniques develop at a rate that precludes intervention, even by an army of diagnostic–remedial specialists. Unless the special educator can become a viable resource to the regular educator, the overall effects of the remedial program may be insignificant, for problems will develop faster than they can be solved.

Fifth, the diagnostic–remedial mystique associated with special education programming has had the effect of creating unrealistic expectations on the part of regular educators, namely that special education experts will independently solve learning problems that are disrupting the status quo of the educational scene. Essentially, special educators have been accepting the sole responsibility for curing the ills of regular education, a task which cannot be successfully accomplished regardless of the time, effort, and money spent trying. Obviously, regular educators must also be involved and must accept their share of this responsibility.

The difficulties associated with providing services for the large numbers of children currently being referred to special education programs make it essential that plans be prepared for the future direction of the field. Several obvious alternatives are available. First, special educators could discontinue services to "minimally handicapped" children on the grounds that their learning problems are caused by the inadequacy of regular education, are rooted in the home or community, or are otherwise beyond the special educator's sphere of interest or capacity. Conceivably, special educators could deal only with children whose learning problems are primarily related to internal pathology — blindness, deafness, brain-damage, autism, among other "hard-core" groups whose learning disabilities could not be prevented by manipulation of regular education programming. In other words, special educators could, probably through self-contained programs, serve the "truly handicapped" who simply cannot learn in regular classes. Although the adoption of this alternative might simplify what has become an increasingly unwieldy educational operation, it ignores certain realities. With the exception of a small minority of children who are easily identifiable, special educators have difficulty agreeing on the definitive characteristics of those who should constitute each disability category. Consequently, there is confusion as to whom should be served. Despite attempts to define specific populations of children more clearly in order to delinate the "truly handicapped," it is impossible to avoid conflict over borderline cases. Retrenchment to programs which deal only with severely handicapped children would reduce the special educator's options for programming for children with less obvious handicaps.

The second alternative is to share with the regular educator responsibility for working with many of these children and operate primarily in the arena where the crux of their learning difficulties lies, that is, in the regular classroom.

Thus, special educators could expand operations by altering their emphasis from the exclusive provision of diagnostic–remedial services in isolation to acting as teacher consultants. Needless to say, there are many problems involved in establishing this type of program since the special educator must have the competencies necessary to relate to regular educators, in addition to those required to act as a diagnostic–remedial specialist.

THE TEACHER CONSULTANT MODEL

In the teacher consultant role, the special educator functions for the most part inside the regular classroom. Although his duties still primarily involve educational planning for children experiencing learning and/or behavior problems, he does not function exclusively as an independent specialist but coordinates his activities with those of the regular educator. In other words, both teachers are involved in planning and implementing strategies, techniques, and methods to resolve learning problems and, in a more general sense, in improving the climate for learning within the classroom. The special educator's ultimate goal is not to remediate a particular child's learning problems, but to prevent certain problems from developing and provide the regular educator with the additional skills and competencies required to undertake remedial activities independently.

The principal difficulty in establishing a teacher consultant program is that it involves a redefinition of the special–regular education relationship, since the model cannot operate unless regular educators are committed to change. Regular educators must be willing to reject their traditional tendency to consign problem children to the exclusive domain of the special educator, realizing that a teacher consultant program requires a cooperative, interactive effort. In other words, regular educators must accept the fact that changes in their behavior may be necessary to produce changes in children's behavior. The optimum time to establish these commitments is during the program planning stage. It is critical that the entire regular education staff be consulted so that they clearly understand the nature of the program. Regular classroom teachers will work openly and undefensively with the teacher consultant insofar as they feel and expect to feel involved in the program.

Despite these precautions at the planning stage, some regular educators may initially be resistant to this model. The idea of permitting another individual to observe possible inadequacies in job performance is threatening to most people. They might also justifiably resent the fact that special educators, after many years of creating the impression that they would solve all learning problems, are now increasingly maintaining that the solution to many of these problems must be found within the realm of the regular classroom. In any event, the special educator should expect initial resistance.

Essentially, the success of a teacher consultant program will depend on several factors. It is important that the special educator offer practical, meaningful suggestions for reducing problems within the classroom. For example, if he can help implant a token economy which will increase learning and reduce disruption, his suggestions will be welcome. A more important skill involves the manner in which these suggestions are offered. Specifically, the teacher consultant must avoid appearing as an expert who is critiquing the regular teacher's performance. Communication between professionals must be undertaken tactfully and must deal specifically with the strategies and techniques related to good teaching. In other words, the successful implementation of this model will require that the special educator possess a broad spectrum of competencies.

First, he must be proficient as a teacher in all specific academic skill areas. He must, for example, understand such components of reading as sound–letter associations, word recognition, and comprehension. He must be familiar

4. EDUCABLE MENTALLY RETARDED

with the developmental instructional programs in all content areas, as well as with remedial programs. Finally, he must be able to use task analysis to modify instructional programs and adapt them to the needs of individuals. This includes creating supplemental materials which may not be available commercially.

Second, the special teacher must be able to assess student academic competencies with appropriate formal and informal diagnostic instruments. For example, he must know how to administer and interpret standardized tests of reading ability and how to devise and use criterion-referenced tests to diagnose specific academic weaknesses.

Third, the special teacher must be able to demonstrate the tactics and strategies of good teaching. He should be able to employ classroom management techniques, such as token economy and contingency contracting; employ specific observational and interviewing techniques, such as baseline charts and anecdotal records; use social factors for the children's advantage through such means as grouping strategies and peer tutoring.

Fourth, the teacher must display these competencies in the regular classroom so as to evoke modeling on the part of the regular educator. In other words, the regular teacher must eventually acquire many of the competencies demonstrated by the teacher consultant. Thus, the regular educator must be involved in all operations enacted to remediate a child's learning problem. Both professionals should plan alternate strategies and cooperate in attempting to implement them.

It should be clear from the above set of competencies that this program is not designed for situations in which one special educator must serve large numbers of regular teachers. A realistic ratio for services might involve one special educator with five regular teachers per week. Obviously the teacher consultant must spend most of his time in the classrooms of the teachers he is assisting. Stretching services invariably results in a "pop-in, pop-off, and pop-out" role, which is one objection many regular educators harbor against those who "assist" them as consultants.

Although many more significant classroom behaviors which promote learning might be discussed, this paper is not designed to deal with specific components of effective teaching. Rather, it would suggest a new role for special educators, focusing on teacher–child classroom interaction as opposed to the current emphasis on diagnosis and remediation of children's pathology in isolation.

All things considered, several distinct advantages may be gained from using a teacher consultant model: (a) Improved instructional techniques can be used with all children in a classroom who share particular learning problems. Attention need not be focused specifically on one particular child who has been designated atypical. (b) Since children are helped within the classroom when they demonstrate learning weaknesses, and since formal diagnostic testing is unnecessary, no disability labeling need occur, and the stigma related to such labeling is avoided. (c) Instructional competencies are shared among teachers rather than remaining the exclusive domain of one expert. (d) Regular educators' increased ability to individualize instruction should reduce the number of potential learning problems. (e) Children's learning problems may be conceived of as normal educational phenomena, rather than deviant conditions.

Lest there be objections to special educators undertaking an operation of this magnitude, it is fair to point out that this interaction model is no more ambitious than an operational design which assumes the ability to remediate in isolation those learning problems which are closely related to classroom activity.

SUMMARY

This paper has dealt with some of the problems which special educators face when they attempt to help children who are essentially poor academic achievers. It has discussed some limitations of certain diagnostic–remedial operations and presented certain supportive arguments for increased teacher consultant services. In conclusion, it seems appropriate to note that if special educators continue to perceive nonachieving children as deviant and administer to them much as an education first-aid department, they will assuredly never lack for patients. Regardless of the service model used, e.g., self-contained class, resource room, itinerant, etc., special educators will remain perpetually passive and defensive by having to devise programs to diagnose and remediate children who may basically suffer from weaknesses inherent in an inefficient instructional system. By perpetuating the premise that these children are disabled, special educators become an integral part of that system. Extending special education services to the regular classroom shifts emphasis from the child's pathology to the multitude of factors in the educational environment which frequently cause poor scholastic achievement. Intervention which focuses exclusively on the child's problem is often simply insufficient to provide a solution. Realigning priorities would de-emphasize certain aspects of assessment in isolation and emphasize the teacher consultant role. These new priorities should not only help many children with their difficulties in academic achievement but should refocus the attention of regular educators on problems which are insolvable without their cooperation.

References

Christopolos, F., & Renz, P. A critical examination of special education programs. *Journal of Special Education,* 1969, *3,* 371–379.

Drew, D., Freston, C., & Logan, D. Criteria and reference in evaluation. *Focus on Exceptional Children,* 1972, *4,* 1–10.

Dunn, L. M. Special education for the mildly retarded — Is much of it justifiable? *Exceptional Children,* 1968, *35,* 5–22.

Elkins, J., & Kirk, S. *Characteristics of children in resource rooms.* Unpublished manuscript, Leadership Training Institute in Learning Disabilities, University of Arizona, 1974.

Farber, B. Family organization and parent-child communication. Lafayette, Ind.: Child Development Publication of the Society for Research in Child Development, 1963, No. 7, Serial No. 91.

Frostig, M., Lefever, D. W., & Willesey, J. R. *Marianne Frostig Developmental Test of Visual Perception.* Palo Alto, Calif.: Consulting Psychologist Press, Inc., 1964.

Glavin, J. P., Quay, H. C., & Werry, J. S. Behavioral and academic gains of conduct problem children in different classroom settings. *Exceptional Children,* 1971, *37,* 441–446.

Hammill, D. D., & Larsen, S. C. The relationship of selected auditory perceptual skills and reading ability. *Journal of Learning Disabilities,* 1974, *7,* 429–436.

Hammill, D. D., & Wiederholt, J. L. Review of the Frostig test and training program. In L. Mann & D. Sabatino (Eds.), *First review of special education* (Vol. 1). Philadelphia: JSE Press, 1973.

Iano, R. P. Shall we disband our special classes? *Journal of Special Education,* 1972, *6,* 167–177.

Jastak, J., Bijou, S., & Jastak, S. *Wide Range Achievement Test.* New York: Psychological Corporation, 1965.

Kirk, S., McCarthy, J., & Kirk, W. *The Illinois Test of Psycholinguistic Abilities.* Urbana, Ill.: University of Illinois Press, 1968.

Lee, L. *Northwest Syntax Screening Test.* Evanston, Ill.: Northwestern University Press, 1969.

McCarthy, J. Personal communication, 1974.

Newcomer, P., & Hammill, D. *The relationship of the ITPA and academic achievement.* Unpublished manuscript, University of Texas, Austin, 1975.

Sedlak, R. A., & Weener, P. Review of research on the Illinois Test of Psycholinguistic Abilities. In L. Mann & D. Sabatino (Eds.), *First review of special education* (Vol. 1). Philadelphia: JSE Press, 1973.

Thorpe, L., Clark, W., & Tiegs, E. *California Test of Personality.* Monterey, Calif.: California Test Bureau, 1963.

Wepman, J. *Test of Auditory Discrimination.* Chicago, Ill.: Language Research Associates, 1958.

Wechsler, D. *Wechsler Intelligence Scale for Children,* New York: Psychological Corporation, 1949.

"I think I can"

It isn't just that she's relearned how to walk and talk and see. It's her unbeatable spirit that makes brain-injured Karen Breisky such a very special child

William Breisky

Karen was two when her brain suffered a massive assault. She was four when she had regained enough vision to comprehend the ocean; five when she learned to take a step without holding on to anything; 7½ when I started my book about her (also called "I Think I Can").

Now she is nine and she is not yet able to skip rope or ride a bike—or even to button her buttons or pull her chair up to the table or look toward the sun. Yet in the past seven years Karen has accomplished more than most people achieve in a lifetime. For, once she was blind, and now she can read. Once she was speechless and now she can sing. Once she was immobile, and now she and her younger sister, Gretchen, can join hands and walk down the road together. Once, locked in a secret world, she used to rage in frustration; now she is a dauntless, buoyant little girl and an inspiration to all of us.

Until the night of Sunday, May 21, 1967, my wife, Barbara, and I had never had a sick child, had never consulted a pediatrician for anything other than routine checkups and shots. We really weren't prepared for the trouble that lay ahead.

Karen was slightly feverish that evening, so Barbara gave her a dose of baby aspirin, and put her to bed early. By half past five in the morning, Karen's breathing had become disturbingly labored. Frightened, we phoned our pediatrician for advice.

"Croup" was his telephone diagnosis.

He told us to raise some steam for her to inhale, and, when she was breathing more readily, to put her back to bed. We followed his instructions and soon Karen was asleep in her crib. Then, moments later, she suddenly stiffened and turned bluish. Barbara sensed immediately what had to be done, and gave Karen "the kiss of life," until she began to gulp mouthfuls of air for herself.

Four-year-old John was awake, and wide-eyed with worry as we phoned the police department for emergency help. A police cruiser pulled into our driveway within minutes, and an oxygen mask was fitted over Karen's face. I placed her in Barbara's lap for the race to Hartford, Conn., 18 miles to the south.

The police siren was wailing as the cruiser sped through the town of Windsor—but not loudly enough. The officer driving the cruiser jammed on his brakes, but couldn't avoid plowing into a car which had crossed his path at an intersection. No one was injured by the impact, but both vehicles were immobilized. Precious minutes were lost while Barbara stood in the road with Karen, agonizing over how —or if—they would reach the hospital in time.

The police officer flagged down a passing car, but the elderly driver elected not to help and drove on. Then a young man, who saved Karen's life, came along. We never learned his name —but he wore the clothes of a factory worker, and with Barbara and Karen beside him, he drove his red hardtop like a man possessed.

As Karen lost color and seemed to lapse into unconsciousness, Barbara

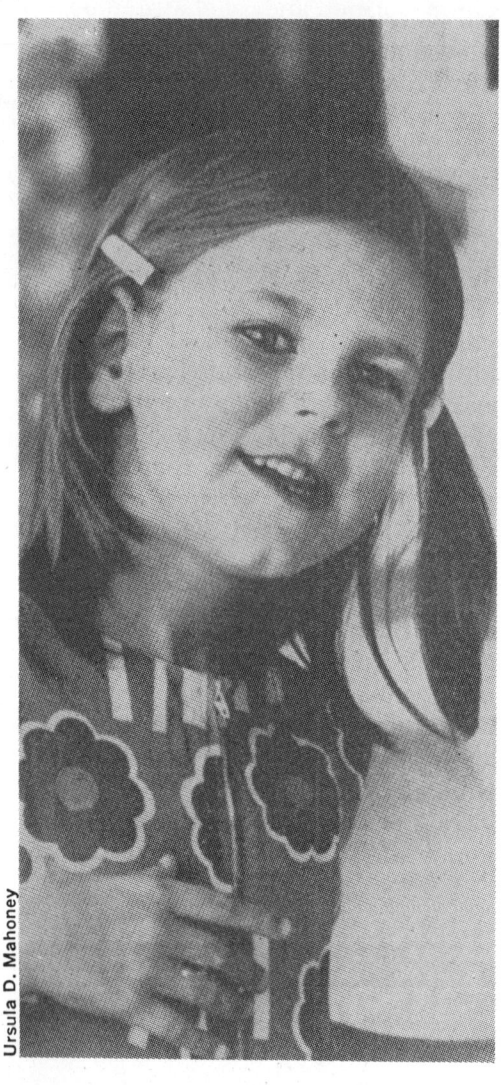

This is Karen Breisky, a courageous little girl whose triumph over massive brain injury is described here by her father.

"I Think I Can." *Good Housekeeping,* September 1974. ©1974 Hearst Corporation, New York, N.Y.

30. "I Think I Can"

screamed her name over and over, and begged her not to die—while the young man floored the accelerator, cut through service stations, bounded over lawns, and finally delivered Barbara and Karen at the emergency entrance of St. Francis Hospital.

Karen, by then, seemed lifeless. Barbara ran with her into the emergency room.

Before long, our doctor was preparing Barbara for the worst. He began to say that sometimes, with the best of facilities and noblest of efforts, doctors and hospitals fail. At that point a member of the hospital's emergency-room team broke in. Karen, he reported, was breathing again.

She had suffered a typically sudden onset of a rare illness—*epiglottitis*, cousin of croup. Her epiglottis, the lid of her voice box, had swollen quickly, closing off her windpipe. She had suffocated and her heartbeat had been arrested—for how long no one could say.

A rubber tube was forced into her lungs, but it was hours before she was strong enough for a surgeon to make an opening in her windpipe which would enable her to breathe easily. And it was a week before a consulting neurologist would confirm our worst fears—that her brain had suffered a very serious trauma and that, for the time being at least, she had lost virtually all ability to perform voluntary and involuntary functions. She was sightless, speechless, immobile. And her chances of survival were not good.

Karen lived for a week in the hospital's "fog room," her life sustained by tubes and needles and clouds of cool, swirling fog. She seemed, in those first days, totally alone and helpless. Her eyes looked through us as we held her hand; we seemed unable to reach her with our voices. She was racked periodically by seizures, and her only response to anyone or anything was an occasional cry. But her cry was soundless because the air that would have created a sound in the larynx was being diverted through the tracheal tube.

The magic reawakening we had hoped for never came, and three weeks later we brought a totally helpless little girl home to Enfield, Conn. She was mute and miserable—in many ways like a new baby.

I carried her to the sofa bed Barbara had made up in the living room and John came in to see her. John, her beloved brother, whose footsteps she had proudly dogged, stood at her bedside, puzzled by her lack of response to him.

"She's looking at me," he said, "but she doesn't talk."

We couldn't bring ourselves to tell him, just then, that Karen was cortically blind: Although her eyes were wide open, they weren't receiving a clear signal from her brain, and she wasn't really "looking" at him at all. Nor could we explain his sister's screaming spells. Were they fits of rage? Pain? Frustration?

The doctors gave us nothing more positive to do for her than to keep her well nourished and to give her a few simple passive exercises—and that, of course, was painful to accept.

Wanting desperately to be able to do more than that, we wrote to an organization in Philadelphia which works exclusively with brain-injured children—The Institutes for the Achievement of Human Potential. Our neurologist said we very likely would be wasting our money, but friends, and friends of friends, told us they knew of youngsters who had been helped there.

When The Institutes replied that it would be months before they could see Karen, Barbara's parents, then living in Philadelphia, sent us some IAHP literature, which we devoured, searching for leads we could follow. We read that brain-injured children could be helped by keeping them on their stomachs, on the floor, and urged to crawl. From that time onward Karen was to spend most of her waking hours not propped up on soft pillows but face down on the playroom floor.

A host of friends joined Barbara, her mother ("Nana," to the family) and me in an IAHP-inspired stimulative program. We rubbed Karen's arms and legs first with ice cubes, then with a warm towel. We put her face-down on a table and tried to manipulate her legs in such a way that we reproduced a crawling motion—"patterning" was The Institutes' word for it.

And we talked endlessly to her, always urging her to respond. Barbara worked especially hard on "hi."

"Hi, Karen. . . . Hi. . . . Can you say 'hi,' too? . . . Hi, Karen."

Karen's first success was in producing an audible h-sound, but at first she couldn't connect it to the "i." She was *trying* to talk—Barbara was certain of that—but her tongue would get in the way. Sometimes she would squeeze her lips together, then part them slightly, as if trying to shape a word. But she'd succeed only in producing some very wet bubbles and a faint sound.

Then one day, softly, without advance fanfare, the "hi" did come.

"Hi," said Karen.

One lone word had been uttered, but to Barbara that one word meant, "Hi, Mommy. . . . Hello, world. . . . Remember me?"

"Why don't you learn to say 'Johnny?'" her brother asked—almost demanded—weeks later. And "Johnny" was the next word Karen uttered.

We took Karen to The Institutes five months after we had applied. Of our first day there we remember one thing above all else: These people *understood*. They knew, almost intuitively, what we had been through. They had already seen all of the problems Karen had, or would have in her future. And they didn't waste time on sympathy; instead they offered their minds, and their eyes, ears and hands, to formulate a massive battle plan that Barbara and I and our friends might carry out.

Karen's mobility, we were told, was hardly better than that of a newborn infant. As for her vision: she was suffering "a severely alternating divergent strabismus"—her eyes were "looking" but not truly seeing, and certainly were not working together. Her eyes reacted reflexively to strong light but she had little or no outline perception.

"We haven't learned everything about the brain," said The Institutes' medical director, "but we think we can help Karen."

The brain, he told us, is like a computer. To get better output you must improve the input. By putting Karen through her paces on a patterning table, we were in effect doing her crawling for her, sending sensory messages to her brain, establishing a pattern which the brain eventually would learn, so that it might send out the right signals to her hands, arms and legs.

We were to stimulate her eyes night and day with a variety of flashlights and light boxes, to build an indoor slide which would encourage forward motion, and to feed more oxygen to her brain by putting a plastic "re-breathing" mask over her nose and mouth periodically.

Karen's response to the program The Institutes prescribed for her was all we could have asked. By mid-December her eyes were able to follow flashlight movements and shortly before Christmas, she succeeded in moving herself forward on her stomach.

Previously, when placed on the floor on her tummy and urged to go somewhere, she had been able to do no more than lift her head, push up on her hands a bit, and do a lot of futile kicking. Prodding her with visual goals was not possible at first, so after each patterning session Barbara or one of our friends had knelt on the floor calling to her—"Come on, Karen! Come over here for a hug." After a few weeks' practice, with an outstretched hand for her to push her foot against, and a tiny pinch to give her something to escape, Karen began, ever so slowly, to move forward.

Early in the new year, she began to call herself "Kan" and one day, eavesdropping on her early-morning chirping, we heard her ask herself, "Why Kan wake up?"

On April 1 we knew springtime had come for Karen. After her one P.M. patterning session she was making her way across the playroom floor, pushing one foot and then the other against her mother's hands, when suddenly she stopped. Her face was about a foot and a half from a pot of artificial red geraniums Barbara had been using to stimulate her visually. Now the geraniums sat alone on the floor, bathed in a strong shaft of sunlight. Karen had not touched them that day, and no one had mentioned them. So we were not at all prepared for her historic announcement.

"I see the flowers!"

Pandemonium.

The Day Karen Saw the Geraniums was a milestone in our lives, holding

4. EDUCABLE MENTALLY RETARDED

out the promise that Karen was to be liberated from cortical blindness. For some time after that she continued to "see" most things with her hands—but we had many an opportunity to share her excitement as she made new discoveries with her eyes.

June 17: Karen is held up to the mirror in the downstairs bathroom. "I see the baby!" she cries. There is a pause, then a second discovery. "It's Karen Luise!" Yet even then she can't quite believe that she is looking at her own image, for she says, "I want to touch the baby."

August 26: It is late evening, well past the children's bedtime, and we are returning home from a church bazaar. As we pause at a traffic signal, a street lamp creates a play of light and shadow in the front seat. I give Karen's hand a squeeze and she says sleepily, "I see you, Daddy."

Karen has seen me before, in the daylight, but here in the semidarkness, I assume, she is seeing me once again with her fingertips. "I know, Karen," is my only response.

Karen realizes that I haven't understood. "No, Daddy," she says, more urgently this time. "I see you with my eyes, not my hands."

In early October of 1968 I received a phone call from the mid-Atlantic. I had been approved for the managership of the Bermuda News Bureau, and we were invited to move family and furnishings to subtropical Bermuda as soon as I could settle our affairs in Connecticut. The sun and sand would be marvelous for Karen, The IAHP's doctors had told us. That was enough reason for us.

While we were loading a rented station wagon to drive to New York and board the S.S. *Franconia*, Karen decided to present everyone a farewell gift: She got up on her knees by herself, for the first time.

On our first Christmas in Bermuda, we rejoiced in knowing that Karen, who could not crawl on her tummy a year before, was now able to creep on her hands and knees for several feet before collapsing. At the age of three her fingers were becoming more skilled at holding a cup, or distinguishing a thruppence from a shilling. And most significant—one Christmas ago she barely reacted to the lights on the tree, and colors meant nothing to her; this year she could fish through a pile of cards in search of "Santa in the red suit."

She began to reassume her role as big sister to the youngest member of our family ("Now tell us what you want, Gretchen—we can't help you unless you tell us what's the matter") and even found a new identity for herself—the Little Blue Engine. Like the heroine in the children's classic, *The Little Engine That Could*, she chugged and chugged and puffed and puffed to the chant of "I think I can . . . I think I can"—but instead of carting a trainload of toys, she was struggling to master hands-and-knees creeping.

Creeping is the key, said The IAHP, because mobility and seeing are interlocking brain functions, and creeping introduces a child to a three-dimensional visual world.

Karen's visual world had widened considerably by our first springtime in Bermuda. "I see the blue water," she announced matter-of-factly during a family picnic one Sunday.

On many previous occasions we had stood on some promontory overlooking the sea and said, "See the ocean, Karen?" Her reply had always been a simple "No," or pursed lips and a bowed head turning slowly from side to side, as if she were ashamed that she couldn't comprehend the vast ocean which everyone else saw so effortlessly. But during that historic Sunday picnic she suddenly announced that she now was able to see the blue Atlantic and, furthermore, that she was intrigued by the wind-whipped surf which came crashing over the sandy beach. "I see the blue ocean. . . . There's some white stuff in it!"

We were overjoyed by Karen's progress—yet her vision continued to puzzle us. She could focus on a horse tethered in a nearby field, but if that same horse were cantering down the road he would disappear from view before she could get a fix on him. And even large, stationary objects eluded her when placed against a confusing background such as a patterned rug.

A month after Karen conquered the Atlantic, Institutes' Director Glenn Doman gave Barbara a prescription to help her walk and to make her eyes and hands work together.

"We want you to build an overhead ladder," he said, "parallel to the ground, with dowel rungs she can grip. We think it will help her move on to walking on her knees, and from there to walking on her feet."

At first Karen would collapse after advancing only two or three rungs, but before long she could knee-walk under the length of the ladder. The neighborhood kids would join us in applauding as she performed, and Karen basked in the applause—provided it was deserved. If the applause seemed premature she would insist, "Don't clap now!" Only when she had completed a self-imposed quota of rungs would she say, "*Now* clap."

As John returned to school in the fall of 1969, we had to face the fact that one year hence Karen would have to be ready to start school, or be left behind.

Only one more year to catch up? She was then barely able to scribble—but perhaps she could get along for a while without the skill to manage a pencil. She had scarcely learned knee-walking, but her mobility was improving steadily. It was reading that could be the real stumbling block. What if a switched signal in Karen's brain wouldn't permit her eyes to read? Barbara had been trying to teach her to recognize a few simple words, but with discouragingly little success.

But failure didn't dampen Karen's boundless optimism. Big books with big pictures became a special treat for her. If the stories in these picture books were short enough, and were read to her often enough, she could virtually commit the text to memory, and by turning the pages and reciting memorized words she could give the illusion of reading. She would, in fact, cheerfully announce that "I'm reading," and could fool anyone who didn't know the limitations of her eyesight.

One rare downbeat day Karen did say, wistfully but with no bitterness, "I wish I could get rid of these eyes and have Gretchen's eyes."

But Lincoln's Birthday, 1970, was not such a day. It was a day when Barbara's determination to help Karen paid off handsomely. Holding a length of pipe in front of Karen, Barbara let her grasp it lightly, and then told her to step out. Miraculously, Karen responded with a series of rigid, puppet-like—but enormously satisfying—steps. When I arrived home from work that evening I was greeted by Karen telling me, quick, to fetch the notebooks in which I kept a record of her progress.

"Put it in my book," she said. "A brand-new thing from Karen Breisky." Then she told me of the historic steps, and of the resultant fireworks, applause and cries of "Do it again!"

After three more weeks of such balancing acts, I said to Karen one evening, "We haven't had anything to put in your book for a while. Isn't it time you did something new?"

Karen agreed it was high time, but couldn't think of anything to try; so I suggested, "How about getting your balance, then taking a couple of steps without holding onto anything?" Her eyes widened as she considered this enormous suggestion; then suddenly she sucked in her breath, took three quick, brave steps and fell into my arms.

Question: When does a baby step become a giant step?

Answer: When you have lost your ability to creep, much less walk, and have spent three long years undoing the damage.

The IAHP had told us repeatedly that success in one area stimulates and reinforces success in others. We found out for ourselves how true that was when the long-awaited breakthrough in reading finally came, following on the heels of the walking achievement.

The Institutes had suggested we try a technique which had worked for another youngster in the program. The boy's father had transferred some printed words onto 35-mm transparencies, with white letters against a black background. He had then projected them onto the wall of an inky-dark room.

We converted our guest-room closet into a projection room, and began with the word "ball."

"What's this word, Karen?"

30. "I Think I Can"

Pause. Then, "Spell it," she asked.

"B-a-l-l."

"Ball!"

"Good, Karen." Good she remembered that b-a-l-l spells ball, but not good that she was unable to identify the word by sight.

But after six more weeks of twice-daily closet shows she was reading.

"What's that letter on the right?" she asked one day.

"G."

"Bag!"

"Great. See if you can get this next one."

"Water?"

"Beautiful! And this one?"

"I see a 'j' with a moon over it . . . jelly!"

Another "brand-new thing from Karen Breisky!"

Before long, Karen had graduated from projected words to two-inch-high printed words and was reading short sentences made up of word signs strung out on the playroom floor. She also progressed from two or three timid steps to the number of steps needed to get her from one room to the next—"real walking" she called it.

Because of her assorted handicaps, however, she wasn't nearly ready for school when she reached Bermuda's school-starting age of five. When September came along, Barbara decided to inaugurate a private school for Karen and Gretchen in our playroom. "Our School" was the girls' name for it. Barbara—the family's arts-and-crafts instructor, choreographer, gardener, repairer of bruised knees and feelings—claimed she was given far more attention and respect as "Teacher" than she ever had received as "Mommy."

Teacher made an alphabet book for each girl. Gretchen, at three, demonstrated real ability in copying and coloring pictures and words in the book; Karen could think up words for each letter more quickly, but her hand couldn't direct a crayon to make anything as difficult as a circle or a square.

Then, during a visit from Nana and Grandpop, we discovered chalk. White chalk marks on black slate proved relatively easy for Karen to make, to erase, and to see. After a week of chalk work with her grandmother, Karen had conquered "x" and "o," and declared herself ready to try "f"—"so we can make 'fox!'" Her x's didn't always cross where they should; the o's sometimes resembled c's lying on their backs; her letters trooped up hills and down into valleys when they should have been marching in a straight line. But she was on her way.

The more Karen achieved and the more interested she became in the world outside the playroom, the more the monotony of "the program" was becoming a problem.

Adela, then a 17-year-old neighbor and Saturday-morning programmer, recalled recently, "I don't think Karen ever said, 'I don't want to do a program'—full stop. But what she would do was stall awhile. If I arrived when she was playing with a pile of blocks, she'd say, 'But if the castle isn't finished, the dragon will take the princesses away.' And how could I argue?"

We had to become more inventive about making Karen's program more challenging. We began, for instance, to play counting games with her as she progressed on her ladder.

By her sixth birthday, in the spring of 1971, Karen could count by ones to 30, by fives to 25, and by tens to 100. By midsummer she was able to produce a reasonable facsimile of K-a-r-e-n on her slate, and was able to draw recognizable facial features instead of scribbles which only she could identify. That fall, the headmistress of John's school approved our plan to give Karen a try as a mornings-only student, with afternoons free for her program.

"Real school," Karen said when we made it official. "Oh, boy!"

Barbara echoed that "Oh, boy!"—and at the same time began taking a mental inventory of last-minute school-readiness projects she and Karen should undertake. Steps, for instance. Karen needed a crash course in step-climbing if she was to negotiate even the few pairs of steps at Somerset Primary.

For the first weeks of real school, thanks to her perseverance, our once word-blind daughter was the best reader in her class. The older girls in the school competed for the privilege of lending her a hand in the schoolyard. On one of the very few occasions when she was deliberately cut out by a classmate, Karen responded by using her reading skill as a weapon and thus demonstrated that she was learning how to defend herself in a give-and-take situation.

The incident took place at a toy playhouse in the school, where a posted sign declared, "Three may play." Karen saw a twosome heading for the playhouse and decided to be number three, but one of the children barred the door to her when she arrived. At first Karen didn't know how to react, "so (as she related the story that evening) I just stood there." But finally she remembered the "Three may play" sign on the playhouse, and in a rare display of spitefulness declared, "*You* can't read!" —which happened to be true.

"A lively and interested member of the class" was her teacher's comment on her first-year report card. That was all that we could ask—but no more than we had come to expect—from our boundlessly determined daughter. She was still unsteady on her feet (her knees were perpetually scuffed from schoolyard spills) and she was still unable to turn her left hand palm up, or keep her place in a book without a reading card, or change into her gym clothes with the other kids. But her good report card was a tremendous victory. And there was more to come.

She was to receive a singular honor before a gathering of men who play a large role in supporting The IAHP's work—the United Steelworkers of America. Every second year, two of The IAHP youngsters who have "made it" are invited to appear with their parents before the steelworkers' convention. 1972 was Karen's year.

After summarizing Karen's heroic five-year struggle against cortical blindness and paralysis, IAHP Director Glenn Doman told the convention a story of Karen and of Sports Day.

Sports Day, he related, is a big annual event at Bermuda schools, and Karen Breisky, who had been looking forward to it, had been terribly disappointed when informed that she and her mother would be away for Sports Day 1972 because she would be in Philadelphia.

"That's okay, Karen," her sister, Gretchen, had said, hoping to console her. "You couldn't win anything anyway."

"I don't care," Karen had replied. "I just wanted to be in the race."

After quoting Karen, Director Doman called her forward and presented her a trophy which seemed almost to have been designed for her—a Wedgwood plate commemorating the 1972 Munich Olympics. A raised figure of a runner was at the center of the plate, and at the top was a paraphrasing of Karen's Sports Day retort—"NOT THE WINNING BUT THE TAKING PART."

The 8,000 steelworkers rose in a body to applaud. They had no difficulty understanding the message implicit in Glenn Doman's presentation: For Karen, taking part *was* winning.

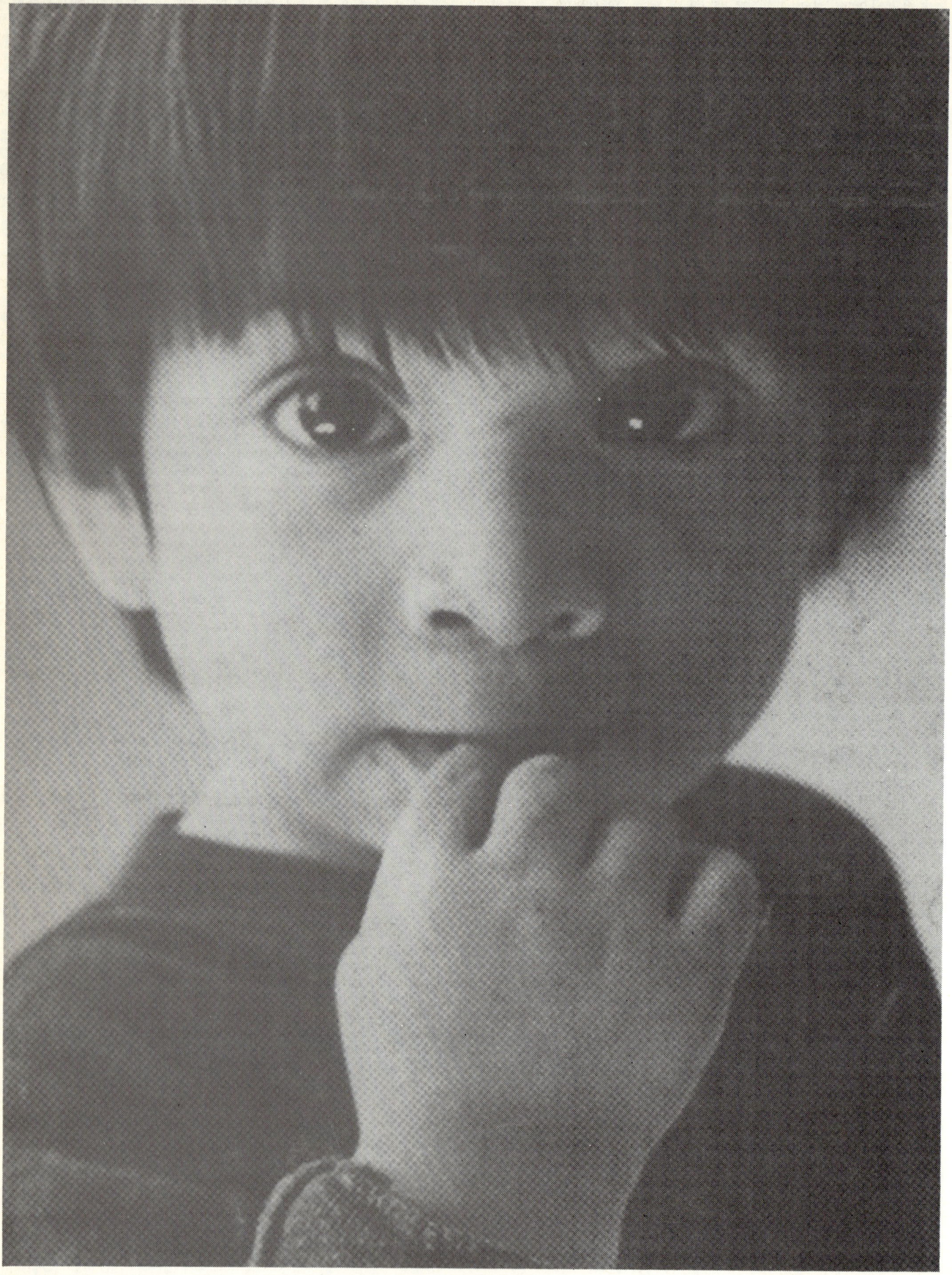

Trainable Mentally Retarded

In 1957, a study completed by Dr. Gerhart Saenger in New York, revealed that 25 percent of trainable mentally retarded children died before reaching adulthood because many suffered from health problems such as heart disease or seizures. Approximately half remained at home, and one quarter were institutionalized.

Since that date, drastic changes have taken place in educational services for the trainable retarded.

The I.Q. has in the past been one of the major distinguishing features in setting the trainable child apart from other degrees of mental retardation. Those generally within the range of 25 to 49 are considered trainable. Defects in maturation and development appear noticeably in the motor development area, especially in speech. The trainable child will respond to training in various self-help activities. In the area of training and education this child can learn simple communication skills, elementary health and safety habits, and simple manual skills. The trainable child will, as a rule, not progress to a great degree in functional reading or mathematics. As an adult, the trainable mentally retarded person can perform simple tasks under sheltered conditions, enjoys participating in simple recreation activities, may travel alone in familiar places, but however, may be incapable of self-maintenance.

Despite the fact that advances have been made in the provision of services for these children, some experts have argued that trainable retarded children should not be educated in the public schools. The major arguments in defense of this position are that first, the public schools should not be concerned with pupils who will not be able to learn academic subjects, and second, the schools should not assume the burden of training those who will not eventually become economically independent. On the other hand, those who advocate public school classes for the trainable argue that the parents of these children pay taxes and the schools are publicly supported and each child deserves the opportunity to best develop his potentialities. Recent federal legislation has resolved this debate, placing the responsibility for the education of all handicapped children into the hands of the public school systems.

In looking at a typical course of study within a public school trainable class framework, one would find the child learning appropriate hygiene and self-help skills. Basic manual tasks are instructed in preparation for the child to obtain social acceptance in later life.

With the ever increasing number of sheltered workshops, group homes, and transitional homes for the retarded opening up nationally, the road to normalization for the trainable becomes easier. As society continues to open their minds and place preconceived prejudices aside, the young trainable retarded adult, can begin to lead personally gratifying lives while making worthwhile contributions to their world.

Assessment of Counseling Practices at the Birth of a Child with Down's Syndrome

SIEGFRIED M. PUESCHEL AND ANN MURPHY
Harvard Medical School

> An attempt was made to analyze 414 parents' perceptions of their experiences at the birth of their child with Down's syndrome. The interpretation of the results and the parents' comments suggest that the counseling of parents with a newborn Down's syndrome child demands tact, truthfulness, and empathetic guidance. The parents should be informed of the child's condition in a kind and sensitive manner as soon as the diagnosis of Down's syndrome has been made. Appropriate terminology should be employed, and both parents should be present when the physician tells them of their misfortune. Unconditional recommendations of institutionalization of the child with Down's syndrome should be practices of the past. The professionals' thoughtful considerations and mature counsel should assist constructively in shaping the child's future.

Parents invariably experience profound emotional distress when they are told that their newborn infant has Down's syndrome. Acute anxiety, desperation, disbelief, and confusion become manifest in the shocked parent, often leading to cognitive dysfunction and disturbance of personality integration. This initial stage of emotional disorganization is followed by the process of reintegration when psychological defense mechanisms become increasingly mobilized. Later, during mature adaptation, the majority of parents are able to face most of the presenting realities (Garrard & Richmond, 1963). This evolution can be enhanced by the physicians' sensitive guidance and genuine support that will bring about a more realistic adjustment of the family and will avoid maladaptive coping. While some physicians are skillful in conveying the diagnosis to parents and offering empathetic counsel, other professionals do not respond appropriately to the needs of parents and often do not provide the assistance asked for in this critical period of stress.

In order to gain more insight into the parents' life experiences after the birth of their Down's syndrome child, to study the professional's approach to counseling, and to analyze possible attitudinal changes over time, we solicited respective pertinent information from parents of children with Down's syndrome.

Method

Subjects and Procedure

The names of 511 parents with Down's syndrome children from 1 to 18 years of age were obtained from the following six sources: the Developmental Evaluation Clinic and the Division of Clinical Genetics, Children's Hospital (Boston); the Massachusetts, Hartford, and Oregon Associations for Retarded Children; and Crystal Springs Nursery, a residential facility in Assonet, Massachusetts. A detailed questionnaire was forwarded to these parents asking for their cooperation in completing the forms. The principal questions submitted were:

What terminology was used when the parents were told of their child's condition?
Who was first informed of the child's diagnosis?
Who notified the parents of the child's condition?
When were the parents informed of the child's diagnosis?
How was the diagnosis presented to the parents?
What kind of recommendations were made by professionals?

What plan did the parents prefer?
What influenced the parents in making their final decision?

The parents were invited to make comments pertaining to each question and present their views of how to best inform other parents who have a newborn child with Down's syndrome.

Results

Of the 511 parents who were sent questionnaires, 414 (81 percent) returned the completed forms. The analysis of the results showed that the total number of responses often differed from the number of completed questionnaires, since in some instances several correct responses were appropriate while on other occasions a specific question appeared to be not applicable.

The following terminology was used by professionals when the diagnosis was conferred to the parents. Three hundred and three physicians (65 percent) had utilized the term "mongolism." The term "Down's syndrome" was used by 70 physicians (15 percent), and 75 doctors (16 percent) employed the term "retarded." Eighteen professionals (4 percent) used other terms (such as slow muscular development, abnormality, something wrong with glands, brain damage, hydrocephalus) and in five instances the child was referred to as a "mongoloid idiot."

Answers to the question, "Who was first informed of the child's diagnosis?" are summarized in Table 1. In 76 percent of the cases, one parent was present when the child's diagnosis was discussed, and in 2 percent families were never told by professionals of their child's condition. These parents either had made the diagnosis themselves or were made aware of their child's problem by friends.

Table 2 shows the results of the inquiry, "Who notified the mother and father of the child's diagnosis?" It is of note that in 35 percent of the cases the father was informed by his spouse of their misfortune. In the category "Other," parents mentioned that medical students, interns, consultants, and friends had communicated the diagnosis to them.

There was no appreciable difference between the time when mother and father were told of the child's condition (see Table 3). In one-third of the cases, the diagnosis was conferred to the parents after the child was older than 30 days; in 10 percent, parents were told of their child having Down's syndrome 1 to 5 years after the birth of their child.

Nearly one-half of the parents reported that professionals had presented the diagnosis in a sympathetic manner (see Table 4), while 25 percent of parents said that their physician was abrupt and blunt. Some parents commented that they were given very little information and that their physician was evasive; two parents were told of the child's condition by mail.

In the attempt to study a possible change of the obstetricians' and pediatricians' recommendations over time, we divided parents' responses as shown in Table 5 into three time categories according to the

TABLE 1
PERSON(S) FIRST NOTIFIED BY PROFESSIONALS OF THE CHILD'S DIAGNOSIS

Person	Number responding[a]
Both parents	82 (20)
Mother alone	196 (47)
Father alone	123 (29)
Sibling of child	2 (0)
Grandparents	3 (1)
Other relatives	3 (1)
Not told	8 (2)

[a] Percentage in parentheses.

TABLE 2
PERSON WHO NOTIFIED MOTHER/FATHER OF THE CHILD'S DIAGNOSIS[a]

Person notifying	Mother	Father
Family physician	78 (19)	76 (19)
Obstetrician	67 (17)	57 (14)
Pediatrician	161 (40)	102 (26)
Nurse	2 (1)	3 (1)
Social worker	2	0 —
Spouse	62 (15)	138 (35)
Relative	0 (0)	3 (1)
Other	32 (8)	18 (4)

[a] Percentage in parentheses.

TABLE 3
AGE OF CHILD WHEN MOTHER/FATHER WERE NOTIFIED OF THE DIAGNOSIS[a]

Age of child	Mother	Father
At birth	35 (9)	51 (13)
1st day	78 (19)	70 (18)
2nd day	48 (12)	47 (12)
3rd day	33 (8)	36 (9)
4th to 7th day	30 (7)	22 (5)
8th to 30th day	36 (9)	36 (9)
> 30th day	138 (34)	129 (32)
Other	8 (2)	7 (2)

[a] Percentage in parentheses.

5. TRAINABLE MENTALLY RETARDED

child's date of birth. As noted in the table, recommendations of home care have markedly increased in recent years. A reverse relationship was observed concerning the recommendation of permanent placement into an institution; this type of recommendation had declined significantly over the past two decades.

Table 6 presents responses of the parents with regard to the plan for their child; there was no appreciable difference between mother's and father's preference. While the majority of parents preferred home care for their child, only 6 percent chose permanent placement.

There were several factors influencing the parents' decision in planning for the child. In most instances (218, 54 percent), the decision was based on both parents' feelings. In 27 cases (7 percent), the decision was based on the mother's feelings while in 18 (4 percent), it was based on the father's. Professional advice was reported by 78 respondents (19 percent), relatives and friends by 16 (4 percent), and reading materials by 17 (4 percent) as being the most important influence in the decision-making. Thirty-two respondents (8 percent) reported other factors.

Discussion

When parents who have joyously awaited the birth of their child are informed that their infant has Down's syndrome, they are facing an emotional, traumatic experience. During this initial period of disorganization, parents look for support and counsel from their physician. His ability to provide positive assistance to the parents in this stressful situation will be a vital influence on the parents' subsequent coping and adjustment (Berg, Gilderdale, & Way, 1969).

In preparing himself for the counseling session, the physician should become familiar with the particular circumstances of this family and should be aware of the general

TABLE 4
PARENTS' PERCEPTION OF THE PRESENTATION OF THE CHILD'S DIAGNOSIS BY THE PROFESSIONAL

Presentation	Number responding[a]
Sensitive, information given, and assistance offered	80 (20)
Sympathetic and factual—placement in institution	38 (9)
Sympathetic and factual—home care recommended	78 (19)
Inadequate information—placement recommended	26 (6)
Inadequate information—home care recommended	18 (4)
Abrupt, unsympathetic—placement recommended	68 (17)
Abrupt, unsympathetic—home care recommended	33 (8)
No information given	23 (6)
Other	43 (11)

[a] Percentage in parentheses.

TABLE 6
PLAN PREFERRED BY MOTHER/FATHER[a]

Plan	Mother	Father
Further study	39 (10)	38 (9)
Home care	254 (63)	245 (61)
Home care, later placement	25 (6)	23 (6)
Temporary placement	10 (2)	12 (3)
Permanent placement	23 (6)	25 (6)
No plan	14 (3)	16 (4)
Undecided	27 (7)	28 (7)
Other	14 (3)	15 (4)

[a] Percentage in parentheses.

TABLE 5
RECOMMENDATIONS MADE BY OBSTETRICIANS (OBS) AND PEDIATRICIANS (PED)[a] TO PARENTS AT THE BIRTH OF THEIR DOWN'S SYNDROME CHILD

Recommendation	Before 1960 Obs	Before 1960 Ped	1960–1970 Obs	1960–1970 Ped	After 1970 Obs	After 1970 Ped
Further studies indicated	10 (8)	13 (10)	12 (8)	20 (14)	1 (1)	1 (1)
Home care recommended	14 (11)	33 (25)	29 (20)	47 (32)	63 (70)	69 (77)
Home care, later placement	7 (5)	9 (7)	7 (5)	6 (4)	0 (0)	1 (1)
Temporary placement	1 (1)	4 (3)	1 (1)	4 (3)	2 (2)	2 (2)
Permanent placement	22 (16)	28 (22)	16 (11)	13 (9)	3 (3)	3 (3)
No plan	62 (46)	31 (24)	72 (50)	36 (24)	17 (19)	8 (9)
Undecided	1 (1)	2 (2)	0 (0)	3 (2)	0 (0)	0 (0)
Not applicable	11 (8)	5 (4)	5 (3)	5 (3)	0 (0)	0 (0)
Other	6 (4)	4 (3)	3 (2)	13 (9)	4 (5)	6 (7)

[a] Percentage in parentheses.

needs and possible reactions of the distressed parents. He should also know of the processes of adaptation and the application of defense mechanisms in stress. Furthermore, the physician should carefully consider the following questions: What terminology should be employed? Who should be notified first? Who should talk to the parents? When and where should the parents be notified? How should they be told? What recommendations should be made?

We investigated these questions from the affected parents' point of view and found that many physicians adhered to the misnomer "mongolism" when introducing the diagnosis to the parents. Some physicians used the most inappropriate term "mongoloid idiot," a term that is demeaning to the child and an insult to the parents. While the term "mongoloid" or "mongolism" might be more familiar to some parents, it conjures up unfortunate stereotypes and has a definite negative connotation. Evasive answers and usage of a variety of "other" terms as mentioned above are no substitute for proper terminology and truthfulness. Because of lack of a more precise and descriptive term, personnel in this clinic prefer "Down's syndrome"; but parents are also told that some other people might use synonyms such as mongolism. Though the parents are made familiar with the terminology, it is emphasized that their child is looked upon first and foremost as a human being with characteristics apart from the "stereotype."

Many parents stressed the fact that both parents should be present during the initial discussion with the physician, as they could offer support to one another. We found that both parents were told together of the child's condition in only 20 percent of the cases, while in most instances the diagnosis was made known when only one parent was present. Some physicians talked to the mother since she was "available" in the hospital when they made rounds. Other professionals assumed the father to be the "stronger" of the two parents and found it easier to inform him first. Yet the physician should avoid having one parent bear the stressful load alone or even being responsible for telling the misfortune to the spouse.

Since the physician primarily is involved in making the diagnosis, he will also, in most instances, be informing the parents of the child's condition. Many parents were displeased because their obstetrician did not participate in the initial counseling. A mother giving birth to her first child might never have met the pediatrician, but a trust relationship with the obstetrician had been established during the antenatal period. Therefore, a combined counseling effort of obstetrician and pediatrician might relieve some of the parental anxieties. Yet the initial contact should not be made by an uninformed medical student or even by mail, as had happened to some parents in this study. In the process of counseling, the physician might also want the assistance of a social worker, who is likely to be more knowledgeable in aspects of family dynamics, adjustments in stress situations, and resources in the community.

Since in most instances Down's syndrome can be diagnosed at birth and since parents have a basic right to all available information concerning their newborn child, they should be notified as soon as the diagnosis has been made. The question arises then why, as found in this study, did physicians disclose the diagnosis in one-third of cases after the child was older than 1 month? Many parents commented that they would have preferred to be told of their child's condition soon after birth. Should parents find out about their child having Down's syndrome from inappropriate sources or in a distorted way, the trust relationship with the physician is undermined.

The most vital aspect of the initial counseling session concerns the manner in which the parents are approached and informed of their child's condition. While one-half of the parents in this investigation expressed satisfaction since their physician was sensitive and sympathetic, the remaining 50 percent could not make such a statement. Although the physician might engage in appropriate counseling, some parents might react negatively and display anger toward him because *he* is giving them the distressing news. At other times the parents' anger might be justified when physicians are blunt, disconcerned, and unsupportive. This most difficult task of discussing the child's condition with the parents demands tact, understanding, and compassion.

Since during the first encounter many parents can only assimilate some of the presented facts, follow-up visits should be forthcoming when more details can be communicated. The parents should be informed of the many aspects of Down's syndrome, including physical features, developmental delay, chromosomal aberration, and other important concerns regarding the child and the whole family. During these subsequent meetings, parents will also be able to express their feelings and

5. TRAINABLE MENTALLY RETARDED

formulate their questions more realistically.

While the counseling process will have a profound impact upon parents, it cannot be an end in itself; unless subsequent support and guidance are forthcoming, the counseling will have failed in the main objective of ensuring a realistic future for the child. The physician is in a unique position to help the parents to a positive beginning and, in doing so, he should attempt to mobilize existing parental strengths.

In past decades, due to prevalent attitudes within society and due to respective teaching in medical schools, physicians often recommended residential placement to the parents when a child with Down's syndrome was born. Since they felt that the child "will have to leave the family sooner or later," proponents of early institutionalization often argued that attachment of the mother to the child could be prevented by disallowing the maternal instincts to surface. In an attempt "to protect" the family, some physicians told parents that the child with Down's syndrome would never do anything since he is profoundly retarded, would be a menace and destructive force within the family, and would have a negative influence on brothers and sisters (all of which are incorrect assumptions).

As can be seen in Table 5, we found that today only a few physicians adhere to these irrational recommendations of institutionalization. Physicians today are better informed of the nonavailability, the poor quality, and the high cost of institutionalization (Farrell, 1956). They realize that a dictum for immediate institutionalization will have profound and lasting negative effects on the child's development. Many parents commented that institutionalization of their child, which had been recommended, would have deprived them of the joy, enrichment, and satisfaction they experienced rearing the Down's syndrome child in their home.

There are only rare situations where placement out of the home is indicated. Should certain medical, social, and psychological conditions not permit the child to stay with the family, foster home placement might be presented as an alternative.

It is of importance that professionals should never make the decision for the parents to place a child or influence parents so that they feel no choice other than sending their child to a residential facility. The physician should offer guidance and counsel and give adequate information so that the parents can arrive independently at an acceptable solution. Whatever decision parents make after careful consideration of the multiplicity of factors involved then deserves thoughtful support of the involved professional.

Since institutionalization of newborn children with Down's syndrome is undesirable and generally should not be pursued, appropriate services should be made available in the community. Families with a mentally handicapped child often will be in need of assistance in making adequate adjustment to community life (Olshansky, 1966). In order to care for their child, parents often need encouragement so that they can see positive aspects they can relate to that will then help them to overcome their fears and anxieties. Furthermore, parents are in need of professional guidance relating to general child care and special services for the handicapped child. They will also benefit from instructions of appropriate sensorimotor stimulation and other environmental enrichment in order to foster their child's progress (Zausmer, Pueschel, & Shea, Note 1). Thus, by getting involved and contributing to their child's development, the parents experience a sense of satisfaction that fulfills their own needs while at the same time they respond to the child's needs.

Your Down's Syndrome Child...

...you can help him develop from infancy to adulthood

DAVID PITT, M.D.

Introduction

This article has been prepared as an aid to parents. There is need for such aid since supportive services for these parents may be patchy and sometimes non-existent.

Many parents have had wise initial advice and continuing support from an interested person such as a pediatrician. Others have had a diagnosis presented to them shortly after the birth and, after the first shock of learning that they have a handicapped child, find themselves left all on their own.

These parents have many questions to ask about their child's future, many of which can only be answered as the child's development is studied.

If there is no professional follow-up, parents may be left bewildered and resentful. The difficult question of home or institutional care may be presented to them in a clumsy or unbalanced way, and they are frequently subjected to pressures from well-meaning but uninformed relatives and friends to part with their child. This article is intended to assist, but not to replace, the personal counsel which is the right of every parent. It is intended to assist by providing supportive reading, and so help to fill gaps that may exist in services to families.

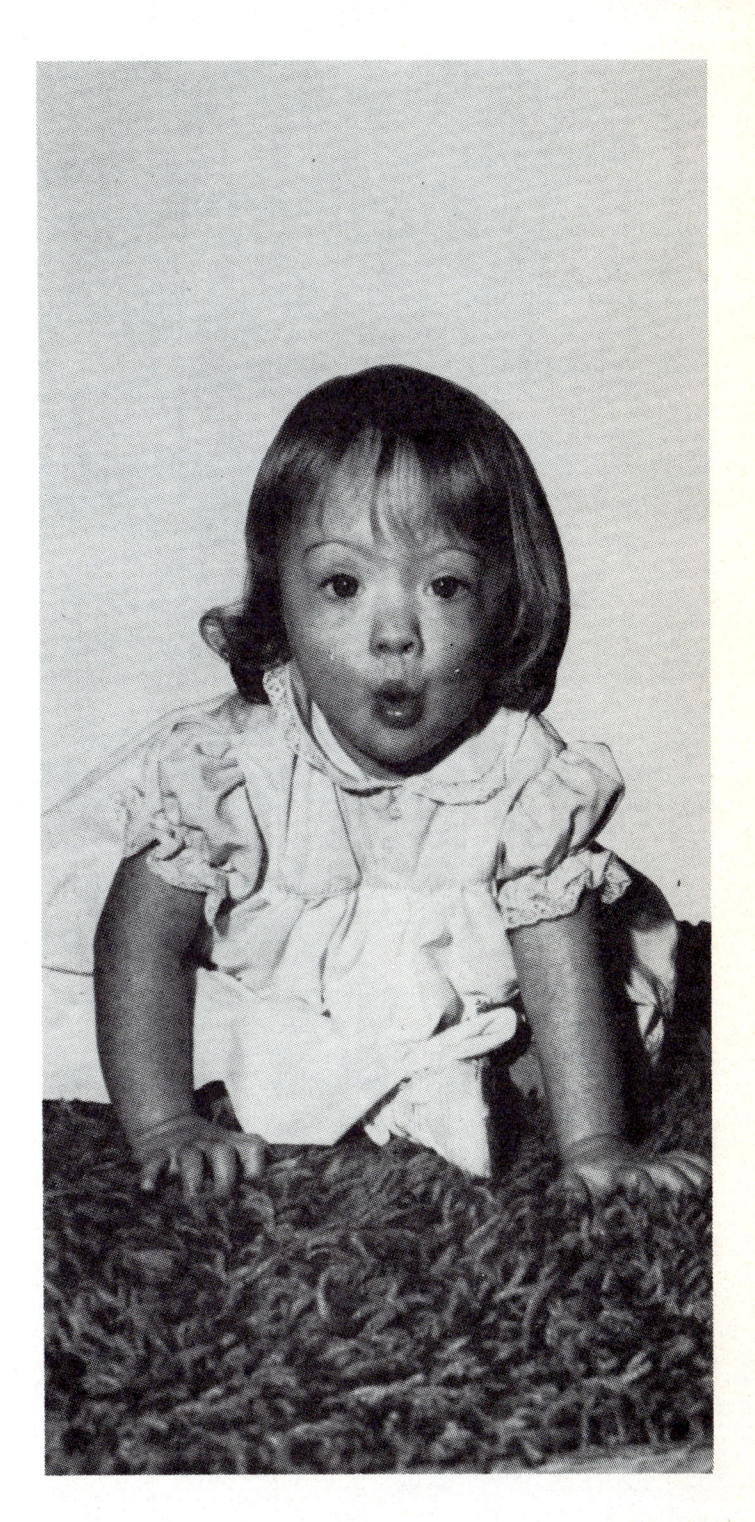

Your Down's Syndrome Child... You Can Help Him Develop from Infancy to Adulthood, David Pitt, M.D. (booklet). ©National Association for Retarded Citizens, Arlington Texas.

5. TRAINABLE MENTALLY RETARDED

What is Down's Syndrome?

Dr. Langdon Down first described this syndrome about 100 years ago, and it came to bear his name — Down's syndrome. Because of a vague resemblance in the face of such a child to the Asian races, he was described as a "mongol," and hence the old terms "mongolism" and "mongoloid." However, it is incorrect to associate the condition with Asians, who are indeed offended by the term. It is considered demeaning and developmentally inappropriate to refer to a child as a "mongoloid."

A Down's syndrome baby is "born different," it is often said. He is different both physically and mentally from a normal baby. The physical differences consist of some reduction in body and head size, and some physical characteristics which can usually be recognized at birth. The eyes are a little different, particularly in their upwards and outwards slope, the ears may be small, the tongue may be big, the hands and feet may have distinctive shapes. These characteristics, especially the small head, often become more obvious as the child grows older.

A child with Down's syndrome, aged five years, may have the mental capacity and abilities of a child of perhaps two years. And there are similar differences from the average developmental rate all through life.

The cause of Down's syndrome is not clearly understood. It is extremely rare for it to be hereditary and to occur more than once in a family. Usually it is a single event, occurring most often at the end of a family of children, when the mother is approaching the end of her child-bearing days. It occurs in about one in every 700 births.

Accident of cell development

Parents who have studied biology at school will remember what a chromosome is. It is a microscopic rod-like structure which carries the hereditary units called genes. The tiny cells of the human body each carry 46 chromosomes, which can be studied under a microscope. Each chromosome is made of hundreds of genes. The 46 chromosomes, which in varying sizes exist in pairs, are present throughout life, even from conception, when the fertilized egg contains its 46 chromosomes. Half of these are derived each from the parents' sex cells, the ovum (maternal) and sperm (paternal), which each contain 23 chromosomes. The 23 chromosomes of the ovum are derived from the splitting into two of an earlier cell, carrying 46 chromosomes, that comes from the mother's ovary.

If this splitting is uneven, for reasons ill-understood, then the ovum may contain 24 instead of 23 chromosomes. When fertilized by a sperm with 23 chromosomes, a child is formed with 24 + 23 = 47 chromosomes. If the extra chromosome is a particular one (number 21), then this child will have Down's syndrome. Somehow the extra gene material in the extra chromosome disturbs the orderly development of the body and brain, which is controlled by genes. This is no fault of the mother, as there is no evidence that any act or omission on her part is related to what is purely an accident of cell development.

This accident of cell development happens in about 95 per cent of children with Down's syndrome. In the remaining five per cent there are other disorders of chromosomes, also resulting in extra chromosome material that causes Down's syndrome.

The Down's Syndrome Baby

At first the baby may look like any average baby, and the special features may not be noticed until seen by an alert nurse or doctor. He may have a low birth weight (one-fifth are premature), and sometimes may not suck as strongly as the average baby; a few have to be fed with a tube, especially the smaller ones. A few also are troubled with heart defects, which may have some effect on their physical health. For these reasons, a Down's syndrome baby may sometimes have to stay in the hospital a little longer than usual, until feeding and sucking is well established. The baby can then go home with its mother, and be cared for and loved like any other baby.

Feeding

Some babies with Down's syndrome feed well at the breast, provided sucking is vigorous. Otherwise, bottle feeding will be necessary. The baby should be as upright as possible during feeding to prevent any tendency to inhale the milk. For the same reasons the baby should be laid down on his right side after feeding and not on the back. The nurse at the public health department or "well-baby clinic" will help with feeding difficulties, and if these are troublesome will suggest a suitable doctor.

About the age of six months is the time to introduce semi-solid food — usually mashed natural or prepared vegetables, or cereal — on a spoon. If the child seems unable to cope with swallowing it, force should not be used. The attempt should be deferred a couple of weeks for another trial; when he is ready to swallow, he will do so, and a baby-mixed diet can be built up from this point. A gradual introduction of semi-solid food helps the baby learn to accept the different food. Bottle and spoon feeding will be necessary for a much longer time than with the average child, who can usually abandon the bottle by 12 months and use a spoon between 18 and 24 months.

32. Down's Syndrome

"... in about one in every 700 births."

169

5. TRAINABLE MENTALLY RETARDED

It is important when the appetite is well established to avoid over-feeding — a natural reaction on some mothers' part — as obesity can make a baby or child sluggish and unable to make the best of his abilities.

An adequate vitamin intake is just as important as in any baby.

Development

Because of his retardation, it will be found that the baby stages of development are much slower. Thus, an average baby will hold up his head well at about three months, be able to sit without support at about seven months, be able to crawl at about nine months, and be able to walk at about 14 months. Although there is a great variation from baby to baby in reaching these "milestones," a baby with Down's syndrome will usually take longer to reach them.

In spite of these delays, it is important to stimulate learning in the Down's syndrome baby rather than merely feeding and caring for him in a passive way. For example, if he does not lift his head or turn his eyes toward objects by the fourth month, he should be picked up with his head held firmly, so that he sees objects about him. For a few minutes each day, a light or bright color should be moved before his eyes to attract his attention to follow its movement. If at the same age he is making no attempt to grasp objects or toys, his hands should be curled firmly around them, enclosing things of various shapes such as a square block, round ball, rattle, etc.

If over the age of six months he does not move his legs or arms much, this should be done for him each day, e.g., at bath time or during a short sun-bathing session, so as to teach him the pleasures of movement.

Mother-child relationship

Experiences and stimuli to which the growing baby is exposed are essential for the greatest development of his mind. These come naturally from the attitudes and actions of a mother, and are just as necessary for the handicapped child as for the average child. There are many research studies which have shown that children deprived (for various reasons) of a mother's care and stimulation are found on psychological testing to be duller than those who have had the full opportunities of a good mother-child relationship. This rich relationship brings many stimuli to the infant — stroking and cuddling, feeding, the sound of her voice, a rattle, a ball, a doll, and all the other things that most mothers naturally produce to give full early experience of the world to the baby.

Sitting without support is usually achieved by about 13 months of age, but may be delayed in some cases to 30 months. This can be actively encouraged by propping the baby up with pillows from about the age of 10 months, or by the use of little baby chairs.

Exercises should be given at changing times — raising the feet to encourage leg movements; moving all four limbs to encourage active resistance and, therefore, movement; pulling the baby (after four months) into a sitting position, to exercise the back and neck muscles, and so on.

Teaching the meaning of speech should be attempted from about the time he learns to sit without support. Simple words should be repeated directly to him, which have a direct relation to obvious things, such as himself, "Mamma," "Daddy," "bath," etc. Any child, whether average or mentally retarded, learns to speak only from a flood of conversation around him. This needs, of course, to be related to common objects about him, so that gradually a vocabulary of simple words is built up. Thus we say, "kitty, kitty," pointing to it, letting him hear the sound and see how we use our lips.

Baby's health

There may be physical problems of health in the Down's syndrome baby. Many are subject to colds and bronchitis, which may call for medical help. Antibiotics such as penicillin may be prescribed for such an acute illness, and may also be used in a low dose as a preventative measure. Coughing may be troublesome, and may sometimes be relieved at night by a sedative cough mixture. In general, cough mixtures are otherwise fairly useless, and the best relief is obtained by removing the cause, which is mucus irritating the lung tubes. By upending the baby over the knee with the head down ("postural drainage") and patting the back firmly, this mucus is encouraged to flow out of the lungs. This is best done before meals, and at night if sleep is disturbed. Cod liver oil and other sources of extra vitamins are traditional helps in colder climates, but are unnecessary in warm climates.

Nasal discharge may also be troublesome even at this age. Nasal discharge calls for the frequent use of tissues — and sometimes nasal drops — if there is much infection. The nose should be cleared first, and then the baby held on his back on the lap, with the head wedged down between the mother's knees, so that the baby's nose is almost upside down. One hand can control the baby's two hands, while the other administers the drops. In difficult cases, and in older children, repeated mild suction inside the nostrils may help to clear the nose, but this means obtaining a suitable suction apparatus and taking antiseptic precautions. However, the family doctor should always be consulted and asked to demonstrate the treatment for the parent of a child who has severe problems.

Skin, nose and teeth

The skin of the young baby with Down's syndrome is usually good, but towards the end of babyhood it starts to roughen and becomes less pliable, and is more prone to cracks and infections such as boils. The roughening may be helped with the use of lotions and creams — especially on the lips, which are apt to dry and crack. Prevention of infections is achieved by the use of antiseptic soap and by the proper care of the nose, which in infected cases can act as a nest, spreading germs both outwards to the skin and inwards to the lungs. From the end of the first year of life, the teeth should be cleaned daily by the mother, either with an ordinary or electric toothbrush.

Immunization against diphtheria, tetanus, whooping cough, poliomyelitis, and measles should be arranged through the well-baby clinic or doctor, just as with any baby.

Heart problems, from congenital defects, are common in Down's syndrome babies, and if present will call for regular medical supervision.

Mother's health

The mother's own health might be mentioned here. She is a busy person and for everyone's sake, including her own, must keep fit. This means a good diet, fresh air, regular exercise and, if possible, a holiday occasionally away from the baby.

Her mental health is just as important. After recovering from the initial disappointment of having a handicapped baby, it is vital that she face the world confidently, and on no account must she hide herself or her baby from ordinary human contact. This may lead to initial difficulties with well-meaning people who may show annoying pity or criticism, but this can be overcome usually by cheerful firmness and tact. It helps the mother's morale, too, to join a parents' group, even at this early age, where she can discuss her problems freely with other mothers, and learn something of the baby's future. These groups can be contacted through the local mental health/mental retardation center, through the state association for retarded citizens, or the nearest training center or school for mentally retarded children. A visit to the latter can be very rewarding.

Down's syndrome from two years

A child with Down's syndrome may be able to stand with support by the age of two years (again, this can be helped with training). When he can do so well, he should be encouraged to take his first steps by holding his hands and pulling him forward gently. If he collapses, he is not ready to walk, and the attempt should be postponed for a few weeks. When he is able thus to take a step or so, he is ready to be put into a little walker. By propping himself on the top part with his hands, he gradually learns to push himself forward with his feet. Eventually he is ready for separation from the device and independent walking, which takes place on an average of 27 months, but may be delayed in some cases to four years.

Self-feeding is generally achieved by the fourth year (sometimes earlier), and may be encouraged in the same way as training the average one to two year-old child — by holding both hands and spoon from behind the high chair during plate feeding, by encouraging the use and eventual holding of a cup, etc.

Toileting

Bladder training in Down's syndrome children is usually achieved during the third or fourth years of life, or sometimes later. It cannot be achieved before the child can walk, though this is sometimes enthusiastically attempted. After walking, he may be gradually introduced to the pot or lavatory when it is thought his bladder should be full, and involuntary passing of urine on these occasions leads eventually to voluntary control.

Just after this stage, bowel control may be achieved — at an average age of 40 months, though in some cases it may be delayed to about five years. As a bowel motion most often occurs after a meal, it is usual to place the child on the toilet for a short period after a meal, until eventually voluntary control follows. It is useless and harmful to prolong the time of sitting on the toilet, or to use it too early, before voluntary control of urine is achieved. Some months after toilet scheduling becomes successful, the child will be able to indicate his needs by gesture, grunts or even speech.

Night control of the bladder — an accomplishment which is variable in all children — is often very delayed, and mothers should not be overly concerned about bed wetting, which is common.

Speech

An average child uses single words at about one year of age, phrases (two words) at about two years, and short sentences (three-four words) at about three years. This is delayed in the Down's syndrome child, particularly if the child has had to be placed in an institution, where opportunities for speech stimulation are so much less than in the home. Some speech is generally present by the age of four years. If speech delay seems excessive, compared with the child's progress in other ways, a doctor should arrange for a test to check the possibility of a hearing defect.

In teaching speech, it is important to be patient and not to expect the child to repeat words before their meaning is clear. This means that taught language must be planned and simple, with the use of

5. TRAINABLE MENTALLY RETARDED

"...activities to capture his interest."

Personality

The child's individual personality will have been developing throughout his babyhood. Like all children, he usually shows acceptable characteristics which are also common in Down's syndrome children. These are cheerfulness, enjoyment, humor and fondness for imitation. He may be mischievous. Most children are pliable, though some are stubborn and may need firm handling. He may be shy with visitors, though some are over-affectionate towards strangers. There are differences between child and child, and resemblances to parents, both physically and in personality. Many are fond of music and games. Some develop bad habits, such as tongue thrust, rocking, or finger-sucking. These are usually the result of boredom; correction consists of relieving the boredom by gentle distraction with games and introduction of other activities to capture his interest.

Preschool contacts

At about this age the parents should be in contact with the nearest day training center or special school—the name varies from state to state. These centers or schools provide appropriate education and training for children with various degrees of mental retardation. They may have a waiting list on which the child's name should be enrolled and the parents will also have the opportunity of meeting the teachers who can give much useful advice. Other parents will also be met, and many centers have a parent group where the problems of their preschool children can be discussed. There will also be the chance of watching activities at the school, and seeing other children with a similar handicap, which deepens the mother's understanding of her child's future.

Down's Syndrome from Four Years

The personality will now be more apparent and varies from child to child. Most of these children are active, full of curiosity and possess a considerable power of mimicking. This is true also of their social graces, which often outstrip their actual intelligence. This, of course, is a good thing and helps to make them more able to live in the community.

Exercises

Muscular development needs to be stimulated by exercises, by marching to music, and by the use of trampolines, on which many Down's syndrome children become very expert. Likewise, swimming is an enjoyable and helpful pastime that can also be taught to these children, even from an early age.

key words over and over again to give the basis of speech. Mentally retarded children are often called "slow learners," and one must therefore prolong the teaching process accordingly, and not give up too soon. The child should be talked with frequently, and common objects and parts of the body named. These can be made into verbal games.

The size of the tongue may cause some speech difficulty, especially if there is a "tongue-thrust" and it protrudes excessively. This should be corrected if possible by tongue exercises, with gentle but frequent reminders to "close your lips."

32. Down's Syndrome

Training and education

Training in this age group should continue just as with an average younger child. Use of the toilet and self-feeding, if not already achieved, need to be stimulated; speech also will still need to be helped. Color discrimination may be taught by presenting brightly colored objects; ribbons, balls and brightly colored building blocks are excellent for this purpose. As many of these children have poor vision, it is wise to have an optometrist check the eyes at this age.

Much of this training by parents is a responsibility which they have to assume in order that the handicapped child may develop as much as possible. Fortunately, in most advanced communities, public facilities for training ("training centers" or "special schools") are available, as was mentioned earlier, so that this task is taken over by trained teachers. The child benefits from more intensive training and simple education, and the parents have the advantage of being able to share their responsibilities of both care and training. They should, therefore, neglect no opportunity of making the most use of these facilities, both for their child's and their own sakes. Parents are often surprised when the teacher shows some knack in handling the child in some respect which has eluded them. They should not be upset about this, but remember the teacher's special experience and training in this field.

Self-care

The child should be taught to clean his teeth during this period. An electric toothbrush is efficient for the parent to use prior to this stage. Cleansing of the body is also learned at this time. Dressing in part or in whole should be encouraged, and the temptation to hurry things by doing these things for him must be resisted.

Safety

In modern urban society, safety is a most important subject for training in all children, and should not be overlooked in the handicapped child. It is, of course, a special feature in programs in centers and schools, but should also be taught in the home. Caution with fire and hot objects should be taught, so that the child learns to avoid them and other obvious dangers.

At the same time a careful scrutiny of the home should be made to eliminate hazards for the grasping little hands — accessible drugs, faulty electrical equipment, open flames, pots of boiling water, etc.

Parent relationships

There should be by this age (four to eight years) good relationships and interaction between mother

"... should be taught to clean their teeth."

and child. The father is equally important, and he should be playing a significant part in home games and general stimulation of the handicapped child.

Down's Syndrome from Eight Years

Except for the few who are more severely handicapped, most children with Down's syndrome who live at home are now attending a public school for

5. TRAINABLE MENTALLY RETARDED

"The Down's syndrome child of eight to twelve years..."

"In school, the child will now be in the middle range..."

mentally retarded children. Although a great deal has been done by both parents to bring out the best in the handicapped child, the job still continues out of school hours, and the parents' duty of teaching remains. Not only do they have to teach the handicapped child, but also they should influence others who are in daily contact with him. From an early age the brothers and sisters need to be helped to understand and accept their slow brother or sister. It is wonderful to see many families in which love and understanding flourish, so

that the handicapped child is neither over-protected on the one hand, nor neglected on the other. Relatives also need to be informed of many elementary truths, e.g., that the child is not insane, that he will not become dangerous or sexually aggressive, etc. They will need to be taught tactfully the need for kindness and stimulation, if they do not already realize this.

The Down's syndrome child of eight to twelve years has of course grown, but is probably shorter than normal children of the same age. In other

32. Down's Syndrome

respects, e.g., his personality, he is very likely to be much the same as he was earlier, but of course has more accomplishments, usually those of a three to four-year-old child. However, social accomplishments may be better. He will probably be toilet-trained, be able to help with dressing, have simple but useful language, and be able to care for himself in most respects except for free movement in streets and traffic. This is a complex accomplishment that often comes a little later, and forms part of training programs.

Down's Syndrome from 12 Years

The child is now advancing towards adolescence. Puberty may be somewhat delayed. Contrary to the expectations and fears of many parents, sexual problems seldom exist.

In the school, the Down's syndrome child will now be in the middle range, preparing soon for workshop activities, and it is remarkable how expert he later becomes in both repetitive and creative manual tasks. In some places you will see young adolescents or adults doing skilled work comparable to that of average workers. Many such children learn to express themselves quite well, and in one instance a book, "The World of Nigel Hunt," has been published by a youth with Down's syndrome.

In the home he will probably have a definite role by now — the cheerful helper. Simple tasks about the home, suitable for a mental age of about five years upwards, such as washing dishes and helping in the garden, are usually enjoyed. He will probably be able to be trusted in the street, go on simple errands and even handle money. He will have useful speech.

Home Care or Institution

In former years it was a common custom to place infants with Down's syndrome in an institution shortly after birth. Often the making of the diagnosis was followed swiftly by the committal. The child was often not seen by the mother, but was transferred to an institution. The unfortunate custom of early placement is still occasionally known.

The reasons given for early institutionalization include:

• *Disadvantage to other children in the family. It is said to be unfair to the other children to keep a handicapped child at home, that they will get less of the parents' attention, and that they will be exposed to*

"Simple tasks about the home . . . are usually enjoyed."

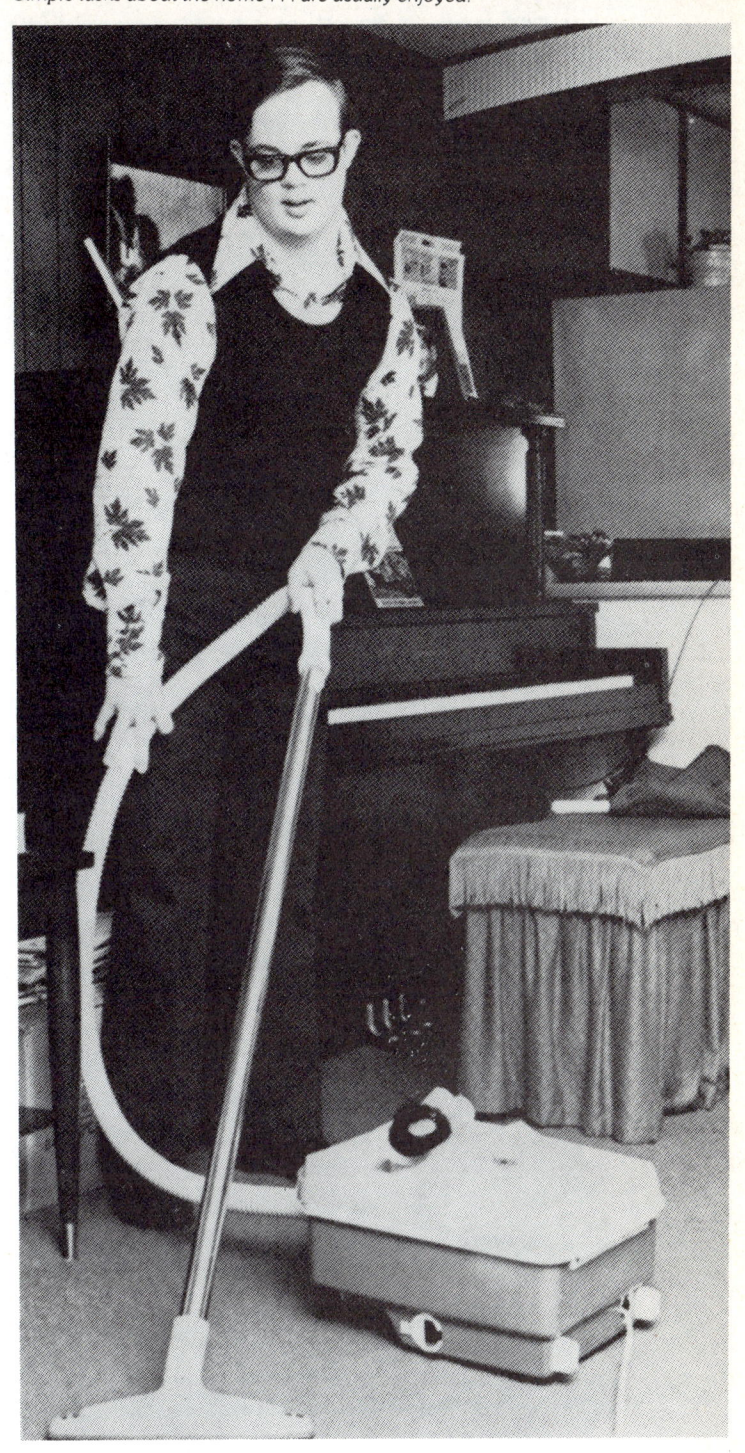

ridicule by neighbors and friends. These things do happen sometimes, especially with other varieties of mental handicap that are severely affected or disturbed. They are unusual with Down's syndrome. In surveys of families that had kept their child at home, it has been found that in about three-quarters there was good family adjustment.

• *In the other quarter there were problems and stresses, and perhaps placement would have been the best solution for these. Of course, shortly after birth,*

5. TRAINABLE MENTALLY RETARDED

there is no way of looking into the future and foretelling how such things will turn out; and many parents decide that, as home placement is obviously best for the child himself, they will try to keep their handicapped child and teach the rest of the family to love and care for him.

• *Another reason sometimes given is that since placement will be inevitable some time in the future, it is best to "get it over now," to "make a clean break," so that later pangs of separation are avoided for both child and parents. Parents are even sometimes advised never to see the child again. This point of view overlooks the grieving that inevitably strikes a mother who puts aside her baby, and also deprives the child of the early years of mother love and stimulation, which might be said to be a right of the child, even though in later years placement away from home may be wise.*

• *"These children are happiest living with children of like ability." Again, this point of view overlooks the great value of family life, and the lessened stimulation often received by young children in residential institutions. Some of the happiest Down's syndrome children I have seen are those found in the special day centers or schools, where they have a jolly and interesting period with other mentally retarded children before they go home to their families.*

Nevertheless, there are many families who have considered all these factors and have decided to place their child in a residential institution. However, they cannot do so for quite a time nowadays, due to the long waiting list for admission to most institutions.

If there is a choice of institutions, the parents should certainly look carefully at them before deciding where to apply. They should inquire about facilities for stimulation, training, occupational therapy, and medical and nursing care. A good guide to the quality of the institution is to look at the children already there, and to observe whether they are sitting around sullen and bored, or whether, as they should be, they are both busy and happy. The parents should also discover if the residential facility is accredited.

After admission it is important for the parents to keep visiting their child, and to arrange outings and holidays. Again, opportunities exist in most of these residential facilities for parents' groups and activities in which parents should join.

Later Placement:

Not all children with Down's syndrome turn out to be the happy placid people I have described. A few children are found later either to be so grossly handicapped as to be unable to look after themselves, or to have behavior abnormalities such as restlessness and aggression. These children put too much strain on family life, to which they have little or nothing to contribute. Placement may be wise in these rare cases.

Residential placement of older children may be considered for other reasons. Parents' advanced age, ill health or fatigue are obvious reasons; and provided family contacts are maintained by regular visits and holidays at home, the stress to the child caused by the change in circumstances need not be severe.

The view is gaining ground that small residential hostels, in preference to large institutions, provide a more suitable home for older mentally retarded people who are employed in "sheltered workshops." Such hostels are gradually becoming available in many places in the United States.

Conclusion

The birth into a family of a child with Down's syndrome raises special problems, but need not be the great tragedy that it is often described. With proper support in the earlier years, and the later help of the day centers or special schools, the rearing of a handicapped child with Down's syndrome can be a rewarding experience. Toleration and understanding are both requirements of the fruits of this rearing, and these gifts can flow from the parents to their other children. In many instances, with everything in their favor, parents can care for the child for years. In other cases, good reasons may impel parents to put their child into a residential center for the handicapped. In all cases, parents will be wiser and more mature for having faced the problem honestly and squarely, and for having done the best for all parties concerned in this problem of the child with Down's syndrome.

Further Reading

Mentally Handicapped Children, A Handbook for Parents and **Your Mongol Baby** (1968), National Association for Mental Health, 39 Queen Anne Street, London, W.1.

Improving Mongol Babies (1969), by Rex Brinkworth and Dr. Joseph Collins, Melbourne Observer Press, Newcastle, Co. Down, Northern Ireland.

Caring for Intellectually Handicapped Children (1962), by Ralph Winterbourn, New Zealand Council for Educational Research; reprinted by Mental Health Authority, Victoria.

The Subnormal Child at Home, by Shonell, F.J., Richardson, J.A., and McConnel, T.S. (1958), MacMillan and Company, Melbourne.

To order these books or for more information on these and other college and professional books, contact Joseph Logan, Special Learning Corporation.

SPECIAL LEARNING CORPORATION
42 Boston Post Rd. Guilford, Connecticut 06437 (203) 453-6525

Cooking Activities for the Retarded Child
Ellen House Kahan, illustrated by Nancy Deyhle.

A cookbook for the trainable and educable retarded child. The purpose is to allow retarded children to become more independent in the kitchen with adult supervision.
AB/Price $2.75

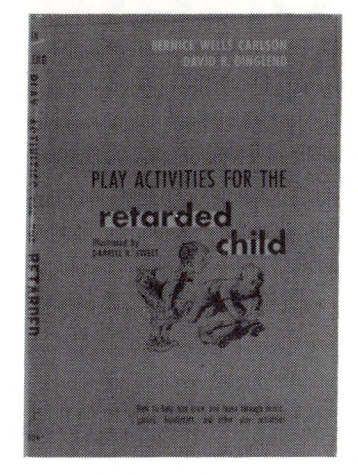

Play Activities for the Retarded Child
Bernice Wells Carlson and David R. Ginglend,

This book of special recreational activities is a psychologically and an educationally sound aid to help parents and teachers plan beneficial play for the retarded child.
AB/Price $7.65

Music Activities for the Retarded Child
David R. Ginglend and Winifred E. Stiles.

This book has been planned to assist the special music teacher, classroom teacher, recreation or volunteer leader to initiate a developmental beginning music program for retarded children. The selections have been planned to appeal to children with mental ages from three to eight years.
AB/Price $6.30

New Directions
Robert Perske, illustrated by Martha Perske

This is a book on attitudes, pointing out new directions. It will be most helpful to parents who elect to keep their retarded child in their own home, or in residential facilities very near to home. This book deals with regular family interactions which include the retarded child.
AB/Price $2.15

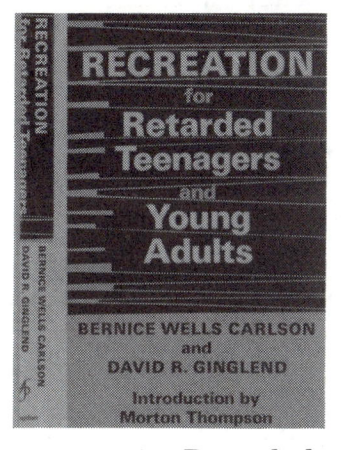

Recreation for Retarded Teenagers and Young Adults
Bernice Wells Carlson, David R. Ginglend, introduction by Morton Thompson

This book suggests new avenues of recreation that will strengthen existing programs and stimulate new programs for making the lives of retarded teenagers and young adults meaningful as well as pleasant.
AB/Price $5.45

Help Them Grow
Jane Blumenfeld, Pearl E. Thompson, Beverly S. Vogel, illustrated by Beverly S. Vogel

This book will help parents start on a program for their retarded child. It should give them some ideas for home-program development and lead them to good professional help and counseling.
AB/Price $3.00

Review Of Drug Treatment for Down's Syndrome Persons

Jack B. Share

A review of drug treatment for Down's syndrome individuals was presented. Drugs used to modify behavior, as well as drugs used with the goal of affecting cognitive processes, were discussed. Some observations were offered as to the effectiveness of past and current drugs on Down's syndrome and some methodological problems relating to drug studies presented. There have not been any drugs that have demonstrated remarkable improvement in the status of Down's syndrome individuals that have been widely accepted as effective.

After initial flurry and enthusiasm by its proponents, drug therapy for persons with Down's syndrome has for many years been a fertile area for disappointed hope. Specific drug studies in which individual medications are dealt with can be readily separated in terms of reported effect largely on the basis of the degree of experimental control employed. As might be anticipated, researchers reporting controlled studies have generally been far less enthusiastic than have those reporting uncontrolled studies.

In this paper data on the use of drugs to modify behavior will be presented, as well as on those drugs employed in the hope of affecting cognitive processes, and then some of the methodological problems associated with studies of this kind will be discussed.

Great success in using drugs with persons having psychiatric disorders led to experiments with mentally retarded persons. In general, efforts to modify with drugs the behavior of retarded children began long ago with the use of sedatives and hypnotics, proceeded to stimulants and anticonvulsants in the late 1930s, antihistamines by the end of World War II, minor tranquilizers in the early 1950s, and then passed on to the major tranquilizers in the mid 1950s. While no known drug can "cure" mental retardation presently, there are many medications that doctors feel can significantly improve the life of the mentally retarded patient. It appears that drugs of this type would be most beneficial in the treatment of retarded children when psychotic disorders or symptoms such as aggressiveness or agitation are present. Freeman (1970), reporting on a survey of psychotropic drug usage in institutions for mentally retarded persons, revealed a high percentage of patients receiving drugs. The major tranquilizers chlorpromazine and thioridazine were overwhelmingly the most popular. Where apathy, inhibition, and autistic behavior dominate, stimulant and antidepressant drugs may be helpful (Claghorn, 1969).

There are potential hazards, though, in using these drugs, and many researchers have warned of side effects such as psychological difficulties and physical problems. Lipman (1970) reviewed the current literature and concluded that the sedative phenothiazines (chlorpromazine and thioridazine) are effective in improving the behavior of the "acting-out" child, but probably at the price of reduced alertness and cognitive efficiency. Amphetamines have been credited with enhancing learning and performance. In evaluating the overall efficacy of psychotropic drugs with retarded patients, it seems important to weigh the behavior problems of the individual with possible side effects of the drug treatment.

Some drugs have been employed in research studies in hopes that they will provide direct help for Down's syndrome in-

---

Special acknowledgment is given to Liberato Salandanan and Nancy G. Leveson for their assistance with this manuscript.

The author is now at California State University Northridge.

dividuals. Beginning with Smith in 1896, many physicians have given thyroid extracts, but without startling results. Koch, Share, and Graliker (1965) studied a sample of 73 noninstitutionalized Down's syndrome children in a 6-year longitudinal study on the effects of thyroid therapy. The sample was divided into three groups in a double-blind study. One group was placed on sodium lyothyronine (Cytomel), one on placebos, and a control group on no drugs or placebos. Pediatric, psychological, social case work, and nursing services were provided for all groups. Subjects were matched and active drug treatment was prescribed according to chronological age (CA). The Gesell Developmental Scales for Infants were used for subjects up to 3 years of age. The Stanford-Binet, Form L-M, was used for subjects over 3 years of age. Height was plotted and judged, according to the Iowa Grid. Protein-bound iodine and skeletal age were determined, according to the method of Gruelich and Pyle (1950). At the end of 6 years, no significant differences were found among groups, although the parents of thyroid and placebo groups thought that improvement had taken place. Clinical examination by a physician resulted in only 50 percent correct judgments between the drug and placebo groups.

Pituitary extract has been claimed by Benda (1959), Carter (1958), and Blumberg (1959) to improve Down's syndrome individuals both physically and mentally. However, it has been proven to be ineffective in controlled studies by Berg, Kerman, Stern, and Mittwoch (1961) and Diamond and Moon (1961). Freeman (1970) concludes that no benefit seems to accrue from hormonal therapy, except in early childhood in cases of hormonal deficiencies.

Like the hormones, there seems to be no good evidence to indicate usefulness of vitamins, except in cases of deficiency. Houze, Wilson, and Goodfellow (1964) reported some improvement in the behavior of 20 retarded boys (who had failed to improve on other drugs) upon the administration of alphatocopheral (vitamin E). No control subjects were used, and no changes were noted on IQ test scores. White and Kaplitz (1964) treated Down's syndrome children with a vitamin-mineral-hormonal preparation used by Haubold, Loew, and Haefele-Niemann (1960) in Germany. There were no real changes toward normalcy in any of the subjects. Coleman (1973) is presently studying the effects of vitamin B_6 with Down's syndrome children. Her results were not available at the time of this publication.

5-hydroxytryptophan is a precursor of serotonin (5-hydroxytryptamine, which has a role in brain metabolism). Because of evidence of lowered blood level of 5-hydroxytryptamine in infants with trisomy 21 Down's syndrome, Bazelon, Paine, Cowie, Hunt, Bouck, and Mahanand (1967) treated 14 patients with oral administration of the precursor. They initially reported improvement in hypotonia, tongue protrusion, and activity level. The treated patients had significantly higher scores on the Bayley Infant Scales and achieved motor milestones at earlier ages than usual for these children. However, in a follow-up study Bazelon failed to find any long-range differences. Weise, Koch, Shaw, and Rosenfeld (1974), in a study replicating Bazelon et al.'s study, treated 26 Down's syndrome infants with 5-hydroxytryptamine from early infancy until 3- to 4-years of age. It was found that the long-term systematic use of 5-hydroxytryptamine is not effective in increasing the overall rate of development, as measured by the Gesell Developmental Schedules, of Down's syndrome children.

Glutamic acid and its salts and metabolites have been highly controversial since their introduction as anticonvulsants in 1943. Glutamic acid is a nonessential amino acid (i.e., it can be produced by the body from its precursors) which, like serotonin, has a role in cerebral metabolism. Generally favorable reviews on the use of glutamic acid in improving the intelligence of retarded persons were published by Gadson (1951), Kugelmaas (1959), and Zimmerman, Burgemeister, and Putman (1949), but Lombard, Gilbert, and Donofrio (1955), in a controversial study, reported no such benefit. Astin and Ross (1960) reviewed a large number of previous investigations and concluded that most positive reports were based on uncontrolled studies, whereas the preponderance of controlled studies showed negative results. Glutamic acid had passed out of usage until interest was revived by a more positive review by Vogel, Broverman, Draguns, and Klaiber (1965). One subsequent positive report on a small number of patients has been made by Babcock and Drake (1967). After 25 years of work with glutamic acid and its derivatives, the issue of this drug's effectiveness remains unsettled.

Siccacell therapy has been widely advertised as producing definite improvements in Down's syndrome children (Goldstein, 1956; Griffel, 1957; Haubold et al., 1960). This treatment was developed by Niehans in the late 1940s (Niehans, 1964) and consists of injecting embryonic cells into muscles in order to stimulate the activity and growth of the corresponding cellular tissues in the

5. TRAINABLE MENTALLY RETARDED

body. Most of the studies have been done in Europe as the Federal Drug Administration and American Medical Association forbid this type of injection preparation in the United States. Claims of successful results have included physical, behavioral, intellectual, social, and maturational improvements. However, the published reports include no objective criteria of improvement and no controls. Griffel (1957) dismisses the lack of controlled studies as unimportant since "the possibility of a psychic effect does not come into the question at all because such children are of course quite unaware of what is going on" (p. 333). Bardon (1964) ran a controlled study of siccacell treatment on five matched pairs of children and failed to demonstrate any effect with Down's syndrome children. In a double-blind study in 1966, Black, Kato, and Walker (1966) also found no evidence that siccacell therapy had any benefit on retarded children. Freeman (1970) describes the treatment as widely regarded as "an expensive form of quackery" (p. 338).

Turkel has treated over 350 Down's syndrome individuals with his mixture of about 48 vitamins, minerals, enzymes, and common drugs which he claims corrects the genetic flaw in Down's syndrome (Turkel, 1961). His "U" series of medication includes thyroid and glutamic acid which, as described earlier, have been used independently in attempts to treat Down's syndrome. Turkel claims that the mental and physical retardation of the Down's syndrome individual is due to an accumulation of harmful metabolics in the tissues and that under his treatment these are removed, thus freeing the retarded organs and tissues to develop according to their heredity. While Turkel has many pictures and parental testimonials as to the efficacy of his U series, he has done no controlled studies.

Bumbalo, Morelewicz, and Berens (1964) conducted a double-blind study to test the effects of the U series of drugs in the treatment of Down's syndrome. Except for improvement in socialization, which Bumbalo et al. attribute to the supervision of these children by an experienced staff, no improvement was observed. Turkel has replied that the children in the Bumbalo et al. study were given other medication, which was not recorded by the investigators, were taken off the U series for intermediate periods of time, also not recorded by the investigators, and that the dosage of the U series of drugs given was not correlated according to weight, severity of abnormalities, age, etc., but rather one dosage was given to all 12 children. No other studies of the U series have been done although Turkel indicates it is being used in several foreign countries. The use of the U series in the United States has not been approved by the Federal Drug Administration, but many parents of Down's syndrome children continue the treatment by traveling to Turkel to obtain the medication.

It seems apparent, from the preceding discussion, that methodological considerations in drug studies are crucial in establishing the effectiveness of a particular treatment method. One important consideration is the degree of control in the study. Claghorn (1969) warns that the evident placebo effects of staff attention and study do result in an improvement in children:

Most patients who have been under long-term treatment are placed in a position of helplessness and dependency. When approached with a new treatment, the opportunity is created for the patient to hang on and cling, and his wish to please and placate the therapist will result in a deceptive appearance of benefit from drug treatment—a particular disaster in the case of uncontrolled experimentation.... The danger in all these instances is that events relating primarily to personality patterns will be seen as drug effects. (p. 290)

Wolfensberger and Menolascino (1970) stress three important experimental design considerations. First, instead of having a "magic bullet" effect, a development-enhancing drug is more likely to work gradually, additively, directionally, and selectively. Therefore, any drug treatment that makes a "just noticeable difference" in a positive direction should be considered to be effective. Finally, the effectiveness of a drug in accelerating development cannot be demonstrated, or only very poorly so, unless the child is exposed to an environment and to experiences that are stimulating and appropriate to his developmental level. The interaction between drug and experience should be considered to be the crucial experimental variable.

Freeman (1970) offers some excellent guidelines on factors influencing drug studies and some common flaws in experimental designs which are listed below.

Factors influencing drug studies:

Drug factors
1. Is the patient taking the drug?
2. Route of administration.
3. Dosage: single, multiple; standard, individualized; short- or long-acting form.
4. Interaction with drugs previously or concurrently administered.
5. Individual metabolic differences may affect timing of peak action.
6. Duration of study and "washout" period between drugs.

7. Interactions with diet.

Nondrug factors in the subject
1. Severity of symptoms, level of anxiety, degree of stress in experimental factors.
2. Constitutional, physiologic, ethnic-cultural, social and personality factors.
3. Expectations and fantasies may enhance or obscure pharmacologic effect.
4. Previous experiences with drugs.
5. Relationship between subject and experimenter.
6. Motivation of subject: preparation (or lack of it) for treatment.
7. Clinic patients may be "atypically unresponsive."
8. Practice effects of testing.

Factors in experimenter and staff
1. Attitudes and expectations which may influence observations; if separate rating sheets are not used, seeing previous ratings may bias current ones.
2. Attitudes and expectations communicated for subjects.
3. Expectations of staff dealing with the patient (or parent if child is at home).
4. Investigator and staff can often guess who is on drug, and who on placebo.
5. Physician's attitude toward "blind" research and use of placebos may be negative.
6. Improper choice of rating scales or statistical methods of analysis.
7. Failure to specify uncontrolled conditions which might have influenced results.

Common flaws in experimental designs:

1. Failure to utilize placebo and "blind" procedures.
2. Failure to test for "blindness" by having investigators guess who is on placebo, and who is on drug.
3. Tests may be needed to be sure patients are actually taking drug.
4. Duration of treatment may be unequal across subjects or insufficient.
5. Failure to select sample or analyze data so as to control for possible developmental (age) differences in reactions to drugs.
6. Dosage is often fixed regardless of age or weight, or flexible, which may break the code by identifying subjects with side-effects. Several fixed levels according to body weight may be best plan.
7. Failure to choose (and specify) reasonable time between drug administration and assessment.
8. Failure to control for variations in behavior at different times of the day, and for sequence (order) effects.
9. Inappropriate sample size and matching, including symptom severity as opposed to mere presence.
10. Failure to assign subjects randomly to conditions after matching.
11. Practice effects of repeated testing on the same or similar instruments are often not "partialled out" (taken into statistical account).
12. Rating scales are frequently nonoperationalized, unreliable, invalid, or not provided in the report. Testing of raters for consistent bias is needed.
13. Failure to utilize (and report) appropriate statistical techniques.
14. Confounding of results by the regression effect (not taking into account the selection of a sample because of its extremeness on a variable).
15. Global assessments alone, without target symptoms, are often employed.
16. Other drugs or forms of therapy may be applied concurrently.

In summary, although there have been many claims of effective drug treatment for Down's syndrome children, methodological problems in the studies, along with lack of confirmation by independent researchers, tend to discredit these reports. However, psychotropic drugs do seem to be able to eliminate some behavior problems and improve the lives of many of these children. So far, there have not been any medications that have demonstrated any remarkable improvement in the status of Down's syndrome individuals that have been widely accepted as effective.

It is hoped that information reported in this paper may serve to stimulate further research in the use of drug treatment with Down's syndrome individuals and that the results of such studies not be cancelled out by poor design and/or monitoring.

NO STARS, PLEASE
for teaching the retarded

MAXINE MAYS, *associate professor, Exceptional Children Education Division, State University College at Buffalo.*

□ **"You deserve a star in your crown for the wonderful work you do!"...."You must have all the patience in the world!"...."I couldn't do that for a minute; how do you stand it?"...."You certainly are to be admired for working with *those* children."**

Is there a teacher of the retarded who hasn't heard similar exclamations of exuberance from those around him? Is there a teacher of the retarded who hasn't received these declarations with a bit of embarrassment and a degree of disdain? "A star in your crown." Why? What crown?

How strange that simply because one teaches the retarded it should automatically be assumed that he is doing "wonderful work." He may or may not be; the fact that he is *there* has little to do with the quality of his work. Yet comments such as these are made so frequently that teachers sometimes begin to believe them, even though they know better.

Why is there a general feeling that a teacher of the mentally retarded should be tremendously admired (or even pitied) for working with "those" children? Why indeed? As with all misconceptions and generalizations, several explanations are possible.

One clue may lie in the words "those children." Who are "those children"? The tone of voice with which the reference is made leads one to believe that the general concept of a retarded child often leaves something to be desired. Unfortunately, the public seems to have an image of the retarded child as an unattractive oddity, despite the diligent efforts of teachers, parents, and volunteer organizations to convince them otherwise. Typically, the first-time visitor to a class for the retarded is incredulous: "Why, I'm so surprised! They look so much like other children!" We often hear such comments, and they indicate that there are those who still view the retarded as unmanageable, pitiful, forlorn, depraved, deprived, deaf, dangerous, and mentally ill.

No wonder, then, the "valiant" teacher who dedicates himself to working with these creatures is frequently viewed as a shining angel of mercy.

Another explanation, perhaps, might lie with the teachers of the retarded. Possibly, as we talk about our work, we convey the impression that we work harder than other teachers; that our children require patience beyond human limits. Endlessly we discuss the inadequacies and failures of the retarded child—to let others know that our work is really pretty tough. By our attitudes, our choice of words, our

34. No Stars, Please

subtle hints that teaching "Johnny Retarded" is next to impossible, we may project the idea that we are really tremendous to go on with this heart-rending work. Consciously or not, perhaps we are seeking the "stars" bestowed upon us. But, because we haven't genuinely earned them, we are uncomfortable about receiving them and sometimes wish they would "go away."

The false image of the tireless, admirable, wonderful *special education* teacher should be destroyed. Images built on false premises are damaging and destructive. We can destroy the illusion and build a true picture by remembering that we are teachers, not martyrs; that our pupils are children, not monsters.

Of course we must speak about the children. We can help others see them as we do. We must erase the notion that these children are all alike. They are neither all miserable moppets nor all adorable dolls; neither all difficult nor all sheer delight. We have an obligation to share our "secret" with others. Incidents that reveal the children as they succeed and fail not only provide insights and humor but can also illuminate the dark corners of misunderstanding so many people have about these children. In our school for children who are trainable, we've encountered these:

One class happened to see a picture of the Liberty Bell in the morning paper. Their teacher asked, "Does anyone know what this is?" "A bell," answered one boy. "That's right, but this is a special bell. Don't you remember anything about this bell? Remember, I told you I saw this bell when I went to Philadelphia. Remember? I told you I even touched it. I *touched* this very bell." The boy looked carefully at the picture once more, then back to his teacher, and said accusingly, "Yeah, and you *broke* it, too! That's what happens when you don't keep your hands off things."

"Why do you color all the faces brown in the pictures you draw?" one girl was asked. "That's easy," she answered. "It's because my best friend is that color!"

A trainable boy was overheard to say, as he put his coat on to go home at the end of his school day, "Oh, boy, I got 100 on my paper today, and I get to join a Scout troop. I guess I'm the luckiest kid in town!"

A teen-aged girl carefully observed her teacher as she came into the classroom one morning. "I know what you're going to do today," the girl sang out. "You're going to a meeting after school." "Why, yes, that's right. How did you know?" "I can tell," the girl answered, "because you have on your high heels and your shiny stockings today." Observant, like other children?

"Growing up is hard," wailed a 15-year-old trainable boy. "Yes, it is," agreed his teacher. "What's bothering you today?" "Well, I keep trying not to get mad when the kids tease me. I keep trying and trying, cause you told me big kids shouldn't get mad and cry about things like that. Well, I don't cry any more, but I still get mad. It's awful hard not to." Feelings, like other children?

A retarded teen-ager had been arrested during an unfortunate incident in his neighborhood. As a result, he had become terrified of the police and hostile toward them. A year later, after a series of units in his classroom on the consequences of breaking laws, the implications of arrest, the reasons for law enforcement agencies, and what it means to respect authority, another incident occurred.

While on a fishing expedition, the boy found a radio buried in the sand by the lake. He could have kept it, but he didn't. He took the radio and rode his bicycle 30 miles to give it to the police. He had learned to be unafraid, to obey the law, and to practice good citizenship. He also learned, as he proudly accepted a $5 reward, that we sometimes benefit from our good behavior. Success, like other children?

These are the sorts of experiences that should be shared with your colleagues. Keep to yourself your once-in-a-while feelings that Betsy never catches on to anything, that Frank will never learn to talk, that Judy's drooling is driving you wild!

In addition to letting our children speak for themselves, we can correct the illusion that they are a sorry lot by curbing our penchant for showing off the children and our program in well-meant demonstration programs.

It is sheer illusion to believe that the public is attracted to our overlong, overprepared "assembly" programs, which often extend beyond sensible limits the capacities of these children to perform. The applause following such programs often spells relief that they are over, not proof that they were enjoyed or appreciated.

In addition to the work of revealing a more satis-factory picture of the retarded child, we can focus some attention on the image of the teacher who teaches him. We can be more honest about ourselves and our work. We can point out that, in fact, work with a retarded child who is trying his very best often requires much less patience than does work with a bright child who is using only half of his potential. We can explain that teaching retarded children, *like all other teaching*, is hard work, but that it is also good work with many compensations.

Some of our admirers might be shocked to learn that teaching the retarded offers a greater variety and flexibility than does most other teaching. In what other field are there so few required children's texts, so few rigidly prescribed course outlines and directives on precisely how to teach? Where is there equal tolerance for the variety of creative approaches in teaching that our work permits? Where is there so likely a commitment to the teaching of children as opposed to subject matter alone?

Furthermore, we must remind the world and ourselves that we are indeed paid for our work; sometimes more than other teachers are.

In short, "that" classroom with "those" children is really a pretty good place to be. So, if there are to be "stars for our crowns," let us give them to the children who have made possible the joys we find in our work. □

"Accept her as she is," the doctor said. "Don't think about what she is not." I did, and in learning to accept her differences, I have learned to be myself

THE GIFT OF SUSY

Nancy Lee Riffe

Another trip down the hall to stand at the window through which I could stare yearningly at Susanna in her isolette, surrounded by the gadgetry that fed her through the veins in her tiny head, a long rubber tube protruding from her stomach through her side, two large surgical wounds in her abdomen and under her arm. She was only a few days old. And although all of this had been done to save her life, the apparatus looked like instruments of torture, so opposite to the life she should be living at home in great-great-great-grandmother's baby bed, surrounded by soft, handmade blankets and excited siblings, being rocked and fed warmly at my breast.

Until now, mine had been a world of schools—the school we lived in because my father was its superintendent, the lifelong list of schools I attended until I earned a Ph.D. degree, the public schools in which my husband, Bill, had taught or been supervising principal, the colleges and universities in which I had taught English—a world of highly educated relatives and friends for whom education and intellectual achievement are the measures used to evaluate a person's worth. "Don't be stupid!" I was told as a child, stupidity being the cardinal sin. But the schooling and values on which I had based so much of my life were of no help to me now; if anything, they were a hindrance, for they had taught me that reason could solve life's problems, and here was one that reason and all my education couldn't solve.

Our babies had always come easily and quickly, but with Susanna, the fifth, things were different from the start. I had more nausea and tiredness during pregnancy. Also, soon after the baby was conceived, we moved from Philadelphia "back home" to Kentucky. The other four children had been born in medical-college hospitals under supremely modern conditions. Bill had been able to stay with me throughout the deliveries. Now we lived in a log house on a farm two miles outside a town of 5,000, dependent on a small-town hospital, 45 miles from the nearest medical center.

Another complicating factor was that we didn't know exactly when the baby would arrive. As luck would have it, she picked a particularly inconvenient time, during a week in which guests from Washington were all over the house while they attended a Teacher Corps meeting in which Bill too was very much involved. While they met, I realized suddenly that the time was *now* and ran around frantically doing all the last-minute things: mail-ordering diapers from Sears, laying in groceries for the family, making a button-down-the-front gown to expedite nursing. We all went to the final banquet and heard (I only half heard for my ear was cocked to inner things) a discussion of the future of Appalachian education.

I dragged Bill away as soon as I could, but we had waited just a bit too long for comfort. Panic and fear took hold of me in the car and increased at the hospital when the doctor explained

The Gift of Susy, Nancy Lee Riffe, *McCalls Magazine*, Vol. C11 No. 2, November 1974. ©1974 McCalls Publishing Company, New York, N.Y.

35. The Gift of Susy

that Bill could not stay with me because he had a bad cold. The hour and a half of labor, an unusually long siege for me, seemed interminable. I had enjoyed other deliveries but somehow everything felt vaguely wrong about this one. The panic and fear abated only when they showed me my baby girl and I could hear her cries.

She was born just after midnight on a Saturday morning. Bill came to see me and bring greetings from the other children as soon as he had given them breakfast. We discussed names and decided on Susanna Jestine, both old family names very dear to us. Then friends began to come in or send flowers. I was incredibly happy.

I had breast-fed my other babies in hospitals that let mothers take charge of their babies almost immediately, but here I wasn't even allowed to try to feed her. In two days I was permitted to hold the baby only twice.

Susanna had taken in a lot of mucus at birth, they told me, and although it was nothing serious, she must stay under watch in the nursery. I thought the nurses were taking the easy way out, not knowing then that the head nurse worked two consecutive shifts to be sure the baby had proper care when another nurse fell ill and no experienced relief could be found.

By Monday morning all my panic and fear returned. She had been in the nursery too long. There was definitely no Rh problem. But something must be wrong. What was it? My doctor was avoiding me. The staff worked very hard to soothe me, but their remarks were disturbingly vague. That night, at last, the head nurse brought Susanna in and stayed with us while the baby tried to nurse. Her head was frightfully wobbly, and Miss Pierson had to steady it. And although she sucked away nobly, my milk came dribbling back.

Then on Tuesday morning, when she was three and a half days old, the doctor called an ambulance to take her to the medical center; the mucus no longer seemed a sufficient explanation for her inability to keep food down. I dressed and went with her, becoming ever more alarmed by the serious way in which everyone moved, by the oxygen tent and the nurse hanging over her in the ambulance, by the furious hurry of the screaming vehicle, by the way in which her admittance had been set up and she was whisked out of sight in the big, strange, pediatrics wing. As yet no one had said anything.

The nurses were extremely thoughtful, despite the big-hospital atmosphere. Knowing that I should still be in my own hospital bed rather than a waiting room, they allowed us the privacy of an unoccupied room. Even so, the general tension began to work on me, though I fought hard to keep calm. At last the pediatrician arrived; she explained that she thought she had located the problem but preferred to discuss it with us after the pediatric surgeon had made his diagnosis. A very matter-of-fact woman, almost brusque at times, she now stopped and assured us that Susanna was in good condition and being fed intravenously in an isolette under the constant watch of a nurse.

Two hours slowly passed. Still we knew almost nothing; the tension was growing. For a mother who has given birth, the fact of motherhood is still a very physical one: I couldn't move my body without a total reminder, from my sagging, empty belly, my full and dripping breasts, that I had a baby—and that she and I were separated.

Finally the waiting was over. The surgeon entered accompanied by his assistant and two young interns who hovered respectfully behind him. I wondered later about their presence. Had he said to them, Come along and see how to handle a professionally tough situation?

Susanna had a tracheoesophageal fistula, he said. Although fairly rare, occurring only once in 10,000 live births, it was easily recognizable and a clear diagnosis was possible. Her esophagus ended in a blind pouch rather than in the stomach and thus she was born destined to starve. He operated on such a fistula about once a year and the baby's chances following surgery would be extremely good. However, and he turned to me, there were complicating factors. For instance, had I noticed anything unusual about the baby's appearance?

My mind went blank; then I forced it into focus. No need to mention her yellow skin, a very common jaundiced condition that all my babies had had. She was even yellower than the others had been, so much so that I had remarked that she looked almost Oriental. So I searched further. In the delivery room when I first saw her, she had appeared different—much weaker and more helpless somehow, a very purplish red, her skin very mottled. So I described this to him. No, he said, that was a normal reaction to cold. Hadn't we noticed anything about her face, particularly her eyes? In short, he said, he felt she was mongoloid.

Bill immediately moved close and, with his arm around me, I buried my head on his shoulder. Words flowed on around me but I was only half aware. Then, and for the next several hours, I was paralyzed mentally and emotionally by the realization of what the doctor was trying to say. A frozen scream went round inside me: *He wants us just to walk away and leave her.*

Now Bill, who has a master's in physiology, tried almost frantically to talk this thing away. She couldn't be mongoloid; so many of the characteristics were lacking. Yes, the surgeon admitted, the whole thing was difficult to pin down—just an expression and the set of her slightly slanted, slightly wide-spaced eyes and his feeling, trained in him by experience, that this was so. Did we want to take 15 minutes to think it over? He'd be back.

We turned to each other, clung and wept. Bill said he'd been so afraid of this. He'd thought she was mongoloid when the nurse brought her to him from the delivery room but had fought down the suspicion when no one had mentioned it, and she lacked the characteristic deformed hands and protruding tongue that textbooks describe. My God! he said, you wouldn't do that to a kitten or puppy—just let it starve. She *couldn't* be mongoloid, he said. And for the first time he told me he'd been afraid our second child was mongoloid when he saw him delivered and had seen the doctor do a double take and check the little hands. But Mat was *not* and so Susanna couldn't be.

I had never seen a mongoloid. I barely recognized the word. All I could summon up was a vague impression of a textbook picture, something about "vegetable existence" and a dim, conditioned response from God knows where that one was supposed to think what this would do to the whole family.

Then the surgeon returned. Well, he said, what did we think?

What did we think? Had he really thought that 15 minutes would solve anything? After nine months of loving hope and expectation, after four days of joy and love and growing fear?

Gently, the doctor went on to say that he could feel for us, that he had a family of his own, that he knew this was very hard. And gently again: What did we think?

My tongue and my mind and my vocabulary felt thick with the fuzz of heavy emotion but words finally came out and I heard myself saying, If one could think, then one would probably have to say that there should not be an operation. He seemed to lean forward, for I suppose my words sounded as far away to him as they did to me. Laboring with them, having to force each one to get it out of my mouth, I went on, But one couldn't think, it was a matter which one could only *feel*. And he settled back, for obviously I had not given an answer.

Bill mentioned that Mat had looked mongoloid and wasn't; mentioned again all the characteristics she didn't have; mentioned that I had said she sucked well when I had nursed her, an instinct a retarded child often lacks. The surgeon only listened. Then Bill asked, If there were no operation, how long would it take? Slowly the doctor answered: About two weeks.... *They want me just to walk away and leave her.* Two weeks of baby whimpers, tiny sobs. Later, when we were alone, Bill said savagely, If it *has* to be, I'd strangle her with my own two hands if they'd let me, but I can't let her starve.

Slowly, still very objectively, the surgeon told us there was another possibility. The fistula called for two separate operations: the first to install a stomach tube to allow for drainage

185

5. TRAINABLE MENTALLY RETARDED

and for feeding her, the second to correct the fistula itself. It would be possible to do the first one now so that she could be fed and kept alive until a chromosome study (requiring a rather large sample of blood and about six weeks) could be made to determine whether or not she was mongoloid, and thus whether or not to proceed with the second operation.

I think Bill saw immediately what this suggestion meant. It dawned on me only slowly during the course of the next few hours, and with the realization came a sense of abysmal darkness, a horror greater than the grief of Susanna's mongolism, greater than the possibility of her death. For this was a suggestion that we should not just let her die naturally but that we should calculate her death. After six weeks of feeding and care and then unfavorable results from the study, we would say: Pull the tube out, sew her up, forget it. Even if our leaving her now to die might not be murder, I felt sure that this alternative would have been.

I was torn apart by shock and grief and uncertainty. I couldn't say: Let her die. The words wouldn't form in my mind or my heart or my mouth. I wanted her to live, and yet I felt enormous guilt for wanting her to live, because all I had been taught suggested that the "stupid" were not fit for life. At that moment, I could not say, either: She's mine, save her for that alone, who cares whether she's retarded or not, *I love her!* It would have been so natural and—I am now convinced of it—so right to have said it. But I couldn't.

Why? Because it ran counter to our societal and intellectual pressures that urge that reason is the one characteristic by which man can be identified as human, that urge that we should not give credence to feelings but only to reason, that anyone whose ability to reason is impaired has no valid place in society and that for her good, for the family's good and for society's good, Susanna had no right to life because she would not be what we consider normal, she would not be like us.

My ability to deal rationally with this big decision was handicapped because I was at this time ignorant of what can be expected in mongoloid children, what life is like for them, though I was too stunned to realize this. I was too busy listening to my learned responses to let my heart cry out, Save her! And I couldn't ignore my heart to say, Let her die. So I said nothing.

Well, said the surgeon, we would want to see the pediatrician again and discuss the matter with her. I should certainly be taken home, he added kindly. He had a meeting the early part of the evening, but as soon as it was over he would rejoin Bill and the pediatrician at the hospital and they could reach a decision.

At the conference with the doctors that night, Bill mainly talked in terms of the great possibility of Susanna's being normal. The surgeon said she was mongoloid, the pediatrician said there was reasonable doubt and the doctor who delivered her was convinced that she was not. The bent of their discussion seems very much to have centered around the thing that most bothers me now: that if she were mongoloid she should not live, that if she were to be saved it should only be because of the chance that she might be normal. This rational approach seems to have been the only way in which, in our reason-centered culture, the question could be considered.

Yet while Bill pleaded with them (although I assume that as a parent he had no need to plead, only to demand the operation) on the grounds of the possibility of normalcy, in his heart I do not think that for him was the issue. To him Susanna simply deserved her chance. He did not see her as a puppet for others to do with as they willed, but as a life, a soul, a little person. She had not asked for this life but we had given it to her. The very fact of her life entitled her to all we could do to preserve that life for her, with no strings attached specifying how or with what abilities she should live it. Because a six-weeks' delay would lessen her chances of survival, he flatly discarded the idea of delaying the ultimate decision for the results of the chromosome study. It then became a question of whether or not *Susanna as herself* should live, not whether she should live only if she were normal. So that night at 11:30 the life-saving surgery began.

The operations, two days apart, were successful, and the stamina that marked her recuperation gave us all heart. For a month the closest I could get to her was the window, and we drove over once or twice a day to stand there and see her progress.

It was hard to know what to tell the other children (who were nine, eight, four and two and a half years old) and the rest of the family and friends. We decided to cross only one bridge at a time, and did not mention the possible retardation. I wanted everyone to want *her* to live, not want her to live in the hope she was "normal." If she died, I didn't want to hear: "What a blessing—she might not have been normal . . ."

Her surgeon was the one who christened her "Susy." I'd always loved the name Susanna and had intended to use it. But he immediately called her Susy, and the nurses followed suit—and their tenderness with her was so apparent that "Susy" seemed just right.

And then one day the surgeon sat me down and said, "Susy has done her part very well. Now your part begins. From here on out it's up to you." So I now came regularly and learned to feed her, as she was reluctantly learning to be fed. After a month of being fed through a stomach tube she had little urge to suck, little understanding that hunger pangs could be assuaged by pulling milk from a bottle.

Soon she came home, and every three hours, night and day, I tried, often unsuccessfully, to give her two ounces of milk. It was weeks before she drank with enthusiasm, but slowly, slowly she progressed and grew.

Eventually we had the chromosome study made. Susy was definitely mongoloid. I had thought I was prepared, but I broke down again in the surgeon's office. As always he was kind. "Accept her as she is," he said. "Don't think about what she is *not*."

From her first arrival home, even before her mongolism was confirmed, we drew the other children into helping with Susy. This wasn't easy to do, because her stomach tube had to remain in until she was totally out of danger and I was the only one allowed to handle her. But I put her playpen in the middle of the house and urged the children to stop and talk with her each time they passed. Every time you get her to smile you are helping her to grow, I told them. And they loved her.

The day I brought her home without the stomach tube, everyone flocked to the car to greet us. Everyone but four-year-old Dan Lee. I wondered where he was, but when I got to the house he was sitting on the couch with arms held out. "I've already washed my hands, Mommy, and you said I could hold her as soon as the tube was out!" So of course he held her, and then all took turns. It's been that way ever since. She's *our* baby.

We have never at any time considered putting Susy in an institution. We didn't want her to live only to assure that she would eat and draw breath. Human life consists of more than animal existence, just as it consists of more than rational existence; it also consists of having loving relationships with other human beings who accept us as we are, and these begin with the family. Unless problems arise regarding her health or education that we cannot possibly handle at home, so that keeping her with us would be to deprive her of what she needs, her life will be with us.

I had trouble in the early months dealing with the few people who gave advice to put Susy "away." I felt they meant well, but I also felt they knew very little about what they were saying. The last person who mentioned an institution to me is a special-education professor at my university; Susy was then 18 months old. I mentioned her progress and how I couldn't understand why so many people feel institutionalization is appropriate. "That's all right for now," he said, "but I advise you to send her away when your other children get to be dating age." "What?" I said, totally unable to see any connection. "Why, desirable mates won't want to marry them if they see a retarded child in the family," he explained. I was temporarily floored. "Well—good!" I finally replied. "If that's what they're like, I'm glad to have a good

35. The Gift of Susy

screening device. I wouldn't consider their sort really 'desirable'!"

I have tried at times to feel bitter and resentful about the surgeon's opening the possibility of letting Susy die, but I can't. For I think it was a decision we had to face squarely, no matter how hard it was. If the surgeon had simply operated and saved her life, and then later we had learned that she was mongoloid, we might have rejected her, might even have resented his having saved her. Or if we had faced the problem simplistically, preserved her life because human life at the animal level ought to be preserved, but preserved it without love and sent her off immediately to an institution, I am convinced she would have been better off dead and the surgeon morally culpable for having kept her alive. When Bill decided that Susy should live, he was making a real choice, not a simplistic one, based on a realization that she is entitled to all the opportunities that life and a loving family can afford her to develop her unique human capabilities, whatever they may be. Her rational capacities may be limited but we will help her develop them as fully as possible; similarly, she will have our love and the opportunity to develop her capacity to give as well as receive love. Her rational capacities are still hard to measure; her capacity for love, as she demonstrates daily, is enormous.

All this is very easy to see now. But at the time the specter of having a retarded child menaced my sanity, leaving me totally unable to see how Susy could fit into our nice, upper-middle-class, intellectual environment.

The surgeon, seeming to speak for all of my past experience, had seemed to me to be saying: This is right, and that would be wrong; this is reasonable, and that is not; which do you want to choose, the right or the wrong? But in actuality he never once suggested which course to choose. He simply presented the alternatives and allowed us to make the choice. His kindliness and concern for Susy suggest to me now that he would have been personally horrified if we had chosen not to operate.

I wish somehow each of you could meet Susy. In the five years since her birth I have met many retarded persons, and for some of them, those who are severely handicapped, I can wonder if life is really a favor to them, much less their families. No matter how much I wonder, though, I can never quite reach an answer; such questions defy absolute answers because they depend so strongly on the feelings and needs of the individuals involved. But no one meeting Susy would wonder if she should have lived, for she is as much a blessing to life as life is a thrill and a blessing to her.

How can I describe her? She is joyous, responsive to everything and everybody near her, totally lovable. People find it hard to resist picking her up, she is so cuddly; in fact, people find it hard to resist her in any way. "C'mon," she'll say to a stranger who has just met the family, and she'll lead him off to play blocks or read her a book. At five, she is like a typical two-and-a-half-year-old, with all of the typical charms and virtually none of the typical negative behavior. She is teeny-tiny in size, so she even looks like a two-and-a-half-year-old. Her social and motor development are greater than a two-and-a-half-year-old's, though her speech is not as advanced. She has been in a training program since she was 22 months old, which has doubtless helped her development; she also seems to have a higher IQ than the typical mongoloid's 40 to 50. She is toilet-trained, can dress herself (except for buttons and tying shoes), can draw circles and turn somersaults. She helps make the beds and is much neater than the rest of us, following us around shutting drawers and doors. She has developed a highly effective pantomime, so it is hard to hold out and insist that she talk; most of her talk is only an isolated word, but she is beginning sentences ("I want out," meaning "outdoors," for instance). However, she comprehends an enormous vocabulary, far, far more than she can verbalize. When the other children were doing "knock-knock" jokes at the table the other night, the first time she'd been subjected to this particular form of entertainment, she finally horned in by rapping on the table: "Who's there, Susy?" they asked. "Me!" she announced proudly.

Susy is like all other children in that she is uniquely herself. She is sweet and loving, often throwing me a kiss when she leaves the room, as well as on more serious occasions. She is sturdily independent, helping herself to snacks, looking at books or drawing with a pencil and any old scrap of paper, rather than needing constant attention. She is also docile and patient, more willing to compromise in her demands than a "terrible two" usually is, more apt to respond sensibly if she is given a reasonable explanation of why she cannot do as she wishes. And she is a natural comic, the funniest and happiest little one you can imagine, delighted with life and seeking to provide the same delight for others.

Susy won't get a Ph.D. like Mommy; she may never be able to do many things like the other children. And so what? She is Susy—not me or anybody else. She's different—and that is what makes her so delightfully herself. And because she is herself and I have accepted her and love her and see what she is, instead of what she is not, somehow I find that I am a better "me."

Going back over the past five years, I am startled by the changes I can see in myself. I had tried to write a few poems through the years, but recently I have written a lot and one has been published. After four years of wanting but not daring to, I have summoned the courage, in the teeth of all the great scholars in my field (the Renaissance) who have already said so much about *Hamlet,* to write an article reinterpreting that well-known play and to write it firmly and with self-confidence as though I were a great scholar too. It may never reach publication, but I have asserted—to myself—my right to think uniquely and say my say. Instead of avoiding discussion of matters about which I am no expert, I am willing now to search within for my own opinions and impressions and feelings; it seems to me that more people enjoy talking with me than before. My students used to seek me out only to find answers to questions; now some of them drop by to chat, even to discuss world or personal problems, and I think we are growing and learning from each other.

Susy has helped me in other ways, too. Because there was no program for trainable retarded children in our county, four years ago I joined a new group of volunteers and we have organized a school. I have learned through commitment and necessity how little I know about life. I've taught myself about publicity and "educating the public" and fund raising. I've learned how to share with others my feelings about Susy and my experiences with mental retardation. I've learned about human psychology and behavior modification, and not just as they relate to retarded children. I've met all sorts of people, ranging from the governor of the state to the illiterate parents of a retarded child, and have learned to listen to and communicate with them all. I've learned about human need of all sorts, and something of how to get some of these needs met. I've learned about human dignity and integrity and strength and compassion, and having found them outside my former narrow world, I no longer confuse them with intelligence and educational prowess but recognize each quality for what it is.

Susy has brought me out of the ivory tower and into the real world. Through efforts to establish and continue her school under our local Association for Retarded Children, I have become involved in the total community around me. And this past year, through a series of accidents, I became governmental affairs chairman for our state Association for Retarded Children. I, who previously wouldn't have walked two blocks out of my way to visit the capitol and somehow assumed that politics was too "fixed" for anyone to waste time trying to deal with, spent several days a week testifying to legislative committees and pulling every string I could discover in my political innocence. The result: No school-age child in Kentucky can now be denied his right to a free public education. (We also worked successfully for bills lowering the cost of institutionalization

5. TRAINABLE MENTALLY RETARDED

and on the problems of the retarded in the corrections institutions.)

So Susy has helped not only me but, through me, some 88,000 exceptional children in our state, herself included. In order to develop myself and much of my potential, I needed more than all my formal education had given me. I needed Susy and her differences to bring me awareness of myself and my world, and an ability to appreciate and enjoy life itself.

And who's to say the world doesn't need Susy as much as I did? Because she is not like most of us, because she is retarded, she presents us with the opportunity to rethink our values and, having thought, to reach out to fulfill our unrealized humanity.

WE WELCOME YOUR COMMENTS

Only through this communication can we produce high quality materials in the Special Education field.

Special Learning Corporation
42 Boston Post Rd. Guilford, Connecticut 06437

"My Twin Sister Isn't Just Like Me"

Sandra Ann Lambert

How one girl learned a very special lesson in love

"One...two...three....We can talk now, Ann!" Those words will always bring back memories of my childhood. I can remember my father telling my twin sister and me to go to sleep. His final threat was a spanking if we didn't quiet down. My sister would close her eyes, fold her arms, count to three, and then, sitting up in bed, would exclaim: "We can talk now, Ann!" It seemed to her that counting to three was all that was needed to make things right. And so, through the years, counting to three has made things all right for Susan. My sister doesn't understand numbers very well. She's mentally retarded.

I don't remember the first time my parents told me about Susan. I guess I just always accepted it as if it were something that was supposed to be. I knew what other families were like, of course, but as Dad used to say, "Ours is a little bit different."

As the years went by, I noticed these differences more and more. There were times when I would ask, why? Why did it have to be us? Why couldn't we be like all the other twins? Why did Susan have to be different? I still ask questions now, though I hope I understand my sister a little better. The only real answer I've found is that God needed a messenger to send to our family to tell us of His love. He sent Susan, knowing that through her, we would learn to care more for the people around us, and for Him. For by understanding her and accepting her handicaps, we can now help others by learning to accept theirs too. We can see that we are all God's children, and that He cares for each of us in His own way. We have already learned a great deal about people and God's love for man, and through Susan's example we are hoping to learn more each day.

At nineteen, Susan is severely retarded. She functions at the level of a nine- or ten-year-old child. When she was born, anoxia occurred, which means that because of a premature birth and a hard delivery, there was a deficiency of oxygen going to the brain. This resulted in damage to the brain cells, which, once destroyed, can never be replaced. There are two hundred *known* causes of mental retardation, and anoxia is only one of them.

As with all other infirmities, the problems entailed vary from one individual to the next. Some mentally retarded persons have no physical disabilities at all, whereas others, like Susan, may have trouble walking, speaking or eating, because the part of the brain controlling these functions has been impaired.

When Susan was very young, she was considered a spastic. With training, however, and a lot of loving care and work on the part of my parents, she learned to walk when she was three. Susan was a slow starter and she will never be able to catch up completely.

When I was younger, I couldn't accept her limitations. I didn't understand why she couldn't ride a bike or run as fast as I. Consequently I began looking down on her and treated her like a little girl. Often I would tease her about not being able to run, but she would always have an answer for that: "I can walk, can't I?"

Before I started going to school, Susan attended a special kindergarten where we lived in Battle Creek, Michigan. It was part of the Ann J. Kellogg School, and designed for children with disabilities, like the deaf, blind, physically handicapped and mentally retarded. I can still remember Susan coming home with the pictures she had drawn. They were always taped to the refrigerator, and everyone made a big fuss over them. When I started bringing mine home too, they were pinned up also, but it always seemed as though hers were more special. I don't know why, but I used to feel cheated and jealous.

I can remember my girl friends coming over to play. We would often leave Susan and go off on our own. We did this mainly because she couldn't keep up, but inside I would feel very mixed up. Should I leave her or should I take her along? I kept thinking of her at home while I was having a good time, and this would make me very guilty. But when Mother asked me to take her along, I would feel resentful and still a little jealous, because she seemed to take away some of my fun. I have often thought about these feelings. Finally, after talking to my parents and friends and searching myself, I have come to realize that she needed, and needs, the extra attention. The feelings are still there sometimes, but I'm more able to cope with them now. I know I have so much more potential than Susan and can do so much more.

There are two major classifications of mental retardation—educable and trainable. Educable refers to the mild or borderline group, who usually have an IQ of fifty to seventy-five and can adjust to society with a little help or training. As they grow older, they often leave home, get jobs, marry and have children if they desire.

The trainable retardate has a few more problems (although both groups, because of greater research and technology, can now live an average lifetime, and many exceed the normal life expectations). Their IQ is below fifty, and they usually need the care of a "supervised" environment—whether home, school, sheltered workshop, nursing home or institution. Susan is considered a trainable MR.

When I reached junior high school, I realized that for a long time I had been looking at my sister only from the standpoint of intelligence. Susan has many fine qualities, but for thirteen years of my life I had seen her only in terms of her limitations in learning. At last I became aware of her personality. Susan could best

"My Twin Sister Isn't Just Like Me" - How One Girl Learned a Very Special Lesson in Love, Sandra Ann Lambert, Seventeen, December 1972. ©1973 Triangle Communications, Inc., New York, N.Y.

5. TRAINABLE MENTALLY RETARDED

be described as the girl with the "curl in the middle of her forehead." When she's good, she's outgoing, tries to please everyone and has a way of making people like her from the start. But when she's bad—watch out! Most of the time she's happy and affectionate at home, but sometimes she can become moody and cold in a flash. She is a constant worrier. Will the bus be on time for school? Will the "leftover" work be safe in class?

Physically, Susan is about five feet two, has reddish-brown hair, brown eyes that twinkle, and a rather large frame. I'm two inches taller and about ten pounds heavier; I don't wear glasses and she does. But when we were younger, we were recognized as twins all the time. In fact, we have what I like to call "twin ESP." It seems that when something goes wrong for her, I can either sense it or something goes wrong for me too. Once at school I had a feeling that something wasn't right at home. A quick phone call told me that Susan had missed her bus for school and was all upset. Episodes like that make me marvel at how very special our relationship is.

After I discovered the "real" Susan, I would play with her a lot and try to teach her things. I often tried to teach her to swim, but she just couldn't coordinate her arms and legs properly. One day while we were swimming at a neighbor's pool, Susan was trying to push someone in and fell in herself. We were all scared to death she would drown and jumped in after her, but she rose to the surface, laughing and doing the dog paddle. "I can swim, right, Ann?" she asked.

During my eighth-grade year, we moved from Battle Creek to Delavan, Wisconsin. My sister had become too old for the school she was attending, and my parents felt that the Lakeland School, near Delavan—a special county school for retarded children through the twelfth grade—would be ideal. At the time, I resented everyone for having to move. After all, I kept asking myself, after living thirteen years in one place, how can you just pick up and leave? Would my whole life now change? Would people accept me after learning my sister was retarded? I guess I just didn't want to leave my old secure friendships, but for Susan's sake it was necessary.

My sister responded well to her new surroundings. She liked her school, fell in love with her teacher, and everybody in the neighborhood was friendly and willing to help. I, too, fell in love with my school and made some great new friends, so I guess everything worked out for all of us.

In my junior year in high school, I became interested in an organization called Youth Association for Retarded Children. This group, made up of young people, is dedicated to making life a little easier for the retarded.

I don't know why I joined at first —I guess because I wanted to make others think I was sacrificing my life for my sister. But soon I met other young people who really cared about the mentally retarded and wanted to help them, and they gave me new strength and support. They taught me to see that I didn't really have to sacrifice my life for Susan, but that I could be giving more of my time to her needs. Susan has many problems that people don't realize unless they understand mental retardation. How do you explain to her, for instance, that she can never learn to drive a car? That she can never play tennis? That she can never go out on dates? These questions need answers, and these young people understand that, not only because they have been working with the retarded, but because many of them have retarded brothers and sisters, too.

By being in this group, I also learned about the different types of mental retardation, and how to cope with each. I was able to see that the term involved many degrees and levels of ability, and that while some retarded persons were perfectly capable of holding down jobs and earning their living, others weren't even able to get out of bed. I was amazed again and again at some of the skills and expertise they acquired—sewing, typing, factory work, even playing the trumpet! I realized then that Susan could be accomplishing more. So we went to work. I started to accept her as a young adult, one who was beginning to learn about the world.

Two summers ago Susan and I had what was probably the most wonderful time of our life. It lasted only one week, but in that week, we began to understand each other a little better. We went to a camp specially designed for retarded children and adults, and run by YARC volunteer counselors. It was the first time Susan and I had ever been away from home together, so it was a new experience for both of us.

There were about thirty retarded campers there, ranging in age from fourteen to fifty. Each day we explored and discovered new things. For Susan it was horseback riding. We had tried for years to get her to ride, but she had always refused. At camp, however, she was always the first in line. Of course, she was scared, but once she was on, it was hard to get her off. Why? Maybe because for the first time she was experiencing something for herself.

I think Susan and I will always remember talent night. We lived in a cabin with five other girls. Our cabin's name was Mouse House, and we called our kids the "Mouseketeers." We made ears and tails out of balloons, and they sang the Mickey Mouse song. I don't think we could have laughed more than when one of the girls got up and her balloon popped. "That's show biz!" said one camper.

We had so much fun the week went by too quickly. I know that both of us will carry memories of that summer for a long time. Awards were given the last night, and my sister received one for "best giggler." There may never be such an award again, but for Susan it was very special, and she will cherish it all her life.

Then I went away to college, and the separation was difficult for both of us. It was harder on my sister, of course, because when I left, she had no one to play with, or to be her friend. The YARC in our county realized this, and now Susan has a special buddy, a youth volunteer, who comes over to play.

Because **of Susan and children like her, I am now pursuing a major in Special Education at the University of Wisconsin at Whitewater. I have also joined a national organization called the Student Council for Exceptional Children, which works with young people with all different kinds of mental and physical problems.**

I also try to go home or call there each week. This gives Susan something to look forward to. When I arrive, she takes me by the hand and we walk around the neighborhood so everyone can see that her sister has returned. This makes Susan very happy and me feel very special.

Like all brothers and sisters, we too have our differences. Susan likes certain TV shows which I can't stand—*I Love Lucy, The Three Stooges*—and we usually end up fighting over which one to watch. Who wins? Well, usually by the time we're through arguing, the program is over!

But no matter how much we fight, a closeness is always there. When she comes to me for comfort and I'm holding her tight, I often wonder what I would do if I ever had a retarded child. Would I be able to accept her as I have grown to accept my sister? I also wonder about Susan's future. What will happen to her? Who will look after her when we no longer can take care of her?

Counseling Parents After The Birth Of An Infant With Down's Syndrome

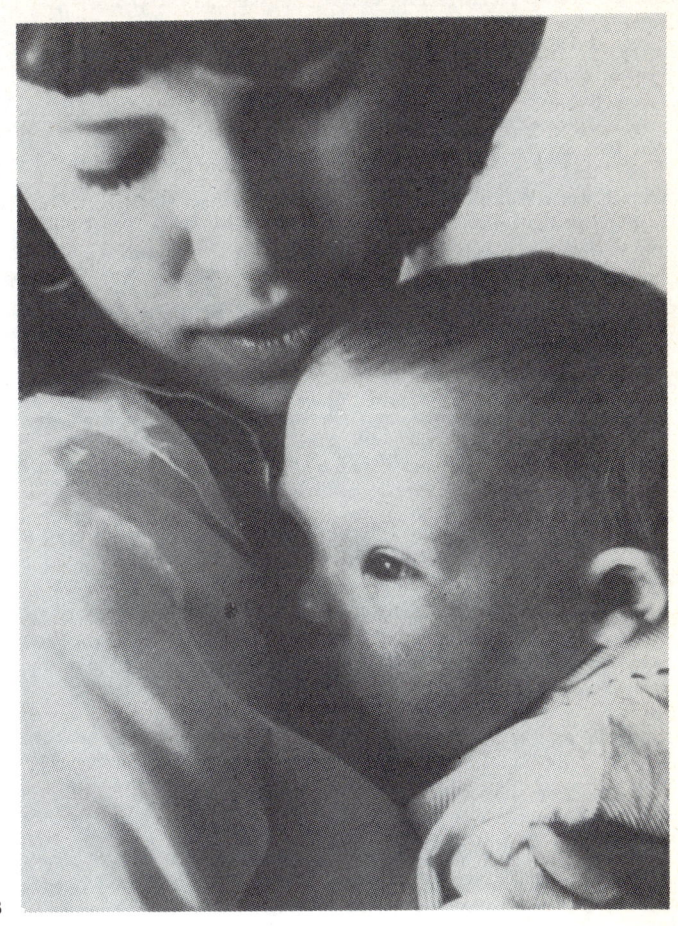

Deborah A. Golden and Jessica G. Davis

Approximately one in every 600 babies born in this country is diagnosed as having Down's Syndrome. The condition has lifelong implications for physical appearance, intellectual achievement and general functioning. It is usually suspected at the time of delivery or shortly thereafter. The clinical diagnosis must be confirmed by chromosome studies for the child with this syndrome has extra genetic material, usually in the form of an entire extra chromosome.

The physical characteristics that a doctor generally finds in a baby thought to have Down's Syndrome may include upward-slanting eyes, simple ears, somewhat protuberant tongue, short stubby fingers and, sometimes, an unusual crease in the palm of his hand. Although babies with mongolism seem to have more heart defects, as well as more colds and respiratory infections than normal infants, the use of antibiotics and the development of modern heart surgery have increased the life expectancy of these children.[1]

The intellectual functioning of the children varies but a majority will be moderately retarded and trainable. A small proportion of individuals with this condition function in the range of mild retardation, while others are severely retarded.

The birth of an infant with Down's Syndrome—mongolism—represents a major crisis for physicians and parents alike. We believe that it is crucial at this time that doctors and other involved professionals view each child as a human being and each family as unique. We also believe that frightened, hysterical and grieving parents should not be offered stereotyped solutions or be pressed for lifetime decisions.

5. TRAINABLE MENTALLY RETARDED

At a time when they have not yet begun to come to terms with the diagnosis, or to understand what the child-rearing alternatives are or might mean to them in the future, parents should not be urged, as they so often are, to place their child in an institution. Rather, we believe that they should be given initial and ongoing medical support and be helped to reach community resources that can aid them. With this kind of help, many families can care for young children with Down's Syndrome at home and those who subsequently decide to place their children in residential care will have done so in a more thoughtful and rational frame of mind.

This article is based upon our clinical experience at the Genetic Counseling Program of the Rose F. Kennedy Center for Research in Mental Retardation and Human Development, Albert Einstein College of Medicine, and on a series of 100 structured interviews held with families of children with Down's Syndrome. The interviews were conducted with parents and sometimes other relatives who had come to the Center for genetic counseling and to discuss other concerns about the children. They took place after we knew the families and had asked them to "think back about your experiences" and then discuss them with us and other doctors, nurses, social workers and counselors at the Center. Since our purpose was to study and evaluate the informing process, we talked about how and when they were told of their children's defect. We also learned what information and advice had been given to them regarding the care of their children and the effect this advice had had on their lives then—and now.

Professional Response To The Birth

The discovery of an affected infant is disturbing to the obstetrician, the pediatrician and the nurse. Any one of them may be immediately confronted with decisions as to when and what to tell the parents about their new baby.

Most doctors tend to give the diagnostic information as soon as possible after the time of delivery. This approach would seem to be a good one, rooted as it is in the recognition that parents have a right to know about their infant. Moreover, delays in relaying the information can lead to misunderstandings and, since information is disseminated and distorted quickly in hospitals, the likelihood that the parents will learn about their child from some unexpected and inappropriate source increases as each day passes. If a couple learns about their infant's condition from another person, the family's relationship with their doctor and with any others they might consult may be jeopardized.

Informing the family early of the diagnosis of Down's Syndrome, however, does have one major pitfall that causes several difficulties: the family does not yet know their infant as an individual. In addition, they may know nothing about children with this medical problem or have only scanty and often incorrect information about it. Therefore, their view of the child—of what he is like now and how he will be in the future—will be very much determined by the doctor's statements regarding cause, manifestations of the condition and his prognosis. Since he may be viewed as an omnipotent figure whose recommendations the family frequently feels compelled to follow, the doctor's opinions and advice are often crucial.

In their initial discussions of Down's Syndrome with parents, physicians often give specific advice regarding planning for the baby's immediate and eventual care, in addition to their explanation of the infant's condition. The experiences of the patients known to our facility confirm findings that the recommendations of many physicians constitute an "unqualified dictum for institutionalization."[2] Such a suggestion on the doctor's part, regardless of the family's eventual decision about placement, can have profound, long-lasting implications for the life of both the child and his family.[3,4]

Why do physicians in such large numbers continue to press automatically for immediate institutionalization of newborns with Down's Syndrome? First, perhaps because some doctors perceive the baby's condition to be a hopeless one. They may know little about this disorder or how children with it develop. The physicians initially consulted by parents now active in our clinic often indicated that the child essentially would be a vegetable and reach few, if any, milestones. They implied it would not be worth the family's effort to bring up the baby. Children with Down's Syndrome were frequently portrayed as presenting overwhelming management problems and parents were told their presence would be destructive to other members of the family unit. Unaware of the guilt, denial and struggle present even in parents who appear to have completely rejected the child, physicians may also tend to focus on the child's possible eventual need for special care and on arranging for this before everyone becomes involved with and attached to him or her.[2]

Placement may also be advised because the physician is transmitting his own negative feelings. Recommendation of institutionalization may become a way of obliterating a situation he considers unbearable.[4]

Parents' Reactions

Whatever their race, religion or socioeconomic background, families are devastated to learn their new baby has Down's Syndrome. Frightened by the implications of this disorder with respect to the child's appearance, intelligence and capacity for independent function, their joy in the new baby is compromised. When placement is mentioned at this juncture, there are several characteristic responses.

Some families seize on the idea, welcoming the apparent opportunity it offers to escape the problem. They then proceed to place their child. However, many such families often find that their problems only begin once the infant is institutionalized. Since they never knew their child, they may now wonder whether he would have done better had he been kept at home. They find their sorrow at having produced a retarded child is still present, as is the attachment to the infant which began long before birth.[4] The Allen family, with whom we spoke, clearly illustrates the difficulties which can arise from premature placement.

Polly was born when the Allens were in their mid 30s. They were told immediately that Polly was "Mongoloid," a condition which meant, they understood the doctor to have said, that she would not develop at all and should be "put away." The Allens responded to the physician's "order" by arranging for immediate institutionalization, despite the great financial burden it would impose. The

37. Counseling Parents

baby developed poorly. However, despite the seeming confirmation of the doctor's dire predictions, the Allens kept wondering if their child would do better at home. Finally, when she was five years old, they decided to take Polly home, even though she could not stand, feed or toilet herself and had no language development. Within six months, Polly was walking, feeding herself and beginning to comprehend what was said to her. She was then accepted into a day school program for severely retarded children.

While the Allens know that residential placement will probably be necessary eventually, they feel Polly will now function better in such a setting. Moreover, they have benefitted from having Polly at home to love and nurture. The Allens feel betrayed by the doctor who urged placement initially and they wonder how their child might have developed had she been with them from the start.

For various reasons, many families reject the recommendation for placement. Nevertheless, the fact that such a plan was proposed often has a substantial and continuing deleterious effect on their relationship with the child and the professionals who deal with him. Parents may view the child as unworthy and useless or at least believe that others perceive him this way. Such an attitude may inhibit them from giving the child needed attention, stimulation and discipline. Other parents may be very surprised when their baby achieves certain milestones and then feel that they have been misled by those who were supposed to know better, a feeling that is often translated into a generalized hostility toward physicians and other professionals.[4] Thus their necessary future relationships with doctors and others often become uncomfortable, unproductive, or cease to exist. The Brandon family story illustrates such a sequence of events.

The Brandons are a young couple whose first child was diagnosed immediately after birth as having Down's Syndrome. Immediate institutionalization of the baby was recommended because, they were told, Robert had no future and would bring them only unhappiness. Although distraught, the Brandons instinctively felt that their son should be with them. They took him home and located a new pediatrician to oversee his routine care.

Robert achieved virtually normal milestones. By age two he was walking, toilet trained, and saying a few words. As the Brandons realized the capacities of their youngster, they became increasingly angry with the physician who had recommended placement. Later they transferred their negative feelings about their first doctor to all physicians, believing that they could not risk discussing Robert with anyone. By chance, when Robert was four, the Brandons learned about the local Association for Retarded Children and then sought services through that agency.

Gradually these parents began to feel comfortable enough to trust professionals by consulting with them in relation to Robert and their decision to have another child, a decision they had postponed until then.

Robert is now a sociable, verbal 7-year-old who is learning to read. The Brandons are still very angry with the doctor who pressed them to institutionalize him, and they are frightened by the thought that they might have heeded his advice.

The Carrs are another family that remains disturbed by

This little girl with Down's Syndrome is growing up at home

Photos: Howard Bennett

5. TRAINABLE MENTALLY RETARDED

an early recommendation for placement of their child, even though the parents rejected the advice.

The Carrs were told that their third child had Down's Syndrome soon after their daughter was born. Both the attending obstetrician and the pediatrician advised that they place the child and the Carrs were on the verge of acceding to this pressure when they sought another opinion. At this point, the way in which the Carrs talked about their infant and handled her showed the consulting doctor that placement was really the last thing the family desired. Once they were encouraged to keep their baby at home, the Carrs were enormously relieved and they assumed their parental roles confidently. Their daughter is now an alert, active toddler whose developmental milestones are only slightly delayed.

The Carrs are delighted with their youngest child, as are her 10- and 12-year-old siblings. However, they still become distressed when they consider that they might have followed their first doctors' advice and placed the child in an institution.

Discussing Down's Syndrome With Parents

How can the physician, who usually has primary responsibility for communicating with the family, and other professionals enable parents to deal with the crisis that occurs when a baby is born with Down's Syndrome?

First, all involved have to recognize and understand their own feelings about the affected infant. The professional must strive for an objective approach to each separate family situation. The parents need support and assistance so that they can get to the point of planning rationally for their child. The eventual solution, such as placement, may not be appropriate at this time. Rather, the major goal then is to help the family deal with the acute grief and chronic sorrow that invariably accompany a diagnosis of Down's Syndrome. This obligation cannot be discharged in one or two discussions with the family.[3,4] If the doctor tries to deal with what has happened, the family will usually try to cope also. It helps, whenever possible, if the doctor (obstetrician, pediatrician or general practitioner) knows and is trusted by the family.

Any information about Down's Syndrome should be discussed in the presence of both parents. The physician may first wish to discuss his impressions with the child's father before they go in together to talk with the mother.[5] If the father is not available, arrangements should be made for a relative or close friend to be present when the doctor initially conveys the diagnosis. The vulnerable new mother should not be alone during this time, as she so often is.

The physician can begin his talk with the family by voicing his concerns and suspicions about the baby. If possible, he should be holding the infant in a respectful and caring way during the discussion. His willingness to hold the infant so will help convey to the family that the baby is human and capable of being accepted. The doctor may wish to demonstrate some of the clinical findings directly in order to support his belief that the baby probably has Down's Syndrome. He should talk about confirmatory studies that need to be made. In addition, he must mention the possible presence of any other medical problems, such as congenital heart disease, and explain what can be done about them. He should indicate that such a child can be born into any family, regardless of their circumstances, and that genetic counseling is available for parents like them.[6]

In speaking about the baby, the doctor should point out that the young infant with Down's Syndrome has the same needs as most babies and that it is anticipated that he will respond to those who care for him and show development over time. The doctor should explain that the baby is not expected to remain in a vegetative state, although his or her achievement of normal psychomotor milestones will probably be delayed. The parents should also know that there is absolutely no way to predict any baby's exact course of development at the time of birth and that this fact also applies to those with Down's Syndrome.[1,3,6] Parents should also be reassured about the baby's physical appearance; in particular, that the infant will not be a "freak" or a "monster."

After the doctor completes his explanation, he should be prepared for and encourage questions. It is important that he demonstrate his willingness and capacity to accept the upsetting behavior parents may exhibit. When he finally leaves the couple to talk alone, he should promise to come again the next day to continue the discussion. This second visit is essential because many parents are unable to communicate effectively so soon after hearing the diagnosis.

No attempt should be made at this time to keep the baby from the mother unless specifically requested.

Much of the initial information should be reviewed when the doctor returns to talk with the family. The parents are certain to have more questions, including some regarding the long-term prognosis for their infant. The family must be told that the child with Down's Syndrome will almost certainly be slow or retarded. Simultaneously, the parents need to hear that there is no cure for this disorder and that their child will not outgrow his difficulties. Again, however, it must be stressed that at birth there is no way of measuring a child's ultimate capabilities. These are dependent both upon endowment, which in this condition sets known upper limits on the individual's development, and on the child's environment. Nevertheless, although there is a wide range of possible functioning, a child with this condition will need special education and supervision throughout his or her life.[6]

Upon learning about the lifetime implications of Down's Syndrome, families usually fall into one of two groups. Some parents will begin to accept their fate and commence the necessary mourning process; at the same time, they will begin to mobilize themselves to care for the baby. These parents need to know that their doctor and other appropriate professionals, such as a public health nurse or social worker, will be there to help them through the very difficult period of adjusting to having a Down's Syndrome baby and telling other family members about his condition, as well as dealing with any medical or management problems the baby presents.

The Duncan family was introduced to their baby's condition in the manner described and the way they were informed seems to have had a great deal to do with the quick progress they were able to make in adjusting to the infant's problems.

37. Counseling Parents

Mark was the Duncan's first child. Mr. Duncan was told first about the baby's difficulty and he then told his wife in the doctor's presence. The physician gave them a positive but realistic view concerning their son's probable development during his first few years of life and later. In discussions with the Duncans, the doctor indicated his belief that Mark could be raised at home and that all concerned would profit from his presence there. The Duncans left the hospital with good feelings about their baby, correctly anticipating his slow but steady development. Moreover, they felt a strong bond with the pediatrician who respected the child and their feelings for him.

Other groups of parents, as they begin to come to terms with the fact their child is irrevocably retarded, will ask about placement. In response to their questions, they should be told that this is one alternative and that it has specific implications for both the infant and his parents. Unless a child needs continual medical attention, the doctor may tell them, "Most mongoloid infants can be cared for at home in the interest of both the child and the family—and many such children in the past have been inappropriately placed." [2,3,7,8,9]

Since the overall needs of a child with Down's Syndrome do not differ greatly from those of other children during infancy, there is no reason why a young mongoloid child should make undue demands on its parents or other family members. The parents can be told they can always place their child later on if they can't manage but that they and their child will probably never be able to regain what is lost if the infant is in an institutional setting during his early years. Parents, as well as their children, lose a great deal when they are unable to nurture their child.

It is also vital for physicians and families to understand that public institutions in the United States may not accept infants and that private facilities which often have long waiting lists can be very expensive. Doctors often suggest institutionalization as an alternative to home care without having any knowledge of the availability, quality or cost of such care. Doctors may also fail to mention other options that may be open, such as foster care or small group nursing home placement for children. Once again, when families subsequently discover that their doctor offered them unrealistic and unacceptable solutions in this area, their confidence in him and in physicians generally can be seriously undermined.[4]

A major issue often raised by parents and professionals alike concerns fears that unless a child is placed in an institution immediately, the family will become so attached to him or her that it will never be ready to place the child, even when such a step becomes imperative. However, families can be told that they were involved with the baby long before his birth and that once they have tried to raise him, they will be able to make whatever plans are necessary for their child with considerably fewer and less destructive feelings of guilt than if they had never made any effort at all. Perhaps most significantly, parents and professionals should plan for a child on the basis of their knowledge of each child and his particular needs and not on the basis of a stereotyped image of children with Down's Syndrome. Such awareness is not possible at the time of the child's birth. For many families who realize this, such an approach will result in a decision to take their baby home, even though they realize that institutionalization may become necessary later.

The Arthur family, for example, first considered placement of their daughter Barbara immediately after she was born. After discussing the alternatives, however, they decided to take her home and soon became very attached to her.

Barbara developed exceptionally poorly, and at 18 months she was functioning at the level of a 3-month-old. She required such constant attention that an older son was neglected. Consequently, when a social worker suggested that Barbara's name be placed on the waiting list of the state institution, the Arthurs agreed. However, they stated that whatever happened in the future, they were glad that they had taken their daughter home and tried to help her.

We recognize that some families, to whom the idea of knowingly raising a retarded child is intolerable, will have to place the child immediately. However, such a plan should be the result of discussion and the decision should be made after all other possibilities have been fully explored.

If the parents do choose institutionalization, they will require support during the process of arranging for the baby's care and afterwards. The feelings and conflicts aroused by the birth of a defective child and its placement are not resolved simply when the institution doors close behind the baby. The following case eloquently pinpoints these issues.

When his second child was born with Down's Syndrome, Mr. Frank, a very immature man, perceived the condition of the baby as an assault on his masculinity. Mrs. Frank was even more upset. She had a severely physically handicapped sister who, she felt, had destroyed her childhood and she could not contemplate living again with another abnormal person. As a result, the Franks' infant went directly into placement from the hospital.

After several months Mrs. Frank became extremely anxious and phobic. Preoccupied with the fear that she would do something to hurt her normal son, she required long term psychotherapy to help her function.

TRAINING THE MENTALLY RETARDED
A Progress Report

VIVIAN HEDRICH

OLD MYTHS ARE BEING CHALLENGED BY DOWN-TO-EARTH METHODS AT THE UNIVERSITY OF WASHINGTON'S MODEL PRESCHOOL CENTER FOR HANDICAPPED CHILDREN

Of all the handicaps that humanity faces, mental retardation may be the most widely misunderstood. In particular, children with Down's syndrome (mongolism) face a world in which people first wonder what on earth to do with them and then may not expect enough from them.

One encouraging new effort to improve the outlook for Down's and other mentally handicapped children is under way in Seattle at the University of Washington's Model Preschool Center for Handicapped Children. In serving nearly 190 children with a wide range of problems—including more than 60 Down's children, from newborn to six years of age—the program concentrates on reaching the youngsters early to get a jump ahead of the adverse effects of retardation.

The children at the Model Preschool are part of approximately three percent of the total population of the country who are mentally retarded. The most commonly recognized form is Down's syndrome, a chromosome "accident" that causes mental retardation in about one out of every 640 live births. The statistic leaps higher among mothers over 45 (an estimated one in 50). Today more of these children survive the first difficult months and years of life, even though many suffer from additional serious handicapping conditions.

In addition to the altered brain development, most Down's syndrome children share certain physical characteristics, including poor muscle tone, smaller than normal ears, noses, and hands, eyes that tend to slant upward, and shorter than normal linear growth beginning at about age four. They usually learn to sit, walk, speak, and are toilet trained later than normal, but can learn to dress and feed themselves, play on a swing, swim, and do many other activities typical of childhood. As they grow older their social development tends to be more advanced than their mental development, and they can deal more easily with people and their environment than has traditionally been expected of them.

"We are challenging some persistent myths about mentally handicapped children," Seattle project director Alice Hayden points out, "and attempting to demonstrate that much can be done to accelerate the development of the retarded, especially when intensive help arrives soon after birth. We are especially encouraged about the progress possible when experts in a number of disciplines get together with parents in the proper setting."

The Seattle setting moves toward that ideal. Initially funded by the early childhood education program of OE's Bureau of Education for the Handicapped, the Model Preschool is part of the University's Experimental Education Unit, one of four components of the Child Development and Mental Retardation Center, one of the largest and most comprehensive facilities of its type in the country. The rustically modern structure, located on the shores of a scenic ship canal at the south end of the campus, welcomes more than 10,000 visitors each year.

More than six years ago, while the center was still in the planning stage, careful consideration was given to all aspects of chil-

---

Training the Mentally Retarded: A Progress Report, *American Education*, November 1975. ©1975 American Education, U.S. Department of Health, Education and Welfare Office of Education, Washington, D.C.

38. Training the Mentally Retarded

A Progress Report

dren's welfare and safety. All-weather instruction and recreation areas promote both indoor and outdoor activities. The latest in multimedia equipment helps to monitor each child's progress. Viewing areas with one-way glass adjoin each classroom. Above all a most important criterion has been met—the center has the atmosphere of a school and not a hospital.

Even the casual visitor soon recognizes that this is an "action place." A large wooden go-cart loaded with clapping and singing toddlers is pushed down the hall by teachers' aides. The group is bound for a play period in the covered courtyard. Classrooms overflow with color displays of childrens' artwork, huge building blocks, and other manipulative materials. Teachers enthusiastically encourage children— "That's right!" "Good boy!" "Fine, try again!"

In one room a teacher sits with several children and unwraps an orange popsicle for them to examine. The three- and four-year-olds quickly name the color of the treat and confirm that it is smooth, cold, and sweet. They enthusiastically join in making orange juice popsicles for the class. Just in doing that, they have demonstrated the ability to discriminate color, texture, temperature, taste, and the motor control needed to pour liquid into special molds without spilling.

"We believe that these children need a well-balanced program," Dr. Hayden explains. "We have large-group and small-group sessions, teacher-and-child-initiated activities, art, music, prereading, and even science. Everything that takes place, however, has a specific objective and each child receives a minimum of ten minutes of concentrated one-to-one instruction every day."

In a small conference room a therapist works with a six-year-old Down's syndrome boy referred to the center by his suburban school district for screening and placement. During the first few minutes the child successfully identifies primary colors by dropping colored tablets into correspondingly colored plastic cups. He also matches animal shapes with pictures on a chart. However, the process is frequently interrupted as his attention wanders and he moves about the room waving his arms and rolling his head aimlessly from side to side. Such random movements probably stem from poor motor control and some emotional complications. According to Dr. Hayden, they are rarely seen among the very youngest children who have been able to get to the center early. Systematic exercise and training has helped them develop control of such movements at a rate that is close to that of normal children.

In the past, children with Down's syndrome were virtually ignored. Their physical characteristics labeled them immediately and everyone assumed they would not live long (many did not survive adolescence), so they were simply tagged non-educable. Today, dismissing any group of children as merely trainable seems unthinkable, says Dr. Hayden.

While most Down's syndrome children are categorized as moderately retarded, J. Doris and S. B. Sarason in their book, *Psychological Problems in Mental Deficiency*, show that IQ scores for this population cover a wide range—from severely retarded to dull-normal. However, data gathered on institutionalized Down's children indicate a tendency for IQ scores to decline with age.

Until recently, the prevailing recommendation for many such children was institutionalization to spare families the burdens involved in long-term care. "Although institutions now emphasize group homes and smaller units, it is still apparent that such placement is not the answer to the problems that face society," Dr. Hayden says. She believes that there are a number of reasons for that regression shown by institutionalized children, one of them being separation from their families, from society, and from an environment that promotes normal behavior. Another reason is a failure on the part of society to render early and continuous help.

Following the birth of a Down's syndrome baby, many households are virtually in mourning. Families have to adjust to the embarrassed silence of friends and relatives as well as face their own emotional turmoil. "Parents may feel awkward and fearful of even such elementary tasks as holding the baby," Dr. Hayden says. "One of our first concerns is to encourage interaction with the infant constantly during his waking hours. Enthusiasm is contagious."

In Seattle, parents are involved from the moment their child is seen by the staff. They are trained in many of the instructional procedures used at the school to help their child develop motor and social skills. Parents work in classrooms at least one session each week as observers, data takers, and teaching assistants.

"Being part of the University's Down's syndrome program has really helped me," one mother says. "I have learned specific ways that I can work with my child at home to help him with the skills he is developing at school—matching and sorting, identifying shapes and colors, and so on. Our kitchen provides most of the teaching materials I need. Also, I have a chance to share problems and ideas with other mothers of children the same age as my own. It helps me to be more objective about my child's behavior."

At regular group meetings held at the center, parents may air their concerns, plan programs, and listen to authorities from such fields as nutrition or pediatrics. Videotapes made in the classroom are of-

5. TRAINABLE MENTALLY RETARDED

ten shown and followed by group discussions; parents may review tapes of their children over several months to see what progress has been made.

Currently 63 Down's children, including 14 infants, are enrolled in the five year-round classes offered by the preschool. Children are admitted at different ages depending upon when parents first hear of the program. The word usually reaches them through their physician, friends, the news media, or referral by the local school district. All children who apply are admitted at no charge. However, parents are expected to provide transportation for those under three years and to participate in classroom sessions and parent meetings.

While some children are seen as early as two weeks, intensive training does not begin until they are five weeks old. In weekly 30-minute sessions, parents learn about early motor and cognitive development, particularly how to stimulate their young child in the areas of sight and sound. When the baby is about six months old, training turns to self-help skills that require eye-hand coordination. Special aids include crackers and other "finger foods" that the infant can grasp.

"We observe our Down's syndrome children systematically," Dr. Hayden says. "We identify goals for each child and work on step-by-step activities for each child's development." She stresses that everyone must be alert to other handicapping conditions. These sometimes develop slowly and might be missed in periodic clinical examinations. But if parents and teachers systematically observe a child's behavior, they can often spot potential problems and thus begin remedial procedures.

Children move through five levels of instruction as they meet the developmental requirements—infant, early preschool, intermediate preschool, advanced preschool, and kindergarten. Each class is staffed by a teacher and an assistant, who helps the teacher identify problems and plan individual programs. Other support personnel assist with physical therapy and communication skills. Children are tested regularly and their progress measured against the general goal of performing a target skill with 85 percent or better accuracy.

Dr. Hayden points out that the longer children stay in the program, the greater the progress they demonstrate toward developmental norms. But the newcomers also evidence steady improvement. As an example, data from tests given a year apart showed five children new to the kindergarten program had a mean lag of 21 months behind normal development of certain skills, while five children who had been in the program for six to twelve months had a lag of only 5.6 months. The second tests, a year later, showed all of the children had maintained gains or accelerated in their development. The mean IQ for the children who had been in the program over the longer stretch increased from 84.8 to 88. The gain for the other children was from 61 to 74.7. *(Note: Tests used included the Peabody Picture Vocabulary Test, the Denver Developmental Assessment Battery and Screening Test, and inventories developed by the staff and validated in field settings.)*

A kindergarten class added to the Down's syndrome program during the fall of 1973 offers instruction to children in two-hour sessions four days each week. These children not only work on skills they have already learned, but also receive individual instruction in reading, math, and speech. Some specific goals for children in this group are printing their own first names, understanding number concepts from one to five, discriminating and naming all upper and lower case letters of the alphabet, throwing a ball, and walking up and down stairs, alternating feet with each step. In their speech exercises, children are expected to use correctly at least half the words they have shown they understand.

Lessons the project people learned since the beginning make new directions possible. "In the summer of 1974, we successfully phased-in a few normal children to serve as models," says Dr. Hayden. "Their speech, social behaviors, and attention to tasks give handicapped children useful 'clues' that adults cannot so readily provide. Parents of normal children enrolled have been enthusiastic about their children's opportunity to participate.

"A major question in our minds is how well the program will 'travel' to public school special-education classes without the support system we have at the demonstration center," Dr. Hayden continues. "We are concerned too with how well our children will continue to fare in other surroundings and to what extent our approach may be able to serve children who have never had the benefits of intensive early training." Toward that end the center hopes to follow its Down's children as long as it can to ensure appropriate education.

A testing ground for such questions is Seattle's Green Lake Elementary School. There a new primary program was established for Down's children last fall with research funding from the Office of Education's Bureau of Education for the Handicapped. This fall, two classes are made up of Model Preschool graduates with five comparison groups of Down's syndrome children from regular district special-education enrollment.

Ann Sweet, special-education instruction at Green Lake, feels that only "time

38. Training the Mentally Retarded

will tell" how the University-developed techniques will adapt to the public school setting. "As a teacher I have been especially impressed with one aspect of the University program that requires only rearranging time," she says. "Each day the teacher or paraprofessional selects target skills from the Down's Syndrome Assessment Form (a list of competencies possible of attainment by the children and developed by the center staff) and concentrates on teaching them to one child for half an hour. This strengthens the child's skill and confidence and helps the teacher get to know individual children well and keep daily records of their progress."

Ms. Sweet feels another worthwhile "spinoff" from the program has been the training of paraprofessional workers. Now a growing number of persons at the school are able to make a substantial contribution to the education of the handicapped.

Currently, the model preschool center serves children from 23 surrounding school districts in the Puget Sound area and many more through the staff's outreach efforts in consultation and training. More than 1,500 undergraduate and graduate students have participated in the University training program and thousands of teachers, paraprofessionals, and parents have attended workshops and received on-site training. Last spring the center's staff helped establish new Down's syndrome programs for children in several States, Canada, and Australia.

Many unanswered questions remain for researchers on the "how and why" of mental retardation and no immediate miracles for easily dealing with it seem likely. Educators like those in Seattle, however, are finding success in a combination of hope and hard work.

For further information, write to Dr. Alice H. Hayden, Project Director, Experimental Education Unit WJ-10, Child Development and Retardation Center, University of Washington, Seattle, WA 98195.

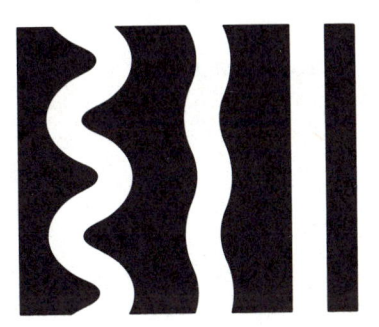

Behavior Modification

The origins of behavior modification and therapy techniques are looked at in addition to methods of behavior assessment and future directions.

For more information about this book and other special education materials, contact Joseph Logan, Editor, Special Learning Corporation.

Special Learning Corporation
42 Boston Post Rd. Guilford, Connecticut 06437 (203) 453-6525

FOCUS ...

Types of Mental Retardation	Characteristics	Causes	Preventions
Apert's Syndrome	webbing of fingers and toes, cleft palate, premature closure of cranial sutures	not known	syntosis must by surgically treated
cretinism	small in stature, rough dry skin, dry, sparse hair	absence of thyroid hormone	administration of thyroid extract to infant before m.r. becomes pronounced
Down's syndrome	there are approximately 50 characteristics including slanted eyes, shortness of stature, stubby fingers; flat nasal bridge, small mouth w/drooping corners and protruding tongue, white speckled iris	one extra chromosome	can be identified in the prenatal period through the technique amniocentesis
phenylketonuria	most cases have blond hair and blue eyes, uncontrolled body movements and convulsions, hyperactive, irritable and musty body odor	a recessive gene causes the absence of certain enzymes necessary to convert phenylalanine to tyrosine	blood test at birth; if detected a diet which eliminates harmful proteins; no treatment for the defective gene
Tay-Sach's Disease	manifested by 4 months of life; convulsions, spasticity and progressive blindness (marked by cherry red spot on retina) associated with optic atrophy	hereditary disease which occurs in children of Ashkenazi Jewish descent	early detection (amniocentesis); no treatment
galactosemia	progressive physical and mental degeneration; may develop seizures, no speech, non-ambulatory	through metabolism error a defect in the enzyme that converts galactose to glucose	detected by blood test and treated with diet
Hurler's Disease (gargoylism)	dwarf stature, shortness of neck and trunk, depression of bridge of nose, clouding of corneas of eyes	not known	no treatment, preventable only by prenatal diagnosis

Types of Mental Retardation	Characteristics	Causes	Preventions
hydrocephalus	exceptionally large head	the growth of a tumor or subdural hematoma; fluid blocked at base of brain and collects in ventricles (abstructive). This is caused by meningitis, brain tumor, birth injury during breech delivery.	correct by surgery: obstructive connecting a tube above and below the obstruction to form a by-pass communicating hydroventriculo-cardiac shunt
hypothyroidism	lethargic, puffy eye lids, protuberant abdomen and history of jaundice	underfunctioning of thyroid gland	blood and bone test at age 2 months, treatment with oral administration of thyroid hormone
leucine-sensitive hypoglycemia	seizures	low blood sugar induced by amino acid leucine	diet low in leucine
maple syrup urine disease	see galactosemia, patients urine smells like maple syrup	defect in recessive gene; protein can not properly be metabolized	dietary treatment
methylmalonicaciduria	see galactosemia	inability of the body to use vitamin B12	dietary treatment and vitamin B12
microcephalus	abnormally small head	pre-natal exposure to high levels of radiation; pre-natal exposure to rubella	
Lowe's Syndrome (oculo-cerebral-renal syn.)	cataracts, poor muscle tone	metabolic disease in which certain proteins cannot be assimilated	none

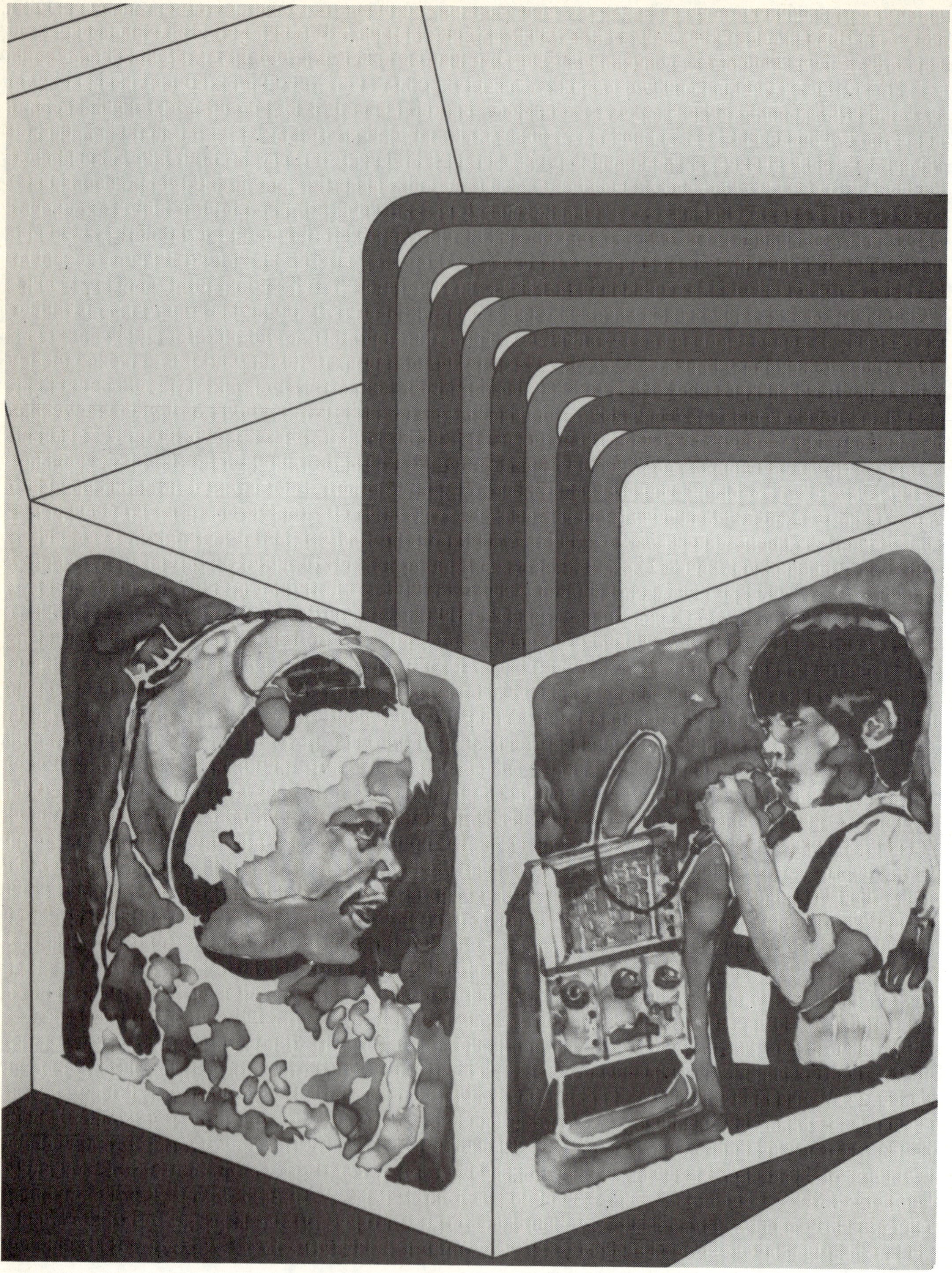

Severely and Profoundly Mentally Retarded

Until recent years, the severely and profoundly mentally retarded consisted of a group of people who could generally be found hidden in back wards of institutions. With an average IQ range of 0 to 30, the severely retarded were often placed in cribs in which they would respond very little to whatever stimuli was available. In 1973, following an extensive study, Sontag, Burke, and Young described children placed within this category as those who often "self-mutilate, regurgitate, ruminate, aggress towards others, display stereopathics, manifest durable and intense temper tantrums, have serious seizures, and/or have extremely brittle medical existences."

This segment of the mentally retarded population has been labeled an assortment of titles in the past, from untrainable to profoundly retarded, seriously disturbed, multiply handicapped, crib cases, and custodial. Whatever label is assigned to these children, one common characteristic is a high mortality rate among them, due to the fact that they usually suffer from serious health problems such as kidney disease, heart disease, and skeletal abnormalities, including spina bifida. In 1973 Gerry Strickland and Richard Koch at Children's Hospital in Los Angeles completed a seventeen year longitudinal study of severely retarded children. It was discovered that 20 percent had died. Of those still living, half were being cared for out of the home.

Not until behaviorists began conducting research with this population was their learning potential recognized. Currently, as more educational provisions are emerging for the severely retarded, appropriate training programs are being created. In several developmental centers across the country the severely retarded learn basic skills such as self-feed, toilet-training, and self-discipline. The enactment of federal legislation that will mandate a right to education for the severely and profoundly handicapped is on the horizen. Goldberg and Lippman, in 1974, projected into the future of the severely and profoundly retarded with the statement, "The right to education, if it is implemented, will bring into our special education orbit those children who were not previously considered to have the necessary academic potential or even to be capable of acquiring the basic skills for community living or who are not of the traditionally prescribed age for education. Many special educators never before saw them. . . they were invisible."

THE SEVERELY/PROFOUNDLY HANDICAPPED: WHO ARE THEY? WHERE ARE WE?

Ed Sontag, Ed.D.
Bureau of Education for the Handicapped

Judy Smith, M.S.Ed.
University of New Mexico

Wayne Sailor, Ph.D.
San Francisco State University

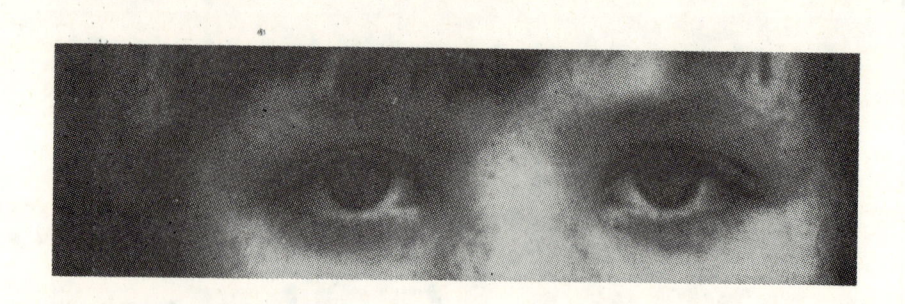

The misunderstanding and misuse of the label "severely/profoundly handicapped" may appear to call for the possible creation of yet another special education category. To create a new category would be a serious error, since it would tend to remove these children from the educational and social mainstream; it also would obscure the fact that the severely/profoundly handicapped exist across all of special education. This article examines various approaches to the problems of definition and categorization of the severely/profoundly handicapped, proposing a service-need definition, with emphasis on teacher competencies. Finally, the authors review what must be done within the profession to make it possible to achieve such a classification system.

THE CHILDREN BEHIND THE LABEL

Children with severe or profound handicaps are children who are divergent in degree, not in kind. The very label "severely/profoundly handicapped" may, however, contribute to the notion that such children are somehow different in kind, since it refers to a very low level of intellectual functioning and therefore suggests that those children so labeled have a homogeneous pattern of neurological impairment. On the contrary, they form an extremely heterogeneous group, comprising not only the organically impaired but also those whose serious emotional disturbance, deafness, blindness, or severe orthopedic impairment renders them *functionally* retarded. These seriously disabling conditions occur with a low incidence in the general population. Thus, when we speak of the severely/profoundly handicapped, we are referring not simply to the severely mentally retarded but to a population of multiply handicapped persons, including the severely emotionally disturbed, the severely health-impaired, and so on.

Inasmuch as a severe or profound handicap is a matter of degree of disability, it follows that children with such impairments may start out both in life and in education at relatively the same point, but their individual potentials will vary spectacularly. An excellent example of a child with a profound functional handicap is the young Helen Keller who, without proper education and training, manifested extreme intellectual impairment but, with enlightened help, became quite another person. Although it now appears that few of the severely/profoundly handicapped (or, for that matter, the gifted) will duplicate the achievements of Helen Keller, these students can make very significant educational gains, and the demonstration of this by special educators has provided the impetus for their intensified public education.

The fact remains, however, that the misunderstanding and misuse of the label severely/profoundly handicapped may appear to call for the possible creation of yet another special education category. To create a new category would be a serious error for two reasons. First, it would promote the placement of these children in settings away from the educational and social mainstream. In some states, trainable mentally retarded students are finally being included in the regular schools, while severely/profoundly handicapped children are being excluded. By creating another category of students outside the educational mainstream, we may find ourselves in the near future fighting to place them in regular schools, much as we have sought and are still seeking regular school placement for trainables. In the past, placement of the trainable mentally retarded in special schools was partially a result of low expectations concerning their abilities to develop traditional academic skills. However, such current work as that of the University of Washington's Experimental Education Unit has dramatically shown that the trainable mentally retarded, as well as children with far more severe impairments, can indeed acquire primary level reading skills.

Second, use of the label severely/profoundly handicapped has already prompted universities and state departments to create new divisions of special education for a category that we believe cannot and should not be given categorical status. The most crucial step that professionals can take at this juncture is to focus on a group of children who do not fit existing educational labels and who must not be trapped in still another educational classification. The severely/profoundly handicapped exist across all of special education. To view them otherwise is to deny their individuality, their special needs and, most unfortunate of all, their educational potential.

IDENTIFYING A NONCATEGORY

Perhaps, then, we need to take a totally new stance toward the entire issue of defining the population of severely/profoundly handicapped children. To do so, we shall first critically examine three current propositions which reflect various approaches to the problems of definition and categorization. We shall briefly pose arguments for rejection of each of these propositions and conclude with a fourth proposition which represents our position on the issue of determining who are the severely/profoundly handicapped.

Proposition 1. *There is a new disability category entitled "severely and profoundly handicapped" (SPH), or variants thereof.*

According to the proposition, this disability category has specifiable parameters, and through diagnostic assessment procedures, children who are appropriate to a disability class of this type can be identified. This concept reflects the position taken by the Bureau of Education for the Handicapped and by university special education departments in 1974 when services for the severely handicapped began their rapid expansion. Parameters were spelled out: e.g., disabilities so severe or complex that they restrict ambulation or locomotion by means of typical transportation modes; behavior characteristics that are injurious to self or others; hyperactivity, impulsivity; frequently uncontrolled bowel or bladder functions; epilepsy, grossly inadequate communication skills; mixed or multiple sensori-motor disabilities.

When parameters to define a population are necessarily subjective and when no adequate standardized instruments exist, then parameters must include such qualifiers as "*must* be characterized by" or "*may* be characterized by." The first qualifier necessarily creates the possibility of a false negative: A child who is severely handicapped will be rejected for services because of failure to display one or more of the descriptors. The second qualifier can easily produce a false positive: A child who is not severely handicapped is mistakenly identified because he displays one or more of the parametric descriptors. Thus, Proposition 1, in our opinion, should be rejected as a basis for defining the severely handicapped in the absence of a reliable diagnostic classification system based upon standardized observation and assessment. Moreover, there are already too many rigidly defined disability categories. The addition of still another category

6. SEVERELY AND PROFOUNDLY RETARDED

compounds an already difficult problem in educational service delivery.

Proposition 2. *The severely handicapped do not represent a new disability category. They represent the lower limits of functioning in the continuum which exists in each established disability area.*

This solution to the definition problem represents a current effort by several state education agencies to handle the problem of certification. It represents, in part, a reaction to the pressure to create a new disability category.

Proposition 2 must be rejected on the basis of the inadequacies that exist in the established system of disability categorization. A child who is *very* orthopedically disabled (who represents the lowest extreme of the continuum of crippled and other health-impaired children) would be considered severely handicapped by this definition and placed with children from the lowest strata of the mentally retarded population, even in the absence of any indication that he was academically retarded. The same would hold true for the emotionally disturbed, the deaf, the blind, and others. The potential for misplacement of children in service settings is probably greatest when this solution to the definition problem is adopted.

Proposition 3. *The severely handicapped belong in one of three global instructional areas, under a reorganization plan which would include early childhood education, general special education, and severely handicapped education. Assignment of children to the new areas would consist of reassignment of the existing disability categories.*

This proposition represents a current thrust in solving the definition problem by many state education agencies. Through this solution, the existing disability categories would be collapsed into a dichotomy of general special education and severely handicapped education, with early childhood education, determined primarily by age, representing a broad new component of special education under Public Law 94-142.

The problem with Proposition 3, and the reason that it too should be rejected, rests again with the inadequacies of the existing disability category system. General special education would encompass, for example, the learning disabled, educable mentally retarded, orthopedically disabled, emotionally disturbed, deaf, speech-impaired, and so on. Severely handicapped education would include the trainable mentally retarded, seriously disturbed, deaf–blind, and others. The potential for misplacement of children in terms of homogeneity of services is great. Trainable mentally retarded children typically do not belong in an educational program designed to benefit the profoundly retarded nonambulatory child; their curriculum requirements are substantially different. Nor does the profoundly retarded deaf child belong in a program designed for disturbed children who can deal with an academic curriculum. New subgroupings within each of the areas would no doubt become necessary at the local education agency level, and these subgroupings might well provide less functional service than the existing system of disability categorization provides.

Proposition 4. *Severely handicapped education represents one of three global instructional areas under a reorganization plan which would include early childhood education and general special education as the other two areas. Assignment of children to the new areas would be according to the nature of the children's service requirements and, indirectly, on the basis of the competencies of teaching personnel.*

This proposition resembles Proposition 3, except that reclassification into either the general special education or severely handicapped education categories (with assignment to early childhood education based on age) would be determined by the type of service required. It assumes a clean slate from the outset, as far as disability categories are concerned. Regardless of his handicapping condition, if a child or young (school-aged) adult requires instruction in basic skills, this proposition specifies that the individual belongs in a program for the severely handicapped. If a child, regardless of handicap, primarily requires academic instruction, then he belongs in a program of general special education. Children in need of both types of service would divide their time between programs. Indeed, a prime goal would be to move students gradually from severely handicapped education to general special education programs and, further, into the mainstream of regular education to the maximum extent. Exceptional children below school age would enter early childhood education programs in which the emphasis would also be divided between services for the severely handicapped (basic skill development) and general special education (preacademic instruction).

In addition, teachers whose training has produced competencies in basic self-help, motor, perceptual, social, cognitive, and communication skill development areas would teach classes for the severely handicapped. Teachers whose competencies lie in preacademic and academic instruction would teach general special education.

With this service–need definition we may cut across disability areas and create a truly programmatic and need-centered model of service delivery. Equally important, this manner of identification, placement, and programming should facilitate a progressive inclusion of the low-incidence population into the mainstream of school and community.

HANDICAPS WITHIN THE PROFESSION

Various teacher training and public education programs focusing on low-incidence children are in operation across the United States, in different stages of development. These programs differ in their degree of emphasis on this population's longitudinal needs and problems and on the competencies needed by teachers to deal with these problems: e.g., training to compensate for severe sensori-motor deficits; beginning verbal and nonverbal communication; home management and living skills; parent involvement; use of prosthetic, orthotic, and adaptive equipment to enhance general development; basic social skill mastery; basic self-help and maintenance (including feeding and toileting); behavior management; community mobility skills.

Although these models are in the process of evolving, there continue to be problems that hamper our professional efforts. We need programs that focus not just on one or two longitudinal areas but on all educational requirements of the severely/profoundly handicapped population. We need the kind of information exchange that would enhance work in all aspects of educational programming. And we need coordination and quality control on a national scale.

High on the list of priorities for dissemination is the creation of a matrix of teacher competencies and a means for measuring the attainment of those competencies. Continued research, as well as the full sharing of information among programs, is a requirement in developing competency-based training programs. Moreover, until a full spectrum of those proficiencies can be developed, we must have a system for refining and updating what is currently known. In the meantime, an exchange program for doctoral students, mutual doctoral training programs, and a national exchange of professionals at all levels may encourage programs to impact on one another.

Evident needs exist for coordination: to create skill sequences; to match existing curricula to assessed skill deficiencies; to evaluate existing curricula through systematic measurement for effectiveness; to create curricula where none exist through task analysis; and to evaluate and control the quality of these curricula. The pressing need for national curriculum and assessment programs can be met if we make a concerted effort in identification, evaluation, development, and dissemination.

From a base of such activities, it may well become possible to develop quality control for our training programs. In view of the requirements of Public Law 94-142, standards of quality and continuity become more than ever a pressing issue. We need continuous evaluation and decision making regarding relevant course content and performance skills, as well as the cost-effectiveness of our

6. SEVERELY AND PROFOUNDLY RETARDED

personnel preparation programs. Many existing evaluation systems simply do not cover both the courses and the experiences designed to provide competencies. We need to generate statements of standards for preservice training in terms of practicum sites, staff qualifications, student–staff ratios, competency statements, evaluation procedures, and professional standards that are exclusionary in the sense of admitting only the most highly qualified people to the task of educating the low-incidence population. A permanent data-monitoring system must also be established as an aid to planning for the rapidly accelerating demand for service delivery. Such a system should generate up-to-date printouts of all enrollment information from state departments, thereby supplying the nation with standardized needs-assessment figures on a current basis.

As we move toward an objective content evaluation system to measure acquisition and toward a series of skill-assessment systems to be administered by independent evaluation teams, we must ensure that the evaluation system reflects child-change data, as well as teacher acquisition. In directly measuring performance change, the trained teacher must be able to assess his own effectiveness in terms of reliable and demonstrable progress on the part of his class.

Related to the evaluation of our training programs, our graduates, and the educational progress of the children they serve is the matter of certification. Several years are required for teacher trainees to complete the typical university training sequence. Yet there is currently a considerable nation-wide demand for people who can work with the severely/profoundly handicapped in public school settings. To fulfill this demand we cannot continue to provisionally certify surplus teachers from other areas of education. While provisional certification may help alleviate the teacher shortage, we cannot expect that it will promote high-caliber educational programming for children. An additional danger is the certification of too many teachers who have an inappropriate range of competencies to serve severely/profoundly handicapped children, thus glutting the market with a surplus of inadequately trained teachers.

To provide a broader certification program for trainees in preservice programs, consistent with Proposition 4, we might consider the merits of a state plan that calls for two types of special educators: those with competencies for high-incidence populations of exceptional children, and those with competencies for low-incidence populations. With the addition of training for preschool programs, certification would follow the attainment of specifiable competencies in one of three areas: general special education, severely/profoundly handicapped education, and early childhood education.

In order to meet the immediate need for staffing, however, we should consider controlled inservice training, in which universities with preparation programs for teachers of low-incidence populations develop a close link with state departments in a coordinated training effort. Two critical factors are the selection of highly qualified professionals to provide such inservice training and the assurance that programs for severely/profoundly handicapped children and their prospective teachers take place within the mainstream of education.

An additional way to meet the demand for personnel is to elevate the paraprofessional within the educational strata. Educational systems have traditionally resisted financing personnel beyond the teaching staff on a local level, and the paraprofessional has been viewed as an assistant, rather than as a therapist or educator in his own right. However, programming for the severely/profoundly handicapped population engenders a teaching situation in which the ratio of professionals to children is optimally around one to three. To help meet this requirement and fulfill a greatly expanded role, paraprofessionals must be trained or retrained, must have professional status as teaching associates, and must be paid in accordance with their contributions, which are often considerable. We must continue, in addition, to make fuller use of occupational, physical, and speech therapists (as well as professionals trained in deafness, blindness, and other specialty areas) as resource persons, teacher consultants, and trainers of children.

For all of these personnel, there must be an effective licensing mechanism, such as peer review or certification by state education agencies, with cooperation from universities. Specialized support personnel (e.g., consultants to programs for the blind) and allied health professionals (e.g., occupational therapists) should be given a coordinated opportunity to enter the competency-based training model. Consortia of training colleges and medical schools, for example, could provide an integrated training program across all the multidisciplinary training components of quality education for the severely/profoundly handicapped. State licensing agencies for specialty educators and support therapists should be encouraged to consider specialized licensing requirements. These would reflect the highly differentiated competencies and expertise acquired by those therapists who complete relevant components of university education preparing them to become effective members of the educational team.

Finally, through the competent people we now have, we must provide technical assistance to localities whose leaders have shown the potential for integrating low-incidence children into the community and into the public schools. That leadership must be reinforced by solid professional support and by the extensive sharing of expertise. Indeed, mutual support and sharing of information are the best and perhaps the only means we have to meet the needs of all professionals who are working to raise the potential of the severely/profoundly handicapped child. Then, perhaps, we will make sure that no Helen Keller goes unrecognized.

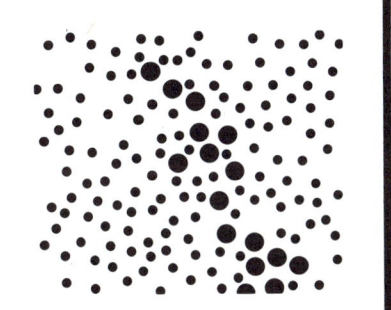

Mainstreaming

Taking an in depth look at the controversy of mainstreaming versus special education classes for the exceptional child, this book presents an overview of the problems and methods involved. The history of mainstreaming, along with future trends are discussed.

For further information concerning this book and other special education materials, contact:

Joseph Logan, Editor
Special Learning Corporation

Special Learning Corporation
42 Boston Post Rd. Guilford, Connecticut 06437 (203) 453-6525

Training Teachers for the Severely and Profoundly Handicapped: A New Frontier

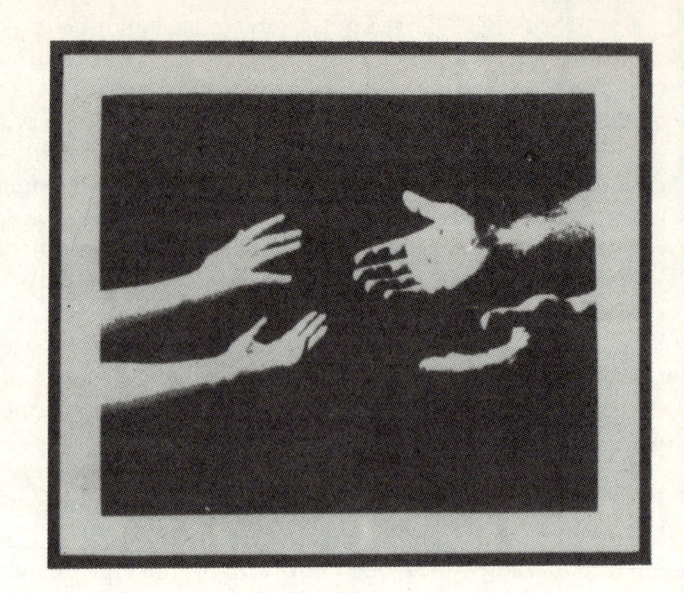

SUSAN STAINBACK
WILLIAM STAINBACK
STEVEN MAURER

Abstract: Due to recent litigation and legislation, there will be an influx of severely and profoundly handicapped individuals into community based public education programs. As a result, teachers who possess the knowledge and skill to foster the growth of these individuals will be needed. The onus of responsibility is on the universities to prepare competent teachers. This article examines the basic components that will have to be integrated into the existing structures of teacher training programs to adequately prepare teachers of the severely and profoundly handicapped.

SUSAN STAINBACK *is Assistant Professor,* WILLIAM STAINBACK *is Associate Professor, and* STEVEN MAURER *is Graduate Assistant, Special Education Division, University of Northern Iowa, Cedar Falls, Iowa. The preparation of this paper was supported in part by HEW Special Project Grant No. 451AH50558.*

The severely and profoundly handicapped consist of a group of individuals who until recently could generally be found on the back wards of large state institutions. They were frequently found in cribs responding very little to the limited stimuli present. Sontag, Burke and York (1973) describe these children as those who self mutilate, regurgitate, ruminate, aggress towards others, display stereopathics (rocking, handwaving), manifest durable and intense temper tantrums, have serious seizures, and/or have extremely brittle medical existences. Included are those who do not suck, swallow or chew, imitate, ambulate, speak, see, toilet themselves, respond to simple verbal commands and/or those who do possess multiple handicaps. They have been labeled untrainable, profoundly retarded, seriously disturbed, multiply handicapped, crib cases and custodial.

It was not until behaviorists (Bensburg, Colwell & Cassel, 1965; Fuller, 1949; Rice & McDaniel, 1966) began conducting research with this population that the learning potential of the severely and profoundly handicapped was recognized. While the necessary initial research was being conducted, parents of these individuals began lobbying through such strong parent groups as the National Association for Retarded Citizens (NARC). They worked to gain for their children educational and training opportunities to enable them to develop their full potential. This parental pressure resulted in several major court decisions (e.g. Pennsylvania Association for Retarded Children v. The Commonwealth of Pennsylvania, 1972) that have expanded public educational services to include the severely and profoundly handicapped.

Along with this emphasis on the right to education for these individuals, the "deinstitutionalization philosophy" has evolved which postulates that equal education for this group should come under the jurisdiction of public education. It is noted that education is the job of public educational agencies, not of social services in an institutional setting. As a result of this philosophy, court decisions, and parental pressures, laws have been passed in many states (Education Commission of the States, 1972) that place the responsibility on the public schools for the education and training of the severely and profoundly handicapped.

Other events have signaled a growing commitment to the education of this group.

1. In March/April, 1975, the NARC held a national training meeting on the education of the severely and profoundly retarded,
2. A new American Association for the Education of the Severely and Profoundly Handicapped has been formed (Haring, 1975a)
3. The Bureau of Education for the Handicapped has cited as one of its top priorities the education of the severely and profoundly handicapped (Martin, 1975).

The Need for Trained Teachers

As the focus changes from custodial care to education and training for the severely and profoundly handicapped, highly trained teachers will be needed in public education.

> Here the onus of responsibility rests on teacher training institutions to design and implement teacher education programs specifically aimed at preparing persons to further develop multiply handicapped, severely retarded children. (Smith & Arkans, 1974, p. 501).

The number of trained teachers needed will be substantial, especially if one accepts a teacher/student ratio of no more than 1:5. This ratio is tenable when the learning, behavioral, and physical characteristics of the severely and profoundly handicapped are considered.

When estimating the number of teachers needed, the necessity of early intervention should be considered also. Even the more profoundly handicapped preschooler has the potential for learning, among other things, visual and auditory awareness, motor control of the head and trunk, and a rudimentary understanding of vocabulary. It should also be noted that early intervention can prevent the development of abnormal body structure from prolonged periods of bed rest (Luckey & Addison, 1974). In many cases early correct body positioning can prevent physical deformities frequently found in older handicapped individuals (Robinault, 1973).

On the other end of the life continuum, continued education and training during adulthood is imperative to maintain and expand the skills of work productivity and daily existence. It has been recently demonstrated that the markedly handicapped can learn to participate in work activities (Gold, 1973) previously thought beyond their capabilities.

In essence, a teacher/student ratio of 1:5 and the necessity of life long intervention will require that institutions of higher education train teachers competent to aid the growth of severely and profoundly handicapped individuals. In addition, it should be noted that (a) recent medical advances are keeping many children with serious handicaps alive who would otherwise not have lived, and (b) today there is virtually a void of trained teachers of the severely and profoundly handicapped.

Training Requirements

Universities have focused their teacher training in special education toward the mildly and, in some cases, the moderately handicapped. The potential special education teacher has received more diagnostic techniques and remediation approaches than the regular classroom teacher. With few exceptions, the basic techniques and materials presented teachers of the mildly handicapped and teachers of so called "normal" students have been the same with changes mainly of emphasis.

The functioning level of the severely and profoundly handicapped will require a wide deviation from what has been the mainstay in university teacher training. The following is a discussion of the training needs of prospective teachers of the severely and profoundly handicapped to provide an impetus for critical evaluation of the content of some elements necessary in teacher training. Discussed here are: (a) diagnostic evaluation, (d) curriculum, (c) methodology, (d) interdisciplinary team work, (e) field experience, (f) parent training, and (g) prosthetic aids.

The standard diagnostic and evaluation tools presently employed with the mildly handicapped such as readiness and achievement tests will generally be of little use to teachers of the severely and profoundly handicapped. Even the social maturity tests at the preschool level are frequently too high and/or have too large a gap between skills to accurately assess the functioning level of many severely or profoundly handicapped individuals for training purposes.

Due to the infantile functioning level of

6. SEVERELY AND PROFOUNDLY RETARDED

some of these individuals and the small achievement increments made over time, it is imperative that teachers of the severely and profoundly handicapped have a thorough working knowledge of human growth and development patterns from birth through beginning preschool as well as the basic readiness and early academic learning process. A high degree of insight into child development during the infancy stage such as visual tracking, responding to stimuli, lifting head, reaching for objects, grasping objects and turning over is needed since it is within this range of functioning that teachers will find many of the severely and profoundly handicapped.

These diagnostic evaluation needs require going beyond the present educational literature. Teachers must become aware of the psychological and medical information concerning infancy and early childhood development. Developmental instruments such as the Gesell Developmental Schedules (1947), the Cattell Infant Intelligence Scale (1940), the Bayley Infant Scales of Development (1969), the Denver Developmental Screening Test (1970), and the Piagetian based Albert Einstein Scale of Sensory-Motor Intelligence (Corman & Escaloma, 1969) will need to be closely examined. Most teachers are not aware of, for example, the developmental sequence for evaluating and/or teaching such skills as ambulation.

It is obvious that educational diagnosis and evaluation as we know it for the mildly handicapped and normal student will need modification for teachers of the severely and profoundly handicapped. It should be noted that a few special educators and psychologists (Balthazar, 1971; Sailor & Mix, 1975) have already begun developing diagnostic and evaluation instruments for the severely and profoundly handicapped.

Curriculum

As in all educational situations, the goal of the curriculum for the severely and profoundly handicapped is to move each individual to higher levels in the developmental sequence. The major differences relate to the range of the developmental functioning levels of concern. In the education of mildly handicapped and normal students, the major focus is on readiness for and achievement in reading, writing, arithmetic and social skills. With the severely and profoundly handicapped the curricular emphasis is on response to environmental stimulation, head and trunk balance, sucking, swallowing and chewing, grasping, movement of body parts, vocalizations, and at higher levels, imitation, language acquisition, self feeding, ambulation, dressing skills, toilet training, social/recreational behaviors and functional academic skills.

Vocational skills, as with any individual, are important. When individuals reach this level, the bagging of golf tees, stapling packages, or more complex tasks such as the assembly of 14 piece bicycle brakes (Gold, 1973) are a few of the possible additions to the curriculum.

The curricular needs are widely divergent from the mildly handicapped or normal child. Despite the newness of this area, ideas and materials for curricular development are becoming available (Ball, 1971; Meyers, Sinco & Stalma, 1973.)

Methodology

Presently educators and psychologists are finding that the behavior modification methodology is very effective with the moderately and severely handicapped (Haring & Phillips, 1972) with many implications for teaching the most profoundly handicapped.

When classroom teachers have used behavior modification, the stress has been on the manipulation of stimuli that occur after the response to increase or decrease the intensity, duration, or frequency of responses.

With the severely and profoundly handicapped, teachers must continue to apply reinforcement principles. They will need only to become more sophisticated. The concepts of reinforcement sampling, discrimination training, generalization, stimulus control, shaping, backward chaining, contingent aversive stimulation, prompting, fading, modeling, etc. will have to not only be understood, but also incorporated into daily teaching sessions. In addition, the manipulation of antecedent stimuli will be essential. With the severely and profoundly handicapped, responses will not only have to be shaped but elicited. The teacher who waits for the emission of a particular response in order to apply reinforcement principles will waste much precious learning time. Also, knowledge of the most efficient methods for modifying behavior is imperative in controlling severe management problems. Finger chewing, head-banging, aggressing toward others, and feces throwing can quickly and totally disrupt classroom learning.

The precise measurement of behavior will take on new importance. Progress with the severely and profoundly handicapped may not always be easily recognizable. The morale of the teacher as well as plans for the next teaching session will depend upon correct identification of progress.

Perhaps the most important skill that teachers must have is the ability to task analyze behavior. It has been found that breaking down tasks into small sequential steps enhances the speed and quality of response acquisition in the severely and profoundly handicapped (Brown, 1973).

40. Training Teachers

Interdisciplinary Teamwork

The importance of interdisciplinary teamwork becomes evident when the daily life of the severely and profoundly handicapped is examined. Many severely and profoundly handicapped individuals live an extremely brittle medical existence. They frequently are under the supervision of medical staff; sometimes gaining nourishment through tubes, urinating through catheters and/or living with reduced spasmodic seizures by continuous medication. (These children will challenge the literal meaning of "zero reject." Here we are referring to community-based education in hospital wards or schools as well as special classes, special schools, and residential centers.)

Due to multiple handicaps, the activities of these individuals must be carefully considered by physicians as well as by physical and/or occupational therapists in terms of strenuousness, bone and muscular involvement, and body positioning. Misunderstanding or overlooking an individual's needs may cause irreparable damage. In addition, these individuals may suffer from partial or total blindness, deafness, and/or paralysis which further complicates the communication process to which opthalmologists, audiologists, and speech clinicians can contribute their expertise. No one person can be expected to possess all the expertise required to facilitate the development of a profoundly retarded child who is also blind, deaf, and/or cerebral palsied.

Some supportive and ancillary personnel may be unfamiliar with the characteristics of the severely and profoundly handicapped. The school counselor, assistant principal or itinerant art teacher, for example, may never before have worked with children who eat their crayons, self mutilate, stare at their left hand for hours, and/or indiscriminately wail throughout the day (Sontag, et al., 1973).

Receiving medications is a frequent occurrence with the severely and profoundly handicapped. A child who is alert and responsive one day may be docile and unresponsive the next. In their teacher training sequence, teachers will need to be made aware of the reasons certain drugs are administered and their side effects.

These and other aspects will have a bearing on how the teacher works with such individuals. The teacher will be required to design an educational program, but not be the sole contributor. The element of interdisciplinary teamwork is mandatory.

Because of this need for teamwork, it is important that teachers be trained to communicate efficiently and effectively with other disciplines. Courses in speech acquisition and psychology will be needed. Exposure to clinical syndromes and the medical aspects of physically handicapping conditions will also enhance the teacher's ability to communicate.

Finally, it is imperative that teachers be thoroughly aware of their own and other team members' roles. They must know their particular areas of competency as well as the compentencies possessed by other professionals and be able to conduct their duties in terms of them.

Extensive Field Experience

Teachers of the severely and profoundly handicapped will be faced with a population previously considered untrainable. Gains may be slight and tediously slow in coming. This combined with the precise skill application required to effect gains emphasizes the need for immediate feedback and support while actually working with children.

Field experiences will permit prospective teachers to determine if they have the abilities and attitudes required. The enhanced precision required in the teaching process will be too difficult for some; the development of appropriate attitudes will be impossible for others. For example, an attitude that permits *normal* risk taking is essential. As for any child, the severely and profoundly handicapped must be allowed to experience pleasure from self discovery even at the risk of minor bumps and bruises. Field experience can assist prospective teachers in developing attitudes that will avoid overprotection.

A teacher training program which includes curriculum, methodology, and field experience may help us avoid some of the pitfalls experienced in the earlier training of teachers for the mildly and moderately handicapped (e.g. knowledge of definitions and characteristics, but no teaching skills). Hopefully, we can reduce the frequency of the first teaching day syndrome: "I know the definitions and characteristics, but what do I do?"

Parent Training

With the severely and profoundly handicapped the training of parents and/or parent surrogates by the teacher is an important factor. Without the necessary information and support, home care will be beyond the abilities and tolerance level of many parents.

Since the teacher is most closely involved in the overall daily planning and training he/she will be called upon to provide information and support to the parents or parent surrogates. With strong lines of communication between the school and home, a consistent and comprehensive 24 hour program can be devised and implemented.

In order for teachers to assume the role of parent trainers, they must become knowl-

6. SEVERELY AND PROFOUNDLY RETARDED

edgeable in several areas. This constitutes another component not previously emphasized in many teacher training programs. A few of the specific competencies needed by teachers to be effective in parent or parent surrogate training include:

1. Explaining student abilities and progress to help parents overcome the problems of under or over protection and inappropriate expectations (either too high or too low);
2. Training parents to deal with explosive, stereotype, self stimulative behaviors as well as appropriate motor responding and verbalization behaviors. This, of course, will make home living a more realistic alternative for the handicapped child, siblings and parents;
3. Being a source of information concerning community resources that can provide health care, social interaction, recreation, etc. This will also include knowledge concerning foster and group home alternatives for parents who are unable to cope with their handicapped child within the existing family structure;
4. Providing parents with knowledge of sources of special clothing and equipment that can aid in easing home care problems and encourage greater independence and self care;
5. Training parents in lifting, carrying, and positioning the nonambulatory;
6. Training parents in techniques for fostering sensory awareness, motor development, communication, eating, toileting, bathing and dressing, etc.
7. Explaining the importance of having the nonambulatory child up and correctly positioned for part of each day in a chair, even if strapped in, rather than flat on his back in a crib or bed. (In addition to enhancing motor development, the child can see and respond to stimuli in his environment other than the ceiling.)

Use of Prosthetic Aids

In order to successfully deal with the severely and profoundly handicapped population, teachers must be well versed in the use of modification tools such as prosthetic aids. A prosthetic aid is a device used to modify an individual or environment so a previously handicapping condition can be bypassed or eliminated in a given set of situations. Smith and Neisworth (1975) list five broad categories of prosthetic devices. These are locomotion, life support, personal grooming and hygiene, communication, and household aids. It can be observed from these categories that the use of prosthetic aids can permeate almost every phase of life from breathing to brushing teeth to recreation.

Due to the high incidence of multiple handicapping conditions in the severe and profound population, many of them use one if not several prosthetic devices in their daily lives. Teachers of these children will find themselves in classrooms with such items as creepers, walkers, standing tables, cut out trays, splints, motorized beds, wheelchairs, built up and/or modified spoons, knives, and forks. In addition, special prosthetic devices will be used in getting some of these individuals to and from school (e.g. adjustable base lifter). Teachers, when helping children load or unload from the transportation vehicle, will need to be familiar with these devices in order to avoid possible accidents. Potential teachers of the severely and profoundly handicapped should be provided the opportunity to acquire a strong working knowledge of prosthetic aids. They should know how to use and maintain the devices so maximum efficiency and effectiveness can be achieved in the classroom setting.

New devices are being designed to help modify the results of the handicaps of blindness, deafness, paralysis, and voice, muscular, and bone aberrations. As research, development, and use of these devices continues, the need for teachers to become familiar with them will increase.

Source of Expertise

We have discussed why and in what areas teachers of the severely and profoundly handicapped should be trained. Now the question is where will the universities get the expertise to train prospective teachers of the severely and profoundly handicapped?

Educators are rapidly gaining the legal right to provide education and training for the severely and profoundly handicapped. With or without this expertise, public schools will establish classes for the most profoundly handicapped. Colleges and universities will begin training teachers. We will accomplish the task of providing education and training for the severely and profoundly handicapped. However, if we are to do the most efficient and effective job, we must recognize our current lack of knowledge of training procedures and begin to correct it.

The recent work of Blatt and Garfunkel (1973), Bricker (1972), Brown (1973), Gold (1973), Haring (1975), Hayden (1975), Lent (1975), Sailor and Mix (1975), Tawney (1974), and others should serve as prime sources of reference for the identification of materials, techniques, and procedures found effective for training the severely and profoundly handicapped. In addition, the excellent work of prominent institution personnel (Azrin & Foxx, 1971; Bensburg, et al., 1965; Gardner, Brust & Watson, 1971; Luckey, Watson &

Musick, 1968; Watson, 1967) should be closely examined.

This focus on available expertise does not minimize the need for further research and study to update and expand what is currently known. It is only to insure that these relatively early efforts are not ignored.

Although we are for the most part inexperienced in dealing with the severely and profoundly handicapped, public education does provide real advantages for this population. Through public education the severely and profoundly handicapped will receive, by the nature of the organizational arrangement, a considerable increase in environmental stimulation by such aspects as living in a community setting, being transported to and from school, and exposure to many normal activities throughout the day. For example, the simple act of being transported back and forth to school provides a wide array of experiences (e.g. active and/or passive interaction with people). It is this involvement in ordinary daily living (normalization), not our current expertise, that largely justifies community based public school education for the severely and profoundly handicapped.

Conclusions

Laws and court decisions have been and are being enacted that will mandate a right to education for the severely and profoundly handicapped.

> The right to education, if it is implemented, will bring into our special education orbit those children and adolescents who were not previously considered to have the necessary academic potential or even to be capable of acquiring the basic life skills for community living or who are not of the traditionally prescribed age for education. Many special educators never before saw them ... They were invisible. (Goldberg &Lippman, 1974, p. 331).

Few teachers are trained to teach these children and few professors of special education are prepared to instruct teachers in educating the severely and profoundly handicapped. This is not to say we cannot do the job. We can and should. However, careful planning will have to occur, if we are to meet this new challenge.

Although laws are being passed to insure public school education for the severely and profoundly handicapped, little money is being appropriated for personnel training. This, of course, enhances the risk of repeating the same mistake made when we first began trying to meet the needs of the less markedly handicapped in regard to the use of ill prepared and unprepared teachers. Because of the pressure to provide special services to the mildly and moderately handicapped, many teachers were not prepared for their jobs. Unfortunately, some handicapped children have suffered, as well as the overall reputation of special education. Although some states are just beginning to overcome the critical lack of trained and certified personnel for the mildly and in some instances the moderately handicapped, we will be faced with new demands for trained personnel for the severely and profoundly handicapped.

Unless adequate support is forthcoming for personnel training, classrooms for the severely and profoundly handicapped are likely to be staffed by untrained teachers. If this happens, these children may fail to progress in an educational environment. This could happen if untrained teachers establish babysitting centers or a watered down curriculum. The severely and profoundly handicapped do not need this kind of educational programing. They need well planned and designed programs developed by rigorously trained special education teachers.

References

Azrin, N. H., & Foxx, R. M. A rapid method of toilet training the institutionalized retarded. *Journal of Applied Behavior Analysis,* 1971, 4(2), 89-99.

Ball, T. (Ed.). *A guide for the instruction and training of the profoundly retarded and severely multi-handicapped child.* Santa Cruz CA: Santa Cruz County Board of Education, 1971.

Balthazar, E. E. *Balthazar scales of adaptive behavior for the profoundly and severely mentally retarded.* Champaign IL: Research Press, 1971.

Bayley, N. *Bayley infant scales of development.* New York: Psychological Corporation, 1969.

Bensburg, G. J., Colwell, C. N., & Cassell, R. H. Teaching the profoundly retarded self-help activities by behavior shaping techniques. *American Journal of Mental Deficiency,* 1965, 69(5), 674-679.

Blatt, B., & Garfunkel, F. Teaching the mentally retarded. In R. M. Travers (Ed.), *Secondary handbook on research on teaching.* Chicago: Rand McNally, 1973.

Bricker, D. Imitation sign training as a facilitator of word-object association with low-functioning children. *American Journal of Mental Deficiency,* 1972, 76, 509-516.

Brown, L. Instructional programs for trainable level retarded students. In: L. Mann and D. A. Sabatino (Eds.), *The first review of special education,* 2. Philadelphia: Ise Press, 1973.

Cattell, P. *The measurement of intelligence of infants and young children.* New York: Psychological Corporation, 1940.

Corman, H. H. & Escalona, S. K. Stages of sensori-motor development: A replication study.

Language Training for the Severely Retarded: Five Years of Behavior Analysis Research

LEE K. SNYDER
THOMAS C. LOVITT
JAMES O. SMITH

LEE K. SNYDER is a doctoral student and research associate, and JAMES O. SMITH is Professor and Chairman of Special Education, George Peabody College, Nashville, Tennessee; THOMAS C. LOVITT is Professor of Special Education, the University of Washington, Seattle.

In the past 20 years, an increasing amount of research has focused on the complex questions related to language development. This trend is reflected in both journals and texts on mental retardation, and has been documented by several thorough reviews of the literature (e.g., Schiefelbusch, 1969; Smith, 1962). Such an emphasis is not surprising in light of the high incidence of language disorders reported among the retarded and considering the central role which language plays in almost every aspect of our daily lives.

Recently, parents, professionals, and legislatures have exerted pressure on the public schools, as well as on state institutions, to provide a meaningful and appropriate education for all handicapped students, including those who are severely retarded. Certainly, language training must play an important part in any such educational program. Behavior analysis researchers have been especially prolific in their response to this new urgency. In the past few years, so many relevant and promising studies have been offered by the behavior analysts, and in such rapid succession, that it has become difficult for the educator to keep abreast of the latest developments in this area. Thus, the need has become apparent for a brief review of the most recent work in this rapidly expanding field of research.

The Focus

The research to be discussed here deals specifically with subjects who have been identified by the investigators as severely retarded, or whose reported levels of functioning and IQ would indicate such a classification. The term "severely mentally retarded," according to the 1973 American Association of Mental Deficiency (AAMD) classification system, refers to persons whose measured intelligence is at least four standard deviations below the mean.

Although adaptive behavior criteria are somewhat more ambiguous, Dunn (1973) suggests that severely retarded individuals "have the ability (1) to walk, toilet, dress and feed themselves; (2) to speak in a very elementary fashion; and (3) to perform simple chores in the home or in a very protective environment" (p. 86). This population has been selected as the focus of concern because (a) for the first time, large numbers of these students are being enrolled in the public schools, requiring new instructional programs and techniques, and (b) it seems at least possible that these students may exhibit qualitatively, as well as quantitatively, distinctive patterns of learning and responding. Therefore, in limiting the focus of this review, it has been decided to exclude the many interesting and exciting language development studies which employed subjects who are "high level retardates" (e.g., McLean, 1970) or extremely disturbed children (e.g., Lovaas, 1968).

Additionally, the scope of this article has been limited to studies of language behavior. Specifically, only those studies dealing with language as meaningful, symbolic communication (both oral and aural) will be considered. Thus, related research in such areas as articulation, audiometry, and motor imitation are not included here.

Finally, this article covers only those studies which have employed a behavior analysis research design. Each of these studies met the following criteria: (a) the behavior under study (the dependent variable) was clearly defined in observable terms; (b) this behavior was directly and precisely measured on a continuous basis with data reported accordingly; and (c) the research analyzed the effects of systematic manipulation of specific environmental factors (the independent variables). There has been an obvious trend in recent educational research toward this methodology. This seems to be a particularly promising approach to the study of language acquisition.

So many studies of this type have appeared in the literature of the past two decades that it would be impossible to discuss all of them here. Therefore, only those studies published since 1968 are included. The 23 studies which were found to meet the above criteria are characterized in Table 1.

The first section of this article will be a summary and comparison of the specific language behaviors investigated in these studies. Several aspects of the research methodologies employed will be considered next. Finally, the implications for classroom or clinical practice, as well as for future research will be discussed.

Target Behaviors (Dependent Variables)

In all of these studies, the behavior under analysis was the subject's performance on specific language tasks. These tasks may be classified along two dimensions—type and level. There are two main types of language: receptive (auditory perception, "input") and expressive (usually vocal production, "output"). Tasks in either of these modes may be at one of three levels—initial acquisition (if the subject lacks prior reception and/or expressive language), appropriate use of language, or, use of correct grammar or syntax.

Another feature which may be incorporated in a study of language development is the generative property of language; that is, the ability to produce and receive "an unlimited number of utterances which share a limited number of regularities" (Lahey, 1973, p. x). This concept is illustrated by the following statement by Twardosz and Baer (1973),

> Several studies have shown that when a child is taught to use specific examples of a grammatical rule, he also produces novel examples of this rule that have never been trained, i.e., the rule is generative, (p. 655).

Elsewhere, this phenomenon is referred to as "generalization to untrained stimuli" (p. 660). It has been suggested by Baer and Guess (1973) that, "So conceptualized, these rules of morphological grammar appear equivalent to the behavioral concept of response class" (p. 498). This suggestion, that "generative" and "response class" may actually be equivalent concepts, seems supportable in light of the definition of a response class as "a set of responses so organized that an operation applied to a relatively small subset of their members produces similar results in other members as well" (Garcia, Guess, & Byrnes, 1973, p. 299). Therefore, in the present discussion, those studies which dealt with the generalization of responses to untrained stimuli, or with the formation of a linguistic response class, are all considered analyses of the generative property of the language behavior under investigation.

Receptive Language

Only three of the studies under consideration dealt exclusively with receptive language. Two of these dealt with initial acquisition of the ability to receive (i.e., respond to) verbal instructions (Whitman, Zakaras, & Chardos, 1971; Striefel & Wetherby, 1973). The generative property of this ability was assessed in both studies, with very different results. In the earlier study (Whitman, et al.), the subjects learned to respond correctly to 11 specific verbal commands and generalized this ability to a set of 11 similar, but untrained, instructions. However, Striefel and Wetherby (1973), working with an older and more severely retarded subject, found no generalization to similar instructions, or even to variations of the same 20 instructions which had been successfully trained.

Baer and Guess (1971) assessed the effects of training the receptive discrimination of comparative and superlative forms of adjectives (concepts of which had been previously trained as opposites). All three of their subjects learned to point correctly to pictures representing the superlative and comparative forms of specific adjectives and generalized this ability to similar, but untrained, adjectives.

Expressive Language

Seventeen studies focused exclusively on the modification of expressive language, and nine of these were concerned with the initial acquisition of the ability to imitate and produce specific words or phonemic elements. Four studies (Sloane, Johnston, & Harris, 1968; Kircher, Pear, & Martin, 1971; Stewart, 1972; Jeffrey, 1972) simply demonstrated the effectiveness of operant conditioning in developing and maintaining verbal responses to specific stimuli (e.g., pictures or adult model). The work of Peine, Gregersen, & Sloane, (1970) and Lawrence (1971) was similar in nature, but additionally demonstrated successful manipulation of spontaneous speech through contingent reinforcement. The generative nature of imitative vocal responses was investigated by Garcia, Baer, & Firestone (1971) and by Schroeder and Baer (1972). In both these studies, subjects who had been operantly trained to imitate specific types of motor and vocal responses generalized this ability to the imitation of topographically similar, but untrained, responses. Griffiths and Craighead (1972) successfully trained a specific response class (pronunciation of 10 words with the initial phoneme /l/) which generalized across three different types of stimuli (all evoking the same 10 words), but not across two different settings.

The appropriate use of language was successfully manipulated through contingent reinforcement in three studies. Barton (1972) increased the amount of social speech (verbalization directed toward others) in four severely retarded women. In 1970, Barton reported the success of operant training techniques in increasing the number of appropriate responses made to magazine pictures by an 11 year old institutionalized boy. However, she found that this behavior did not generalize to similar, but untrained, tasks. In contrast, Twardosz and Baer (1973) succeeded in training two institutionalized adolescents to ask a specific class of questions ("What letter?") in one setting, and found that this did generalize to similar stimuli within the same setting.

Five studies in recent years dealt with the operant training of grammar or syntax in expressive language. Guess, Sailor, Rutherford, & Baer (1968), Sailor (1971) and Garcia, et al. (1973) successfully trained subjects to correctly use singular and plural forms of nouns and, through the use of probes and experimental reversals, clearly demonstrated the generative nature of these learnings. Similarly, Schumaker and Sherman (1970) trained three subjects to produce verbs of the appropriate tense (past or present progressive) in response to verbal stimuli, and demonstrated the generation of appropriate tense use in untrained verbs. Baer and Guess (1973) reported successfully teaching four severely retarded adolescents to produce noun suffixes ("__er" and "__ist") and generalize this skill to untrained words.

Receptive and Expressive Language

Finally, three studies analyzed both receptive and expressive language behaviors. MacAulay (1968) reported on her work with 11 severely retarded students, between the ages of 9 and 15, at the Rainier State School in Buckley, Washington. These studies were discussed rather informally in an article intended to give an overview of the procedures employed, and no complete list of the specific behaviors was provided. However, the data which were presented demonstrated successful operant training of vocabulary reception ("point to the ___"), phoneme production, and morpheme production in response to verbal, pictorial, and, in some cases, written stimuli.

Two more studies dealing with pluralization (Guess, 1969; Guess and Baer, 1973) explored the interrelationships, in terms of generalization, between receptive and expressive training. The earlier study demonstrated that successful training to discriminate receptively between the singular and plural forms of a noun did not generalize to the production of the appropriate form of that noun. In the followup study, four subjects were trained to receptively discriminate one class of plurals and expressively use another class. Probes revealed no generalization across modes.

Research Methodology

Subjects and Settings

The 23 studies discussed here involved a total of 64 subjects. With very few exceptions, these subjects had either been officially diagnosed as severely retarded, according to the AAMD classification system, or could be so classified on the basis of their reported functioning and IQ. Four of the studies, employing a total of 9 subjects, involved children under 8 years of age. Fifteen subjects, in 7 different studies, were over 14 years of age. The remaining 36 subjects, involved in 15 of the studies, were all between the ages of 8 and 13. (Several studies employed subjects of widely varying ages and so were counted twice in these figures.)

Nineteen studies, involving 52 of the subjects, were conducted within residential institutions for the retarded. Only 5 studies, involving 12 children, were carried out in noninstitutional settings. These included one public school, one preschool, one day care center, and two clinics.

Intervention Techniques (Independent Variables)

Most of these studies involved more than one independent variable. Without exception, all of the studies included the use of some tangible reinforcement (12 using primaries and 11 using tokens) for desired verbal behavior. In two studies, the relative effectiveness of different reinforcers was assessed. Lawrence (1971) found that the use of social reinforcement, alone or paired with a consumable primary, was more effective with three adolescents than the use of the consumable alone. In a study with four retarded women, Barton (1972) found that token reinforcement produced dramatically greater increases in verbal behavior than did primary reinforcement.

Several of the studies placed the subject(s) on a continuous or fixed ratio schedule of reinforcement only until the verbal behavior attained a predetermined criterion level (Sloane, et al., 1968; Guess, 1969; Garcia, et al., 1971; Baer & Guess, 1971; Sailor, 1971; Schroeder & Baer, 1972; Garcia, et al., 1973; Guess & Baer, 1973; Twardosz & Baer, 1973). The behavior was then placed on a variable ratio schedule (VR) of reinforcement (usually VR 2 or VR 3) to facilitate the interjection of nonreinforced probes designed to assess generalization of learning.

In many of the studies, a time out contingency (ranging from 10 to 30 seconds in most cases) was arranged for incorrect responses or nonattending behavior (Sloane et al., 1968; Schumaker & Sherman, 1970; Barton, 1970; Baer & Guess, 1971; Kircher et al., 1971; Lawrence, 1971). No evidence is provided in any of these studies to support the effectiveness of this technique, and one might question its appropriateness with this population. As Lawrence (1971) has observed, time out from reinforcement is the usual state of affairs for most institutional residents. In fact, Kircher et al. (1971) demonstrated the relative ineffectiveness of time out, as contrasted with contingent mild shocks, in decreasing inappropriate behavior.

In 11 of these studies, antecedent modeling of desired responses was provided. Usually, if this failed to elicit the correct imitation or verbalization, the response was shaped through reinforcement of increasing approximations as physical prompts were gradually faded out. In two studies (Whitman, et al., 1971; Striefel & Wetherby, 1973), this process of shaping and fading was the central intervention technique under study.

The relative effectiveness of two different training procedures on generalization to untrained response types was assessed by Schroeder and Baer (1972) in their study of vocal imitation. Two subjects were taught to verbally imitate groups of three words (through modeling and shaping) with two

6. SEVERELY AND PROFOUNDLY RETARDED

TABLE 1   Characteristics of 23 Behavior Analysis Studies of Language Training for the Severely Retarded

Author/date	Target behavior Type	Target behavior Level	Antecedent events	Reinforcement	Nonreinforcement	Research design employed
Guess, Sailor, Rutherford, & Baer (1968)	Expressive [a]	Grammar, Syntax		Primary		Reversal of contingency
MacAulay (1968)	Receptive, Expressive	Initial Acquisition [b]	Shaping/fading; Modeling	Token		
Sloane, Johnston, & Harris (1968)	Expressive	Initial Acquisition [b]	Shaping/fading; Modeling	Primary	Time out	Noncontingent reinforcement
Guess (1969)	Receptive, Expressive	Grammar, Syntax		Token		Reversal of contingency
Schumaker & Sherman (1970)	Expressive [a]	Grammar, Syntax	Modeling [c]	Token	Time out	Multiple baseline
Barton (1970)	Expressive [a]	Appropriate Usage		Primary	Time out	Reversal of contingency
Peine, Gregersen & Sloane (1970)	Expressive	Initial Acquisition [b]		Token [d]		Reversal of contingency
Garcia, Baer, & Firestone (1971)	Expressive [a]	Initial Acquisition [b]	Shaping/fading; Modeling	Primary		Multiple baseline
Baer & Guess (1971)	Receptive [a]	Grammar Syntax		Token	Time out	Multiple baseline
Kircher, Pear, & Martin (1971)	Expressive	Initial Acquisition [b]	Modeling	Token	Time out	
Whitman, Zakaras, & Chardos (1971)	Receptive [a]	Initial Acquisition [b]	Shaping/fading	Primary		A-B-A design
Sailor (1971)	Expressive [a]	Grammar, Syntax	Modeling	Primary		Multiple baseline
Lawrence (1971)	Expressive	Initial Acquisition [b]		Primary [d]	Time out	A-B-A design; Pretest/posttest
Stewart (1972)	Expressive	Initial Acquisition [b]	Modeling	Primary		
Jeffrey (1972)	Expressive	Initial Acquisition [b]	Shaping/fading; Modeling	Primary		
Schroder & Baer (1972)	Expressive [a]	Initial Acquisition [b]	Shaping/fading; [c] Modeling	Primary		
Barton (1972)	Expressive	Appropriate Usage		Primary/token		
Griffiths & Craighead (1972)	Expressive	Initial Acquisition [b]	Modeling	Token		Multiple baseline
Garcia, Guess, & Byrnes (1972)	Expressive [a]	Grammar, Syntax	Modeling	Primary		Reversal of contingency
Guess & Baer (1973)	Receptive, Expressive	Grammar, Syntax		Token		
Twardosz & Baer (1973)	Expressive [a]	Appropriate Usage	Shaping/fading; Modeling	Token		Multiple baseline
Striefel & Wetherby (1973)	Receptive [a]	Initial Acquisition [b]	Shaping/fading	Primary		
Baer & Guess (1973)	Expressive [a]	Grammar, Syntax	Modeling	Primary/token		Reversal of contingency

[a] Study included analysis of generative property of specific language behavior trained.
[b] Initial acquisition of specific words or phonemic elements.
[c] Optional: Used only if other interventions failed to elicit desired response.
[d] Systematically paired with social reinforcement.

alternating procedures: In one condition, each of the three words would be trained to criterion before the next was introduced; in the second condition, the three words would be trained concurrently until all three had reached criterion. The two procedures were equally effective in producing correct imitations of the words being trained. However, generalization to probe items was significantly greater following concurrent training.

In 7 studies, contingent reinforcement of responses was the only intervention employed. In these studies, no antecedent events preceded the presentation of the stimulus to which the subject(s) responded (Guess et al., 1968; Guess, 1969; Barton, 1970; Peine et al., 1970; Baer & Guess, 1971; Barton, 1972; Guess & Baer, 1973).

Experimental Control

Several research designs were employed in these 23 studies, the complexity of which probably reflects the complexity of the language behaviors being investigated. Behavior analysis researchers commonly use an A-B-A design (baseline—intervention—return to baseline) to demonstrate the effectiveness of their interventions. However, in most of the studies reported here, such a design was either not practical or not desirable.

The method of reversing contingencies was employed by several of these investigators and involves the switch of contingent reinforcement to a previously unreinforced, and usually incorrect, response after the correct response has been successfully trained. In the studies which used this design, reestablishment of the normal contingencies for correct responding consistently succeeded in reinstituting the previously established patterns of correct responding. In a multiple baseline design, experimental control is demonstrated through successive application of the intervention to two or more subjects, behaviors or settings. As the intervention is applied to each, a change in the pattern of responses is interpreted as indication of the effectiveness of the technique employed.

Implications

Suggestions for Classroom and Clinical Practice

In the past five years, a large amount of behavior analysis research has appeared dealing with the language development of severely retarded subjects. Perhaps the most striking implication to be drawn from all these studies is that it is definitely possible to improve the language skills of severely retarded children and adults through the application of systematic instructional techniques and reinforcement contingencies. However, for the teacher or clinician who is applying such behavior management techniques, some more specific inferences can be made.

In order for a response to be reinforced, it must first exist in the student's repertoire. This is an obvious fact, but one we can easily forget in our enthusiasm for behavior modification. In several of the studies discussed here, the investigators found it necessary to develop a systematic shaping procedure in order to initially establish the desired behaviors. The use of modeling and physical prompting, which could be gradually faded out as the behavior came under reinforcement control, was reported as a successful approach in several of these studies.

Several implications for the scheduling of consequent events can be drawn from the research reviewed here. The selection of effective reinforcers is certainly one critical component in a program designed to strengthen or extend a desired behavior once it has been initially acquired. While we frequently assume that primary reinforcers are the most potent, the study by Barton (1972) demonstrated that tokens were significantly more effective than primary reinforcers in modifying the social speech of the four severely retarded women included in that study. In selecting a reinforcer for any one student, the teacher or clinician should experiment with a wide variety of reinforcers—both primary and secondary—to determine which is most reinforcing for that particular person. Similarly if a time out procedure is to be used effectively, it must take the form of time out from a truly reinforcing reinforcement, not just time out from the activity or attention.

The conflicting findings regarding generalization which were reported in these studies indicate clearly that we should not expect generalization to occur automatically. The practice of gradually fading from a one to one to a variable ratio schedule of reinforcement, employed in many of these investigations, may prove to be a useful practice for the clinician or teacher who wishes to promote generalization across settings, as well as maintenance over time. Although it may be possible to reinforce a desired response every time it occurs, in a clinical or classroom setting, this behavior will disappear if it is not reinforced when it occurs in other settings. If the behavior is placed on an intermittent schedule, it will be more resistant to the inevitable instances of nonreinforcement in uncontrolled situations.

One potential means for fostering generalization to new responses is indicated by the findings of Schroeder and Baer (1972). In their study, generalization was found to be greater after several words had been trained concurrently, as opposed to a sequential teaching procedure. Certainly, this would be an easy technique to apply in both clinical and classroom settings and one with which the teacher or clinician may wish to experiment.

Directions for Future Research

From the results of the studies discussed here, it would seem that the possibility of modifying the language behavior of severely retarded subjects through the use of operant procedures has been clearly established. Far from exhausting the need for research in this area, however, these studies have revealed many unanswered questions which call for further investigation.

Certainly, there is a need to extend the range of ages and settings involved in future language training research. With the current trend towards early screening and intervention for handicapped children, more studies involving severely retarded subjects under the age of seven would be relevant. Similarly, as the move towards deinstitutionalization progresses, we look increasingly towards research conducted in public school, group home, foster home, and natural home environments.

It is somewhat surprising that every study discussed here involved the use of some tangible reinforcement. It would seem worthwhile to investigate the possible application of purely social reinforcement in the form of contingent praise or physical contact (e.g., hugging, patting). As has been noted earlier, this type of reinforcement has all too often been lacking in the environments of institutionalized subjects. It seems possible that this might provide a source of very potent reinforcement. Similarly, the effects of different antecedent events, without any elaborate reinforcement contingencies, would seem to merit investigation. Certainly, in studies of language *acquisition*, the efficiency of waiting for the subject to emit a desired response, which has not yet been mastered, and then reinforcing it, may be questioned. Although most studies have employed antecedent strategies as a "last resort," it is hoped that future investigators will focus more direct attention on these antecedent instructional interventions.

It should be noted that only a few of the studies described here have reported data on either maintenance over time or generalization of learned responses to new settings. Since the reason for training language skills is to have those skills applied in the subject's daily living, it is hoped that future investigators will analyze intervention strategies employed in training or modifying specific language behaviors in order to identify those variables which are most effective in promoting maintenance. Similarly, analyses of data obtained through the systematic manipulation of antecedent or consequent events are needed to determine the efficacy of different intervention strategies in terms of response generalization—both to untrained responses *and* to new settings.

The 23 studies which have been discussed here represent an exciting avenue of research which holds great promise for the severely retarded individual. As future investigators find answers to the many new and difficult questions raised by the present studies, we may hope to see this promise realized and the door of two-way communication finally opened to those who have been shut out for so long.

Breaking Down the IQ Walls
Severely Retarded People Can Learn to Read

The Ball-Stick-Bird reading program avoids rote learning to provide the excitement of forming words with the first few letters the person learns. Using three basic figures, he can form all the letters of the alphabet. The result is not only the magic of reading, but a general increase in happiness.

Renée Fuller

EIGHTEEN-YEAR-OLD JANE is a mongoloid with an IQ of 35. A few years ago she had little spontaneous speech, threw tearful tantrums, and spent a good deal of time rocking back and forth. Today she talks about her frustrations and disappointments, no longer rocks, and the tantrums are rare. Jane has developed a sense of humor that helps her get along with others. She now reads and understands complicated fiction and answers printed letters from home. Totally unexpected for one labeled "severely retarded."

The story of Jane and 25 other retardates began more than 10 years ago when I began to develop a reading system intended for normal and superior toddlers. Its use with the retarded was accidental, and their success with the system was totally unexpected.

The Ball-Stick-Bird method developed from my own learning disabilities. I was not able to read until I was 12. Much later, after I earned a doctorate in psychology, it became apparent why reading had been so difficult for me. My deficit covered several areas, in sight, sound, and the ability to remember what I had seen or heard unless it made sense (associational memory). Because letters or sounds by themselves make no sense, many children are stymied by rote memorization and the mechanics of learning to read.

With this initial insight, I began to put together a reading program based on principles of perceptual and developmental psychology. The first task was to simplify the process of recognizing letters. Using three basic forms—a line, a circle and an angle—one can make all the letters of the alphabet. Even a two-year-old can build letters this way. To make the figures stand out clearly, I gave each a different color; to make them amusing, I gave them fun names. The circle became a ball, the line a stick, and the angle a bird. With these three basic forms children can build letters themselves. Thus the student has tactile and kinesthetic feedback as he learns.

The human brain is not a computer with an unlimited ability to absorb bits of information, so it seemed logical to reduce the initial memory load. For this reason, the first reader, *Go Go Vooroos*, begins by teaching letter sounds rather than letter names. And so, "I" is "ī" as in "icky," and "V" is "vuh" as in "vanishing vampire." The child learns words after he knows only two letters. He forms words with the second letter; the story begins with the fourth. This allows him to utilize immediately what he learns, and tells the student the truth about reading: that the hieroglyphs, when unlocked, can tell marvelous stories.

Words in Action. From the first book on, action adventures begin, and the student gets so involved in trying to find out what happens next that he does his utmost to decipher the code. He sees firsthand that the purpose of the code is to tell a story, not to produce a series of disjointed words that do not make sense. In this way the system avoids "word calling," or reading without comprehension.

Another way to reduce initial memory load is to teach reading in capital letters only. The student must learn only 26 different configurations, rather than 52 or 104, if handwriting is also taught. Once he learns to read in capitals, we find he quickly transfers his skill to lower-case letters or handwriting.

There is another way to simplify initial learning. One of the reasons so many children have trouble learning to read English is that the vowels have many possible sounds. It has become fashionable to try to teach first-graders to discriminate between these sounds, a difficult task for many of them. However, we can use this difficulty to advantage: if the different sounds of "A" appear the same to the child, he will not be disturbed that these get the same symbol. Our system takes into account the inaccuracies of childish speech, using them to benefit the reading process, and thus no child feels that he has failed. The method also avoids failure because it does not require immediate mastery; it allows for overlearning in the context of action-packed stories as a substitute for boring drills. Students learn the alphabet in two consecutive books, and other reading principles in at least three. If the pupil has not mastered what was presented in the first book, he can learn it in the second book, and so on, always in the context of a fast-moving action story. He can't miss.

The student starts deciphering sentences and paragraphs almost immediately, and then we teach him another

42. Breaking Down the I.Q. Walls

truth about English: a particular letter does not always make the same sound. We tell him that the letter sounds may indicate what the word will be, but that he cannot be sure except in the context of a sentence or a paragraph; he learns to play detective and use the letters as his clues. But like all clues, the letters make sense only in the context of a story. So the student learns a flexible approach to the alphabet code, one that demands feedback from the content of the whole. This kind of sophisticated intellectual feedback is not what either the psychologist or the layman presume to be within the capacity of low-IQ students.

Reading As Fun, Not Failure. The vocabulary of Ball-Stick-Bird is multisyllabic, deliberately difficult, and current. The first reader includes words like *electricity, antenna, planet, rocket, comet*. By the second book, the child reads:

VAD PULLS PLUG OF MATTER TRANSMITTER. VAD OPENS HIS KIT, PULLS OFF BAD BUTTONS OF MATTER TRANSMITTER, STICKS ON BUTTONS FROM HIS KIT, SENDS CURRENT FROM HIS KIT INTO MAGNETS OF MATTER TRANSMITTER.

By book number five he has even more fun:

AT LAST THEY GET TO PLUTO, THE LAST PLANET OF THE SOLAR SYSTEM. PLUTO IS NOT A PLANET OF DOGS. PLUTO IS A PLANET OF FISH. BUT ALAS! WHAT HAPPENED TO PLUTO, THE PLANET OF FISH? GREEDY WEEDS SLITHERED INTO THE WATER, GOBBLED UP THE FISH FOOD, AND SMASHED THE DAMS.

The space odysseys are cliff-hangers. In order to find out what happens next, the student must learn a new letter or reading principle. Yet if he has not mastered the principles on the first reading, they appear in book after book. We emphasize the overall concept of reading; the student acquires a framework onto which he attaches the details (the rote-memory material).

All but the mechanical aspects of Ball-Stick-Bird should have precluded success with low-IQ groups. Even though Ball-Stick-Bird is highly entertaining and marvelously "now," we expected that this abstract system would not work with them. The first experiments done with Ball-Stick-Bird and retardates were designed to see whether the system really simplified the mechanics of reading, not to see whether the retardates could comprehend. We taught the alphabet to one group using the Ball-Stick-Bird method, while another group received traditional instruction. The first group learned some of the letters, the second did not.

Students can form all the letters of the alphabet with little yellow and big red balls, bright blue sticks, and light blue birds.

6. SEVERELY AND PROFOUNDLY RETARDED

Next we wanted to find out whether the new system simplified the word-building process. If it did, we hoped retarded students would learn mechanical reading, even though we presumed they would not understand what they read.

And then it happened—the teaching staff claimed that the students were understanding what they were reading. My reaction was total disbelief. The staff insisted that I watch through the one-way mirror. After viewing a few lessons, I had to admit that it seemed as if the students understood the Ball-Stick-Bird stories. It was impossible; these students had a history of reading failure. Their institution had exposed them to a multitude of reading systems, individually and in groups, yet through all this effort they had not learned even the alphabet. It seemed totally out of the question that such a group could learn to read with comprehension.

Life had not been kind to these 26 students. Their IQs ranged from 33 to 72; nine had IQs below 40. Their ages ranged from 11 to 49. They had a wide range of physical deformities and diseases. Many had abnormal EEGs. Most of them had been in trouble with the law for juvenile offenses, arson, indecent exposure, threats to kill, or breaking and entering. Staff psychiatrists suspected that five were schizoid or schizophrenic. That such students in a matter of months understood what they were reading, even if it was only on the book number two level, must have been an experimental accident. But experimental accidents must be investigated.
IQ Makes No Difference. And so we developed a series of tests to measure what was happening and to try to find out why. We gave the students word-list tests and the same words embedded in a paragraph. If they could read more words correctly in the paragraph than in the list, they were using contextual clues. This meant they understood at least part of what they were reading. In fact, the students did significantly better with the words in context than with those on the list. Curiously, the students with higher IQs did not do any better than those with lower IQ scores.

The next question was whether these low-IQ students understood the difficult vocabulary of Ball-Stick-Bird, which appeared too difficult for anyone but superior children. Yet how could the students understand the stories if they could not understand the words?

We gave each student a vocabulary test. The students did so well that they created a methodological embarrassment—many of them scored 100 percent, making it im-

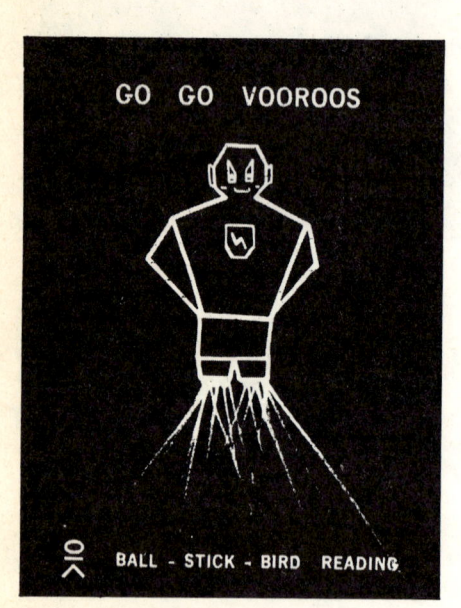

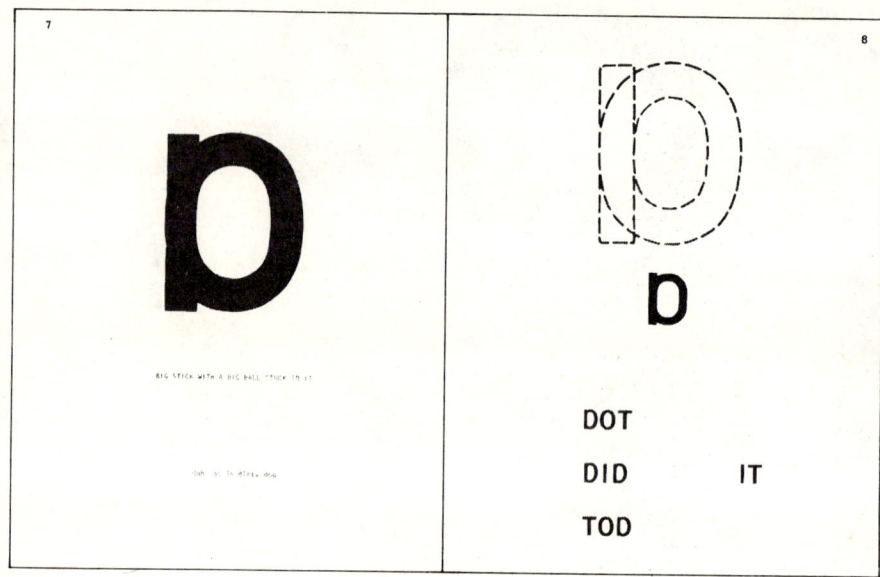

In the first reader students can read after they have learned their fourth letter. By the end of the book they have learned the entire alphabet.

3. MENTAL RETARDATION

42. Breaking Down the I.Q. Walls

possible to differentiate between the students. Indeed, the same number of low- and higher-IQ students got perfect scores. We had to use more difficult scoring standards than those used on standard IQ tests, because their responses were so sophisticated:

IQ 62 *doctor* "You mean in the medical profession? Someone who helps you get well—usually."

IQ 38 *funny* "Jokes, laughing, when people tell stories, funny stories particularly. It means somebody gets a kick out of something."

IQ 64 *chilly* "Chilly is midway between hot and cold, but it's more like cold."

IQ 33 *speed* "When you're going too fast."

We had now established that our students were comprehending what they read and that they understood the difficult Ball-Stick-Bird vocabulary. To measure their story comprehension, I wrote a story called *Tommy the Green Cat* that the students could read within one session. After they finished, each student answered 15 questions on both the implicit and explicit content of the story, rated by readability formulas from third- to the eighth-grade level. Although scores on *Tommy the Green Cat* correlated positively with IQ scores, the relationship was not significant. Our low-IQ students frequently were able to answer the questions as well as those with higher IQs.

By this time, the explanation for the success of the retarded students seemed to be in the nature of the fast-moving space odysseys. Perhaps the students performed so well because man is the animal who understands stories. Even if a person is badly brain damaged, story comprehension may be so basic to our species that he still maintains that ability.

Of Cats and Comprehension. To determine how well our students could comprehend material that was not story bound, we developed a fourth type of comprehension test, called the "following written directions test." It uses the same vocabulary and very similar sentence structure as the story-comprehension tests, but differs in content and presumed intellectual demand. The students scored almost as well on this test as they did on the *Tommy the Green Cat* test. They could read with comprehension and transfer that ability to material not presented in stories.

Most of our students taught themselves to write. One place that replicated our findings is the Orange County Chapter of the New York Association for Retarded Children in Middletown, New York. They

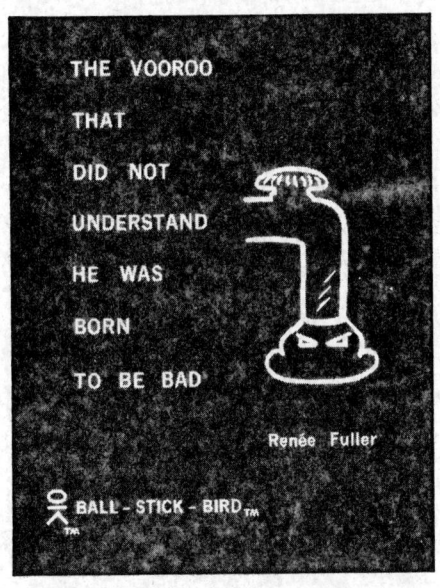

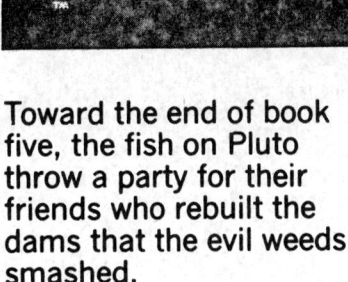

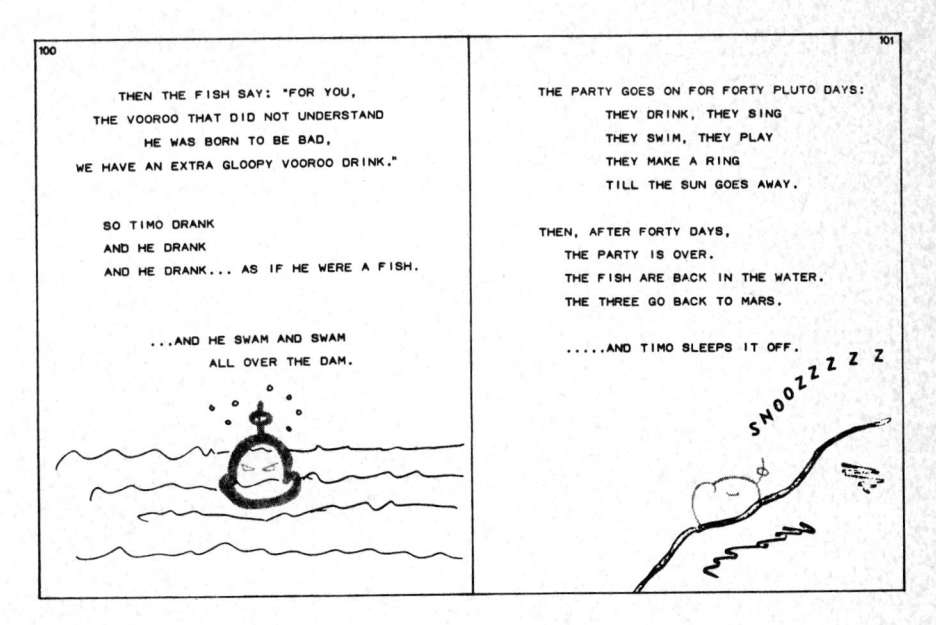

Toward the end of book five, the fish on Pluto throw a party for their friends who rebuilt the dams that the evil weeds smashed.

THE VOOROO THAT DID NOT UNDERSTAND HE WAS BORN TO BE BAD

Renée Fuller

BALL-STICK-BIRD

AT LAST, THE DAMS ARE FINISHED.

HAPPY FISH SET A BIG, BIG TABLE
IN THE MIDDLE OF THE LAKE.
FISH MAKE ALL SORTS OF GOODIES FOR:
WONDERFUL COMETS
COOL CATS
SPACE VADS
AND THE VOOROO –
THAT DID NOT UNDERSTAND
HE WAS BORN TO BE BAD.

THE FISH SING THEIR DRINKING SONG:

"DRINK, DRINK, DRINK OF THE WATER –
FROM SPARKLING LAKES AND PLUTO'S PONDS.

DRINK, DRINK, DRINK OF THE WATER –
BACK FROM THE WEEDS THAT DRANK IT UP.

DRINK, DRINK, DRINK TO THESE SPACEMEN,
FIXERS OF FISH AND PONDS AND DAMS !"

(FISH ARE GOOD DRINKERS
BUT NOT GOOD SINGERS.
THEY ARE VERY BAD POETS.)

THEN THE FISH SAY: "FOR YOU,
THE VOOROO THAT DID NOT UNDERSTAND
HE WAS BORN TO BE BAD,
WE HAVE AN EXTRA GLOOPY VOOROO DRINK."

SO TIMO DRANK
AND HE DRANK
AND HE DRANK... AS IF HE WERE A FISH.

...AND HE SWAM AND SWAM
ALL OVER THE DAM.

THE PARTY GOES ON FOR FORTY PLUTO DAYS:
THEY DRINK, THEY SING
THEY SWIM, THEY PLAY
THEY MAKE A RING
TILL THE SUN GOES AWAY.

THEN, AFTER FORTY DAYS,
THE PARTY IS OVER.
THE FISH ARE BACK IN THE WATER.
THE THREE GO BACK TO MARS.

.....AND TIMO SLEEPS IT OFF.

SNOOZZZZZ

21. Breaking Down The IQ Walls

have taught students with IQs in the 20s to read with comprehension. Just as unexpected as these findings is the lack of a correlation between IQ and reading performance. Some of our students with IQs in the 30s learned to read as rapidly and performed as well on the tests as other students with IQs in the 60s. Obviously our students came from the lower part of the IQ continuum; our sample stopped at 72, not 200. Results from using Ball-Stick-Bird with normal and superior children who have learning disabilities show they learn considerably faster than retarded students. Evidently the total IQ range is needed before the IQ correlation becomes apparent.

The lack of correlation between IQ and performance has implications in the classroom. It means that teachers may see some low-IQ students outperform youngsters with higher IQs. It also means that once the classroom teacher has had the experience of being successful in a matter of months with one low-IQ student, she becomes impatient when it requires two years with another, even though in the past she would have gotten bursitis patting herself on the back for such a success.

Finally, we wondered whether the changes we observed in reading were reflected by changes in IQ scores. All but two students showed a slight increase in IQ, but this was not large enough to explain the success of our students. Ironically, Jane, one of our faster learners, dropped from 39 to 35, and our poorest student gained nine points. Inadvertently we had stumbled on a phenomenon that questions IQ tests and their meaning.

Straightened Backs and Happy Smiles. But more striking than the cognitive development were the changes in personalities and self-concepts. These advances were visually obvious. Film records showed that slumped postures changed to straightened backs; continual rocking ceased. People who had never been concerned with their appearances began grooming themselves. These changes cannot be attributed to success in itself, because several students had been gold-medal winners in the Special Olympics for retarded children. It was the *nature* of the success that was important.

Their increased verbalization made communication with others, both fellow residents and staff, much easier. Because the students looked and acted differently, their peers and the staff perceived them as different. But above all, their new ability to verbalize allowed for greater self-communication; they could think thoughts that had not been possible before. Changes in Paul's behavior were typical of those in other patients.

Paul was a detached and withdrawn 12-year-old when he entered the reading program. He has an abnormal EEG. Psychiatric evaluations had stated that his "autisticlike behavior" was an "inhibiting factor in his intellectual development." His parents had been institutionalized mental defectives. In foster homes he was beaten and neglected, then returned to the institution. The institution's school reported that in spite of individual attention, "Paul is unable to learn new material."

After entering the reading program Paul gradually became more docile and less prone to tantrums, and he began to trust people. Verbal communication replaced his autistic withdrawal, and he learned to interpret and follow directions. Often Paul coached other patients in the reading program. He helped them with difficult words and concepts and took pride in their accomplishments. While he waited for reading lessons, he picked up books to read on his own.

From Nonpersons to Human Beings. Educators, psychologists, and mental-health officials have assumed that most of the cognitive and behavioral changes we have described are out of the reach of severely retarded patients. Yet people who were labeled as going no place suddenly have new opportunities. Seven of our students have been discharged from the institution, and several others are employed in semiprotected environments.

The students were not the only ones who changed. At first, to us—never mind how much we knew about retardation—the students represented a group of nonpeople. We dutifully extended ourselves to them, but as a gesture of generosity, not as one person to another. But as our students learned to talk to us as people, we came to see them as people. And so what began as an experiment to test the dimensions of a reading system became something totally different. We learned that the human being begins not at an IQ of 100, or an IQ of 70, not even at an IQ of 30. But what we are as people is something that can be developed. Unexpectedly, an amusing reading system for superior toddlers triggered this development.

By now, Ball-Stick-Bird has been used successfully with almost every conceivable group. Normal three- to five-year-olds not only learn to read with it, they also show the same calming reaction and increased verbalization that we saw in the hospital population. Apparently the subtitle of Ball-Stick-Bird is valid. It is: "a scientific system of teaching for those who are ready or not."

In 1960, Renee Fuller was in charge of psychological evaluation for the New York Study of phenylketonuria, a genetic disorder frequently associated with mental retardation. She was also working on a Ph.D. in physiological psychology at New York University. After she received her degree, she developed the Ball-Stick-Bird method, and in 1967 she took up duties as chief of psychological services at Rosewood Hospital Center in Maryland. There she conducted an in-depth study of her reading system with mentally retarded patients. She left Rosewood last year, and now consults with school districts and other agencies that are studying the cognitive changes that accompany the use of Ball-Stick-Bird.

Optimizing Test Performance of Moderately and Severely Mentally Retarded Adolescents and Adults

Milton Budoff and James L. Hamilton

> This study provided further evidence for the validity of a learning potential assessment procedure with institutionalized moderately and severely retarded adolescents and adults. Significant positive correlations were obtained between psychometric and learning scores, attendants' and teachers' ratings of ability, and the posttraining scores on the modified Kohs Extended Learning Potential procedure. In addition, performance on this test-train-test procedure was compared with a train-within-test format for two different tasks: training embedded within the administration of the Leiter International Performance Scale and a formboard version of Raven's Coloured Progressive Matrices. The students responded equally to the two formats. Stanford-Binet IQs were least predictive of performance on the three learning potential measures and were unrelated to teachers' and attendants' ratings of ability. The implications of these data were discussed with particular attention to the potential advantages of the train-within-test model.

Although intelligence tests[1] such as the Stanford Binet Intelligence Scale (SB) (Terman & Merrill, 1960) and Peabody Picture Vocabulary Test (PPVT) (Dunn, 1959) have been widely used with moderately and severely retarded persons for placement and other purposes (Silverstein, 1963), numerous investigators have questioned the validity of these tests with this population for several reasons: (a) the response requirements of many assessments penalize moderately and severely retarded persons, a population replete with multiple handicapping conditions (O'Connor, Justice, & Payne, 1970); (b) the single administration format of standard tests untenably assumes that the person's initial responses are reliable (Barrett, 1965; Jensen, 1963; Zeaman & House, 1963) and that the person has a normal experiential background from which he has spontaneously learned knowledge and skills common to persons of the same age (Clarke & Clarke, 1967); and (c) data from conventional tests are frequently inadequate as predictors of learning ability (Gardner, 1945; Talkington, 1967).

What is required is an assessment format which could be used to indicate the ability of moderately and severely retarded persons to learn and profit from instructional experiences. Because of the high incidence of speech and language problems among these persons, the assessment should be nonverbal. The expectancy of failure in evaluative situations dictates that the procedure be couched in a supportive, nonpenalizing context to maximize the person's efforts. To minimize the negative effects of the differences in these persons' experiences on their efforts, many investigators (Luria, 1961; Penrose, 1934; Tobias, 1960; Vygotsky, 1934/1962) have suggested the incorporation of instruction within the assessment procedure so that the person's familiarity with the task can be assured and the implication of imminent failure minimized. With the exception of Schucman

---

This research was supported by Grant No. OEG-0-8-080506-4597 from the Bureau of Education for the Handicapped, U.S. Office of Education, and Grant No. NE-G-00-3-0016 from the National Institute of Education, U.S. Department of Health, Education, and Welfare.

The second author is now at the Bureau of Education for the Handicapped, U.S. Office of Education.

[1] The first author (as opposed to the Editor) prefers the use of the term "IQ tests" since the thrust of the learning potential research is to show that traditional intelligence tests do not measure intelligence in children from non-Western, non-middle-class backgrounds.

6. SEVERELY AND PROFOUNDLY RETARDED

(1960) and Hamilton and Budoff (1974), this testing paradigm has not been applied with moderately and severely retarded persons, although it has proven useful in predicting learning potential with educable mentally retarded individuals (Budoff, 1975; Haywood, Filler, Shifman, & Chatelanat, 1975; Feuerstein, Note 1).

Hamilton and Budoff (1974) applied the learning potential test-train-test model to moderately and severely retarded adolescents by adapting Budoff's modification of the Kohs learning potential task (Budoff & Friedman, 1964). They reported that the trained students did improve their competence on the task more than the nontrained group. Following training, some students markedly improved their scores, while others did not. Consistent with the findings for mildly retarded persons, the moderately (IQs from 32 to 51) and severely and profoundly (IQs from less than 10 to 31) mentally retarded gainers performed better on a simple learning task and were perceived as more effective learners by their classroom teachers than those who did not improve their score following training. The first purpose of the present study was to obtain additional validity data for this test-train-test assessment approach with moderately and severely mentally retarded persons.

Hamilton and Budoff (1974) also observed that some subjects could correctly solve nontrained instances of problems during or immediately following training but failed to apply the strategy to similar items during the posttest session on the following day. They apparently understood the problem during training since they solved it successfully with a minimal lapse in time, but they had difficulty retaining and/or spontaneously invoking it after a 1-day interval. Since the intent of learning potential assessment is to ascertain a person's ability to learn and apply problem-solving principles under optimal conditions, an alternative procedure was developed appropriate to these persons' cognitive level of mental functioning. This procedure incorporated training within the ongoing assessment process to allow the person to apply a newly acquired understanding to nontrained instances immediately, rather than on the following day, by working with new instances of the same problem. The second purpose of this study was to compare the performance of moderately and severely retarded persons on the two learning-potential formats: when training is embedded within the testing procedure (train-within-test) or presented in separate sessions (test-train-test).

Method

Subjects

The sample consisted of 38 mentally retarded persons (20 males, 18 females) drawn from the same institution as in the previous study (Hamilton & Budoff, 1974). From information drawn from the institutional records, the subjects ranged in chronological age (CA) from 12 to 22 years (mean CA = 204.5 months, standard deviation [SD] = 32) and in IQ from untestable up to the low 50s (mean mental age [MA] = 46.11 months, SD = 15.9). As indicated by their correct responses to the easiest modified Kohs test items, the subjects' visual, motor, and color discrimination abilities were sufficient for them to perform the kinds of tasks used in this study. Length of institutionalization ranged from a minimum of 1 to a maximum of 20 years.

Instruments

The test-train-test procedure for measurement of learning potential consisted of a modification of the Kohs block designs used by Budoff and Friedman (1964). Items were developed which constituted a logical downward extension of the Kohs designs, so that moderately and severely retarded students could successfully complete the easiest items. This extended Kohs test was composed of 12 difficulty levels with three test items at each level. The test can be characterized as a match-to-sample task with block design pictures serving as the sample and concrete objects (2.5 cm blocks) available for construction of the match. Test problems ranged in difficulty from simple color discriminations to complex four-block pattern constructions.

Thirteen demonstration-training items were developed to correspond to each difficulty level on the test. These items were used in the two testing sessions and the training session. During testing, these items were used by the examiner to demonstrate equivalent design constructions at particular difficulty levels. During the training session, the same items were used to teach the subject strategies for solving problems at a given difficulty level. Each subject was trained on four of these nontest items: the training item which corresponded to the highest level of difficulty he successfully completed during pretraining followed by the training items which corresponded to the next three difficulty levels. (See Hamilton [1972] for more detailed presentation of training procedure.)

The Extended Kohs Test was administered individually twice: prior to and 1 day after training. During each testing session, the examiner constructed a demonstration item prior to each problem level. After viewing this demonstration, the subject was required to construct two of the three test items correctly from the designs to achieve credit at that problem level. Testing was discontinued when the subject failed to attain this criterion for three successive difficulty levels.

On the day prior to the second test administration, an individual training session which lasted no more than 30 minutes was interpolated. The training procedure consisted of several steps: (a) assisting the subject initially in his construction of the design, (b) calling attention to the separateness of the blocks making up the design, (c) requiring the subject to point actively, block-by-block, to his constructed design and the corresponding "blocks" on the design card, and (d) repeating the process so that he could practice and become familiar with the materials.

Train-within-test procedures were developed pertinent to the tasks included on the Arthur adaptation of the Leiter International Performance Scale (Arthur, 1952) and Raven's Coloured Progressive Matrices, Sets A, AB, B (Raven, 1956). Both tasks appeared suitable because they include problems which range over a broad span of difficulty and can be responded to nonverbally.

The Arthur adaptation of the Leiter International Performance Scale was also modified so as to provide a correction and training procedure when an item was missed.[2] The examiner immediately removed an incorrectly placed block, pointed to the correct one, and encouraged the subject to correct his error. After this correction, the subject was given a maximum of three trials to complete the item with no assistance from the examiner. If the subject missed the item on any of the following trials, the correction procedure was repeated.

A weighted scoring system was used in which 1 point was awarded for each item correct on the first trial, .75 for each item correct on the second trial (corrected once), .50 for each item correct on the third trial (corrected twice), .25 for each item correct on the fourth trial (corrected three times), and .00 for each item that required more than four trials. Testing was discontinued after six successive incorrect responses.

The Raven Coloured Progressive Matrices used in this procedure consist of three sets (Sets A, AB, B), each containing 12 items. The test was modified in three ways. First, the items were presented as formboards mounted on pieces of cardboard, so that the individual could physically place the correct item correctly oriented in the missing space. Second, the test items were arranged in order of difficulty within the factor structures described by Corman and Budoff (1974): Simple Continuous Pattern Completion, Discrete Pattern Completion, Continuity and Reconstruction of Simple and Complex Structures, and Reasoning by Analogy. The order of presentation was: A1, A2, A3, A4, A5, A6, AB3, AB2, AB1, B1, B2, A8, AB7, B3, A7, AB4, B4, A9, A10, AB5, AB10, AB6, B5, AB9, AB11, B6, AB8, B9, B10, A11, B7, B11, B8, AB12, A12, B12. The purpose of presenting the items in this order was to maximize the probability that the training effect would transfer to subsequent, similar test items. Third, the test was modified by providing a correction and training procedure during the test for each item missed. The examiner removed the incorrect choice, placed the correct choice in the space, and pointed out the relevant features of the pattern in an attempt to demonstrate the appropriateness of the choice in completing the design. The correct choice was then removed and placed with the distractors, all of which were then rearranged randomly. The subject had three additional trials in which to complete the item correctly. If, however, the subject missed the item on the following trial(s), the correction procedure was repeated. The same weighted scoring system used with the Leiter Scale was used in scoring this test. Testing was discontinued after five successive incorrect responses.

The validity measures included two intelligence tests (SB and PPVT), a simple measure of learning (an adapted version of the Knox Cubes Test [Arthur, 1947]), and ratings of student competence in classroom learning and in their dormitory. Each subject's classroom teacher was asked to indicate on the basis of his experiences whether the student tended to retain information or skills mastered in the classroom on a previous day.

The Resident's Functioning Questionnaire (Decker, Note 2) was completed by attendents familiar with the subject's abilities as observed in the ward environment. The scale consists of 22 items covering several areas: 7 items relating to self-

---

[2] From this point, this modification of the Arthur Adaptation of the Leiter International Performance Scale will be referred to as the Leiter Scale.

help skills, 4 items on physical skills, 4 items on social skills, and 1 item for each of the following areas: language use, attention span, task performance, safety, destructive/assaultive behavior, self-injury, and anxiety. The format for each item permitted the attendant to choose one of five descriptive statements. The SB, the PPVT, and the Knox Cubes Test were administered individually by two trained examiners using the standardized instructions. All tests were administered to each subject in the same order as follows: PPVT, Extended Kohs Test, Knox Cubes, SB, Leiter Scale, and Raven Matrices. Concurrently, the teachers' ratings and the Decker scale ratings were obtained from the subjects' teachers and ward attendants, respectively.

Results

The analyses relating to the validity of the Extended Kohs Test included the scores derived from the Raven and Leiter learning potential procedures so that comparisons would be available among all the variables.

Table 1, which presents the intercorrelations of all variables, indicates that following the Extended Kohs pretest, the zero-order predictors of the Extended Kohs posttraining scores in order of magnitude were the weighted Leiter score (.82), Knox Cubes (.71), SB MA (.61), weighted Raven score (.59), teacher rating (.51), PPVT MA (.49), ratings of dormitory behavioral competence (.47), and SB IQ (.39). All were significantly correlated with Extended Kohs posttraining scores above the .05 confidence level. The moderately and severely mentally retarded person's response to the training experience on the block design task clearly provides an indication of the level of competence the person displays in learning, whether measured by laboratory tasks, classroom performance, or estimates derived from dormitory behavior. These results provide support for this measure of learning potential with these kinds of persons. Length of institutionalization, which was included in this correlation matrix, did not correlate with any variable and was omitted from the table and subsequent analyses.

The intercorrelation matrix was then used in a multiple regression analysis, employing the least squares solution, with the posttraining Extended Kohs score as the dependent variable. Independent variables in the equation were the remaining array of measures. The order of entry of independent variables in the stepwise regression was by the amount of variance accounted for by each variable.

The regression analysis on posttraining scores (see Table 2) indicated that the significant predictors of posttraining scores, with the variance due to pretraining level removed, were the Knox Cube ($t = 3.37, p < .01$) and the Leiter scores ($t = 3.16, p < .01$) (total equation $R^2 = .895$, $F = 26.52$, 9/28 df, $p < .001$). Although in this equation the Raven Matrices was not a significant predictor of a subject's responses to training, inspection of the zero-order correlations reveals that the Raven Matrices score was highly correlated with pretraining Kohs

TABLE 2
REGRESSION ANALYSIS ON POSTTRAINING KOHS SCORES

Independent measure	Standard error of coefficient	Standardized coefficient
Kohs pretraining	.158	.606
Knox Cubes	.107	.331
Leiter Scale (weighted)	.077	.443
SB[a] MA	.049	−.237
Teacher rating	.601	−.088
Raven Matrices (weighted)	.038	−.059
Resident's Functioning Questionnaire	.035	−.051
PPVT[b] MA	.024	−.035
SB IQ	.043	.028

[a] Stanford-Binet Intelligence Scale.
[b] Peabody Picture Vocabulary Test.

score, Knox Cubes, and Leiter Scale scores, and these four independent measures were significantly related to posttraining Kohs score. Since a large portion of the variance in the posttraining score was shared among the pretraining Kohs score, Knox Cubes, and Leiter Scale, the Raven Matrices was not a significant predictor of posttraining Kohs score with the other performance tests entered into the equation. As indicated by the rationale for a training-based learning potential measure and consistent with previous findings (Budoff & Corman, 1974), the simple learning task and the learning potential scores, both of which provide practice and positive feedback (unlike the measures derived from the traditional intelligence test procedure) constituted the significant predictors of the Kohs posttraining score, when the variance attributable to the pretraining competence was removed.

Performance on the Raven Matrices and Leiter Scale train-within-test learning potential procedures were summarized by calculating means and SDs across all subjects on total items attempted, items correct without training (Trial 1), items correct

TABLE 1
INTERCORRELATIONS OF EXPERIMENTAL VARIABLES ($N = 38$)

Variable	\multicolumn{9}{c}{Intercorrelations}
	2	3	4	5	6	7	8	9	10
1. SB[a] MA	.787***	.830***	.702***	.257	.518***	.717***	.565***	.485**	.609***
2. SB IQ	—	.558***	.467**	.191	.160	.473**	.380*	.428**	.393*
3. PPVT[b] MA		—	.569***	.050	.442**	.600***	.426**	.297	.491**
4. Kohs pretraining			—	.454**	.620***	.820***	.635***	.511**	.904***
5. Teacher rating				—	.261	.466**	.606***	.350*	.505**
6. Raven Matrices (weighted)					—	.712***	.411*	.426**	.590***
7. Leiter Scale (weighted)						—	.519***	.549***	.824***
8. Knox Cubes							—	.410*	.710***
9. Resident's Functioning Questionnaire								—	.469**
10. Kohs posttraining									—

[a] Stanford-Binet Intelligence Scale.
[b] Peabody Picture Vocabulary Test.
* $p < .05$.
** $p < .01$.
*** $p < .001$.

with successive training (Trials 2, 3, 4), and total items correct over four trials. Comparisons of these persons' performance on these train-within-test procedures were made by dichotomizing the subjects on the basis of their performance on the Kohs test-train-test procedure into high and low learning potential groups. Table 3 presents those data as well as means and SDs for high and low learning potential groups. High learning potential was defined as an increment of two or more difficulty levels on the Extended Kohs Test following training or attainment of difficulty level 4.0 or higher on Extended Kohs pre- or posttest.

The results indicate that as a total group the subjects attained approximately half the items attempted with no training (Trial 1) and substantially benefited from training. They responded correctly, over all four trials, to 93 and 78 percent of the Raven Matrices and Leiter Scale items, respectively. It is interesting that on both tests most of the increment occurred after only one training experience (Trial 2) and that the pattern was consistent for high and low learning potential groups. Converting the mean Raven Matrices raw score for the total group before training (11.71) and after successive training (21.97) to corresponding MAs yielded 5.5 and 8.16 years, respectively. Leiter Scale raw scores before (11.74) and after (17.79) training converted to MAs of 4.5 years and 5.0 years, respectively. For both tests, the MA equivalents were higher than the PPVT and SB MA estimates of approximately 4.0 years. High Kohs learning potential persons were correct on a greater number of items prior to training on the Raven problems than the low Kohs learning potential group ($t = 2.47$, 37 df, $p < .05$). None of the other differences between high and low learning potential groups on the Raven Matrices were significant. On the Leiter Scale the high Kohs learning potential group performed significantly higher than the low learning potential group on number of items attempted ($t = 4.88$, $p < .001$), number of items correct without training ($t = 4.73$, $p < .001$), and total items correct over four trials ($t = 4.82$, $p < .001$).

Discussion

The results of this study provide further support for the earlier findings of Hamilton and Budoff (1974) that a learning potential approach to the assessment of abilities of moderately, severely, and profoundly retarded persons provides a fairer estimate of their capabilities than traditional intelligence measures. Since these persons lead markedly atypical lives and experience the world quite differently from the persons on whom the standardized tests were normed, valid attempts to measure their abilities must, at a minimum, ensure that these persons have (a) the physical capabilities to perform the task and (b) some direct or related experience(s) with the task(s) in question. Due to the interaction of the dis-

6. SEVERELY AND PROFOUNDLY RETARDED

TABLE 3
RAW SCORE MEANS AND STANDARD DEVIATIONS (SDs) OF TOTAL, HIGH AND LOW LEARNING POTENTIAL (LP) GROUPS ON THE RAVEN MATRICES AND LEITER SCALE OVER TRIALS[a]

Scale	N	Items attempted Mean	SD	Trial 1 Mean	SD	Trial 2 Mean	SD	Trial 3 Mean	SD	Trial 4 Mean	SD	Total correct Mean	SD
Raven													
Total	38	23.13	8.70	11.71	6.71	7.39	3.77	2.07	1.36	.79	1.08	21.97	8.83
High LP	21	24.57	8.34	13.90	6.94	7.57	3.69	2.10	1.41	.48	.59	24.05	8.27
Low LP	17	21.35	8.80	9.00	5.28	7.18	3.87	2.06	1.30	1.18	1.38	19.40	8.84
Leiter													
Total	38	22.32	6.39	11.74	6.06	3.39	1.84	1.87	1.40	.79	.92	17.79	7.11
High LP	21	25.81	5.74	15.05	4.86	3.86	1.70	1.95	1.43	.90	1.02	21.76	5.28
Low LP	17	18.00	4.10	7.65	4.75	2.82	1.85	1.76	1.35	.65	.76	12.89	5.92

[a] Trial 1, items correct without training; Trials 2 through 4, items correct with successive training.

tortions in their life experience and the biological complications that accompany these severe levels of mental retardation, these persons frequently do not sustain their attention for extended periods, do not critically attend to the distinctive features of a stimulus display, and do not spontaneously develop a work-oriented stance to problems set before them.

These findings with learning potential assessment provide support for Schucman's (1960) statement that learning scores with these types of persons are stable and consistent indicators of ability to learn and profit from experience. They are also in essential agreement with Gold (1972), who has reported similar results with such manipulative tasks as bicycle brake assemblies. Training on a simple brake assembly resulted in more rapid and successful learning of a more complex brake assembly and in more rapid mastery of an electronic circuit board assembly.

Within the context of this study, none of the commonly used measures (SB MA and IQ, PPVT MA) were positively correlated with the teachers' ratings of these persons' learning and retention behavior. By contrast, posttraining scores were correlated with the teachers' ratings and the ratings of dormitory behavioral competence in their living situations. In two "real-life" situations, persons who have extended contacts with these mentally retarded individuals perceive differences in their ability to cope with the school and dormitory environments, which are also predicted by posttraining scores. These findings provide further support for a learning potential assessment in which the judgment of ability to perform is made following training, rather than following a single test administration. Persons with extended contact with these residents appear to use different indicators of these persons' abilities than those measured by the PPVT and SB.

This study failed to provide empirical evidence to support a choice of either the test-train-test or train-within-test assessment formats. The data provided support for a training-based model, regardless of the format utilized. Both formats were equally effective when evaluated against the predictive criteria.

Intuitively, a training-embedded-within-test format should be a means of overcoming some of the problems that appeared to be evident on the test-train-test (on separate days) paradigm. In the latter procedure, test-related anxiety does appear during the pretraining session, which, however, gets handled within the train-within-test procedure at the first point at which the child errs. More important, the individual can demonstrate his ability to master and apply a principle within the context of the ongoing assessment, unlike the test-train-test format when the principles he learns must be retained to be applied at a subsequent session.

The introduction of training in the assessment procedure changes a number of features of the test situation for the participant. The most evident change is affective. The person changes his perception of the situation from a purely evaluative one, with the negative affect he attaches to such situations, to one in which he perceives the role of the examiner as helping him become competent. This change was reflected in the evident pleasure with which these persons approached the learning potential assessment sessions. While the social reinforcement value of the contacts (Zigler, 1966) must be considered, these persons enjoyed the contacts and came repeatedly without qualms, although their initial response to tests usually evokes negative affect and avoidant behavior. The active intervention of the examiner in his role as trainer helps the person learn to focus on the critical features of the stimulus display, helps him to structure an attack on the problem, and encourages the person to test actively his hypotheses regarding the critical features of the problem without fear of the negative judgment. The procedures stimulate and sustain an active work-oriented address to these problems, which probably can be extended to other situations when this type of context for learning and doing is established.

Training procedures for more able mentally retarded persons utilizing a learning potential assessment model to test the child's capability have focused on helping them understand processes more clearly related to reasoning, as it is commonly defined from the vantage point of "normal" functioning. Demonstrating increased capability of moderately and severely retarded persons to solve problems requires helping them learn to sustain attention to the critical elements of the problems. Though these students did start with simple discrimination problems, on all three tasks there were persons who successfully solved problems that require reasoning, e.g., double classification problems. What is interesting is that the largest increment in performance occurred after one helping trial using the train-within-test model, suggesting the possibility that the more able of these persons may require simple orienting information primarily and then can solve problems they initially failed. Further research is required to understand more clearly the manner in which the information acquired by this learning potential assessment procedure can be translated into suitable plans for education and training of these persons.

Reference Notes

1. Feuerstein, R. *The dynamic assessment of retarded performers: The learning potential assessment device, theory, instruments, and techniques. Studies in cognitive modifiability* (Report No. 1, Vol. 1, Clinical LPAD Battery). Jerusalem, 1972.
2. Decker, H. *A system for planning and achieving comprehensive health care in residential institutions for the mentally retarded.* Ann Arbor: Department of Health Development, School of Public Health, University of Michigan, 1970.

References

Arthur, G. *A point scale of performance tests.* New York: Psychological Corporation, 1947.

Arthur, G. *The Arthur Adaptation of the Leiter International Performance Scale.* Washington: Psychological Service Center Press, 1952.

Barrett, B. H. Acquisition of operant differentiation and discrimination in institutionalized retarded children. *American Journal of Orthopsychiatry,* 1965, 35, 862-885.

Budoff, M. Measuring learning potential: An alternative to the traditional intelligence test. In G. R. Gredler (Ed.), *Ethical and legal factors in the practice of school psychology: Proceedings of the First Annual Conference in School Psychology.* Philadelphia: Temple University, 1975.

Budoff, M., & Corman, L. Demographic and psychometric factors related to improved performance on the Kohs Learning Potential procedure. *American Journal of Mental Deficiency,* 1974, 78, 578-585.

Budoff, M., & Friedman, M. "Learning Potential" as an assessment approach to the adolescent mentally retarded. *Journal of Consulting Psychology,* 1964, 28, 434-439.

Clarke, A. M., & Clarke, A. D. B. Learning transfer and cognitive development. In J. Zubin & G. A. Jervis (Eds.), *Psychopathology of mental development.* New York: Grune & Stratton, 1967.

Corman, L., & Budoff, M. Factor structures of retarded and nonretarded children on Raven Progressive Matrices. *Educational and Psychological Measurement,* 1974, 34, 407-412.

Dunn, L M. *Peabody Picture Vocabulary Test manual.* Minneapolis: American Guidance Service, 1959.

Gardner, L. P. Response of idiots and imbeciles in a conditioning experiment. *American Journal of Mental Deficiency,* 1945, 50, 59-80.

Gold, M. W. Stimulus factors in skills training of retarded adolescents on a complex assembly task: Acquisition, transfer, and retention. *American Journal of Mental Deficiency,* 1972, 76, 517-526.

Hamilton, J. L. *Application of the learning potential paradigm to severely mentally retarded adolescents.* Unpublished doctoral dissertation, University of Missouri-Columbia, 1972.

Hamilton, J. L., & Budoff, M. Learning potential among the moderately and severely retarded. *Mental Retardation,* 1974, 12, 33-36.

Haywood, H. C., Filler, J. W., Jr., Shifman, M. A., & Chatelanat, G. Behavioral assessment in mental retardation. In P. McReynolds (Ed.), *Advances in psychological assessment.* San Francisco: Jossey-Bass, 1975.

Jensen, A. Learning ability in retarded, average, and gifted children. *Merrill Palmer Quarterly,* 1963, 9, 123-140.

Luria, A. R. An objective approach to the study of the abnormal child. *American Journal of Orthopsychiatry,* 1961, 31, 1-14.

O'Connor, G., Justice, R. S., & Payne, D. Statistical expectations of physical handicaps of institutionalized retardates. *American Journal of Mental Deficiency,* 1970, 74, 541-547.

Penrose, L. S. *Mental defect.* New York: Farrar & Rinehart, 1934.

Raven, J. C. *Coloured Progressive Matrices: Sets A, AB, B.* London: H. K. Lewis, 1956.

Schucman, H. Evaluating the educability of the severely mentally retarded child. *Psychological Monographs,* 1960, 74(Whole No. 501).

Background Music for Repetitive Task Performance of Severely Retarded Individuals

JOEL S. RICHMAN
University of Illinois at Chicago Circle

> Environmental manipulation in the form of specific tempo background music was used to assist in the habilitation of severely retarded persons. Thirty institutionalized retarded males were tested on a repetitive manual performance task judged to be similar to the type of tasks found in sheltered workshops. Each subject received each of the background treatments noncontingently: no music, slow tempo music, regular tempo music, fast tempo music. The results indicated that the regular tempo of background music facilitated the greatest improvement in performance, suggesting that the effect of music on performance is more complex than the issue of contingent presentation.

Severely mentally retarded individuals may exhibit many kinds of behavior that make it extremely difficult for them to adapt to a work or work-training situation. Among these are distractibility and poor attention span, poor coordination and body control, and difficulty in social and emotional adjustment (Weigl, 1959). Facilitating the extensive habilitation process would benefit the individual's growth and development in deinstitutionalization and normalization within the community. Intervention through environmental manipulation may be a valid means to aid these achievements.

The use of music as an aid for retarded persons in learning tasks and activities has been widely demonstrated. Music has been used to increase activity level (Alvin, 1959; Reardon & Bell, 1970; Rieber, 1965; Stevens, 1971), facilitate manual dexterity (Fitzpatrick, 1959; Harrison, Lecrone, Temerlin, & Trousdale, 1966), improve coordination (Sheerenberger, 1953), aid cognitive task performance (Fraser, 1960; Ross, 1971; Sternlicht, Deutsch, & Siegal, 1967), and aid social and emotional adjustment (Luckey, 1967; Murphy, 1957; Podolsky, 1966; Weigl, 1959). Music has been shown to be an effective reinforcer with mentally retarded persons (Seale, 1969; Zimny & Weidenfeller, 1962) and specifically functional in increasing productivity when used in established contingencies (Cotter, 1971; Madsen & Madsen, 1972; Steele & Jorgenson, 1971). In addition, it has been found that retarded individuals can be trained in rhythm skills (Ross, Ross, & Kuchenbecker, 1973) that have been shown to function as prerequisites to successful performance on gross (Ross, 1969) and fine (Ross & Ross, 1971, cited in Ross et al., 1973) repetitive movement tasks. Ross demonstrated with educable mentally retarded persons that temporal attention is task specific (Ross, Note 1) and is determined in part by task characteristics (Ross, 1970a, 1970b). In addition, musical tempo has been recognized as a key variable in affecting the activity level of retarded persons (Reardon & Bell, 1970) and stereotyped rocking behavior of severely retarded individuals (Stevens, 1971).

The present study was designed to determine the efficacy of four background treatments on repetitive manual task performance by severely retarded males. The treatments were no music and three varied tempos of the same musical selections. Available evidence offered no definite basis for predicting the effects of musical tempo variation on task performance. If presented as background music noncontingent upon performance, it was equally likely that performance rate would vary with tempo or that there would be an optimum tempo for a

---

The author would like to express gratitude to Dr. James V. Kahn, University of Illinois at Chicago Circle, for his consultation and assistance in the data analysis.

particular task. Therefore, this study was designed to determine whether differences in performance exist as a function of tempo of noncontingent background music.

Method

Subjects

The subjects were 30 severely retarded institutionalized males who were free from visual, auditory, and bimanual disabilities. Potential subjects were selected on their ability to comprehend verbal instructions and perform a repetitive manual task. The 30 subjects were randomly assigned to three groups of 10 each (A, B, C). These groups did not differ significantly in either age or IQ (see Table 1).

TABLE 1
MEANS AND STANDARD DEVIATIONS (SDs) OF AGE AND IQ FOR SUBJECTS IN EACH GROUP

Group[a]	Age[b] Mean	SD	IQ[c] Mean	SD
A	218.20	53.10	38.60	9.74
B	210.00	35.70	42.20	13.96
C	195.60	50.28	43.60	10.72

[a] $N = 10$ for each group.
[b] In months.
[c] Based on the Stanford-Binet Intelligence Scale.

Repetitive Task

A manual performance task was chosen for its repetitive nature and for its resemblance to the type of task a mentally retarded individual might encounter in a sheltered workshop. The task was envelope filling. The subject was to insert an IBM card measuring 18.73 × 8.25 cm into a plain white envelope measuring 19.30 × 9.99 cm and drop the filled envelope into a wooden bin. Five hundred envelopes and 500 IBM cards were provided, each card having a pink stripe on the upper horizontal edge for increased visibility. The subjects were seated in a high work chair at a work table adjustable for height. For each trial the subject's score was recorded as the total number of envelopes filled in a 10-minute period.

Experimental Treatments

There were four treatment conditions: no music, slow tempo, regular tempo, and fast tempo. Tempo refers to the relative rapidity or rate of movement of a musical selection, not the rhythm or pattern of regular or irregular pulses caused in music by the occurrence of strong and weak melodic and harmonic beats (American College Dictionary, 1966). The three musical tempo treatments were fabricated from the same musical selections. Because of the high degree of similarity in instrumentation, harmony, melodies, pitch, timbre, texture, rhythm, and tempo of each selection, four John Philip Sousa marches ("Sound Off," "Nobles of the Mystic Shrine," "Sabre and Spurs," "The Picador") as recorded by the Eastman Wind Ensemble (*Sound Off*, Mercury MG 50264) were chosen. After 10 minutes of continuous regular tempo music was recorded on a high-fidelity master tape, the master tape was converted to the slower and faster tempos on a Speech-Time-Compressor-Expander. This is a taping device used in speech therapy to expand or compress speech. It repeats or discards parts of audio signals such as vowels, consonants, pauses in speech, and retransmits the signal so that complete intelligibility is retained. As used in this study, the regular music was expanded (slowed down) to two-thirds of the regular tempo and compressed (speeded up) to 1½ times the regular tempo. Thus, the slow and fast treatments were created from the original music, with high intelligibility and no distortion of pitch due to tempo change. Expressed in beats per minute (bpm), the three tempo treatments were: slow (85 bpm), regular (121 bpm), and fast (168 bpm). An edited experimental tape consisting of 10 minutes of each of the three tempos was created for use on a portable tape recorder.

Procedure

A visitors' lounge located between two wards of a large Connecticut state training school for mentally retarded persons was closed off and used as the testing room. Subjects were tested individually under each treatment. Data collection took place daily from 9:30 A.M. to 4:30 P.M. for 6 weeks, with each subject being tested only once on any test day. The experimenter went to the ward, selected the subject, and escorted him to the testing room. The subject was instructed where to sit and was read a set of standardized instructions. The treatment was then delivered on a Sony-o-matic portable tape recorder while the subject performed the task. For all trials the volume was set at three and the tone at seven. This was a mildly audible background level. Once each subject began the task, the experimenter sat in a chair that was placed so as to preclude visual contact with the subject. After a 10-minute trial, the subject was told to stop work, and the music was terminated. The measure was taken and recorded, the subject thanked, and escorted back to the ward where another subject was selected. This procedure was repeated until all subjects were tested under each treatment.

Design

Since this study was designed to test for significant differences in manual task performance under no music and three varied tempo music treatments, a 4 × 3 Latin Square design was selected because it permits assessment of main effects due to the sequence of treatments as well as due to treatments. In addition, it was chosen for its advantages in requiring relatively few subjects and removing between-subjects variability due to temporal effects (Meyers, 1966).

Results

The results provide support for the efficacy of matching the tempo of background music with the repetitive task it is to accompany. An analysis of variance showed no significant differences between groups as well as no significant Group × Treatment interactions. However, significant differences due to tempo treatments were found ($F = 8.51$, 3/75 df, $p < .01$). Tukey's HSD test was used to determine which of the tempo treatments differed significantly (Kirk, 1968). From this test, it was found that the mean number of envelopes filled during the regular tempo treatment (31.12) was significantly greater than the mean (23.36) during the no music condition (HSD = 6.96). Although the mean number of envelopes filled during the slow and fast treatments (28.71 and 28.00, respectively) were also higher than the no music treatment (mean = 23.36), the differences were not significant. Of the three musical tempo treatments, although the mean number of envelopes filled during the regular tempo was consistently highest, differences were not statistically significant.

Discussion

The presence of noncontingent background music is an environmental manipulation that can improve the performance of severely retarded persons on a repetitive manual task. This is in agreement with previous related research that documents the use of music to improve manual dexterity (Fitzpatrick, 1959; Harrison et al., 1966) and fine repetitive movement tasks (Ross & Ross, 1971). Other researchers have shown that music can be used in contingency as a reinforcer to improve performance (Cotter, 1971; Madsen & Madsen, 1972; Steele & Jorgenson, 1971). However, the present investigation on the effects of noncontingent backgrounds of music has brought out an interesting finding, namely, that the effect of music on performance is more than just an issue of contingency. Three tempos and no music were tested, and only one, the regular tempo condition (4/4 time = 121 bpm), was significantly better than all other conditions. This finding may indicate that tempo and task can be matched to facilitate performance. This can be supported in part by previous research with retarded individuals in which investigators demonstrated that temporal attention is task specific (Ross, Note 1), in part determined by task characteristics (Ross, 1970a, 1970b), and that varying the musical tempo can effect changes in activity level (Reardon & Bell, 1970) and stereotyped rocking behavior (Stevens, 1971).

There are several explanations for the effect of music and optimum tempo music on improving task performance of severely retarded males. It may be that music effects a condition of narrowed attention by masking extraneous auditory stimuli due to electrophysiological occurrences in the brain (Hernandez-Peon, Brust-Carmona, Penoloza-Rojas, & Bach-y-Rita, 1961). Another explanation not discordant with the first is that music serves as an attention-directing variable and facilitates the organization of information through rhythm (Isern, 1960). In addition, Fitzpatrick (1959) demonstrated that tempo alone (a nonmusical metronome beat) does not appear to be responsible for reported differences in performance output or regularity. The present results support previous research indicating that tempo via music appears to be integral. In arousal theory, another explanation, it is stated that music has an activating effect, and any procedure incorporating music that increases vigilance should also facilitate learning (Semmel, 1965). It may appear from this explanation that faster music must necessarily facilitate greater learning; however, Pick and Pick (1970) demonstrated in other investigations with retarded persons that input presented at a rate or level exceeding the subjects' receptive capacity is associated with a resultant loss of attention. The results of the present study, which showed that severely retarded subjects can significantly improve performance on a repetitive manual task under one tempo of noncontingent music and not others, may lend support to a merger of these explanations. The relevance of the results lies in the possibility that certain music may prove more effective in yielding lasting improvement when used in contingency than other music. This variable must be studied in the noncontingent situation to eliminate the confounding factors of reinforcement. Yet, there are at least two important areas remaining to be investigated. These are the relationship between learning and performance under matched task and musical tempo conditions (contingent and noncontingent) and the relationship between loss of attention and performance under similar conditions. However, the implications for educators and trainers of severely retarded persons are clear. Background music of specific tempo may be effective in assisting severely retarded individuals to perform certain meaningful tasks.

Reference Note

1. Ross, D. M. *Imitation of a television model by young mentally retarded children.* Unpublished manuscript, Stanford University, 1965.

References

Alvin, J. The response of severely retarded children to music. *American Journal of Mental Deficiency*, 1959, 63, 988-996.

American college dictionary. New York: Random House, 1966.

Cotter, V. W. Effects of music on performance of manual tasks with retarded adolescent females. *American Journal of Mental Deficiency*, 1971, 76, 242-248.

Fitzpatrick, F. K. The use of rhythm in training severely subnormal patients. *American Journal of Mental Deficiency*, 1959, 63, 981-987.

Fraser, L. W. The use of music in teaching writing to the retarded child. In E. H. Schneider (Ed.), *Music therapy.* Lawrence, KS: Allen Press, 1960.

Harrison, W., Lecrone, H., Temerlin, M. K., & Trousdale, W. W. The effect of music and exercise upon the self-help skills of nonverbal retardates. *American Journal of Mental Deficiency*, 1966, 71, 279-282.

Hernandez-Peon, H., Brust-Carmona, H., Penoloza-Rojas, & Bach-y-Rita, G. The efferent control of afferent signals entering the central nervous system. *Annals of New York Academy of Sciences*, 1961, 89, 866-882.

Isern, B. Summary, conclusions, and implications of the influence of music upon the memory of mentally retarded children. In E. H. Schneider (Ed.), *Music therapy.* Lawrence, KA: Allen Press, 1960.

Kirk, R. *Experimental design: Procedures for the behavioral sciences.* Belmont, CA: Brooks/Cole, 1968.

Luckey, R. E. Severely retarded adults' responses to rhythm band instruments. *American Journal of Mental Deficiency*, 1967, 71, 616-618.

Madsen, C. K., & Madsen, C. H. Selection of music listening or candy as a function of contingent versus non-contingent reinforcement and scale singing. *Journal of Music Therapy*, 1972, 9, 190-198.

Murphy, M. M. Rhythmical responses of low grade and middle grade mental defectives to music therapy. *Journal of Clinical Psychology*, 1957, 13, 361-364.

SPECIAL EDUCATION

Designed to follow the introductory course in special education, it is also a book which can be used as the first course book for Exceptional Children, Foundations of Exceptional Children, and the overview course for students entering special education departments.

For more information about this book and other materials in special education, contact Joseph Logan, Editor, Special Learning Corporation.

Special Learning Corporation

42 Boston Post Rd. Guilford, Connecticut 06437   (203) 453-6525

Teaching the Unteachables

JOHN FLEISCHMAN

A group of caring people in Oregon are proving that the profoundly retarded can learn to lead happy and useful lives. Yet the mind of the retardate is full of the human mystery. How does one survive and another fail?
John Fleischman is an assistant editor of HUMAN BEHAVIOR.

In Oregon's Willamette Valley, rain is what falls with very little interruption from November to May. If this is October, the drizzle frosting the windshield can't be rain. Some locals put on hats for the autumn storm clouds scudding east into the Cascades, but the army surplus ponchos, the rubberized trousers, the L.L. Bean's moosehunting shoes are held in reserve. In the fall, moss gathers strength on the northern exposures.

Picking up the McKenzie River highway heading northeast out of Eugene, Dan Close is trying to reconstruct a dry July Sunday last summer when a year's work almost died on a highway bridge 48 miles up into the Cascades. Close was then the director of a new group home in Eugene for 10 severely and profoundly retarded adults. He had been off that Sunday climbing Three Sisters Mountain while three of his weekend staff had taken the "folks" for a carefully planned hike along the McKenzie River. The folks were becoming accomplished walkers. Graduating from walks around town, the group-home residents were taken hiking at least every other weekend, usually along logging roads or major trails. The week before, a staff member had driven up to the tiny town of McKenzie Bridge to alert the rangers and to scout the trail.

It was a flawless summer day—so clear that when Close reached Three Sisters' summit he could see the snowy top of Mount Rainier to the north and, faintly but unmistakably, Mount Shasta over 200 miles south. He took color slides to prove it.

Tired from the day's climb, yet still exhilarated by the view, Close drove home along the river road—unaware that two of his folks had walked away from the hike. In the long July daylight, it was still bright when Close crossed the river above the little village of McKenzie Bridge and continued down the twisting valley towards home. He didn't know that less than two hours before, one of the missing residents had been struck and killed on the bridge itself by a woman motorist who told police that the man had lunged out into the roadway in front of her. When Close reached home, the phone was ringing. John Collier was dead, and Jim Clay had disappeared into the rugged woods.

Jim Clay was a strong, healthy 30-year-old with a measurable IQ below 20. He had almost no language and was wearing no coat. At about the same time that John Collier was run down on the highway bridge, Jim was spotted not very far away on the other side of the river. Crossing the McKenzie on a ramshackle log bridge, Jim encountered a local boy. The boy spoke to him, and Jim became frightened and bolted up a power-line break. The boy's father called the ranger station to report that his son had seen a strange man who looked to be on drugs.

By morning, Close was on his way back up the river road for the first of a dozen runs that July to join a search force of rangers, deputy sheriffs, group-home staffers, state police and volunteers backed by helicopters and light planes. A nearly equal force of television camerapersons and reporters—as well as the curious—turned up to watch the operation. The news media were very helpful, Close says, by emphasizing that Jim was not dangerous but only hungry and frightened. In their zeal to be of assistance, the people of McKenzie Bridge phoned in every report of an overturned garbage can or mysterious thump in the night. These false reports turned the search away from the rough hills and back towards the village.

Seven days after Jim disappeared, a man hiking up to his remote cabin spotted Jim standing in the cabin's doorway holding a jug of water. The man ran for help, and when the group-home staff came back with him, they found Jim sitting up in bed with his clothes neatly folded at the foot. He was 30 pounds lighter, spotlessly clean and very hungry.

In October, the mountains are black walls of thick fir and pine; the rainclouds, white dragons snuffling eastward up the narrow valley. The tires hiss on the asphalt. "I used to think these were the ugliest hills in the world," Close says, staring off into the wet wilderness, "because I thought Jim was up there." Close remembers the police conducting the hunt with thoroughness, gallons of coffee and the idea that Jim was "escaping." It was the only way they could conceptualize Jim's elusive behavior. As misconceptions go, it was very minor. But while the search continued, there was an unspoken fear in the minds of Close and the others connected with the group home—the fear of much larger misconceptions.

"People think the greatest risk in group homes is the risk of death," says Close. They had had a death. But while the search for Jim continued, the reality

236 Reprinted from *Human Behavior*, Vo. 5, No. 5, May 1976. Copyright © 1976 by Manson Western Corporation.

6. SEVERELY AND PROFOUNDLY RETARDED

of John's loss didn't have time to sink in. But what if Jim was never found or was found dead? If the police saw Jim as an escapee, would the public see the group-home staff as delinquent custodians? What were two such helpless men doing hiking around in a wilderness area? Surely the severely and profoundly retarded had to be protected from themselves and the outside world.

A death seemed a disastrous way to introduce the public to a novel treatment for the severely and profoundly retarded. The very label makes professionals wince. The severely and profoundly retarded are those with IQs below 35, the bottom limit of the trainable mentally retarded (TMR) category. That sounds splendid except that it is very difficult to accurately measure an IQ below 50. The subjects have little or no language, and often cannot hold a pencil in a way that could possibly be construed as functional. Behavioral-inventory tests are the only way to measure their IQ. You find out if the subjects can eat with a fork. Do they wash behind their ears? Can the men close their own flies? Are they toilet trained?

The severely and profoundly retarded don't do very well on these kinds of tests, either. Which may explain why most of the severely retarded, especially the adults, are stored in institutions where attendants close their flies, cut their food, wash behind their ears and clean them up when they forget their toilet training. These custodial institutions are filled with severely retarded adults because their natural parents wear out or die or are told to do the "best thing" or throw up their hands in despair once the impact of their child's condition sinks in. Also children, even retarded children, are cute. Children are symbols of hope, but a 20-year-old man with three days of stubble and an IQ estimated below 20 looks neither cute nor hopeful.

"The adult severely and profoundly retarded population is not in the forefront of the public consciousness. The attitude is 'Let's get the children and prevent them from ending up like this,'" says Close. "They've lived in institutions all their lives. They're those retarded people you've heard about. Maybe you've seen one on the street with his mother, but you've never thought about them." In institutions and nursing homes, the severely and profoundly retarded exist out of sight and out of mind. "This group has been kissed off," says Close.

The group Close talks about is larger than we like to think. A 1972 HEW

"They've lived in institutions all their lives. They are those retarded people you've heard about. This group of people has been kissed off."

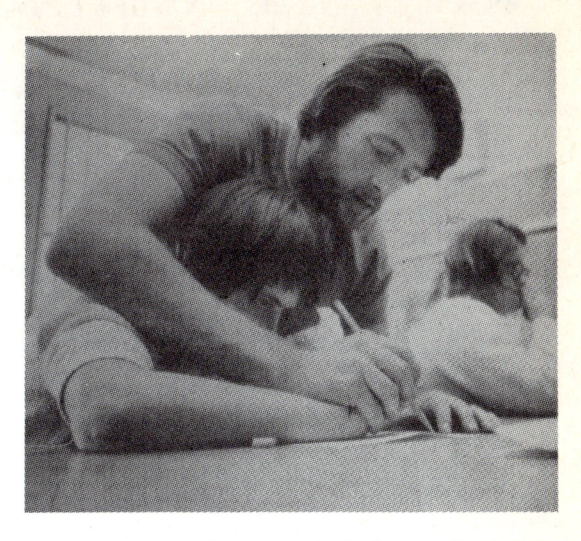

study shows that there were 200,000 mentally retarded Americans of all ages and levels in institutions. Dr. Richard Eyman, a demographic researcher at Pacific State Hospital in Pomona, California, has looked at it more closely. His studies have shown that in a hypothetical community of 100,000, there are 25 profoundly retarded adults (measurable IQ below 20) and 100 severely retarded adults (measurable IQ below 35). He points out that these figures can be extrapolated for the nation as a whole, giving a figure of 275,000 severely and profoundly retarded Americans.

A 1970 study conducted by Eyman in Riverside, California, showed that the severely and profoundly retarded have a "well over 80 percent" probability of being committed to an institution at some point in their lives. In particular, the profoundly retarded are likely to be institutionalized—a probability of 95 percent. "The place you are going to find the profoundly retarded is in an institution," says Eyman. "There are not many homes that can stand up to that kind of thing."

The Eugene home wanted to try. The idea of group homes for the handicapped and the retarded has been around for years. But as far as Close or any of the others involved in the Eugene home could discover, it had never actually been attempted with this class of retarded adults. The low level of the subjects' intelligence, combined with their adult strength and size, had discouraged this kind of treatment.

The problem with a group home is what to do with the residents during the day. Retarded children can be sent off to special schools. Moderately retarded adults can work in sheltered workshops. But here was a group seemingly too old to educate or too slow to work. Still, the last 10 years have seen a revolution in the behavioral sciences that seemed to promise both a solution to the daytime problem and the means to operate a group home for so difficult a population.

Tom Bellamy, a young doctoral candidate in special education at the University of Oregon, started a workshop for severely and profoundly retarded adults in Eugene. He adapted some of the techniques pioneered by Marc Gold, whose work at the University of Illinois had opened up the whole field of vocational training for the severely retarded. Through a method called task analysis and sequential training technique, Gold divided the assembly of a 15-piece bicycle brake into its smallest discriminations and successfully taught the steps to a group of 64 moderately and severely retarded individuals in sheltered workshops. Gold had opened the door to useful and commercially valuable work for the retarded.

Bellamy set up a shop to subcontract the assembly of electronic subunits. Bellamy's severely and profoundly retarded workers were able to put together a 52-piece cam switch actuator at a rate close to industry standard and with quality equal to or higher than that of industry. Bellamy's first workers lived at home, but there simply weren't enough uninstitutionalized potential subjects living in Eugene to give his program a meaningful sample. The population Bellamy wanted was living outside town at the state hospital, Fairview.

Meanwhile, Dan Close was working with Gold in Chicago. Initially, Close worked with severely and profoundly retarded adults at Camarillo (California) State Hospital as a psychology undergraduate at California Lutheran College. Pursuing a master's degree at Idaho State University in Pocatello, he became involved with a sheltered work-

237

6. SEVERELY AND PROFOUNDLY RETARDED

shop for TMR adolescents and adults. Marc Gold was consultant to the project; and the first time Close heard him speak, he knew this man was onto something. Gold invited him to Chicago to run the research on a vocational-skill training experiment. Close says flatly of Gold, "He taught me everything I know."

Close had become interested in the community-living approach; and when he heard about the proposed Eugene group home, he came out to Oregon to join Bellamy.

Bellamy found a sponsor through the Alvord-Taylor Homes, a nonprofit organization operating a group home for the mildly retarded and another as a respite care center in Eugene. Through the state Mental Health Division, he found money and access to the patients at Fairview.

In the fall of 1974, Close drove out to Fairview for an initial look at his future residents. He knew what institutions were like, but he was momentarily overwhelmed by the scene. Fairview is an excellent institution of its kind with a cooperative director backed up by a progressive state mental health establishment. Still, the first encounter unnerved Close. "They looked bizarre," he recalls. "You go out to a state hospital, and you'll find people sitting around in white shirts and pants and bowl haircuts. Some with shoes, some barefoot, some with snot running down their faces. I thought there was no way we were going to be able to work with these people."

Institutions teach institutional behavior. Stereotypical institutional behavior for the mentally retarded is head banging, floor searching, hand rubbing and throwing tantrums. After 20 years in institutions, the patients often curl into a permanently stooped posture, the shoulder blades half-folded around the chest. Sitting aimlessly in wards, the retarded become addicted to self-stimulation, or "self-stim" as it is called—crotch rubbing, earhole grinding and endless rocking back and forth. The line between the symptoms of the retardation itself and the institutional stereotype is blurred.

The journey from the institution to the normal world is a cultural ocean as frightening and as wide as the one many Europeans crossed seeking a New World. Close likes the metaphor: "Our people are like that—immigrants from another land. They don't understand our language, and their culture is the culture of the institution."

In a ward of endless rockers and shriveled men, Dan Close found 27-year-old John Collier sitting immobile in front of a TV set. John hated to move, and he had discovered that if he parked himself in front of a TV, no one would disturb him. But Dan Close had plans to disturb him. "The thing about John was that he acted as if he knew nothing, but then he would come out with things like counting to 10," he explained.

For his generation, John's case was unusual. The cause of his retardation was unknown, and it was only after he started school that he was given the dread label of mentally retarded. He lived with his parents until he was 19, when the strain of caring for and supervising him every minute became too great. But even after he was committed to a state institution for the retarded, his family stayed in contact—coming to visit, sending presents and asking about his living conditions. Most of the severely and profoundly retarded John's age were committed early, and their families lost touch with them. "It becomes pretty unrewarding to visit a child who is unresponsive," says Close.

Because of his parents' attention and his relatively short period of institutionalization, John had the most going for himself of the eight chosen in the fall of 1974 for the new group home. John was selected by the toss of a coin from a group of 17 retarded adults at Fairview Hospital and Training Center outside Eugene. The "target" population was made up of those patients who were over 18, able to walk and use a spoon and who tested out as "severely or profoundly retarded." Because of the funding through the Oregon Mental Health Division, the target group had to have been committed from Eugene or the surrounding Lane County. Eight were arbitrarily picked for the group home, and nine people remained at Fairview as a control group. Subsequently, two more residents were added to the home, but they remained outside the "experiment."

Less than a year before his death, John Collier emigrated to a new world. He was in the first group brought to the electric-blue house at 670-16th Street, the group home that would much later be called the John Collier House.

* * *

A few minutes before nine, they struggle up 16th Street on their way to work. There is no mistaking the six women and four men. Some walk fast, intent on their goal. Others shuffle, looking lost to the world. Louie, the "Big L," lopes along in great strides, then stops to survey the scene, then bounces forward again. Jim, clad in a bright yellow windbreaker, brings up the rear. His hand is clenched just in front of his eyes, his fingers working up and down like a trumpet player's. When the front of the group reaches Alder Street, Jim screws his eyes tight and waits, his fingers marking time.

At every corner, Jay Buckley, who has taken over after Close went back to school to get his doctorate, puts the folks through the street-crossing program one at a time. Buckley takes Alice's hand and points down the street. "Car's close," says Jay. "Car's close," says Alice. She tracks the car with her outstretched finger as it speeds past. "Car's far away," Jay says. "Car's far away," she repeats. Under his direction, she tracks both directions and then steps off on her own. In ones and twos, the group repeats the corner drill.

Alder Street borders the University of Oregon campus. On the far side, the folks turn right and follow a sidewalk past the tennis courts and up a small rise to the new special-education building where the workshop is located. The university is a hotbed of behaviorism, where the first tenet is "Show me the

> "Our people are like new immigrants from another land. They just don't understand our language, and their culture is that of the institution."

45. Teaching the Unteachables

data." The special-ed building was designed for data collection. A darkened gallery runs above the classrooms. Beveled one-way windows look down into the workshop. Directional microphones are positioned in the ceiling. Perched on hard metal stools, "coders" sit in the shadows watching the scene below. Disembodied voices from the wall speakers echo in the gallery. A beeper sounds every 10 seconds, and the coders dutifully mark down on special sheets what their subject is doing at that moment—looking around, "self-stim," attending to directions, working and so on.

Graphed and computerized, the results are empirical, tangible and comparable. Can "self-stim" be decreased in X? Code the behavior and find out its exact rate of occurrence. Design a program to change the behavior. Code the subject's behavior during the correction program and afterward. Then compare the numbers. Has there been a change? Is the program effective? Behavioral science marches on to the beep of a 10-second timer.

The workshop is an ordinary-looking classroom furnished with evenly spaced trapezoidal tables. Each table has a row of shallow bins and the necessary forms and tools for the task. The folks manufacture cable trusses, plugs and switches for oscilloscopes. The key to the workshop is task analysis. A job is broken down into its tiniest steps, and the necessary discriminations are plotted. Then the job is taught tidbit by tidbit, and the worker is reinforced every step of the way.

Assembling a switch becomes a series of small discriminations and simple operations. Take one piece out of a bin. Fit it in a wooden form. Place the second piece on top. Screw the two together. Lay the unit on a marked card. Repeat the process until the card is filled. Call for a supervisor to count the units and check the quality. Start another card.

Louie has been institutionalized for 34 of his 38 years. His hair is long and lank, and he has grown a full beard that, at first glance, gives him a vaguely sinister air. It is a false impression. Louie fits the first piece into the form. He studies the result with melancholic concentration; then he snatches the second piece and slaps it carelessly into place. The workshop surpervisor squats at his elbow. She puts the second piece back into the bin. "Fix it, Louie," she says.

His frustration boils over, his arms jerking back at his head, the forearms locked at the wrists. "Fix it, Louie," she says. His locked arms slowly uncoil. He snaps up the returned piece and slaps it back. She puts it back. "Fix it, Louie." His arms fly up again, his head twisting backward. Suddenly he pulls his arms down again and quickly fits the piece correctly. "All right, Louie," she congratulates, "all right, Louie. Very nice." He races through the card, assembling the units with spasmodic intensity. He jerks his head away and throws one arm up in triumph.

"Hey, Louie, you've got your one hand up." She comes over to inspect the card, poking the pieces to make sure they are screwed tightly. Satisfied, she offers Louie a penny, an immediate reward for the job. "Let's trade," she suggests. Louie studies the coin. "What did you get, Louie?" she asks. "What did you get?" "Penny," says the bearded man in the softest of voices. "Way to go, Louie, way to go." He slips his reward into a plastic cup taped to his workbench and starts another card.

The pennies are the basis of a token economy to reinforce correct behavior. Besides pennies, everyone earns a flat piece rate. Some exceed minimum wage because of high productivity. But for many, paychecks and even tokens are too remote. They work for the constant verbal and social reinforcements the supervisors lavish on them.

Barry is on the token economy. All day he works at his station screwing plugs together, shaking them at his ear and tapping them against his face to insure they are tight. The pennies mount up. At 4 p.m., he grasps his money tightly in his fist and goes to the "store," a table spread with small plastic boxes of raisins and cookies. The boxes are arranged by price, and he walks up and down the row, deciding. He settles on a box of animal crackers, which he takes to a table and opens with great care. Satisfied, Barry munches his day's earnings.

The house on 16th Street comes alive when the folks come home. Sam, the house mongrel, barks like crazy. Mark heads straight for the stereo, stuffs "The Who" into the machine, and Friday night is off and running. Soon there are dancers in the living room and vegetable choppers in the kitchen, where Jeanne Bell is patching together a dinner without a stove, since the old one gave up the ghost that morning. Jay Buckley is out in the driveway wrestling a donated replacement off a pick-up truck.

Jeanne started out as an elementary school teacher and then became interested in "exceptional" children. Together with Dan Close, she helped to set up the group home. When Close left, she stayed on to work with Jay. They are supposed to work a roughly normal Monday-through-Friday week. When stoves burn out, or other problems mount, the week becomes longer.

Two other staff members come in first thing in the morning, and two more after dinner. There is also a different weekend staff. The night manager is the only staff member who lives in, in a room in the basement. The group home also has a stream of volunteers and practicing students from the university.

"At first, we hired a man to stay up all night. We didn't have any idea what would happen," Jeanne remembers. "But it turned out that they sleep like anybody else."

The folks do most of the work—the cooking, the laundry, the housecleaning, the dishwashing, the yard work, the table setting and emptying the garbage cans. They feed the pets and make the beds—just like in a real home.

Barry is methodically slicing up apples for a salad while a staff member half-watches him and half-watches two sandwichmakers. One of the sandwichmakers has changed her clothes twice since she came home from work. Changing your clothes when you want is an example of the distance between the institution and 670-16th Street. Jeanne says, "In an institution, they slept in a large room. There was another room where their clothes were kept locked up. But when they came here, suddenly they had bedrooms, dressers and drawers with clothes in them."

The house on 16th Street is not just a bunch of nice people being nice to retarded people. The ideology of the group home is behaviorist, and the methodology is thumbtacked to the pantry wall. The wall is covered with programs for problems great and small —to get Bonnie to say certain sounds, to teach shoe tying, to toilet train Alice. For example:

Name: Barry. (Desired) Behavior: Keeping his clothes to himself. Objective: Barry will tell Louie to take off any article of clothing that is rightfully Barry's.
If Louie has Barry's clothing—
(1) Get Barry, point at Louie and at the article of clothing, say, "Barry, Louie has your ——— on."
(2) Nudge Barry and get him involved.

6. SEVERELY AND PROFOUNDLY RETARDED

"Many of the folks had no idea how to show elementary affection. It's hard to believe, but some of them didn't know how to hug and kiss."

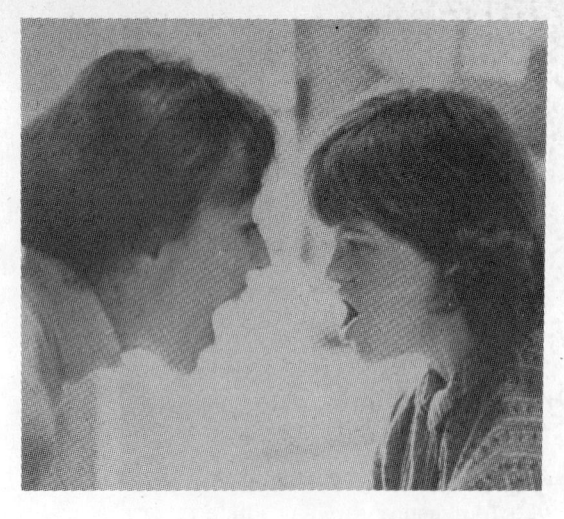

(3) Tell Barry to tell Louie, "Hey take my pants, etc., off."
(4) Wait for Barry's verbalization.
(5) Then tell Louie to take off Barry's article of clothing.
Note: This is especially important for you morning folks.

Another part of the group home's behaviorist approach is the use of systematic coding observations to generate data for the experiment and also to analyze specific behavior problems.

When Louie first came from Fairview, he spent hours on his hands and knees searching the floor. The behavior showed up on the community-living observations as a form of "self-stim" because of the way Louie rubbed the carpet with his fingers. A program was written up to "overcorrect" the searching. Anytime a staff member found Louie searching, Louie was made to wash his hands and was then given paper to scribble on. Now Louie collects pencils like a magnet. He scribbles intently and then stops to study the circles. Then he returns to scribbling.

The Friday night excitement is heightened by the news that Alice is going out to dinner with Bob Johnson. Bob is a severely retarded young man from a foster-care home. Alice, who is 10 years older chronologically but his equal mentally, is beside herself with anticipation. "You're going out to dinner with Bob Johnson?" asks Jeanne. "Bob Johnson," blushes Alice, tucking her chin under.

Just as the group sits down to dinner, Bob arrives. Bob is delighted to be there, delighted to be going out to dinner, delighted to be going out with Alice and delighted to see Jeanne. He shakes everybody's hand. Along with two staffers, they are off to Mama's Truckstop. Bob is slipped a few bucks to pay for the outing and with much handshaking and at least two complete sets of farewells, the couple sets out.

Jeanne seems almost as delighted as Bob. Sex has never been a problem, she says. Quite the contrary, many of the residents have little idea how to show even elementary affection. "It's hard to believe, but some of them don't know how to hug and kiss." Hugging and kissing are an unofficial priority. There is no program on the pantry wall, but the staff teaches it, anyway.

Eating is a big part of the official program. Institutions don't spend a great deal of time on table manners; they don't even teach chewing. Since institutional food is soft and bland, the patients only have to master the spoon. The severely and profoundly retarded often choke on foods such as apples that require chewing. Louie is a chronic choker. He eats with the same wild abandon with which he walks. Once he was surprised stealing a potato from the kitchen. He jammed the whole thing down his throat and was nearly asphyxiated.

Eight residents sit at the main table while two others work on eating programs with Jay at the small "training table." Jeanne presides at the main table. "Isn't everyone sitting up straight? Isn't Sally sitting up straight? Good, Sally, really good." Sally beams from her seat. In institutions, the patients slump at the table, their noses in their plates, shoveling the food into their mouths. In the group home, everyone sits up straight to eat. After a few meals spent reinforcing the residents, staffers find themselves eating with the carriage of ballet dancers.

Louie eyes an extra sandwich. "Would you like another sandwich, Louie?" Jeanne asks, offering him the plate. He picks up a half and takes one small bite. "Good chewing," says Jeanne. "Isn't everyone sitting up straight?" Everyone, staff included, is sitting bolt upright.

Saturday morning, staff member Tama Levine sets out for the local Y with five of the folks. Underlying the group home's philosophy is the principle of normalization; retarded people should lead as normal a life as possible in the least restrictive setting. The folks go bowling. They go to movies and to concerts. Three nights a week, the folks study rudimentary arithmetic, handwriting and reading at a local school. Normal people go to baseball games, so the folks go see Eugene's minor league Emeralds. Whether they understand the rules is not important; they cheer from beginning to end.

Normal people like to work out, and so do the folks. They play a unique brand of basketball. Jan, who is 24 and suffers from Down's syndrome, can barely manage the ball. She seems frozen; yet slowly she coils her body for a two-handed cradle shot straight from the knees. Jim has a different approach: shouldering the ball one-handedly, he advances on the basket with one eye screwed shut, his free hand working its continual trumpet-playing routine. At 15 feet, he pops the ball through the hoop with the assurance of Wilt Chamberlain. He squeezes both eyes shut in delight.

Tama puts the group through calisthenics. Down's people are incredibly limber. Jan drops easily into a full leg split, then tucks both legs behind her head. Then they all jog around the gym. Barry, who is the state champion in the Special Olympics 50-yard dash, leads the way, squealing in a high voice, his left hand raised over his head.

It is too late for a swim, but Tama takes them down to the weight-lifting room. As the group enters, the lifters look up in amazement. Tama soon gets everyone lifting something, and the body builders go back to the serious business at hand. Fifteen minutes later, the folks have blended into the strange rituals of weight lifting. Jim kneels before an iron bar connected through a pulley to a stack of iron discs. As he pulls, his face continues its perpetual grimacing. Next to him, a weight lifter staggers under an immense barbell resting on a foam-rubber backpad. The lifter's face is contorted with strain as his buddy shouts encouragement:

"Work it, work the weight." Tama urges Jim on: "Pull, Jim, pull. All right, Jim. All right." Jim lets the pulley down with a clang. He shakes his wrists wildly. "All right, Jim. Way to go," says Tama.

45. Teaching the Unteachables

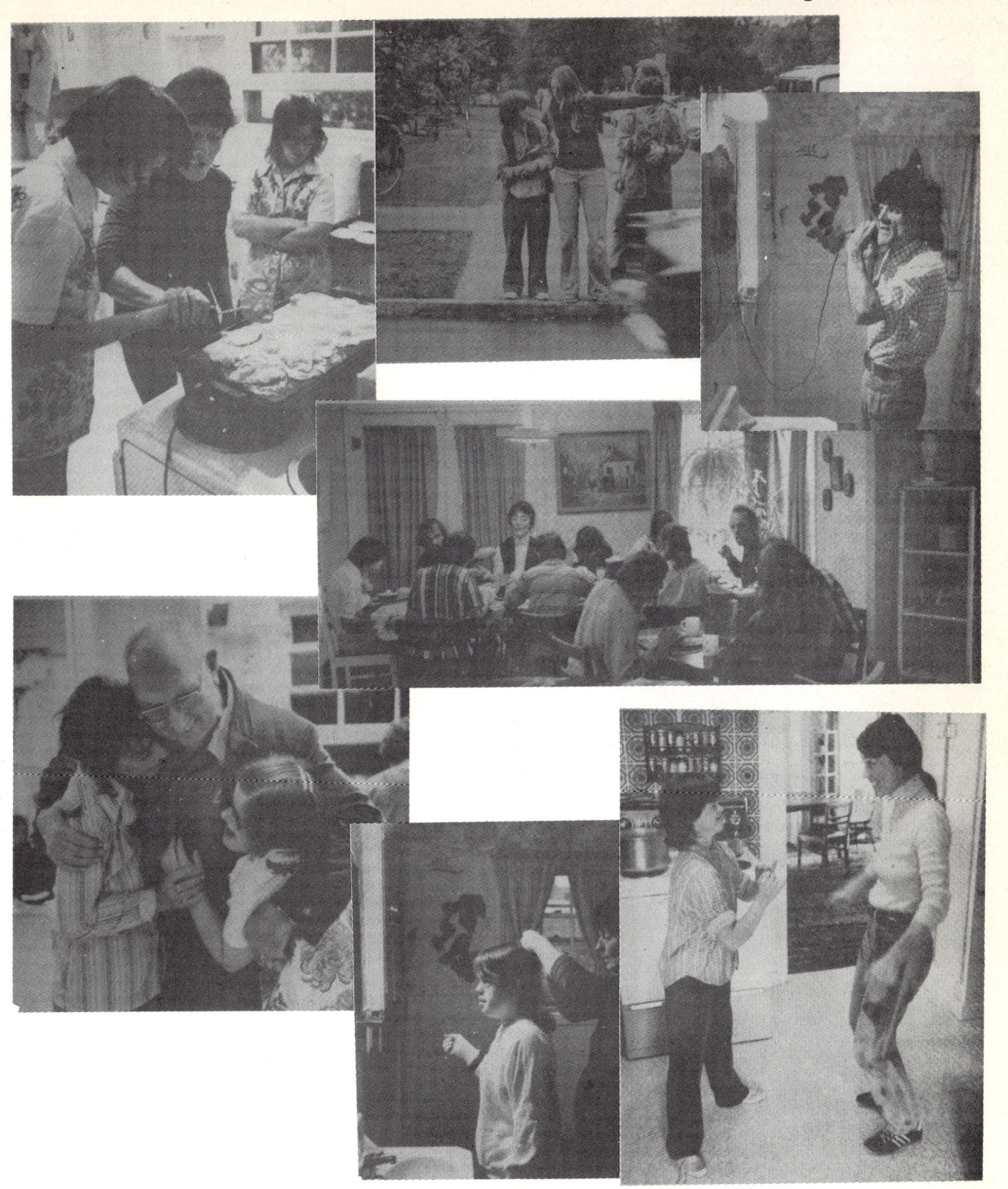

Having spent most of their lives stored in various state hospitals, 10 severely and profoundly retarded adults now have their own home. It's a place (clockwise from lower left) where one can stand at the front window watching for the paperboy, and where codirector Jeanne Bell can share a hug with a visiting father and his stepdaughter. Bell and the staff teach such basic how-tos of living as frying an egg, crossing a street, shaving, tripping the light fantastic in the kitchen, amateur hairstyling and minding one's table manners at dinner.

241

6. SEVERELY AND PROFOUNDLY RETARDED

"On a pantry wall, there is a little slogan taped up, saying, 'How come you've never spoken before?' 'How come you've never asked?'"

* * *

In the pantry of the John Collier House on 16th Street, there is a little inspirational slogan taped up. It says:

"How come you've never spoken before?"

"How come you've never asked?"

* * *

Close eases the car off the McKenzie highway into the gravel parking lot where the group hike set out that July Sunday. A hundred feet behind is the bridge where John Collier died. The puzzle is why John perished and Jim survived. John Collier was the star performer of the group. From the first day he came to 16th Street, John Collier discovered that he wouldn't be allowed to curl up in front of a TV until he died. He became the tester of new programs, the pioneer of skills. "This guy had it all together," Close remembers. "He walked with a normal gait. He rode the bus alone. He was the first graduate of the travel training program. He walked to work by himself for seven months. He had the best verbal skills. He learned the tasks faster than anyone else." Of all the group, John Collier had the most experience with traffic; yet he apparently walked out into the middle of a busy highway.

The survivor, Jim Clay, was one of the slowest in the group, a man with virtually no language who would be unable to cross Eugene on his own.

Nearly everything between the moment of Jim's disappearance and the moment of his rescue is assumption, says Close. Some of those connected with the group home don't even think it is right to speculate on what happened in between or why. But the riddle teases the mind.

Close sees all behavior as a matter of cues. The job in teaching a skill is to break it down into its component cues. The last known cue the two men received that July was verbal. The group had hiked along the river trail and then cut back to the highway opposite the ranger station. Half the group had already crossed the road when a staff member became involved in untangling Barry's zipper. John and Jim were standing behind her when she said, "Go see Paulette. We're going home."

When she looked up, John and Jim were gone, and she assumed they had crossed over to where Paulette had parked the station wagon. Instead, the two had disappeared back down the trail they had just hiked.

Close is sure it was John Collier who led the way. "No one knows what he processed," says Close, but he believes that somehow John was convinced that he had fallen behind the hike and was trying to catch up. The logical way to go "home" is to go back the way you came. Whatever the cue, John covered the four miles back to the starting place at top speed. He was run down an hour and 20 minutes after he left the ranger station.

Retracing his steps was no small achievement. Close pulls an orange poncho over his head and plunges down the narrow track from the parking lot to the river trail. In the summer, the underbrush would have been heavier, says Close, and the trail even harder to follow. At the junction with the river trail stands a marker post. In the first sweep down the trail after John, Close himself had missed the turnoff and had walked 100 yards past it before realizing his mistake. But John Collier must have found it the first time in his rush to his fate.

Under the great canopy of the Douglas firs, the October rains stop. Close strips off the poncho and looks back down the river trail. For some reason, Jim did not follow John Collier. Probably he fell behind and after passing several inviting cross trails and side roads, Jim turned left on a rutted road and crossed the river where he encountered the boy. In his fright, Jim followed a power-line cut up a steep ridge and then picked up the ridge trail. That trail led to the cabin where he was found all those days later. Incredible luck or instinct?

Jim could not tell his rescuers how he survived. Close has a few good guesses and many blanks. For one thing, says Close, the July skies clouded over, reducing the risk of heat prostration. Then Jim probably has no clear concept of a personal death. For Jim, danger is an immediate and direct threat such as a verbal challenge from a strange boy. But once Jim ran off into the deep woods, he was blissfully unaware of his very real danger. Panic is the greatest danger in getting lost. Aside from the weight loss, Jim was in fine condition when he was found. His clothes were untorn and clean. He wasn't covered with scratches and bruises. He didn't look like a man who had been running about in a panicked frenzy. He looked like a man who had kept calm, found shelter, saved his energy and waited in one place for rescue. It was almost textbook survival technique.

Yet the blanks resist simple explanation. In teaching behavior at the group home, cues are made specific and uniform. Generalized or vague cues only confuse the folks. Close feels that is might have been the vagueness of the instruction "We're going home," and the lack of a clear physical prompt such as pointing that set John Collier off on his fatal walk.

In surviving, Jim performed skills he had never been directly taught. He selected a good path and then recognized shelter. He carried stream water back to the cabin in a jar. The water jar is a prime puzzler. Jim had filled plastic water jugs at the group home from a tap, but the connection between water from a running stream and water from a tap was his own discovery.

The river roars in the distance. Close starts back to the car. Up until the moment he lost John Collier on the trail, Jim's every waking moment had been programmed, the cues selected and presented in a uniform fashion. Then for seven days, Jim Clay ran his own life. "When he lost our cues, he found his own," says Close.

Behavioral training strategies in sheltered workshops for the severely developmentally disabled

Paul Wehman
Adelle Renzaglia
Richard Schutz

This paper is a behavioral analysis of learning and behavior problems which may be expected of severely developmentally disabled persons in vocational settings. The behavioral analysis includes three major sections: (1) a categorization and description of primary problems encountered by a severely handicapped population, (2) a logically arranged hierarchy of behavioral procedures which can be used to treat different types of problems, and (3) a general set of management strategies. It is recommended that the hierarchy of behavioral procedures be empirically validated.

In recent years, applied behavior analysis is one training methodology which has been used successfully in the amelioration of emotional and learning handicaps found in several deviant populations (e.g., Haring & Brown, 1976). Behavioral training techniques have also been effective in training complex assembly skills in moderately, severely, and profoundly retarded adolescents and adults (Bellamy, Peterson, & Close, 1975; Crosson, 1969; Gold, 1972; Hunter & Bellamy, 1976).

Much of the vocational research and programs with the severely developmentally disabled has been directed toward instructional strategies to facilitate the acquisition of complex manual tasks. Basic tenets of discrimination learning (Gold & Scott, 1971; Zeaman & House, 1963) and task analytic skill sequencing have been used when difficult job skills are required (Crosson, 1969).

Although research completed on acquisition of complex tasks, such as assembling cable harnesses, drill presses, or bicycle brakes, has demonstrated that the severely handicapped can learn if material is presented in a logically arranged sequence, relatively few efforts have been directed toward developing innovative techniques and strategies for accelerating work performance. Typically, efforts at increasing production have included some manipulation of reinforcement contingencies (Brown & Pearce, 1970; Schroeder, 1972). However, other behavioral treatment practices have not received attention by researchers in vocational programming for the severely retarded. This paper provides a behavioral analysis of work problems which may be expected of severely developmentally disabled clients, and identifies and discusses a logically arranged sequence of behavioral procedures available to overcome specific vocational problems.

6. SEVERELY AND PROFOUNDLY RETARDED

PRESENTING PROBLEMS

Work behavior may be subdivided into learning a skill (acquisition), and then performing it accurately at a high enough rate (production) to meet competitive employment standards. These two processes can be analyzed more closely, however, through a specific description of the client's vocational behavior excesses or deficits.

Acquisition Problem—Discrimination Deficits

A problem typical of severely handicapped workshop clients is failure to attend to the salient cues (size, color, form) of a task. The person ignores relevant variables and instead may try to assemble or sort materials without watching what he or she does or while attending to the wrong cue in the task. As Gold (1973) notes, this is the main obstacle for the mentally retarded in acquiring complex manual skills. Gold (1972) has found that retarded people can master a difficult job at a rate similar to nonretarded peers when they attend to relevant dimensions.

Acquisition can also be impeded by a client's failure to attend to verbal cues of the supervisor. A common characteristic of severely handicapped adults is noncompliance behavior and inability or unwillingness to follow simple instructions. Even though a worker may attend to the learning task, his failure to follow instructions can interfere with acquisition rates, particularly if job requirements or materials vary slightly from day to day.

Acquisition Problem—Sensory-Motor Deficits

Many severely developmentally disabled persons receiving vocational programming services also display sensory-motor deficits. For instance, clients with cerebral palsy, loss of limb, and spasticity or athetosis may require prostheses or specially arranged environmental support.

Certain clients may be visually handicapped or hearing impaired, thus prohibiting the use of standard training procedures. The rare combination of both aural and visual handicaps in retarded workers is perhaps the most difficult disability to overcome for the acquisition of complex work skills. Yet some workers have found that such disabilities need not impede learning progress on difficult tasks such as bicycle brake assembly (Gold, 1976).

Low Production—Slow Motor Behavior

Once a vocational task is mastered, high rate performance becomes important. This is a serious problem with many severely and profoundly retarded workers, particularly those with a long history of institutionalization. Slow motor behavior is one characteristic of severely developmentally disabled workers who have not previously been required to meet a work criterion for success. Clients may be persistent and stay on task, but their actual motor movements are lethargic and at far too low a rate to be competitive (Hollis, 1967a, 1967b). Often such clients are unresponsive to the commonly used workshop incentives such as praise or money.

Without objectively established work criteria, it is difficult for workshop supervisors to determine which clients are performing competitively. Workers who stay on task and do not disrupt workshop routine are often viewed as performing adequately. This view is based on a popular vocational training model of "work activity" or "keep busy" rather than a developmental model which looks to expand the client's work skill repertoire.

Low Production—Interfering Behaviors

Equally problematic in accelerating production rates with the severely and profoundly retarded are interfering or competing behaviors, such as high levels of distractability and hyperactivity, out-of-seat behavior, excessive looking around, making bizarre noises, and playing with the task.

Similarly, the work performance of severely developmentally disabled clients may be highly susceptible to changes in the work environment. Fairly commonplace alterations in setting or routine, e.g., furniture rearrangement, can upset work behavior, thus making continuity of programming extremely difficult. A worker may display criterion-level work rates, but only for short periods of time. Interfering or competing behaviors interrupt the work level required for successful community placement.

46. Behavioral Training

SPECIFIC TRAINING TECHNIQUES FOR ALLEVIATING WORK PROBLEMS

To meet these various workshop problems with severely developmentally disabled clients, a logically arranged sequence of training and behavior management procedures is required. This section provides a hierarchy of techniques and guidelines for alleviating these workshop problems. Workshop staff members may draw on the techniques which are the most effective, the least time consuming, and the most economical. The sequence is affected by traditional methods of alleviating problems within the world of competitive employment. The less severe or more typical training and management procedures are listed as most desirable for use.

For example, giving a verbal reprimand would be preferred (Schutz, Wehman, Renzaglia, & Karan, in press) to using restraint if both procedures were equally effective in alleviating the problem. However, it may be necessary for a trainer to use his or her own discretion with each individual client in determining the most appropriate procedure. If a trainer has had previous experience with a particular client and has found that a verbal reprimand *increases* inappropriate behaviors (e.g., Madsen, Becker, Thomas, Koser, & Plager, 1970), it would be beneficial to begin with the next technique in the hierarchy to ensure success.

Table 1 contains a summary of the proposed hierarchy of training and behavior management procedures for ameliorating workshop problems. These are arranged for each problem area.

Acquisition Problem—Discrimination Deficits

The most frequently used training method in competitive employment is verbal instructions. Many times a new task will be presented with only a verbal explanation. Thus, this should logically be the initial method used to train a new task. If unsuccessful, a trainer must attempt to train a task through alternative methods.

Alternatives include verbal instructions paired with modeling of the correct movements (Bellamy et al., 1975; Clarke & Hermelin, 1955), priming the response, and physical guidance (Williams, 1967). Breaking a task down into small measurable components (task analysis) is also effective in aiding acquisition (Crosson, 1969; Gold, 1972), as is presenting learning material in an easy-to-hard sequence (Gold & Barclay, 1973; Irvin, 1976). For clients who fail to attend to relevant cues or task dimensions, cue redundancy, e.g., color-coded parts, facilitates acquisition (Gold, 1974).

Acquisition Problem—Sensory-Motor Deficits

In meeting the needs of clients with sensory-motor deficits, the trainer must first consider the clients' physical capacity. For clients with poor motor coordination due to cerebral palsy or loss of limb, the first four suggested strategies in the hierarchy do not differ from those used with clients whose acquisition problems are due to discrimination deficits. However, if the client's physical limitations are extensive, the arrangement of materials or the use of prosthetic devices such as specially designed jigs may be crucial in the acquisition of vocational skills (Hollis, 1967a). It may be necessary for a trainer to modify the task so that clients can complete a task with the least effort and most speed.

Low Production—Slow Motor Behavior

As clients become more proficient at performing a task, increasing the rate of production to competitive employment standards becomes a focal point. The severely developmentally disabled must produce at a competitive level to obtain and maintain community workshop employment. A verbal prompt to "work faster" appears to be the least time consuming and most efficient technique, providing that it is effective (Bellamy et al., 1975). Peer modeling (Brown & Pearce, 1970; Kazdin, 1973b; Kliebhahn, 1967) and trainer modeling have also increased production rate.

The manipulation of reinforcing events is another extensive area of possible techniques. Increasing reinforcer proximity, increasing the frequency or the amount of reinforcement, and increasing the number of redemptions of token reinforcers in a work period all are logical techniques for increasing production rates (e.g., Schroeder, 1972). Furthermore, our experience indicates that mixed schedules of reinforcement, such as continuous social reinforcement for each unit completed and penny or token reinforcement for every ten units completed, can be extremely effective in altering production rates with the severely handicapped (Wehman,

6. SEVERELY AND PROFOUNDLY RETARDED

Renzaglia, Schutz, & Karan, 1977). Intermittent schedules of reinforcement are a means of programming for response maintenance and approximating competitive employment work situations.

However, if the problem of low production rates still persists, it may be necessary to provide aversive consequences. Once a trainer has established a minimum criterion for production rate, the use of aversive consequences may be necessary. Implementing a verbal reprimand procedure and no reinforcement (Schutz, et al., in press), or a response cost procedure for low production, may be effective if used in conjunction with positive consequences for acceptable work rates. With an established minimum criterion for performance, an isolation-avoidance procedure may also be used successfully (Zimmerman, Overpeck, Eisenberg, & Garlick, 1969). (An isolation-avoidance procedure entails removing the client from the work area if a designated criterion is not met.)

Because low production is often a result of slow motor behavior, which is characteristic of the severely developmentally disabled, implementing a positive practice overcorrection procedure with the intent of teaching fast motor behavior is a feasible alternative (e.g., Rusch & Close, 1976). This procedure requires guiding the client through a task a number of times (so that it constitutes an extended duration) quickly, and therefore, teaching a client to move with speed. If positive practice is implemented, a trainer must take care to make the physical guidance sufficiently unpleasant that it is not socially reinforcing.

This procedure was recently applied to a profoundly handicapped adolescent who was performing at a very low production rate (Wehman, Schutz, Renzaglia, & Karan, 1977). When positive reinforcement for meeting criterion work levels was combined with positive practice, the trainee rapidly reached the target rate. In this situation, the client increased the rate of on-task behavior to avoid positive practice training.

Low Production—Interfering Behavior

Low production rate as a result of nonfunctional competing behavior poses a somewhat different problem. A trainer must not only increase a client's work rate, but also decrease or preferably eliminate the amount of time a client engages in the interfering behavior. Manipulating different parameters of reinforcement may also be effective here; unfortunately, little or no published research is available describing efforts to overcome excessive distractability by severely developmentally disabled clients in vocational settings.

To decrease many interfering behaviors, it may be necessary to implement aversive consequences. The use of response cost (Kazdin, 1973a), time-out (MacDonough & Forehand, 1973), restraint, and positive practice (Azrin, Gottlieb, Hughart, Wesolowski, & Rahn, 1975; Wehman, Schutz, Renzaglia, and Karan, 1977) procedures as immediate consequences for engaging in interfering behaviors may successfully decrease stereotypic behavior, aggression, out-of-seat behavior, and bizarre noises. These techniques have been effective with handicapped populations in different settings (Gardner, 1969), and should be seriously considered in workshops for the severely developmentally disabled.

GENERAL STRATEGIES FOR TREATMENT

To facilitate specific sequences of training and management techniques, a number of general strategies for treatment may be employed. The general intervention strategies discussed in this section include changing-criterion methodology, isolated treatment programs, and self-control strategies.

Changing-Criterion Design

A changing-criterion design may be used when work behaviors are gradually shaped to a competitive level (Axelrod, Hall, Weis, & Rohrer, 1974; Bates, Wehman, & Karan, 1977; Hartmann & Hall, 1976; Kazdin, 1975). Employing this design, a client must meet a minimum criterion or level for production rate to earn reinforcement. As a client's productivity consistently meets the criterion, the criterion is gradually increased or made more stringent. Thus, over time and with the use of effective behavior shaping methods, productivity may greatly increase from the initial criterion.

This design may be used with specific operant techniques to alleviate low production due to slow motor behavior or competing behaviors. In the case of low production behaviors, a changing time contingency may be introduced. This procedure requires setting a specific time limit for the completion of a task; it places the client under a time limit to receive reinforcement. A timing device, such as a kitchen timer or sports time-clock, may be used as a cue for the client and a subsequent indicator that a time limit was not met. As the client consistently meets the required time limit, the time allowed can be gradually decreased. This procedure has been successfully demonstrated and evaluated in a changing criterion design in a recent study performed with an institutionalized profoundly handicapped adult (Renzaglia, Wehman, Schutz, & Karan, 1977).

Isolated Treatment

Low production rates resulting from a client's excessive interfering behaviors poses a difficult remediation problem. Operant techniques employed within the work environment, such as manipulating different parameters of reinforcement, may not obtain successful results with particularly distractable or disruptive clients. With such clients, it may be advantageous to implement a treatment program in a relatively stimulus-free environment. Previously discussed training techniques may be enhanced by reducing the number of environmental cues to which a client might attend. As a client demonstrates increased on-task behavior, the treatment program may be gradually faded back into the work environment.

A general strategy of behavior control which may be used in an isolated treatment program is differential reinforcement of other behavior. With this approach, the trainee might be reinforced for instances of *not* being bad (Repp, Dietz, & Dietz, 1976; Wehman & Marchant, Note 1), for instances where he was performing only the appropriate behavior (Thomas, Becker, & Armstrong, 1968), or for low rates of responding (Dietz & Repp, 1973). Differential reinforcement is used in most training efforts when the trainee is taught fine discriminations and also in the reinforcement of high work rates. It is certainly not limited to an isolated treatment program. However, in an isolated, relatively stimulus-free environment, it may be easier to use differential reinforcement of the target behavior.

Self-Management Strategies

The operant techniques and procedures discussed thus far pertain to external control on the part of a significant change agent, such as a workshop supervisor. These techniques involve staff-administered contingencies; if relied on entirely, they present potential disadvantages to self-sufficient vocational behavior (Kazdin, 1973b).

One major problem is that an external control approach precludes the development of self-directed choice behaviors on the part of severely developmentally disabled clients. Many rehabilitation professionals recognize this deficit as a primary obstacle in the community transition process for these clients (Wehman, 1975). Secondly, an external control approach presents a number of inherent drawbacks. Since it is difficult to notice all instances of an appropriate response, a workshop supervisor or counselor usually misses many opportunities to reinforce a client. Furthermore, the change agent himself may become a cue for a behavior rather than a natural environmental stimulus (Redd & Birnbrauer, 1969). This drawback relates also to the problem of transfer of training and durability of program progress. Thus, whenever possible, external control must not be viewed as an end itself, but rather as a means to train a client to control his or her *own* behavior and achieve self-selected goals.

Self-control has been defined in reference to "those behaviors an individual deliberately undertakes to achieve self-selected outcomes" (Kazdin, 1975, p. 192). Self-control training procedures which are applicable to the severely developmentally disabled include self-observation, self-reinforcement, and stimulus control.

Self-observation has been successfully implemented with mentally retarded clients through the use of behavioral graphs (Jens & Shores, 1969) and daily feedback of work performance from a videotape (DeRoo & Haralson, 1971). With this procedure, a client is trained to become aware of his or her work performance through immediate external feedback and through a visual record of work behavior. Gradually a client's self-observation can be faded to pictures of improvement in work performance.

Self-reinforcement is another strategy which holds potential, particularly in

6. SEVERELY AND PROFOUNDLY RETARDED

workshops that use a token economy as a motivational system. Two concepts of self-reinforcement are self-administered reinforcement and self-determined reinforcement. An important requirement for both self-administered reinforcement and self-determined reinforcement is that the individual is free to reward himself at any time, whether or not he performs a particular response (Skinner, 1953).

Self-administered reinforcement refers to a client taking a reinforcer himself, but under an externally determined criterion. Once a client's self-administered reinforcement response is shaped, it is possible to move toward *self-determined* reinforcement. This broader concept of self-reinforcement allows clients to determine their own work criteria (e.g., Glynn, 1970). It may be possible for contingency contracts to be set up between clients and workshop supervisors. Within such a contract would be a set rate of work and social skills which a client agrees to perform. In return, he or she can self-select reinforcement preferences for performance of the contract.

How severely handicapped trainees can manage their own work behavior was illustrated recently (Wehman, Schutz, Bates, Renzaglia, & Karan, 1977). The workers' production rates were assessed under no reinforcement, externally administered reinforcement, and self-administered reinforcement, with pennies used as reinforcers. Treatment conditions were presented in a Latin Square sequence to control for order effects. Results indicated that through modeling and physical priming initially the trainee was able to reinforce himself and maintain a high level of production. Other research in workshop settings also supports the development of self-management skills in the severely handicapped (Helland, Paluck, & Klein, 1976; Nelson, Lipinski, & Black, in press).

Another self-control strategy which may be employed is stimulus control. *Stimulus control* refers to specific behaviors performed in the presence of specific stimuli which serve as cues and increase the probability that the behavior will be performed. For example, self-observation may function as a reinforcing consequence initially, but may also function as a discriminative stimulus for subsequent task-related behaviors.

Possible applications of the stimulus-control strategy, in workshops for the severely developmentally disabled, include altering stimuli which consistently lead to frustration-aggression situations, modifying cues that presumably contribute to task failure, or pairing positive stimuli with low preference tasks. Social behaviors such as eliciting social greetings, being on time, or appropriately using leisure time might also be developed through stimulus control.

CONCLUSION

This paper has attempted to provide direction in treatment strategies for workshop personnel who work with the severely developmentally disabled. It pointed out that a severely handicapped population presents a unique set of learning and behavior characteristics which can make traditional training and management techniques less applicable. It is strongly suggested that the hierarchy of strategies proposed for treatment be systematically examined with different learning/behavior problems to validate which methods are most effective with which workshop problems.

It should be apparent that the behavioral training and management procedures identified and sequenced in this paper can also be applied to behavior problems and deficits found in students or clients in other settings than workshops. It may be advantageous for parents, teachers, clinicians, and other practitioners to adopt a more planned approach to selection of behavior change procedures. Hopefully, the presentation in Table 1 takes one step toward a more systematic approach to ameliorating instructional and behavior problems in any setting.

Table 1 *A logically arranged hierarchy of procedures for Alleviating Work Problems*

I. Learning or Acquisition Problem—Discrimination Deficits

1. Give verbal instructions.
2. Model and give verbal instructions.
3. Give verbal and physical guidance.

46. Behavioral Training

    4. Break task down into simpler steps (easy-to-hard sequence) and repeat steps 1–3.
    5. Use cue redundancy or stimulus fading, depending on task.
    6. Always accompany steps 1–5 with positive reinforcement for correct response.

II. *Learning or Acquisition Problems—Sensory-Motor Deficits* (Assess handicap to be sure there is a physical problem)

  A. Poor motor coordination
    1. Give verbal instructions.
    2. Model and give verbal instructions.
    3. Give physical and verbal guidance.
    4. Break task down into simpler steps (easy-to-hard sequence) and repeat steps 1–3.
    5. Use prosthetic device or physical arrangement of materials.
    6. Use cue redundancy or stimulus fading, depending on task.
    7. Always accompany steps 1–6 with positive reinforcement for correct response.

  B. Visually handicapped
    1. Give verbal instructions (detailed).
    2. Give physical guidance and verbal instructions.
    3. Use tactile cue redundancy and repeat steps 1–2.

  C. Acoustically handicapped
    1. Use gestural instructions.
    2. Use physical guidance.
    3. Break task down into simpler steps (easy-to-hard sequence) and repeat steps 1–2.
    4. Use cue redundancy or stimulus fading, depending on task.

  D. Deaf–blind
    1. Use physical guidance.
    2. Use tactile cue redundancy.

III. *Low Production–Slow Motor Behavior*

    1. Use verbal prompt (e.g., "work faster").
    2. Use verbal prompt plus model.
    3. Use physical prompt (paired with verbal)
    4. Increase reinforcer proximity.
      a. Pennies present.
      b. Back-up present also.
    5. Increase frequency of receiving pennies.
    6. Increase number of pennies and/or back-ups.
    7. Increase frequency of redemption of pennies.
    8. Give verbal reprimand plus no reinforcement.
    9. Use response cost.
    10. Use isolation-avoidance.
    11. Use positive practice.
    12. Present aversive stimuli.

IV. *Low Production—Interfering or Excessive Behavior*

  Representative classes include:
    a. nonfunctional competing behaviors,
    b. bizarre noises,
    c. out-of-seat behaviors,
    d. aggression against objects,
    e. aggression against people.

    1. Use verbal reprimand and prompt.
    2. Use verbal reprimand and physical prompt.
    3. Increase reinforcement proximity (pennies, then back-up).
    4. Increase frequency of receiving reinforcement (pennies).
    5. Increase amount of pennies and/or back-up.
    6. Increase frequency of redemption.

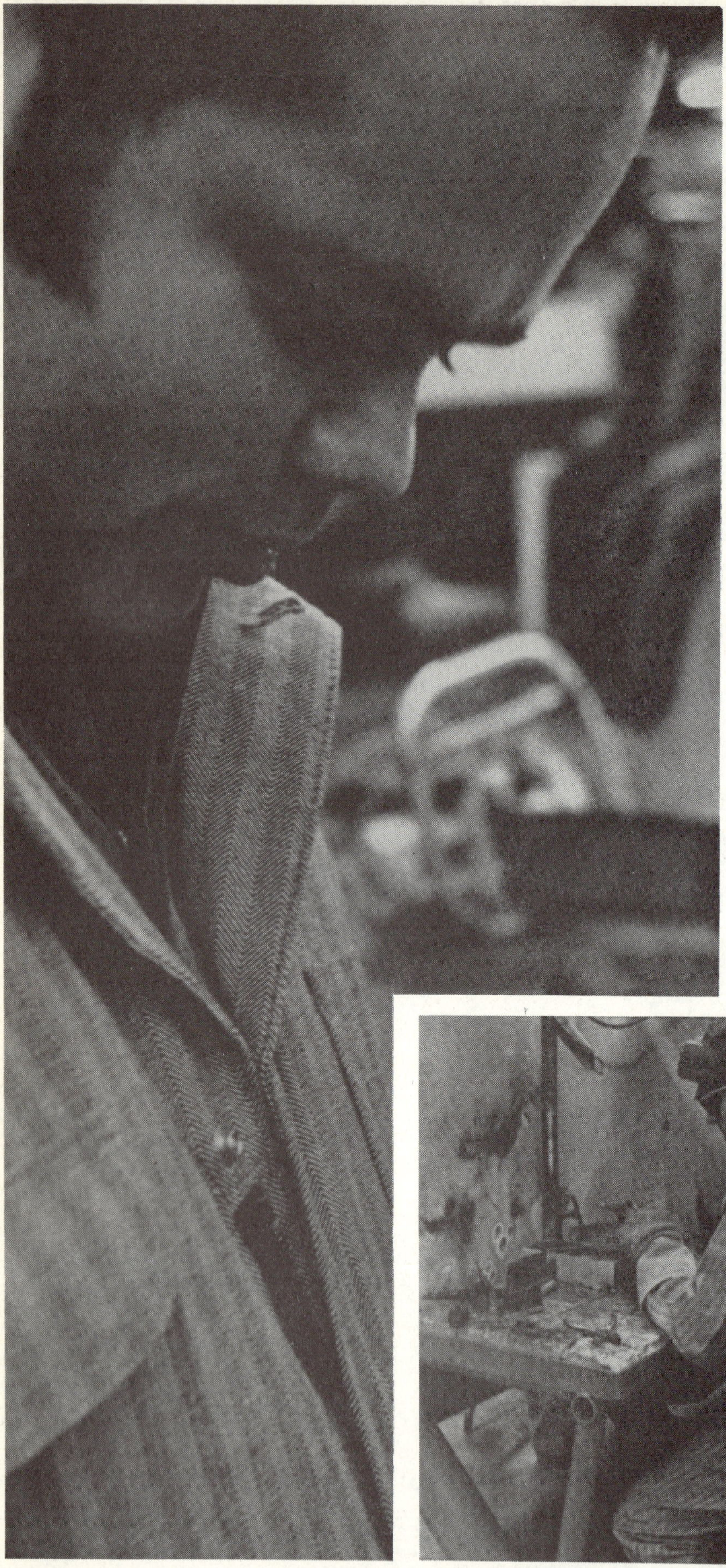
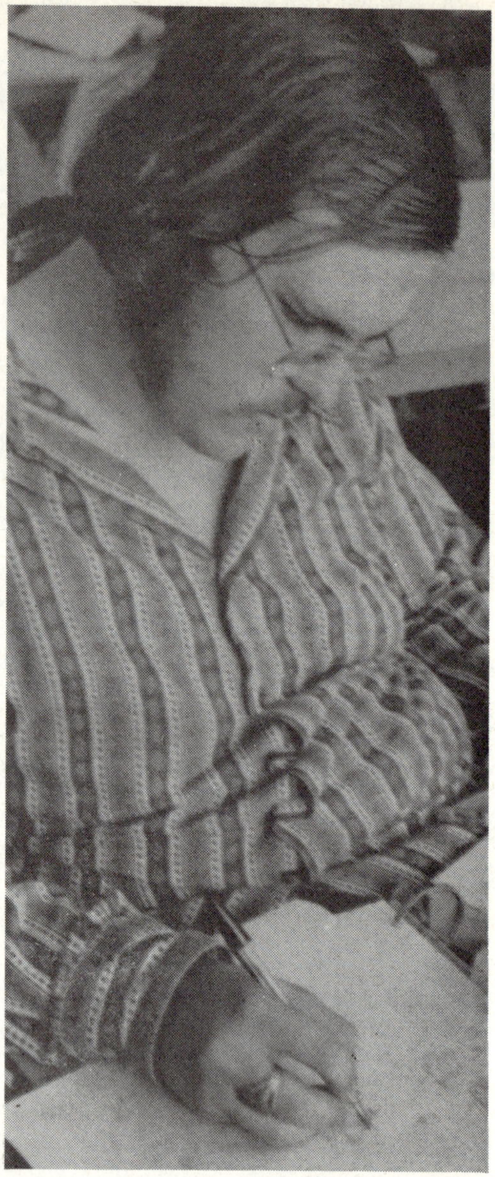
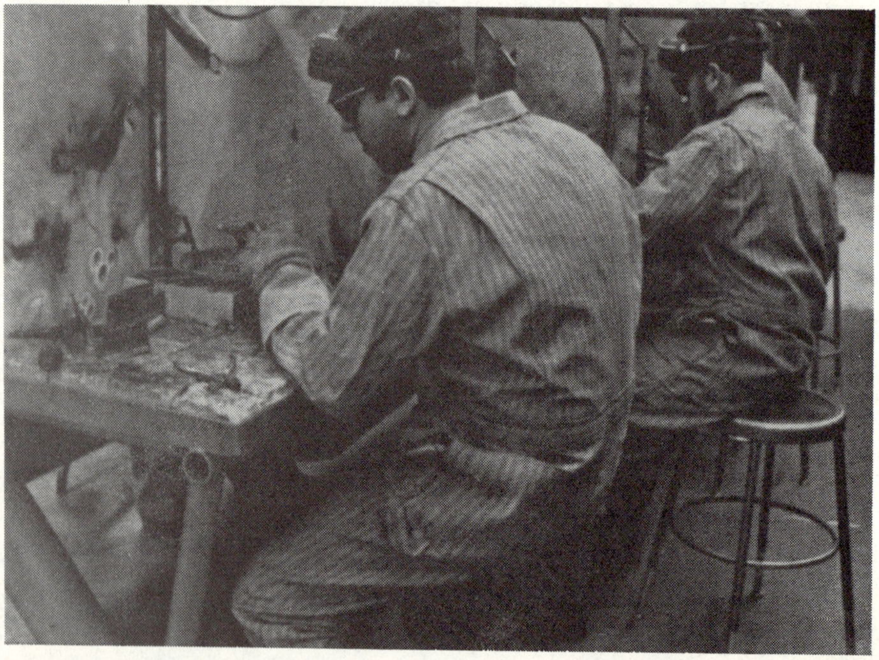

Emerging Directions

Despite two centuries of national history, only within the past few years has the acceptance of the mentally retarded into society taken place. The evolution of educational provisions for the mentally handicapped has been marked by steady progress, however. Looking back, the progression basically began with the neglect of public education of the handicapped between 1776 and 1817. Beginning in 1817, the solution for the problem of retardation was seen in the creation of asylums and residential institutions. Not until 1869, were day school classes established, offering the parents of mentally retarded children the alternative of home care. The expansion of a dual system of residential and day schools took place between 1869 and 1913. To follow was the establishment of state programs for the retarded, supported by state subsidies beginning about 1900, and the eventual expansion of public school programs starting in about 1950.

Since that time, progress has been greater during the past decade than during the past two centuries, due largely to a combination of Federal legislation and precedent-setting court cases. Behind this has been a great change in attitudes toward the mentally retarded since our nation's founding. Initially rejected, with standard practice being to remove them as far from society as possible, in time this rejection gave way to a sense of pity. Though pity can be viewed as a gain over hostility, in reality the mentally retarded remained in isolation.

Only in recent years has there begun to emerge the recognition that the retarded deserve the rights and opportunities equal to those enjoyed by all other Americans. Though a strong beginning has been made, this point of view is not yet universal. Serious gaps still remain, the number of mentally handicapped people receiving appropriate services is still not as large as those who are not. Regardless, progress has been steady. By every sign, the nation seems firmly on the way to achieving the goal of providing full opportunities for all mentally retarded citizens in the near future.

OPENING MORE DOORS FOR THE NATION'S RETARDED

A new world is at hand for many retarded persons as they learn to live and work in the broad community—and earn some of its rewards.

More and more of the nation's 6.4 million mentally retarded—children and adults—are moving into an outside world that, until recently, largely shunned them.

Waning is the old practice of segregating the retarded in institutions "for their own good." Today the emphasis is on keeping them in the mainstream of community life and enabling them, with appropriate help, to lead as normal and useful an existence as possible.

Experts in the field say that the new approach is opening new vistas to the retarded and their families. Comments Dr. Louis Brown of the University of Wisconsin:

"We have proven that when we isolate the retarded in institutions, they do not improve. When we allow them to be members of a complex, heterogeneous society, using public rest rooms, crossing streets and going to school along with the rest of us, they do improve—often remarkably."

From 1970 to 1975, the number of retarded who were confined in public institutions dropped from 187,000 to 168,000. The goal, according to Fred J. Krause, executive director of the President's Committee on Mental Retardation, is to cut that number by another 50,000 by 1980.

Reformation paying off. In California, the number of hospitalized retarded is down to 1 in every 60, from an earlier peak of 1 in every 30. The other 59 are obtaining services of some kind in their communities.

In New York City, thousands of mentally retarded inmates at the Willowbrook Developmental Center are being relocated gradually into homes that are operated by private agencies or by foster parents.

Throughout the country, mentally retarded children are being assisted in leading normal lives in schools with other children, while group homes and sheltered workshops are providing opportunities for retarded adults to live and work in the community.

Institutions themselves are being reformed with the purpose of releasing inmates for reintegration into the community as soon as possible.

Coming into wide use is an "early intervention" technique. As typified by the Daytime Development Center in Fairfax, Va., run by the county health department, mentally retarded infants are diagnosed at birth and undergo training, together with their mothers, from the age of 6 weeks onward.

"We begin the socialization process far earlier than textbooks say," remarks co-ordinator Joy Chance. "There are 2-year-olds here who are more independent than my normal 2-year-old."

Also in Fairfax County, a private organization provides specialists who will baby-sit mentally retarded children at either their own homes or at the homes of the parents.

In Arlington, Va., another organization provides emergency help for the parents of mentally retarded children on a 24-hour basis.

The trend of recent court decisions and State laws has been to affirm the right of handicapped children—including the mentally retarded—to equal educational opportunities. Most of the States have laws that require education of the handicapped, and 20 States include the preschool handicapped in this provision.

The Federal Government is assisting the States in providing education for the handicapped by making annual grants that may escalate to more than 3 billion dollars by 1982.

Already, 90 per cent of the country's 1,057,000 mentally retarded children are being served by public schools, according to the U.S. Office of Education.

In New York State, for example, public schools were ordered in 1973 to educate all children, including the severely retarded and those with multiple handicaps who had previously been left to private agencies to care for.

Three public schools in New York City have early-childhood programs for 5 to 7-year-olds. One Manhattan school has a "hot line" over which parents of the retarded can discuss their problems among themselves.

Public schools in the city are operating a retrieval and redirection program aimed at the retarded, aged 15 to 17, who have quit school. These teen-agers are given training in workshops, aid in locating jobs and a $1-an-hour stipend.

School officials in Madison, Wis., have set up the Zero Reject Plan, designed to educate all developmentally disabled children from birth to age 21.

Under this plan, children whose

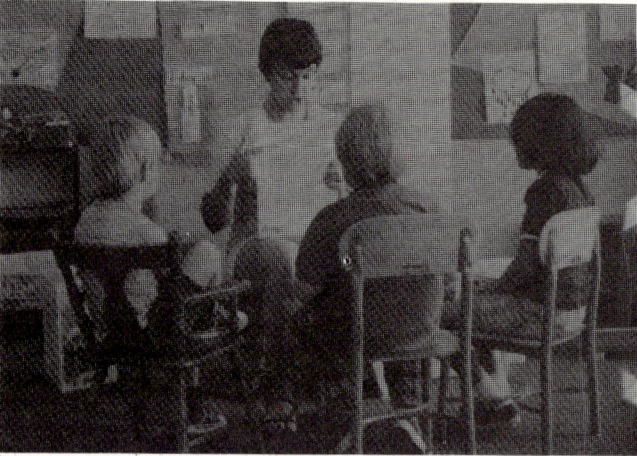

Zero Reject Plan at Madison, Wis. public schools provides instruction for all developmentally disabled children.

handicaps are judged not to be excessively severe attend regular schools. They go to normal classes for subjects they can handle, such as art or physical education, and attend special classes for subjects that they cannot cope with. The other retarded go to a special school for the mentally handicapped.

The University of Oregon's Center on Human Development in Eugene is instructing mixed classes of 10 retarded and 30 normal preschool children. The Oregon experiment is reported to be so successful that there is a waiting list for the Center's services.

Springing up everywhere are group homes where mentally retarded persons of different ages are living together under the supervision of specially trained "house parents" and staff.

In Georgia, for example, the first group home was opened in 1972; the present total is 29. "We have about 1,500 persons currently in institutions whom we would like to move into a community-living situation," reports Budd Hughes, in charge of the State's mental-retardation program.

One such home is in Marietta and

47. Opening More Doors

University of Oregon conducts mixed classes for retarded, normal children. Retarded child wears protective helmet.

houses eight men aged 20 to 36, who between them had previously spent 102 years at institutions. The oldest had been an inmate for 28 years.

In most cases, points out social worker Maggie Smith, the men were institutionalized only because they had nowhere else to go.

"These people are more like us than unlike us," says Mrs. William D. McSwain, the housemother, who lives in the Marietta home with her husband and two sons.

The men participate in making the home's rules, such as lights out at 11 p.m. and restriction of smoking to certain hours. They pitch in with the chores on an informal basis. They go to movies or shopping or church on their own.

Churches and civic groups in the community are helping to organize trips and other activities for them.

Seven of the eight attend workshops where they are taught such basic skills as counting change.

One works full time as a dishwasher in a cafeteria. Some also contract for such jobs as packaging fishing tackle and making planters for sale through nurseries. Pay, based on proficiency, averages $10 a week. They spend their earnings as they please.

Only one man has had to leave the Marietta home to return to an institution because of adjustment problems.

Mr. Hughes's hope is that after further progress is made, some of the men will be able, with some assistance, to take apartments, or live with families on a more or less independent basis.

Wisconsin has about 100 group homes housing 800 individuals, of whom 600 would otherwise be in large institutions. According to Gerald Dymond, director of the State's bureau of mental health, it costs only $450 a month to keep one person at such a home, as opposed to $1,500 a month at a full-care institution.

The Federal Government is contributing not only money but incentives in this trend.

Finding them jobs. Federal regulations require any company having Government contracts of $2,500 or more to take "affirmative action" to secure employment for handicapped individuals, including the mentally retarded.

Under modified examination procedures, more than 7,400 mentally retarded persons have been hired for minor positions by the Federal Government itself since 1964.

An on-the-job training program, funded at about 2 million dollars a year by the Federal Government and administered by the National Association for Retarded Citizens, has placed some 14,000 retarded in competitive jobs at private firms since 1967.

Many others find employment in sheltered workshops. For example:

At workshops run by the Chicago Association for Retarded Citizens, 500 individuals make lamps and candles for department stores and pillowcases for airlines, fill tubes with glue, stuff envelopes and shred polyester. They are supervised by employes of the companies who have hired them and earn a minimum wage based on piecework.

Otto Whitehall, executive director of the association, makes the observation that these people are being returned to communities where "they feel productive and worthwhile."

Within institutions, increased efforts are being made to train retarded inmates so they can eventually return to the community.

One example is Stockton State Hospital near Sacramento, Calif., where student volunteers from the University of the Pacific are teaching retarded children simple behavioral skills that may enable them eventually to return home.

California officials estimate that, for each youngster between the ages of 5 and 18 who can be trained and released to his home, the State would save in the neighborhood of $14,000.

Experts point out that all this does not mean that every retarded person in institutions can, or should, be released.

"Some very handicapped people have more freedom in a hospital than they can have in the community," observes Harold Schmitz of Pacific State Hospital in Pomona, Calif. He reports that some parents are fighting legal battles to keep their children hospitalized because they want to be sure that they are getting good care.

Problems of budgeting. At the same time, in one community after another, officials are reporting money and other shortages that make it impossible for them to provide all the retarded on the outside with the supportive services they need to lead near-normal lives in their communities.

In New York City, public-school programs for the retarded suffered budget cuts during the city's fiscal crisis, and there are not enough small community residences for retarded adults.

In Montgomery County, Md., a critical shortage of trained and specialized staff is reported to be making it difficult to comply with a State law which mandates special educational programs for all mentally retarded from birth to age 20.

North Dakota, officials say, has only eight group homes for the mentally retarded, whereas 150 are needed.

Another major obstacle to the mainstreaming of the retarded, according to experts, is the persistence of adverse community attitudes. Some instances:

Near Washington, D.C., a major bank until recently refused to allow the residents of a home for the mentally retarded to open savings accounts.

Notes Thomas T. Crowner, director of special services at the Madison, Wis., public schools: "We have had people ask us why we spend money on kids whom they call 'wet noodles.'"

Says Samih Ismir, assistant director of Mental Health and Retardation Services for North Dakota: "Our main problem is neighborhood resistance. People are afraid to have the retarded living next door to them."

Increasingly, however, officials and ordinary citizens are pushing ahead to offer America's mentally retarded the kind of "normal" life in the broad community that many of them are capable of leading.

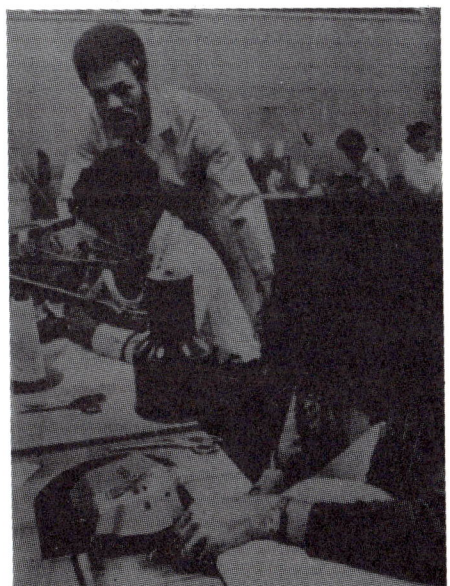

Instructors at workshop in Chicago teach retarded to make pillowcases for airlines.

253

New Hope for Retarded Children

SARA D. STUTZ

Child psychologists are proving that infants of *any* intelligence level can develop and learn if the special training they need is set in motion soon enough

JORDY is mongoloid. When he was born, the pediatrician suggested that his parents put him in an institution. Fortunately for Jordy, his parents ignored the doctor's advice and took him home. Within a few months they enrolled him in the Infant Development Program of the Exceptional Children's Foundation in Los Angeles. At three, he's functioning so well that he has been accepted in a pre-school for normal children.

• Linda, normal at birth, suffered massive brain injury in an auto accident when she was two. Pronounced "hopeless," she was sent to Pacific State Hospital in Pomona, Calif., where her parents expected her to be a crib case for the rest of her life. But now, through special sensory motor training, Linda is learning to walk and talk again. She'll never return to normal, but she'll soon function in a manner her family can manage at home.

• At nine months, Christy was hospitalized with malnutrition and other evidences of parental neglect. She was unresponsive and slow for her age. Now, enrolled in the Developmentally Delayed Infant Education Project at the Nisonger Center in Columbus, Ohio, she is, at 13 months, feeding herself, crawling, and trying to talk. It looks as if Christy is going to catch up.

Jordy, Linda and Christy aren't miracle babies. They are typical of the youngsters being served by infant intervention programs, a new and highly promising concept in education. "With early intervention, many developmentally delayed children may be entered in regular classes or helped so that their disabilities require less extensive special services," says James J. Gallagher, former associate commissioner of education for the handicapped, at HEW.

There are an estimated five million retarded persons in the United States. Dr. George Tarjan, professor of psychiatry at U.C.L.A., testifying before the President's Committee on Mental Retardation, estimated that as many as 50 percent might have been classed as "normal," had they had the benefit of early training. Not only could they be leading more satisfying lives, but society could be spared the expense of their lifetime institutional care. The cost of such care for a person from age six can be $300,000 to $800,000.

Babies learn from experience. If they can take in what's happening around them, and if their surroundings contain an average amount of stimulation, they develop to their full potential. But, if their ability to absorb their environment is limited, they don't get the experiences they need for mental development. These are the babies who need help, says Eugenia Vogt, who supervises the infant program at the Exceptional Children's Foundation.

"Any infant suffers if his original capacity to inquire, to seek, to explore, is stifled. Sterility of the early childhood environment, especially the absence of daily conversational exchange with the mother and others in contact with the infant, seems to impose a permanent limitation on intelligence," notes John W. Kidd, president of the Council for Exceptional Children.

When a profoundly retarded infant is put in a crib and given only the necessary custodial care, as was common practice until recently, he merely lies there, explains Clara Lee Edgar, the psychologist who has developed a training program at Pacific State Hospital. He has no way of making anything happen.

48. New Hope

He cannot learn anything.

But if that same child is taken out of the crib and strapped to a scooter board on wheels with his toes hanging down on the floor, he can, with the slightest amount of wiggling, make the board move. He seems to say to himself, "Hey, I can go somewhere." In subsequent periods on the board he learns to scoot across the room. Eventually, he begins to hold his head up while doing it and even use his arms and hands to guide him. He's having experiences that will increase his intelligence.

Now, with the new intervention programs which have sprung up in the past ten years, babies with developmental delays are being helped to have the experiences they need to make mental and physical progress. Most programs are open to *any* developmentally delayed baby—the preemie, the baby having difficulty relating to people, the child of overanxious parents, the slow walker—not just children with known physical or mental impairment.

Babies enter programs through a variety of channels. Some, usually low-birth-weight preemies or babies who have experienced unusual difficulties at birth, become part of a program while in the newborn nursery. Many are referred to programs by their pediatricians or public-health nurses because of obvious medical conditions such as Down's syndrome (mongolism), hydrocephaly (enlargement of the brain because of an abnormal drainage of cerebral fluid), microcephaly (abnormally small skull) or spina bifida (open spine). "Others," reports Lee Ann Britain, director of the two-year-old Infant Development Center in Kansas City, Kan., "don't get to us until after somebody notices that they aren't walking or talking when they should. That's too bad, and we're trying to find them earlier."

Babies who have developmental problems evident at birth may cry all the time or they may be very "good." They might not cry or fuss for attention for a variety of reasons. Without being neglectful, a mother could leave such a child in the crib all day except for feeding and changing him. Yet this is the baby who most needs an environment that provides a maximum of social and sensory experience.

Directors of infant programs usually request mothers to bring their babies once a week to a center where special equipment is available, and where trained personnel can show them how to teach their babies. Group activities are offered when babies are old enough to work on the self-help and language skills necessary for entry into pre-school.

At the new Early Childhood Intervention Center in Dayton, Ohio, I followed a group of seven mongoloid youngsters, one-and-a-half to three years old, through a morning's activities that would be almost unbelievable to the person conditioned to think of Down's syndrome as a totally incapacitating handicap. After a period of free play with specially chosen toys to improve coördination, the children sang songs that helped them to identify their own names. Then they divided up, one group going to draw with crayons and play simple ball games while the other had a lesson in identifying colors and matching shapes. At snack time, all the children fed themselves. In half-hour discussion periods, the mothers were told what the children would be learning next and how to reinforce it at home.

Rural areas, as well as cities, can have such special services. Six years ago, the Bureau of Education for the Handicapped, a part of HEW, provided funds to develop a model rural program in Portage, Wis. "We expected at first to build a special school and bring in children for classes," says David Shearer, director of the project. "But we soon rejected that. The area we're responsible for covers 3600 square miles of farms and villages. Since youngsters with problems may live 100 miles apart, we use 'home trainers' instead."

The home trainers—women who either have had instruction in special education or are paraprofessionals—come once a week for an hour-and-a-half lesson. They show parents how to conduct similar lessons the other days of the week, and leave any equipment that is needed.* Results? The average child in the Portage project gained 13 months in an eight-month period.

Pacific State Hospital at Pomona, Calif., is showing that there is *no* level at which children are "hopeless." There Clara Edgar now administers a federally funded Hospital Improvement Program that is taking severely retarded youngsters—ones who are often crib cases for life—and training them so well that they can return to their families.

Edgar is taking severely retarded children through the developmental stages that the normal child experiences. For a variety of reasons, the retarded youngster cannot effectively use his body to deal with the world around him. Edgar's research has shown that by improving his balance and other sensory motor skills the child can be helped toward more normal behavior. I watched the most advanced group go to the dining room for lunch, where one bright-eyed little girl carefully set the table and served the rolls to her classmates. It was hard to imagine that she had been a crib case.

Will the community be ready to accept these children? The teachers and parents I talked with said yes, if the public is given adequate information about developmental problems. I heartily agree.

My youngest child, Eric, is afflicted with Down's syndrome. He has been a much-loved member of the family ever since he was born. Friends and acquaintances with whom we have openly discussed his condition are interested in his development and are rooting for him in a truly heartwarming way.

Several months ago, when Eric was not quite three, I took him on one of our routine trips to the supermarket. I held his hands as he walked into the store for the first time. As we passed through the turnstile, we were startled by the sound of loud applause. The checkers were clapping for him and his small chest swelled with pride.

At that moment the thought of what might have been crossed my mind. Even with early stimulation and training, Eric is slower than the "average" mongoloid child. He could easily be a hopeless, unresponding hospital patient instead of a lively happy little boy embarking now on a program of special public education. Where he was born and the kind of advice we were given have made that much difference in his life.

Role Playing and Behavior Modification: A Demonstration with Mentally Retarded Children

L. GERALD BUCHAN, SALLY TEED, and CRAIG PETERSON

Within the last few years a "new wave" of therapeutic techniques for teaching the mentally retarded has emerged in this country. Two techniques which have been useful to the teaching professional are role playing and behavior modification. Not only do these methods modify learning behavior of the retarded, but also research has suggested they serve to improve adaptive behavior (Edwards and Lilly, 1966; Bryer, 1963).

Role playing procedures for the retarded have given them an actional dimension which is important in the total learning spectrum. Also, the "here and now" quality of role playing activities doesn't require a time perspective, yet specific situations can help the retarded plan for future events.

Behavior modification has been labeled variously as operant conditioning, reinforcement therapy, and behavior therapy. A primary principle involved is that of using reinforcement or reward to increase the probability of a response occurring again (Skinner, 1953). Operant conditioning also involves the principles of shaping or successful approximation where a response approximating the final desired response is rewarded. Another important principle is chaining responses. Gagne (1965) states that chaining is a matter of connecting together in a sequence two or more previously learned responses before reinforcement is presented. Eensburg (1965) has shown that chaining is an important technique for the severely retarded. Through chaining it is possible to have an individual learn complex and sometimes very difficult maneuvers in succession.

The mentally retarded individual should be prepared to the best of his or her ability to compete in society as an economically independent person. In the primary grades this involves learning experiences in the academic area. In junior and senior high levels, learning centers around practical application, prevocational, vocational, and avocational skills, and the utilization of academic subjects to assist in these skills. The teacher's job is to effectively prepare the students for the roles they will take in society.

In any classroom total individualized instruction between teacher and pupil is impossible. Therefore, when utilizing the principles of behavior modification, it is necessary to find a way to reinforce all children and yet allow this reinforcement to be as individualized as possible. Some goals of behavior modification in the classroom are to develop procedures whereby motivation, good study habits, cooperation, perseverance, and concentration can be developed (Birnbrauer, Tague,

---

Dr. Buchan is School Psychologist, Multnomah County Intermediate Education District, Portland, Oregon.

Mrs. Teed, high school teacher of EMR individuals, Highland High School, Pocatello, Idaho.

Dr. Peterson, School Psychologist, Vancouver Public Schools, Vancouver, Washington.

et al., 1965). If these goals can be established early in the child's academic career, then the possibility exists that these same principles will carry over into his or her adult life.

Combining Role Playing and Behavior Modification

Role playing situations and techniques can be adapted for use with the mentally retarded. Since many retardates exhibit a short attention span, as well as a limited verbal ability, situations with an actional base for the participants are preferable to those that are conversational in nature.

Two procedures will be examined which can be used with the mentally retarded: skill training and problem solving. These two procedures are the outgrowth of combining role playing and behavior modification.

Skill Training: When the director's purpose is skill training, guidance helps retarded individuals focus on acquiring skill in various tasks. If the situation is learning telephoning procedure, the teacher may provide the children with a model of appropriateness in using the phone. Later, the children may practice with other children or be given opportunity for "live" phoning.

Problem Solving: When the major purpose is problem solving, the director may focus on problems, feelings about handling these problems, and alternatives. More time may be spent delineating the problem or probing alternative proposals in an effort to get brief enactments and alternatives, and then helping the group choose one or two alternatives to explore in further detail. Time will also be spent in summarizing proposals for behavior and discussing the enacted sequences (Shaftel and Shaftel, 1967).

Both of these procedures are effective with the mentally retarded. They offer alternatives to problem areas in the classroom, as well as prepare the older retarded individual for experiences in the social world they will eventually encounter. An example of this would be to conduct a job interview and thereby give the student a chance to practice without fear of failure.

With a retarded individual, it is necessary to keep role playing situations relatively simple, especially at first. The individual needs to experience success and if the situations are too complex this is not possible.

Classroom Applications

This section will show how concepts of role playing and behavior modification can be utilized with the mentally retarded individual. The examples noted are for demonstration purposes only. It should be noted that the unfolding of role playing is generally spontaneous and consequently does not lend itself to orderly procedures, sequences, and so forth.

Two groups of mentally retarded individuals were selected for the demonstration. [The authors wish to thank the administration of the Pocatello public schools for providing time and space to conduct this demonstration.] Group one consisted of prevocational mentally retarded students; chronological age twelve to sixteen, mental age six to nine. Group two was composed of ten primary age trainable mentally retarded students; chronological age nine to twelve, mental age four to six. One day observation was given to each group to help identify the individual to be used in the demonstration, and also to decide which students in the group could be used as reinforcers. Peer reinforcements were used for both groups.

GROUP I: Robin is an educable mentally retarded individual, fourteen years of age. She has adequate verbal skills for a girl of her intellectual capacity. However, she is shy and withdrawn. She is easily intimidated by other class members and prefers to let them speak for her. This pattern of behavior was evident during the warm-up for role playing. It was noted that she would rather follow others than make any type of decision for herself. On the first day of the role playing situations several introductions were made, and as a role playing situation, students were given an opportunity to make applications for a job. Robin had an opportunity to view other students in this "pretend" situation and to get a feel for the mechanics of entering an interview situation.

She was then chosen to serve as an interviewee. Two students were chosen to reinforce Robin for appropriate interview behaviors; she was praised when she shook hands, asked questions in a clear voice, and when she left the office in an appropriate manner at the close of the interview. She was also reinforced verbally for not fidgeting with her hands while in the interview situation. During these particular enactments, several individuals were given an opportunity to serve as both interviewer and interviewee. Role reversal as a technique helped increase the reality of the situation. This also provided an opportunity for the individual to get a feel for the other persons point of view and also served to reduce anxieties in future job interview situations.

It was necessary for the director to serve as an auxillary and assist the individuals when they temporarily experienced difficulty in phrasing questions or responding to questions. It should be

7. EMERGING DIRECTIONS

noted that Robin was the only individual reinforced during this role playing situation.

On the second day of the role playing situation, additional interview-type situations were conducted in the classroom during a reading period. It was noted that Robin spoke loudly and clearly to the audience and to the teacher during this occasion in spite of a fellow student who spoke out of turn and exhibited rude behavior. As on the first day, Robin was the only individual reinforced in terms of techniques used during the two sessions. They included warm-up, role reversal, and mirroring.

Results with the group one students indicate that they had some difficulty in reinforcing Robin. They wanted to reinforce the model who initially gave appropriate ways to conduct the interview, and in the process the students became so involved in the role playing situation that they forgot their tasks. It was necessary for the director to signal them when she wanted Robin to be reinforced. As peer reinforcement was a vital part of this demonstration, the director stood behind Robin and nodded to the reinforcers when praise was to be given. Since immediacy of reinforcement is critical it was necessary to anticipate what Robin would say or do so adaptive behavior could be shaped. With reinforcement Robin did speak more loudly and clearly as she seemed to gain confidence each time she was placed in a role.

Using peer reinforcement techniques is necessary because behavior may be extinguished with little carry over value unless reinforcement and practice are frequent. In the author's opinion there was not an adequate amount of time to allow intermittent and secondary reinforcers to produce the desired behavior. With this particular age group, the lack of cohesiveness which prevailed and the factor of peer reinforcement did not appear to be entirely satisfactory. The group's lack of acquaintance with role playing techniques and the novelty of the situation may have caused some disorganization.

GROUP II: With the younger mentally retarded children, the director concentrated on one individual who had difficulty participating in group activities. Jane is a mongoloid child who appears to function much like an isolate in the class. Two of Jane's classmates were chosen to serve as reinforcers. The director talked to each of them independently and explained that when she nodded to them they were to praise Jane. They were to say, "That's good Jane," "Fine Jane," or "You're doing O.K. Jane".

Role playing for this class was more active than for group one. For warm-up, a story was told with each child taking part. The role playing situation centered around animals in the jungle (the children played the animals) and one individual was chosen to be king. In this particular story the children decided on their own to band together and manage a lion. The lion's behavior was dependent on the child who was portraying him. Jane was reluctant initially to enter into the story. However, when she did make moves or gestures indicating an interest, she was given pats on the back by peer reinforcers. With the use of successive approximation, she gradually became more interested in the story. During the first day of the demonstration, she did join in the group. However, this was all in a nonverbal manner.

On the second day of the demonstration, warm-up consisted of mirroring, and the students were given a chance to tell about vacation plans. Jane participated actively in mirroring (acting out facial grimaces pretending to be a tree, eating a banana, and so forth) but would not discuss vacation plans. A role playing situation was then developed with the activities centering on a "physical education classroom," with one individual being a leader and the rest of the class becoming participants. Jane was verbally reinforced for joining the group and participating actively. During this particular session, she did take part and even became leader for approximately thirty seconds.

Results of the demonstration with group two indicates that Jane's behavior changed dramatically. Jane had never before taken part in games at recess or worked with other individuals in the class, nor had she demonstrated a willingness to join a group. Verbal praise was reinforcing for Jane and reinforcement by her peers seemed to create more interest in group activities.

Results of these two demonstration groups suggest that mentally retarded individuals can utilize the accomodations of role playing and behavior modification to develop more appropriate social skills. Role playing gives the individuals freedom because it is like pretending while positive reinforcement gives incentive to go on and improve.

As the demonstration classes were only two sessions each, it is apparent that intermittent and secondary reinforcements had not become prominent. It is difficult to assess the long range value of role playing and behavior modification because of the brevity of the demonstration. However, it seems apparent that utilizing the peer group as reinforcers provided positive behavior changes in the mentally retarded individuals.

As the result of this demonstration, the teachers involved with these retarded individuals gained

49. Role Playing

additional tools to utilize in reaching the growing, developing individual. Both role playing and behavior modification are important in the teacher's curriculum, and as professionals we have achieved only a modicum of the potential possible in helping students teach each other.

REFERENCES

BOOKS

Bandura, Albert, and Walters, Richard A. *Social Learning and Personality Development.* New York: Holt, Rinehart & Winston, 1963.

Buchan, L. Gerald. *Role Playing and the Educable Mentally Retarded,* Belmont, California: Fearon Publishers, 1972.

Chesler, Mark, and Fox, Robert. *Roleplaying Methods in the Classroom.* Chicago: Science Research Associates, Inc., 1966.

Shaftel, F.R., and Shaftel, George. *Roleplaying for Social Values: Decision-Making in the Social Studies.* Englewood Cliffs, New Jersey: Practice-Hall Inc., 1967.

ARTICLES—BEHAVIOR MODIFICATION

Edwards, M., and Lilly, R.T. "Operant Conditions, An Application to Behavioral Problems in Groups." *Mental Retardation.* 4, No. 4 (1966): 18-20.

Skinner, B.F. "The Science of Learning and the Art of Teaching." *Cumulative Record.* New York: Appleton-Century-Crofts, Inc.

ARTICLES—ROLE PLAYING

Bryer, S.J., and Wagner, R. "The Didactic Value of Role Playing for Institutionalized Retardates." *Group Psychotherapy.* 16 (1963): 177-181.

Long, Wilma J. "An Exploratory Study of the Use of Roleplaying with Severely Retarded Children." *American Journal of Mental Deficiency.* 3 (1959): 784-791.

Pankratz, Loren D., and Buchan, Gerald. "Techniques of 'Warm-Up' in Psychodrama with the Retarded." *Mental Retardation.* (May 1966): 12-15.

WE WELCOME YOUR COMMENTS

Only through this communication can we produce high quality materials in the Special Education field.

Special Learning Corporation
42 Boston Post Rd. Guilford, Connecticut 06437

A New Life For The Retarded

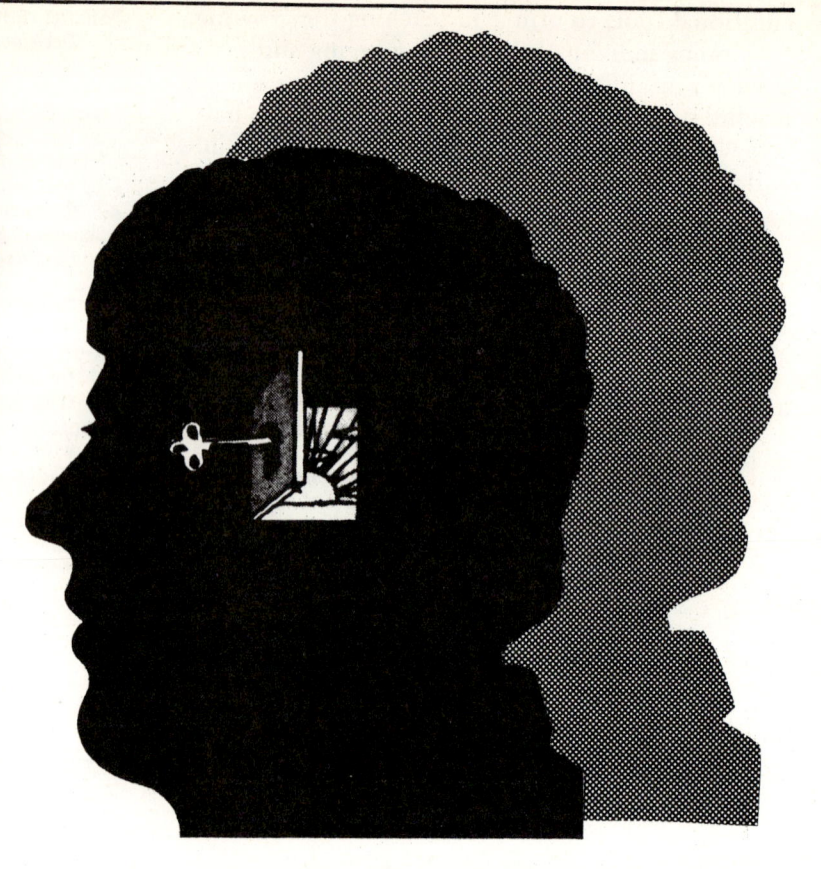

Susan Charnelle

A little less than a year ago, 21-year-old Paul was living in a Massachusetts home for the mentally retarded. Today he earns $2.45 an hour at a full-time job in a commercial laundry. He banks his money and shares an apartment with three other young men—also mentally retarded. With some help from a counselor, they shop for food, cook their own meals, keep their rooms cleaned up. If all goes well, in about six months Paul will be ready to go back home and live as a self-supporting member of his family. He will always need some help and care, but his family's worst fear—that he would have to live out his days in some grim state institution—will probably never come true. For Paul should be able to take care of himself with minimal assistance even after his parents are dead.

What intervened in Paul's life was an experimental project called Community Group, located in the Boston suburb of Wakefield, Massachusetts. The project trains moderately to mildly retarded young adults to live in the community and take care of themselves on whatever level they are able to function. Paul is one of 35 people living in ten apartments in downtown Wakefield. Seven chaperons live with them and help them to learn such important skills for survival as shopping, meal planning, housework and, more importantly, getting along with their peers and holding a job. Other apartments in the same buildings are inhabited by "normal" people.

To qualify for the community, participants have to be able to dress, wash and feed themselves and take care of other basic personal needs without assistance. Under their administrator, the former head of a school for the retarded, counselors try to cultivate a sense of self-respect and decency among the participants. No accomplishment is ever denigrated. All must take turns shopping, cooking and doing the laundry, so each learns reading, writing and arithmetic in a practical way.

In a central workshop both men and women get vocational training. As they gain skill, they may move on to jobs or school. One girl attends a public high school; 17 others—like Paul—hold simple factory and laundry jobs. Sometimes the step into the outside world doesn't work at first. One girl who held a job at a local electronics plant managed the work well but unaccountably broke into fits of crying. She will wait until she develops more self-confidence before she tries another job.

As a resident progresses, he can either return home to his parents or graduate to Community II—a cluster of four apartments where residents have their own keys and live more independently, even though they too are supervised by counselors. Two young people will go home this month, and by the end of the year several more will be ready to leave. Not everyone will be as financially self-sufficient as Paul. One girl will live with her parents and attend a day-care center in her community—an arrangement that will relieve them of constant supervision while giving her a life outside institutional walls.

The man behind this experiment is not a social worker but a dynamic businessman, David Slater, formerly president of Mr. Donut Corporation. Slater became interested in applying business-management techniques to social-welfare programs and wanted to try out his theory that moderately retarded adults could be taught to help sustain themselves—and lead happier lives in the process—at far less cost than it takes to institutionalize them. Modeling his project after work being done in Denmark, he started out by hiring a counselor and renting one apartment for two retarded adults, gradually adding apartments as the project succeeded. Parents pay $575 a month to maintain their children in the community. Slater would like to find a way to create an annuity plan that would pay the cost of a resident in case his parents die.

The experiment has been under way for a year and a half, and so far the rate of improvement has been nearly 100 percent. Only one resident had to be sent back to an institution. The rest, within their own limitations, are taking steps back into the community.

One Person Makes a Difference

Eunice Kennedy Shriver

FRANCIS BACON wrote, "In this theater of man's life, it is reserved only for God and for angels to be lookers-on."

This is still the best rationale for voluntarism I know. So much work remains to be done in this unfinished and imperfect world that none of us can justify standing on the sidelines. Especially in a society like ours, volunteering is an expression of democracy in its purest form. For the volunteer is a participant, not a looker-on, and participation *is* the democratic process.

In a world full of problems, it is tempting to ask, "What can one person do?"—and do nothing. But each of us can cure an ill, teach a child to play, to run, to read. Each of us can reveal to a child the beauty and wonder of nature. Each can reach out and touch another human being. Give something and receive something.

That is what volunteering is all about—you and another human being. It is about understanding another's needs. It is a commitment. It is acting—sometimes boldly, sometimes unconventionally, sometimes quietly—but acting.

For, as my brother Robert said, "In our country it is no longer enough to count the poor, to sympathize with the struggle for equality, to watch with sadness the decay of our urban life. We must *do* something to change the facts of our present life."

It is no accident that the sports and recreation programs sponsored by the Joseph P. Kennedy, Jr., Foundation are among the largest volunteer efforts of their kind in the world—over 150,000 in Special Olympics and 20,000 in the foundation's new Families Play to Grow program.

Without volunteer support, without willing hands and caring hearts, the mentally retarded would not be able to take part in those activities we have historically reserved for the "normal."

It requires volunteer participation almost on a one-to-one basis to organize and put on a Special Olympics meet. Volunteers must coach and train the young athletes, accompany them to the games, make certain they get to the starting line at the right time, cheer them on as they take part in their events, help organize and coach clinics and demonstrations, serve as timers and judges, present medals and ribbons, serve and supervise meals, chaperone dances and other social events, and just be there with their athletes throughout the games to lend a hand and speak an encouraging word.

The Fourth International Special Olympics Games held August 7-11, 1975, in Mount Pleasant, Michigan, produced a new kind of volunteer who played a most significant role in the success of the games. These were the "huggers"—hundreds of boys and girls, men and women, who stood at the end of every lane at every race and gave each athlete a warm, enthusiastic hug as he or she crossed the finish line.

You will not find this position listed on any table of organization, but the hugger is essential to the spirit of the Special Olympics, which places effort above win-

Ms. Shriver is executive vice-president of the Joseph P. Kennedy, Jr., Foundation and president, Special Olympics, Inc.

7. EMERGING DIRECTIONS

ning and caring above competition.

It used to be that the mentally retarded were shut away in huge, impersonal institutions where an overburdened staff herded them into barnlike dayrooms where they sat out their lives in empty isolation.

Now, thanks to volunteers, the mentally retarded are breaking out of this imprisonment. Thousands are returning to society, to halfway houses in their own communities where volunteers are helping them to get jobs, enjoy community facilities, take part in social and recreation activities.

Because of programs like Special Olympics, communities are opening their playgrounds, school yards, gymnasiums, and swimming pools to the physically handicapped and mentally retarded. And schools and institutions themselves are letting the world into their classrooms and back wards and bringing the retarded out into the world.

At Western Carolina Center, a marvelous state institution for the retarded in North Carolina, volunteers have organized horseback riding classes, camping, skiing, and outdoor recreation programs of all kinds for the retarded. There are even lovely cottages built in the pine woods surrounding the center, where parents, the most important volunteers of all, can spend weekends with their youngsters playing games with them and taking them on nature walks through the countryside.

At the Military Road School, a public school for the retarded in Washington, D.C., the absence of large playing fields has not been an obstacle to recreation for the children. Teachers, parents, and volunteers have taken advantage of nearby Rock Creek Park for horseback riding, nature walking, and outdoor games. They have used the Kennedy Foundation's Play to Grow program as the basis for these activities.

In Maine, Vermont, Utah, and many other states, winter Special Olympics are now held each year. Children who only got the chance to be outdoors on nice days, if at all, are now joyfully competing in snowball throwing contests, "flying saucer" slaloms, ice skating, and skiing. Volunteers make these opportunities possible.

Celebrity volunteer Sally Struthers salutes a Maryland Special Olympian.

Examples of volunteer activities in Special Olympics are legion. Great athletes like George Foreman, Muhammad Ali, Chris Evert, Arthur Ashe, Bart Starr, and Franco Harris are just a few of the devoted celebrities who work with the Special Olympians to improve their skills and are there with a handshake and a "well-done" when they have run their race or played their game. All the team members and coaches of the National Basketball Association, the American Basketball Association, and the National Hockey League are involved in an international program which supports the basketball and floor hockey activities of the Special Olympics. Olympic medalists Rafer Johnson, Bill Toomey, Mark Spitz, Lillian Watson, and Diane Holum are volunteer members of one of the most impressive coaching staffs in the world. And they do not just talk voluntarism. They have put in thousands of hours and traveled thousands of miles to let Special Olympians everywhere know that they are admired and respected by the world's finest athletes.

On a different level, high school students all over America are taking part in the "Train-A-Champ" program through which Special Olympians are coached in sports events on a year-round basis. How many parents have heard their teenagers complain, "There is nothing to do?" There is always something to do—a hundred outlets in every community for the energies and dedication of our youth.

Special Olympics provides a challenging opportunity for youngsters who have been blessed with gifts of normal intelligence and physical capacity to enrich the lives of boys and girls, much like themselves, who have been less fortunate than they. They will find almost immediately that the handicapped have great gifts to bestow on them in return—gifts of love and loyalty, gifts of improved skills and growing self-esteem.

As President Kennedy so often said, "Oh, the difference one person can make."

Although 400,000 mentally retarded youth are already taking part in the Special Olympics, more than 1 million are still standing on the sidelines. Volunteers everywhere, young and old, are needed to bring them onto the playing field, to give them a chance to expand their abilities and explore the unknown limits of their potential.

51. One Person

Eight years ago, there were no volunteers in Special Olympics and very few volunteers anywhere bringing sports and recreation to the retarded. Now, more than 150,000 are joined together in a great movement that started simply because, one by one, human beings cared for other human beings. And that is all it takes—especially to bring the blessings of the outdoors and the benefits of recreation to the handicapped. You do not have to leave your own block or your own community. You do not need to involve large groups of people or organize a complicated bureaucracy. All you have to do is *do* somethings.

And in the doing, you will have started a great movement—"harnessing for God," as the philosopher said, "the energies of love."

Huggers greet Special Olympics runners.

PSYCHOLOGY OF EXCEPTIONAL CHILDREN

Designed for the introductory courses of study in special education, this book provides an overview of the exceptional child. The social, emotional, linguistic and cognitive development of handicapped children are looked at, along with a special section dealing with support systems for the exceptional child, specifically family relationships.

For more information about this book and other materials in special education, contact Joseph Logan,

Special Learning Corporation
42 Boston Post Rd. Guilford, Connecticut 06437 (203) 453-6525

Sex Education of The Mentally Retarded Child in The Home

Evalyn S. Gendel, M.D.

Evalyn S. Gendel, M.D., *Chief, School Health Section, Division of Maternal and Child Health, Kansas State Department of Health, Topeka, Kansas 66612*

Education About Sexuality—A Concept of Sex Education

The growth and development of a human being is a non-computerized phenomena of life. The great and never-ceasing wonder to me is that the intricacies of cellular maturation, of genetic codes of DNA and RNA, of the physical and human environment do not go awry more often. The programming of every individual, through time, follows certain patterns but is never exactly the same for any two people—normal or otherwise. When the blueprint or program is disrupted either genetically or by the environment, only certain elements are altered and growth, in general, continues to follow these basic patterns.

There are numerous causes and degrees of mental retardation which are related to these disruptions, but the developmental phases from infancy to maturity follow the over-all principles. Physical, emotional, mental and social growth inevitably take place—more limited in some children depending on the etiology and extent of their mental retardation.

The sexual component of this growth and development is so closely interwoven with the other segments that they cannot be separated. Yet, it is this sexual component which is so frequently ignored, or when recognized, is treated in such a distorted manner that it becomes unbalanced in its direction.

I make these observations because they are a key to a concept of sex education which I will be using in this discussion: which is—that sex education is more descriptively termed education *about* human sexuality—that it defines sex as something we are—not something we do and that it is a process of learning about being male and female, about the totality of being human. It is intimately tied to self-understanding based on recognition of one's own growth and development from childhood through later life.

Many existing home and school programs for the general population equate sex education with sex instruction, and focus their attention on reproductive and genital anatomical facts, usually beamed to junior high school age children who describe the programs as too little, too late and too shallow to be meaningful.[1] A similar situation also exists in a number of the institutional and school programs on sex education for the mentally retarded. These may be even more superficial, stressing exclusively social behavior, dating and boy/girl relationships; suddenly initiated at adolescence.[2] Although these are important skills and should be taught, by themselves and at the age at which they are introduced—they may be distressing and confusing for the child. Concerns about the quality of sex education in these settings are pertinent to the concerns in the home.

Motivation for sex education of the retarded (or any children) should be carefully evaluated, whether for home or school, or institution. It can determine also, the quality and tone of the education provided.

Where the motivation is directed toward controlling sexual behavior by fear of venereal disease, pregnancy or other consequences—the tone will be punitive. The attitudes which are developed are often ones of deceit and disrespect for self.

If the motivation is to develop a panacea for socio-sexual ills, those programs too, will be restricted in their scope. Rather than encompassing the broad concept of maleness and femaleness, the concentration is on specific problems of the *sex act* and demeans sexuality as wholly instinctual. Even when the concept is more expanded the expectations are unrealistic and misleading.

Instead, we can seek motivations which stem from a belief in the learning process as essential to life—that all human beings have the urge to know about themselves and

Sex Education of the Mentally Retarded Child in the Home, Evalyn S. Gendel, M.D., (booklet). ©National Association for Retarded Citizens, Arlington, Texas.

52. Sex Education

about the world around them. One's own sexuality is a segment of that learning which deserves the same attention as any other area. It encompasses the provision of material self learning which will later determine the retarded adult's ability to discuss sterilization where indicated or desired, as a means of strengthening his marriage or increasing his own potential to work or study without the added responsibility of parenthood *and* marriage. Or to limit the number of children where one would be accommodated but several might be overwhelming. Parents, too can be more open when their deliberations with the young adult are based upon a known foundation of prior understanding by the child of his worth as a person with the same sexual needs and aspirations as others in the society.

Those who oppose education about sexuality also have a motivation which grows out of the belief that knowledge in this area causes experimentation and stimulation of sex impulses. The scientific method tells us that the reverse is true—that the more information and dialogue on a subject, the less is the experimentation and "glamor" or daring associated with it.

Education about sexuality for all children begins when the new infant enters the family. The manner in which he is received, the affectional climate in which he is cared for; these factors influence his own self-concept and may determine the character of his future interpersonal relationships. Parents need to know that this atmosphere is in itself the beginning of their child's sex education. The principle is no different for parents of retarded children—but their own early adjustments to the impact of retardation make it a more difficult realization.

Parents should be advised that verbal and non-verbal communications are equally important and that this involves, for them, an evaluation of their feelings and attitudes about their own sexuality. Whatever their family habits are in regard to such things as privacy, the states of dress or undress, they should not be radically changed because of the presence of a retarded child. If the normal activity around the house is relaxed in these matters they should continue to be so—if they are somewhat more restricted, they should not become increasingly so. Where there is great inhibition and fear in questions of sex, frank discussion should be encouraged to help prepare parents for facing sexual issues between themselves and for their effect on children.

They should be helped to recognize that the retarded child does not need overprotection *or* overexposure to the sexual implications of family life—but that a natural acceptance of sexuality as one part of the totality of the individual is a reasonable goal for themselves and for the child. Just as parents are hopefully receiving anticipatory guidance on intellectual, social and physical growth expectations for their child—they should know what to expect in related early and ongoing sexual development. They should be acquainted with the variations in physical development among children in general. The mildly retarded, depending on etiology, probably approximates the most normal, chronological developmental pattern, and sexual maturation and its concomitant interests and physiological changes will follow. These are also the children most likely to be kept at home, to enter community school special classes, to progress to job training and to marry.[3]

There Is No Single Formula

For children in the trainable or the severely retarded categories, the same guidelines apply for the period they remain with the family. More of these children move on to institutionalization and their sex education will be discussed in another paper. Although their problems are different: they mature biologically much more slowly for instance, according to the severity of their retardation, their levels of comprehension also decreasing with severity; but the fundamental approach to their sex education is the same. Regardless, then, of the degree of retardation, whether they remain with the family or are institutionalized; parents and helping personnel need to know the expected patterns of the child's physical and mental development—that a range of differences may occur from a toddler crawling several months later than normal in mild retardation, to a child with a congenital brain anomaly, with extreme retardation where he never leaves the prone position and is tube fed and totally cared for.

Even though the group we will discuss is primarily at the less extreme end of the range of mental retardation, these background factors are essential to parents in education about sexuality. They emphasize that there is no single formula which will be fitting for each type of child at a particular age and time. Certain suggestions can be helpful and apply to a wide spectrum of individual differences of children. They include:

1. The idea that love and affection nurture a sense of self-worth for the child and enhance his life experience at whatever level it occurs.

2. The concept of responding to a child's curiosity and questions about sex to be answered at any age. Parents should not evade or dismiss them but should answer directly and honestly. When the parent truly does not know the answer he should let the child know it and proceed to find the information he needs and share it.[4] Concise, brief answers are the most meaningful, and will have to be repeated many, many times. The main point to stress is that learning about sexuality is a part of the general learning process, no matter how slowly it may progress or how poorly it seems to be comprehended. Granting the child the dignity of receiving an answer to his query helps to create a healthy attitude—whereas discomfort and evasion by the parents is interpreted by the child as rejection of himself as a person. It also places a special connotation on sexuality associated with the rejection.

3. Parents must also feel free to initiate discussion on sexuality whether or not questions are ever asked. Having acquainted themselves with expected developmental tasks they can make use of discussion of neighborhood and family pregnancies or other events as they occur, to bring about the dialogue they wish to elicit. Animal families are not as good for discussion as the retarded child has limited capacities in relating one subject to another—or in interpreting concepts from one area to another.

4. A knowledge of sex-related behaviors such as masturbation, which may begin for the younger 4-6 year old as a pleasurable exploration of the genitals along with other body areas represents one example of the confrontation parents must experience.

They need to know that this activity is normal and

7. EMERGING DIRECTIONS

not limited to mentally retarded children. That it cannot harm the child physically or mentally. When practiced to an excess of total preoccupation for most waking hours, it is a symptom of anxiety and other problems—it is not a problem per se. Ordinarily as children grow, their interests broaden, and they may not experience this intense urge to self-manipulation for release and pleasure until puberty and thereafter. As their socialization with peers and with adults outside of the family expands, they can be taught that masturbation, like toilet needs must be taken care of in private. Most retarded children who are adapting to the culture, recognize, for instance, that it is not acceptable for them to urinate in public. The same kind of learning or training can be acquired concerning masturbation. Parents of both normal and retarded children are asked to follow the most difficult advice which can be given—to ignore the masturbatory activity, to overcome their own reactions of fear, or shame, and to resist punishing or threatening their children, or "falling apart" themselves.

5. Earlier reference was made to keeping the family patterns of modesty, privacy and/or openness about sex, or about states of dress, or bathroom habits unaltered in any radical way. Only where excessive over stimulation or frightening restriction are the family styles should parents be counselled toward changes.

6. Creating a feeling of trust of the child's abilities as they manifest themselves is critical to his concept of being male or female.

7. Listening to his concerns about family roles, to the impressions he has received about sex from other children is an important part of the parents' support. Much of the peer-group gossip will have little meaning for the mentally retarded child but the manner in which the other children relate it, the vulgarized responses often displayed by them, will influence his impressions of sexuality. He cannot be shielded from these contacts as they are the experience of living—but parents' sensitivity and anticipatory explanations are helpful in maintaining respect for the human body and its functions, and for people as individuals.

8. Parents also cannot isolate the child from the mass media sex messages of our time. Rather than bemoan their influences—especially since we do not know their effect, we must accept them as the "real world" and assist the child in strengthening his positive responses to the sexual scene.[5]

9. At puberty the tasks which are universal to all children must also be met by the retarded adolescent—assuming independence, identifying self, choosing a vocation and maturing sexually. Parents of normal and retarded children are equally concerned about this period. The mentally retarded child must have information and understanding of these changes to whatever degree he can absorb them. This is why simple information on body characteristics in a context of appreciation of self must be given as early as 4 or 5 years of age chronologically, to strengthen the child's self-concept.

Material presented objectively and in the early years of healthy curiosity, can help to stabilize the social and emotional factors later. The adolescent boy hears about sexual intercourse, and experiences his own nocturnal emissions and penile erections. The more prepared he is for the impact of these happenings the better he will cope with his own feelings. For girls, the circumstance of menstruation is so concrete that there is no hesitation in informing and training them for this event—but even here we often wait too long and we narrow the idea to the mechanics of the menstrual cycle. A sequential pattern of repetition and reinforcement is needed which will provide a foundation for both boys and girls upon which future discussions of social behavior, dating, marriage and family planning can take place.

10. We are all familiar with the case of a child who has been living at home and has become accepted in the neighborhood and by friends for a number of years. At sexual maturity and the teen years he is suddenly looked upon by a previously accepting group as a less desirable associate because they suddenly recognize that the slow, pleasant child is now a sexual person whose judgement and impulses are limited. Their fears may not be justified but the child should be helped to understand the possibility of community reaction. He should learn that his sexual feelings are part of his makeup as an individual, and that everyone has them—they are not to be feared or characterized by shame or guilt, but to be understood to the degree possible.

11. In the post adolescent years, parents who have tried to expand the knowledge of sexuality for themselves and their child are in a position to help them make the life decisions which lie in the future. Depending on the condition of retardation—but certainly in the mild cases—many retarded wish to consider marriage.[6] They need all of the background and experience which they can handle to reach the most realistic and happy conclusions. The comfort and communication of marriage enhance the lives of many couples. Even the most successful adjustments, however, cannot tolerate the extra burden of children to care for. They need opportunities to be advised on contraception and sterilization. These decisions affect job aspirations, possibilities for independence from the family and for the further growth of potential as an individual.

For the subnormal adult, in the few studies which are available, marriage is common.

Promiscuity and prostitution were slightly more frequent in the mildly mentally retarded, 6%, to 3% in a control group of normals. The frequency of pregnancy out of wedlock was 7% for this group compared to 1% in the normal controls.[4,7]

What Parents? What Children?

The generalized suggestions just reviewed pertain primarily to mild retardation and to normally intelligent, accepting families who are completely aware of their own adjustments, accepting of their child's limitations, and willing to seek counsel and guidance.

Many parents of retarded children are not this way—as with the normal population, they *may* be caring or they may be indifferent, neglectful, abusive or retarded themselves with limited capabilities. Since sex education in the home is difficult at best for most parents—then the efforts we make as teachers, nurses, physicians, ministers, or counsellors must be highly individualized for each family.

Recognizing that most causes of mental retardation are not known, that over 65%, in some classifications,[8,9,10] are considered to be environmental and socio-cultural in origin with only scarce evidence of a genetic factor—we know we are dealing with different elements and potential within each category of retardation. Our advice on genetic counselling, family planning, sterilization, and sexual development will shift as better diagnoses are made. The expectations for a child with Mongolism and one who is retarded due to post measles encephalitis *may* be different—but the advice on marriage will most certainly differ since genetic factors will not be a consideration in the encephalitic condition.

The same would be true in mild brain damage caused by poor obstetrical management. The variations are as unlimited as are the prenatal factors, the damaging diseases and intoxicants in the perinatal period, the disrupted genetic combinations, trauma at birth and delivery, disorders of metabolism and nutrition, tumors and other growths, congenital defects, and the deprivations of infancy—maternal, cultural and economic.

In other words, the bulk of mild and moderate retarded who marry will not have retarded children. The problem is not marriage, but whether or not there should be children—for though they are not retarded at birth, their chances for normal intellectual development may be hampered by the atmosphere of the environment. In a recent study in Kansas at the Kansas Neurological Institute, out of 153 girls who had left the institution over a three year period and returned to work in the community, sixteen were married, 130 were single and seven had been divorced at the time they came to the institution.

In working with the girls age 13 - 18 in residence in the same institution, we were in the midst of a discussion about human reproduction. The girls had requested some informational sessions and a film strip which could be stopped and held for narrative by the teacher had been shown. The girls were all at varying levels of development into mature women—one or two had been pregnant and given up their babies. Questions were on specifics of anatomy, how much love does a baby need from mother and father, questions about nursing and many observations such as, "If my folks had loved me more, I might have been smarter."—or "I gave up my baby cause I was too dumb to raise him." Although these girls had learned much about themselves and these thoughts had meaning for them, they were very critical of some of the educational material which made many references to animals as well as humans, and which these girls thought was confusing. Second and third meetings with them indicated that as with younger children, questions were repeated—and answers reexamined over and over again. The simpler the explanations and the more tied to the incidents and insights of the girls, the better remembered.

The comments from these girls, who had come far in their own sexual comprehension and the majority of whom had been abandoned by their homes, illustrate to me the very hopeful aspect for development of responsible understanding of human sexuality that could be possible with the added education in the home.

If parents seek the resouces of compassionate medical, psychological, educational, public health and welfare services, the combination of their efforts with the schools and day care institutions can contribute constructively to the conservation of human potential. These hopes are dependent, however on close communications and exchange among the disciplines involved. Often the human barrier between professionals themselves obstructs the full development of what is possible. Each of us needs to learn the words to the same theme song—which might be "Call Me"—but, then, that is the subject of another discussion.

REFERENCES

1. Gendel, Evalyn S., "Sex Education Patterns and Professional Responsibility," Southern Medical Journal, Volume 59, #4, April, 1966, p.p. 411 - 16
2. Gendel, Evalyn S., "Education About Sexuality For Retarded Children," TRACKS, Volume XI, #2, October, 1966
3. Peck, J. R., Stephens, Will Beth, "Marriage of Young Adult Male Retardates," American Journal of Mental Deficiency, Volume 69, #6, May, 1965, p.p. 812-827
4. Gendel, Evalyn S., "Parents Are Human Beings," Journal Of The American Medical Women's Association, February, 1968
5. Gendel, Evalyn S., "Sex Education Is Character Education," Kansas Teacher, March, 1968, p.p. 23 - 28
6. Bass, Medora Steedman, "Marriage, Parenthood and Prevention of Pregnancy," American Journal of Mental Deficiency, Volume 68, #3, November, 1963, p.p. 318-331
7 & 8 Harper, Paul A., *Preventive Pediatrics*, Appleton, Century-Crofts, 1962, p.p. 486 - 518
9. "A Manual On Terminology And Classification On Mental Retardation"—Monograph Supplement to the American Journal of Mental Deficiency, second edition, 1961
10. Mental Retardation—A Family Crisis—The Therapeutic Role of the Physician, Report #56, Group for the Advancement of Psychiatry, 1963

HOW RETARDED CHILDREN CAN BE HELPED

EVELYN HART

Evelyn Hart, author of the Public Affairs Pamphlet Making the Most of Your Years, *was formerly woman's editor of the Dayton, Ohio Daily News . . . The illustrations are by Elizabeth D. Logan.*

She was not prepared for the doctor's verdict. There has never been a parent prepared for hearing a doctor say: "I'm genuinely sorry, but there's no way to tell you gently. Your child is mentally retarded."

The black despair that rolls over the mind, the cold fear that numbs the heart are thoroughly understood only by a parent who has heard those cruel words crashing down the years, destroying all the carefully made plans, all the dreams of happiness. She had known for a long time, as most parents know, that her child was not like other children, yet she had kept hoping.

How would she tell her husband? Whose fault was it? His? Hers? What a shameful thing! Of all the children in the neighborhood—why hers? She could never let those other mothers know . . . she'd persuade her husband to move away, out of the neighborhood, out of the city, some place where no one would find out. They'd put the child in an institution . . . but, how could she give him up? He belonged to them! What had gone wrong? Was it something she did — or didn't do — during pregnancy that had brought this on?

Anything that damages the lives of 5 million residents of these United States is a thing to be reckoned with. Studies have revealed that approximately thirty out of every 1,000 persons are mentally retarded, a truth that in our democracy cannot be casually brushed under the rug. As a matter of fact, during the past twenty years, the rug has been removed, the strong, warm light of scientific and public interest and concern has been played on all phases of this problem.

parents no longer alone with problem

Thirty, even twenty, years ago parents of retarded children were often isolated by their misfortune. Today, these parents find tremendous comfort in the knowledge that they are not alone, that many other parents are facing and coping with the same problems and that, in many areas, they can work with other parents toward making a better world for their handicapped youngsters. What a relief to be able to talk about one's frustrations, worries and problems with those who have had similar experiences and thoroughly understand one's reactions.

This is not to say that the serious problems attendant on mental retardation have been solved, nor that parents today who are told that their child is mentally retarded can dismiss this knowledge with a shrug or can rely on some strange kind of magic to erase the heartbreak.

It *is* to say, however, that we are entering a period of higher hope and more substantial, practical help than has ever existed for the retarded and their families. It is to say, with certainty, that no parent need be tortured by feelings of guilt. Scientific research has found many causes over which parents have no control. No parent need be ashamed of having produced a mentally retarded child, for studies reveal that mentally retarded children are the product of families rich or poor, families socially prominent or obscure, families highly educated or illiterate, families of any and all races and religions.

children can be helped

A national movement on behalf of the retarded child has adopted the slogan, "Retarded Children Can Be Helped." This statement of fact is the password that is already opening doors down the corridor of the future leading to undreamed-of-possibilities for the retarded. It is indeed heartening to hear Dr. Howard A. Rusk, noted pioneer in rehabilitation, declare that "retarded children resemble normal children more than they differ from them."

As we said above, about thirty children out of every 1,000 are retarded. Authorities report that at least twenty-five of the thirty can be educated, can be taught the basic skills of reading, writing and arithmetic, can learn to manage their own affairs. Four more of every thirty retarded children can be trained to do simple tasks under supervision and will, as adults, be only semidependent. Only one is so seriously retarded that he requires nursing attention, preferably in an institution. This is a much

53. Retarded Children

more hopeful picture than was believed possible a few generations ago.

retardation in history

A quick glance backward shows mankind achieving great victories over nature, ferreting out secrets deeply hidden in the universe he inhabits. Yet, over the ages, he has been reluctant to investigate the dark corners of the human brain and, in his perplexity, has accepted outrageous interpretations of the things he did not understand. In ancient Greece, while the great minds of Plato and Socrates were formulating basic concepts of a new and enduring philosophy, any of their countrymen who were mentally retarded were abandoned and left to die. For many centuries, the mentally deficient were considered incapable of human feeling, were neglected, ostracized, persecuted. During the Middle Ages, public opinion swung far in the opposite direction and these unfortunate human beings were regarded as sacred creatures meriting reverence and even worship. In some areas, they were court fools and jesters, earning the protection and patronage of royalty.

modern developments

Not until the beginning of the 19th century was anything resembling an educational and medical approach made to this problem. Through long-range experimental methods, Dr. Jean Itard of France who had worked with the deaf and dumb and with the insane, proved beyond any doubt that the mentally retarded were capable of some degree of education. His work influenced other educators and medical scientists in Europe and America and the study of mental retardation in an objective, practical, scientific manner was on its way. In this country, the record shows that the period 1850-1900 gave rise to the development of institutions for care of the mentally retarded; the next half-century, 1900-1950, saw the development of intelligence and personality tests and establishment of special classes for the retarded in public schools; the period beginning in 1950 is marked already by an increasing emphasis on research and rapid expansion of community resources.

myths still exist

We like to think that we have at last overcome the superstition and ignorance which marked our treatment of the retarded. But have we really?

Let's ask Mrs. Davis who is struggling valiantly to help her retarded child adjust to a complex world he did not devise and cannot control. What about your friend next door, Mrs. Davis — the one who told you angrily yesterday after Tommy pulled up two of your freshly planted marigolds, "What that child needs is a good spanking!"

And the neighbor across the street who saw Tommy hit a boy who was teasing him . . . what was it she said? "You'd better put that child in an institution before he kills somebody!" Strange . . . the neighbors never said those things about Ronald, your other son, and he was forever getting into fights.

Then there's Mrs. Adams in the next block. You know, of course, what she thinks of Tommy, Mrs. Davis. How could you not know? Whenever she sees the child, she grabs her Marilyn and runs into the house. She has told everyone who would listen that she'd think you'd do something about Tommy— "anyone can see he's a sex delinquent — that kind always is!"

Be patient, Mrs. Davis. We are living in an age of enlightenment, but it has not yet filtered down to your neighborhood . . . to so many neighborhoods. Perhaps you, Mrs. Davis, can help to correct the misconception of your neighbors who are nearly as emotional and uninformed as were the people of the Middle Ages, and with far less excuse.

information vital

Dislodging firmly rooted, traditional beliefs fed and watered by emotion and fattened by popular acceptance is not an easy task. Nor is it quickly achieved. Yet, it must be done. The mentally retarded can learn to function within their limitations and to the fullest extent of their capacities only in a climate of understanding and acceptance. Many of the problems faced by Mrs. Davis and Tommy would be far easier to handle wisely with the help of informed and sympathetic neighbors. It is difficult indeed for a parent to be patient when she sees the welfare of her own child threatened by outmoded superstitions. This is one more situation proving the fallacy of "what you don't know can't hurt you" — it can and does hurt untold numbers of people.

One mother, after receiving the doctor's diagnosis that her four-year-old had been brain-damaged and was mentally retarded, spent the next two years frantically searching out information about retardation, working long hours with the parents' group in her community to enlist support for research and for services designed to help the retarded. Later, she wrote, "Part of my feverish activity (during that period) came because I was angry. I was getting at the facts and I was angry. Indignant. Indignant toward a crude, uncultured, ignorant, arrogant society that had caused my family and other families to suffer unwarranted stigma, shame, fear and cruelty. Right here in our own U.S.A. I guess I was indignant at just about everybody . . . (But) you can't be mad at people when they don't understand and particularly when no one has bothered to tell them. My role became very clear. 'The man who knows must tell!' So, I started really trying to learn how to tell it at all levels."

FACTS ABOUT THE RETARDED

It must be told and retold. It must be stated again and again that:

1. *Most mentally retarded need not be confined in institutions*
2. *They have no more criminal tendencies than the rest of us, probably less*
3. *They are not predetermined sex delinquents*
4. *They can be trained and educated*

The opposite views are now properly tagged as old wives' tales. Experience and careful study have disproved these traditional assumptions and they must be discarded before the problems of the retarded can be viewed with any degree of objectivity.

7. EMERGING DIRECTIONS

One authority has observed that "to no other form of human inadequacy have so many social blights been attributed — crime, delinquency, degeneracy, poverty, vagrancy, immorality . . ." He follows with the statement that today the retarded are looked on less as liabilities and more as potential assets, calling on society not for control but for skilled help.

role of institutions

Some institutional training may be valuable, it is true, for many of the retarded. And there are a few who cannot be taught to function without constant supervision. But the latter constitute a very small percentage of the retarded. It was found early in this century, through experiments prompted by necessity, that the less severely retarded fared far better outside of institutions, provided proper controls were set up and adequate supervision was available and effective educational opportunities existed. With the development of institutions for mental defectives toward the end of the 19th century, most people assumed that this was the answer to a bothersome and serious social problem. However, those working in the field soon became aware that institutional care could not serve as the answer to this problem because there could not possibly be constructed and maintained throughout the country enough institutions to accommodate all of the retarded who would benefit by institutional training.

It became necessary for those charged with responsibility for the care of mentally retarded to cast about for other methods of dealing with the problem. Interestingly enough, the search for substitute ways of caring for the retarded gave rise in the early 1900's to establishment of farm "colonies" where residents enjoyed a greater degree of freedom and received more realistic and practical preparation for return to the community. The value of this type of approach was quickly recognized and the idea was put into practice in many areas. Industrial colonies were set up in some towns where patients could be employed in certain kinds of factory jobs. At this time, too, public school systems were persuaded to include in their curriculum special classes for the mentally retarded. Family care, similar to foster care for other kinds of dependent persons, was tried successfully and still serves as a vital part of the network of services for the mentally retarded.

most retarded adjust satisfactorily

A recent study made in New York City of former pupils in special classes for the severely retarded in the public schools discloses some surprising facts relevant to the potentialities of even the severely retarded for adjustment to family, neighborhood and community life. The study was based on a sample of 520 cases, a cross-section of about 2,600 cases. All had I. Q.'s between 40 and 50, and family backgrounds representative of the population of New York City. The individuals studied ranged in age from 17 to 40 and their attendance in special classes varied from less than three years to more than six years. It was found that 66 per cent or 343 of the former pupils studied were still living at home and that 43 per cent of that number were getting along quite well with their families and, according to their parents, had no major personality difficulties. One-third of the group living at home could venture outside their own neighborhoods, taking buses and subways by themselves, asking directions if they got lost. They had, of course, far more freedom than they might have enjoyed in an institution and they handled it surprisingly well.

This follow-up study did much to bring the picture into sharp focus, to correct the misconceptions listed earlier. It underscored the fact that the adjustment of a mentally retarded individual depends not so much on degree of retardation as on the devotion of parents, the understanding of neighbors, the acceptance of the community. A study of the retarded in any given community serves as a reliable index to family cohesion and solidarity, to community attitudes in that area. It is, in a sense, an accurate measure of a community's social conscience.

no criminal tendencies

To those who believe that the retarded have criminal tendencies, it will come as something of a shock to learn that of the group of former pupils of special classes living in the community at the time the New York study was made (1957), only 11 per cent had gotten themselves into any kind of trouble, only 7 per cent had been involved in or created problems that might have been of concern to the neighborhood, and a still smaller percentage were involved in criminal activities. The percentages were much smaller than those of normal children who got into trouble in the same neighborhoods.

Authorities agree that, ordinarily, the retarded do not initiate; they are led by others. The severely retarded rarely get into trouble. True, the majority of retarded are easily led. But if they are led into criminal behavior, then chances are that the criminal intent may be found in the leader.

little interest in opposite sex

As for sex delinquency, the record shows that as mental retardation increases in severity, there is marked reduction in interest in the opposite sex and in sexual activity. The New York study shows that only one out of four of the severely retarded group had friends of the opposite sex and it was estimated that only 4 per cent of the sample had ever had sex relations.

can be trained

Follow-up studies of educable children tagged all through their school years as mentally retarded reveal that, on leaving school after age 16, many of these individuals adjusted to life in the community, obtained employment and supported themselves, and were no longer reported as retarded. In one county in New York state, one out of every four children referred to an agency for suspected mental retardation was found later to have an I. Q. of 90 or more, well within the range of normal or average intelligence.

Evidence is piling up to suggest that we still have a lot to learn about measuring native intelligence. Perhaps you're thinking, "What difference does it make, if the end results are the same? What does it matter whether the cause is physical, cultural, emotional or social?" It matters a great deal. It is a vital factor in determining treatment for the individual child, perhaps in effecting basic changes in our public school systems, and in re-directing public attitudes. The whole field of psychological testing is itself relatively new, techniques and procedures are being constantly revised and improved, and chances are that one day the present-day tests will be replaced by other tests which will be more definitive and reliable.

However, until that day arrives, it must be noted again that the retarded, unless so severely handicapped that they cannot take care of their own bodily needs, can usually be trained to live comfortably in our society, to hold employment and to lead reasonably normal lives. The degree of adjustment attained by the retarded depends chiefly on other people — on his parents and other members of his family, on the neighbors, on his employer and fellow workers, and on the community at large.

COMMUNITY SERVICES VITAL

Meanwhile, this is a situation where we cannot serve if we only stand and wait. Of the estimated 5 million retarded persons in this country, many need the kind of help that can be provided only through the close cooperation of individuals and groups and various public and private agencies.

After completing his education or training, the retarded must have a place to live and a place to work before he can find his place in the community. Usually this will be his own home. But for some this is impossible. In some instances, a job may be found near an institution and he will remain there until he is ready for discharge. In other instances, a home as well as a job must be found where he will have proper supervision.

family care program

The development of an organized program of family care has shown that it is neither necessary nor desirable for the majority of retarded persons to spend their lives behind institution walls. In communities across the country there has been increasing recognition of retardation as a community problem and of the need to provide a variety of services and facilities in the fields of health, education, recreation and counseling. Development of community services is especially important because institutions for the retarded still have long waiting lists.

The services available in most communities are still far from adequate, but the prospects for improvement are bright. There are too few clinics, for example, but the number is growing. Many child guidance clinics refuse to accept retarded children even for diagnosis, and of those that do accept them too many provide diagnosis only. There is urgent need for clinics that offer therapy for personality disorders, speech defects and other accompanying physical handicaps as well as professional guidance for parents.

clinics and training centers

In the entire country there are only some 70 clinics that specialize in help for the retarded. But a number of states have set aside substantial funds for clinical services tailored to meet all the needs of the retarded.

In some states, community care for the retarded is promoted and coordinated by the state department of mental health or some other appropriate department. There is no uniformity in state operations, as each state has set up its own pattern. In New Jersey, for instance, a Bureau of Mental Deficiency in the Department of Institutions and Agencies is used by workers in all parts of the state as a clearing house for information about the mentally retarded, and their proper care and treatment.

In New York, a bill was passed recently to establish a community center in the western part of the state to provide services for retarded adults and all retarded children who are neither institutionalized nor attending public school classes. The plan calls for day training centers, recreation, sheltered workshops and vocational counseling for adults, guidance for parents and a residential halfway house for those entering or leaving an institution. There will be the closest cooperation with the public schools and other public and private agencies concerned with problems of retardation.

Minnesota has worked out a rather complicated but very flexible and comprehensive system whereby the state controls admissions to institutions, classifies applications and establishes a waiting list according to needs. In Minnesota, primary responsibility for service rests on agencies in the community where most of the mentally retarded actually live, and welfare agencies give service to the retarded as part of general casework without singling them out as a separate group.

The quantity and quality of services for the retarded vary from state to state and from community to community. One area may have a broad program of excellent services available, including up-to-date diagnostic clinics with all supporting services, recreation programs especially designed for the retarded, vocational guidance and placement, visiting teachers, special classes in the schools and all the rest — while another area, not far away, hasn't even a decent clinic where parents can take a child for examination.

One might expect that more and better services would be available where the need is greatest, but this is not necessarily so. Services have been established where concern for the welfare of the retarded is greatest, where the demand is loudest, where community leaders or educators or medical authorities feel a keen responsibility for the well-being of this segment of our population. There are large and serious gaps that must be filled, and this requires long-range, coordinated planning.

role of parent groups

There are nearly a thousand local groups abroad in the land, whose members not only believe this will happen but are working hard to make it happen. They know what can be achieved for their retarded youngsters through the combined efforts of federal, state and community agencies . . . and their voices are being heard. They know the value of home teaching services to reach parents who cannot cope, on their own, with the problem of training their retarded child. In a Pennsylvania county, a parents' group appealed to the local Visiting Nurse Association to provide regular home visits for the retarded in that area and the group agreed to pay for each visit. The nurses performed such services as informing parents of local resources available, helping them to accept the child's limitations, instructing them in training techniques, arranging for mental and physical examinations and follow-up treatments for the child. The arrangement worked out so well that the pattern was soon followed in other areas in the state.

In some states, social workers make regular visits to the homes of retarded children to help with training and to plan basic educational programs with the parents. In other states, teachers do the home visiting. This service is extremely helpful in strengthening the morale of the mother who feels isolated by her child's condition. Another advantage is that it reaches a group for whom almost nothing has been done in the past — the retarded youngster in a good home who is perhaps too handicapped for acceptance in school, but does not need institutional care. Every community should manage, somehow, to make home visiting available, for it is an extremely valuable service.

7. EMERGING DIRECTIONS

recreational facilities

Parents groups, which will be more closely examined in later pages, have been responsible also for much of the increase in recreational facilities for the retarded over the past five years. Recreation programs, especially tailored for the retarded by public recreation agencies, have at least trebled since 1954. These programs include such activities as day camps, summer playgrounds, indoor activities, swimming, crafts and dancing. Boy Scouts and Girl Scouts have given serious thought to the needs of handicapped children and have extended their organized activities to include retarded boys and girls. In some instances, retarded youngsters have been assimilated into an established troop and have participated in the regular routine, but, in other situations, retarded children comprise the entire troop and, under the supervision of a well-trained adult leader, they engage in recreational activities especially designed for them. The disadvantages of this kind of segregation are outweighed by the enormous benefits of recreation in which the retarded does not have to compete with the normal child — recreation which is meaningful to him and which gives him genuine satisfaction.

You will find playgrounds here and there — not many, it's true — where special facilities are provided for the retarded, just as in some areas provision is made for the aged. Recreation is not a matter of finding the least common denominator and making it the basis of an overall program. If recreation is to be beneficial, it must be carefully tailored for specific groups. Recreation for the retarded carries great promise, offers unexplored possibilties. Little has been done in this relatively new field. Hopefully, the decade ahead will bring forth a harvest of sound, practical developments.

Perhaps all this talk of planned recreation strikes you as nonsense. After all, when you were a child, your mother said simply, "Go on outside and play" — and you went outside and played. What's all this fuss about today?

Partially, the fuss is about the thousands of children who, because of physical, emotional, social or environmental factors, are wholly incapable of "going outside and playing" on their own. The total pattern of our daily lives has changed over the past half-century, and we are just now becoming deeply concerned with serious lags that have existed for some time in various segments of that pattern. Recreation is one such segment. Education is another.

special education in public schools

The public schools in this country were designed for the so-called average child. Thus, the exceptional child, whether he be toward the top or toward the bottom of the measuring rod, was a misfit in the schoolroom. As a matter of fact, the genius and the retarded individual have always been misfits in society and largely because they are minority groups and our civilization was not developed with their needs in mind. One authority has said flatly that children of superior intelligence and those of low I. Q. present behavior problems that are very similar not only in kind, but in degree.

An educational system adapted to the needs of all grades of intelligence is essential for the development of the individual, the welfare of the community and the progress of society. It is probably the most important service a community can provide. Certainly it is a major factor in the adjustment of the retarded child. In many areas, attendance at school provides the sole opportunity for socialization which the retarded child urgently needs. Exclusion from school has frequently proved to be a fatal blow to a child, making him an outcast in his own eyes and, in the eyes of his family and his neighborhood and the whole community. The majority of retarded children, like all other children, want, above all else, acceptance. Attendance at school, with all the other children, is a form of acceptance. Denial of this opportunity may push a retarded child into anti-social behavior, a logical reaction to his public rejection, and may lead to his removal from society. This is not only unfair to the individual child but is costly to the taxpayer.

How much more sensible — and economical — it is to provide special classes for the retarded in the public school system. Through effective testing techniques, through the services of a school psychologist and a school psychiatrist, through the tireless efforts of a warm-hearted, dedicated, well-trained teacher, the retarded children of a community can be helped immeasurably.

The teacher is the heart of the school program. The qualities of character that he or she brings to it receive professional recognition through specialized training in the field of special education.

The development of special education has spanned the first half of this century, largely through its concern with the mentally retarded child who is considered educable. Such children can learn to read and write, not with great facility, but enough to make their own way in the world. They learn something about their own community, about transportation, and later they learn simple, basic skills that may enable them to find employment which keeps them occupied and content and helps to pay for their support. In special classes they are not competing with normal children, so they are more relaxed and confident and, hence, can learn more easily.

A new development in the field of special education — no more than a decade old in some areas, but with notable forerunners elsewhere — has been its concern with the more severely retarded or "trainable" child, whose I. Q. is within the 25 to 50 point range. The evidence is just now being gathered, but there is reason to believe that it is conclusive. It demonstrates that these severely retarded children can profit from attending special classes organized and designed specifically for them. Here they learn good personal habits and develop some degree of socialization, making it possible for them to continue living at home without creating tensions in family relationships.

home visiting

The school's work with the retarded does not end, however, when class is dismissed at the close of the day. Home visiting by a social worker employed by the school or a cooperating agency is an integral part of the program, for there may be forces at work in the retarded child's home that cancel out the benefits of his school training. Perhaps his brothers and sisters are jealous of the attention he receives or maybe they are ashamed of him and show it. His parents may not understand his limitations, or they may be unwilling to accept them. Whatever the situation, the classroom teacher will be better equipped to do her job effectively if she knows the background of her pupils, and chances are that she can contribute to their adjustment in the home.

Follow-up work is time-consuming and the classroom teacher

53. Retarded Children

cannot be expected to do as much as is required. The social workers and classroom teachers must cooperate closely. The home visiting program is aimed toward easing the lot of parents, as well as helping the retarded child, and it is hoped that one day it will be found in all public school systems. Helping parents handle their emotional problems is an indirect, but very effective, way to help retarded youngsters.

An intelligent parent of a retarded child must have a tremendous reservoir of courage, endless patience, staunch faith and enduring love if she (or he) is to help the child adjust to a world for which he is poorly equipped. The parent's role is made even more difficult by our society's emphasis on achievement in the school situation. While the neighborhood is applauding little Johnny next door for winning prizes and getting his name on the honor roll, it is heartbreaking for a mother to agree that *her* child should be enrolled in the special class for retarded children. And yet, if she is more concerned with her child's happiness and future welfare than with her own pride and ego, that mother will insist that her child be admitted to the special class. This is not easy.

It may help, however, for parents to know that all studies made to date of graduates of special classes in public schools make it clear that the majority of these pupils have been able to make their own way socially and financially and have been accepted as decent, hard-working citizens in their communities. They are not, in any sense, community liabilities. The results of these studies should serve as some consolation to parents and as a mandate to residents of all communities to see to it that training facilities are made available to all retarded children.

Statistics tell a sorry story. Of an estimated 1,000,000 mentally retarded children of school age, the most recent count indicates that only 110,000 are in special classes. All but two states have some provision to assist and encourage communities to offer special education to the more capable retarded, those with I. Q.'s above 50. Programs for "trainable" children whose I. Q.'s are below 50 are now evolving and some forty states have given them legal status either through specific regulation or through interpretation of existing education statutes.

Special education classes cannot be organized without teachers, specially trained and qualified to teach them. The federal government recognized this in 1958 when it passed a bill authorizing that funds be granted to colleges, universities and state departments of education for the training of teachers of the mentally retarded. Recognition of the educational rights of the mentally retarded child is leading to steps to make the right a reality.

In some states, communities are required by law to set up public school classes for pupils whose I. Q.'s are 50 or below.

In a recent, informal discussion of the value of such classes, an elementary school teacher commented that she doubted the trainability of such children and felt that it would be better for them and their families if they were placed in institutions. "It's a waste of taxpayers' money," she said. "What we need to do is improve our institutional care."

financially sound

Her argument is refuted by the 1957 New York study referred to earlier which disclosed that 27 per cent of the former pupils of special classes who were living at home were working for pay. They had been trainable to the point of holding employment. The taxpayers' money had definitely not been wasted on these pupils who, instead of living out their lives in an institution at the expense of the state, had been able to work at jobs that made them at least partially self-supporting. Institutional care is being constantly improved in all its phases, but there is just no comparison between the cost of special classes and the cost of institutionalization for the same number of retarded individuals. And regardless of economic factors, children who are able to live at home and receive the benefits of special education usually do as well as those trained in institutions.

The fervent hope of every parent is that his retarded child may achieve a reasonable degree of social adjustment and financial independence. In most cases, this is not a vain hope. The situation is changing so rapidly these days in the field of mental retardation that one hesitates to make any kind of flat statement.

But, today, the retarded child may be placed in a special class in the public schools. He may have the advantage of home visiting which vastly improves his family relationships. He may participate in special recreation programs. He may later be helped to find employment in industry or he may be employed in a sheltered workshop. He is protected, too, by legislation. If there were space here even for brief enumeration of the bills enacted into laws in recent years to safeguard the rights and the welfare of the retarded, the reader would be amazed. The Social Security Act, for example, was changed in 1956 to insure benefits for retarded children beyond the age of 18 who became disabled before age 18, who are not married, and who are at least semi-supported by a parent entitled to old-age benefits.

Social Security agencies refer applicants to divisions of vocational rehabilitation. If applicants are judged capable of gaining through vocational training, they receive it. Social Security benefits are reserved to those severely retarded youngsters who are incapable of supporting themselves even were they offered specialized services.

This is an example of cooperation between two federal agencies and their state and local counterparts. When the federal government designed its comprehensive program for the mentally retarded in 1956, it implied that practically every agency within the Department of Health, Education and Welfare would be involved. Practice has borne out this assertion.

Through its maternal and child health functions, the Children's Bureau has stimulated the organization of diagnostic clinics in cooperation with state health departments; the Office of Vocational Rehabilitation has provided funds to establish sheltered workshops and occupational training centers; the Office of Education has sponsored research on how the mentally retarded learn and how they might be taught; the National Institutes of Health have supported research on causes and prevention of mental retardation. The list is long and in a few short years, the benefits have been many.

funds for research and rehabilitation

Not only the federal, but many state legislatures and even local governments are showing an increasing inclination to appropriate funds for research and for rehabilitation projects in this field. Last year, for example, an Ohio county set aside $2 million of tax money to provide better schooling for retarded children in that area. Congress, in 1958, authorized $1 million for training of special teachers for retarded youngsters. Appropriations in the health, education and welfare fields, with specific relationship to mental retardation, have been increasing consistently over the past several decades. One of the major objectives of the National Association for Retarded Children is to promote necessary legislation to insure the best medical, educational, vocational and recreational facilities for today's retarded youngsters and to hasten the day when more of the mysteries of retardation will be revealed and prevention will be possible.

important survey

Much of the money appropriated by legislative bodies is going

7. EMERGING DIRECTIONS

into medical and psychological research. The most definitive work completed to date is presented in an impressive volume titled *Mental Subnormality*. The book is divided into two sections, one describing and evaluating current research into causes of mental retardation where damage or injury to the nervous system is involved, and the other examining the role of psychological and cultural factors. The combined survey was sponsored by the National Association for Retarded Children.

The most striking fact that comes out of this round-up of research into the physical, psychological and cultural factors in mental retardation is that we know so very little about so prevalent a disability. And some of the most important discoveries have been made by researchers not in the field of mental retardation, but in related fields. There is urgent need for close cooperation among workers in all areas related to retardation. Every city should have a diagnostic and a research center affiliated with a medical center. Training schools and universities and teachers training centers should be in close enough proximity that their work can be coordinated.

At Johns Hopkins Hospital, where the NARC established its first research professorship in mental retardation, scientists are conducting research projects in pediatrics, psychiatry, biochemistry, human genetics, neurology, virology — and progress achieved by any one scientist is shared by all. There is need, throughout this country, for many more centers which see relevance of their research to mental retardation as is the case at Johns Hopkins.

An ambitious, collaborative study is being made at Johns Hopkins (and 14 other medical centers) which, when completed, will have involved 40,000 pregnant women. Detailed records are kept of each woman during pregnancy, during labor and birth of the baby — and careful follow-up studies are made of mother and child. The project will cover a span of 10 years and is expected to establish important findings about causes of mental retardation, cerebral palsy and other neurological disorders. The medical centers are collaborating with the National Institute of Neurological Diseases and Blindness, a federal agency, in the long-range study. The project is unique, for nearly all previous attempts to find causes for retardation began with the handicapped child and worked backwards. Most of the 40,000 births in the current study will produce normal, healthy babies, but when a retarded child is born there will be his carefully written history in which, somewhere, may be found the cause of his handicap.

The second section of *Mental Subnormality*, dealing with environmental factors, leaves no doubt that the problem of mental retardation is social and cultural as well as biological and psychological. This relatively new concept needs a great deal of examination and clarification. A strong appeal is made to social scientists and to young and talented psychologists and psychiatrists to consider this as an important research area, for there is much vital work to be done.

It becomes increasingly clear that mental retardation is an extremely complex problem, a symptom that may result from a countless number of underlying causes. It must be approached from a variety of angles by experts in many specialized fields. And while this work is going on, society, viewing the problem with broad vision, must provide a many-faceted program of services to assist retarded individuals to make their own way in a so-called normal world.

Ironically, advances in medical science which have sharply reduced infant mortality and added years to the average life-span have, thereby, added another complication to the already difficult lot of the retarded adult. He, too, is living longer these days, much longer. Society may soon be faced with the problem of caring for large numbers of severely retarded individuals who have outlived their parents and no longer have someone to look after them in their own homes. Some agencies are already investigating the possibilities of providing foster home care for these adults, similar to the foster home care made available to homeless children and, in some areas, to the aging. Workers in the field realize that some form of responsible guardianship must be arranged for these individuals so that they can remain in the community. Institutionalization is not a satisfactory answer, for our institutions are already overcrowded and custodial care is usually not required.

the NARC

The National Association for Retarded Children consists of thousands of parents banded together in nearly 700 local groups in communities all across the country. It includes parents, physicians, teachers, other professional lay workers and citizens interested in mental retardation. These are the people who know the problem best because they have lived with it and worked with it. Formed as recently as 1950, the national organization and its local groups have helped to create dozens of diagnostic clinics, hundreds of recreation programs, thousands of special schools and classes. These are providing essential services for hundreds of thousands of children and adults — out of the millions who need such services.

goals

The NARC, with headquarters at 2709 Avenue E. East, Arlington, Texas 76011, is dedicated to:

1. Promote the general welfare of mentally retarded children everywhere — at home, in the community, in institutions and in public, private and religious schools.

2. Further the advancement of all ameliorative and preventative study, research and therapy in mental retardation.

3. Develop better understanding of mental retardation by the public, and to cooperate with all public, private and religious agencies, international, federal, state and local, and departments of education, health and institutions.

4. Further the training and education of personnel for work in the field of mental retardation.

5. Encourage formation of parents' groups, to advise and aid parents in solution of their problems, and to coordinate the efforts and activities of these groups.

6. Serve as a clearing-house for gathering and disseminating information regarding the mentally retarded, and to foster the development of integrated programs in their behalf.

The local groups, composed of parents and other socially-minded citizens, are the life-blood of the NARC. The national office was set up in full recognition of the fact that nothing can be done effectively at the national level unless it is applied and interpreted locally. The NARC has created its Scientific Research Advisory Board with the hope that many small advances may be made across the broad front that makes up the field of

53. Retarded Children

research in mental retardation. A NARC Research Fund has been established, a research professorship in mental retardation has been founded, and studies are being supported in university and medical centers across the nation. Members of the local groups, as they labor for each small gain with the child of today, cannot help thinking sometimes, with sadness, of what might have been, and then with faith and hope of what some day will be.

It must be kept in mind at all times, of course, that retarded children are only a portion of America's children. Their needs must be considered in the perspective of the total needs of all children. But now that we know that their special needs can be met to the benefit of society as a whole, the community can no longer dodge its responsibility for this handicapped segment of the population.

WHAT TO READ

Chamberlain, Naomi H. and Moss, Dorothy H. *The Three R's For the Retarded — A Program for Training the Retarded Child At Home.* National Association for Retarded Children, 2709 Avenue E. East, Arlington, Texas 76011.

Davies, Stanley Powell, in collaboration with Ecob, Katherine G. *The Mentally Retarded in Society.* Columbia University Press, New York.

Dittmann, Laura L. *The Mentally Retarded Child at Home.* U. S. Children's Bureau Publication #374. Supt. of Documents, Washington, D.C. 20402.

Hill, Margaret. *The Retarded Child Gets Ready for School.* Public Affairs Pamphlet No. 349.

SPECIAL EDUCATION

Designed to follow the introductory course in special education, it is also a book which can be used as the first course book for Exceptional Children, Foundations of Exceptional Children, and the overview course for students entering special education departments.

For more information about this book and other materials in special education, contact Joseph Logan, Editor, Special Learning Corporation.

Special Learning Corporation
42 Boston Post Rd. Guilford, Connecticut 06437   (203) 453-6525

TO DEFEND THE RIGHTS OF THE HELPLESS

EUNICE SHRIVER

"Until we see the common value of all people," says one of the most dedicated and hard-working members of the Kennedy family, "we fail to honor the essential American idea"

Eunice Kennedy Shriver races through life, looking back to pull those behind along with her, inviting them to catch up and match her own exuberance. Daughter of an ambassador to Great Britain, sister to a President of the United States, married to a candidate for the Democratic Presidential nomination, she always has been a strong individual in her own right.

I first met her on the campaign trail in 1960, when she, Lady Bird Johnson and Ethel Kennedy were proving to the Bible Belt that being a Catholic did not disqualify one for election to the office of President.

At every stop the most conservative churchgoers turned out to see these women in action. Four thousand handshakes in Dallas, 5,000 handshakes in Houston and 2,500 in Wichita Falls. But the three were more than handshakers. They stood before the microphones, speaking out for the Kennedy-Johnson ticket—Eunice sounding and looking like her brother Jack.

Between stops, while we waited for our plane to carry us on to the next city, Eunice would stride back and forth on the runway to get her exercise. En route, her head was in a book. No wasted time. Alighting from a plane, she immediately made contact with the crowd somehow, with her eyes, her handshakes—and they were bone-crunching handshakes.

The fifth of nine children born to Joseph and Rose Kennedy, Eunice was graduated with a degree in sociology from Stanford University, in California. Consistently active in social work and in a wide range of community programs, she is now executive vice-president of the Joseph P. Kennedy, Jr., Foundation, which supports research and related programs for the handicapped; and she is president of the Special Olympics for the mentally retarded, which she organized in 1968.

I think she was created to take on impossible dreams. Her missions—whatever they may be—never exhaust her, never wind her down emotionally or physically. At 50 plus she still plays touch football with her kids. She'll be doing it at 80, I suspect.

That vitality, that undaunted exuberance, is what she pours into her efforts to help the thousands of people, here in the United States and overseas, who are mentally handicapped—the victims of one of life's deepest cruelties. She finds life in being their friend. —LIZ CARPENTER, PRODUCER
REDBOOK'S BICENTENNIAL SERIES

The experience that made me proudest to be an American had nothing to do with politics, power or patriotism.

It happened last summer. At 6 P.M. on August 7, 1975, I was in Mount Pleasant, Michigan, to attend the Fourth International Special Olympics for the mentally retarded, most of them children, some of them adults. I stood outside Perry Stadium, greeting some of the 3,200 competitors who were massed there under bright flags and banners, waiting for the ceremonies to start. They had come from 30 states and eight countries. I saw many in wheel chairs, dozens on crutches. Some had cerebral palsy, many were mongoloid; all were slower in thought than what we have decreed to be "normal" in our society.

I thought about the great courage of these people, the agonizing effort and determination that had brought them all the way to this Michigan town. I hoped fervently that the Special Olympics would somehow prove to be an exciting, significant and memorable experience in their lives.

Then as I walked into the brightly lighted stadium I saw something I'll never forget: 20,000 people—total strangers to the mentally retarded—had filled every seat. They had come to tell the contenders that they were loved, wanted, admired. This was no condescending "benefit" audience. Here were farmers, factory workers, storekeepers, housewives—most of them con-

276 To Defend the Rights of the Helpless, Eunice Shriver, *Redbook Magazine*, Vol. 146, No. 6, April 1976. ©1976 The Redbook Publishing Co., New York, N.Y.

54. To Defend the Rights

servative Midwesterners who do not readily show their emotions. But as the band began to play and the competitors entered the stadium these people cheered their heads off.

"They like us!" exclaimed a ten-year-old girl from Connecticut as she marched in with her delegation. It was true. For the next four days the cheering never stopped.

Away from the stadium, moreover, the people of Mount Pleasant pitched in to make the retarded children and adults welcome in every way. They took them into their homes, exchanged names and addresses, gave them souvenirs, assisted them in the Olympic events. One thousand Mount Pleasant teen-agers adopted as "brothers and sisters" boys and girls whose differences from their hosts were startling and even disturbing. Fifty nearby communities made them guests of honor for a day.

When it was all over, one young Michigan woman wrote to me: "I saw and heard and did things that I shall never forget as long as I live. It was the most satisfying thing I have ever done in my life." Another young volunteer told me, "I got so excited when I saw one boy running the two-twenty-yard dash on crutches that I ran along with him for the whole race. I felt I was a part of him."

President Kennedy once said that a nation's greatness can be measured by the way it treats its weakest citizens. At Mount Pleasant I saw and felt how great America can be.

Still, I know that in many places in our country we have not yet learned to accept people who are different. We have not learned that the rights of the helpless must be defended even more vigorously than those of the powerful. Not every community is Mount Pleasant, and mentally retarded individuals are not cheered or welcomed everywhere. They are often rejected by their community, isolated, put in institutions, experimented upon, forgotten. Until we see clearly the common value of all people—bright or dull, strong or weak, fortunate or deprived—we fail to honor the essential American idea; and more deeply, in denying the humanity of others we are destroying it in ourselves.

But Mount Pleasant, Michigan, was different, and in that joyous stadium on that August night I saw America at its greatest, and I was deeply proud.

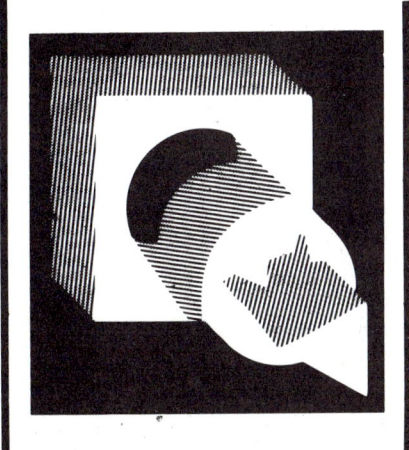

Diagnosis and Placement

Current trends in diagnostic procedures, along with a detailed look at medical assessment of exceptional children are discussed. The controversy of mainstreaming versus placement in self-contained special education classes is also featured.

For further information about this book and other special education materials, contact:

Joseph Logan, Editor
Special Learning Corporation

Special Learning Corporation
42 Boston Post Rd. Guilford, Connecticut 06437 (203) 453-6525

Classroom Techniques

LOU BROWN *is Associate Professor, Department of Studies in Behavioral Disabilities, University of Wisconsin, Madison.*

BARBARA HUPPLER, LAURA PIERCE, *and* NANCY SCHEUERMAN *are classroom teachers, Badger School, Madison Public Schools.*

ED SONTAG *is Branch Chief, USOE, BEH, Division of Training Programs, Washington, D.C.*

Language behavior, at least as the phrase is used here, refers to behavior on the part of a student that communicates information to another person, or behavior on the part of a student that indicates that information has been received. Language behavior deficits are probably the most crucial, pervasive, and salient deficits confronted by teachers of trainable retarded students (Brown, 1972). Unless a teacher can develop a behavioral repertoire in her students that can communicate information to others or that can demonstrate that information has been received, the role of a teacher will be essentially that of a custodian concerned with little more than arranging for physical needs. That is, without language it is extremely improbable that a teacher can develop math, reading, social, and vocational skills (McLean, Yoder, & Schiefelbusch, 1972).

The program described here represents an attempt by classroom teachers to develop and/or improve basic communication skills of young trainable students. The program evolved from the observations of the teachers, and for that reason it might be of interest to present a brief account of the teachers' preprogram experiences.

At the start of the school year the teachers attempted to provide a series of varied interesting and educational activities. Puppet shows, animal displays, historic demonstrations, films, and filmstrips were some of the activities provided in class; nature walks and trips to the police and fire stations were some of the activities provided away from the school. After the students had been exposed to an activity, the teacher often would quiz the students as to where they went, what they noticed, what they did, etc. It soon became obvious either that the students did not want to or did not know how to communicate what they experienced or that they did not obtain information from the experiences and therefore had nothing to communicate.

Attempts at obtaining information from the students concerning the experiences to which they had been exposed consisted of questions such as: What did we do? Where did we go? What animals did we see? What happened? What did I first do? Unfortunately, few, if any, appropriate responses were given and most of the responses provided were incoherent or unrelated to the experiences provided.

Thus, it was decided to arrange an instructional environment that might contribute to the development of skills that would allow the students to communicate information provided by another person.

While there are many approaches to the development of communication skills, it was decided that the program should (a) include

Classroom Techniques, Lou Brown, Barbara Huppler, Laura Pierce, Nancy Scheuerman, Ed Sontag, *Education and Training of the Mentally Retarded.* ©The Council for Exceptional Children, Reston, Virginia.

clearly discriminable events; (b) include a large number of training trials; and (c) at least initially, be conducted in the classroom by teaching personnel.

As the ability to learn from observing the behavior of another person is a crucial cognitive skill that all students must acquire, it was decided that the information to be communicated to the students would come from the teacher. Thus, a series of "behavioral events" were delineated. Since verbal communication skills are particular deficits of young trainable students it was decided that a verbal response would be required as a vehicle for determining whether the student obtained information contained in the behavioral events. Thus, we have a situation whereby a teacher would carry out an action (e.g., comb his hair) and then require the students to respond verbally in such a way as to demonstrate that they obtained information from observing the action.

Initially, the behavioral events were quite simple in that they involved a small number of actions (one-component behavioral events) on the part of the teacher, the actions were performed immediately in front of the students, and the verbal responses required were relatively simple. Subsequently, the behavioral events became more complex (two-component behavioral events), the events were removed from the immediate presence of the students, and concommitantly the verbal responses required became more complex.

Program Phases

The entire program was divided into the following 11 phases:

Phase 1. Two sets of 5 one-component behavioral events were performed by the teacher, and the students' ability to report verbally characteristics of the events was measured.

Phase 2. The students were taught to report verbally characteristics of one set of one-component behavioral events but were not taught to report verbally the characteristics of the other set.

Phase 3. The ability of the students to report verbally characteristics of the one-component behavioral events not taught in Phase 2 was measured.

Phase 4. The students were taught to report verbally characteristics of the one-component behavioral events not taught in Phase 2.

Phase 5. Three sets of 5 two-component behavioral events were performed by the teacher, and the students' ability to report verbally characteristics of the events was measured. Two of the three sets of two-component behavioral events were performed by the teacher while she was seated at a table. The third set of two-component behavioral events was performed by the teacher as she walked about the classroom.

Phase 6. The students were taught to report verbally characteristics of one of the two sets of two-component behavioral events performed at the table but were not taught to report verbally characteristics of the remaining two sets of two-component behavioral events.

Phase 7. The ability of the students to report verbally characteristics of the second set of two-component behavioral events performed at the table, and the set of two-component behavioral events performed about the classroom was measured.

Phase 8. The students were taught to report verbally characteristics of the second set of two-component behavioral events performed at the table.

Phase 9. The ability of the students to report verbally the characteristics of the three sets of two-component behavioral events was measured.

Phase 10. The students were taught to report verbally characteristics of the set of two-component behavioral events performed while the teachers were walking about the classroom.

Phase 11. Retention measures of the students' ability to report the characteristics of two-component behavioral events were obtained.

Method

Students

The four students were enrolled in a public school program for trainable retarded students. The two girls and two boys ranged in CA from 8 to 10 years and psychological reports contained test scores suggesting IQ's in a 34 to 40 range. Evaluation reports contained such labels and descriptions as Down's Syndrome, severe retardation, severe learning disability, delayed speech, and emotional disturbance.

Materials

The materials used in the program were common objects found in the classroom; these objects were incorporated into one- and two-component behavioral events. The behavioral events (and the required objects) are presented .

7. EMERGING DIRECTIONS

Set I

1. Laura squeezed clay.
2. Laura combed hair.
3. Laura cut paper.
4. Laura clapped hands.
5. Laura colored balloon.

Set II

1. Laura dropped pencil.
2. Laura read book.
3. Laura ate cookie.
4. Laura rolled ball.
5. Laura drank water.

Set III

1. Laura piled blocks; Laura blew feather.
2. Laura drew circle; Laura tore napkin.
3. Laura buttoned shirt; Laura tied shoe.
4. Laura rang bell; Laura folded towel.
5. Laura opened box; Laura zipped pants.

Set IV

1. Nancy wiped table; Nancy cleaned hands.
2. Nancy threw cup; Nancy blew nose.
3. Nancy turned pages; Nancy pushed truck.
4. Nancy wrote name; Nancy erased board.
5. Nancy raised hand; Nancy sharpened pencil.

Set V

1. Nancy got food; Nancy fed fish.
2. Nancy got water; Nancy watered plant.
3. Nancy got coat; Nancy put on coat.
4. Nancy walked to chart; Nancy read story.
5. Nancy closed door; Nancy turned off lights.

Pennies were used as rewards for each correct response and were saved in paper cups. At the end of each teaching session, each penny was exchanged for one M&M. Data sheets were constructed that provided easy recording of responses to each behavioral event.

Instructional Setting

Two instructional arrangements were utilized. The first arrangement was used for the two sets of one-component behavioral events and for the two sets of the two-component events which occurred at the teaching table. Teaching was conducted at a table in a corner of the classroom by a student teacher while the six remaining students in the class were involved in activities with the teacher. The four students sat directly across from the teacher at the table.

The second instructional arrangement utilized also had the four students seated directly across from the teacher at the table in the corner of the classroom. In this setting, however, the teacher performed the third set of two-component behavioral events as she moved about the classroom at a distance of 10 to 20 feet away from the teaching table.

Testing and teaching sessions were conducted from 10:20 a.m. to 10:40 a.m. daily.

Teaching Procedures

Phase 1. When students and teacher were seated around the table, the teacher performed the first behavioral event of Set I (squeezed clay) and said to student 1, "What happened?" The response of student 1 was then recorded on the data sheet. The teacher then performed the second behavioral event in Set I (combed hair), said to student 2, "What happened?" and recorded the response. This procedure was followed until each of the four students had the opportunity to witness and label each of the five behavioral events in Sets I and II on three consecutive occasions.

Phase 2. Students were taught to report the behavioral events in Set I but not the events in Set II. The students were taught to report the events in Set I in the following manner:

In step 1 the teacher said, "John, watch what I do," while performing the first behavioral event (squeezed clay) in Set I. She then said, "What happened?"

In step 2 if student 1 responded correctly the teacher said, "Good, Great, etc.," and gave student 1 a penny.

In step 3 if student 1 did not report or responded incorrectly (e.g., "Laura, clay, squeezed" or "Laura clay"), the teacher said, "John, watch what I do," performed the event a second time and said, "What happened?" If student 1 responded correctly, the teacher said, "Good, Great, etc.," and modeled a correct response ("Laura squeezed clay") so the four students could easily hear her but did not present the student with a penny.

In step 4 if student 1 did not respond correctly to the second performance of the first behavioral event in Set I, the teacher modeled a correct response ("Laura squeezed clay") and said, "Now say it." If student 1 matched the verbal behavior of the teacher, the teacher said, "Good, Great, etc." If student 1 did not match the behavior of the teacher, the teacher said, "No, I am sorry, you did not say the right words."

Subsequently, the same procedures were applied to students 2, 3, and 4 respectively until all four students correctly reported the five behavioral events performed by the teacher in Set I on three consecutive occasions.

Phase 3. The procedures described in Phase 1 were used to measure the students' ability to report the behavioral events of Set II.

Phase 4. The procedures described in Phase 2 were used to teach students to report the behavioral events in Set II.

Phase 5. The procedures described in Phase 1 were used to measure the students' ability to report the events in Sets III, IV, and V with two exceptions. First, the behavioral events in Set III involved two components rather than one component. Second, the behavioral events in Set V were performed by the teacher as she walked about the room.

Phase 6. The procedures described in Phase 2 were used to teach students to report the behavioral events in Set III.

Phase 7. The procedures described in Phase 1 were used to measure the students' ability to report the events in Sets IV and V.

Phase 8. The procedures described in Phase 2 were used to teach students to report the events in Set IV.

Phase 9. The procedures described in Phase 1 were used to measure the students' ability to report the events in Sets III, IV, and V.

Phase 10. The procedures described in Phase 1 were used to teach students to report the events in Set V.

Phase 11. The procedures described in Phase 1 were used to measure the students' ability to report behavioral events of Sets III, IV, and V two weeks after Phase 10 had been completed.

Results

Correct responses to questions related to one-component behavioral events (Phases 1 through 4) were operationally defined as follows: A response on the part of a student that included (a) a subject (e.g., Laura), a verb (e.g., squeezed), and an object (e.g., clay); (b) a subject (e.g., Laura) and a verb (e.g., combed); and (c) a verb (e.g., drank) and an object (e.g., water).

Correct responses to questions related to two-component behavioral events (Phases five through ten) were operationally defined exactly as the one-component behavioral events except that the student was required to meet one of the criteria listed above in each of the components. For example, if the two-component behavioral event was "Nancy raised hand; Nancy sharpened pencil," a response was not considered correct unless the student included a subject, verb, and object; a subject and a verb; or a verb and an object when reporting each of the two events.

In any given trial each student could make from 0 to 5 correct responses to any given set of events and the four students combined could make from 0 to 20 correct responses.

As can be discerned from Figure 1, during Phase 1 students made 1, 4, and 1; and 3, 4, and 0 correct responses to questions related to Sets I and II respectively.

As can be discerned from Figure 1, during Phase 2, 12 teaching trials were required before each student could report the behavioral events in Set I on three consecutive occasions.

In Phase 3, students made 5, 7, and 5 correct responses to questions related to Set II. When performance on Set II in Phase 3 is compared with performance on Set II in Phase 1 a slight increase in correct responding can be discerned.

In Phase 4, five teaching trials were required before each student could report the behavioral events in Set II. Obviously, students learned to report the events in Set II in substantially fewer trials than the events in Set I.

As can be discerned from Figure 1, during Phase 5 students made 0, 0, and 0; 0, 0, and 0; and 0, 0, and 0 correct responses to questions related to Sets III, IV, and V, respectively.

In Phase 6, 11 teaching trials were required before each student could report the behavioral events in Set III on three consecutive occasions.

In Phase 7, students made 2, 3, and 2; and 0, 0, and 0 correct responses to questions related to Sets IV and V respectively. When performance on Set IV, in Phase VII is compared with performance on Set IV in Phase 5, a slight increase in correct responding can be discerned. There is no difference in performance on Set V between Phase 7 and Phase 5.

In Phase 8, 12 teaching trials were required before each student could report the behavioral events in Set IV on three consecutive occasions. Therefore, the same number of trials was needed by students to learn to report the events in Set IV as in Set III.

In Phase 9, students made 19, 20, and 19; 20, 19, and 20; and 1, 1, and 1 correct responses to questions related to Sets III, IV, and V, respectively. Obviously, there was almost perfect retention of the correct re-

7. EMERGING DIRECTIONS

sponses to the behavioral events in Set III. Students also maintained performance on Set IV. There is no apparent difference in performance on Set V between Phases 5, 6, or 9.

In Phase 10, eight teaching trials were necessary before each student could report the behavioral events in Set V on three consecutive occasions. It can be discerned that students learned to report the events in Set V in fewer trials than were required to learn Set III or Set IV.

In Phase 11, students made 20, 17, and 17 correct responses to the behavioral events in Sets III, IV, and V after a two week retention period.

Discussion

Inspection of Figure 1 strongly suggests that, in accordance with the definition offered, four young trainable students acquired the skills necessary to report verbally both one- and two-component behavioral events which occurred in their immediate presence and two-component behavioral events which occurred in their classroom.

In addition, it appears that as the program progressed and thus became more difficult, the students became more efficient at learning the required response patterns. For example, in Phase 2, which involved teaching responses to the one-component behavioral events, the students reached criterion after 12 teaching trials whereas in Phases 6 and 8, which involved teaching responses to two-component behavioral events occurring immediately in front of as well as around the room, a total of 11 and 12 teaching trials respectively were required.

When the components of the program described thus far had been completed, it was decided to attempt to investigate whether the skills acquired could be made to occur during more natural school activities. Six activities were selected: handwriting, chart reading, math, milk break, auditory training, and gym, and two sets of three two-component behavioral events were arranged. While these activities were in progress, the teacher would say, for example, "Ricky, watch," and then secure the pointer and read the chart, or get a container of milk and open it, or get a basketball and shoot it. Only two of the four students were selected for this extension and three different teachers (teacher, aide, and student teacher) asked the questions and scored the responses. Using the same criteria of a correct response to the two-component behavioral events, a total of five teaching trials were required before the two students performed perfectly on the two sets of two-component behavioral events. Thus, it would appear if environmental demands are made on the students that require them to report behavioral events in the natural environment, they are capable of meeting such demands.

The criteria used to define correct responses were quite arbitrary and in retrospect appear to have been inhibiting. The rationale for the definition was: Here is a group of children who apparently are not communicating well with people in their immediate environment. It is crucial that they be taught to communicate. If it is crucial that they be taught to communicate, it is of sufficient importance that their ability to communicate be verified empirically. The demands that the existence of the communication skills in question be verified empirically placed, at least temporarily, constraints upon the structure of the program. For example, it was decided that both the behavioral events as well as the responses required be held constant. That is, the behavioral event was repeated until each student responded in a manner prescribed by the teacher.

Ultimately, all students met the prescribed response criteria. However, there were situations where the constraints of the program seem to have prevented individualized responses. For example, in the extension to the program the students were taken to the gym. During the gym period the teacher said, "David, watch" and then picked up a basketball, walked to the basket, shot the ball, missed, and said to the student, "What happened?" The program required that the student say, "Nancy got ball, Nancy shot basket" in order for the response to be scored correct. The student's response, which had to be scored incorrect, was, "Ha, Ha. Nancy missed." Obviously, the student attended to the behavioral event and communicated what he felt was the substance of that event. The incorrectness of the response was a function of the program rather than of the ability of the student to communicate. While it is quite doubtful that the student would have made that particular response before he received the training in the program, his response clearly indicates that the response criteria of future programs must be improved. Programs are now being designed that hopefully will provide the students with basic expressive skills and yet allow for more individualized responses.

In addition to the quantitative changes there seemed to have been qualitative changes in the students' behavior as well. For example, prior to the start of and during the initial stages of the program, it would have been difficult to claim that the students were attending to the teacher. That is, often

55. Classroom Techniques

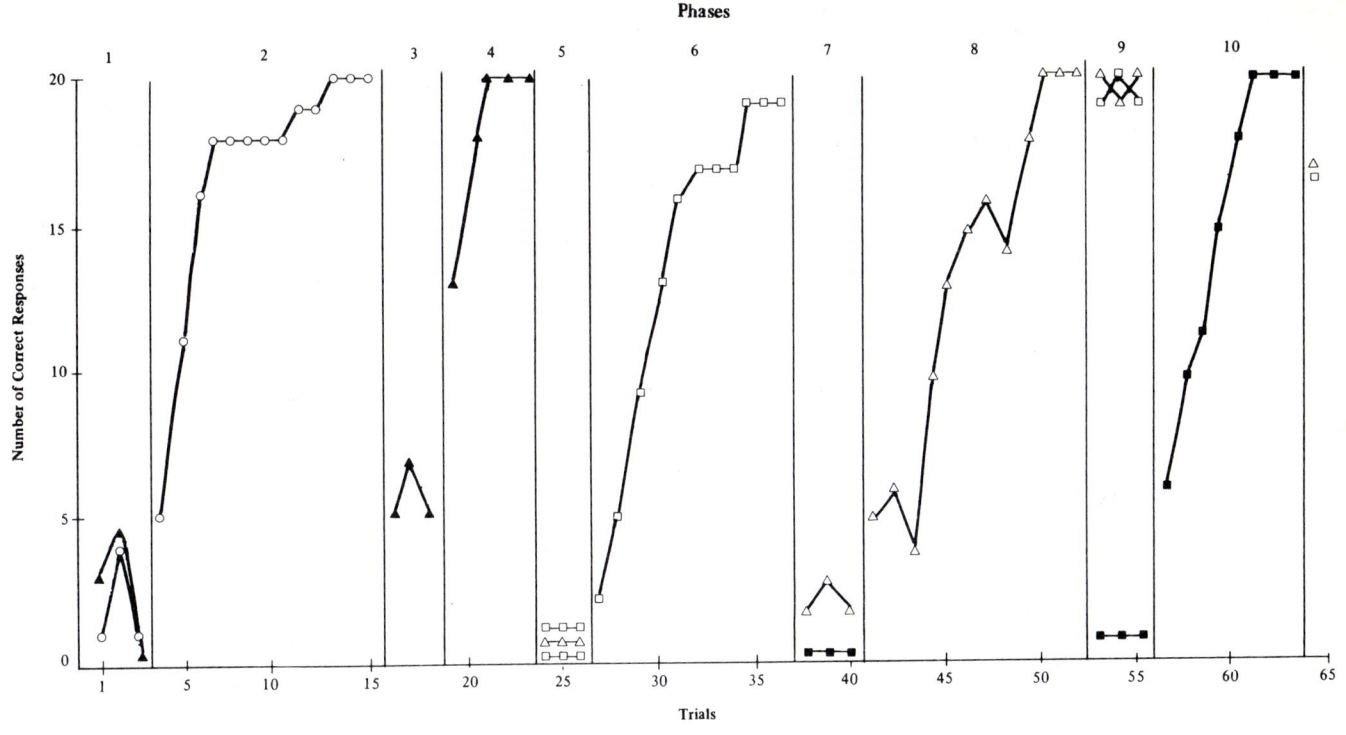

FIGURE 1. Total Number of Correct Responses Made by Four Students During Phases 1 through 10.

SET I — ○
SET II — ▲
SET III — □
SET IV — △
SET V — ■

they would look out of the window, down at their hands, or at one another instead of at the teacher. By the end of the program a dramatic change in their attending and tracking skills had occurred. According to subjective reports of the teacher these improvements in attending and tracking skills seems to have generalized to other instructional programs.

Qualitative improvements in the verbal repertoire of the students seemed to have occurred also. For example, at the start of the program the students responded often with a blank stare, incoherent verbiage, irrelevant words, and monosyllables. During the final phases of the program the students rarely responded with less than five intelligible words.

Two glaring examples of qualitative changes in verbal behavior were demonstrated by two students, Ed and David. First, during an unstructured period at the beginning of the day, students were asked such questions as, "What did you do last night?", "What did you eat for dinner;", or "What happened at your house?" In the initial phases of the program, Ed would respond with blank stares or irrelevant verbalizations ("fire engine") to such questions. At the end of the program Ed was making relevant responses using complete phrases. For example, when asked one day, "What did you do at home?" Ed responded, "Daddy chase dog, throw stick, dog run to stick."

One day David was absent. When he arrived at school the following day the teacher asked him why he was not in school the previous day. He responded with, "Me sick, Mommy take me nurse, Nurse shot butt." Such complete verbalizations had not occurred before the program had been initiated.

Finally, it appears that an instructional procedure has been delineated and applied by classroom teachers that has resulted in young trainable students acquiring basic communication skills. This, in itself, provides a much needed note of optimism to public school programs for young trainable students.

A Haven for Steve

—Veronica Dolan

Questions haunt the parents of all retarded children: Will we be able to care for our child when he grows to adulthood? Is he doomed to live in a state institution after we're gone?

In the past there were few happy answers. But now, some good things are happening to create more attractive alternative residential facilities for the mentally retarded.

One such development is the hostel program, which has recently begun in Colorado and several other states. Hostels are small, homelike residences for six to eight retardates. "The idea," explains William Crosby, of the state Department of Institutions, Division of Mental Retardation, "is to make life for the retarded person more normal than it has been in the past."

Colorado's program is still in the embryonic stage with only 35 mentally retarded persons currently living in hostels in Denver, Grand Junction, and Pueblo. But the future seems hopeful and, therefore, the present merits a closer look.

Denver's Garfield Street hostel houses five mentally retarded men in a five-bedroom rented house just off a busy street. The men, who range in age from their early twenties to early forties, are supervised by a married couple, who also live in the hostel. With the help of counselors and vocational rehabilitation specialists, all of the men have found jobs outside the home; their salaries range from $1.01 to $1.80 an hour.

The twenty-four-year-old housemother, who holds a degree in psychology, does most of the cooking for the hostelers. The men help her set the table and wash dishes. They are also responsible for making their own beds and cleaning their rooms. In fact, they do all the heavy cleaning; household training is considered an essential part of the program because, ideally, many hostelers will eventually "graduate" into apartments of their own. Toward that end, the men are also taught to handle money and manage a budget.

One of the hostelers, twenty-three-year-old Steve Benson (not his real name), is delighted with life on Garfield Street. Unlike two of the other men, Steve had never been institutionalized, but he had been growing increasingly frustrated with his life at home. Retarded since birth, he has gone through numerous special programs. His mother estimates the family has spent the equivalent of two college educations in tuition to private schools and summer programs, for transportation and medical expenses. Fees for a special weekdays-only boarding school were $150 per month, every month for five years. (The Bensons pay no fees now; the Garfield Street pilot program is financed for three years by a federal grant.)

The hostel has brightened Steve's future. But if the concept of "normalization" is to work over the long haul, professionals say, quality support services—resident and family counseling programs, workshops or work stations in industry, apartments for the graduates—must be made available. Important, too, is the cooperation of the community. Some retardates, for instance, will always need a volunteer citizen advocate, who will represent the rights of the retarded as if they were his or her own.

Proponents know that much depends on how hostels like Garfield Street work out. The large institution is not likely to disappear in some cases, since many professionals still believe it can best care for the profoundly retarded or those with multiple handicaps. But, in the future, other retardates may be able to share Steve's luck. "The hostel has given Steve new goals and a different attitude," Mrs. Benson says. "He feels he's equal to the rest of the family now."

"The Six Point Program"

A Modern Plan for Modern Services to the Mentally Retarded

INTRODUCTION

For the past 3 years, the Division of Mental Retardation and its predecessor programs have been seeking to help in the building of services which will truly meet the needs of America's 6 million retarded citizens. To recite the history of those 3 years here would be beside the point. Suffice it to say that they have been active—and educational.

We have, in the nature of things, put great emphasis on planning and coordination of programs at State and local levels. And out of this emphasis have come most of the lessons we have learned.

We have discovered, for example, that what we have known to exist—a severe shortage of trained manpower—not only exists, but threatens to get worse before it gets better.

We have found ourselves in a difficult competitive position for our full share of the community resources.

We have not found a solution to the problem of provision of services. The generalist's approach which is comprehensive still vies for our attention with the specialist's higher quality but more fragmented approach.

We have learned that development of services for the retarded must proceed in keeping with the general development of all personal services in the community and yet must maintain the identity of the mentally retarded.

Summing up our lessons learned, and perhaps most important of all, we have discovered that means must be found to extend services to all the retarded with those resources which are available.

The lessons I have outlined underscore the fact that we cannot expect, simply by developing a number of programs for the mentally retarded in a community, that these shiny new programs will then automatically fit together into a dynamic structure. It is difficult enough for the community to plan concretely for all the needs of the retarded in the beginning. Precise data are lacking. There is little or no definition of function. Philosophies change. And if planning for the present is difficult, planning for the future is nearly impossible. Yet it must be done. It has to be done in the full knowledge of the difficulties involved: The financial and manpower problems, the changing missions of programs and agencies, the lack of specific treatment and preventive programs, and the uncertain future in which the only certainty which exists is the certainty of change and the development of new trends.

Planning in a vacuum is no planning at all. We have to work with what we have. Attempts to develop mental retardation service programs in a vacuum can only result in isolated programs without community understanding, backing, or support.

It is with these factors in mind that we have devised a model 6-point program for the proper balance and coordination of community services.

POINT 1
OPEN EVERY GENERIC COMMUNITY AGENCY TO THE RETARDED INSOFAR AS THESE AGENCIES' COMPETENCE AND ABILITY PERMITS

A definition is in order here. By generic agency, I am referring to any health, welfare, educational, rehabilitative, or employment agency in the community whose purpose is not for the specific care of the mentally retarded. An example might be an orthopedic clinic not specifically for the mentally retarded, which would be considered a specialized service in other circumstances, but would be considered generic in our conceptual model. Our reasoning is that if we are to provide the quantity of care necessary, we have to consider the fact that most retardates do not require complex and specially trained assistance in every situation throughout their lives.

Most retardates fit into the mildly retarded grouping and can cope with most situations without help or, at least, without the help of specialized agencies. We should not be thinking so much of types of retardation. Rather, our attention must be directed to the situations which retardates are apt to encounter. Thus, a child may be mildly

---

The 6 Point Program. ©U.S. Government Printing Office, U.S. Department of Health, Education and Welfare, Social and Rehabilitation Services.

7. EMERGING DIRECTIONS

retarded yet have complex genetic problems or learning difficulties while a far more seriously retarded individual may have such comparatively slight problems (or at least uncomplicated ones) as a toothache or a fractured leg. Actually most of the services the retardate needs are—or should be—available in the community.

Moreover, it takes time for the service worker to develop a rapport with the family of the retardate, learn its strengths and weaknesses, and know the community and its full range of services in order to determine the most practical treatment plan. These are factors which argue persuasively for local rather than distant care and for care given by agencies and professionals who already know this family.

Just as the individual cannot be split into separate parts for treatment, we are coming to the understanding that close inter relationships which bind the family together require that it be treated as a unit. Thus the development and mushrooming of specialized agencies which isolate the retarded individual from his family must be carried out only after careful consideration.

There is still another factor which inhibits the retardate from receiving the treatment he needs in the generic agency. Too often, the mentally retarded person is refused service because he is identified as a retardate. Furthermore, the presence of specialized agencies available for the retarded tends to encourage referral to them almost automatically. Thus begins to develop a mysterious aura of specialization supposedly required for this exotic and difficult condition. The retardate quickly moves beyond the scope of the generic agency regardless of his true need—a need which most often could be supplied in the very agency which shuts him out. This develops into the concept of mental retardation as an all-or-none condition rather than one with graduated problems.

Again arguing for the greater use of generic services is the logistical problem of distance. Local agencies are simply easier to get to. Why send the retardate miles from his home unnecessarily when by doing so we also send him away from the service which has been treating his family for years, which knows his family and its problems, and which by all reasonable standards, should be best equipped to treat him?

Today the mental health field is moving towards family unit treatment and away from child guidance and adult mental health clinics. Social workers are moving again toward family unit treatment, and there are strong recommendations that medical schools should be developing a new specialty—the family specialist—to handle the majority of medical situations for the entire family and act as the family's fixed point of referral for its full complement of service. We who are interested in the retardate should be thinking in these same terms.

POINT 2
THE PROVISION OF BASIC TRAINING IN MENTAL RETARDATION FOR EVERY HEALTH WORKER

I would go further than that and say that every personal service worker should have such training. This would not be so vital for such technicians as the X-ray or laboratory worker, but is a must for every personal service worker who offers services in a health, welfare, educational, rehabilitative, or employment situation.

With such training, the generic agencies would be more easily persuaded to open their doors to the retarded. This would greatly facilitate the understanding needed for satisfactory case-finding, referral, and timely intervention.

This basic knowledge would not have to be very extensive. It should be enough to enable the worker to know the essential concepts of retardation along with the major problems and possible relationships. Thus he would be able to identify most retardates or at least to refer cases for proper identification, would be able to handle basic questions, and could be aware of the relationship of specific services to the problems of the individual retardate.

With the ability to make logical referral at the appropriate time, the health worker or other personal service worker will be able to avoid passing the retardate and his family around haphazardly to inappropriate services, wasting usable professional time, and perhaps missing the optimal period when intervention of the right kind would do the most good.

POINT 3
THERE IS A NEED FOR ROLE DEFINITION AND CRITERIA FOR UTILIZATION OF SPECIALIZED SERVICES, AGENCIES, AND FACILITIES

This is another point which would broaden our quantity of services and manpower greatly, thereby permitting more retarded people to be served while not subverting the manpower and funds available to the community.

Although we must recognize the value of generic services and agencies, we do not propose an either-or situation in regard to generic vs. specialized services. Both are needed for a balanced program but must be properly fitted into the overall community services structure.

One of the major problems facing the field of planning for services to the retarded is the lack of definition of role of the various agencies. Unless this definition is made, it is most difficult to fit the various service roles together into the total spectrum of services which alone can guarantee the continuum of care the retarded require.

Needless to say, the confusion and loss of time for both professionals and patients created by this lack of definition is considerable—and far more than we can tolerate.

Another very important factor is poor utilization of the specialized agency or facility. Simpler cases are not usually appropriate for the specialized agency. When they are referred to it, two things happen. The agency receiving these cases is prevented by the very volume of need from performing its principal mission—provision of service to the more complex or difficult case, training, research, and demonstration of new techniques.

In addition, the generic agency which should be handling the simpler cases is prevented from doing so and, as a result, may not shoulder its responsibilities for handling even simpler levels of care for the retarded. Thus we defeat the purposes which we are trying to propagate, and the results of evaluation of previous planning become distorted and meaningless. Thus even future planning for such important factors as manpower is made useless.

It is disturbingly true that at present, only a small percentage of our retarded population is being provided services which are truly comprehensive both in variety and in time. Yet we are committing tremendous sums of money and numbers of people to just such programs.

In order to justify the continued presence of these services, we must use them to a more efficient end than we are currently doing. That is why it is so pressingly important that we sort out the missions of various kinds of services and make certain that problems are referred to services where they can be handled as simply as possible.

What we have been talking about in the first three points relates primarily to quantity of services for the retarded and to those services directly working with the retarded. We need to be concerned about quality, and the next two points refer to this.

POINT 4
THE PLACEMENT OF A MENTAL RETARDATION SPECIALIST, EITHER FULL-TIME OR PARTTIME, IN EVERY GENERIC AGENCY OF ANY SIZE OR SIGNIFICANCE

This accomplishes several things. First of all, it provides better distribution of specially trained manpower, putting professionals in positions where they can best utilize their skills in behalf of the greater number of retardates, thus relating to another great problem today which is the inequality of levels of service in different areas throughout the Nation.

More than that, point 4 provides a backup service enhancing staff competency in the generic agency. The mental retardation specialist in the generic agency acts as a consultant and inservice educator offering greater likelihood that the generic community service and health worker will accept the retarded patient. This, in turn, contributes to the quantity of services offered in the community, but it also can upgrade considerably the quality of those services. Furthermore, it satisfies another important problem concerned with the information explosion and the lag in the use of new knowledge.

It is obviously impossible for everyone to keep up with all the new developments today. We keep up with only those areas in which we have a special interest. The inclusion of the mental retardation specialist, either full or part time, in each sizable generic agency thus adds a professional with one special field of interest in which he keeps currently informed.

Since this specialist is trained in the multidisciplinary approach, though not necessarily skilled in every specialty contributing to it, he would be expected to have some knowledge of new developments as they relate to the other disciplines. Thus he becomes the intake channel for new knowledge and new techniques keeping the quality of care at a high level, and reducing the lag time between new knowledge and the implementation of that knowledge.

POINT 5
WE MUST DEVELOP STANDARDS FOR SERVICES AND TRAINING

"Standards" can have a very specific meaning. We are talking more generally at this point. Here, I am using the word to include those standards established nationally by a variety of groups, and all those established for various reasons by State and local groups. In addition, authoritative statements, guidelines, and regulations should be considered. Those to be utilized are determined by the community when appropriate to control and justify the expenditure of tax dollars, to help in program evaluation, to stimulate program improvement, and to use in determination of the need for continuance or modification of various programs. Standards are a quality control factor for the good of the community, the family, and, most important, the patient.

This discussion has centered to date on quality and quantity of programs. We need to say a

7. EMERGING DIRECTIONS

word for efficiency, for any discussion of a model for services of any kind is incomplete without consideration of this factor.

POINT 6
A COORDINATING MECHANISM WITHIN THE COMMUNITY IS A REQUISITE FOR BALANCED SERVICES AS WELL AS FOR MENTAL RETARDATION PLANNING

The coordinating mechanism should relate to the services existing in the community, and would probably be utilized best if based upon a service such as an information and referral center. Such a center would have the added advantage of offering a positive service to the generic or specialized agency. Thus it would be better able to enlist the cooperation and use of its coordinative role by existing agencies.

This would result in such needed side effects as an agreement on terminology, bringing improved communications, better data collection, and more unemotional and rational planning. The coordinating mechanism should be concerned with finding and eliminating those barriers which prevent the retarded from access to community services.

More than that, the center should serve in the coordination of inservice education and training and should be a meeting ground for planning across agency lines. This service might also be part of a community coordinating mechanism with a far wider role than merely mental retardation. If this is to be the case, however, the community agency should have an identifiable subsection responsible for retardation.

The coordinating body should be concerned, then, in bringing together all the fragments for the continuity of services needed by the retarded, assuring balance in the development and delivery of services, and making sure that the retarded get their fair share in both quantity and quality of the services available in the community.

CONCLUSION

This, then, is our 6-point model for a community service program. Individually, these points have been enunciated before. But that is not the point. The six points must be considered in a group in order to produce the various checks and balances necessary to the development of a balanced program.

Embodied in the whole model is the idea of economy—a very basic concept indeed—and vital since the amount of new knowledge available and still developing will stretch our resources to the bursting point. We have to recognize that in our field of mental retardation we cannot expect to obtain the ultimate in services when none of the other problem areas facing the community can do so. After all, we are not alone. Other conditions find the same lag between knowledge and implementation and have to compete for their fair share of the financial and manpower resources.

But under the system I have suggested, we have a fair fighting chance of obtaining our share of available community resources for the retarded. This fact plus the flexibility of the model enables us to bring the retardate together with his community's resources in an equitable, adequate manner.

We do not suggest—and for good reason—that these six points are unyielding and not to be adjusted. Quite the contrary. If a community needs to put more emphasis on specialized services and facilities, this can be done by lowering the criteria which determine their use. If the need is to channel more retardates into generic community agencies, we can always raise the criteria. The coordinating mechanism can and should be given a wide latitude in such areas as developing communications systems for the community. All this serves to give the community the basic control it needs to insure the best services compatible with the total availability of services.

There is one other important point which should be considered. We are here interested in the problem of mental retardation—one categorical problem which requires consideration in the total community framework. Nothing we have said here, however, could not with modification be applied to other categorical problems. In this age of comprehensive care, all of us must be thinking in terms of service to these various categories. But we must be concerned that we do not swing full circle. We moved from generalized services to specialized services in order to improve the quality of care. We achieved this improvement, but we also developed a degree of fragmentation which is not so desirable. Now, in the attempt to avoid fragmentation, we must be careful not to go back to the lower quality which generalization might bring.

We must use the elements of both systems, providing comprehensive care without too much decrease in quality. The great movement we are seeing toward the neighborhood health center—the center which will eventually become in effect, if not in fact, a personal services center—brings us closer to the time when health, welfare, educational, rehabilitative, and other services will be recognized as closely intertwined and when services to the family unit in all these areas will be closely coordinated.

What we really are dealing with, it seems to me, is a system—or a model of a system—in which, already, communities are beginning to participate. Many communities today have one

57. The 6-Point Program

or more elements of the 6-point model I have discussed. As the complete models are put together in more and more communities, we will indeed be reaching the day when the retarded member of our society does in fact receive something approaching his fair share of the services he so desperately needs.

MAINSTREAMING LIBRARY

BY
SPECIAL LEARNING CORPORATION

- Special Education
- Learning Disabilities
- Mental Retardation
- Autism
- Behavior Modification
- Speech and Hearing
- Deaf Education
- Emotional and Behavioral Disorders
- Psychology of Exceptional Children
- Diagnosis and Placement
- Dyslexia
- Visually Handicapped Education
- Mainstreaming
- Physically Handicapped Education
- Gifted and Talented Education

NOW $120.00

*individual books $8.75

For Teachers
For Administrators
For School Librarians

This set of highly useable professional books is published by Special Learning Corporation--a publisher of high quality special education materials.

The mainstreaming library provides the concerned professional a comprehensive resource for exceptional children. Each book deals extensively with a specific disability; providing a concise perspective and insight into the area.

Innovative methodology techniques are provided as an aid for the teacher concerned with providing quality education for the special child.

To order these books or for more information on these and other college and professional books, contact Joseph Logan, Special Learning Corporation.

SPECIAL LEARNING CORPORATION
42 Boston Post Rd. Guilford, Connecticut 06437   (203) 453-6525

Enabling the disabled

For many young students, selecting a college involves considerations far beyond curriculum, location or the ratio of men to women. A growing number of students are looking for schools with elevators in every building, automatic doors, wide bathroom stalls and lowered drinking fountains. These factors are essential for students confined to wheelchairs.

California State University, Hayward credits itself with a history of architectural design that accommodated handicapped students. When the school moved to its present location in 1963, the majority of the new buildings were constructed to be readily accessible to the disabled. But by the late 1960's, school administrators began to realize that even with the campus's modern facilities, there were still problems for students who were extremely handicapped or disabled.

"The commitment, the interest and the grass roots effort and desire to help disabled students has always been present at Cal State," says Jean Seavey Thomas, director of special programs. "Five years ago, however, was a turning point for us. That's when we started to take a serious look at what we were doing for our disabled and began to coordinate our efforts."

At that time, Thomas began working with other administrators to establish a disabled student services program for the entire university. Every department able to provide a service to the handicapped student was invited to participate, including library personnel, job placement officers and the director of health services. Their monthly meetings concentrated on consolidating disabled students services and establishing an open line of communication throughout the university. It became apparent, however, that major changes could not be undertaken without the assistance of outside funding.

In 1973 the university received its first financial aid in the form of a $8,300 state grant. The money was used in lowering all drinking fountains and increasing the number of curb cuts and ramps throughout the campus. Later, a combination grant of $38,400 from the Federal and state government was awarded. Again, a formal study was made by students, staff and administrators via the advisory committee. It was decided that the funds would be spent for four major projects.

1. The university's training swimming pool was made accessible for the disabled with the installation of a movable hoist to raise and lower handicapped swimmers in and out of the pool.
2. A sonar system in both the training and olympic pools will be installed. The sonar system will provide assistance to blind swimmers.
3. A ramp was constructed near the bookstore to provide better access to the bookstore and main campus. (20% of the costs were provided by the Auxiliary Foundation.)
4. A ramp to the second floor of the gymnasium was constructed. This was previously the only portion of the campus deemed totally inaccessible to the disabled.

Besides costly new construction and special programs demanding outside funding, the university initiated a number of other changes without exceeding its normal fiscal budget. A drop-in center for disabled students has been organized, offering support services in counseling, registration and tutoring.

All pay phones have been converted to touchtone and lowered. Also, courtesy phones have been installed so disabled students can call for assistance when needed. For blind students, every room on campus is identified with a braille number. There are also braille directories in each campus building.

Campus restrooms have been updated to accommodate the disabled by widening the entrances and stalls. Assistance bars were added. Priority medical parking is enforced strictly through the assistance of the university's campus patrol. Medical parking permits are issued through the office of special programs.

And is Cal State succeeding in its goal of giving equal education to the handicapped? Most of the school's 180 disabled students think that it is. Many of the students are quick to point out that accessibility means more than just the removal of architectural barriers. As one student points out, "What good is it if you can physically get into the classroom, but once you're there, your professor or classmates are ignorant or insensitive to your special needs?"

New hope for the retarded child

Walter Jacob

Dr. Jacob is director of the American Institute for Mental Studies in Vineland, New Jersey, a private, nonprofit center specializing in diagnosis, treatment, education, and care of the intellectually handicapped.... Illustrated by Anna Marie Magagna.

JOHNNY was the Bensons' first child. Because Sally and Bill Benson had been married for eight years before Johnny was born, they were unusually thrilled at his birth. They made great plans for him. Not only was he to go to college but to the best college in the land. After that, graduate school and a professional career.

Johnny was a sweet, happy baby. But somehow he didn't seem to develop as rapidly as the children of their friends and neighbors. He was slow in learning to sit up, slower in learning to walk, and at two years of age he still could not speak.

The Bensons were frightened and bewildered. They felt as if it was somehow their fault that Johnny did not seem quite like other children. They read all the child-rearing books they could lay their hands on, but they were still ashamed. Finally their fears drove them to seek professional help.

The Bensons' experience is not an unusual one. Over a hundred thousand parents each year have children who prove to be slow. There has been so much confusion as to what a retarded child is, so much guilt connected with retardation, that many parents have been reluctant to seek the help they need.

Part of the trouble has been confusion between mental retardation and mental illness.

A person with normal mental faculties may become mentally disturbed at any age. Worry, frustration, shock, and dozens of pressures all too common in the complexity of present-day living can precipitate mental illness. Such illness may afflict a child as well as an adult. If the condition is diagnosed soon enough, mentally ill patients can often be successfully treated.

what is mental retardation?

Mentally retarded persons are quite different. Theirs is a case of incomplete mental development, which limits their ability to learn. Since learning is cumulative from one set of items to the next, theirs is a progressively worsening problem in a society geared to achievement. So far, no pill or inoculation or other specific treatment has been discovered which can promise to lift such persons to normal or average intellectual advancement. But there is much that parents and others can do to help the mentally handicapped child learn as much as he is capable of.

There are no accurate census figures on the number of mentally retarded persons in this country or elsewhere. The best we can do is to make rough and rather arbitrary estimates. If we were to make a chart of the intellectual abilities of the entire population, we would have a bell-shaped "normal probability" curve. Most people would fall in the high, wide section in the center of the curve, with relatively few at each extreme. The severely mentally retarded, probably amounting to some 2 million persons, are at the lowest end. Another 4 to 6 million are less retarded but still seriously handicapped; yet today many of them may find their way in the community in a semi-dependent status.

Above this group, included in the broad term "mentally retarded," are those of milder handicap and of borderline intelligence. As we approach "normal" intelligence, it becomes difficult to say whether a person is retarded or "dull normal"; and as we rise along the scale, the curve of normal probability encompasses many more individuals. If we include all these persons with relatively mild handicaps, we are able to say that over half of the mentally retarded can find a place in the world at large.

These estimates indicate that the problem is a serious one in terms of numbers alone. In terms of heartache and emotional frustration, the impact on the families of those afflicted cannot be measured. And mental retardation presents a social problem too, for a considerable number of the retarded will need continuing help throughout their lives.

Mental retardation is not a single entity like measles or diphtheria. It is a condition resulting from many causes. Some of the causes have shown promise of correction or amelioration. All of them need further study.

what are the causes?

For many years it was generally assumed that 60 to 80 per cent of all mentally retarded persons had inherited their condition. This view received seeming substantiation from the "Kallikak Family" study published in 1912. The Kallikak study attempted to show the effects of blood inheritance in tracing the offspring of a Revolutionary War soldier who had had children by a mentally subnormal woman, and who later reared another family in marriage with an intellectually normal woman. The descendants of the subnormal mother were generally problems to society and to themselves, while those of the normal mother were generally contributing members of society. The conclusions of this one study became so entrenched in peoples' minds that even today the real causes of mental retardation are not widely understood. The Kallikak study did not stress environmental influences enough for present-day investigators.

"brain damage"

More recent studies have brought to light ample evidence that most mental retardation results from causes that have little to do with inheritance. Many cases involve children of average or superior parents, children whose handicap is the result of injury to the brain before birth or during the first few years of life.

"Brain damage" is a term at present loosely used. It may be applied to children with normal intelligence who have been injured in games or accidents, or to children with a number of types of retardation. When such damage is evident primarily in motor handicaps, sometimes accompanied by certain speech prob-

7. EMERGING DIRECTIONS

lems, the child is generally described as cerebral palsied — although many cerebral-palsied children are not mentally retarded.

The causes of mental retardation are grouped into major classifications: blood incompatibility, infection, exposure to poisonous substances, trauma (injury caused by a physical agent), metabolic disorder (the inability of the body to change protein into the elements it needs), new growths in the brain, genetic irregularities, environmental factors, and a large group of still unknown conditions. While research on causes and treatment has multiplied greatly in the past decade, a quick review of a few conditions emphasizes the continued need for effort.

blood incompatibility

Mental retardation may occur in the child of a mother with Rh negative blood and a father with Rh positive blood. Rh negative mothers may become sensitized to Rh positive blood by having an Rh positive baby or an Rh positive miscarriage. Today many state laws require a test for Rh factor at the birth of a baby.

Repeated blood transfusions for the baby before or at birth can wash out the sensitized blood and prevent brain damage. An injection of Rh immune globulin, given to an Rh negative mother within 72 hours of *each* Rh positive birth or miscarriage, prevents the mother from becoming sensitized and protects future children from blood incompatibility.

infections

Rubella, commonly known as German measles, is usually a mild disease, but it is very serious when it occurs early in pregnancy and is transmitted from the mother to the unborn child. Partial loss of hearing or vision, major heart defects, and mental retardation frequently result. It is estimated that at least 15 to 20 per cent of women who contract German measles during the first 12 weeks of pregnancy (and possibly just before conception) give birth to infants with serious handicaps. In 1964-1965, for instance, the nation experienced an epidemic of rubella, and 20,000 to 30,000 infants were born with congenital defects as a result.

Fortunately, since then an effective rubella vaccine has become available. The vaccine is given to children between one year old and puberty to prevent the disease from being transmitted to adult women. It is not usually given to mature women, since they may be pregnant and we do not know the vaccine's effect on an unborn child. Also, side effects of the vaccine can cause discomfort to adults.

Other infections that cause mental retardation are congenital syphilis, toxoplasmosis, and other prenatal conditions, as well as viruses and bacteria that may affect a child before or after birth.

poisonous substances

Brain disease (encephalopathy) is associated with toxic or poisonous substances in the mother's blood. These are not very common and usually can be detected during pregnancy.

The child himself may be exposed to lead, carbon monoxide, or other toxic substances. Of these, lead poisoning is the most frequent cause of brain damage; counter-agents are available. More important, many communities are conducting programs aimed at eliminating lead poisoning.

Kernicterus (bilirubin encephalopathy) may follow severe jaundice in the newborn. It is frequently due to Rh incompatibility between the unborn baby and the mother but may be caused by other conditions.

Inoculation of a child with serum or vaccine to prevent diseases like smallpox, rabies, and typhoid may occasionally result in nervous-system reactions or, in rare instances, encephalitis.

trauma or physical injury

Prenatal injuries such as those caused by excessive irradiation and lack of oxygen can cause brain damage in an infant, as can complications during birth — malposition, poor presentation for delivery, disproportion, and excess use of drugs or anesthetics. While the effects of birth injury tend to diminish somewhat with time, many subtle disorganizations and defects of motor, sensory, perceptual, emotional, and integrative behaviors may result.

In a small number of cases brain damage may result from falls — from highchairs, cribs, and the like — that cause severe injury such as fractured skull or prolonged unconsciousness.

metabolic disorders

Metabolic (blood chemistry) errors also may damage a baby's brain. Some of the more recognized forms are described here.

Cretinism is caused by insufficient secretion of the thyroid gland and reveals itself in underdeveloped physical growth. In early life it is often confused with Down's syndrome (mongolism). Early treatment with thyroid extract can produce rapid improvement. But, while in some cases the physical signs of cretinism nearly disappear, there is rarely a complete disappearance of mental retardation. To prevent possible cretinism in their children, pregnant women may be advised to take supplemental iodine.

Galactosemia, which is due to a missing enzyme that is necessary to produce useful blood glucose, may cause severe retardation in a baby. It is a rare condition, but a strict diet makes normal health and mentality possible. In suspected instances the diet should be followed in pregnancy and continued for the baby after birth.

PKU (phenylketonuria), characterized by a "musty" smell in the urine, can produce convulsions and mental retardation. It is caused by lack of an enzyme which can be detected at birth by a simple blood test, now mandatory in many states. A special diet, carefully supervised by the physician, helps to prevent brain damage in PKU babies.

Other metabolic diseases that occur frequently are: gargoylism (Hurler's disease), a form of dwarfism with no definite treatment known at present; Gaucher's disease (familial splenic anemia), a family disease which is found particularly in Jewish families and for which there is no known treatment at present; Niemann-Pick disease (lipoid histiocytosis) and Tay-Sachs disease (cerebromuscular degeneration), both related to defects in the metabolism of fats, for which there are as yet no specific treatments; maple syrup urine disease, so named because of the characteristic odor, which can be prevented by a special diet; and Wilson's disease (hepatolenticular degeneration), an inherited defect in the body's use of copper or protein, which usually shows up between 10 and 25 years of age, and which can be controlled by diet.

Of the many biochemical disorders that can cause mental retardation, there is hope in the fact that a few can now be prevented, a few can be treated, and research is pursuing answers to others.

new growths

Neurofibromatosis (Von Recklinghausen's disease) is a hereditary condition characterized by such things as tumorous growths on nerve trunks and skin, calcium growths in the brain area, small nodule growths throughout the brain and central nervous system, and other manifestations including seizures, skin discoloration, and paralysis of one side of the body.

There are several other conditions too, discernible by a physician, in which new growths cause retardation and seizures.

genetic irregularities

Every cell in the body contains a lump of matter called chromosomes, each one of which holds hundreds of genes. These genes hold the hereditary elements that decide everything from the color of our eyes to the chemical processes of our bodies. We are just beginning to learn how these chromosomes and genes are formed and grouped.

Down's syndrome (mongolism) dramatically illustrates this. The term "mongolism" or "mongoloid," formerly used to describe these children, is misleading and is giving way to "Down's syndrome" in recognition of the pioneer identification of these children by a British physician, John Langdon Down, some 70 years ago. In 1959 the first scientific identification of the cause came with the discovery that a person with this condition has an extra chromosome. Where normal humans have 46 chromosomes, a person with Down's syndrome has 47. In some cases, the 47th chromosome is free and distinct, and in others it is attached to another chromosome.

It is estimated that Down's syndrome occurs in about one out of every 700 births and is unrelated to the race, economic level, or intelligence of the parents. It can be diagnosed while the fetus is developing within the mother. If the 47th chromosome is unattached, the possibility of having another child with this condition appears remote for a young mother — but much higher when the mother is over 40 years of age. When the 47th chromosome is attached to another, the chances of having a second child so afflicted are about 33 per cent.

Although personality disturbances are not infrequent among them, children with Down's syndrome tend to be happy, affectionate, and lovable. Sometimes they have difficulty in establishing satisfactory social relations, and few seem able to learn to read. They seem to be more susceptible than most children to disease, especially respiratory ailments, and in mature years many lack sufficient stamina to pursue a vocation. Modern medicine, however, has extended their lives into adulthood.

other causes

The origins of several conditions leading to mental retardation are not yet understood. Among these conditions are microcephaly (undersized skulls), hydrocephaly (oversized skulls containing excess fluid), and other skull malformations — generally attributed to unidentified prenatal influences. Brain diseases, usually degenerative, can also cause retardation.

In some cases, when there is no clear clinical indication of physical disease or abnormality, mild mental retardation may be caused by environmental or cultural conditions.

emotional disturbance

Many mentally retarded children are also emotionally unstable. This may be caused by parents' excessive pressure on the child or by the derision of playmates, for example.

In other cases, prolonged emotional disturbance may cause a normal child to function as if he were retarded. Although the disturbance and the mental handicap must be handled at the same time, easing the emotional problems makes it easier to attack the retardation. How long the condition has existed and the degree of retardation reached before treatment is started affect the child's chances of performing at higher levels.

multiple handicaps

Autism is a type of childhood schizophrenia. The autistic child does not respond normally to those taking care of him; he does not cuddle. Because he is more responsive to objects than to people, he may not learn to talk and so resembles a retarded or an aphasic child (one who is unable to speak). Many times prolonged reactions of this kind lead to true retardation. The hope is that correcting the psychological condition can make way for clearing up the retardation. But a high degree of retardation, existing over a relatively long time, added to the general difficulty of treating schizophrenia, works against a very hopeful prognosis for an autistic child.

Confusion between autism and aphasia is common. Generally an autistic child is apathetic, while the aphasic child is very active. An autistic child usually shows some indication that his capacity to form ideas is higher than that represented by his speech level. In both instances, however, communication with the child is difficult.

Partial loss of some sensory mechanisms limits a child's comprehension of his environment. Deafness of some tones may make it difficult to hear the same word in the same way twice. Oversensitivity may make it difficult for him to select impressions from his surroundings; this can lead to a loss in ability to concentrate. Inability to share ideas, experiences, and emotions deadens intellectual development, thus leading to the child's functioning at a mentally retarded level.

Although some forms of seizures — epilepsy, convulsions, psychomotor disturbances — frighten those who are unfamiliar with them, the intelligence of most victims is much the same as that of the general public. Seizures themselves are not inherited, although a predisposition toward them may be. Nobody should be institutionalized just because he is epileptic. In most cases, drugs are effective in controlling the seizures; and help can be obtained from clinics throughout the country.*

However, brain damage may cause seizures, and they are not uncommon among mentally retarded individuals.

Those who work with children who are multiply handicapped — who are not only mentally retarded but also suffer from emotional disturbance, sensory disabilities, seizures — must use the knowledge and resources of many different fields.

HOW CAN WE LOCATE THE VICTIMS?

With so much information about mental retardation constantly accumulating, it is obvious that diagnosis is a highly technical matter involving numerous professional specialties. The key to such diagnosis is the competent observer, one who has had considerable experience with many different kinds of mentally retarded children.

Tests should be used to corroborate observation; they should not be used alone. Conducted by inexperienced persons or those in positions removed from actual work with these children, tests draw a picture of a child and his problems and a label of his handicaps which can be highly suspect. Unfortunately such reports can lie in record files of the child for years, only to be restated by later workers, thus giving a stamp of approval to a diagnosis that may have been made on weak bases.

Some retarded children, such as those with Down's syndrome, cretinism, or hydrocephalus, usually have symptoms so readily recognizable at birth or infancy as to leave little doubt about their condition. But even with them differences in the degree of their handicaps can affect future levels of development.

Other children have symptoms such as physical handicaps and convulsive disorders which may be noted early in life. But most retarded children may not show obvious handicaps. Particularly in such instances the causes and degree of retardation must be determined in order to help them, and the physician must consider many things before reporting his suspicions to the parents and recommending treatment.

Terminology varies over the years as words become distasteful to parents or as new ones seem to describe conditions more accurately. At present, two of the most popular terminologies that attempt to grade levels of retardation are those used by educators and psychologists. Both professions base their gradations on intelligence quotients derived from a series of individual psychological tests — as a convenient method — but both will admit readily that IQ's hardly make a satisfactory yardstick for

7. EMERGING DIRECTIONS

such determinations.

By studying the growth of average children, scientists have been able to classify stages of physical growth by such factors as the child's ability to balance his head, to grasp objects within reach, to roll over, and to sit up unsupported. Social growth status may also be discernible and is graded by such tests as the Vineland Social Maturity Scale.

Social growth involves such things as the ability of a young child to occupy himself, to play while unattended, to demand personal attention, to follow simple directions, and later to play with other children. Scales for measuring social growth depend on the levels of self-help, locomotion, occupation, communication, self-direction, and socialization which are achieved at various stages of maturation.

Even without obvious physical evidence, infants who are seriously retarded may show developmental signs that suggest their problems: unusual placidity, extreme fretfulness, lack of interest in surroundings, no attempt to sit up or grasp at objects, are some of these. They may have seizures, which are not uncommon; if they do, a careful record should be kept. In less severe cases there are far fewer easily discernible signals.

If by the time a child is 3 years old he is obviously backward in a number of growth stages by as much as a year, mental retardation should be suspected and the parents should be informed. Such factors as poor environment or ill health should be corrected, if feasible, to eliminate them as further contributors to the lack of development.

The whole matter of sound diagnosis has become very complex. For a parent to attempt to diagnose his child without a trained worker at hand is, at best, questionable. Long experience with the signs and problems of mental retardation is necessary. Even with all available tools at hand, it is difficult enough for professional workers to achieve an accurate diagnosis.

steps in diagnosis

By the time a child reaches the age of 4, there should be little remaining doubt about the seriousness of any physical or neurological condition. Sometimes, however, in the absence of conclusive signs, intellectual retardation may not be clearly established before the age of 5 or 6. Some parents have their first awakening after the child has been refused promotion from kindergarten or first grade. Then, after a succession of examinations and consultations, they begin to remember slownesses in development during the earlier years. Passed over as unimportant at the time, these signals become significant when they are viewed collectively.

This is not meant to frighten parents of normal children into six years of anxiety and worry. Children may be slow in several areas, but a normal child is not slow in as many areas as a retarded child.

Parents who become concerned about their child usually seek help by consulting their family physician or the school teacher first. They may then move through a succession of clinics, psychologists, and medical specialists — some of whom may have had little day-to-day experience with mental retardation. The ideal situation provides a number of specialists from different fields in one place. Such a resource lets the parent obtain a comprehensive competent diagnosis of his child's condition — and at the lowest possible cost, since traveling to see many specialists is usually expensive. It also enables better research. The national organizations listed on page 27 and the Referral Service, American Institute for Mental Studies, Vineland, New Jersey 08360 can help parents select the appropriate diagnostic facilities.

A sound diagnosis should cover at least these six elements:

1. *A study of background and history* includes family history as well as that of the child.

2. *A general medical examination* concerns itself with not only the general well-being of the child but also evidence of the potential command of his faculties.

3. *Physical tests* include the muscular development, height, weight, and head and chest measurements of a growing child.

4. *A neurological examination* tests the responses from the brain and the spinal cord (the so-called nervous system), with a view to gaining a better understanding of the child's perception and memory functions. This may include electroencephalograms, a screening for errors in metabolism and nutritional deprivation, and, where necessary, pneumoencephalograms.

5. *Speech, hearing, and vision tests* are conducted, since damage to brain tissue or nerve fibers often affects speech, hearing, and vision centers as it does the intellectual centers of the brain.

6. *Psychological and psychiatric evaluations* cover not only mental age and IQ but also social and emotional elements.

These six kinds of examinations are essential. While various other tests can be made in genetic, endocrinological, and biochemical areas, *it must be emphasized that all of them are not needed for all children.* Only when there are sufficient grounds for uncertainty should a test be given. If a condition can be readily diagnosed after some study, superfluous examinations are irresponsible; specialists' time and energy may be needed elsewhere.

Double checking of the diagnosis, however, especially if made for a child before his fifth or sixth year, is often desirable. Levels of retardation apparent in tests early in life are not necessarily permanent indicators of levels of achievement in later life. Under good programs, checks are made as often as thought necessary in as many areas as necessary to trace progress or lack of it until the child reaches maturity.

WHAT CAN BE DONE?

A clear idea of the type and degree of retardation, and the accompanying speech, hearing, vision, and emotional problems, is necessary before a program can be drawn up for the retarded child. Also to be considered are such factors as the home, the parents, the number and age of brothers and sisters in the home, and the family income.

A good program not only will provide the greatest possible help to the child but also will give the comfort so needed by the parents. Since such a program involves special decisions in each individual case, it demands serious deliberation.

For example, Mary is 6 years old and severely handicapped intellectually. She needs constant supervision and much physical care. But her family is unable to meet the demands that her presence makes on all its members. Mary needs a place where she will be helped to function — and to be happy. Whether it should be a private or state-operated institution will depend on the availability of the services and on family finances. In any event she needs a place where whatever abilities that may be dormant

59. The Retarded Child

within her can be drawn out through an understanding educational program, where she is kept from regressing, and where her life is given a purpose.

Mark is an 8-year-old child with Down's syndrome, happy and lovable, with not a care in his little head. The "degree" of his retardation is less than in many children with Down's syndrome, and the prospects for his future development are better than most. His present level of development is that of a nursery school child. He can be trained in a day or residential school. He presents little problem in care — except for his childishness, and the fact that, because children with Down's syndrome are so susceptible to disease, any sign of illness should be brought to the immediate attention of a physician.

Paul, an emotionally disturbed 11-year-old, functions on a subnormal level, but no diagnosis has ever clarified the true mental ability beneath his disturbance. Undoubtedly, he would not be classified as "normal." He needs a 24-hour atmosphere of regularity, steadiness, and peace wherein he can experience the feeling of success in personal relationships, in learning new skills, in developing physical prowess. When his emotional disturbance eases or disappears, his subsequent development may be impressive.

A good diagnosis of these children's problems would recommend not only education and training but various kinds of therapy, such as psychotherapy, behavior therapy, physiotherapy, speech therapy, play therapy, and the like, each working to improve performance in a specific area and each affecting performance in other areas.

the beginnings of special education

Although the cause of retardation — and future prevention — is primarily a problem for scientific teamwork, the basic elements in the rehabilitation of the child are educational. Since he learns slowly we must refine our methods of teaching him and evaluate the usefulness to him of what we ask him to learn.

The first American school for retarded children was established in July, 1848, in Barre, Massachusetts. Later that year, another school was opened in Boston and after two successful years became the Massachusetts School for Idiotic and Feeble-Minded Children. In October, 1851, an experimental school was opened in Albany, New York. A private school was opened in Millville, New Jersey in 1887, moved a year later to Vineland, New Jersey, and became known as The Training School at Vineland — now a unit of the American Institute for Mental Studies. As time passed more residential schools, public and private, were established.

In 1949, in *The Child Who Never Grew*, the well-known novelist Pearl S. Buck wrote about her own child at The Training School at Vineland. She helped parents realize that mental retardation is often accidental, is no fault of theirs, and exists in many normal and superior families.

private facilities

Many schools and institutions were established by private citizens who were concerned about the problems facing mentally handicapped children and their families. Originally most of these were residential schools.

Under favorable circumstances, residential schools, because they deal with smaller numbers of children, may offer more individual attention to each child. The quality of the staff determines the quality of the services at a particular school; advertisements and furnishings are no indication of the quality of programs. Visits to schools, personal contacts with staff, and talks with other parents who have children in a school are essential in selecting the best school for the particular child.

Small residential cottages, closer staff relationships with the children, a full range of professional workers — either full-time or available for consultation and services — are hallmarks of good schools. Programs for individual children are tailored to the needs of the child and his family; a good portion of attention is given to the family unit. Educational programs leading to vocational and social training which can carry the child to the limits of his abilities are indispensable.

Facilities for research and training of professional workers may be taken as additional evidence of professional alertness.

Day services, ranging from preschool classes up, may also be offered by private schools. Some offer clinical services for diagnosis and therapy. Some conduct vocational training, from workshops to actual employment inside the school and in the neighboring communities.

Private schools may be either nonprofit or proprietary. Nonprofit schools, often referred to as voluntary organizations, have no owners or stockholders, and excess funds at the end of the year are applied to the school's needs as determined by its board of trustees, usually unpaid volunteers. The board of trustees are responsible for control and guidance; they help keep the schools alive and give them permanence comparable to that of public institutions.

Most private schools are proprietary, which means that their profits go to owners or stockholders as in any other business. The fact that a private school is proprietary does not limit its quality, but it may limit its continuance if the owner decides to close the school.

In our society, private schools, being relatively free of the complexities of larger organizations, have had the opportunity to develop and demonstrate new methods of helping children. Unless the schools use this opportunity, there is little reason for their existence. The day of the "plush" private school for social purposes has passed.

public facilities

Public resources support numerous types of organizations that serve the mentally retarded. The President's Committee on Mental Retardation has outlined the desirability of a life program in the community for these children. Increased federal support has done much to bring many of these services into being.

During the late 1950s and 1960s innumerable programs and millions of dollars were provided for the mentally retarded. Never before had such support been given these children. The President's Committee on Mental Retardation in its 1969 report pointed to a decade of accomplishments such as these:

- The development of a national network of diagnostic and evaluation centers;
- The development of a national network of research in mental retardation;
- The development of teaching and professional centers;

7. EMERGING DIRECTIONS

- The development in every state of plans for mental retardation services;
- Some mandatory testing for PKU and vaccines for rubella;
- Increasing acceptance of the mentally retarded in vocational rehabilitation programs;
- Dramatic growth in the number of volunteers to help retarded persons;
- Attention to poverty areas and their effect on retardation;
- Programs of total life support in communities;
- Greatly increased attention to the retarded in public schools.

Obviously all these are in no way finished projects, but their very existence on the national scene is impressive.

Public schools. In recent years most states have dramatically expanded special education programs in public schools. The establishment of these classes has brought more services to more retarded children than ever before, and has allowed many more to remain at home instead of being institutionalized.

In some cases the classes for mentally retarded children are separate; in some, whole buildings specialize in such services; while in most the aim is to return as many children as possible to regular classes as soon as possible.

Grants support the establishment of Head Start classes for some children below school age. Day care centers care for children of working mothers. Visiting nurses demonstrate techniques of child care to selected groups of families that have young retarded children. Homemakers' services help families through a crisis period. Counselors and other social workers offer services to retarded children and their parents.

Public institutions. State institutions offer longer-term residential care for those who need it, rates adjusted to the parents' ability to pay, and ever-improving organization and quality of service. Of necessity they handle greater numbers than do private institutions. But centralized eating and large dormitories are gradually disappearing. In most institutions the orientation is toward the child's return to society, although in severe cases this may not be possible.

As in all agencies, the staff determines the quality of the programs, and in the long run is vastly more important than the physical plant. Parents should make personal visits to these institutions and consult with the staff just as they would if they were selecting a private school.

Mental health clinics. In the past ten years mental health clinics have proliferated throughout the country. Their services may cover the community or whole counties. They supply diagnostic services and as much treatment as they can. Supported mostly by public funds, they offer their services at a minimum fee. Most of them will handle mental retardation, emotional disturbance, and many other problems.

Vocational centers — habilitation. Although since 1943 handicapped persons have been eligible for special vocational training programs sponsored by state and federal governments, it took almost twenty years before much service was offered to the mentally retarded. In a sense, since these children never had vocational competency and therefore never lost any skills, we are dealing with "habilitation" programs that train for original vocational skills.

Various agencies, private and public, sponsor sheltered workshops, work-activity centers, and other training organizations of many kinds — from those where the child is taught motor manipulation and coordination on work models, to those where he earns money by actually completing jobs often provided by the workshop on a subcontract basis with a producer or factory. A vocational center will try to follow a person until he has shown his ability to hold a job with minimum or no further supervision. The centers help socially deprived and physically handicapped persons of all ages as well as the mentally handicapped.

Vocational Rehabilitation Commissions, federal and state, coordinate such efforts, which are heavily supported by federal funds. Schools or local or regional vocational rehabilitation offices can help the parents seeking these services for their child.

how can we teach these children?

The teacher must study the child, observe his problems in approaching a learning situation, and attempt to interpret the underlying attitudes and disabilities. For this the teacher needs competent support from many other services in order to utilize everything possible to increase the child's learning.

Traditionally the teacher of the retarded child has had little such additional help. The most common methods brought vocabulary and subject matter down to the mental level of the child and adopted teaching strategies appropriate to this level — usually in an attempt to train the senses. If a child was 12 years old with a mental age of about 7 years (approximately second grade in regular school), the teacher used first- or second-grade material. Some students do not respond satisfactorily to such a program but, as with almost any system, some do.

It is doubtful if simple generalizations concerning the learning characteristics of the retarded can be considered adequate today. Yet, although some progress has been made in understanding the mental processes of various types of mentally handicapped children, there is still no accumulation of satisfactory techniques to help the teacher in the average situation; the traditional generalities are still applied in many instances.

The direction of most training is vocational — with the hope of eventual community employment. Success is closely related to the child's ability to keep at a task until it is completed, his motor coordination, his ability to understand what is wanted of him, and his sense of pride in turning out a good job; these are the same demands made of normal workers everywhere.

Parallel to vocational training must be training in socialization: habits of personal hygiene, how to dress, how to make change, how to handle oneself on the job and in the community, and a multitude of other things to help the child live successfully with others.

Of major importance in any learning situation is the ability of the teacher to motivate the child. This implies an ability to understand him and his personal problems.

For the less handicapped, where communication is easier, response to motivation may approximate that of "normal" children. For children with less intellectual ability, the teacher selects shorter terms and more modest goals; often a child is immediately rewarded with candy or privileges.

Because there are so many different kinds of mental handicap in most special classrooms — even though they cannot be too specifically diagnosed — the teacher's tasks in motivating and teaching require special knowledge, ability, and energy. The enthusiasm of the teacher and the degree to which she gives individual attention to the child are still most important.

As the retarded child reaches adolescence, it may be more difficult to work with him. And many services for the retarded or emotionally disturbed prefer to work with younger children. As the child passes the legal age for inclusion in the public school system, and if he is not yet able to take some part in community life and employment, parents are confronted with further problems. Every effort should be made to keep the child in ordinary community life.

If an adult is not able to carry on even semi-dependent living in the community, he may profit by *living* in an institution with its many supports and *working* in the community with as many social activities as possible. Whether this is feasible or whether complete institutional protection of some sort is required, much grief can be avoided for the child and his parents if proper counseling has led to realistic expectations.

home still vital

The *home* is still a vital place for mentally retarded children. It should be an environment where a young child is loved and feels that he is wanted. So many of his future reactions and concepts depend on this.

Children capable of profiting from community offerings such as pre-school classes, special classes in the public school system, community mental health clinics, vocational training, and the like

59. The Retarded Child

can continue living at home.

Some may benefit from "home instruction" programs where instructors make home visits to teach the parents how to care for and train the child in the home and offer workbooks, games, and recreational suggestions.

It is hoped that as the more capable child reaches maturity he may be involved vocationally and socially in his community to a greater or lesser degree, depending on his abilities. Here the home is still his bastion of security and guidance. A collection of specialists to aid him — even though more knowing and skilled in their specific field — can rarely supplant a mother and father. If necessary, foster parents sometimes may meet the need for a good home.

community integration

All efforts to absorb a retarded child into the community depend on the willingness of the neighborhood to accept him. At present this presents a serious problem to the child and parents. Gradually all types of handicapped persons are being accepted more readily by others, but the mentally handicapped seem to be having more difficulty than the physically handicapped.

It is not uncommon to find that some persons turn away or involuntarily recoil from an obviously retarded child — perhaps out of fear or, almost worse, an unwillingness to admit that such problems exist. On the other hand, the large numbers of retarded children without apparent physical or emotional symptoms may initially be accepted, only to be rejected later. This leads to special problems during the courtship ages.

The steadiness of mentally retarded workers often begins to win grudging appreciation and sometimes admiration from employers and other workers. And nationally the numbers of mentally retarded are so great as to represent a large pool of manpower and citizenship which cannot be overlooked. The President's Committee on Employment of the Handicapped states that records of the mentally retarded show that:

- They work harder than most, for they want to make good on the job; accident and loss rates are lower.
- They stay on routine tasks much longer than other workers.
- Their attendance record usually is better than average.
- Their job stability is better than average; they "job hop" less.

Yet it is doubtful if America has matured sufficiently to allow the retarded person a place in society commensurate with his abilities.

At the same time, the many classes in schools for the retarded, the mental health clinics, vocational workshops, and recreation programs appearing on the scene bring these children out into the open and other youngsters grow up with them, more aware and therefore more understanding of their condition. This personal contact will do much to bridge the gap.

recreation

A mentally retarded child is not usually as physically active as a normal child. His sense of competition is not as strong, and in general he is not as robust. Highly organized team sports may attract some less retarded children, but they do not usually appeal to those of lower intelligence. There are exceptions: once in a great while a "natural" appears, obviously not too able mentally but outstandingly capable in a sport.

Less highly organized sports and games are activities in which these children are better able to participate. Dancing, music, arts and crafts, hobby collections, are within the range of most, are enjoyed thoroughly by them, and are necessary for their wellbeing. Schools and local recreation commissions, churches, YMCA's, Boy Scouts, and other organizations are steadily developing programs for these children. The Associations for Retarded Children and similar groups often sponsor recreational activities for them. The Joseph P. Kennedy, Jr. Foundation has provided funds to set up demonstration camps in 23 states. Family outings, fishing trips, nature walks, camping, and the like are as satisfying and beneficial to a retarded child as to others.

Basic to all recreation for the retarded child is the understanding that he need not "star" in any activity, particularly to satisfy a parent's longing for something to compensate for the child's mental slowness. Recreation can give the child a feeling of success, something he does not experience too often. Parents and friends can organize weekend events, club programs, hikes, and other activities through many of the organizations to which they belong. And they can encourage retarded and normal children to work and play together in these groups.

research and demonstration

Usually conducted by teams of specialists, today's research is costly and requires numerous facilities and staff, which not many centers can maintain. Most research is in either physical or behavioral fields. The physical specialist, usually in a medical field, tries to find actual organs or body functions which are malfunctioning. The behavioral specialist, usually a psychiatrist, psychologist, or educator, is concerned with behavior aberrations and learning ability. Both try to find ways of ameliorating or correcting conditions, but perhaps their greatest triumphs lie in learning how to prevent the conditions. As their efforts clarify the different kinds or different causes of mental handicaps, the tempo of progress in eliminating the problem will increase.

To *see* improvement achieved with new techniques is as exciting and inspiring to professional workers as it is to parents. Every center dealing with the problems of mental handicap — be it educational, clinical, or recreational, public or private — should set itself up as a demonstration center for all who wish to see, to learn, and to be inspired to greater effort.

WHAT CAN YOU DO?

Mental handicaps of all sorts present a challenging personal problem to parents. They must live with and love their child for so many years in a world that puts such emphasis on mental facility. To do this they must understand their child and his condition. This takes more than sympathy. It takes *empathy*, putting oneself in the child's place and observing what the world looks like from there. It takes mature judgment to balance the effect of this child's presence on the rest of the family. It takes patience above all things.

Understanding mental retardation means more than reading books or listening to speeches about it. It means living with it and fitting the life into the society in which it has found itself. It means acceptance rather than rejection. It means freeing oneself from feelings of guilt for having had such a child, or fear of the consequences. In that understanding, the parent grows in social maturity. Iron never becomes steel without heat.

keep contact with others

As their own understanding grows, parents are in a better position to influence others to help improve the lot of the handi-

297

7. EMERGING DIRECTIONS

capped child. At first, contact with others proves a source of comfort. There is satisfaction and help in being able to talk freely about personal problems with others who face similar ones. It helps to talk with professional people who are in daily contact with these children. Meetings of all kinds are excellent means of contact and learning.

Later these experiences breed realization of the desirability of group action toward larger goals for the good of the retarded children, and parents become leaders in community projects and legislative efforts in this direction.

One significant result of such activity was the formation in 1950 of the National Association for Retarded Children, which now has local chapters almost everywhere across the country. It has had a tremendous effect on the rest of the nation, and the retarded child has benefited beyond estimation. Other results are represented by the many local services a parent finds available to the child within his community.

improve present facilities

Happily no one is ever satisfied with present conditions. Whether concerned with private or public facilities, parents can organize to help improve programs in schools, agencies, institutions, and research. These activities are created to serve the parents and the child, and enlightened parents can do much to orient them in directions most helpful in meeting the child's needs. Even the best of agencies must revise its procedures periodically.

encourage public and private responsibility

Because of the large numbers of children involved and the fact that today most parents of retarded children are oriented to social welfare, many people think in terms of public responsibility for the help and services they need. Taxes have risen greatly to pay for these services. And the individual citizen expects and gets a return for his taxes in facilities such as those previously described. But establishment of a facility by government is no more assurance of quality or efficiency than if it had been established under private auspices. A facility that finds itself the beneficiary of the efforts of parents vitally interested in retarded children is fortunate. As "owners" of the activity, they can do much to help improve its services.

Similarly, parents can do much to encourage voluntary services. Although it seems increasingly difficult to establish new voluntary facilities to help retarded children, or even to maintain the existing ones in the face of higher taxes and few donors, the amount of private philanthropy is still imposing. Tax laws that give advantages to donors have much to do with this.

Parents can also help by acting as volunteers or by enlisting volunteers to assist in centers and workshops that train or employ the retarded. They can watch for opportunities for retarded persons and help to match persons to jobs. They can help their school systems develop services for the retarded.

It should be realized that the cost of maintaining a retarded person for a lifetime inside or outside an institution, especially with steadily increasing life spans, can run to $500,000. Any earnings on his part to offset this cost would be welcome, to his family, to society, and to himself. Parents can help develop preschool programs, evaluation centers, day care centers, and additional classes and programs in regular schools. They can help provide more trained teachers and other professional workers and aides. They can help provide special equipment. And all these can be supported by both public and private sources.

spread the story

Every act of informing others about mental retardation is a step in the right direction. Education leads to understanding, understanding to effort, and effort eventually leads to success.

Speeches, printed articles, television, motion pictures, labeled collection cans, and posters — all can help to spread the story, and all benefit both the public and private programs for prevention of mental retardation and help for the retarded. Local and state educational agencies and private centers and universities are natural dispensers of knowledge. And one should not forget the many social agencies and private industries that can help.

Since the problem respects no race, creed, or economic level, and continues into adult life, all of us have a personal interest in its solution. Preventing future mental retardation, and turning wasted lives into useful ones, would add millions of responsible and productive citizens to the nation and the world.

associations, societies, and foundations

This is a partial listing of national organizations directly or indirectly concerned with the welfare of exceptional children. Many of them issue helpful publications and offer guidance on services.

American Association on Mental Deficiency, 5201 Connecticut Avenue, N.W., Washington, D.C. 20015.

American Speech and Hearing Association, 9030 Old Georgetown Road, Washington, D.C. 20014.

Association for Children with Learning Disabilities, 2200 Brownsville Road, Pittsburgh, Pennsylvania 15210.

The Council for Exceptional Children, 1201 West 16th Street, N.W., Washington, D.C. 20036.

Epilepsy Foundation of America, 111 West 57th Street, New York, New York 10019.

The National Association for Mental Health, Inc., 1800 North Kent Street, Rosslyn, Virginia 22209.

National Association for Retarded Children, Inc., 2709 Avenue "E" East, Arlington, Texas 76011.

National Easter Seal Society for Crippled Children and Adults, 2023 West Ogden Avenue, Chicago, Illinois 60612.

National Epilepsy League, 203 North Wabash Avenue, Chicago, Illinois 60601.

National Institute of Neurological Diseases and Stroke, National Institutes of Health, Bethesda, Maryland 20014.

United Cerebral Palsy Associations, Inc., 66 East 34th Street, New York, New York 10016.

what to read

Adler, S. *The Non-Verbal Child.* Springfield, Ill.: Charles C Thomas Publishing Company, 1964.

Allen, R. M., and Cortazzo, A. D. *Psychological and Educational Aspects and Problems of Mental Retardation.* Springfield, Ill.: Charles C Thomas Publishing Company, 1970.

Buck, Pearl S. *The Child Who Never Grew.* New York: John Day Publishing Company, 1950.

Chess, S., and Thomas, A. *Annual Progress in Child Psychiatry and Child Development.* New York: Brunner and Mazel, Inc., 1970.

Hutt, Max L., and Gibby, Robert Gwyn. *The Mentally Retarded Child — Development, Education and Treatment.* Second Edition. Boston: Allyn and Bacon, Inc., 1965.

Jones, R. L. *New Directions in Special Education.* Boston: Allyn and Bacon, Inc., 1970.

INDEX

abnormal body structure, 211
abused children, 9, 10, 102
acceptance of the retarded, 9, 44-45
accidents, 101
acting out, 178
activity level, 179
adolescence, 264, 296
affective domain, 86
Aid to the Permanently and Totally Disabled, 69
Albert Einstein Scale of Sensory-Motor Intelligence, 212
alcoholism, 91
alphatocopheral (vitamin E), 179
Alpert's syndrome, 59
altered brain development, 204
American Association of Mental Deficiency, 51, 68, 143 216
American Medical Association, 180
American Psychiatric Association, 68
amniocentesis, 92, 100
anxiety, 162
Ann J. Kellogg School, 189
anoxia, 48, 189
antecedent modeling of desired responses, 217
antibiotics, 191
antibiotic lozenges, 49
antisyphilitic therapy, 95
apathy, 178
applied behavior analysis, 243
asphyxia, 48
audio signals, 233
audiologists, 213
Australia, 199
autism, 50, 178, 293
aversive consequences, 246
avocational skills, 256

backward chaining, 212
Ball, Stick-Bird method, 220-224
Baltimore Early Childhood Learning Continuum, 52, 53
Barr's syndrome, 59
Bayley Infant Scales of Development, 212
behavioral graphs, 247
behaviorism, 238
behavior handicaps, 48, 72, 129
behavior modification, 18, 50, 119, 256-259
behavior management, 207
Bender Visual Motor Gestalt, 134, 135, 136
Benzedrine, 137
bilateral congenital cataracts, 59
blindness, 4, 5, 11, 15, 64, 92, 152, 158, 204, 290
blood incompatibility, 292
Boy Scouts, 272
Braille, Louis, 11
brain damage, 14, 27, 34, 36, 38, 57, 90, 156-159
brain disease, 292

Brigham, Dr. Amariah, 18
Buck, Pearl S., 295
Bureau of Education of the Handicapped, 204, 205, 255
Bureau of Mental Deficiency, 271

California State University, Hayward, 290
Canada, 199
captodiamine hydrochloride, 137
case studies, 193
Cattell Infant Intelligence Scale, 212
causes, 14, 27, 48, 49, 57, 90-93, 94, 291
  abused children, 9, 10, 102
  accidents, 101
  alcoholism, 91
  anoxia, 48
  brain damage, 14, 27, 34, 36, 38, 57, 90, 156-159
  cerebral palsy, 13, 15, 26, 48, 57, 92 134
  chicken pox, 14, 95
  chromosomal abnormalities, 98
  Down's syndrome, 14, 20, 27, 57, 58, 59, 60, 61, 92, 98, 99, 162-166, 167-177, 184-188, 191-195
  encephalitis, 14, 101
  environmental factors, 9, 14, 25, 49, 56, 90
  genetic irregularities, 14, 27, 57, 90
  heavy smokers, 91
  herpes simplex, 95
  lead poisoning, 14, 27, 28, 92, 94, 102
  maple syrup urine disease, 92
  malnutrition, 14, 28
  measles, 14, 15, 27, 28, 48, 92, 95
  meningitis, 14, 27, 101
  mumps, 95
  parental causes, 19, 27
  polio, 14, 26
  poverty, 91
  prematurity, 27, 91, 100
  scarlet fever, 14
  seizures, 92, 157
  tumors, 57
  whooping cough, 14
cerebral gigantism, 59
cerebral metabolism, 179
cerebral palsy, 13, 15, 26, 48, 57, 92, 134
changing criterion, a design, 246
chicken pox, 14, 95
child advocacy, 8
child development, 73
child find, 52
childhood schizophrenia, 293
Children's Bureau, 273
chondrodystrophy, 58
chromosomal abnormalities, 98, 168
chronological age, 9
Cincinnati Public Schools Curriculum Bulletin No. 119, 114
Clintest, 61
cognitive development, 73-74, 82, 86
color discrimination, 173
communal living, 22, 28
communication skills, 278
community involvement, 276-277
community mobility skills, 207
community services, 271
competency based programs, 84-86

Connecticut Asylum for the Education and Instruction of Deaf and Dumb Persons, 4
contraception, 266
contingent aversive stimulation, 212
continuing medical education, 51
cost factors, 29
Council for Exceptional Children, 7, 8, 10, 68, 254
counseling practices, 162-166
counting in sequence, 54
court action, 8
craniosynostosis, 15, 27, 92
creative play, 39-43, 45
creative potential, 119-123
creepers, 214
cretinism, 59, 292
criminal tendencies, 270
curiosity, 172

day care centers for retarded children, 20, 28
day school classes for the blind, 5, 16
deafness, 15, 18, 64, 92, 152, 204, 214
degrees of mental retardation, 9, 10, 14 17, 24-25, 26, 27, 91
deinstitutionalization, 232
deLange's syndrome, 59
Delayed Infant Education Project of the Nisonger Center of Columbus Ohio, 254
dental diagnosis, 60-61
  hypoplastic pits, 61
dental research, 49
Denver Developmental Assessment Battery and Screening Test, 198
Department of Health, Education, and Welfare, 273
Development Center of Kansas City, Kansas, 255
Development Disabilities Services and Facilities Construction Act of 1970, 29
developmental delay, 58, 170
develomental psychology, 220
Dexedrine, 137
diagnosis, 56-63, 148, 162, 192, 194, 294
  age, 57-58
  biological syndrome, 58
  dental, 60-61
diagnosis by age, 57-58
diagnosis by biological syndrome, 58
diagnostic clinics, 29
diagnostic techniques, 211
Dialantin, 102
discrimination, 6, 212
discrimination deficits, 244
discrimination learning, 243
Discrete Pattern Completion, 227
dissemination of information, 207
distractability, 244
DNA, 48, 264
Down's syndrome, 14, 20, 27, 57, 58, 59, 60, 61, 63, 92, 98, 99, 162-166, 167-177, 184-188, 191-195, 255, 267, 292
  assessment form, 199
  counseling parents, 191-195
  characteristics, 191, 196
  diagnosis, 192
  drug treatment, 178
  vitamin B6, 179
Down's Syndrome Assessment Form, 199
Down's Syndrome, causes, 168

Down's Syndrome, definition, 168
drugs, 8, 102, 137
    benzedrine, 137
    dexidrine, 137
    dialantin, 102
    phenobarbital, 102
    thioridazine hydrochloride, 137
    tranquilizers, 178
drug therapy, 178
Dyslexia, 138

early childhood education, 206
early identification, 8, 15, 27, 49, 52-55, 56, 57
educable mentally retarded (EMR), 31, 50, 56, 78, 80, 108-113, 114, 115, 119-123, 125-127, 189, 257, 285
Education for All Handicapped Children Act, (Public Law 94-142), 10
EEG, 49
Elwyn Training School, 18
embryonic cells, 179
emotionally disturbed, 147, 149, 293
emotional lability, 132
employment, 142-145
encephalitis, 14, 101
encephalopathy, 292
environmental factors, 9, 14, 25, 49, 56, 90
epilepsy, 15, 205
equal education opportunity, 4, 26, 38
equivocal neurological signs, 132
erythroblatosis, 100
evtomegalic inclusion disease, 48
exceptional children, 4, 12
Exceptional Children's Foundation of Los Angeles, 254
expressive language skills, 40, 49, 52, 54, 217
Extended Kohs Test, 226
external feedback, 246

facilities for care, 67-71
fading, 212
Fairview Hospital and Training Center, 238
family care program, 271
Families Play to Grow Program, 261
family relationships, 184-188
family roles, 266
family unit treatment, 286
faulty teaching techniques, 152
Federal Drug Administration, 180
feeding, 168
fetal monitoring, 99
field experience, 213
Fisher's Exact Probability Test, 32
fistula, 185
foster homes, 28
Frostig Developmental Test of Perception, 148
frustration-aggression situations, 248
fuberous sclerosis, 59
functional retardation, 56, 204

Gallaudet, Rev. Thomas H., 4, 9, 11
generalized gangliosiodosis, 59
generic agencies, 286
genetic codes, 264

genetic irregularities, 14, 27, 57, 90
genetic research, 49
Gesell Developmental Schedules, 212
gifted children, 9, 10
Girl Scouts, 272
glutamic acid, 179
guilt denial, 192
Gray Standardized Oral Reading, 133, 135

habitation, 142-145
halfway houses, 8
Handicapped Children's Early Education Assistance Act (Public Law 90-538), 143
Hartford, Connecticut, 4
head start program, 143, 296
Hear-Touch Subtest, 54
hearing vocabularies, 49
heart surgery, 191
heavy smokers, 91
herpes simplex, 95
high energy radiation, 48
home nursing programs, 28
home visitation, 272
hormonal deficiencies, 179
hormonal therapy, 179
hostels, 284
Howe, Dr. Samuel Gridley, 4, 5, 9, 18
Hunter's disease, 59
Hurler's disease, 59, 292
hydrocephalus, 15, 27, 59, 255
hydroxytryptophan (5), 179
hyperactive children, 94, 205
hyperkinesis, 131, 138
Hypoplastic pits, 61
hypotonia, 179
hypoglycemia, 59

impulsivity, 132
incoherent verbiage, 283
individualized instruction, 256
infections, 292
instructional arrangements, 280
intellectual development, 40
intercorrelation matrix, 228
interfering behaviors, 244
intermittent schedules of reinforcement, 246
International Special Olympics, 276
intervention techniques, 217
IQ, 13, 17, 19. 32, 38, 49, 57, 61, 62, 65, 74, 77, 78, 79, 81, 82, 83, 109, 117, 126, 133, 136, 148
Illinois Test of Psycholoinguistic Abilities, 148
impulsivity, 205
inadequacies and failures of the mentally retarded, 182
inadequate communication skills, 205
Infant Intelligence Scales, 64-66
Institutes for the Achievement of Human Potential, 157
isolation avoidance, procedure, 246
institutionalization, 175, 192, 195, 228, 270
Itard, Dr. Jean, 18, 269

Johns Hopkins Institute of Neurological Diseases and Blindness, 274
Joint Commission of Accreditation of Hospitals, 70
Joseph P. Kennedy Jr. Foundation, 261, 297

Kallikak Family Study, 291
Kansas Neurological Institute, 267
Keller, Helen, 11, 204
Kennedy, John F., 20, 29
Kernicterus, 292
kinesthetic modalities, 53
Klinefelter's syndrome, 92, 98, 99
Knox Cubes Test, 227
Kohs learning potential task, 226

labeling, 6, 9, 14, 17, 24, 26, 27, 56, 57, 91
    educable, 31, 50, 56, 78, 80, 108-113, 114, 115, 119-123, 125, 127
    gifted 9, 10,
    mildly, 9, 14, 17, 24, 26, 27, 56, 91, 146-155
    moderately, 9, 14, 17, 24, 26, 27, 56, 57, 90, 91
    profound, 15, 24, 26, 27, 56, 57, 91
    severely, 9, 15, 17, 24, 26, 27, 38, 56, 57, 64, 90, 91
    totally dependent, 56
    trainable, 38, 50, 56, 77, 82
labor unions, 145
language behavior, 278
language development, 216
L'Arche (the ark)-in Trosley-Brevil, France, 22
lead poisoning, 14, 27, 28, 92, 94, 102
Leiter International Performance Scale, 227
learning disabilities, 9, 13, 34, 52, 56, 62, 110, 140-141, 147
life expectancy, 27
longitudinal study, 179

mainstreaming, 7, 151, 207
malnutrition, 14, 28, 254
malposition, 292
mandatory education laws, 64
manipulative materials, 197
Mann-Whitney U-Test, 111
maple syrup urine disease, 92
Martens, Elsie, 7
masturbation, 266
Matching Colors Subtest, 54
measles (rubella), 14, 15, 27, 28, 48, 92, 95, 296
media, 266
median cleft face syndrome, 59
medication, 213
Mendelian Laws of Heredity, 19
meningitis, 14, 27, 101
Menke's syndrome, 59
menstruation, 268
mental age, 77
mental health clinics, 296
mental retardation, 13, 19, 24-25, 26-30, 48, 56, 75, 90-93, 114, 147, 182, 189-190, 269
mental retardation definition, 13, 24-25
mental retardation history, 4-12, 17-21, 269, 295
Merrill-Palmer Scale of Mental Tests, 65
metabolic disorders, 96, 100, 292
methodology, 49, 52-55, 64-66, 72-83, 90-93, 109, 125, 126, 137, 212
Metropolitan Readiness Test, 53
Michigan Picture Test, 135
microcephaly, 59, 255

microfiche readers, 11
mildly handicapped, 9, 14, 17, 24, 26, 27, 56, 91, 146-155
mimicking, 172
Minnesota, 271
minimal cerebral dysfunction, 56, 128-139
modeling, 212
moderately handicapped, 9, 14, 17, 24, 26, 27, 56, 57, 90, 91
monilethrix, 59
monosyllables, 283
mother-child relationship, 170
motor imitation, 216
motorized beds, 214
motor skills, 31, 41, 52, 131, 141
multiply handicapped children, 64, 213
mumps, 95
muscular development, 172
music, severely retarded, 232-235

National Association for Gifted Children, 8
National Association for Retarded Citizens (NARC), 20, 30, 68, 145, 193, 210, 253, 273, 274, 297, 298
National Institute of Neurological Diseases and Blindness, 48
need-centered model of service delivery, 207
needs, 29, 68
New England Asylum for the Blind of Boston, 4
New Jersey, 271
New York City, 270
New York State Idiot Asylum in Syracuse, 50
neonatal care, 93
neurodegenerative disease, 59
neurofibromatosis, 292
neurological examination, 58
neurological impairment, 204
non verbal tasks, 49
normalization, 240, 284

occulo-cerebral-renal syndrome, 59
occupational therapists, 208
OPTICON reader, 11
optimum tempo music and task performance, 234
operant conditioning, 256
operant procedures, 219
optiscope enlarger, 11
oral-facial-digital (OFD) syndrome, 59
Orange County Chapter of the New York Association for Retarded Children, 223
organical impairment, 204
orthopedic clinic, 285
orthopedically disabled, 206
overlearning, 220

parental causes, 19, 27
parent counseling, 28, 102
parental involvement, 207
parental neglect, 254
parent's organizations, 50
parent relationships, 173
parent training, 213
Peabody College for Teachers, 65
Peabody Picture Vocabulary Test, 198
pediatric care, 15

perceptual psychology, 220
perceptual skills, 27, 131, 149
Perkins Institution of Boston, 5
personal hygiene, 296
personal services center, 288
personality, 172
personnel, 208
pharmacologic problems, 100
physical deformities, 211
physical problems, 178
physical therapists, 208
physically handicapped, 9, 10
physiological method, 18
Piaget, Jean, 72-83
phenobarbital, 102
pituitary extract, 179
PKU (phenylketonuria), 14, 48, 49, 61, 91, 96, 97, 101, 292
placement, 192, 197
polio, 14, 26
political issues, 50
Porter-Sargent Directory, 68
port-wine hemangioma, 59
post adolescence, 266
postural drainage, 170
poverty, 91
precise measurement of behavior, 212
pre-doctoral education of the physician, 50
prematurity, 27, 91, 100, 168, 189, 255
prenatal care, 90, 93, 95
pre-school classes, 16, 28, 172
President's Committee on Mental Retardation, 14, 30, 252, 295
prevalency, 13, 19, 24-25, 26-27, 56, 92
prevention, 15, 28 90-93, 94, 95-103
prevocational skills, 256
private facilities, 295
problem solving, 257
problems at birth, 14, 27, 91
problems during pregnancy, 14, 27
profoundly retarded, 15, 24, 26, 27, 56, 57, 91, 204-209, 236, 254
progress, 9
Project on the Classification of Exceptional Children, 8
promiscuity, 266
prompting, 212
prosthetic device, 8, 214
prostitution, 266
psychological difficulty, 178
psychological reports, 279
psychological tests, 61-62, 170
psychomotor development, 194
psychomotor disturbances, 293
psychomotor domain, 86
psychomotor skills, 27
psychotherapy, 195
psychotic disorders, 178
puberty, 175, 266
public law 94-142, 206
Public School No. 2 of New York City, 5

Rand report, 8
Raven Coloured Progressive Matrices, 227
reading comprehension, 54, 114-118, 223
receptive language skills, 40, 49, 52, 217
recreational programs, 8, 16, 28, 39-43, 272, 297

Rehabilitation Act of 1973, 10
repetitive manual task performance, 232
research, 48-50, 72-83, 119
Resident Functioning Questionnaire, 227
residential services, 16, 18, 28, 50, 68, 176
response-cost procedure, 246
response patterns, 282
reversing contingencies, 219
Ring-chromosome, 18, 59
Rh-factor incompatibility, 15, 27, 28
RNA, 48, 264
role playing, 256-259
role reversal, 257
Rose F. Kennedy Center for Research in Mental Retardation and Human Development, 192
Rubinstein-Taybi syndrome, 59

Sanfilippo's syndrome, 59
scarlet fever, 14
schizophrenia, 222
School Behavior Profile, 53
See-Say Letters Subtest, 54
See-Say Numbers Subtest, 54
See-Write Letters Subtest, 54
Sequin, Edouard, 18
seizures, 92, 157
self administered reinforcement, 248
self care, 173
self control, 247
self-management strategies, 247
self-stimulation, 238
sensory-motor deficits, 244
sensory skills, 27, 49, 66
sensory training, 18, 49
sequelac of traumata, 57
serotonia, 179
severely handicapped, 9, 15, 17, 24, 26, 27, 38, 56, 57, 64, 90, 91, 204-209, 232-235, 255, 265
sexual delinquency, 270
sex education, 264-267
shaping, 212, 256
sheltered workshops, 8, 16, 28, 142-145, 237, 273
short attention span, 132
Shriver, Eunice, 276
siblings of mentally retarded, 189-190
sign language for the blind, 11
Silver's syndrome, 58
Simple Continuous Pattern Completion, 227
skill acquisition, 244
skill sequences, 210
skill training, 257
skull malformations, 293
slow motor behavior, 244
Smith-Lemli Opitz syndrome, 59
social adjustment problems, 13
social development, 40, 52
social growth, 294
Social Security Act, 69
social skills, 248
special diet, 8, 15
special education, 4, 5, 6, 10, 16, 24, 26, 28, 29, 31-32, 38, 39-43, 50-51, 52, 84-86, 108-113, 114-118, 119-124, 128-139, 146-155, 173, 182-183, 196-199, 295, 296
Special Olympics, 159, 224, 261
special playground, 39-43, 45

specific learning deficits, 131
specific language tasks, 216
speech and language problems, 225
speech disability, 34
speech therapy, 38, 49, 170, 171, 208
Stanford-Binet Intelligence Scale, 109, 225
St. Coletta Schools Reading Curriculum for the Mentally Handicapped, 114
standing tables, 214
State of Washington Screening Booklets, 53
sterilization, 266
stimulus control, 212, 248
Strauss syndrome, 140
Sullivan, Anne Mansfield, 11
surgical techniques, 15

"Talking Calculator," 11
task analysis, 212
Tay-Sachs disease, 59, 92, 93, 96, 97, 292
tax laws, 298
teacher consultant model, 153-154
Teacher Corps, 184
teacher training, 211
teratogenic agents, 96
Terman-Merrill Scale, 77
terminology, 293
test-related anxiety, 230
therapy, 8
The American Association for the Study of the Feebleminded (1906), 18
The American Association on Mental Deficiency, 18
The Boston Way-1924, 7
The Wild Boy of Aveyron (1801), 18

thioridazine hydrochloride, 137
thyroid extracts, 179
toilet training, 58, 171
tokens, 219
tongue, 172
    protrusion, 179
totally dependent, 56
toxic medications, 48
toxoplasmosis, 95
train-within-test procedures, 227
Trainable Mentally Retarded (TMR), 38, 50, 56, 77, 82, 189, 237, 260, 265, 273
Training School at Vineland, The, 295
translocation Down's syndrome, 98
tranquilizers, 178
trauma, 292
Trisomy, 13, 59
Trisomy 17-18, 59
tumors, 57
Turner's Syndrome, 92
two-component behavioral events, 279

United Cerebral Palsy Association, 68
University of Oregon Center on Human Devlopment, 252
University of Washington Experimental Education Unit, 205
University of Washington Model Preschool for Handicapped Children, 196

Vanier, Jean, 22
venereal disease, 264

verbal praise, 258
verbal tasks, 49, 53
Vineland Social Maturity Scale, 294
Visiting Nurse Association, 271
visual contact, 233
vitamin B6, 179
vocabulary development, 125-127, 149
vocabulary test, 222
vocational rehabilitation, 16, 25, 28, 29, 142-145, 260
Vocational Rehabilitation Commissions, 296
vocational skills, 212

Waardenburg's syndrome, 59
Wallin, Wallace, 6
Wechsler Intelligence Scale for Children, 148
Wepman Test of Auditory Discrimination, 148
wheelchairs, 214
White House Conference on Children and Youth of 1930, 7
whooping cough, 14
Wilbur, Dr. Harvey, 50
Willowbrook Developmental Center, 252
Wilson's Disease, 292
Wizard of Oz Preschool Screening Program, 53
World Health Organization, 17, 49
word calling, 220

YMCA, 297
Youth-NARC, 30

STAFF

Publisher	John Quirk
Editor	Joseph Logan
Director of Production	Maureen Luiszer
Director of Design	Donald Burns
Photographer	Richard Pawlikowski
Research Asst.	Rod Mulock
Staff Consultant	Dona Chiappe
Editorial Asst.	Helen Flynn

Cover Design — Li Bailey of Enoch and Eisenman Inc. New York City.

Appendix: Agencies and Services for Exceptional Children

Alexander Graham Bell Association for the Deaf, Inc.
Volta Bureau for the Deaf
3417 Volta Place, NW
Washington, D.C. 20007

American Academy of Pediatrics
1801 Hinman Avenue
Evanston, Illinois 60204

American Association for Gifted Children
15 Gramercy Park
New York, N.Y. 10003

American Association on Mental Deficiency
5201 Connecticut Avenue, NW
Washington, D.C. 20015

American Association of Psychiatric Clinics for Children
250 West 57th Street
New York, N.Y.

American Bar Association
Commission on the Mentally Disabled
1800 M Street, NW
Washington, D.C. 20036

American College of Obstetricians and Gynecologists
79 W. Monroe Street
Chicago, Illinois 60603

ACLU Juvenile Rights Project
22 East 40th Street
New York, N.Y. 10016

American Diabetes Association
18 E. 48th Street
New York, N.Y. 10017

American Foundation for the Blind
15 W. 16th Street
New York, N.Y. 10011

American Medical Association
535 N. Dearborn Street
Chicago, Illinois 60610

American Orthopsychiatric Association
1790 Broadway
New York, N.Y.

American Psychological Association
1200 Seventeenth Street, NW
Washington, D.C. 20036

American Speech and Hearing Association
9030 Old Georgetown Road
Washington, D.C. 20014

Association for the Aid of Crippled Children
345 E. 46th Street
New York, N.Y. 10017

Association for Children with Learning Disabilities
2200 Brownsville Road
Pittsburgh, Pennsylvania 15210

Association for the Aid of Crippled Children
345 E. 46th Street
New York, N.Y. 10017

Association for Education of the Visually Handicapped
1604 Spruce Street
Philadelphia, Pennsylvania 19103

Association for the Help of Retarded Children
200 Park Avenue, South
New York, N.Y.

Association for the Visually Handicapped
1839 Frankfort Avenue
Louisville, Kentucky 40206

Boy Scouts of America
North Brunswick, New Jersey 08902
(Scouting information for boys with handicaps)

Camp Fire Girls, Inc.
1740 Broadway
New York, N.Y. 10019

Career Service, Rehabilitation/World
20 West 40 Street
New York, N.Y. 10018

Center on Human Policy
Division of Special Education and Rehabilitation
Syracuse University
Syracuse, New York 13210

Center for Sickle Cell Anemia
College of Medicine
Howard University
520 "W" Street NW
Washington, D.C. 20001

Child Fund
275 Windsor Street
Hartford, Connecticut 06120

Children's Defense Fund
1520 New Hampshire Avenue NW
Washington, D.C. 20036

Civil Rights Division
United States Department of Justice

Closer Look
National Information Center for the Handicapped
1201 Sixteenth Street NW
Washington, D.C. 20036

Clifford W. Beers Guidance Clinic
432 Temple Street
New Haven, Connecticut 06510

Committee to Combat Huntington's Disease
200 W. 57th Street
New York, N.Y. 10019

Child Study Center
Yale University
333 Cedar Street
New Haven, Connecticut 06520

Child Welfare League of America, Inc.
44 East 23rd Street
New York, N.Y. 10010

Children's Bureau
United States Department of Health, Education and Welfare
Washington, D.C.

Children's Center
1400 Whitney Avenue
Hamden, Connecticut 06514

Council for Exceptional Children
1411 Jefferson Davis Highway
Arlington, Virginia 22202

Epilepsy Foundation of America
1828 "L" Street NW
Washington, D.C. 20036

ERIC Document Reproduction Services (EDRS)
P.O. Box 190
Arlington, Virginia 22202

Gifted Child Society, Inc.
59 Glen Gray Road
Oakland, New Jersey 07436

Herner and Company
Clearinghouse on Programs and Research in Child Abuse and Neglect
2100 M Street NW
Suite 316
Washington, D.C. 20037

Highland Heights
651 Prospect Street
New Haven, Connecticut 06511

Institute for the Study of Mental Retardation and Related Disabilities
130 South First
University of Michigan
Ann Arbor, Michigan 48108

International Association for the Scientific Study of Mental Deficiency
Ellen Horn, AAMD
5201 Connecticut Avenue NW
Washington, D.C. 20015

International League of Societies for the Mentally Handicapped
Rue Forestiere 12
Brussels, Belgium

Joseph P. Kennedy, Jr. Foundation
1701 K Street NW
Washington, D.C. 20006

League for Emotionally Disturbed Children
171 Madison Avenue
New York, N.Y.

Little People of America, Inc.
P.O. Box 126
Owatonna, Minnesota 55060

SISU mathematics

SISU is a new math program designed for children with learning problems. Its purpose is to give individual training in readiness in order to improve a student's mathematical ability. The SISU program contains materials that are very basic, self-instructing, self-correcting and easy to use.

The objective of SISU is to help students to learn the basic skills of mathematics. Students work at their own pace with the student booklets and cassette tapes. The cassettes provide detailed instructions and the student performs a given task in his booklet. Answer sheets attached to each page offer the student immediate reinforcement and the opportunity to see how a task is properly completed.

- Field-tested for 10 years
- Basic skills
- Individualized instruction

The Complete Program Includes:

25 Student books
25 Cassettes
5 Diagnostic/Remediation books
5 Teacher's Guides
1 Set of Cuisenaire rods
1 Counting frame
Reading In Learning Disabilities/SISU Supplement

TITLES

Strand I - Numerations of whole numbers
Strand II - Addition of whole numbers
Strand III - Subtraction of whole numbers
Strand IV - Multiplication of whole numbers
Strand V - Division of whole numbers

For more information on SISU and our inservice workshops contact:
Dessie Boras

Special Learning Corporation
42 Boston Post Road
Guilford, Connecticut 06437
phone: (203) 453-6525

- PRE-TESTS
- PRACTICE SHEETS
- POST TESTS

trains the pupil in basic skills

CUSTOM PUBLISHING

CUSTOM-PUBLISHED BOOKS FOR YOUR COURSE OF STUDY

TEXTS DESIGNED FOR YOUR COURSE

Special Learning Corporation publishes books that are particularly tailored for a specific course and that fit a professor's specific needs. Special Learning Corporation will compile a book of required readings based on a bibliography selected by the professor teaching the course. These selected academic readings serve as the required course of readings and in some cases the major book for the course. It also benefits other small enrollment areas at various other colleges. Originally designed to serve small course areas in special education, e.g. *Readings for Teachers of Minimally Brain Damaged Children*, the idea spread to larger course enrollments in Special Education, Psychology, and Education.

HOW DOES CUSTOM PUBLISHING WORK?

- A professor selects a list of articles relevant to his course from a bibliography. These articles usually come from scholarly journals, magazines. The professor can also suggest other articles, unpublished papers, and articles he has written.
- Special Learning Corporation does all editoral work, clears permissions and produces the book--using the facsimile reproduction of the articles.
- The book is then used in the professor's course of study.

Pages: 192 to 224 or about 50 to 70 articles.
Price: $5.95 to $6.95 (Hardback available to libraries for $12.00).

For more information please contact:

Joseph Logan
Editor
Custom Publishing Division,
Special Learning Corporation

> Excellent for the many different courses in mental retardation and the many types of mental retardation.

Special Learning Corporation
42 Boston Post Rd. Guilford, Connecticut 06437

1978 Catalog
SPECIAL LEARNING CORPORATION

Programs in Special Education

Table of Contents

Basic Skills

I.	Language Arts
II.	Self-instructional Special Education Math
III.	Mathematics
IV.	Special Education Materials
V.	Early Childhood Education
VI.	Bi-lingual Programs-L.A. and Math
VII.	College and Professional Books
VIII.	Media-cassettes, films filmstrips
IX.	Social Learning
X.	Science
XI.	Testing Materials
XII.	Mainstreaming Library

- special education ● learning disabilities ● mental retardation
- autism ● behavior modification ● mainstreaming ● gifted and talented
- physically handicapped ● deaf education ● speech and hearing
- emotional and behavioral disorders ● visually handicapped
- diagnosis and placement ● psychology of exceptional children

Special Learning Corporation
42 Boston Post Rd. Guilford, Connecticut 06437 (203) 453-6212

SPECIAL LEARNING CORPORATION
COMMENTS PLEASE:

Does this book fit your course of study?

Why? (Why not?)

Is this book useable for other courses of study? Please list.

What other areas would you like us to publish in using this format?

What type of exceptional child are you interested in learning more about?

Would you use this as a basic text?

How many students are enrolled in these course areas?

_____ Special Education _____ Mental Retardation _____ Psychology _____ Emotional Disorders

_____ Exceptional Children _____ Learning Disabilities Other _____

Do you want to be sent a copy of our elementary student materials catalog?

Do you want a copy of our college catalog?

Would you like a copy of our next edition? ☐ yes ☐ no

Are you a ☐ student or an ☐ instructor?

Your name _____ school _____

Term used _____ Date _____

address _____

city _____ state _____ zip _____

telephone number _____

CUT HERE ● SEAL AND MAIL

M/R

COMMENTS PLEASE:

SPECIAL LEARNING CORPORATION
42 Boston Post Rd.
Guilford, Conn. 06437

SISU MATHEMATICS — Packaging

Component	Net Prices

1) **STRAND ONE: NUMERATIONS OF WHOLE NUMBERS**
   Six student books, six cassettes, one diagnostic test/remediation book, one Teacher's Guide, one set of Cuisenaire rods, one counting frame.. $119.00

2) **STRAND TWO: ADDITION OF WHOLE NUMBERS**
   Five student books, five cassettes, one diagnostic test/remediation book, one Teacher's Guide, one set of Cuisenaire rods, one counting frame.. $102.50

3) **STRAND THREE: SUBTRACTION OF WHOLE NUMBERS**
   Five student books, five cassettes, one diagnostic test/remediation book, one Teacher's Guide, one set of Cuisenaire rods, one counting frame.. $102.50

4) **STRAND FOUR: MULTIPLICATION OF WHOLE NUMBERS**
   Four student books, four cassettes, one diagnostic test/remediation book, one Teacher's Guide, one set of Cuisenaire rods, one counting frame.. $ 86.00

5) **STRAND FIVE: DIVISION OF WHOLE NUMBERS**
   Five student books, five cassettes, one diagnostic test/remediation book, one Teacher's Guide, one set of Cuisenaire rods, one counting frame.. $102.50

6) One individual student book
   One accompanying cassette
   One diagnostic test/remediation book
   (includes pre-tests, practice sheets and post tests)
   One Teacher's Guide
   One set of Cuisenaire rods
   One counting frame.. $ 36.50

7) **TOTAL KIT** — Five complete strands
   Twenty-five student books, twenty-five cassettes, five diagnostic/remediation books, five Teacher's Guides, five sets of Cuisenaire rods, five counting frames: Readings in Learning Disabilities/SISU Supplement.. $521.00

8) 15 copies of a single book... $127.50
   15 copies of a single cassette.. $120.00
   Total for 15 books and 15 cassettes.. $247.50

Individual Replacement Components

   Student book... $8.50
   Cassette.. $8.00
   Teacher's Guide.. $5.00
   Diagnostic test/remediation book.. $9.00
   Cuisenaire rods (one set)... $3.00
   Counting frame.. $3.00
   Readings in Learning Disabilities/SISU Supplement.................... $8.60

Special Learning Corporation
42 Boston Post Rd. Guilford, Connecticut 06437   (203) 453-6525

STRAND FOUR:

MULTIPLICATION OF WHOLE NUMBERS

M-1 Multiplication Facts, Part 1
M-2 Multiplication Facts, Part 2
M-3 Multiplication: No Regrouping
M-4 Multiplication: Regrouping

STRAND FIVE:

DIVISION OF WHOLE NUMBERS

D-1 Preparing for Division
D-2 Division: Dividends Multiples of 10
D-3 Division: Dividend 99 or Less, Part 1
D-4 Division: Dividend 99 or Less, Part 2
D-5 Division: Dividend 150 or Less

**For additional information
please contact:**

**Dessie Boras
Phone: (203) 453-6525**

Special Learning Corporation

42 Boston Post Rd. Guilford, Connecticut 06437   (203) 453-6525

SISU MATHEMATICS — TITLES

STRAND ONE:

NUMERATIONS OF WHOLE NUMBERS

    N-1 Numbers and Numerals 0-5
    N-2 Numbers and Numerals 0-9
    N-3 Same Number, More Than, Less Than
    N-4 More Numbers and Numerals 0-5
    N-5 More Numbers and Numerals 0-9
    N-6 Place Value: Tens and Ones

STRAND TWO:

ADDITION OF WHOLE NUMBERS

    A-1 Addition: Sums of 10 or Less
    A-2 Addition: Sums of 18 or Less
    A-3 Addition: No Regrouping
    A-4 Addition: Regrouping, Part 1
    A-5 Addition: Regrouping, Part 2

STRAND THREE:

SUBTRACTION OF WHOLE NUMBERS

    S-1 Subtraction: Sums of 10 or Less
    S-2 Subtraction: Sums of 18 or Less
    S-3 Subtraction: No Regrouping
    S-4 Subtraction: Regrouping, Part 1
    S-5 Subtraction: Regrouping, Part 2

Flow Chart

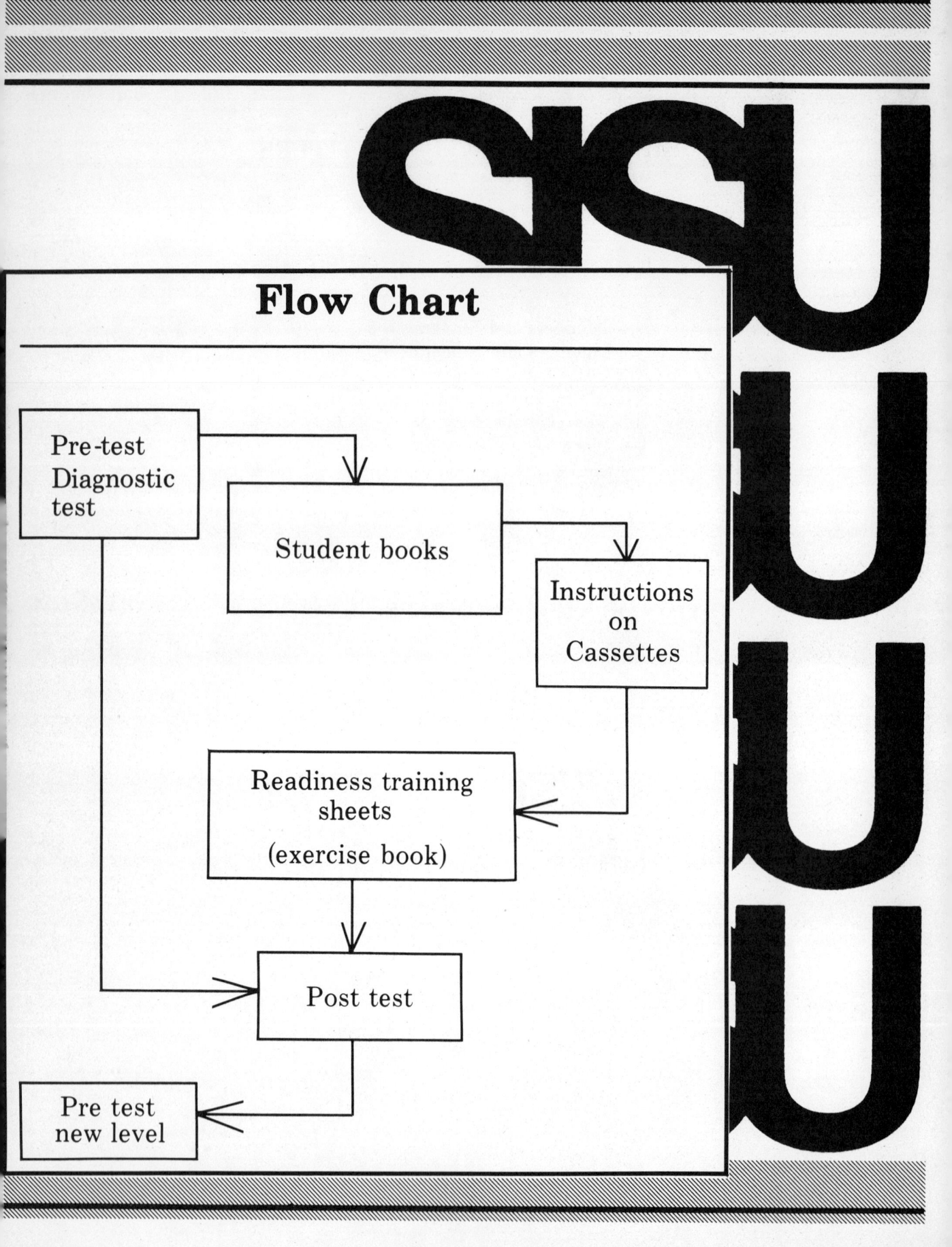

- Pre-test Diagnostic test
- Student books
- Instructions on Cassettes
- Readiness training sheets (exercise book)
- Post test
- Pre test new level

How To Use SISU

A. A diagnostic test is administered to decide whether the pupil needs extra training in a certain skill.

B. The result of the pre-test shows if the pupil needs training or not. Less than 80% correct answers means that the pupil is offered remedial material.

C. The pupil writes his answers in the notebook.

D. By covering the page with an answer sheet showing the correct answer, the student can decide whether his own answer is right or wrong.

E. When the pupil has finished the notebook, he erases his own answers from the sheets. This makes the notebook ready for use by the next pupil.

F. After each practice period the student gets a post-test showing the result of the training.

G. If the pupil does not reach a minimum of 80% right, the same training materials can be used again later on.

H. After the test the pupil gets further training.

I. After practicing with the SISU material the pupil generally goes back to his ordinary textbook.

J. Adequate instructional materials are of great help in individualizing the learning activities.

K. If the teacher can use self instructional teaching aids, she will be more able to distribute her time among the pupils.

The level of difficulty within each of the various strands mandates that the teacher let the student work at his own pace within 1) a book or 2) within a strand or 3) between strands. The student will have many assignments to work at; while students are working the teacher will have more time to work with individual students.

By reviewing each of the different strands the teacher decides if the student should work with or without the tape recorder. The teacher also has the option of challenging students to work through different strands or to try strands that the teacher feels the student might be ready for.

The strands of SISU all lend themselves to preliminary tests and to readiness assignments. Preliminary tests can also be used as supplementary examinations to reveal if the student understands what the work in a specific strand means---specifically what the readiness training assignment was intended to bring out through exercises. These tests are excellent for the teacher to see if the lesson objectives are being accomplished.

EACH OF THE STRANDS CONTAINS

1. Diagnostic Tests
2. 4 - 6 Student Books
3. Cassette Instructions
4. Readiness Training Assignments

HOW TO USE SISU THE BEST WAY

A. First administer the pre-tests (Diagnostic tests). Give each of your students the book in the strand the student should begin. Each student's needs are different and the student should begin at a strand he can work at comfortably. This placement into a specific strand is accomplished by using the diagnostic tests.

B. Make sure the student understands the work and the way in which the self-correcting is done.

C. Teach the student to use the recorder.

D. Let the student practice and work within the correct strand by himself at his own pace--

--LET THE STUDENT REVIEW AGAIN AND AGAIN BY SELF-INSTRUCTION.

E. Talk about and discuss with each student their progress and what they achieved---compare the pre-test with answers in the book and post-tests.

HOW TO BEGIN

The teacher should instruct the student how to do the following:

HOW THE CASSETTE IS PUT IN

HOW THE CASSETTE IS TURNED ON AND OFF

HOW TO USE FAST SPEED FORWARD AND BACK

HOW THE VOLUME ADJUSTS

HOW THE EARPHONES (HEADSETS) HOOK UP

When the student masters the use of the cassette recorder let him demonstrate each of the above steps for the teacher. When the student has learned the technique and procedure in using the books and cassettes, he or she can begin at once to test himself. The student then lifts up the answer sheets to see if his answers are right or wrong. Corrections are made by raising the sheet with the answer, writing the answer, then checking the answer. The sheet with the answer can be placed down to check the answer. In this way the correct answer is found either beside or above the student answer and the student can tell immediately if his answer is right or wrong. Certain students---especially those with learning disabilities---might have problems with self-correcting and thus it is very important that the teacher aids the student in seeing the differences in their own answer and the correct answer.

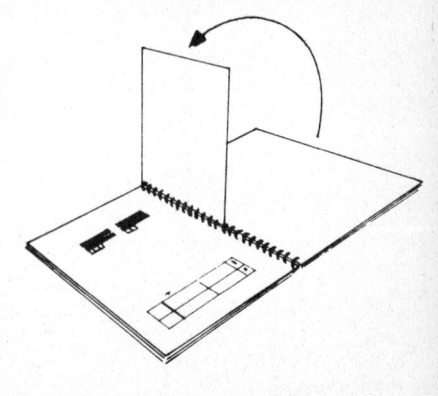

HOW TO WORK WITH SISU

The teacher's guide gives a description of the lesson objectives, goals, the readiness approach, the testing procedures, and the text-to-tape (script) instruction. The work with SISU can be done working with the following model:

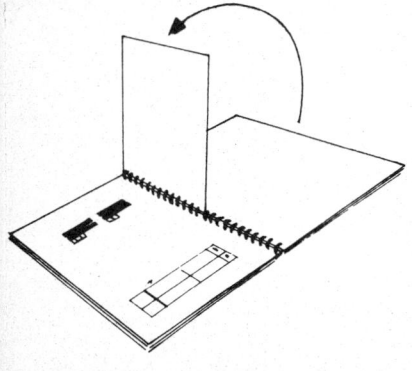

Pre-test Administered

Post-test Administered

SISU student book used

Diagnostic tests that accompany each of the student book levels indicate whether a student needs additional training. The training or remediation first occurs by using the student books; then by using the readiness training sheets in the exercise book. The instructions on tape also correspond to the work in the student books. Each strand (there are 5) consists of student books, instructions on cassettes, and remediation sheets. When a student is beginning a book the side with the answer should be UP. In this way the student will not see the answer before he works with each page. If the student has not worked with SISU before or any material with cassette instructions the teacher should instruct the student in how to use the booklets. The student should then proceed through the materials by testing himself---then writing---and then testing himself again. This self-instruct approach is designed to free the teacher for more individualized teaching and instruction.

WHAT IS SISU?

SISU is a remedial mathematics program designed for the early or beginning stages of mathematics. SISU can be used either as an additional training program for students with learning problems or a remedial alternative for re-learning. SISU was developed out of a research group within the Department of Mathematics, the Teacher-Training Institute, and the School of Education in Goteborg, Sweden. The goal was to create a set of materials that would significantly improve a student's mathematical abilities---it was to be a set of materials that would be very, very, basic. The material is designed so that it can be used independently of basal books. It is also superb for remediation---especially in order to learn specific concepts from curriculum. By using SISU the student might be able to return to the basal program. Moreover, by using SISU he will be able to get steady remediation while continuing to work within the basal program. The material is self-instructional and self-correcting.

FIELD-TESTING AND DEVELOPMENT

The work-groups SISU was used with consisted of experienced mathematics teachers with low achieving students. SISU material was first developed and field-tested with 600 students in 100 classes and resource centers in Goteborg. It was expanded to 3000 students, and then 12,000, and then 20,000 students throughout all of Sweden---just for field-test purposes. During the next five years field-test and revision sites were set up in Norway, Germany, the United Kingdom, Cuba, and the United States. Field-test data was cleared, analyzed, and incorporated into the final products by the Teacher-Training Institute in Goteborg. The final materials you see are the result of this large field-test analysis.